KU-781-909

COMPANY LAW

Fourth edition

COMPANY LAW

Fourth Edition

By

Nicholas Grier, MA, LLB, WS, *Solicitor*
Senior Lecturer in Law at Edinburgh Napier University

W. GREEN

 THOMSON REUTERS

First Edition 2002 by Nicholas Grier
Second Edition 2005 by Nicholas Grier
Third Edition 2009 by Nicholas Grier

Published in 2014 by W. Green, 21 Alva Street,
Edinburgh EH2 4PS
Part of Thomson Reuters (Professional) UK Limited
(Registered in England & Wales, Company No 1679046.
Registered Office and address for service: Aldgate House, 33 Aldgate High Street, London
EC3N 1DL)

Typeset by YHT Ltd, London
Printed and bound in Great Britain by CPI Antony Rowe, Wiltshire

No natural forests were destroyed to make this product;
only farmed timber was used and re-planted.

A CIP catalogue record for this book is available from the British Library.

ISBN 978-0-414-01892-1

Thomson Reuters and the Thomson Reuters logo are
trademarks of Thomson Reuters.

© 2014 Thomson Reuters (Professional) UK Limited

Crown copyright material is reproduced with the permission of the Controller of HMSO
and the Queen's Printer for Scotland.

All rights reserved. No part of this publication may be reproduced or transmitted in any
form or by any means, or stored in any retrieval system of any nature without prior written
permission, except for permitted fair dealing under the Copyright, Designs and Patents Act
1988, or in accordance with the terms of a licence issued by the Copyright Licensing Agency
in respect of photocopying and/or reprographic reproduction. Application for permission
for other use of copyright material including permission to reproduce extracts in other
published works shall be made to the publishers. Full acknowledgement of author, publisher
and source must be given.

PREFACE TO THE FOURTH EDITION

Five years after the bringing into force of the final parts of the Companies Act 2006, it is possible to have an objective view of how well it is operating. Did the Act have the effect that its proponents desired? Did it make the United Kingdom a country where entrepreneurs would wish to set up or maintain their companies? Did the codification of directors' duties concentrate directors' minds on what they should or should not be doing?

As for the first two questions, the answer is that it is hard to tell. The Companies Act 2006 did away with many unnecessary rules, and many of the procedural rules, at least for private companies, are simpler and more convenient than ever before. Certainly, the Act did no harm when it came to attracting entrepreneurs, though it is arguable that the United Kingdom is a good place for business anyway, since its taxation levels are not too high, there is little corruption at governmental level, the rule of law is obeyed, and the country is politically stable.

As for the codification of directors' duties, while the codification itself may be welcome, in the sense that the rules on directors' duties are now at least relatively easy to find, there are still doubts about conflicts of interest and how they are to be managed. One particular part of directors' duties, the requirement to have regard to a range of stakeholders under s.172 of the Act, has in practice turned out to have been widely ignored by directors, particularly in the major banks. Although the company reports of the major banks indicated that directors and employees duly conformed to the requirements of law, some of the banks had no qualms over money-laundering, tax evasion and mis-selling of insurance policies, while other banks had a culture of sailing close to the wind, particularly in the areas of financial regulation. Had directors really taken the requirements of s.172 on board, none of these should have taken place. If s.172 was meant to make directors run their companies in a more enlightened manner, the evidence is that it didn't.

However, the derivative claim is beginning, perhaps slowly, to have an effect. If a director is tempted to "pull a fast one" on his fellow shareholders, he will find that in general the courts are reluctant to entertain sharp practice. As for any liability towards creditors, and piercing the corporate veil, recent cases, such as *Prest v Petrodel Resources Ltd*, indicate that on the whole company law still protects members and directors from their company's creditors—and rightly so, since that this is the whole point of company law.

I have tried to express the law as at March 2014. Meanwhile the law moves on, with proposals for greater sanctions for rogue directors combined with a requirement to compensate victims of their companies' frauds and changes at European level to auditors' appointments.

I remain grateful to the staff at Greens for their editorial vigilance and help throughout the process of writing this book. Any errors and omissions, however, will remain my own responsibility.

Nicholas Grier
Edinburgh Napier University
March 2014

PREFACE TO THE THIRD EDITION

Since the last edition of this book, the major change to company law has been the gradual implementation of the Companies Act 2006.

Politicians often produce legislation to address a perceived problem, which, by the time the legislation is in place, is the least of everyone's worries. This is true of the Companies Act 2006. Britain's politicians, most of whom have never been in business themselves, had seized the chance to tell businessmen how companies must be run. Now, of course, sheer survival is a far more pressing concern for company directors than promoting "enhanced shareholder value". Nevertheless, the Companies Act 2006 has removed a number of pointless and cumbersome rules and, even if the Act is not as user-friendly as it professes to be, it is clear that the Parliamentary draftsmen have tried to make the law more intelligible and less bewildering than it was before.

Another change to company law is new style administration, as introduced by the Enterprise Act 2002. This was supposed to remove the privileged position of the banks and in a receivership, to promote a rescue culture and to improve matters for unsecured creditors. While the banks' privileged position has on the whole diminished, imposing a rescue culture remains problematic. A rescue culture is not easy to operate in a struggling economy, as witnessed by the collapse of Woolworths. Administrations have also attracted some opprobrium with the rise of pre-packs, whereby a company in difficulties is swiftly sold by the administrator to a purchaser who picks up the company—with its employees—pretty much free of debt but with many creditors, except to the extent of the prescribed part, out of pocket. Although it is good to keep employees in jobs, one wonders how long unsecured creditors, in particular HMRC, will continue to put up with pre-packs.

Meanwhile, the recent collapse of various building societies and banks, including venerable and until then well regarded Scottish banks, appears to have been caused by a sad combination of hubris, ignorance, greed, complacency and a reluctance by those at the top of large organisations to rock the boat. Corporate governance and shareholder democracy did not work as they should have done: either people with large egos and short tempers made it difficult for dissent to be expressed, or a herd mentality took over. If everybody else was either investing in obscure sub-prime instruments, or lending funds for commercial property, it would have looked strange not to join in. Business was ever thus, and no doubt in twenty years time there will be another unforeseen financial scandal for which we shall be equally unprepared

At the end of each chapter I have tried to include some further reading. This has not been possible in some cases, either because the law is so new that no-one has written anything significant about it, or because at the time of writing, further information was required but was not yet available. This book does not discuss limited liability partnerships or the law relating to community interest companies and some of the other, more specialised, types of corporate vehicle. It, also, does not discuss the international dimensions of corporate insolvency law. It would not be possible to do justice to these topics with the "Concise" imprint. For those who wish to have more detailed knowledge of company law, as before I would always recommend Palmer's Company Law, the Scottish sections of which are written by the inestimable David Bennett, W.S.

I have tried to express the law as at October 2009, as far as possible at time of writing. There are still many statutory instruments in the pipeline in the run up to the final implementation date of the Companies Act 2006 of October 1, 2009. Some of these only existed in draft at the time of writing while others have yet to be drafted. The same is true of the new forms from Companies House.

This edition could not have been written without the loyal forbearance of my wife and family who have been a constant source of support during the many hours of writing. I should also like to thank various colleagues and students at Edinburgh Napier University and the University of Edinburgh for all their comments and suggestions. I am grateful to Bruce Beveridge, W.S., Deputy Keeper of the Registers of Scotland, for his advice and help, particularly in the context of registration of charges and to Professor George Gretton for his support and encouragement. Any errors and omissions will remain my own responsibility.

Nicholas Grier
Edinburgh Napier University
July 2009

PREFACE TO THE SECOND EDITION

Since the first edition of this book, there have been various changes to company law, with the most important being the Enterprise Act 2002. The aim of this Act is to encourage enterprise by, amongst other things, protecting unsecured creditors who, before the Act passed, often received a raw deal from receiverships. By setting aside some funds for unsecured creditors, it is hoped that entrepreneurs' (and their employees') livelihoods will be maintained, albeit possibly at the expense of banks' shareholders or indeed the taxpayer. This book explains both the new law of administration, as introduced by the Enterprise Act, and the old law relating to receivership, which is likely to be with us for many years yet.

There have also been changes to the law relating to auditors (with more on the way) and the information that must be provided to them, and to the law relating to the extent to which a company may indemnify directors for the costs of actions being raised against them.

Normally, corporate scandals provoke changes in the law, as has happened in the USA, resulting in the Sarbanes Oxley Act 2002 which introduces significant sanctions against directors and other who attempt to mislead their investors or others. This has imposed a degree of corporate rectitude on American business and perhaps encouraged a culture of greater transparency and accountability towards investors and creditors. As a result recently the UK and particularly the Alternative Investment Market, has attracted a good deal of business worldwide on account of the fact that the UK's rules are not as stringent as the USA's. Ironically, the Sarbanes Oxley Act has given the UK a competitive advantage. A further and future competitive advantage, if the Government gets it right, is that there is a recognition by the government that a new, better set of company laws is needed to replace the UK's current company legislation which in some areas is out of date, unclear, and full of procedural complications which do little to protect creditors or investors. There has been a wide and thoughtful consultation exercise on the future of company law within the UK. The Government is even looking at other areas which over the years have been put back in the drawer marked "Too difficult": these include reform of the law relating to registration of charges, directors' duties generally, and trying to restore some sense of purpose to general meetings. These consultations will eventually result in a new Companies bill: the bill has been promised for many years now, and it is important that when it is finally enacted, it is properly drafted to general satisfaction. The various Government consultation documents, most of which are surprisingly readable, and its White Paper are referred to throughout this book and readers are urged to refer to the relevant websites for further information

At the end of most chapters I have given as list of further reading. Over

and above such reading, I would always recommend, as suggested in the
first edition, Tolleys for the practicalities of company law, and as regards
the precise interaction of Scots law with company law, the contributions
of David Bennett W.S. to Palmer's Company Law.

On a different note, I would like to acknowledge the support I have
received in the writing of this second edition from Dr Valerie Malloch
and Rebecca Standing of W. Green, and of Professor George Gretton of
Edinburgh University, whose helpful advice and encouragement in many
matters has been much appreciated. I would also like to thank my various
colleagues and students at Napier and Edinburgh Universities for their
observations and support for my endeavours. Any errors and omissions
will of course remain my own responsibility.

Nicholas Grier
Napier University
August 2005

PREFACE TO THE FIRST EDITION

This book is written at a testing time for company law. Not only are there many proposals in the UK for a proposed new statute for companies, at present in draft form attached to the Government's White Paper, but there is an Enterprise Bill in the wings which may abolish, in the long run, much of the law and practice relating to receiverships, and a Corporate Responsibility Bill which aims to protect the interest of that amorphous group, stakeholders. At an international level, the recent scandals in the US, such as Enron, Worldcom, and Tyco, not to mention the problems affecting Andersens, have shown the need for company laws and accounting rules that encourage fair dealing, the straightforward presentation of accounts and proper corporate governance. In the long run, anything else is counter-productive. There is also a growing awareness that in the field of commerce, compliance with the spirit of the law, particularly when it comes to matters such as disclosure and transparency, as well as the need to act in good faith, is becoming more important.

At the same time, however, that flimsy rag, the corporate veil, still acts to divide the company from its managers and owners, and still permits directors and members to walk away from their companies' debts or negligence in the overall interest of encouraging commerce. The law, accordingly, has to face both ways: it has to encourage fair dealings but not deter business.

Where does Scots law fit into this? The actual Scottishness of company law in Scotland is minimal. The Scottish rules on insolvency are different to those in England, as are the rules on floating charges and receivers. But in most other respects the law is much the same. There are Scottish versions of, for example, Foss v Harbottle but it seems pointless in a book of this size to refer to them when any practitioners would nowadays refer to the better known English case. In writing this book I have tried to emphasise the commercial nature of company law and to present appropriate cases and legislation from either side of the border. In doing so, it is hard not to be aware of each country's deficiencies. The worst example of this is in the law relating to receiverships and charges. In Scotland, at least until Sharp v Thomson, the law on receivership was relatively clear albeit unsophisticated—but at least you knew what it was. A charge was either fixed or it wasn't, and unsecured creditors knew where they stood. Sharp v Thomson, of course, however humane in its judgement, has done the law no favours.

By contrast, English law, with its ceaseless quest for ever greater flexibility, particularly to benefit the secured creditor, has sometimes made it very difficult to know if a charge is fixed or not, if it ranks ahead of some other charge, or if it is even registrable—it is no wonder that the

Enterprise Bill, proposing the demise of administrative receivers, was drafted. The two national approaches could not be further apart, and yet what ultimately matters is that the law should be effective, easily comprehensible, cheap to operate and fair to all participants. Easy to say: hard to put into practice.

Suggested reading

At the end of most chapters I have included some suggested reading, but some chapters are about matters that are entirely procedural and clear cut and so there are very few relevant published articles about those matters. These matters are often well covered in company secretarial manuals, such as those published by CCH. The White Paper on company law is available from the BIS website (http://www.dti.gov.uk/whitepaper) and is well worth frequent reference. I have included many references to the most readable of the many books on company law, Davies' Gower's Principle of Modern Company Law. Although this is not necessarily the most technical of the books on company law, it has the great virtue of approachability. Readers requiring a more detailed approach should consult Palmer's Company Law, magisterially edited as regards Scottish matters by David Bennett W.S.; while for a day to day practical matters, Tolleys has much to recommend it.

The readership of this book

This book will, it is hoped, be of use to practitioners, accountants, businessmen, students, and anyone else involved in the practice or study of company law. It is not as detailed as a company secretary manual, nor does it cover subjects in quite such depth as the great authorities on company law referred to above. But it is to be hoped that it will provide an overview, a commentary and an explanation of most of the important practical and theoretical matters arising in company law.

Acknowledgements

I have been encouraged in the writing of this book by my editors, Neil McKinlay and Luisa Deas, by the always good advice of Josephine Bisacre of Napier University, by other colleagues and friends at the Schools of Law at both Napier University and the University of Edinburgh, and by the kind of forbearance of my wife, Jean, who put up with my many hours spent writing this book. Any errors and omissions are of course my own responsibility.

Dedication

This book is dedicated to the memory of my late uncle, Francis Martin, who trained as a lawyer in Edinburgh but practised for many years in the Far East. He was a respected and sensitive translator of modern Thai literature and a meticulous legal draftsman, with particular skills in trademark law and company law. This is but a small mark of my gratitude towards him for many kindnesses.

Nicholas Grier
Napier University
October 2002

CONTENTS

		Page
Preface		v
Preface to the 3rd edition		vii
Preface to the 2nd edition		ix
Preface to the 1st edition		xi
Table of Cases		xv
Table of Statutes		xxix
Table of Statutory Instruments		xlv

Chapter 1	Introduction	1
Chapter 2	The Corporate Veil	22
Chapter 3	Company Incorporation	43
Chapter 4	The Articles of Association	75
Chapter 5	Securities	91
Chapter 6	Capital Maintenance	118
Chapter 7	Dividends and Accounts	148
Chapter 8	Directors I: Appointment, Dismissal & Disqualification	175
Chapter 9	Directors II: Powers, Rights, Duties, Liabilities and other Obligations	197
Chapter 10	Company Secretary and Auditor	245
Chapter 11	Minority Protection, Derivative Claims and BIS Investigations	259
Chapter 12	Insider Dealing	288
Chapter 13	Meetings and Resolutions	302
Chapter 14	Takeovers and Mergers	315
Chapter 15	Charges and Receivership	330
Chapter 16	Administration and Company Voluntary Arrangements	355
Chapter 17	Winding Up	384

| *Index* | | 407 |

TABLE OF CASES

7722656 Canada Inc and Beck v Financial Conduct Authority [2013] EWCA Civ
1662 12–26
A and BC Chewing Gum, Re; sub nom. Topps Chewing Gum Inc v Coakley [1975] 1
W.L.R. 579; [1975] 1 All E.R. 1017 4–25
ACGE Investments v House of Fraser. *See* House of Fraser Plc v ACGE Invest-
ments Ltd
ADT Ltd v Binder Hamlyn [1996] B.C.C. 808, QBD 10–17, 10–18
AG (Manchester) Ltd (formerly Accident Group Ltd) (In Liquidation), Re [2008]
EWHC 64 (Ch); [2008] B.C.C. 497; [2008] 1 B.C.L.C. 321 .... 7–25, 7–27, 8–30
Aberdeen Railway Co v Blaikie (1854) 1 MacQ. 416, HL 9–16
Abouraya v Sigmund [2014] EWHC 277 (Ch) 11–35
Acatos and Hutcheson Plc v Watson [1995] B.C.C. 446; [1995] 1 B.C.L.C. 218, Ch
D 6–30
Adams v Cape Industries Plc [1990] Ch. 433; [1990] 2 W.L.R. 657; [1991] 1 All E.R.
929, CA (Civ Div) 2–15
Advocate General for Scotland v Reilly [2011] CSOH 141 2–09
Advocate (Lord) v Royal Bank of Scotland; sub nom. IRC v Royal Bank of Scotland
Ltd, 1977 S.C. 155; 1978 S.L.T. 38, IH (1 Div) 15–55
Aerators Ltd v Tollitt [1902] 2 Ch. 319, Ch D 3–17
Airbase Services International Ltd, Re [2008] EWHC 124 (Ch); [2008] 1 W.L.R.
1516; [2008] Bus. L.R. 1076; [2008] B.C.C. 213; [2008] 1 B.C.L.C. 436 16–34
Airlines Airspares Ltd v Handley Page [1970] Ch. 193; [1970] 2 W.L.R. 163; [1970] 1
All E.R. 29, Ch D 15–37
Allders Department Stores, Re [2005] EWHC 172; [2005] 2 All E.R. 122; (2005)
102(15) L.S.G. 34, Ch D 16–32
Allied Carpets Group Plc v Nethercott [2001] B.C.C. 81, QBD 7–27
Alpha Sim Communications Ltd v Caz Distribution Services Ltd [2014] EWHC 207
(Ch) 9–66
Amaron Ltd (No.1), Re. *See* Secretary of State for Trade and Industry v Lubrani
Anderson v Dickens [2008] CSOH 134; 2009 G.W.D. 1–15, OH 17–26
Anderson v Hogg, 2002 S.C. 190; 2002 S.L.T. 354; [2002] B.C.C. 923, IH 11–29,
11–30
Anglo-Austrian Printing and Publishing Union, Re [1895] 2 Ch. 891, Ch D 9–65,
15–41
Arab Bank Plc v Merchantile Holdings Ltd [1994] Ch. 71; [1994] 2 W.L.R. 307;
[1994] 1 B.C.L.C. 330, Ch D 6–22, 6–26
Archer Structures Ltd v Griffiths [2003] EWHC 957; [2004] B.C.C. 156; [2004] 1
B.C.L.C. 201, Ch D 3–13
Arctic Engineering (No.2), Re [1986] 1 W.L.R. 686; [1986] 2 All E.R. 346; [1986]
B.C.L.C. 253, Ch D 8–25
Armour v Thyssen Edelstahlwerke [1991] 1 A.C. 339; [1990] 3 W.L.R. 810; [1990] 3
All E.R. 481; 1990 S.L.T. 891; [1991] B.C.L.C. 28; 1990 B.C.C. 925, HL 15–09,
15–45, 17–33
Armour Hick Northern Ltd v Whitehouse; sub nom. Armour Hick Northern Ltd v
Armour Trust [1980] 1 W.L.R. 1520; [1980] 3 All E.R. 833, Ch D 6–25
Ash and Newman Ltd v Creative Devices Research Ltd [1991] B.C.L.C. 403 15–37
Ashbury Railway Carriage and Iron Co Ltd v Riche; sub nom. Riche v Ashbury
Railway Carriage and Iron Co Ltd (1875) L.R. 7 H.L. 653, HL 4–04
Association of Certified Public Accountants of Britain v Secretary of State for Trade
and Industry [1998] 1 W.L.R. 164; [1997] B.C.C. 736; [1997] 2 B.C.L.C. 307, Ch
D 3–15

Astec (BSR) Plc, Re [1999] B.C.C. 59; [1998] 2 B.C.L.C. 556, Ch D 4–20, 11–25, 11–27

Atlantic Computer Systems Plc, Re [1992] Ch. 505; [1992] 2 W.L.R. 367, CA (Civ Div) 16–24

Atlas Wright (Europe) Ltd v Wright. *See* Wright v Atlas Wright (Europe) Ltd

Aveling Barford Ltd v Perion Ltd [1989] B.C.L.C. 626; [1989] P.C.C. 370, Ch D .. 7–14, 7–26, 9–19, 9–28

BCCI v MORRIS. *See* Morris v Banque Arabe Internationale D'Investissement SA (No.2)

BNY Corporate Trustee Services Ltd v Eurosail [2013] UKSC 28 17–18

Baby Moon (UK), Re (1985) 1 B.C.C. 99 3–07

Bahia and San Francisco Railway Co Ltd, Re (1868) L.R. 3 Q.B. 584, QB .. 5–20, 5–28

Baillie Marshall Ltd (In Liquidation) v Avian Communications Ltd, 2002 S.L.T. 189; 2000 G.W.D. 27–1057, OH 17–26

Bain v The Rangers Football Club plc [2011] CSOH 158 9–32

Baird, Petitioner; Baird v Lees, 1924 S.C. 83; 1923 S.L.T. 749, IH (1 Div) 17–19

Bairstow v Queens Moat Houses Plc [2000] B.C.C. 1025; [2000] 1 B.C.L.C. 549, QBD 7–27, 9–63

Baku Consolidated Oilfields Ltd, Re [1993] B.C.C. 653; [1994] 2 B.C.L.C. 173, Ch D 5–20

Baltic Real Estate Ltd (No.2), Re [1992] B.C.C. 629; [1993] B.C.L.C. 498; [1993] B.C.L.C. 503, Ch D 11–20

Bamford v Bamford [1970] Ch. 212; [1969] 2 W.L.R. 1107; [1969] 1 All E.R. 969, CA (Civ Div) 9–29

Bank of Middle East v Sun Life Assurance Co of Canada (UK) Ltd [1983] 2 Lloyd's Rep. 9; [1983] Com. L.R. 187, HL 4–13

Banque Arabe Internationale d'Investissement SA v Morri. *See* Morris v Banque Arabe Internationale d'Investissement SA (No.2)

Barings Plc v Coopers and Lybrand [1997] B.C.C. 498; [1997] 1 B.C.L.C. 427, CA (Civ Div) 10–17, 10–18

Barings Plc (In Liquidation) v Coopers and Lybrand (No.5) [2002] EWHC 461; [2002] 2 B.C.L.C. 410, Ch D 8–23, 8–29

Barlow v Polly Peck International Finance Ltd. *See* Polly Peck International Plc (In Administration) (No.4), Re

Barron v Potter [1914] 1 Ch. 895; 83 L.J. Ch. 646 8–01

Barrow Haematite Steel Co, Re [1901] 2 Ch. 746, CA 6–07

Barton Manufacturing Co Ltd, Re [1998] B.C.C. 827; [1999] 1 B.C.L.C. 740, Ch D 17–29

Beattie v E and F Beattie Ltd [1938] Ch.708; [1938] 3 All E.R. 214, CA 9–18

Belmont Finance Corp v Williams Furniture Ltd (No.2) [1980] 1 All E.R. 393, CA (Civ Div) 6–25

Bhullar v Bhullar [2003] EWCA Civ 424; [2003] B.C.C. 711; [2003] 2 B.C.L.C. 241; [2003] W.T.L.R. 1397; (2003) 147 S.J.L.B. 421; [2003] N.P.C. 45 9–18

Biba Group Ltd v Biba Boutique [1990] R.P.C. 413, Ch D 3–17

Bird Precision Bellows Ltd, Re; sub nom. A Company (No.003420 of 1981) (No.2), Re [1986] Ch. 658; [1986] 2 W.L.R. 158, CA (Civ Div) 11–18

Bloomenthal v Ford; sub nom. Veuve Monnier et Ses Fils Ltd (In Liquidation), Re; Veuve Monnier et Ses Fils Ltd Ex p. Bloomenthal, Re [1897] A.C. 156, HL 5–20, 5–28

Blue Star Security Services (Scotland) Ltd, Petitioners, 1992 S.L.T. (Sh. Ct.) 80 ... 17–17

Bluebrook Ltd, Re [2009] EWCH 2114 14–16

Bonus Breaks Ltd, Re [1991] B.C.C. 546 .... 3–13, 9–70

Borland's Trustee v Steel Bros & Co Ltd [1901] 1 Ch. 279 .... 5–02, 5–03

Boston Deep Sea Fishing Co Ltd v Ansell (1888) 39 Ch. D. 339 9–22

Bottrill v Secretary of State for Trade and Industry. *See* Secretary of State for Trade and Industry v Bottrill

Brady v Brady [1989] A.C. 755; [1988] 2 W.L.R. 1308, HL; reversing (1987) 3 B.C.C. 535; [1988] B.C.L.C. 20, CA (Civ Div) 6–25, 6–27

Bratton Seymour Service Co v Oxborough [1992] B.C.C. 471; [1992] B.C.L.C. 693,
CA (Civ Div) 4–20
Breckland Group Holdings v London and Suffolk Properties (1988) 4 B.C.C. 542;
[1989] B.C.L.C. 100, Ch D 4–20
Brenfield Squash Racquets Club Ltd, Re [1996] 2 B.C.L.C. 184, Ch D 11–16
Brian D. Pierson (Contractors) Ltd, Re; sub nom. Penn v Pierson [1999] B.C.C. 26;
[2001] 1 B.C.L.C. 275, Ch D 9–64, 9–69
British and Commonwealth Holdings Ltd v Barclays Bank Plc [1996] 1 W.L.R. 1;
[1996] 1 All E.R. 381; [1996] 1 B.C.L.C. 1, CA (Civ Div) 6–18
British Telecommunications Plc v One in a Million Ltd [1999] 1 W.L.R. 903; [1998] 4
All E.R. 476, CA (Civ Div) 3–17
Brown v British Abrasive Wheel Co Ltd [1919] 1 Ch. 290, Ch D 4–22
Brumder v Motornet Services and Repairs Ltd [2013] 1 W.L.R. 2783; [2013] 3 All
E.R. 412 3–36
Bugle Press, Re; sub nom. Houses and Estates Ltd, Re; HC Treby's Application
[1961] Ch. 270; [1960] 3 W.L.R. 956, CA 14–11
Bushell v Faith [1970] A.C. 1099; [1970] 2 W.L.R. 272, HL 4–20, 5–09, 13–05

CADBURY SCHWEPPES PLC v HALIFAX SHARE DEALING LTD [2006] EWHC 1184 (Ch);
[2006] B.C.C. 707; [2007] 1 B.C.L.C. 497; (2006) 103(24) L.S.G. 29; (2006) 150
S.J.L.B. 739 5–19
Cameron v Glenmorangie Distillery Co Ltd (1896) 23 R. 1092 6–52
Caparo Industries Plc v Dickman Touche Ross [1990] 2 A.C. 605; [1990] 2 W.L.R.
358; [1990] 1 All E.R. 568, HL 10–17
Cargo Agency Ltd, Re [1992] B.C.C. 388; [1992] B.C.L.C. 686 8–32
Centros Ltd v Erhvervs-og Selskabsstyrelsen [2000] Ch. 446; [2000] 2 W.L.R. 1048;
[1999] ECR I–1459, ECJ 1–14
Chandler v Cape plc [2012] 1 W.L.R. 3111; [2012] 3 All E.R. 640 2–18
Charnley Davies (No.2), Re [1990] B.C.C. 605; [1990] B.C.L.C. 760, Ch D 16–28
Charterhouse Investment Trust v Tempest Diesels [1986] B.C.L.C. 1, Ch D 6–18
Chartmore, Re [1990] B.C.L.C. 673 8–32
Chaston v SWP Group Plc [2002] EWCA Civ 1999; [2003] B.C.C. 140; [2003] 1
B.C.L.C. 675, CA (Civ Div) 6–19, 6–26
City Equitable Fire Insurance Co Ltd, Re [1925] Ch. 407; [1924] All E.R. Rep. 485,
CA 9–15
Claybridge Shipping Co SA, Re [1997] 1 B.C.L.C. 572; [1981] Com. L.R. 107; *The
Times*, March 14, 1981, CA 17–17
Cobden Investments Ltd v RWM Langport Ltd [2008] EWHC 2810 (Ch) 9–11
Cohen v Selby; sub nom. Simmon Box (Diamonds) Ltd, Re [2002] B.C.C. 82; [2001] 1
B.C.L.C. 176, CA (Civ Div) 9–59
Commonwealth Oil & Gas Co. Ltd v Baxter (2010) S.C. 156 .... 9–11, 9–16
Company (No.005287 of 1985), Re [1986] 1 W.L.R. 281; [1986] 2 All E.R. 253, Ch
D 11–10, 11–21
Company (No.000789 of 1987) Ex p. Shooter, Re [1990] B.C.L.C. 384 11–16
Company (No.005009 of 1987) Ex p. Copp, Re (1988) 4 B.C.C. 424; [1989] B.C.L.C.
13, DC 8–12
Company (No.004803 of 1996), Re. *See* Secretary of State for Trade and Industry v
Taylor
Continental Tyre and Rubber Co (Great Britain) Ltd v Daimler Co Ltd. *See* Daimler
Co Ltd v Continental Tyre and Rubber Co (Great Britain) Ltd
Contex Drouzhba Ltd v Wiseman [2007] EWCA Civ 1201; [2008] B.C.C. 301; [2008]
1 B.C.L.C. 631; (2007) 157 N.L.J. 1695 9–53
Cook v Deeks [1916] 1 A.C. 554, PC 9–19, 9–28, 11–06
Copp v D'Jan. *See* D'Jan of London Ltd, Re
Corporate Development Partners LLC v E-Relationship Marketing Ltd [2007] All
E.R. 162 6–27
Cottrell v King; sub nom. TA King (Services) Ltd, Re [2004] EWHC 397; [2004]
B.C.C. 307, Ch D 4–20
Coulthard v Russell [1998] B.C.C. 359; [1998] 1 B.C.L.C. 143, CA (Civ Div) 10–18

Craiglaw Developments Ltd v Gordon Wilson & Co, 1997 S.C. 356; 1998 S.L.T.
  1046; 1997 S.C.L.R. 1157; [1998] B.C.C. 530; 1997 G.W.D. 21–1050; *The Times*,
  September 11, 1997, IH 17–26
Cramaso LLP v Viscount Reidhaven's Trustees, unreported, 11 February 2014,
  UKSC 2–18
Craven Insurance Co Ltd, Re [1968] 1 W.L.R. 675; [1968] 1 All E.R. 1140, Ch
  D 17–17
Cream Holdings Ltd v Davenport [2011] EWHC 1287 4–20
Creasey v Breachwood Motors Ltd [1992] B.C.C. 638; [1993] B.C.L.C. 480, QBD ... 2–10,
                                                                                     2–17
Cumana Ltd, Re [1986] B.C.L.C. 430 11–23
Cumbrian Newspapers Group Ltd v Cumberland and Westmorland Herald and
  Printing Co Ltd [1987] Ch. 1; [1986] 3 W.L.R. 26; [1986] 2 All E.R. 816; [1986]
  B.C.L.C. 286 4–21
Cunninghame v Walkingshaw Oil Co Ltd (1886) 14 R. 87 17–17

DHN Food Distributors Ltd v Tower Hamlets LBC [1976] 1 W.L.R. 852; [1976] 3
  All E.R. 462, CA (Civ Div) 2–15
DKG Contractors Ltd, Re [1990] B.C.C. 903, Ch D 9–64, 17–29
DKLL Solicitors v Revenue and Customs Commissioners [2007] EWHC 2067 (Ch);
  [2007] B.C.C. 908; [2008] 1 B.C.L.C. 112 16–39
Daimler Co Ltd v Continental Tyre and Rubber Co (Great Britain) Ltd; sub nom.
  Continental Tyre and Rubber Co (Great Britain) Ltd v Daimler Co Ltd [1916] 2
  A.C. 307, HL 2–14
Dawson International Plc v Coats Paton Plc [1989] 5 B.C.C. 405 9–14
Dawson Print Group Ltd, Re (1987) 3 B.C.C. 322; [1987] B.C.L.C. 601 8–29
Director General of Fair Trading v Pioneer Concrete (UK) Ltd; sub nom. Supply of
  Ready Mixed Concrete (No.2), Re [1995] 1 A.C. 456; [1994] 3 W.L.R. 1249,
  HL 2–33
D'Jan of London Ltd, Re; sub nom. Copp v D'Jan [1993] B.C.C. 646; [1994] 1
  B.C.L.C. 561, Ch D 7–27, 9–15, 9–59, 9–64
Dorchester Finance Co v Stebbing [1989] B.C.L.C. 498, Ch D 9–15
Duckwari Plc (No.1), Re; sub nom. Duckwari Plc v Offerventure Ltd (No.1);
  Company (No.0032314 of 1992), Re [1995] B.C.C. 89; [1997] 2 B.C.L.C. 713, CA
  (Civ Div) 9–33
Dunlop Pneumatic Tyre Co Ltd v Dunlop Motor Co Ltd [1907] A.C. 430; 1907 S.C.
  (H.L.) 15, HL 3–17
Dunstans Publishing Ltd, Re [2010] EWCH 3850 (Ch); [2012] B.C.C. 515 5–28
Duomatic Ltd, Re [1969] 2 Ch. 365 9–18

EDC v United Kingdom [1998] B.C.C. 370, ECHR 8–28
ESS Production Ltd v Sully [2005] EWCA Civ 554, CA (Civ Div) 3–13
Ebrahimi v Westbourne Galleries Ltd; sub nom. Westbourne Galleries, Re [1973]
  A.C. 360; [1972] 2 W.L.R. 1289; [1972] 2 All E.R. 492, HL 11–27, 17–19
Edwards v Halliwell [1950] 2 All E.R. 1064; [1950] W.N. 537, CA 11–06
Electra Private Equity Partners v KPMG Peat Marwick [2000] B.C.C. 368; [2001] 1
  B.C.L.C. 589, CA (Civ Div) 10–17
Eley v Positive Government Security Life Assurance Co Ltd (1875) 1 Ex. D. 20 4–20
Elgindata Ltd, Re [1991] B.C.L.C. 959 11–25
Enviroco v Farstad Supply A/S [2011] 1 W.L.R. 921 .... 3–39, 5–33
Equitable Life Assurance Society v Hyman [2002] 1 A.C. 408; [2000] 3 W.L.R. 529;
  [2000] 3 All E.R. 961, HL 4–20
Erlanger v New Sombrero Phosphate Co; sub nom. New Sombrero Phosphate Co v
  Erlanger (1878) 3 App. Cas. 1218, HL 3–57
Evans (C) & Son Ltd v Spritebrand Ltd [1983] Q.B. 310; [1985] 1 W.L.R. 317; [1985]
  2 All E.R. 415; (1985) 1 B.C.C. 99316; [1985] P.C.C. 109; [1985] F.S.R. 267;
  (1985) 82 L.S.G. 606; (1985) 129 S.J. 189, CA 9–53
Ewing v Buttercup Margarine Co Ltd [1917] 2 Ch. 1; (1917) 34 R.P.C. 232, CA ... 3–17
Exchange Banking Co (Flitcroft's Case), Re (1882) 21 Ch. D. 519, CA 7–27

FERGUSON V MACLENNAN SALMON CO LTD, 1990 S.L.T. 658; [1990] B.C.C. 702, IH (2 Div) 11–16

Fife Coal Co Ltd, Petitioners, 1948 S.C. 505; 1948 S.L.T. 421; 1948 S.L.T. (Notes) 39, IH 6–11

Fildes Bros, Re [1970] 1 W.L.R. 592; [1970] 1 All E.R. 923; (1970) 114 S.J. 301 ... 17–19

Firestone Tyre and Rubber Co Ltd v Lewellyn [1957] 1 W.L.R. 464; [1957] 1 All E.R. 561, HL; affirming [1956] 1 W.L.R. 352; [1956] 1 All E.R. 693, CA 2–17

First Energy (UK) Ltd v Hungarian International Bank Ltd [1993] 2 Lloyd's Rep. 194; [1993] B.C.C. 533, CA (Civ Div) 4–13

First Independent Factors & Finance Ltd v Churchill [2006] EWCA Civ 1623; [2007] Bus. L.R. 676; [2007] B.C.C. 45; [2007] 1 B.C.L.C. 293; [2007] B.P.I.R. 14; (2006) 150 S.J.L.B. 1606; *The Times*, January 11, 2007 3–13

Folkes Group Plc v Alexander [2002] EWHC 51; [2002] 2 B.C.L.C. 254, Ch D 4–20

Foss v Harbottle (1843) 2 Hare 461, Ch D 11–03, 11–04, 11–05, 11–30, 11–39

Fowlers (Aberdeen) Ltd, Petitioners,1928 S.C. 186; 1928 S.L.T. 126, IH (2 Div) 6–11

Franbar Holdings Ltd v Patel [2008] EWHC 1534 (Ch); [2008] B.C.C. 885; [2009] 1 B.C.L.C. 1; [2009] Bus. L.R. D14 11–32

Freeman Lockyer v Buckhurst Park Properties (Mangal) Ltd [1964] 2 Q.B. 480; [1964] 2 W.L.R. 618, CA 8–06, 8–11

Freevale Ltd v Metrostore Ltd [1984] Ch. 199; [1984] 2 W.L.R. 496; [1984] 1 All E.R. 495, Ch D 15–37

Fulham Football Ltd v Cabra Estates Plc [1992] B.C.C. 863; [1994] 1 B.C.L.C. 363, CA (Civ Div) 9–14

GALBRAITH V MERITO SHIPPING CO LTD, 1947 S.C. 446; 1947 S.L.T. 265, IH 17–19

Galoo Ltd v Bright Grahame Murray [1994] 1 W.L.R. 1360; [1995] 1 All E.R. 16; [1994] B.C.C. 319, CA (Civ Div) 9–66, 10–18

Gencor ACP Ltd v Dalby [2000] 2 B.C.L.C. 734; [2001] W.T.L.R. 825, Ch D ... 2–15, 9–13, 9–21, 9–30

German Date Coffee Co, Re (1882) 20 Ch.D. 169; 46 L.T. 327, CA 4–04, 17–19

Gibson Davies Ltd, Re [1995] B.C.C. 11 8–32

Gilford Motor Co Ltd v Horne (1933) Ch. 935 .... 2–13, 2–26, 9–53

Gillespie v Toondale Ltd [2005] CSIH 92; 2006 S.C. 304, IH 11–32

Glasgow City Council v Craig [2008] CSOH 171; 2009 S.L.T. 212; [2009] R.A. 61; 2009 G.W.D. 5–75, OH 3–13, 9–70

Glaxo Plc v Glaxowellcome Ltd [1996] F.S.R. 388, Ch D 3–18

Goldfarb v Higgins and Ors [2010] EWHC 613 (Ch) 17–29

Gray v Davidson, 1991 S.L.T. (Sh. Ct.) 61 9–64

Grayan Building Services Ltd (In Liquidation), Re [1995] Ch. 241; [1995] 3 W.L.R. 1; [1995] B.C.C. 554; [1995] 1 B.C.L.C. 276; (1995) 92(1) L.S.G. 36; (1994) 138 S.J.L.B. 227; *The Times*, November 24, 1994; *The Independent*, December 12, 1994 8–27

Greenhalgh v Arderne Cinemas [1951] Ch. 286; [1950] 2 All E.R. 1120, CA 4–22

Grosvenor Press Plc, Re [1985] 1 W.L.R. 980; [1985] P.C.C. 260, Ch D 6–07

Guidezone Ltd, Re; sub nom. Kaneria v Patel [2001] B.C.C. 692; [2000] 2 B.C.L.C. 321, Ch D 11–29

Guinness Plc v Ward and Saunders [1990] 2 A.C. 663; [1990] 2 W.L.R. 324; [1990] 1 All E.R. 652, HL 8–01

HLC ENVIRONMENTAL PROJECTS LTD, RE [2013] EWHC 2876 (Ch) 9–13

Haig & Co Ltd v Lord Advocate, 1976 S.L.T. (Notes) 16, OH 17–22

Halls v David. *See* Produce Marketing Consortium (In Liquidation) (No.1), Re

Harmer, Re [1959] 1 W.L.R. 62; [1958] 3 All E.R. 689, CA 11–22

Harold Holdsworth Co (Wakefield) Ltd v Caddies; sub nom. Caddies v Holdsworth and Co [1955] 1 W.L.R. 352; [1955] 1 All E.R. 725, HL 8–06

Hawkes Hill Publishing Co Ltd (In Liquidation), Re [2007] B.C.C. 937; [2007] B.P.I.R. 1305; (2007) 151 S.J.L.B. 743 9–68

Heald v Connor [1971] 1 W.L.R. 479; [1971] 2 All E.R. 1105, QBD 6–23

Hellas Telecommunications (Luxembourg) SA, Re [2011] B.C.C. 295 16–39

Hickman v Kent and Romney Marsh Sheepbreeders Assn [1915] 1 Ch. 881, Ch
  D 4–20
Hogg v Cramphorn [1967] Ch. 254; [1966] 3 W.L.R. 995, Ch D 9–10
Holders Investment Trust, Re [1971] 1 W.L.R. 583; [1971] 2 All E.R. 289, Ch D .. 6–11
Hollicourt (Contracts) Ltd (In Liquidation) v Bank of Ireland [2000] 1 W.L.R. 895;
  [2000] 2 All E.R. 45; [2000] Lloyd's Rep. Bank. 21; [2000] B.C.C. 237; [2000] 1
  B.C.L.C. 171; (1999) 96(48) L.S.G. 39; (2000) 144 S.J.L.B. 24 17–22
Hong Kong and China Gas Co Ltd v Glen [1914] 1 Ch. 527, Ch D 5–16
Hopkins v TL Dallas Group Ltd [2004] EWHC 1379, Ch D 4–15
Houldsworth v Yorkshire Woolcombers Association Ltd. *See* Illingworth v
  Houldsworth
House of Fraser Plc v ACGE Investments Ltd; sub nom. ACGE Investments v
  House of Fraser; House of Fraser, Re [1987] A.C. 387; [1987] 2 W.L.R. 1083,
  HL 6–08
Howard Smith Ltd v Ampol Petroleum Ltd [1974] A.C. 821; [1974] 2 W.L.R. 689, PC
  (Aus) 9–10
Hughes v Weiss [2012] EWHC 2363 (Ch). 9–13, 9–56, 11–35, 11–36
Hunt v Edge and Ellison Trs Ltd; sub nom. Torvale Group Ltd, Re [2000] B.C.C.
  626; [1999] 2 B.C.L.C. 605, Ch D 9–10
Hydrodam (Corby) Ltd (In Liquidation), Re. *See* Hydrodan (Corby) Ltd (In
  Liquidation), Re
Hydrodan (Corby) Ltd (In Liquidation), Re; sub nom. Hydrodam (Corby) Ltd (In
  Liquidation), Re [1994] B.C.C. 161; [1994] 2 B.C.L.C. 180, Ch
  D 8–12

IR v LION STEEL EQUIPMENT LTD, unreported, 20 July 2012, Manchester CC 2–32
Illingworth v Houldsworth; sub nom. Houldsworth v Yorkshire Woolcombers
  Association Ltd; Yorkshire Woolcombers Association Ltd, Re [1903] 2 Ch. 284,
  CA 15–06
Imperial Hotel (Aberdeen) Ltd v Vaux Breweries Ltd, 1978 S.C. 86; 1978 S.L.T. 113,
  OH 15–36
Independent Pension Trustee Ltd v Law Construction Co Ltd, 1996 G.W.D. 33–1956
  1997 S.L.T. 1105; *The Times*, November 1, 1996, OH 15–36
Industrial Development Consultants Ltd v Cooley [1972] 1 W.L.R. 443; [1972] 2 All
  E.R. 162 9–20
Inland Revenue Commissioners v Adams and Partners Ltd [1999] 2 B.C.L.C.
  730 16–42
Inland Revenue Commissioners v McEntaggart [2006] 1 B.C.L.C. 476 8–33
Iona Hotels Ltd (In Receivership), Petitioners, 1990 S.C. 330; 1991 S.L.T. 11; 1990
  S.C.L.R. 614 15–45
IRC v Royal Bank of Scotland Ltd. *See* Advocate (Lord) v Royal Bank of Scotland
Item Software (UK) Ltd v Fassihi [2004] B.C.C. 944 9–11
It's A Wrap (UK) Ltd (In Liquidation) v Gula [2006] EWCA Civ 544; [2006] 2
  B.C.L.C. 634 7–26

J & A CONSTRUCTION (SCOTLAND) LTD v WINDEX LTD [2013] CSOH 170; 2013 G.W.D.
  36-703 17–18
Jesner v Jarrad Properties Ltd, 1993 S.C. 34; [1993] B.C.L.C. 1032 17–19
John E Rae (Electrical Services) Linlithgow Ltd v Lord Advocate, 1994 S.L.T. 788,
  OH 17–26
Joint Liquidators of Automatic Oil Tools Ltd, Noters, 2001 S.L.T. 279; 2000 G.W.D.
  6–228, OH 17–31
Jones v Lipman [1962] 1 W.L.R. 832; [1962] 1 All E.R. 442, Ch D 2–13
Jupiter House Investments (Cambridge) Ltd, Re [1985] 1 W.L.R. 975; (1985) 82
  L.S.G. 2817, Ch D 6–07

KENSINGTON INTERNATIONAL LTD v CONGO [2005] EWHC 2684 (Comm); [2006] 2
  B.C.L.C. 296 2–23

Kingsley IT Consulting Ltd v McIntosh [2006] EWHC 1288 (Ch); [2006] B.C.C.
875 9–20
Kingston Cotton Mill (No.2), Re [1896] 2 Ch. 279, CA 10–16
Kinloch Damph Ltd v Nordvik Salmon Farms Ltd, 1999 S.L.T. 106; 1998 S.C.L.R.
496 15–44
Kuwait Asia Bank EC v National Mutual Life Nominees Ltd [1991] 1 A.C. 187;
[1990] 3 W.L.R. 297; [1990] B.C.L.C. 868 8–12

LCM Wealth Management Ltd, Re [2013] EWHC 3957 (Ch) 4–25
Lafferty Construction Ltd v McCombe, 1994 S.L.T. 858, OH 17–26
Laing v Gowans (1920) 10 S.L.T. 461, OH 17–07
Landauer & Co v WH Alexander & Co Ltd (No.1), 1919 S.C. 492; 1919 2 S.L.T.
2 17–17
Lander v Premier Pict Petroleum Ltd, 1997 S.L.T. 1361; [1998] B.C.C. 248, OH 9–47
Lee v Lee's Air Farming Ltd [1961] A.C. 12; [1960] 3 W.L.R. 758, PC   (NZ) 2–02
Lehman Bros. International (Europe) Ltd [2009] EWCA Civ 1161 14–16
Levy v Napier, 1962 S.C. 468 17–19
Lewis v Haas, 1971 S.L.T. 57; 1970 S.L.T. (Notes) 67, OH 17–19
Lexi Holdings Plc (In Administration) v Luqman [2009] EWCA Civ 117 8–08
Lindop v Stewart Noble and Sons Ltd, 1999 S.C.L.R. 889; [2000] B.C.C. 747, IH (2
Div) 15–38
Liquidator of West Mercia Safetywear Ltd v Dodd; sub nom. West Mercia Safety-
wear (In Liquidation) v Dodd (1988) 4 B.C.C. 30; [1988] B.C.L.C. 250, CA (Civ
Div) 9–13, 9–52
Liquidators of PAL SC Realisations 2007 Ltd v Inflexion Fund 2 Limited Partner-
ships [2010] EWHC 2850 (Ch); [2011] B.C.C. 93 16–34
Liquidators of Pattisons Ltd, Noters (Authority to Remunerate Committee) (1902) 4
F. 1010; (1902) 10 S.L.T. 211, IH 17–23
Lloyd v Popely [2000] B.C.C. 338; [2000] 1 B.C.L.C. 19 5–28
Lloyd Cheyham Co Ltd v Littlejohn Co [1987] B.C.L.C. 303; [1986] P.C.C. 389,
QBD 7–05
Lo–Line Electric Motors Ltd, Re; sub nom. Companies Act 1985, Re [1988] Ch. 477;
[1988] 3 W.L.R. 26, Ch D 8–29
Loch v John Blackwood Ltd [1924] A.C. 783; [1924] All E.R. Rep. 200, PC (WI) 17–19
Lonedale Ltd v Scottish Motor Auctions (Holdings) Ltd [2011] CSOH 4 14–03
London School of Electronics Ltd, Re [1986] Ch. 211; [1985] 3 W.L.R. 474, Ch
D 11–19
Lord Advocate v Royal Bank of Scotland, 1977 S.C. 155 15–45
Lubbe v Cape Plc (No.2) [2000] 1 W.L.R. 1545; [2000] 4 All E.R. 268, HL 2–35
Lundie Bros, Re [1965] 1 W.L.R. 1051; [1965] 2 All E.R. 692; (1965) 109 S.J. 470 ... 17–19

MB Group Plc, Re (1989) 5 B.C.C. 684; [1989] B.C.L.C. 672 6–12
Macaura v Northern Assurance Company Ltd [1925] A.C. 619, HL 2–03
McGregor Glazing Ltd v McGregor, 2013 G.W.D. 19-379 9–45
McGuinness v Black, 1990 S.C. 21; 1990 S.L.T. 156, OH 17–04
Mackie v Advocate (H.M.), 1994 J.C. 132; 1995 S.L.T. 110; 1994 S.C.C.R. 277 ... 12–23
Macleod v Alexander Sutherland Ltd, 1977 S.L.T. (Notes) 44, OH 15–37
McLuckie Bros Ltd v Newhouse Contracts Ltd, 1993 S.L.T. 641, OH 17–26
Macplant Services Ltd v Contract Lifting Services (Scotland) Ltd [2008] CSOH 158;
2009 S.C. 125; 2008 G.W.D. 38–577 .... 17–17, 17–18
Mactra Properties Ltd v Morshead Mansions Ltd [2008] EWHC 2843 (Ch); [2009]
B.C.C. 335; [2009] 1 B.C.L.C. 179 5–28
Madoff Securities International Limited (In Liquidation) v Stephen Raven [2013]
EWHC 3147 (Comm.) 9–11, 9–15
Manley, Petitioner, 1985 S.L.T. 42, OH 17–04
Maxwell v Department of Trade and Industry [1974] Q.B. 523; [1974] 2 W.L.R. 338,
CA (Civ Div) 11–46
Medforth v Blake [2000] Ch. 86; [1999] 3 W.L.R. 922; [1999] B.C.C. 771, CA (Civ
Div) 15–36

Meyer v Scottish Cooperative Wholesale Society Ltd [1959] A.C. 324; [1958] 3
W.L.R. 404; [1958] 3 All E.R. 66; 1958 S.C. (H.L.) 40; 1958 S.L.T. 241; (1958)
102 S.J. 617, HL 9–10
Micro Leisure Ltd v County Properties and Developments Ltd, 1999 S.L.T. 1428;
[2000] B.C.C. 872; *The Times*, January 12, 2000, OH 9–33
Migration Services International Ltd, Re [2000] B.C.C. 1095; [2000] 1 B.C.L.C. 666;
(1999) 96(47) L.S.G. 29; *The Times*, December 2, 1999; *The Independent*, Jan-
uary 17, 2000 8–27
Minton v Cavaney (1961) 56 C2d 576 2–06
Mission Capital Plc v Sinclair [2008] EWHC 1339 (Ch); [2008] B.C.C. 866 11–32,
11–34
Mitchell and Hobbs (UK) Ltd v Mill [1996] 2 B.C.L.C. 102, QBD 8–01, 8–06
Moorgate Metals Ltd, Re [1995] B.C.C. 143; [1995] 1 B.C.L.C. 503, Ch D 8–33
Morija Plc, Re; Kluk v Secretary of State for Business Enterprise and Regulatory
Reform [2007] EWHC 3055 (Ch); [2008] 2 B.C.L.C. 313 8–32
Morphites v Bernasconi [2001] 2 B.C.L.C. 1, Ch D 9–66
Morris v Bank of America [2000] 1 All E.R. 954; [2000] B.C.C. 1076; [2000] B.P.I.R.
83, CA (Civ Div) 9–66
Morris v Bank of India [2003] EWHC 1868; [2003] B.C.C. 735; [2004] 2 B.C.L.C.
236 9–66
Multinational Gas and Petrochemical Co Ltd v Multinational Gas and Petro-
chemical Services Ltd [1983] Ch. 258; [1983] 3 W.L.R. 492; [1983] 2 All E.R. 563,
CA (Civ Div) 9–52
Mumtaz Properties Ltd, Re [2011] EWCA Civ 610 8–11

NATIONAL WESTMINSTER BANK PLC v IRC [1995] 1 A.C. 119; [1994] 3 W.L.R. 159;
[1994] 2 B.C.L.C. 239, HL 5–10
Neptune (Vehicle Washing Equipment) Ltd v Fitzgerald [1996] Ch. 274; [1995] 3
W.L.R. 108; [1995] 3 All E.R. 811; [1995] B.C.C. 474, Ch D 3–36, 8–01, 9–48
Naxos v Project Management (Borders) Ltd & K.J. Salmon, 2012 CSOH 158 9–53
New Bullas Trading Ltd, Re [1994] B.C.C. 36; [1994] 1 B.C.L.C. 485, CA (Civ
Div) 15–07
New Cedos Engineering Co, Re [1994] 1 B.C.L.C. 797, Ch D 5–28
New Sombrero Phosphate Co v Erlanger. *See* Erlanger v New Sombrero Phosphate
Co
New Technology Systems Ltd, Re; sub nom. Official Receiver v Prior [1997] B.C.C.
810, CA (Civ Div) 8–28
Newhart Developments Ltd v Cooperative Commercial Bank Ltd [1978] Q.B. 814;
[1978] 2 W.L.R. 636, CA (Civ Div) 15–36
Nicoll v Steel Press (Supplies) Ltd. *See* Nicoll v Steelpress (Supplies) Ltd
Nicoll v Steelpress (Supplies) Ltd; sub nom: Nicoll v Steel Press (Supplies) Ltd, 1992
S.C. 119; 1993 S.L.T. 533, IH (Ex Div) 15–18, 17–26
Nordic Oil Services v Berman, 1993 S.L.T. 1168, OH 9–52
Norfolk House Plc (in receivership) v Repsol Petroleum Ltd, 1992 S.L.T. 235,
OH 15–42
North-West Transportation Co v Beatty (1887) 12 App.Cases 589, PC 9–28
Northern Engineering Industries, Re [1993] B.C.C. 267; [1993] B.C.L.C. 1151, Ch
D 6–08, 6–11
Norwest Holst Ltd v Secretary of State for Trade [1978] Ch. 201; [1978] 3 W.L.R. 73,
CA (Civ Div) 11–45
Nova Glaze Replacement Windows Ltd v Clark Thomson & Co, 2001 S.C. 815; 2001
G.W.D. 13–508, OH 17–26

OASIS MERCHANDISING SERVICES LTD, RE [1998] 1 Ch.170 .... 9–67, 17–29
O'Donnell v Shanahan [2009] EWCA Civ 751 11–29
Official Receiver v Brady [1999] B.C.C. 258, Ch D 8–24
Official Receiver v Prior. *See* New Technology Systems Ltd, Re
Official Receiver v Nixon. *See* Tasbian Ltd (No.3), Re
Official Receiver v Vass and Croshaw [1999] B.C.C. 516 8–10

Official Receiver v Wild [2012] EWHC 4279 (Ch) 8–30
O'Neill v Phillips; sub nom. Company (No.000709 of 1992), Re; Pectel Ltd, Re [1999]
    1 W.L.R. 1092; [1999] 2 All E.R. 961, HL 11–03, 11–27, 11–28
Ord v Belhaven Pubs Ltd [1998] B.C.C. 607; [1998] 2 B.C.L.C. 447, CA (Civ Div) 2–05

PANORAMA DEVELOPMENTS LTD v FIDELIS FURNISHING FABRICS LTD [1971] 2 Q.B. 711;
    [1971] 3 W.L.R. 440, CA (Civ Div) 10–03
Parks of Hamilton (Holdings) Ltd v Colin Campbell [2013] CSOH 67 14–02
Parlett v Guppys (Bridport) Ltd (No.1) [1996] B.C.C. 299; [1996] 2 B.C.L.C. 34, CA
    (Civ Div) 6–18
Patrick and Lyon Ltd, Re [1933] Ch. 786 17–29
Pender v Lushington (1877) L.R. 6 Ch. D. 70 11–06
Penn v Pierson. *See* Brian D. Pierson (Contractors) Ltd, Re
Percival v Wright [1902] 2 Ch. 421, Ch D 9–56
Pergamon Press Ltd, Re [1971] Ch. 388; [1970] 3 W.L.R. 792, CA (Civ Div) 11–46
Permacell Finesse Ltd (In Liquidation), Re [2007] EWHC 3233 (Ch); [2008] B.C.C.
    208 16–34
Pettie v Thomson Pettie Tube Products Ltd, 2001 S.L.T. 473 11–24
Pharmed Medicare Private Ltd v Univar Ltd [2002] EWCA 1569 4–12
Phillips v Fryer [2013] B.C.C. 176 11–35
Phoenicia Asset Management SAL v Steven Alexander [2010] CSOH 71 17–31
Phonogram Ltd v Lane [1982] Q.B. 938; [1981] 3 W.L.R. 736; [1981] 3 All E.R. 182;
    [1981] Com. L.R. 228; [1982] 3 C.M.L.R. 615; (1981) 125 S.J. 527, CA (Civ
    Div) 3–60
Plaut v Steiner (1989) 5 B.C.C. 352 6–25
Polly Peck International Plc (No.3), Re; sub nom. Secretary of State for Trade and
    Industry v Ellis (No.2) [1993] B.C.C. 890; [1994] 1 B.C.L.C. 574, Ch D 8–28
Popely v Planarrive Ltd [1997] 1 B.C.L.C. 8; *The Times*, April 24, 1996 5–28
Portland Place (Historic House) Ltd [2012] EWHC 4199 (Ch); [2013] W.T.L.R.
    1049 8–32
Pow Services Ltd v Clare [1995] 2 B.C.L.C. 435, Ch D 8–15
Power v Sharp Investments Ltd [1993] B.C.C. 609; [1994] 1 B.C.L.C. 111; *The Times*,
    June 3, 1993 .... 16–28, 17–26
Precis (521) Plc v William M Mercer Ltd [2004] EWHC 838 (Ch); 10–17
Precision Dippings Ltd v Precision Dippings Marketing Ltd [1986] Ch. 447; [1985] 3
    W.L.R. 812, CA (Civ Div) 7–26
Prest v Petrodel Resources Ltd [2013] UKSC 34; [2013] 3 W.L.R. 1 .... 2–12, 2–13, 2–15,
                                   2–25, 2–28, 2–29, 2–35, 9–53
Prestige Grindings Ltd, Re [2005] EWHC 3076; [2006] B.C.C. 421; [2006] 1 B.C.L.C.
    440; [2006] B.P.I.R. 844 8–3

Primlake Ltd (In Liquidation) v Matthews Associates [2006] EWHC 1227 (Ch);
    [2007] 1 B.C.L.C. 666 8–11
Produce Marketing Consortium (In Liquidation) (No.1), Re; sub nom. Halls v David
    [1989] 1 W.L.R. 745; [1989] 3 All E.R. 1; [1989] B.C.L.C. 513 9–64
Produce Marketing Consortium Ltd (No.2), Re [1989] B.C.L.C. 520 .... 9–69, 17–29
Prudential Assurance Co Ltd v PRG Powerhouse Ltd [2007] B.C.C. 500 16–42
Purewal Enterprises Ltd, Petitioner [2008] CSOH 127; 2008 G.W.D. 37–555, OH ... 17–22

QUAYLE MUNRO LTD, PETRS, 1992 S.C. 24; 1993 S.L.T. 723; [1994] 1 B.C.L.C. 410, IH
    (1 Div) 6–07
Quin and Axtens Ltd v Salmon; sub nom. Salmon v Quin and Axtens Ltd [1909] A.C.
    442, HL 4–20, 11–06

R. v BROCKLEY [1994] B.C.C. 131; [1994] 1 B.C.L.C. 606, CA (Crim Div) 8–26
R. v Cole [1998] B.C.C. 87; [1998] 2 B.C.L.C. 234, CA (Crim Div) 3–13, 9–70
R. v Creggy (Stuart) [2008] EWCA Crim 394; [2008] Bus. L.R. 1556; [2008] 3 All E.R.
    91; [2008] B.C.C. 323; [2008] 1 B.C.L.C. 625; [2008] Lloyd's Rep. F.C. 385 8–25

R. v Georgiou; sub nom. R. v Hammer (1988) 4 B.C.C. 472; (1988) 87 Cr. App. R. 207 8–25

R. v Goodman [1993] 2 All E.R. 789; [1992] B.C.C. 625; [1994] 1 B.C.L.C. 349, CA (Crim Div) 8–25, 12–06

R. v Hammer. *See* R. v Georgiou

R. v Holyoak, Hill and Morl, Unreported 12–21

R. v JMW Farms Ltd, 2011 NICC 17 2–32

R. v McCredie [2000] B.C.C. 617; [2000] 2 B.C.L.C. 438, CA (Crim Div) 3–13

R. v Omar (Bassam) [2004] EWCA Crim 2320; [2005] 1 Cr. App. R. (S.) 86 2–22

R. v Panel on Take-overs and Mergers Ex p. Al-Fayed [1992] B.C.C. 524; [1992] B.C.L.C. 938, CA (Civ Div) 14–07

R. v Panel on Take-overs and Mergers Ex p. Datafin [1987] Q.B. 815; [1987] 2 W.L.R. 699, CA (Civ Div) 14–07

R. v Panel on Take-overs and Mergers Ex p. Guinness Plc [1990] 1 Q.B. 146; [1989] 2 W.L.R. 863, CA (Civ Div) 14–07

R. v Peter Eaton and Cotswold Geotechnical Holdings Limited [2011] EWCA Crim 1337; [2012] 1 Cr. App. R. (S.) 26 2–32

R. v McQuoid [2009] EWCA Crim 1301 12–06

R. v Randhawa (Charnjit); Randhawa (Jusvir Kaur) [2008] EWCA Crim 2599 8–28

R. v Registrar of Companies Ex p. Att-Gen [1991] B.C.L.C. 476, DC 3–07, 11–20

R. v Secretary of State for Trade and Industry Ex p. McCormick [1998] B.C.C. 379; [1998] C.O.D. 160, CA (Civ Div) 11–46

RA Noble & Sons (Clothing) Ltd, Re [1983] B.C.L.C. 273 11–13

R Gaffney and Son Ltd v Davidson, 1996 S.L.T. (Sh.Ct) 36 .... 15–18, 17–26

Rainham Chemical Works Ltd v Belvedere Fish Guano Co. Ltd [1921] 2 A.C. 645, HL 2–17

Ransomes Plc, Re; sub nom. Ransomes Plc v Winpar Holdings Ltd; Winpar Holdings Ltd v Ransomes Plc [2000] B.C.C. 455; [1999] 2 B.C.L.C. 591, CA (Civ Div) 6–11

Ratners Group Plc, Re (1988) 4 B.C.C. 293; [1988] B.C.L.C. 685, DC 6–09

Red Label Fashions Ltd, Re [1999] B.C.L.C. 308, Ch D 8–11

Redmount Properties Ltd, unreported December 11, 2009 Edinburgh Sheriff Court 17–25

Regal Cinemas (Hastings) Ltd v Gulliver [1967] 2 A.C. 134; [1942] 1 All E.R. 378, HL 9–17

Regentcrest Ltd v Cohen [2002] 2 B.C.L.C. 80 9–11

Revenue and Customs Commissioners v Holland [2010] 1 W.L.R. 2793 8–11

Rhondda Waste Disposal Ltd (In Administration), Re [2001] Ch. 57; [2000] 3 W.L.R. 1304; [2000] B.C.C. 653; [2000] Env. L.R. 600; [2000] 1 E.G.L.R. 113; [2000] E.G. 25 (C.S.); (2000) 150 N.L.J. 227; Times, March 2, 2000; *The Independent*, April 10, 2000 16–24

Riche v Ashbury Railway Carriage and Iron Co Ltd. *See* Ashbury Railway Carriage and Iron Co Ltd v Riche

Ricketts v Ad Valorem Factors Ltd [2003] EWCA Civ 1706; [2004] 1 All E.R. 894; [2004] B.C.C. 164, CA (Civ Div) 3–13, 9–70

Rod Gunner Organisation Ltd, Re [2004] EWHC 316 (Ch); [2004] B.C.C. 684; [2004] 2 B.C.L.C. 110 9–68

Rolled Steel Products (Holdings) Ltd v British Steel Corp [1986] Ch. 246; [1985] 2 W.L.R. 908, CA (Civ Div) 4–12

Romer-Ormiston v Claygreen Ltd [2005] EWHC 2032; [2006] B.C.C. 440; [2006] 1 B.C.L.C. 715; (2005) 102(38) L.S.G. 28 5–28

Royal Bank of Scotland v Bannerman Johnstone Maclay, 2003 S.C. 125; 2003 S.L.T. 181; [2005] B.C.C. 235; [2003] P.N.L.R. 6; 2002 G.W.D. 26-917, OH 10–17

Royal Bank of Scotland v Sandstone Properties Ltd [1998] 2 B.C.L.C. 429; *The Times*, March 12, 1998 .... 5–20, 5–28

Royal British Bank v Turquand (1856) 6 El. Bl. 327; 5 El. Bl. 248 4–14

Royal Scottish Assurance plc [2011] CSOH 2 6–11

Russell v Northern Bank Development Corp. Ltd [1992] 1 W.L.R. 588; [1992] 3 All E.R. 161, HL (NI) 4–25

SALOMON v A SALOMON CO LTD (1887) A.C. 22 2–01
Saltdean Estate Co Ltd, Re [1968] 1 W.L.R. 1844; [1968] 3 All E.R. 829, Ch D 6–10
Sasea Finance Ltd (In Liquidation) v KPMG [2000] 1 All E.R. 676; [2000] B.C.C.
    989; [2000] 1 B.C.L.C. 236, CA (Civ Div) 10–18
Saunders v United Kingdom [1997] B.C.C. 872; [1998] 1 B.C.L.C. 362; (1997) 23
    E.H.R.R. 313, ECHR 11–46
Saul Harrison Sons Plc, Re [1994] B.C.L.C. 475 .... 11–26, 11–27
Scottish Exhibition Centre Ltd v Mirestop Ltd (in Administration), 1993 S.L.T.
    1034; [1993] B.C.C. 529 16–24
Scott's Trustees v Scott (1887) 14 R. 1043 17–32
Scottish Coal Company (in provisional liquidation); sub nom. Scottish Environment
    Protection Agency v Joint Liquidators of the Scottish Coal Co Ltd, 2014 S.L.T.
    259; [2013] CSIH 108 17–24
Secretary of State for Business, Innovation and Skills v Bloch [2013] CSOH 57; 2013
    G.W.D. 13-275 8–31
Secretary of State for Business Innovation and Skills v Din [2013] CSOH 98; 2013
    G.W.D. 22-429 8–31
Secretary of State for Business Enterprise and Regulatory Reform v Sullman [2008]
    EWHC 3179 (Ch); [2009] 1 B.C.L.C. 397 8–28
Secretary of State for Trade and Industry v Baker (No.6); sub nom. Barings Plc
    (No.6), Re [2001] B.C.C. 273; [2000] 1 B.C.L.C. 523, CA (Civ Div); affirming
    [1999] 1 B.C.L.C. 433, Ch D 8–30
Secretary of State for Trade and Industry v Bairstow [2004] All E.R. (D) 333 (Jul)
    Ch. D. 8–23
Secretary of State for Trade and Industry v Creegan [2002] 1 B.C.L.C. 99 8–30
Secretary of State for Trade and Industry v Deverell [2001] Ch. 340; [2000] 2 W.L.R.
    907; [2000] 2 All E.R. 365; [2000] B.C.C. 1057; [2000] 2 B.C.L.C. 133, CA (Civ
    Div) 8–12, 8–24
Secretary of State for Trade and Industry v Forsyth; Helene Plc (In Liquidation), Re;
    Barry Artist Ltd; Re Secretary of State for Trade and Industry v Forsythe [2000]
    2 B.C.L.C. 249 8–25
Secretary of State for Trade and Industry v Gerard [2007] CSIH 85; 2008 S.C. 409;
    2007 G.W.D. 38–662, IH 8–30
Secretary of State for Trade and Industry v Griffiths (No.2). *See* Westmid Packaging
    Services Ltd (No.2), Re
Secretary of State for Trade and Industry v Hall [2006] EWHC 1995 (Ch); [2009]
    B.C.C. 190; *The Times*, August 2, 2006 8–24
Secretary of State for Trade and Industry v Hasta International Ltd, 1998 S.L.T. 73,
    OH 17–21
Secretary of State for Trade and Industry v Hollier [2006] EWHC 1804 (Ch); [2007]
    Bus. L.R. 352; [2007] B.C.C. 11 8–11
Secretary of State for Trade and Industry v Jones [1999] B.C.C. 336, Ch D 8–11
Secretary of State for Trade and Industry v Jonkler [2006] EWHC 135 (Ch); [2006] 1
    W.L.R. 3433; [2006] 2 All E.R. 902; [2006] B.C.C. 307; [2006] 2 B.C.L.C. 239;
    (2006) 156 N.L.J. 273; *The Times*, March 3, 2006 8–24
Secretary of State for Trade and Industry v Laing [1996] 2 B.C.L.C. 324, Ch D 8–30
Secretary of State for Trade and Industry v Langridge [1991] Ch. 402; [1991] 2
    W.L.R. 1343; [1991] 3 All E.R. 591; [1991] B.C.C. 148; [1991] B.C.L.C. 543; *The
    Times*, March 4, 1991; *The Independent*, March 11, 1991; *The Financial Times*,
    February 22, 1991 8–28
Secretary of State for Trade and Industry v Lovat, 1996 S.C. 32; 1997 S.L.T. 124;
    1996 S.C.L.R. 195 8–28
Secretary of State for Trade and Industry v Lubrani; sub nom. Amaron Ltd (No.1),
    Re [1997] 2 B.C.L.C. 115, Ch D 8–30
Secretary of State for Trade and Industry v McTighe (No.2) [1997] B.C.C.
    224 8–31
Secretary of State for Trade and Industry v Reza [2013] CSOH 86 8–30
Secretary of State for Trade and Industry v Rosenfield [1999] B.C.C. 413, Ch D ... 8–32

Secretary of State for Trade and Industry v Taylor; sub nom. CS Holidays Ltd, Re;
  Company (No.004803 of 1996), Re [1997] 1 W.L.R. 407; [1997] 1 B.C.L.C. 341,
  Ch D 8–34
Sevenoaks Stationers (Retail) Ltd, Re [1991] Ch. 164; [1990] 3 W.L.R. 1165; [1991]
  B.C.L.C. 325, CA (Civ Div) 8–31
Shanks v Central RC, 1987 S.L.T. 140, OH 15–36
Sharma v Sharma [2013] EWCA Civ 1287; [2014] W.T.L.R. 111 9–18
Sharp v Thomson; sub nom. Sharp v Woolwich Building Society, 1997 S.C. (H.L.)
  66; 1997 S.L.T. 636; 1997 S.C.L.R. 328; [1998] B.C.C. 115; [1997] 1 B.C.L.C.
  603, HL 1–29, 15–09, 15–47
Sheffield Corp. v Barclay [1905] A.C. 392, HL 5–20, 5–28
Shuttleworth v Cox Bros Co Ltd [1927] 2 K.B. 9, CA 4–20
Simmon Box (Diamonds) Ltd, Re. *See* Cohen v Selby
Site Preparations Ltd v Buchan Development Co Ltd, 1983 S.L.T. 317, OH 17–22
Smith v Henniker–Major and Co [2002] B.C.C. 544, Ch D 4–14
Smith and Fawcett, Re [1942] Ch. 304, CA 5–28
Smith, Stone and Knight Ltd v Birmingham Corp [1939] 4 All E.R. 116, KBD 2–17
Snelling v John G Snelling Ltd [1973] Q.B. 87; [1972] 2 W.L.R. 588; [1972] 1 All E.R.
  79, QBD 4–25
Southard and Co Ltd, Re [1979] 1 W.L.R. 1198; [1979] 3 All E.R. 556, CA (Civ
  Div) 2–16, 2–35
Southern Foundries (1926) Ltd v Shirlaw [1940] A.C. 701 4–20
Spectrum Plus Ltd (in liquidation), Re. [2005] 3 W.L.R. 58 15–07
Speirs (J) & Co v Central Building Co Ltd, 1911 S.C. 330; 1911 1 S.L.T. 14, IH (2
  Div) 17–17
Standard Chartered Bank v Pakistan National Shipping Corporation (No.2) [2002]
  UKHL 43; [2003] 1 A.C. 959; [2002] 3 W.L.R. 1547, HL 2–24, 9–53
Standard Chartered Bank v Walker [1982] 1 W.L.R. 1410; [1982] 3 All E.R. 938, CA
  (Civ Div) 15–36, 15–41
Stephen (Robert) Holdings, Re [1968] 1 W.L.R. 522; [1968] 1 All E.R. 195 (Note);
  (1968) 112 S.J. 67 6–11
Stephen and Hill, joint administrators of QMD Hotels Ltd [2010] CSOH 168 16–34
Stuart Eves (in liquidation) v Smiths Gore, 1993 S.L.T. 1274, OH 17–26
Sukhpaul Singh v Satpaul Singh, Singh Bros Contractors (Northwest) Limited [2014]
  EWCA Civ 103 .... 11–34, 11–35
Supply of Ready Mixed Concrete (No.2), Re. *See* Director General of Fair Trading v
  Pioneer Concrete (UK) Ltd

T AND D AUTOMATIVE LTD, RE. *See* T and D Industries Plc, Re
T and D Industries Plc, Re; sub nom. T and D Automative Ltd, Re [2000] 1 W.L.R.
  646; [2000] 1 All E.R. 333; [2000] B.C.C. 956; 16–28
Tasbian Ltd (No.3), Re; sub nom. Official Receiver v Nixon [1992] B.C.C. 358; [1993]
  B.C.L.C. 297, CA (Civ Div) 8–12
Thomas Edward Brinsmead and Sons Ltd, Re [1897] 1 Ch. 45, Ch D 17–19
Thompson v Goblin Hill Hotels Ltd [2011] UKPC 8; [2011] 1 B.C. L. C. 587 4–20
Thompson Clive Investment Plc Unreported, June 8, 2005 6–11
Thundercrest Ltd, Re [1994] B.C.C. 855 5–19
Tottenham Hotspur Plc v Edennote Plc [1994] B.C.C. 681; [1995] 1 B.C.L.C. 65, Ch
  D 11–24
Towers v Premier Waste Management Ltd [2011] EWCA Civ. 923 9–18
Trustor AB v Smallbone (No.3) [2001] 1 W.L.R. 1177; [2002] B.C.C. 795; [2001] 3 All
  E.R. 987, Ch D 2–26, 9–53
Tudor Grange Holdings Ltd v Citibank NA [1992] Ch. 53; [1991] 3 W.L.R. 750;
  [1991] B.C.L.C. 1009, Ch D 15–36

UBERSEERING BV v NORDIC CONSTRUCTION COMPANY BAUMANAGEMENT GMBH [2005]
  1 W.L.R. 315; [2002] E.C.R. I–9919, ECJ 1–14
Uniq plc, Re [2011] EWHC 749 (Ch); [2012] 1 B.C.L.C. 783 6–26

United Dominions Trust Ltd, Noters (Company: Winding up), 1977 S.L.T. (Notes)
56, OH 17–22
Ultraframe (UK) Ltd v Fielding [2005] EWHC 1638 (Ch); [2006] F.S.R. 17; [2007]
W.T.L.R. 835; (2005) 28(9) I.P.D. 28069 .... 8–12, 9–09

VTB Capital plc v Nutritek International Corpn. [2013] UKSC 5; [2013] 2
W.L.R. 398 2–19
Vale Sewing Machines v Robb, 1997 S.C.L.R. 797 17–33
Veuve Monnier et Ses Fils Ltd (In Liquidation), Re. *See Bloomenthal v Ford*
Weavering Capital (UK) Limited (In Liquidation) v Peterson [2012] EWHC 1480
(Ch) 9–14
Weir v Rees, 1991 S.L.T. 345, OH 11–41
West Coast Capital (LIOS) Ltd v Dobbies plc [2008] CSOH 72 .... 9–10, 9–18
Westmid Packing Services Ltd (No.2), Re; sub nom. Secretary of State for Trade and
Industry v Griffiths (No.2) [1998] 2 All E.R. 124; [1998] B.C.C. 836; [1998] 2
B.C.L.C. 646, CA (Civ Div) 8–29, 8–30, 9–14
White & Osmond (Parkstone) Ltd, Unreported, June 30, 1960 9–68
Williams v Natural Life Health Foods Ltd [1998] 1 W.L.R. 830; [1998] 2 All E.R.
577, HL 2–24, 9–52
Wilson v Inverness Retail & Business Park Ltd, 2003 S.L.T. 301; 2003 G.W.D. 3–60,
OH 11–30
Wilson v Wilson, 1999 S.L.T. 249; 1998 S.C.L.R. 1103, OH 2–21
Wilson and Clyde Coal Co Ltd v Scottish Insurance Corp Ltd, 1949 S.C. (H.L.)
90 6–08
Winkworth v Edward Baron Development Co Ltd [1986] 1 W.L.R. 1512; [1987] 1 All
E.R. 114; (1987) 3 B.C.C. 4; [1987] B.C.L.C. 193; [1987] 1 F.L.R. 525; [1987] 1
F.T.L.R. 176; (1987) 53 P. & C.R. 378; [1987] Fam. Law 166; (1987) 84 L.S.G.
340; (1986) 130 S.J. 954, HL 9–52
Wirecard Bank AG v Scott [2010] EWHC 451 (QB) 8–33
Wishart v Castlecroft Securities Ltd, 2010 S.C. 16; 2009 S.L.T. 812; [2010] B.C.C.
161 .... 11–31, 11–32, 11–35, 11–36
Woolfson v Glasgow Corp. *See* Woolfson v Strathclyde RC
Woolfson v Strathclyde RC; sub nom. Woolfson v Glasgow Corp, 1978 S.C. (H.L.)
90; 1978 S.L.T. 159, HL 2–15
Wragg Ltd, Re [1897] 1 Ch. 795, CA 5–16
Wright, Layman and Umney v Wright (1949) 66 R.P.C. 149, CA 3–17

Yenidje Tobacco Co Ltd [1935] Ch. 693 17–19
Yorkshire Woolcombers Association Ltd, Re. *See* Illingworth v Houldsworth
Yukong Line Ltd of Korea v Rendsburg Investments Corp of Liberia [1998] 1
W.L.R. 294; [1998] 4 All E.R. 82, QBD (Comm) 2–19

TABLE OF STATUTES

1720 Bubble Act (6 Geo. 1) 1–02
1844 Joint Stock Companies Act
(7 & 8 Vict. c.110) 1–02
1856 Joint Stock Companies Act
(19 & 20 Vict. c.47) 1–02
1868 Title to Land
(Consolidation)
(Scotland) Act (31 & 32
Vict. c.101)
s.25 15–47
1890 Partnership Act (53 & 54
Vict. c.39) 1–18
s.1 1–18
s.4(2) 1–19
s.9 .... 1–07, 1–19
1907 Limited Partnership Act (7
Edw. 7, c.24) 1–24
1928 Agricultural Credits Act (18
& 19 Geo. 5, c.43) 15–06
1939 Trading with the Enemy Act
(2 & 3 Geo. 6, c.89) 2–14
1948 Companies Act (11 & 12
Geo. 6, c.38)
s.210 11–03
1961 Companies (Floating
Charges) (Scotland)
Act (9 & 10 Eliz. 2,
c.46) 15–08
1972 Companies (Floating
Charges and Receivers)
(Scotland) Act
(c.67) 15–08
European Communities Act
(c.68)
s.9 4–05
1973 Matrimonial Proceedings
Act (c.45) 2–25
Prescription and Limitation
(Scotland) Act (c.52)
s.6 7–25
1976 Damages (Scotland) Act
(c.13) 17–37
Fatal Accidents Act (c.30) 17–37
Race Relations Act (c.74) ... 3–10
1979 Sale of Goods Act
s.9 15–44
1980 Companies Act (c.22) 11–03
Limitation Act (c.58)
s.5 7–26
1985 Companies Act (c.6) 1–12,
3–02, 6–01, 9–32, 11–03

Pt 14 .... 9–58, 11–42
s.153 6–25
s.226(2) 7–29
s.309 9–06
s.311 9–03
s.330 8–05
s.341(2)(c) 11–43
s.421(2)(b) 11–43
s.431(2)(a) 11–43, 11–48
(b) 11–48
(3) 11–43
(4) 11–43
s.432(1) 11–43, 11–45
(2) 11–44, 11–45
(2A) 11–44
(3) 11–45
s.434 9–58
(1) 11–45
(2) 11–45
(3) 11–46
(5A) 11–46
(5B) 11–46
s.436 9–58
s.437(2) 11–47
s.438 11–47
s.441 11–47
s.442 11–48
(3) 11–48
(3A) 11–48
s.444 11–48
s.447 11–50
(8) 11–50
(8A) 11–50
(8B) 11–50
s.448 11–50
s.452(1) 11–45
(1A) 11–46
ss.454–457 11–49
s.458 9–66
s.459 .... 11–03, 11–17, 11–19,
11–20, 11–23, 11–24, 11–25,
11–26, 11–29, 11–30, 11–39
s.460 11–47
s.462(5) 15–09
s.464(4)(a) 15–07
(b) 15–17
(c) 15–17
(5) 15–17
s.486(1) 15–04
Bankruptcy (Scotland) Act
(c.66)

	s.22(9)	17–31
	Sch.1	17–31
1986	Insolvency Act (c.45)	1–09, 2–07, 16–02
	Pt 2	7–32, 16–02
	ss.1–7	6–21
	s.1	8–03
	(2)	16–42
	(3)	16–42
	s.1A	16–43
	s.2(2)	16–42
	(3)	16–42
	s.3(1)	16–42
	(2)	16–42
	s.4(3)	16–42
	(4)	16–42
	(5)	16–42
	s.4A	16–42
	s.5(2)	16–42
	(3)	16–42
	s.6	16–42
	s.7	16–42
	(3)	16–42
	(4)(b)	16–42
	s.8(3)	16–03
	(4)	16–02, 16–03
	s.9	16–03
	(2)	16–04
	(4)	16–04
	s.10	16–04
	s.11	16–05
	s.12	16–05
	s.14	16–05
	(1)	17–20
	s.15	16–05
	s.17(2)	16–05
	(3)	16–05
	s.19(4)	16–06
	(6)	16–06
	s.22	9–58, 16–06
	s.23	16–05
	(1)	16–05
	(2)	16–05
	s.24(2)	16–05
	(4)	16–05
	(5)	16–05
	s.27	16–05
	s.29(2)(a)	15–06
	s.41	8–25
	s.42(1)	17–20
	ss.50–71	15–23
	s.51	15–42
	s.52	15–33
	(1)(a)–(d)	15–33
	(2)	15–34
	s.53(1)	15–34
	(5)	15–34
	(6)(a)–(b)	15–34
	(7)	15–34
	s.55(3)(a)	15–45
	s.55(2)	17–20
	s.57(1)	15–37
	(1A)	15–38
	(2)	15–37, 15–38
	(2A)	15–38
	(3)	15–37, 15–38
	(4)	15–37
	(5)	15–38
	s.59	15–35
	s.60	15–40
	(2)	15–40
	s.61(1)	15–45
	(1A)	15–45
	(1B)	15–45
	ss.65(1)(a)–(b)	15–34
	s.66	9–58, 15–35, 15–41
	s.67	15–35, 15–41
	(2)	15–35
	(4)	15–35
	(5)	15–35
	s.68	15–35
	ss.72B–72GA	15–23, 16–04, 16–16
	ss.72B–724A	16–07
	s.72B(1)(a)	15–25
	s.72D	15–27
	s.72DA	15–28
	s.72E	15–29
	s.72F	15–30
	s.72G	15–31
	s.72GA	15–32
	s.74(2)(f)	7–25
	s.75	17–20
	s.76	17–20
	(1)(a)	6–48
	(2)(a)–(b)	17–20
	s.77	17–20
	s.79(1)	17–20
	ss.84(1)(a)–(b)	17–07
	(2A)	17–07
	(2B)	17–07
	(3)	17–07
	s.85(1)	17–07
	s.86	17–07
	s.87(1)	17–07
	(2)	17–07
	s.88	17–07
	s.89	8–03
	(1)	17–09
	(2)(a)	17–09
	(4)	17–09
	(5)	17–09
	s.90	17–09
	s.91(1)	17–10
	(2)	17–10
	s.94(1)	17–10
	(3)	17–10
	s.98	17–11

s.99(1) 17–11
    (2) 17–11
s.100(1) 17–12
    (2) 17–12
    (3) 17–12
s.101(1) 17–12
    (2) 17–12
    (3) 17–12
s.103 17–12
s.105 17–13
s.106 16–35
s.107 17–09
s.109 .... 17–07, 17–12
    (1) 17–10
s.110 .... 6–21, 14–14, 16–41
    (1) 17–14
    (3)(a)–(b) 17–14
s.111 17–14
s.114 17–07
s.115 .... 17–07, 17–31
s.120 17–15
s.122(1)(a)–(d) 17–16
    (a) 17–16
    (f) 17–16, 17–21
    (fa) 17–16
    (g) 8–20, 11–08, 11–40,
                          17–16, 17–21
    (2) 17–16
s.123 15–20
    (1) 17–17
        (a)–(c) 17–17
        (e) 17–17
        (f) 17–17
    (2) 17–17
s.124(1) 17–20
    (2)(a)–(b) 17–21
    (3) 17–21
    (4)(a) 17–20
s.124A 11–47, 16–24, 16–38,
                          17–21
    (1) 17–20
s.125(1) 17–17, 17–22
    (2) 8–20, 11–40, 17–19,
                          17–22
s.126 17–22
s.127 17–22
s.129(1) 17–22
    (2) 17–22
s.130(1) 17–22
    (2) 17–22
s.131 17–23
s.133 17–23
s.134 17–23
s.135 17–22
s.138 17–23
s.139 17–23
s.140 17–23
s.142 17–23
s.144 17–24

s.145 17–24
s.148 17–24
s.149 17–24
s.157 9–58
s.165 .... 9–62, 9–66, 17–10,
                          17–13
    (2) 17–29
s.167 .... 9–62, 9–66, 17–13
    (1) 17–29
s.170 .... 8–25, 17–24
s.175 16–33
s.176A(3)(a) 15–32, 16–34
    (b) 15–32, 16–34
    (5) 15–32, 16–34
    (6) 15–32, 16–34
    (9) 15–32, 15–41
s.195 17–17
s.201 17–08
    (2) 16–35
s.204 17–25
ss.206–211 .... 9–58, 9–61, 9–62
s.208 9–58
ss.212–216 .... 1–09, 1–21, 1–25,
                          8–23
ss.212–217 .... 2–09, 9–61, 9–62,
                          16–12
s.212 ... 8–05, 9–30, 9–64, 9–65,
                          15–41, 17–29
s.213 ... 1–09, 5–02, 8–05, 8–26,
      9–15, 9–64, 9–66, 17–20, 17–29
s.214 ... 8–05, 8–26, 9–15, 9–30,
      9–64, 9–67, 9–68, 9–69, 17–20,
                          17–29
    (1) 9–67
    (2) 9–67
    (3) 9–67
    (4) 9–15, 9–68
s.216 .... 3–13, 8–05, 17–29
    (3) 3–13, 9–70
        (c) 3–13, 9–70
s.217 3–13
    (2) 9–70
ss.218–219 9–58
s.218 7–27
s.233 16–05
s.238 17–26
s.239 17–26
ss.242–245 17–05
s.242 .... 2–19, 16–04, 16–20,
                          16–28, 17–26
    (4)(a)–(c) 17–26
s.243 .... 15–18, 16–04, 16–20,
                          16–28, 17–26
    (2)(a) 15–18, 17–26
    (b) 15–18, 17–26
    (c) 15–18, 17–26
    (d) 15–18, 17–26
    (5) 15–18
s.244 .... 16–28, 17–26

s.245 .... 16–04, 16–20, 16–28
  (2)(a)–(c) 15–21, 17–26
  (3)(a) 15–20, 17–26
   (c) 15–20, 17–26
  (4)(a)–(b) 15–20, 17–26
  (5) 15–20, 17–26
s.249 .... 15–20, 17–26
s.386 17–31
  (1) 15–39
ss.423–425 17–30
s.423(2) 2–19
s.426 17–32
s.435 15–20
Sch.1 .... 16–05, 16–28
  para.5 9–63
  para.21 17–20
Sch.A1 16–43
  para.2(2) 16–43
  para.3 16–43
  para.4(1) 16–43
  para.6 16–43
  para.7 16–43
  para.8(1) 16–43
   (6) 16–43
   (8) 16–43
  para.11 16–43
  paras.12–14 16–44
  para.18 16–44
  para.24 16–44
  para.25 16–44
  para.26 16–44
  para.27 16–44
  paras.29–31 16–44
  para.32 16–43
  para.40 16–44
  para.43 16–44
Sch.B1 ...... 16–02, 16–09, 16–9
  para.3(1) 16–10, 16–26
   (2) 16–10
   (3) 16–10
   (4) 16–10
  para.4 16–10
  para.5 16–14
  para.6 16–01
  para.10 .... 16–18, 16–20
  para.11 .... 16–20, 16–22
  para.12(1) 16–20, 16–22
  para.13 16–23
   (1) 16–23
   (2) 16–20
  para.14 16–20
   (2) 16–16
   (3) 16–17
  para.15 16–18
   (1) 16–18
   (3) 16–18
  para.16 16–18
  para.17(a) 16–18
   (b) 16–18

para.23 16–21
para.24 16–21
para.25 16–18
  (a)–(c) 16–21
para.26(1) 16–21
para.27 16–21
  (2) 16–21
para.28(1) 16–21
  (2) 16–21
para.29 16–21
  (3) 16–21
para.35 16–23
para.36 16–20
para.37 .... 16–18, 16–20
para.39(1) 16–20
para.42 16–24
para.43 16–24
para.44 16–24
para.45 16–25
para.46 16–25
para.47(2) 16–25
  (3) 16–25
para.48 16–25
  (4) 16–25
para.49 16–26
  (2) 16–26
  (3) 16–26
para.51(2) 16–27
para.52(1) 16–27
  (2)–(4) 16–27
para.53 16–27
  (2) 16–27
para.57 16–27
para.59 16–28
para.61 .... 16–12, 16–28
para.65 16–33
para.69 .... 16–28, 16–30
para.70 16–28
para.72 16–28
  (2) 16–28
para.74 .... 16–28, 16–30
para.75 16–28
para.76(1) 16–28
para.79 16–38
para.80 16–37
para.81 16–38
para.83 16–35
para.84 16–37
para.99(4) 16–31
  (5) 16–32
  (6) 16–32
para.111 16–28
Sch.2 15–35
  para.21 17–20
Sch.2A paras.1–3 15–25
Sch.4 17–10
  para.3A 9–62, 9–66,
                   17–29
Sch.6 .... 15–32, 15–39, 17–31

Company Directors
  Disqualification Act
  (c.46) 1–07, 1–12, 2–07,
    2–10, 7–27, 8–01, 8–04, 8–14,
    8–21, 8–24, 9–15, 9–69, 11–47,
                              12–06
  s.1 .... 8–14, 8–24
  s.1A 8–24, 8–28
  ss.2–4 .... 8–24, 8–28
  s.2 8–25
  s.3 .... 8–25, 8–26
    (2) 8–25
    (5) 8–26
  s.4 8–25
    (1)(b) 8–25
  s.5 8–26
    (5) 8–26
  s.3 1–07
  s.6 .... 8–24, 8–25, 8–26, 8–27
    (2) 8–27
    (3C) 8–27
    (4) 8–27
  s.7 .... 8–25, 17–30
    (1) 8–28
    (2) 8–28
    (2A) 8–28
    (3) 8–28
      (c) 16–28
  s.8 .... 8–25, 8–28
    (1) 8–28
    (2A) 8–28
  s.8A 8–24
  s.9 8–29
  s.9A 8–26
    (4) 8–26
  s.9B 8–26
  s.10 8–26
  s.11 .... 8–14, 8–26
  s.12 8–26
  s.13 8–33
  s.14 8–24
  s.15 2–10
  s.17 8–32
  s.22(5) 8–12, 8–27
  Sch.1 .... 7–28, 8–26
    Pt I 8–29
    Pt II 8–29
  Building Societies Act
    (c.53) 16–02
1989 Companies Act (c.40) 4–05,
        4–06, 4–08, 4–12, 11–03
  s.112 4–16
    (2) 4–16
    (4) 4–16
    (5) 4–16
    (6) 4–16
1990 Law Reform (Miscellaneous
        Provisions) (Scotland)
        Act (c.40)

       s.14 17–20
1991 the Water Industry Act
        (c.56) 16–02
1993 Criminal Justice Act (c.36)   1–12,
                        12–08, 12–18
  s.52(1) 12–07
    (2)(a)–(b) 12–07
      (b) 12–21
    (3) 12–07
  s.53 12–20
    (1)(a)–(c) 12–21
    (2) 12–21
    (3)(a)–(b) 12–21
    (6) 12–21
  s.55 12–13
  s.56(1) 12–08
    (2) 12–16
  s.57(1) 12–09
    (2) 12–10
  s.58(1) 12–12
    (2) 12–12
    (3) 12–12
  s.59 12–15
  s.60 12–17
  s.62 12–23
    (1) 12–14
      (b) 12–23
  Sch.1 .... 12–20, 12–22
    para.1 12–22
    para.2(4) 12–22
    para.5 12–22
  Sch.2 Pt V 12–11
  Railways Act (c.43) 16–02
1994 Insolvency Act (c.7) 15–38
1995 Requirements of Writing
        (Scotland) Act (c.7) 3–56
    Sch.2 para.3(5) 3–56
1996 Employment Rights Act
        (c.18)
  s.205A 5–08
  Channel Tunnel Rail Link
    Act (c.61)
  s.19 16–02
1999 Greater London Authority
        Act (c.29) 16–02
2000 Financial Services and
        Markets Act (c.8) 1–12,
        3–58, 5–27, 12–19, 14–02,
                              15–23
  Pt VI 5–11, 5–26, 5–27
  Pt VIII 12–26
  Pt XI 12–19
  s.80 5–26
  s.82 5–26
  s.84 5–26
  s.86 5–26
  s.87A 5–26
  s.87B 5–26
  s.87G 5–26

s.90	2–11, 5–26
s.90A	5–27
s.118	12–26
(1)	12–26
(2)	12–26
(3)	12–26
(4)	12–26
(5)	12–26
(6)	12–26
(7)	12–26
(8)	12–26
s.118A(1)	12–26
(4)	12–26
(5)	12–26
s.118B	12–26
s.118C	12–26
s.122(2)	12–26
s.123	12–26
(2)	12–26
ss.132–136	12–26
s.137	12–26
s.144(1)	12–22
s.167	12–19
s.168	12–19
s.169	12–19
s.171	12–19
s.174	12–19
s.175(4)	12–19
(5)	12–19
s.177	12–19
s.367	16–38
s.381	12–26
s.383	12–26
s.384	12–26
s.397	12–26
Sch.10	5–26
Pt 2	5–27

Limited Liability Partnership Act (c.12) 1–20, 1–21

Transport Act (c.38) 16–02

2002 Enterprise Act (c.40) 5–37, 8–26, 9–63, 15–03, 15–23, 15–39, 15–48, 16–02
s.249	16–02
s.250(1)	15–23
s.252	15–32
s.253	9–62, 9–66, 9–67, 17–29

2004 Companies (Audit, Investigations and Community Enterprise) Act (c.27) 1–27

2005 Charities and Trustee Investment (Scotland) Act (asp 10)
s.16	4–20

2006 Companies Act (c.46) 1–06, 1–12, 2–07, 3–01, 3–02, 4–02
Pt 7	1–13
Pt 15	1–13
Pt 27	1–13
Pt 28	1–13, 14–07
Pt 34	1–13, 3–42
Pt 36	2–33
Pt 43	1–13
s.3(3)	3–35
s.4(1)	3–20
(2)	3–20
s.7	3–26
s.8	3–01
s.9	3–01
(2)(a)	3–01
(b)	3–01
(c)	3–01, 4–03
(d)	3–01, 3–02, 4–03
(3)	3–01
(4)(a)	3–03
(b)	3–03
(c)	3–01, 3–04
(5)(a)	3–02, 3–05
s.10	3–01, 3–03
s.11	3–01, 3–03
s.12	1–06
(1)	3–04
(3)	3–04
s.13	3–01, 3–06
s.15(4)	3–07
s.16	3–07
s.17	9–10
s.20	4–19
s.21	5–03
(1)	4–11, 4–20
(3)(b)	4–20
s.22	4–06
(1)	4–23
(2)	4–23
(3)	4–23, 4–24
s.23(1)	4–23
(2)	4–23
s.24	4–24
s.26	4–24
(2)	4–24
s.28	4–06, 4–24
s.29	9–10
s.30	13–24
s.31	9–10
(1)	4–06
s.33	5–02, 11–01
(1)	4–18, 5–03
s.35A	4–14
ss.39–42	4–08
s.39(1)	4–09, 4–10
s.40	8–02, 9–10, 13–17
(1)	4–12, 4–15
(2)	10–03
(a)	4–12
(b)	4–13, 4–15, 4–17
(4)	4–10, 4–11

s.41 .... 4–17, 8–02
  (2) 4–17
  (3)(a)–(b) 4–17
  (4)(a)–(d) 4–17
  (5) 4–17
s.42 4–16
s.48(2) 3–57
s.51 3–60
s.53(a) 3–10
  (b) 3–10
s.54 3–10
s.55 3–10
s.56 3–10
s.58(1) 3–10
s.59 3–10
ss.60–64 3–10
s.66 3–09
s.67 .... 3–09, 3–15
s.68(2) 3–15
  (5) 3–15
  (6) 3–15
s.69(1)(a) 3–16
    (b) 3–16
  (2) 3–16
  (4) 3–16
    (a)–(e) 3–16
s.70 3–16
s.71 3–16
s.72 3–16
s.73 3–16
s.74 3–16
s.75(1) 3–15
s.76 3–15
s.77 .... 3–14, 8–01
  (2)(a) 3–14
    (b) 3–14
    (c) 3–14
    (d) 3–14
s.78(2) 3–14
s.79 3–14
ss.81(1)–(3) 3–19
s.83 3–12
s.84 3–12
s.85 3–12
ss.90–96 .... 3–23, 3–46
s.90(1)(a) 3–47
  (2)(b) 3–47
    (e) 3–47
  (3) 3–47
s.91 3–47
  (1) 3–47
    (b)–(d) 3–47
s.92(1)(a) 3–47
    (b) 3–47, 10–16
  (2) 3–47
  (3) 3–47
s.93 3–47
s.94(3) 3–47
s.95 3–47

s.96 3–47
ss.97–101 3–46
s.97(1)(a) 3–48
  (3) 3–48
s.98(1) 3–48
  (2) 3–48
  (3)–(5) 3–48
s.100 3–48
s.101 3–48
ss.102–104 3–46
s.102(1)(a) 3–49
  (2) 3–49
  (3) 3–49
s.104 3–49
ss.105–108 3–46
s.105(1)(a) 3–50
  (2) 3–50
  (3) 3–50
  (4) 3–50
s.106(3) 3–50
  (4) 3–50
s.107 3–50
ss.109–111 .... 3–46, 3–48
s.109(2) 3–51
  (3) 3–51
s.110(2)(a) 3–51
  (3) 3–51
s.111 3–51
s.112 3–54
  (1) 5–19
  (2) 4–16, 5–10
  (4) 4–16
  (5) 4–16
  (6) 4–16
s.113(1) 5–30
  (2) 5–30
  (3) 5–30
s.114 5–19
  (1) 5–30
  (2) 5–30
s.115 5–30
ss.116–119 5–31
s.116 5–30
  (2) 5–31
  (4)(b) 5–31
    (d) 5–31
s.117(1) 5–31
  (4)(a) 5–31
  (5) 5–31
s.118(1) 5–31
  (3) 5–31
s.119 5–31
s.121 5–31
s.123 5–19
  (1) 3–36
  (2) 3–36
  (3) 3–36
s.125 .... 5–19, 5–28, 5–31
s.126 5–19

s.127 5–19
s.130(2) 6–52
s.136 3–39
s.141 3–39
s.146 5–21
s.149 5–21
s.152 5–21
s.154 .... 3–04, 8–17
  (2) 3–26
s.155 .... 3–04, 8–17
  (1) 8–01
s.157 8–01
  (5) 8–01
s.160 .... 3–25, 8–15
s.162(1) 8–17
ss.162–166 1–06
s.162(2) 8–17
s.163 .... 3–04, 8–17
  (2) 3–04, 8–17
s.164 .... 3–04, 3–05, 8–17
s.165 8–17
s.167 .... 3–05, 8–17
  (1)(a) 8–21
s.168 .... 8–20, 8–22, 9–27,
    11–02, 13–01, 13–15, 13–25
s.169 8–22
  (2) 8–22
  (3) 8–22
  (4) 8–22
  (5) 8–22
ss.170–187 11–31
ss.170–222 11–06
s.170 9–07
  (2) 9–20
    (b) 9–22
  (3) 9–07, 9–08
  (4) 9–07, 9–08, 9–27
  (5) 9–27
ss.171–177 .... 9–06, 9–08, 9–27,
                                      9–56
s.171 .... 4–11, 9–06, 9–09, 9–13
s.172 ... 9–03, 9–04, 9–10, 9–12,
        9–13, 9–63, 11–03, 11–34,
                                    11–35
  (1) 8–03
    (a)–(f) 9–13
    (b) 9–55
    (f) 9–56
s.173 9–14
  (2)(a)–(b) 9–14
s.174 9–15
ss.175–177 14–02
s.175 ... 8–19, 9–16, 9–18, 9–19,
                  9–21, 9–22, 9–24
  (1) 9–18
  (2) 9–18
  (3) 9–18
  (4)(a)–(b) 9–18
  (5)(a) 9–18

  (6) 9–18
s.176 9–22
  (4) 9–22
s.177 ... 3–36, 3–54, 8–19, 9–18,
                                      9–23
  (1) 9–23
  (6)(a)–(c) 9–26
s.178 .... 4–11, 9–27
s.179 9–09
s.180(1) 9–18, 9–19, 9–28
  (2) 9–21, 9–22
  (4) 9–19
    (a) 9–22
s.181 9–18
s.182 9–23
s.184 9–25
s.185 .... 9–25, 9–51
s.186(1) 9–25
ss.188–226 ..... 9–21, 9–22, 9–31
s.188 .... 8–16, 9–32
  (4) 9–32
s.189 9–32
s.190 .... 3–54, 9–33
  (1) 9–33
  (5) 9–33
  (6) 9–33
s.191(2) 9–33
s.192 9–33
s.193 9–33
s.194 9–33
s.195(2) 9–33
  (3) 9–33
s.196 9–33
ss.197–214 9–34
s.197 6–19
  (1) 9–35
  (2) 9–35
  (3) 9–35
  (4) 9–35
  (5) 9–35
s.198(1) 9–36, 9–38
  (3) 9–37, 9–39
  (4)–(6) 9–37
s.199 9–37
s.200 .... 9–35, 9–37
s.201(4)–(6) 9–39
s.202 9–40
  (1)(b) 9–40
s.203 9–41
ss.204–209 9–22
s.204(1) 9–42
  (2) 9–42
s.207 9–34
  (1) 9–35, 9–37
  (2) 9–39
  (3) 9–40
s.208(1) 9–42
  (2) 9–42
s.209(1)(b) 9–43

(2) 9–43
(3) 9–43
(4) 9–43
ss.210–212 9–42
s.213 9–45
  (1)(c) 3–36
  (2) 9–45
  (6) 3–36, 9–45
  (7) 9–45
s.214 9–46
ss.215–217 .... 8–21, 14–02
s.215 .... 8–16, 9–47
s.216(1)(a) 7–35
  (b) 7–35
s.217 9–47
s.218 9–47
  (2) 9–47
s.219(4) 9–47
s.220 .... 8–21, 9–47
s.221 .... 8–21, 9–47
s.222 9–47
s.223(1)(c) 9–45
  (d) 9–47
ss.226A–F 8–16, 8–21, 9–47
s.228 .... 8–16, 9–32
  (3) 9–32
s.229 9–32
s.230 9–32
s.231 .... 3–36, 9–26, 9–48
  (5) 9–48
s.232 9–15
  (1) 9–29, 9–49
  (2) 9–49
ss.233–235 9–15
s.233 9–49
  (1)(b) 9–32
s.234 9–49
  (4) 9–19
s.235 9–49
s.236 9–49
s.237 9–49
s.238 9–49
s.239 .... 4–11, 9–19, 9–29, 9–59
  (3) 4–11, 9–19, 9–29
  (4) 4–11, 9–29
  (6)(a) 9–19, 9–29
ss.242–244 .... 3–04, 8–17
s.243(2) 3–04, 8–17
s.244 .... 3–04, 8–17
s.245 .... 3–04, 8–17
s.246 .... 3–04, 8–17
s.247 9–01
  (4)–(6) 9–01
s.248 .... 3–36, 8–01
  (2) 8–01
s.249 8–01
s.250(1) 8–01, 8–11
s.251 8–01
ss.252–255 .... 9–35, 9–37, 9–38,

9–39
ss.252–257 9–23
s.252 .... 4–17, 9–29
s.253 9–44
  (3) 9–44
s.254 9–44
s.255 9–44
s.256 .... 9–36, 9–38
ss.260–264 11–31
s.263(3)(b) 11–35
  (f) 11–36
ss.265–269 .... 4–11, 9–28,
11–03, 11–06, 11–07, 11–31,
11–37
s.265 11–31
  (1)–(3) 11–31
  (3) 11–37
  (4) 11–31
  (7) 11–31
s.266 .... 11–32, 11–33, 11–34
  (2) 11–32
  (3) 11–32
  (4)(a)–(b) 11–32
s.267 .... 11–33, 11–34, 11–36
  (2) 11–33
  (4) 11–33
s.268 .... 11–32, 11–33, 11–34
  (1) 11–34
    (a)–(c) 11–34
    (a) 11–35
  (2)(a)–(b) 11–35
  (f) 11–36
s.269 11–36
s.270 .... 3–04, 10–01
  (1) 3–36
s.271 .... 3–04, 3–26, 10–01
s.272 10–01
s.273 .... 3–04, 3–25, 3–26
  (1) 10–02
s.274 10–03
s.275 10–03
s.276 10–03
s.277 .... 3–05, 10–03
  (5) 10–03
s.278 .... 3–04, 3–05, 8–17,
10–03
s.280 .... 10–02, 10–03
s.281(3) 13–23
s.283 13–24
  (6) 13–09, 13–14
s.284 13–18
s.285 13–18
ss.288–300 13–07
s.288 13–25
  (2)(a) 8–22
s.290 13–26
s.291 13–26
s.292(1) 13–26
  (2) 13–26

(4) 13–26
(5) 13–26
s.293 13–26
s.294 13–26
s.295 13–26
s.296 13–26
s.297 13–26
s.302 13–08
s.303 .... 8–03, 11–38, 13–09
  (1) 13–09
  (2) 13–09
  (3) 13–09
  (4)(a) 13–09
  (5) 13–09
s.304(4) 13–09
s.305(1) 13–09
  (3) 13–09
  (4) 13–09
  (6) 13–09
  (7) 13–09
s.306 13–10
s.307(1) 13–08, 13–11
  (2) 13–11
    (a) 13–10
  (4) 13–08, 13–10, 13–11
  (6) 13–11
    (a) 13–08, 13–11
    (b) 13–11
s.308 13–14
s.309 13–14
s.310 13–14
  (2) 13–14
  (3) 13–14
s.311 13–14
s.312 .... 10–12, 13–15
  (3) 13–15
s.313 13–14
s.314 13–16
  (2) 13–16
s.315 13–16
s.316(1) 13–16
  (2) 13–16
s.317 13–16
s.318 13–17
  (1) 3–36
s.319 13–17
s.320 13–18
s.321(1) 13–18
  (2) 11–38, 13–18
s.323 13–18
s.324 13–14
  (1) 13–18
  (2) 13–18
s.326 13–14
s.327 13–14
s.328 13–14
s.329 .... 13–14, 13–18
s.336 .... 3–29, 13–07
  (1) 13–10

s.337 13–10
  (2) 13–10
s.341 13–18
ss.342–354 13–18
s.357 3–36
ss.362–379 9–51
s.366 9–51
s.378 9–51
s.382 7–50
  (3) 7–46
s.383 .... 7–49, 7–54
  (4) 7–53
s.384(1) 7–48
  (2) 7–48
s.384A 7–47
s.384B 7–47
s.385 .... 3–28, 7–36
s.386 7–28
  (2) 7–28
s.387 7–28
s.388(1) 7–28
  (4) 7–28
s.390(2) 7–31
  (3) 7–32
  (5) 3–08, 7–31
s.391(4) 7–31
  (5) 3–08, 7–31
s.392 .... 3–08, 7–31, 7–32,
                                13–10
  (2)(b) 3–08
  (3) 3–08
    (a)–(b) 7–32
  (4) 3–08
  (5) 7–32
s.393(1) 7–30
s.394 7–29
s.395(1)(b) 7–05
s.396 7–29
  (1) 7–29
s.397 .... 7–05, 7–29
ss.398–408 7–29
s.400 7–52
  (4) 7–52
s.403 7–29
  (2)(b) 7–05
s.405 7–52
  (2) 7–52
  (3)(a) 7–52
    (b)–(c) 7–52
s.406 7–05
s.409 7–29
s.410 7–29
s.410A 7–29
s.411 7–29
s.412 7–29
s.413 7–29
s.414 8–03
s.414A 7–36
s.414B 7–36

s.415 7–35
s.417 7–46
    (2) 7–36
    (3) 7–36
    (4) 7–36
    (5)(a)–(b) 7–36
s.418 .... 7–38, 9–57, 10–10
    (2) 7–38, 9–57
    (5) 7–38, 9–57
    (6) 7–38, 9–57
s.419(1) 7–40
s.419A 7–36
s.420 7–41
s.422 7–41
s.423 .... 5–21, 7–20
    (1) 7–40
s.424 10–08
    (2) 7–40
    (3) 7–40
s.426 7–45
s.430 .... 5–21, 7–41, 7–45
s.431 5–21
s.432 5–21
s.437 .... 7–20, 7–40, 7–42
s.439 8–16
    (1) 7–41
    (4) 7–41
    (5) 7–41
s.439A 8–16
ss.441–450 7–40
s.441 7–42
s.442 8–25
    (2)(a)–(b) 7–42
     (a) 10–08
    (3)(a)–(b) 7–42
ss.444–447 7–33
s.448 .... 1–07, 3–37
    (1) 7–44
    (2) 7–44
    (3) 7–44
s.448A 7–55
ss.451–453 .... 7–40, 7–43
s.451(1) 7–43
s.454 7–56
s.455 7–56
s.456 7–56
s.463 7–37
s.465 7–51
s.466(4) 7–53
s.467 7–54
    (1) 7–51
    (2) 7–51
s.475(1) 7–50, 10–07
    (2) 7–50, 10–07
    (3)(a)–(b) 7–50, 10–07
s.476 .... 7–50, 10–07
s.477 .... 7–20, 10–07
    (2)(a)–(b) 7–50
s.478 .... 7–49, 10–07

s.479 10–07
s.480 .... 3–38, 7–55
s.482 10–07
s.483 10–07
s.485(3) 10–08
    (c) 10–08
    (4) 10–08
s.486 10–08
s.487(2) 10–08
s.489(2) 10–09
    (3)(a) 10–09
     (c) 10–09
    (4) 10–09
s.490 10–09
s.492 10–11
s.493 10–11
s.495 10–16
    (3) 7–20
     (a)–(b) 7–33
    (4) 7–20, 10–16
s.496 .... 7–34, 10–16
    (3) 10–16
s.498 10–16
    (1) 7–33
     (a)–(b) 7–33
    (2) 7–34
     (b) 10–16
    (3) 7–34, 10–16
    (4) 7–34
    (5) 10–16
s.498A 7–34
ss.499–501 7–34
s.499 10–10
s.500 10–10
s.501 10–10
s.502 .... 10–10, 13–25
s.503 10–16
    (1) 7–33
s.504(3) 10–16
s.506 10–16
s.507 10–16
s.510 13–25
    (1) 10–12
s.511 .... 10–12, 10–13, 13–15
    (2) 10–12
    (3) 10–12
    (4) 10–12
    (5) 10–12
    (6) 10–12
s.512 10–12
s.513 10–12
s.514 .... 10–12, 10–13, 13–15
    (6)(a) 10–13
    (8) 10–13
s.515 13–15
s.516 10–13
s.517 10–13
s.518 13–12
    (2) 10–13

(3)	10–13
(4)	10–13
(5)	10–13
(6)	10–13
(7)	10–13
(8)	10–13
(9)	10–13
(10)	10–13
s.519	10–14
(1)	10–14
(2)	10–14
(3)	10–14
(4)	10–14
s.520(1)	10–14
(2)(a)	10–14
(4)	10–14
(5)	10–14
s.521(1)	10–14
(2)	10–14
s.522	10–14
(5)–(8)	10–15
s.524	10–14
s.525(2)	10–14
s.533	5–16, 10–18
ss.534–536	10–18
s.535(1)	10–18
s.537	10–18
s.538	10–18
s.540(2)	5–01
s.541	5–02
s.542	5–01
ss.549–551	5–12
s.549	3–54
s.550	3–54, 5–12
s.551(3)(a)	5–12
(b)	5–12
(4)	5–12
(6)	5–12
s.555	3–54
s.558	5–10
s.560(1)	5–14, 5–15
s.561	2–11, 3–54, 5–15
(1)	5–14
(a)	5–14
(2)	5–14
(5)	5–14
s.562	2–11
(5)	5–14, 5–22
s.563(2)	2–11, 5–14
(3)	5–14
s.564	5–15
s.566	5–15
s.567	3–54, 5–15
s.569	3–54, 5–15
s.570	3–54, 5–15
(1)	5–15
(3)	5–15
s.571	3–54, 5–15
(6)	5–15
(7)	5–15
s.573	5–15
s.575	5–15
s.578(3)	2–11
s.579(3)	2–11
s.580	5–16
s.584	5–17
s.585(1)	5–17
(2)	5–17
s.586	2–08, 5–17
s.587(1)	5–17
(2)	5–17
s.588(1)	5–17
(2)	5–17
s.592	5–17
s.593	5–17
(1)(b)	5–17
(c)	5–17
(3)	5–17
s.594(2)	5–18
(4)	5–18
s.595	5–18
s.596(2)	5–17
(3)(d)	5–17
s.597	5–17
s.598	5–18
(4)	5–18
s.599	5–18
s.600	5–18
s.601(1)	5–18
(3)	5–18
s.602	5–18
s.605(1)	5–17
(2)	5–17
(3)	5–17
s.610	5–02
s.611	6–53
ss.612–613	6–52
s.612(2)	6–52
s.618	5–25, 6–05, 13–23
s.619	5–25, 13–23
ss.622–628	5–25, 6–05
s.630(2)(a)	5–03
(b)	5–03
(3)	5–03
(4)(a)	5–03
(b)	5–03
(5)	5–03
s.633	11–38
ss.641–657	6–06
s.641	7–11
(1)	6–10, 6–11
(4)	6–10
ss.642–644	6–13
s.642(1)	6–14
(2)	6–14
s.643(1)(a)	6–14
(2)(b)	6–14
s.644(1)	6–15

(2)	6–15
(5)	6–15
ss.645–653	6–16
s.645	6–11
(2)	6–11
(5)(a)	6–11
s.646	6–11
(1)	6–11
(2)	6–11
(3)	6–11
(4)	6–11
(5)(b)	6–11
s.647	6–11
s.648(2)	6–11
(3)	6–12
(4)	6–12
s.649	6–12
s.653(2)	6–11
s.654	6–17, 7–04
(1)	6–17
s.656	6–51, 8–03, 13–13
s.658	6–30
s.659(1)	6–30
(2)(b)	6–30
(3)	6–30
s.659A(6)	15–10
s.660	3–39
s.662	5–34
(3)(a)–(b)	6–31
(5)	6–31
(6)	6–31
s.664	6–31
s.668	6–31
s.676	6–28
ss.677(1)(a)–(d)	6–18
s.678	6–21, 6–25
(1)	6–18, 6–21, 6–28
(2)	6–24
(3)	3–39, 6–21
(4)	6–24
s.679	6–21, 6–25
s.680	6–21, 6–23
s.681	6–21
(2)(a)–(g)	6–21
s.682(1)(a)	6–21, 6–28
(2)(a)–(d)	6–22
(3)	6–22
(4)(a)	6–22
ss.684–723	7–02
ss.684–737	6–21
s.684	5–05
(2)	6–34
(3)	6–34
(4)	5–06, 6–34
s.685(1)	5–06
(a)–(b)	6–34
(4)	5–06
s.686	5–06
(1)	6–34

(2)	6–35
(3)	6–35
s.687	6–41
(2)	6–34
(3)	6–41
(4)	6–41, 6–52
(5)	6–42
s.688	6–34, 6–43
s.689	6–34
ss.690–737	6–30
s.690(2)	6–35
s.691(1)	6–35
(2)	6–35
s.692	6–41
(1)	6–41
(b)	6–41
(2)(a)–(b)	6–41
(3)(a)–(b)	6–41
(4)	6–42
s.693(2)	6–36
(3)	6–36
ss.694–700	6–35
s.694(1)	6–36
(2)	6–36
(3)	6–39
(4)	6–36
(5)	6–36
s.695(3)	6–48
s.696(2)	6–36
(3)	6–36
(4)	6–36
s.698(1)	6–36
(2)	6–36
(3)	6–36
s.699	6–36
s.700	6–36
ss.701–708	6–35
s.701(1)	6–37
(3)	6–37
(4)	6–37
(5)	6–37
(7)	6–37
s.702(3)	6–40
s.705	6–41
s.706	6–40, 6–43
s.707(1)	6–40
s.708	6–40
ss.709–723	6–06, 6–34, 6–41
s.709	6–45
(1)	6–45
s.710(2)	6–45
s.712(4)	6–46
(7)	6–46
s.713(1)	6–48
s.714	8–03, 10–16
(3)(a)–(b)	6–48
(6)	6–48
s.715(1)	6–48
s.716	6–49

(1)	6–48
s.717(2)	6–48
s.718	6–48
s.719	6–48
s.720	6–48
s.720A	6–46
s.721	6–49
(3)–(7)	6–49
(5)	6–49
s.722(1)	6–49
(2)	6–49
(4)	6–49
s.723(1)	6–49
s.724	5–09, 6–34
(1)(b)	6–32
s.725	6–32
s.726(2)	6–32
(3)	6–32
s.733(2)	6–43, 6–44
(3)	6–43
(5)	6–04, 6–44
(6)	6–44
s.734(2)	6–46
(3)	6–47
s.735(2)	6–50
(3)	6–50
(6)	6–50
ss.738–754	5–35
s.743	5–36
s.744	5–36
s.745	5–36
s.755	5–13
(3)	5–13
(4)	5–13
s.756	5–13
ss.757–759	5–13
s.761	3–23, 3–47, 5–18
(3)	3–22
s.762	2–08
(1)(b)–(c)	3–23
(2)	3–23
s.763	2–08, 3–22
s.767	2–08, 3–23
s.768	5–20
s.769	5–20
s.771(1)	5–28
(2)	5–28
s.779	5–01
s.780	5–01
s.781	5–01
ss.793–825	5–32
s.793	5–32
s.794	5–32
s.797	5–32
ss.801–802	5–32
s.803	5–32
s.804	5–32
s.808	5–32
s.817	5–32
ss.820–825	5–32
s.829	7–02
(2)(a)–(d)	7–02
ss.830–832	7–26
s.830	7–14
(1)	7–13, 7–14, 7–23
(2)	7–01, 7–03
s.831	6–07, 7–14
(1)	6–04
(4)	7–24
(5)	7–24
ss.832–833	7–24
s.836(1)	7–34
(2)	7–20
s.837(1)	7–20
(4)	7–34
(a)	7–20
s.838	7–22
(6)	7–22
s.839(2)	7–21
(4)	7–21
(5)	7–21
(7)	7–22
s.841(2)	7–05, 7–06
(4)	7–06
(a)–(b)	7–07
(5)	7–07, 7–08
s.842	7–08
s.844(1)	7–17
(a)–(b)	7–18
(2)	7–18
(3)(a)	7–19
(c)	7–19
s.845	7–14
(2)(a)	7–14
(3)	7–14
s.846	7–14, 7–15
s.847(1)	7–26
(2)	2–11, 7–26
(3)	7–26
s.852	7–26
s.853(4)	7–04
(5)	7–04
s.859A(2)	15–12
(4)	15–10, 15–11
s.859D	15–10
(1)(b)	15–11
(d)	15–12
(2)(b)	15–08
(c)	15–07
s.859E(1)	15–11
s.859F	15–14
(3)	15–10
s.859G	15–12
s.859H	15–14
s.859I	15–13
s.859L	15–16
s.859O	15–17
s.859P	15–15

s.859Q 15–15
ss.895–901 6–11
s.895 .... 6–21, 7–12, 14–01,
    14–14, 14–15, 16–03, 17–35
s.896(1) 14–15
s.897(2) 14–16
   (3) 14–16
s.899(1) 14–15, 14–16
   (3) 14–16
   (4) 14–16
s.900 14–17
ss.919–934 14–05
s.947 14–07
ss.952–956 14–07
s.966(4) 14–22
s.968(6) 14–21
s.974 14–10
s.979(2) 14–11
s.980(4) 14–11
s.981(2) 14–12
   (6) 14–12
s.982(7) 14–12
ss.983–985 11–38
s.983 14–12
s.984(2) 14–12
s.985 16–26
   (2) 14–12
s.986(2) 14–11
s.993 8–25
s.994 ... 4–22, 5–02, 6–06, 7–12,
   9–56, 11–03, 11–06, 11–09,
   11–17, 11–24, 11–25, 11–28,
   11–30, 11–34, 11–36, 11–39,
              11–40
   (2) 11–10
s.996 .... 11–11, 11–16
   (2)(a)–(e) 11–16
s.1000 17–34
s.1001 17–34
ss.1002–1011 17–35
s.1003(6) 17–35
s.1012 17–36
s.1013 17–36
s.1014 17–36
ss.1024–1034 17–37
s.1030(1) 17–37
   (5) 17–37
   (6) 17–37
ss.1035–1038 11–42
s.1113 8–25

s.1121(2) 10–01
s.1136 .... 5–19, 5–30, 6–48,
               9–32
ss.1143–1148 1–13
s.1150(1) 5–17
   (2) 5–17
s.1151 5–17
s.1153 5–17
s.1157 .... 7–27, 9–29, 9–59,
         9–64, 10–18
ss.1159(1)(a)–(b) 3–39
s.1161(1) 3–40
s.1162 3–40
   (4)(a)–(b) 3–40
s.1169 7–55
s.1210 10–07
s.1212 10–07
s.1214 .... 8–14, 10–07
s.1217 10–07
ss.1219–1222 10–07
Sch.4 1–13
Sch.5 1–13
2007 Corporate Manslaughter
   and Corporate
   Homicide Act (c.19) 2–31
   s.2 2–31
     (1)(a)–(c) 2–31
   s.8 2–31
   s.10 2–31
   s.18 2–31
   s.19 2–31
   Bankruptcy and Diligence
    etc. (Scotland) Act (asp
    3)
   Pt 2 15–03
   s.155 15–45
   s.208(2) 15–46
     (12) 15–46
   Sch.5 para.14 15–45
2010 Bribery Act (c.23) 2–34
   s.7 2–34
2012 Financial Services Act
   (c.21) 1–12
2013 Crime and Courts Act (c.22)
   Sch.17 2–34
   Enterprise and Regulatory
    Reform Act (c.24) 9–47
   Growth and Infrastructure
    Act (c.27)
   s.31 5–08

TABLE OF STATUTORY INSTRUMENTS

1972 Mortgaging of Aircraft
       Order (SI 1972/1268) . 15–12
1986 Insolvency (Scotland) Rules
       (SI 1986/ 1915) . 3–13, 17–22
    r.1.23 16–42
    r.2.2(2) 16–23
    r.2.2(3) 16–23
    r.2.3(1) 16–23
    r.2.4(1) 16–23
    r.2.13(2)(a) 16–21
    r.2.13(2)(b) 16–21
    r.2.15 16–21
    r.2.16(3) 16–21
    r.2.18 16–21
    r.2.20(3) 16–21
    r.2.23(2)(b) 16–21
    r.2.25(1) 16–26
    r.2.27(2) 16–27
    r.2.34 16–27
    r.2.36 16–27
    r.2.38 16–27
    r.2.45 16–37
    r.2.46 16–38
    r.2.67(1)(f) 16–32
    Pt 4, Ch.2 17–23
    rr.4.1–4.82 17–22
    r.4.12(2A) 17–23
    r.4.15 17–24
    r.4.16 17–31
    r.4.18 17–22
    r.4.19 17–22
    r.4.22 17–24
    r.4.66 17–31
    r.4.66(4) 17–31
    r.4.67 .... 16–32, 17–31
    rr.4.78–4.82 16–39
    r.4.80 3–13
    r.4.81 3–13
    r.4.82 3–13
    r.7.12(1) 16–42
    r.7.12(2) 16–42
    r.22.1 16–25
    r.22.2(4) 16–25
    Insolvency Rules (SI 1986/
       1925)
    r.4.228 3–13
1989 European Economic Interest
       Groupings Regulation
       (SI 1989/638) 1–15
1993 Merchant Shipping
       (Registration of Ships)

Regulations 1993 (SI
       1993/3138) 15–12
1994 Insider Dealing (Securities
       and Regulated
       Markets) Order (SI
       1994/187) 12–14
1996 Insolvent Companies
       (Reports on Conduct
       of Directors) (Scotland)
       Rules (SI 1996/1909) ... 8–28
2001 Financial Services and
       Markets Act 2000
       (Financial Promotion)
       Order (SI 2001/1335) ... 15–25
2003 Insolvency Act 1986
       (Prescribed Part) Order
       (SI 2003/2097) 15–32,
                                       16–34
    art.1 15–41
    Financial Collateral
       Arrangements (No.2)
       Regulations (SI 2003/
       3226) 15–10
2004 European Public Limited
       Liability Regulations
       (SI 2004/2326) 1–15
2005 Financial Services and
       Markets Act 2000
       (Market Abuse)
       Regulations (SI 2005/
       381) 1–13
    Prospectus Regulations (SI
       2005/1433) 3–27
2006 Cross–Border Insolvency
       Regulations 2006 (SI
       2006/1030) 17–38
2007 Companies (Fees for
       Inspection and Copying
       of Company records)
       Regulations (SI 2007/
       2612) 5–30
    Companies (Cross–Border
       Mergers) Regulations
       (SI 2007/2974) 1–13
2008 Small Companies and
       Groups (Accounts and
       Directors' Reports)
       Regulations (SI 2008/
       409) 7–20, 7–29, 7–46,
                                       7–53
    reg.3 7–46

reg.35 6–04
Sch.1 Pt 2 Section A
  para.10(1), (2) 7–05
Sch.1 Pt 2 Section A
  para.13(a) 7–04
Sch.1 Pt 2 Section C
  para.35(1) 7–04
Sch.1 Pt 3 reg.44 7–08
Sch.5 7–35
Sch.7 Pt 1 reg.12 7–05
Large and Medium–sized
  Companies and Groups
  (Accounts and Reports)
  Regulations (SI 2008/
  410) 7–04, 7–20, 7–29,
        7–35, 7–52, 7–54, 8–16
reg.35 6–04
Sch.7 7–35
Companies (Trading
  Disclosures)
  Regulations (SI 2008/
  495) 3–11
reg.5 3–11
reg.6(1), (2) 3–11
reg.7(1)–(3) 3–11
reg.9 3–11
Companies (Reduction of
  Capital) (Creditor
  Protection) Regulations
  (SI 2008/719) 1–13
Company Names
  Adjudicator Rules (SI
  2008/1738) 3–16
Companies (Reduction of
  Share Capital) Order
  (SI 2008/1915)
  art.3(2) 6–17, 7–04
Companies (Company
  Records) Regulations
  (SI 2008/3006) 5–30
Companies (Registration)
  Regulations (SI 2008/
  3014) 3–02
Companies (Model Articles)
  Regulations (SI 2008/
  3229) 3–05, 4–19
reg.3 .... 8–01, 9–01
reg.4 9–01
reg.14 9–18
reg.15 8–01
reg.16 9–18
reg.17 8–01
reg.18 8–14
reg.20 8–01
reg.21 .... 8–14, 8–15
reg.22 .... 8–14, 8–15
reg.23 8–16
reg.24 8–16
reg.26 5–28

reg.31 7–25
reg.33 7–25
reg.34 7–25
reg.38 13–14
reg.39 13–14
reg.44 13–17
reg.49 3–57
regs 52, 54–61 5–34
2009 Bankruptcy and Diligence
  etc. (Scotland) Act
  2007 (Commencement
  No.4, Savings and
  Transitionals) Order
  (SI 2009/67)
  art.3(a) 15–45
Companies (Disclosure of
  Address) Regulations
  (SI 2009/214) 3–04, 8–17
Companies (Trading
  Disclosures)
  (Amendment)
  Regulations (SI 2009/
  218) 3–11
Business Names
  (Miscellaneous
  Provisions) Regulations
  2009 (SI 2009/1085) 3–09
Overseas Companies
  Regulations 2009 (SI
  2009/1801) 3–42
Overseas Companies
  (Execution of
  Documents and
  Registration of
  Charges) Regulations
  (SI 2009/1917) 3–42
Companies (Share Capital
  and Acquisition by a
  Company of its Own
  Shares) Regulations (SI
  2009/2022) 6–32, 6–46
reg.2 5–14
reg.3 6–11
Company, Limited Liability
  Partnership and
  Business Names
  (Miscellaneous
  Provisions)
  (Amendment)
  Regulations (SI 2009/
  2404) 3–09
Company, Limited Liability
  and Business Names
  (Public Authorities)
  Regulations (SI 2009/
  2982) 3–10
Company, Limited Liability
  Partnership and
  Business Names

(Sensitive Words and Expressions) Regulations (SI 2009/2615) 3–10

2011 Act of Sederunt (Sheriff Court Rules) (Miscellaneous Amendments) (SSI 2010/279) 11–32

Prospectus Regulations (SI 2011/1668) 3–27

Overseas Companies (Execution of Documents and Registration of Charges) (Amendment) Regulations (SI 2011/2194) 3–42

2012 Prospectus Regulations (SI 2012/1538) 3–27

2013 Companies Act 2006 (Amendment of Part 18) Regulations (SI 2013/999) 6–35

Companies Act 2006 (Strategic Report and Directors' Report) Regulations (SI 2013/1970) 7–36

Large and Medium–sized Companies and Groups (Accounts and Reports) (Amendment) Regulations (SI 2013/1981) 8–16

Small Companies (Micro–Entities' Accounts) Regulations (SI 2013/3008) 7–47

CHAPTER 1

INTRODUCTION

MAJOR FEATURES OF COMPANIES

A company's existence

At the heart of company law is a major principle: that the law recog- **1–01**
nises the existence of an artificial legal person, called a registered company, which has a freestanding legal personality, separate from those who
own it (the members) and those who manage it (the directors), and which
only comes into existence on registration. The registered company is
intangible, its existence symbolised by a paper certificate of incorporation. Although without a physical existence, it can do many things that a
human being can do, especially trade, own property, pay taxes, or act as a
servant or employer, but it cannot, for example, commit certain crimes,
such as assault, nor enter into certain civil contracts, such as an ante-
nuptial agreement.

A second lesser principle is this: that the form of a company is more
important than the substance. Provided the requisite paperwork has been
prepared properly, the fee duly paid and the certificate of registration
issued, a company will exist, even if it has no money to speak of and
undertakes no business activity. Although, as we shall see later, the courts
will occasionally look behind the apparent separate legal personality of
the company to investigate the conduct of a company's directors or
members, on the whole, irrespective of the motives, the actions and the
behaviour of the directors, the members or the company's employees, the
company will remain in existence and alone will remain responsible for its
own actions and omissions, own its own assets and be liable for its own
debts.

Incorporation

Until 1844 companies as we know them scarcely existed, and most did **1–02**
so either because a monarch had granted a charter of incorporation, as
with the Honourable East India Company,[1] or because Parliament had
granted a charter of incorporation, as the Scots Parliament did on the
incorporation of the Bank of Scotland in 1695.[2] Other, unincorporated
companies did exist, with a rather uncertain legal identity, and with a

---

[1] This company received a charter from Queen Elizabeth I in 1600.
[2] There are (as at March 2013) 878 companies set up by these methods, with six new
companies set up by royal charter in 2012/13.

1

form of trading in shares, mostly through coffee shops which doubled as
the first stock exchanges. Company law was slow to develop in the United
Kingdom, mainly because of the ill effects of the South Sea Bubble, the
name given to a speculative fever that seized the country in 1720, and in
which many lost fortunes through folly and chicanery.[3] The Bubble Act
1720 was passed to prevent such scandals happening again, but had the
equal effect of frustrating commerce. Later, however, in the mid-nine-
teenth century, the then Chancellor of the Exchequer, Gladstone,[4] saw
that business was leaching to the USA and France, both of which
countries had developed the idea of the joint stock company with limited
liability. Gladstone recognised the importance of incorporation and
registration for giving legitimacy to companies generally, and the commercial significance of limited liability. Thus were passed the Joint Stock
Companies Acts 1844 and 1856.

Inherent in the idea of *incorporation* is a document that sets out the
terms of the corporation by way of a constitution or a charter: in a
company this is nowadays provided by the memorandum and articles of
association.[5] These were originally derived from partnership agreements
which set out the purpose of the company, and the rights and duties of
the individual partners towards each other and towards their partnership.
A further part of incorporation is the idea of public accessibility to its
registered incorporation documents.[6] There are plenty of unincorporated
associations, such as partnerships, which have their own internal bylaws,
constitutions or charters,[7] but these documents are not generally accessible to those who are not members of that association.

1–03   *Registration* requires the setting up of a register, or authorised list,
controlled by a registrar who ensures that registration is granted only on
the fulfilment of certain conditions, namely the correct documentation
and the payment of a fee. Once a company is registered, it is placed on the
register and that company's details may be accessed either in person at

---

[3] The South Sea Company was set up both to buy up the national debt and to trade in the
South Seas (the southern part of the Pacific Ocean), but was hampered by the fact that the
Spanish, who controlled the area, refused permission for such trade to take place. This
fact was carefully concealed from the investors. When the company's share price reached
its highest point, the promoters of the company, who had artfully talked up the share
price, sold their shares and fled to France, leaving many speculators holding worthless
shares. "Bubbles" were not restricted to eighteenth century Britain: contemporaneously,
the French had their own disastrous Mississippi bubble, engineered by the Scots financier
John Law of Laurieston, and in 2001 there was a mini-bubble in technology companies
("dot.com" companies) caused by investors speculating in a new and untried market
without considering the true underlying value of the businesses they were investing in. The
Wall Street Crash of 1929 was another example.

[4] Admirers of Gladstone, Prime Minister for much of Queen Victoria's reign, may inspect
his statue in Coates Crescent in Edinburgh. Gladstone was at one stage MP for Mid-
lothian. His grandparents are buried in the old Leith cemetery.

[5] See Ch.4.

[6] Such accessibility was until recently not in practice very realistic, but now that the Register
of Companies is online it is actually now easier than ever before to access the relevant
documents.

[7] Typical unincorporated associations with charters or constitutions include kirk sessions,
bowling clubs, amateur dramatic societies etc.

the Register of Companies[8] or online by anyone who wishes to do so. As at December 2013 there were 3,186,814 private companies registered in the United Kingdom, of which 173,937 were Scottish, and 7,584 public limited companies, of which 279 were Scottish.

Limited liability

Limited liability is a characteristic of many companies, but not all.[9] **1–04** What this means is that the liability of the members[10] is limited, not that the company's liability is limited. In a company limited by shares, the limit of a shareholder's liability is the amount required to pay up the full *nominal value* of each of his shares. With a neat circularity, the nominal value of a share is the designated value given to a share purely for the purpose of enabling the full liability of the shareholder to be extinguished by payment. So in the case of a company whose shares each have a nominal value of 50 pence per share, provided he has paid the whole 50 pence for each share that he owns, the shareholder will have no further liability to the company, even if asked to pay more by the directors or by the company's liquidator. His liability to the company is therefore limited to the nominal value of each share that he owns. The nominal value bears no relation to the market value of a share, and only exists as part of an accounting convention.[11] Having paid up to the nominal value of each share, the shareholder is only obliged to pay more than the nominal value of his share if he agrees to do so.[12]

If the shareholder chooses for the time being to pay only some of the nominal value of each 50 pence share, say to the extent of 20 pence only, he could subsequently be required by the directors or the liquidator to pay the balance of 30 pence on each share; but again, once he has paid the remaining 30 pence per share, he has no further liability to his company except where he agrees to accept such liability. In practice it is rare nowadays to have partly paid shares, mainly because shareholders will not welcome the possibility of being asked to pay at an uncertain date the unpaid amount of the nominal value of each share.[13]

In the case of a guarantee company, instead of having shares, the

---

[8] The Edinburgh office is at the fourth floor premises known as Quay 2, 139 Fountainbridge, Edinburgh. The main Register of Companies is at Crown Way in Cardiff, but there is also an office in London, at 4 Abbey Orchard Street, Westminster. Northern Ireland has its own register in the Linenhall in Belfast.

[9] For example, it is possible to register an unlimited liability company for which the shareholders are jointly and severally liable. Such companies are discussed further in Ch.3.

[10] "Members" is a global term that includes shareholders. A shareholder only exists in a company if that company has shares, but some guarantee companies do not have shares, and therefore cannot have shareholders. "Members" is by definition a wider term.

[11] For more on the accounting convention and the nominal value of shares, see Ch.5.

[12] This might arise where there is a premium payable on the shares when they are issued. The market price for a newly issued share may sometimes be much greater than the nominal value. The difference between the market price and the nominal value is the premium and reflects the desirability of the share.

[13] In some countries, share capital is seen as an anachronism and it is possible to have shares with no nominal value. These are known as no-par value shares, and will be discussed further in Ch.5.

member's liability is limited by the terms of a guarantee that the member undertakes to pay. The amount required by way of the guarantee will be stated in the company's articles, and if the company requires funds for whatever reason specified in the articles (commonly on insolvent liquidation), each member will have to pay up to the predetermined amount or limit specified in the guarantee, commonly £1.00. Once that is paid, the member has no further liability to the company.

Even if the company's debts are substantial, and the company later collapses, the member's liability still remains limited to the extent of the nominal value of each share that he owns, or to the extent of the guarantee he has offered. The member who has fully paid for each of his shares or paid the sums due on his guarantee may walk away from the insolvent company's debts, leaving the creditors to fend for themselves with such small sums as a liquidator may give them.

1–05 The advantage of the limitation on liability is that investors know exactly how much they will lose if the company loses all its money, and can budget for that loss. There is a predetermined cap on their loss, but no limit to the amount of money they might gain if the company is profitable. Furthermore, unless they have invested a great deal of money in the company, there is little likelihood of their being made bankrupt if the company fails. These advantages make investors more likely to invest in companies generally, and thus promote business.

The promotion of commerce

1–06 Not only does limited liability make investors more willing to invest, but the safety net of limited liability makes entrepreneurs more willing to set up new businesses. This in turn creates employment and creates wealth, out of which taxes may be paid, so that the country benefits as well. A country that did not permit the existence of limited liability companies would find that its best entrepreneurs would flee to countries with a more sympathetic commercial regime. A country that did not have limited liability companies would have few risk-takers and people would be deterred from trying out new commercial ideas, carrying out research or developing new technological ideas. Over a period of time that country would stagnate and become impoverished relative to other countries. Where limited liability is not available, investors are likely to insist on a high return on capital to compensate them for the risk they are bearing. This would result in reduced investment in businesses generally and would drive up the cost of capital. Limited liability also allows investors to pool their wealth together for very large projects. In the nineteenth century, many railways and canals were built by companies. This was because only they could harness the savings of a large number of investors to raise the capital to carry out huge undertakings at limited commercial risk to the investors. Even now, most large undertakings are carried out through limited liability companies to avoid the risk of the undertakings' losses falling on the investors.

The promotion of commerce is a major theme underpinning the Companies Act 2006. Given that all major developed economies have limited companies for the same reason, the promotion of commerce, it was considered important that UK company law should not place barriers in the way of entrepreneurs who wished to set up and run companies here. Consequently, much of the Companies Act 2006 was deliberately drafted to be easily understood and easily accessible. It was written in a more user-friendly manner than its predecessor Companies Acts. It was laid out with an open texture, with helpful cross-referencing,[14] and much breaking down of complex rules into constituent parts. The idea is that this would help non-lawyers and company directors understand the law without too much difficulty.

The Act was also written in such a way that the director of a small company would find the rules relating to his type of company printed before the rules relating to larger companies and public companies, a principle known as "Think Small First". As further evidence of the accessibility of the new rules, the Companies Act 2006 is available on the internet: no longer is it necessary to buy an expensive paper copy of the Act.

At the same time, old drafting habits die hard. There are still parts of the Act that are difficult to follow,[15] and parts where the draftsman was not given the opportunity to express matters as clearly as he might have liked, and where Parliamentary scrutiny was minimal.[16] In addition, many ancillary rules are not included in the Act but are in secondary legislation, known as statutory instruments. These contain the fine detail of regulations which at the time of passing of the Act had yet to be drafted. As these regulations are not in the Act, many people are unaware of them.

The disclosure principle

The economic effect of limited liability is that risk is transferred away from the investor to creditors. Generally speaking, creditors can better suffer a degree of loss from a company's collapse than an investor can suffer the entire loss of his capital, as happens when a sole trader becomes liable for his business's debts. Anxious creditors may nevertheless bargain with companies with which they are dealing, and may ask for personal guarantees from the directors, or ask for performance bonds from the companies' banks. But the best form of reassurance for creditors is that all limited companies must publish their accounts and other information

1–07

---

[14] For example, in s.12, which refers to the register of directors' service addresses, the legislation helpfully indicates that further information about directors' addresses is to be found at ss.162–166.

[15] Few people can read the rules relating to directors' loans, quasi-loans and credit transactions without being baffled by the wording. Even the Government's own Explanatory Notes provide little assistance: they do not even explain in layman's terms what a quasi-loan is.

[16] For example, see Pt 28 (Takeovers) Ch.2 (Impediments to takeovers). There was pressure to get the Bill passed before the end of the Parliamentary session. There is also the suspicion that this part of the Act was so complex that few MPs felt very motivated to look at it carefully.

about the company annually at the Registrar of Companies.[17] Publication is the price of limited liability for the company's members. Unlimited companies, whose members are personally liable for their companies' debts, consequently do not need to publish their accounts.[18] There are sanctions for failure to publish the required documentation, and directors' persistent failure to lodge accounts, annual returns, and other documents is possible grounds for disqualification under the Company Directors Disqualification Act 1986.[19] Publication of its accounts enables potential investors and creditors to have some idea whether or not a company is safe to invest in, or to do business with. Nevertheless it is wise to be cautious even with published accounts: there are ways of disguising a company's true financial state and it is rash to place much reliance on its published accounts. This is because the accounts may not be honestly prepared, or because the accounts of some companies, particularly small private companies, do not need to be published in full or audited. Company accounts are dealt with in greater detail in Ch.7.

By contrast, sole traders and partnerships do not have to disclose anything, except to HM Revenue and Customs, and their business affairs may be as secret as they wish. But equally, sole traders are personally liable for all their business debts, and partners are jointly and severally personally liable for the debts of their partnership.[20]

The maintenance of professional standards

1–08   Historically, certain professions, particularly accountants, doctors and solicitors, were not allowed to incorporate, because it was feared that limiting their liability might lead to a lapse in professional standards; or to put it another way, being personally liable for their mistakes would concentrate partners' minds on doing a proper job. However the increasing costs of professional liability insurance and the ever higher costs of negligence claims, together with the fact that in other jurisdictions other professionals were allowed to limit their liability by incorporation, has meant that most professionals, may, if their professional bodies permit it, now incorporate either as limited companies or as limited liability partnerships. The disadvantage of such incorporation is the visibility of the accounts to both their clients and employees, but the advantage is that where the businesses are prosperous, their healthy balance sheets will give reassurance to their clients that the businesses are well run and well-funded.

---

[17] Companies House joined the European Business Register in 2007. This means that businesses in Europe may find out about British companies, and conversely, British businesses may, through the EBR, find out some information about companies throughout Europe. Although the UK is fortunate to have a well run company registration system, the quality and accuracy of some other European countries' company registration systems can be variable.

[18] Companies Act 2006 s.448.

[19] Company Directors Disqualification Act 1986 s.3.

[20] Partnership Act 1890 s.9.

The danger of fraud

Precisely because limited liability offers investors and directors the **1–09** opportunity to walk away from insolvent companies, leaving creditors and employees unpaid, the law is vigilant to ensure that the opportunities for taking unfair or fraudulent advantage of limited liability and of the company's separate legal personality are restricted. Under certain circumstances directors may be found personally liable for the debts of their insolvent companies,[21] and even when a company is solvent, there are occasions both under common law and statute when directors or others will be liable if they abuse their position.[22] The law has to find a balance between encouraging commerce while preventing fraud; that balance is not always easily found. Registration of a company and regular lodging of annual accounts are no guarantee that a company is operating honestly.

The opportunities for personal wealth creation

It is perfectly possible to make a great deal of money as a sole trader, **1–10** perhaps as an artist, an advocate or a computer consultant. Partners in a successful partnership can become wealthy too. But one typical way to become very rich is to start off as an entrepreneur, with a private limited company, expanding to become a public limited company, and finally having the company's shares floated on the London Stock Exchange. At that point, assuming the company's shares are desirable enough and the entrepreneur runs the company well, he may sell some of his own shares, thereby releasing a great deal of cash, or retain his own shares while the share price climbs, the dividends flow in and his own personal status as a director of a listed company rises. Having a company listed on the London Stock Exchange has its inconveniences, but it can provide excellent opportunities for wealth creation. Over the last few years, this traditional approach has proved less attractive,[23] partly because of the volatility of the stock market, the caution of investors and the high degree of scrutiny to which listed companies are exposed. Private companies, especially if registered abroad, may escape much of that scrutiny.

The universality of the limited liability company

The limited liability company has proved one of the most effective **1–11** economic developments in commerce in the last 200 years. It is probably as significant as double-entry book-keeping or the introduction of universally accepted systems of weights and measurements. Limited liability companies are now to be found all over the developed world, and while they may differ in detail from country to country, they all share a system of registration, with directors in charge and members owning the shares.

---

[21] Insolvency Act 1986 ss.212–216. Under s.213 members may also potentially be personally liable.

[22] See Ch.2.

[23] For example, many of the high street retailers are now owned by private equity companies which bought out the retailers from their former listed company owners.

Some countries have more manager-friendly rules than others, and some states in the USA (Delaware in particular) have set themselves out to attract business by their director-friendly legislation and the skills of their commercial judges; those states attract significant income from the number of companies that choose to register there, paying fees to the state for doing so. Other countries, particularly certain tax haven countries, permit companies to be set up with minimal paperwork and minimal disclosure requirements. Such companies are sometimes used by political despots, money launderers, drug dealers, tax evaders and others who would not care to have their finances investigated too closely. Former communist countries, or at least those reasonably closely allied to Europe, have generally adopted either German or American models of company legislation. China, in its pursuit of socialism with Chinese characteristics, regularly sends experts round the world to garner the best features of company law internationally for their own company laws. Increasingly we shall see company law become more and more similar throughout the developed world, as capital follows legal jurisdictions with which it feels comfortable. The principles of corporate governance, which include transparency, accountability and an adherence to generally agreed standards of best practice, are also gradually being adopted internationally. Those countries which do not choose to follow these principles may in the long run be starved of capital, since without good corporate governance investors will not be confident that their capital will be properly used.[24]

United Kingdom company legislation

1–12   In the United Kingdom the main legislation applicable to companies is the Companies Act 2006 ("the CA 2006"). It replaced the Companies Act 1985. Other significant legislation applicable to companies comprises the Insolvency Act 1986 ("the IA 1986"), which has substantial parts dedicated to Scottish procedure; the Company Directors Disqualification Act 1986 ("the CDDA 1986"); the Criminal Justice Act 1993 Pt V, which deals with insider dealing; and the Financial Services and Markets Act 2000, as amended by the Financial Services Act 2012. This deals with the issue of securities to the public and the regulation of the financial industry. The CA 2006 was the fruit of an exercise in 2002 undertaken by the then Department of Trade and Industry ("DTI"), culminating in the Company Law Review Steering Group's document *Modern Company Law for a Competitive Economy—the Final Report*.[25] Many of the Steering Group's recommendations were carried forward into the CA 2006. A major feature of the CA 2006 is the simplification of the law for

---

[24] The corollary of this is that countries where corporate governance is not much in evidence are also countries where the opportunities for exceptional profits—or indeed losses—arise, Russia being a good example.

[25] Company Law Review Steering Group, *Modern Company Law for a Competitive Economy—the Final Report*, DTI, 2001.

private companies in order to encourage commerce. Another feature of the CA 2006 is the accessibility of the rules applicable to directors' duties. This matter is dealt with in Ch.9.

European legislation

The United Kingdom has an admirable record in introducing Eur- 1–13 opean company legislation and in adopting the rules for the harmoni- sation of company law throughout Europe. Where Directives have been approved, the United Kingdom has taken steps, usually by producing regulations in the form of statutory instruments, but sometimes by sta- tute, to bring them into force.

Many of the original European company law Council Directives have been repealed and been replaced by others, sometimes dealing with much the same issues. The following is a list of the more important Directives:

- Second Directive (77/91): this deals with public limited compa- nies,[26] the net asset rule applicable to dividends of public com- panies,[27] and the rules relating to the raising and maintenance of capital[28];
- Fourth Directive (78/660): this deals with the standardisation of the layout of accounts and the accounting disclosure rules applicable to small and medium-sized companies[29];
- Sixth Directive (82/891): this deals with the scission (also known as division) of public limited companies into smaller companies[30];
- Seventh Directive (83/349): this deals with the preparation of consolidated company accounts[31];
- Eleventh Directive (89/666): this deals with filing and disclosure requirements for branches of foreign companies[32];
- Thirteenth Directive (2004/25): this deals with mergers and takeovers and the protection of minority shareholders.[33]

By this stage the system of numbering the directives was beginning to break down so it became easier to name them instead:

- Employee Involvement Directive (2001/86): this is concerned with the involvement of employees in European companies;

---

[26] To be seen in the CA 2006 Pts 20 and 23.
[27] See Ch.6.
[28] See Ch.5. This was amended by Directive 2006/68 amending Council Directive 77/91/ EEC as regards the formation of public limited liability companies and the maintenance and alteration of their capital and by Directive 2009/109. See also the Companies (Reduction of Capital) (Creditor Protection) Regulations 2008 (SI 2008/719).
[29] CA 2006 Pt 15. See Ch.7.
[30] CA 2006 Pt 27. See Ch.14.
[31] CA 2006 Pt VII Sch.4A.
[32] CA 2006 Pt 34.
[33] CA 2006 Pt 28. This Directive is discussed further in Ch.14.

- Market Abuse Directive (2003/6): this deals with insider dealing and market abuse[34];
- Disclosure Directive (2003/58): this permits the disclosure of company information by electronic means[35];
- Transparency Directive (2004/109): this deals with the harmonisation of transparency requirements for listed companies[36];
- Cross-border Directive (2005/56): this deals with cross-border mergers of limited liability companies[37];
- Single-member company Directive (2009/102): this rationalised the law relating to companies with only one shareholder or member;
- Electronic and cross-border voting Directive (2007/36): this was designed to encourage electronic voting and to prevent companies impeding the casting of votes from abroad;
- Remuneration policy Directive (2010/76): this required the preparation of a report on the effect of high remuneration on certain types of business and also dealt with capital requirements and re-securitisation;
- Public limited company Directive (2012/30): this deals with the formation of public companies, and the maintenance and alteration of capital.

There are also various Directives dealing with listed companies, with banks and with the operation of stock markets. The purpose of the Directives is to ensure that throughout the Europe Union countries have similar rules and requirements about the release of company information, takeovers, capital raising and maintenance, protection of shareholders' interests, audit, transparency of accounting, prevention of market abuse and other matters. There are also regulations for cross-border insolvency proceedings to ensure that proceedings commenced in one jurisdiction may be continued, enforced and transferred to another without difficulty.[38]

1–14 Certain draft Directives have not been passed by the European Parliament. These include a draft Fifth Directive (known as the "Vredeling" Directive), which the United Kingdom would not accept because of the requirement to have worker participation in management of companies above a certain size. It would also have had specific duties relating to directors and auditors. A draft Ninth Directive concerned corporate groups, especially in the context of inter-group liability on insolvency. Drawn from a German model, it was not very effective even in Germany and has since been withdrawn. A draft Fourteenth Directive, which was supposed to deal with the transfer of a company's place of registration

---

[34] See the Financial Services and Markets Act 2000 (Market Abuse) Regulations 2005 (SI 2005/381).

[35] This is covered by ss.1143–1148 and Schs 4 and 5 of the CA 2006.

[36] See Pt 43 of the CA 2006 and the Financial Conduct Authority's ("FCA") transparency rules.

[37] See Companies (Cross-Border Mergers) Regulations 2007 (SI 2007/2974).

[38] Regulation 1346/2000 on insolvency proceedings.

from one EU jurisdiction to another, lapsed. One reason for this is that there has not been much evidence that businesses find the inability to move a difficulty, since they merely set up a foreign subsidiary. Secondly, case law[39] has established that there is no reason why a company registered in, say, England, should not operate its business in Denmark even if in so doing it does not adhere to some of Denmark's company law rules.

Further regulations that are applicable to company law in the United **1–15** Kingdom include EC Regulation 2137/85 on European Economic Interest Groupings,[40] which are non-profit-making cross-border ventures in such fields as research and development.[41] Although each grouping has its own separate legal personality, the members of the grouping are all liable for its debts.

One particular matter, which had been over 30 years in the making, is the European Company Statute, which allows for the creation of a pan-European Company, generally known by its Latin name, *Societas Europaea* ("SE"), which could trade throughout Europe. Following the implementation of the regulation,[42] the European Company Statute and the European Public Limited Liability Company Regulations 2004[43] were introduced in the United Kingdom to facilitate the use of SEs here. It is thought that with a common currency, the Euro, in existence, there should be opportunities for economies of scale with SEs carrying out trades or projects that straddle frontiers. SEs should obviate the need for separate national subsidiaries, thus saving money and reducing prices for consumers. A particular feature of an SE is that there must be regular reports to and consultation with a body that represents its workers' interests, though if the SE is registered in a country such as Britain or Spain, where employee participation is not part of company law generally, it is possible to derogate to some extent from this requirement. There does not appear to be much demand for such companies, possibly because of the employment consultation requirements, the fact that an SE is not quite as portable between different states as the legislation suggests, and because of taxation considerations. As at July 2013 there were 60 SEs established in the United Kingdom. There has also been a proposal for a Private European Company, known properly as *Societas Privata Europaea*. It has been discussed for many years, but EU Member States so far have been unable to agree how it will operate and there does not appear to be any pressing need from business for such companies.

The aim of much of the European law, at least for public companies **1–16** and listed companies, is to have "a level playing field" for all such

---

[39] *Centros Ltd v Erhvervs-og Selskabsstyrelsen* [2000] Ch 446; [1999] ECR I-1459 ECJ and *Uberseering BV v Nordic Construction Company Baumanagement GmbH* [2002] ECR I-9919 ECJ.

[40] The UK regulations that deal with them are the European Economic Interest Groupings Regulation 1989 (SI 1989/638).

[41] As at March 2013, there were 257 of such Groupings.

[42] Regulation 2157/2001 on the Statute for a European company (SE) [2001] OJ L294/1 and the Directive 2001/86 supplementing the Statute for a European company with regard to the involvement of employees [2001] OJ L294/22, both dated October 8, 2001.

[43] European Public Limited Liability Company Regulations 2004 (SI 2004/2326).

companies and on the whole to reduce artificial and national barriers to
commerce. This commendable objective is generally welcomed in EU
countries until individual national and sometimes protectionist interests
are significantly threatened, or some rule is introduced which runs contrary to a nation's culture. For an example of the latter point, Germany
and France traditionally are hostile to takeovers (and particularly foreign
takeovers) because of the threat to employment and the national interest,
while the United Kingdom has a horror of employee participation in
company management.

By having a level playing field it is hoped that companies within the
various countries within the EU will all operate to the same agreed set of
laws. At the same time it is recognised that having "markets" in corporate law is good for countries' corporate legislation as it makes each
country's legislature continually evaluate the effectiveness of its own
corporate legislation relative to other countries' corporate legislation.
For example, all German companies used to require a minimum capital
of €25,000 while a UK registered company could and indeed still can
have a minimum capital of as little as £1.00. Although the capital
requirement of €25,000 was designed to make German businesses take
their corporate responsibilities seriously, for a while it encouraged certain
German entrepreneurs to set up British registered companies, mainly to
avoid the minimum capital requirement. Facing the potential loss of
business, German corporate law was revised to join most other European
countries in permitting companies to have minimal share capital.[44]

Comparison with Other Forms of Trading Organisation

Sole traders

1–17   A sole trader is a person running a business on his own account. He is
responsible for his entire losses, but equally he keeps all the profits
himself and need not disclose his accounts to anyone save HM Revenue
and Customs. It can be a precarious existence, dependent on the sole
trader's continued good health, and there may be no-one with whom to
share the responsibility of running the business. Many small businesses or
occupations, such as farmers, self-employed tradesmen, small shop-
keepers, artists, musicians, freelance journalists and consultants, are sole
traders. One option for sole traders is to incorporate as a single member
private limited company,[45] which combines all the benefit of limited liability and the separate legal personality of the company with the total
independence of running a business alone, not subject to any "boss" or
other interference.

---

[44] This was achieved by the creation of a new type of company known as a UG
haftungbeshränk.
[45] Following the implementation of the CA 2006, it is permissible to have a single member
public limited company.

Partnerships

A partnership is defined in the Partnership Act 1890 as two or more **1–18** persons carrying on a business in common with a view of profit.[46] The business does not necessarily have to be profitable, but it should intend to make a profit; and the business carried on by the partners must have something in common, so that a business of a seamstress and a tree surgeon would not be a partnership, but a partnership of a plumber and a joiner might be.

The principal advantages of partnerships are as follows:

- Partnerships are easy to set up. No paperwork is needed, although a partnership agreement is desirable as it puts beyond doubt the partners' rights and duties to each other. If there is no partnership agreement, the Partnership Act 1890 imposes a series of standard assumptions which are deemed to apply unless there is agreement to the contrary; for example, in the absence of agreement otherwise, each partner has a right of management, and the partners share their profits and losses equally.
- It is relatively easy to close down a partnership, without the formality required for companies.
- A partnership need not disclose its accounts to anyone other than HM Revenue and Customs. This means neither a partnership's employees nor its creditors may find out how much the partners are earning.
- In principle it should be easy for a partner to withdraw his capital from his company, though in practice some partnership agreements restrict a partner's opportunities for doing this.

The principal disadvantages of partnerships are as follows: **1–19**

- Partners are jointly and severally personally liable for the partnership's debts.[47] This means that any creditor may sue the partnership, and ultimately all the partners personally, for a debt owed to him by the partnership. The creditor may even try to extract his debt from any one partner, leaving it up to that partner to reclaim from the other partners, if he can, the sums he has had to pay on their behalf.[48] Partners put their own personal wealth at risk in their business, and may be made bankrupt in the process of trying to pay the partnership's debts.
- In practice in Scotland partnerships may only borrow against the value of the partnership's heritable assets, and cannot, unlike a company or limited liability partnership, borrow against the value of the partnership's moveable assets unless they assign

---

[46] Partnership Act 1890 s.1.
[47] Partnership Act 1890 s.9.
[48] Partnership Act 1890 s.4(2). If any one partner is bankrupt, the other partners have to pay his share for him between themselves.

those assets to the lender or physically deliver them to the lender. Both companies and limited liability partnerships may grant floating charges and may raise funds thereby with greater ease than partnerships.

- A partnership is only as strong as its weakest partner. When a partner enters into a contract on behalf of the partnership he binds the whole partnership, and the partners are supposed to have mutual trust in each other and be confident of each other's abilities. Such trust and confidence may not always be entirely justified. In any large firm of partners, there is commonly at least one partner whom the other partners regard with some disfavour, and who has a reputation for signing letters and deeds on behalf of the partnership which other, more prudent partners, would not. Such a partner may be a liability as far as the partnership as a whole is concerned, unless he has some redeeming feature such as being good at bringing in clients. Although this is also true of a company and its directors, at least in a company the other directors, if they have behaved properly, are not jointly and severally personally liable for the financial consequences of a fellow director's foolish acts.

Features of partnerships that are neither advantageous nor disadvantageous are as follows:

- Partnerships in Scotland have a legal personality separate from their partners. This enables partnerships to sue in their own name, and equally to be sued. The fact that a partnership has a separate legal personality in practice makes very little difference, because the partners are still jointly and severally liable for the partnership debts. Partnerships in Scotland (but not yet in England) may act collectively as directors or company secretaries.[49] In Scotland, it is possible for a partner to be a debtor or a creditor of his own partnership, but this is conceptually impossible in England. In England partnerships do not have a separate legal personality, but court rules have been specially adapted to allow partnerships to sue and be sued in the normal manner. One of the proposed amendments to partnership law is that English law should follow Scots law in giving partnerships a separate legal personality.[50]
- Partnerships are supposed to reconstitute themselves every time a partner dies or retires. But in a partnership, such as some of the large accounting or legal partnerships, with a continuous

---

[49] Although this is permissible it is not generally a good idea: a firm of solicitors, if asked to act as a company secretary for a client's firm, will generally use an in-house limited company owned collectively by the firm to act as the company secretary. This means that if the company secretarial work is not done well, at least it will be the in-house limited company that will be initially responsible rather than the firm's partners individually.

[50] Law Commission and Scottish Law Commission, *Report on Partnership Law* (2003), Scot. Law Com. No.192, paras 3.12 to 3.17.

turnover of partners, it is clearly unrealistic to keep reconstituting the partnership. Accordingly most partnership agreements are drafted to permit the partnership to remain in existence despite the death or retirement of partners.

Limited liability partnerships

Limited liability partnerships ("LLPs") were introduced by the Limited **1–20** Liability Partnership Act 2000, which came into force on April 1, 2001. They combine some of the features of partnerships with most of the features of companies. Confusingly, the "partners" in a LLP are called members. As at March 2013 there were 58,583 LLPs in the United Kingdom, with 2,661 in Scotland.[51] The Registrar of Companies maintains a register of LLPs. LLPs have some of the rights of partnerships, such as equal treatment of members (subject to agreement to the contrary), privacy of internal arrangements (again, usually drawn up in an agreement which is not disclosed to non-members) and the tax treatment of partnerships (this meaning that the members are treated as self-employed).[52]

In the same manner as a limited company, a LLP has to be registered **1–21** with the Registrar of Companies and comply with the disclosure requirements under the Limited Liability Partnership Act 2000; it must publish its accounts; it has the benefit of limited liability, so that the LLP's liability to its creditors generally is limited to the amount of capital in the LLP; it may grant floating charges; and its members will not generally be liable to creditors except on the same terms as directors of companies are liable to creditors.[53] Of the members, some will be "designated" members, who are expected to sign the annual returns to the Registrar of Companies, and others will just be members, with no such duty. The default position is that each member will be a designated member unless otherwise stated.

Many professional firms which used historically to be partnerships are now LLPs. In order to comply with professional requirements imposed by such bodies as the Institute of Chartered Accountants of Scotland and the Law Society of Scotland, LLPs will still need to be insured against losses arising through their members' own negligence or other cause. A LLP's capital may also be used to pay its losses, though after that fund has been exhausted, the LLP will then go into liquidation—but without the members having joint and several liability for the LLP's losses. If, however, after insolvent liquidation the members are found to have breached their fiduciary duties, or otherwise acted in a manner prejudicial to creditors and others in terms of the amended rules under the IA 1986 ss.212–216 (the "clawback provisions"), the members may be liable to make such payments to the liquidator as the court deems appropriate. These reimbursed sums could then be used to help repay the creditors.

---

[51] Companies House Annual Report 2012–13.
[52] At the time of writing there are proposals from HMRC to tax salaried members of a LLP as employees rather than as self-employed, as has previously been the case.
[53] See Chs 2 and 9.

1–22   The individual membership interests in a limited liability partnership may not be traded in the same manner as a share. A member resigns his share on retirement or resignation. The main drawback, as far as existing partnerships are concerned, to the conversion to LLP status is the requirement to disclose accounts, but as stated before, healthy accounts may give confidence to those dealing with the LLP, and therefore bring more business in.

1–23   A significant feature of some LLPs is that the individual members are liable to UK tax (if resident) but the LLP itself is not. If the individual members are foreign entities they will not be subject to UK tax laws, and the LLP itself is not subject to UK tax. This loophole makes an LLP attractive to money launderers, while being registered in the United Kingdom gives the LLP a possibly unjustified respectability.

Limited partnerships

1–24   These are not to be confused with limited liability partnerships, and are regulated by the Limited Partnership Act 1907. The Registrar of Companies maintains a register of limited partnerships.

Limited partnerships are not very common nowadays. As at March 2013 there are 23,828 in the United Kingdom, with about 11,099 in Scotland. In a limited partnership, there are two types of partner, the limited partner and the general partner. The limited partner puts capital into the business and is entitled to a return on his investment. He may take no part in the management whatsoever, or he will lose his limited status, but provided he obeys this rule he is protected to the extent that if the limited partnership goes into sequestration, he only loses the capital he has invested and no more. The other partner, known as the general partner, also puts capital into the limited partnership, but is personally liable for the limited partnership's losses. On the other hand he has all the rights of management. Occasions where limited partnerships are commonly used occur when a tenant of a farm is a limited partnership with the landlord as the limited partner, drawing an income, while the general partner is the farmer who does the work, takes the decisions, bears all the risk and keeps much of the profits. On other occasions the limited partners will be the parents in a farm-owning family and the general partners will be their children. Limited partnerships are also used as investment vehicles, when an investor or business angel will act as the limited partner, restricting his liability, taking no part in management but expecting a good return on his capital, while the general partner bears all the risk. There may be several limited partners and several general partners, but there must be at least one of each.

Limited liability companies

1–25   The main advantages of a limited liability company are as follows:

- A company has a legal personality separate from its members and its managers. Its members and its managers are not normally responsible for its debts unless the company is unlimited.

- The members do not have to bother themselves with the minutiae of managing the company. In general they delegate that power to the directors, instead expecting to receive dividends, capital appreciation in the value of their shares, voting rights for certain major matters (including dismissing directors) and such other rights as are available to the members under the company's constitution and under company law generally.
- Publication of the accounts is advantageous if the accounts show that the company is prospering, as creditors will then be prepared to deal with the company and investors to invest. On the other hand, if the accounts show that the company is not prospering, creditors and investors may feel less inclined to deal with or invest in the company.
- Companies may borrow large sums in a hurry because they can, with relative ease, grant security over their moveable assets by the use of a floating charge. This enables companies to take advantage of commercial opportunities.
- A successful company may ultimately be able to float its securities on a recognised stock market such as the London Stock Exchange. If all goes well and the floated securities are seen to be desirable, the original shareholders may make a great deal of money.
- A company may endure for a long time and retain its assets indefinitely even though its members and directors may change from time to time.
- Holding companies may set up subsidiaries through which to trade in new ventures. Providing the holding companies have not guaranteed their subsidiaries' debts, holding companies may enjoy all the benefits of their investments in the subsidiaries but avoid all the liabilities of those subsidiaries should the subsidiaries turn out to be unsuccessful.
- Some people enjoy the kudos of being a director of a company.

The disadvantages of being a company are as follows:

- Some directors resent the requirement to publish the company's accounts, as this allows competitors to find out too much about their company.
- There are incorporation costs and continual compliance costs, such as auditing and the provision of legal advice. These do not arise in some other forms of trading venture such as sole traders and partnerships.
- It is difficult to withdraw capital from a company except by following certain complicated rules or selling shares, assuming, that is, that the articles permit sale and that there is a willing buyer for the shares—which may not always be the case.
- Directors may believe that they will not normally be responsible for their companies' debts, but it is very common for commercial lenders to insist on personal guarantees by the directors for

insist on personal guarantees

their companies' borrowings. On certain other occasions, particularly in the context of insolvency, directors may be responsible for their company's losses.[54]

- Some directors, particularly of family companies, or if they have built the company up from nothing, find it difficult to accept that they are expected to run the company for the benefit of the whole body of shareholders, not merely for their own interests.

1–26 Features of companies that are neither advantageous nor disadvantageous:

- Perpetual existence is often said to be an advantage of companies, but in practice it makes very little difference.
- Taxation may sometimes favour incorporation or partnership (or limited liability partnership) according to the prevailing taxation rules. Companies do not have the benefit of personal allowances for income tax or capital gains tax but equally do not suffer inheritance tax.

COMMUNITY INTEREST COMPANIES AND CHARITIES

1–27 The Companies (Audit, Investigations and Community Enterprise) Act 2004 allowed certain companies to be set up to promote social enterprises, using their profits for a public good. Such a company is known as a community interest company ("CIC"). In addition to normal incorporation as a company, a potential CIC must also be registered with the Community Interest Companies Regulator, who, if satisfied that it falls within the required guidelines, will instruct Companies House to issue a certificate indicating that it is a CIC.[55] The virtue of a CIC, compared to a charity or even a charitable company, is that CICs may carry on business, whereas there are restrictions on the ways in which a charity may trade if it wishes to take advantage of certain tax benefits. Secondly, charity trustees are not allowed to draw salaries in their capacity as trustees unless the wording of the charity permits it and it is in the best interest of the charity. This means that a person who sets up a charity may not be reward himself from his own enterprise in setting the charity up. By contrast, those who set up and manage a CIC may get paid by their CIC provided that the CIC applies its remaining funds to the purposes for which it is set up. CICs are designed to enable philanthropic entrepreneurs to run businesses with the benefit of separate legal personality and limited liability (if necessary). A community interest company may wish to undertake projects whose aims are broader than the restricted range available to charities, and it is possible to "lock" the wording of the

CIC

---

[54] IA 1986 ss.212–216.
[55] See the website of the Regulator at *https://www.gov.uk/government/organisations/office-of-the-regulator-of-community-interest-companies* [Accessed April 22, 2014].

community interest company so that its profits and gains must be used for the public benefit. They have attracted considerable attention worldwide, in particular in Japan and in Canada.[56]

Charities in both Scotland and in the rest of the United Kingdom now **1–28** need to be registered with the Office of the Scottish Charity Regulator ("OSCR") and the Charities Commission respectively. They have to prepare a report and annual accounts which are sent to the relevant authority. If a charity is also a company, it also needs to comply with the requirements of the Companies Act 2006. A charitable company normally needs to have its articles of association approved by the relevant authority to ensure that the purposes for which the company has been set up are acceptable, and to ensure that any profits or gains of the charitable company will be used for those purposes. Since March 2011 it has also been possible to set up or run a charity through a special body known as a Scottish Charitable Incorporated Association ("SCIO").[57] This has the benefit of separate legal personality, but unlike a charity, the trustees do not carry out the SCIO's activities on its behalf, the SCIO being able itself to enter contracts, hire staff and so on. Although the SCIO has trustees, in general, unless they act carelessly, fraudulently, or beyond their authority, the trustees will not be personally liable for the activities of the SCIO. The SCIO's constitution must conform to certain guidelines and SCIOs may only exist to carry on charitable activities. As with a company, they must publish annual reports and annual accounts.

Scots Law and Company Law

Gladstone ensured that the nationality of a company should be included **1–29** in its incorporation documentation, and it is not, at least at present, possible to change that nationality. At the moment, a Scottish-registered company remains a Scottish-registered company even if its business is all over the world. Company law in Scotland has been strongly influenced by the greater commercial world of England, and while Scots law copes adequately with most areas of company law, one area that has been noticeably unsatisfactory, and has long been recognised as such, is the law relating to floating charges.[58]

Finally, it may be regrettable but no surprise that even major businesses in Scotland, such as construction companies, insurance companies and banks, often conduct their corporate business using English law, because inevitably so many more of the participants know English law, it is the dominant legal system and incoming businesses are unlikely to feel drawn to an unfamiliar and in some respects (as noted above)

---

[56] See the Regulator's annual report for 2012–13.

[57] For more detailed information about SCIOs, see their website at *http://www.oscr.org.uk/about-scottish-charities/scio/* [Accessed April 22, 2014]. The equivalent in England and Wales is known as a Charitable Incorporated Association.

[58] As may be seen in the controversy arising from the case of *Sharp v Thomson*, 1997 S.C. (HL) 66; 1997 S.L.T. 636.

unsatisfactory legal system. To take account of the increasing dominance
of English law, this book will frequently refer to English law. While
technically many English cases may not be binding on Scots law, it is
clearly pointless for a small island to have widely diverging commercial/
legal practices depending on which side of the Tweed one may happen to
be, and consequently much regard is paid to English cases. This book will
follow this precept.

COMPANY LAW AND JURISPRUDENCE *The theory or philosophy of law.*

1–30 Company law is very unsatisfactory from a jurisprudential point of view.
There is some academic discussion about the moral issues for involuntary
creditors of a company, such as victims of the company's negligence[59] or
the environment, whose future degradation at the hands of a company[60]
effectively subsidises the company's current profits. There is also discussion as to whether or not directors ought to pay attention to wider,
non-business considerations when deciding on company policy. This is
discussed in Chapter 9. There are those who think directors should do
this, and those who think that whether or not they choose to do so, they
should not be obliged to do so. As ever, there is a shifting balance to be
found between those companies where there are directors who ignore
wider considerations and see their duty as being owed to their shareholders, and others who are more alert to wider political and social
considerations but do not generate such good returns for their shareholders—but may possibly be better at preserving the long-term interests
of the company. At the moment, UK company law does allow a degree of
unfairness to certain creditors as the price of providing the benefit of
limited liability. But apart from these points, which are ultimately economic matters, company law does not greatly lend itself to philosophic
issues. Company law is about the regulation of power within a company,
and it is about the proper use of money within a company. Company law
is predominantly a pragmatic set of laws to help businesses make money
fairly. It presupposes capitalistic instincts and it is no surprise that former
socialist countries had no company law. Company law is not a deep law,
replete with significance for the rights of mankind: it is down to earth,
commercial, pragmatic and is ultimately about helping businesses work
effectively.

---

[59] See the end of Ch.2.

[60] For example, Exxon (the US name for Esso) caused untold damage to wildlife in Alaska
when its ship, the Exxon Valdez, ran aground. Although eventually some fines were paid
to regulatory agencies, the company has managed to avoid paying much for its
carelessness.

Further Reading

Paul L. Davis and Sarah Worthington, *Gower and Davies' Principles of Modern Company Law*, 9th edn (London: Sweet and Maxwell, 2012), Parts 1 and 2.

Mayson, French and Ryan, *Company Law* (Oxford, Oxford University Press, published annually).

For the texts, etc. of European Directives on company law, see *Butterworth's Company Law Handbook*, edited by Keith Walmsley (published annually).

Company law there to ensure, Business operate, and aid in their financial success.

CHAPTER 2

THE CORPORATE VEIL

THE IMAGINARY BARRIER

The separate legal identity of the company

2–01   Chapter 1 outlined the various commercial effects of the concept of
limited liability and the advantages, relative to other forms of trading
organisation, of the registered company. This chapter analyses the legal
effects of the separate legal personality of the company.

The general principle of the separate legal personality rule is that a
company is separate from those who own the company (the members),
those who direct it (its directors), and those who are employed by it (its
employees). The seminal case for this is the well-known case of *Salomon v
Salomon & Co Ltd*[1]:

> Salomon owned a bootmaking business. He was also the majority
> shareholder and managing director of a limited company, A. Salo-
> mon & Co Ltd, to which he sold his bootmaking business for the
> high but not fraudulent price of £39,000. The company could not
> pay the entire purchase price itself, so in his capacity as managing
> director Salomon arranged that the outstanding balance of the
> purchase price (£10,000) be treated as a loan, though recorded as
> debentures, payable to himself personally by the company, and
> secured over the company's assets by means of a charge.[2] Later
> Salomon transferred the debentures to another businessman, Bro-
> derip. The company suffered various financial difficulties, as a result
> of which the company was unable to pay Broderip the interest on the
> debentures. Broderip sued for his money and the company went into
> receivership and later into liquidation. Broderip received his money,
> and reassigned the debentures to Salomon, but there was nothing left
> over for the unsecured creditors.

---

[1] *Salomon v Salomon & Co Ltd* [1897] A.C. 22 (HL).
[2] In effect he had a mortgage over the company's assets, so that if the loan was not repaid,
he had a prior right to the secured assets ahead of any other creditors and would thereby
be the first to get his money back.

The unhappy unsecured creditors persuaded the liquidator to raise an action against Salomon personally on the grounds that the company was not set up properly,[3] that the debentures in Salomon's favour should be rescinded on the grounds of fraud, and that the contract for the sale of Salomon's business to the company should be rescinded since the value of the business had been overstated. The purpose of the litigation was to make Salomon liable to the creditors. The House of Lords held that as a matter of statutory interpretation, Salomon had complied with all the requirements of the Companies Act 1862 as regards incorporation, that there was no evidence of fraud (either in the issue of the debentures or in the valuation of the business) and that it was perfectly legitimate for Salomon to contract personally with his company both in respect of the debentures and in respect of the sale of his business to the company. The creditors were well aware that they had been dealing with a limited company, not Salomon personally; and if they chose to deal with a company, they had to be aware of the risks of doing so. One of those risks was that a secured creditor was in an advantageous position compared to the unsecured creditors. Salomon was not therefore personally liable to those creditors.

The important issues to be drawn from this are that: (i) Salomon and his company were two separate legal personalities who were free to contract with each other; and (ii) that in the absence of fraud there was nothing wrong with Salomon being a secured creditor of his own company even though he had been in a position, in his capacity as managing director and controlling shareholder, to make the company enter into a contract with himself.

This same principle was followed in *Lee v Lee's Air Farming Ltd*[4]: **2–02**

Mr Lee set up an aerial crop-spraying company in New Zealand with himself as the majority shareholder and governing director. His wife had one share. Following the proper procedures, he, as the main shareholder, caused the company to pass a resolution appointing himself the chief (and indeed only) pilot of the company. A contract of employment was signed, and his wages as company pilot were duly entered into the company's books. He later was killed while crop-spraying, and the question arose as to whether or not his widow was entitled to a payment from the company, under the (New Zealand) Workers Compensation Act 1922, because of his death during the course of his employment.[5] The company asserted that as

---

[3] Of the 20,006 issued shares, Salomon had 20,000 shares and his family had the rest. At the time, seven shareholders were needed for a company to be validly incorporated. The creditors believed that Salomon's arrangements were an abuse of the rules relating to incorporation.

[4] *Lee v Lee's Air Farming Ltd* [1961] A.C. 12.

[5] The action was raised against the company, which was insured, as required under the Workers Compensation Act 1922. It was really the insurers for the company that were trying to resist paying the widow.

governing director and controller of the company he was precluded from being a servant of his company. The Privy Council disagreed, and held that it was acceptable for Lee's company to contract with Lee personally for him to be employed as the company's chief pilot; and therefore his widow was entitled to her payment.

2–03 However, the separate legal personality of the company can work to a person's disadvantage too, as can be seen in the case of *Macaura v Northern Assurance Co Ltd*[6]:

> Macaura grew timber on his farm in Northern Ireland. The Government encouraged the growing of timber for use as pit props in mining, and to hold up trench walls in the event of another war in northern France. As part of the Government's encouragement for timber growing, a tax liability could be avoided by transferring the ownership of the growing timber, at the appropriate stage, to a limited company. Macaura duly did this, but neglected to insure the timber, now owned by the company, in the name of the company, instead keeping the insurance in his own name. The timber mysteriously caught fire, and on its destruction, he (and not his company) claimed the value of the timber from the insurers. The insurers successfully resisted the claim on the grounds that Macaura and the company were not the same, and he had no insurable interest in the timber.

These three familiar cases firmly establish the separate legal identity of the company.

The corporate veil

2–04   The corporate veil is the term given to the imaginary barrier that stands between the company and either or both of those who manage it (the directors) and those who own it (the members). On the whole this barrier prevents the directors and/or members being liable for the company's acts and omissions, but occasionally, the veil is said to be pierced,[7] on which occasion the directors and/or members may be found liable for the company's acts and omissions and lose the benefit of incorporation. Alternatively, the members (particularly if they are a holding company) may be able to have a benefit, attributable to the company, made available to themselves. The veil may also be pierced if a company is being used as a device to avoid honouring a legal obligation or evading the law in some way.

2–05   It is well recognised that the law relating to the occasions when the veil is pierced is by no means clear. Deciding when it should or should not be pierced is a matter of much concern both to disgruntled creditors and to

---

[6] *Macaura v Northern Assurance Co Ltd* [1925] A.C. 619.
[7] In the past the word "lifted" was much used, but following American usage, "pierced" is now the standard word.

anxious directors and shareholders. In principle, our laws make it deliberately difficult to pierce the corporate veil. While this may be infuriating for, say, a pursuer entitled to a payment of damages from a company which is a shell, its assets having been transferred elsewhere and the pursuer's claim now worthless,[8] we have to accept that our legislation occasionally allows this to happen. On an individual basis this can seem unfair and unjust, but it is the price we pay for the wider benefit to the commercial world of limited liability. The difficulty of piercing the corporate veil is a hazard of business life; and, after all, in practical terms it is little different from suing a sole trader who becomes bankrupt before a decree can be enforced against him.

The difficulty of knowing when exactly the veil may be pierced is not **2–06** restricted to the United Kingdom. Almost every country has difficulties with this. Some countries allow for veil-piercing where it would not be allowed in the United Kingdom. For example, in the USA the veil may be pierced where the directors of the company deliberately or otherwise undercapitalise the company so that creditors have no effective remedy against the company.[9] A difficulty for any country that makes veil-piercing easy, perhaps to protect creditors, is that it deters entrepreneurs from setting up companies in that country, thus depriving the country of valuable incorporation fees and corporation taxes. What may be good for consumers and some creditors may be less good for the country's finances.

There are two main grounds for piercing the veil in the United Kingdom, the first being where statute so requires it, and the second being where the courts have permitted it under common law.

Lifting the veil under statute

There is a number of occasions under the Companies Act 2006 ("the **2–07** CA 2006"), the Insolvency Act 1986 ("the IA 1986") and the Company Directors Disqualification Act 1986 ("the CDDA 1986") where this arises. The following demonstrate some of the better known occasions. For many of these, statute is using the threat of personal liability (either to the company itself, to its creditors, to certain members or to prospective investors) as a tool to make directors or members, as the case may be, act properly.

Absence of a trading certificate

When a public limited company is incorporated as a public limited **2–08** company (as opposed to incorporating initially as a private limited company and converting itself into a public limited company), the directors need a s.761 trading certificate from the Registrar of Companies. This can only be obtained if they provide the Registrar with certain forms and a statement of compliance.[10] If they have no certificate, are

---

[8] As happened in *Ord v Belhaven Pubs Ltd* [1998] 2 B.C.L.C. 447 CA.
[9] *Minton v Cavaney* (1961) 56 C2d 576.
[10] CA 2006 s.762.

trading, and having been called upon to obtain a certificate fail to obtain one within 21 days, they will be jointly and severally liable, together with the company, for any unpaid debts of the company.[11] This exists as a sanction for directors to ensure that public limited companies genuinely have the required capital to start trading.[12]

Liability on the insolvency of the company under the Insolvency Act 1986 ss.212–217

2–09   This topic is dealt with in greater detail in Ch.9, but in essence, when a company has gone into insolvent liquidation, a liquidator is entitled to look at the behaviour of the directors in the period leading up to the insolvency of the company. The liquidator may apply to the court for an order to make a director compensate the company[13] for any breach of his duty, statutory or otherwise, to the company, in that period,[14] for fraudulent trading (this applies to members as well)[15] and for wrongful trading,[16] which is where a director continues to accept credit or accept supplies when he knows or ought to know that the company is not in a position to honour its obligations, and fails to take all steps that he ought to take in order to minimise the loss to the creditors. In addition, if a company is put into insolvent liquidation and a new enterprise is created with a very similar name, usually in the same line of business and with the same personnel, the directors will be jointly and severally liable for the debts of the new enterprise if the new enterprise's name is the same or virtually the same as the old company's now prohibited name, and consent has not been granted by the courts for the use of the prohibited name or a name very similar to it.[17]

Liability under the Company Directors Disqualification Act 1986

2–10   If a director has been disqualified from acting as a director for any reason, and if he does then act as a director of a company despite being disqualified, he will be jointly and severally liable, together with the company for which he was acting, for the debts of that company.[18]

---

[11] CA 2006 s.767.
[12] The capital requirement is £50,000 (s.763) though only one quarter of each share needs to be paid up (s.586).
[13] There is no direct liability of the directors to the creditors, but the liquidator would use the money from the directors to help repay the creditors.
[14] IA 1986 s.212.
[15] IA 1986 s.213.
[16] IA 1986 s.214.
[17] IA 1986 ss.216, 217. *Advocate General for Scotland v Reilly* [2011] CSOH 141. This is also known as "phoenix trading" and is discussed in Ch.16.
[18] CDDA 1986 s.15. See also Ch.8.

Other statutory occasions for liability

These include the personal liability for directors where the requirement **2–11** to offer pre-emption rights under the CA 2006 ss.561 and 562 have been ignored by the directors and the deprived members have suffered loss[19]; for directors of a public company where they do not repay share applicants' money within 40 days after the failure to obtain a full subscription for an allotment of shares[20]; for directors of a public limited company where they allot shares although the minimum subscription has not been received by the company[21]; for those providing inaccurate information in a prospectus thereby causing loss to a person relying on that prospectus[22]; for members if they receive an unlawful distribution of profits and know it[23]; and various other occasions dealt with later in Ch.9.

There are also occasions under prevention of terrorism laws, taxation law and money-laundering rules (amongst others) which enable the courts to pierce the corporate veil as may be necessary, but such matters are beyond the ambit of this book.

Piercing the veil under common law

Piercing the veil under statute is relatively clear-cut. Would that the **2–12** same could be said of the common law. Under the common law, the cases collectively suggest that on some occasions the courts may be prepared to pierce the veil, but that on the whole they are very reluctant to do so. It was unfortunate that for many years there was no coherent policy on this matter. This made it difficult for a lawyer to advise directors or members when they might be personally liable for their company's acts and omissions, or to advise clients whether or not they might be able to seek redress against a company's directors or members who might have taken too much advantage of their company's separate legal identity. The very uncertainty of the law every year encouraged a few hardy litigants to see if directors or holding companies may be made personally liable for the acts of their companies or subsidiaries; and once in a while, temporarily, they succeeded,[24] though on the whole they were unlikely to be successful.[25] The position has been substantially altered by the case of *Prest v Petrodel Resources Ltd*[26] (discussed shortly) in which the Supreme Court,

---

[19] CA 2006 s.563(2).

[20] CA 2006 s.578(3).

[21] CA 2006 s.579(3).

[22] Financial Services and Markets Act 2000 s.90 (this is not restricted to directors, but in practice may well affect directors).

[23] CA 2006 s.847(2).

[24] For example, *Creasey v Breachwood Motors Ltd* [1992] B.C.C. 638, later overruled by *Ord v Belhaven Pubs Ltd* [1998] 2 B.C.L.C. 447 CA; but notwithstanding the subsequent overruling six years later, in the meantime Creasey had won his case, mainly because his opponent chose not to appeal.

[25] The issue of directors' personal responsibility to creditors and victims of their negligence will be addressed in Ch.9.

[26] [2013] 4 All E.R. 673; [2013] B.C.C. 571; [2013] 2 A.C. 415; [2013] UKSC 34; [2013] 3 W.L.R. 1.

and Lord Sumption in particular, closely examined the occasions when veil-piercing should, in its view, take place under common law.

One way of looking at the common law cases is to look at certain general categories, even though they overlap to some extent. Only in some of them was the veil permitted to be pierced, and in others a remedy other than veil-piercing would be more suitable.

Evasion of responsibilities

2–13   In *Gilford Motor Co Ltd v Horne*[27] a former manager, Horne, of a car-dealing business, Gilford Motor Co, had a restrictive covenant in his employment contract, preventing him from soliciting his former customers once he had left the business. Aware that he could not solicit his clients himself, Horne arranged for the formation of a new company, run by his wife and a former employee, which then employed him. Through the company he then approached his former customers. Gilford swiftly took out an injunction against both Horne's company and Horne personally to prevent such behaviour. Horne tried to argue that the restrictive covenant was too wide. The Court of Appeal rejected this specious argument, and ruled that the abuse of the corporate form to evade a previous obligation was unacceptable.[28] Indeed, had the court's decision been otherwise, any time anyone felt like evading a personal responsibility, he would merely have had to set up a company to evade his obligation—which would hardly be good law.

Lord Sumption in *Prest* believes that this is a good example of when veil-piercing should take place[29] though Lord Neuberger is not so sure.[30]

Public policy

2–14   In *Daimler Co Ltd v Continental Tyre and Rubber Co (Great Britain) Ltd*[31] which took place during World War I, Daimler was admittedly due to pay Continental a large sum of money. Daimler successfully contended that as a matter of public policy the courts should look behind the registration of Continental to see Continental's underlying predominantly German ownership and management and that Continental should be treated as having "enemy character". If it had enemy character, the debt should cease. As far as a company is concerned enemy character could be established by looking at who controlled it, in this case Germans; and thus Continental was not able to claim its debt.

As a cynical aside, during the First World War anti-German feeling ran high, and in London and elsewhere the homes of people with German names or German sympathisers had their windows smashed. It is unrealistic to think that the highest court in the land would at that

---

[27] *Gilford Motor Co Ltd v Horne* [1933] Ch. 935.
[28] See also *Jones v Lipman* [1962] 1 W.L.R. 832; [1962] 1 All E.R. 442, for the operation of the same principle.
[29] *Prest v Petrodel Resources Ltd* per Lord Sumption at 29.
[30] Per Lord Neuberger at paras 69–72.
[31] *Daimler Co Ltd v Continental Tyre and Rubber Co (Great Britain) Ltd* [1916] 2 A.C. 307.

perilous time have found in favour of Continental. Nowadays were such an issue to arise, the Trading with the Enemy Act 1939 would ensure that the debt would not need to be paid. The point of the case is that as a matter of public policy there may be occasions when it is possible to look behind the corporate veil.

The demise of the group entity theory

In *DHN Food Distributors Ltd v Tower Hamlets London Borough Council*[32] the Court of Appeal held that companies within a group of companies, including DHN, were so closely intertwined that it would have required a simple transfer of the legal title of a piece of land from one company within the group to another to enable certain compensation payments to be paid by the council to DHN. Technically the paperwork was missing, but as it could so very easily have been effected, Lord Denning said that the compensation ought to be paid.

2–15

This case established what is known as the "group entity theory" which presupposes that a group of companies all closely connected may be presumed to be one greater whole, known as a group entity. In this case there was no suggestion of fraud or deceit involved, and, on the face of it, it would have been unjust to deprive the business as a whole of the compensation otherwise payable had the appropriate paperwork been in place. Under these circumstances it was reasonable to have ordered the compensation to be paid. Nonetheless later courts were unimpressed by this decision. The House of Lords failed to follow the *DHN* decision in the Scottish case of *Woolfson v Strathclyde Regional Council*,[33] a case similar to *DHN*, but one in which the courts held that in principle companies should be treated as separate within a group, and that the corporate veil should only be pierced where special circumstances exist indicating that it is a "mere façade concealing the true facts".[34] The decision of the *Woolfson* case, and in particular the phrase "mere façade concealing the true facts", was later referred to with approval in the case of *Adams v Cape Industries Plc*,[35] while the *DHN* decision, while not overruled, was politely disparaged by being said to depend on the statutory provisions for compensation and on being expressed "somewhat broadly". The group entity theory is not, therefore, seen as having any continuing validity.

If a company was being used as a "façade concealing the true facts" it was for many years (until the *Prest* case) seen to be acceptable to pierce its veil, or conversely, the veil would not be pierced if the company was not acting as a façade, instead acting perfectly normally, without any good reason to pierce the veil. In the *Woolfson* case, Woolfson very much wanted the veil to be pierced but the courts refused to do so, more or less taking the view that if he had structured his business through various

---

[32] *DHN Food Distributors Ltd v Tower Hamlets London Borough Council* [1976] 1 W.L.R. 852; 3 All E.R. 462.
[33] *Woolfson v Strathclyde Regional Council*, 1978 S.C. (HL) 90; 1978 S.L.T. 159.
[34] See Lord Keith of Kinkel's speech at 96 (or for S.L.T. at 161).
[35] *Adams v Cape Industries Plc* [1990] Ch. 433; [1991] 1 All E.R. 929 CA.

companies, he had to take the consequences of doing so, one of them being that any compensation payments would be payable to his companies and not to him. In *Adams* the courts saw no reason in the absence of any "façade concealing the true facts" to make a holding company liable to pay compensation for injuries sustained by an employee of one of that company's subsidiaries. The holding company had done nothing wrong and was using the corporate veil entirely legitimately.

If the company really is a "façade concealing the true facts", Lord Sumption in *Prest* suggests that it is acceptable to look behind the concealing façade to see who the true actors are.[36]

Subsidiaries

2–16   As far as a holding company's liability for its subsidiaries' debts are concerned, the position is well expressed in Lord Templeman's famous words in *Re Southard Co Ltd*[37]:

> "A parent company may spawn a number of subsidiary companies, all controlled directly or indirectly by the shareholders of the parent company. If one of the subsidiary companies, to change the metaphor, turns out to be the runt of the litter, and declines into insolvency to the dismay of the creditors, the parent company and the other subsidiary companies may prosper to the joy of the shareholders without any liability for the debts of the insolvent subsidiary."

In other words, holding companies may reap the benefits of dividends and management fees they may obtain from and charge to subsidiaries, but should the subsidiaries become insolvent, the holding company is not responsible for the subsidiaries' debts. If a holding company effectively conducts all its business through its subsidiaries, it can insulate itself from any debt whatsoever.

Agency

2–17   Historically the courts sometimes tried to pierce the corporate veil by saying that the company was acting as an agent for its members, thus making the members liable for the company's actions, and in particular a holding company liable for its subsidiaries acting as the holding company's agents. This approach was favoured in a few cases such as *Firestone Tyre and Rubber Co Ltd v Llewellin*[38] and *Smith, Stone and Knight Ltd v Birmingham Corp*,[39] but then appears to have lapsed. One reason for this is that it may be acceptable to make a company the agent for its

---

[36] *Prest*, per Lord Sumption at 28. As an example of the concealment principle, he cites with approval *Gencor ACP Ltd v Dalby* [2000] 2 B.C.L.C. 734.

[37] *Re Southard Co Ltd* [1979] 1 W.L.R. 1198 at 1208; [1979] 3 All E.R. 556 at 565.

[38] *Firestone Tyre and Rubber Co Ltd v Lewellyn* [1956] 1 W.L.R. 352; [1956] 1 All E.R. 693, affirmed [1957] 1 W.L.R. 464; [1957] 1 All E.R. 561 HL.

[39] *Smith, Stone and Knight Ltd v Birmingham Corp* [1939] 4 All E.R. 116.

shareholders if that is something that has specifically been agreed between the parties,[40] but if the courts start inferring agency and allowing the veil to be pierced merely because the shareholders control the company, there would be almost unlimited opportunities for veil-piercing and the law would become even more complex and unmanageable than it already is.

Assumption of responsibility

In *Chandler v Cape plc*,[41] which at the time of writing is awaiting an **2–18** appeal to the Supreme Court, a holding company which had control of a subsidiary, a subsidiary whose insurance cover had lapsed, was found liable in tort for damages payable to a former employee of that defunct subsidiary. The Court of Appeal was insistent that the issue was not one of piercing the corporate veil but rather one where the holding company has assumed responsibility of the subsidiary and the subsidiary's employees, in particular by the holding company's management of the health and safety procedures that the subsidiary was expected to follow. The case was solely concerned with the extent of the duty of care and not with the piercing of the veil. Conversely, in the case of *Cramaso LLP v Viscount Reidhaven's Trustees*,[42] the trustees tried to maintain that they were not liable for a negligent statement made to an individual by the trustees' employee about the state of a grouse moor. This was because the statement was made to the individual and not to the limited liability partnership (one of whose members was that individual) that eventually took on a lease of the moor as a result of the information in the statement. The Supreme Court did not accept the trustees' view. The court held that it was foreseeable that the benefit of the statement could be extended to a corporate vehicle connected with that individual and which ultimately took the lease. This case is also nothing to do with piercing the veil, but is of interest because of the presence of the corporate body, which though separate from the individual to whom the statement was made, was deemed to come within the ambit of responsibility of the person who made the statement.

Alternative remedy in statute

In *Yukong Lines of Korea Ltd v Rendsburg Investments Corp of Liberia* **2–19** *(No.2)*[43] the director of Rendsburg, realising that Rendsburg would have to pay substantial damages to Yukong for breaching the terms of its charterparty with Yukong, abstracted a substantial sum of Rendsburg's money. He paid it to a company that he controlled personally, and then disappeared, no doubt with the abstracted funds. Although the

---

[40] This happened in *Rainham Chemical Works Ltd v Belvedere Fish Guano Co. Ltd* [1921] 2 A.C. 645 HL.
[41] [2012] 1 W.L.R. 3111; [2012] 3 All E.R. 640.
[42] UK Supreme Court, 11 February 11, 2014.
[43] *Yukong Lines of Korea Ltd v Rendsburg Investments Corp of Liberia (No.2)* [1998] 1 W.L.R. 294.

circumstantial evidence was not to the director's advantage, it was not, in Toulson J.'s view, sufficient to displace the normal rule concerning the corporate veil, and the plaintiffs were not permitted to raise proceedings against the director personally, even though Rendsburg by now had minimal assets. This was partly because the director had never been a contracting party to the charterparty,[44] partly because Yukong too late in the day wanted him to be a defendant, but mainly because what the plaintiffs were expected to do was to have the defendant company wound up. The plaintiffs could then obtain an order under the IA 1986 s.423(2)[45] to enable the liquidator to find the abstracted funds in order to repay them to the company.[46]

2–20   The problem with all this is practical: it is easy for the courts to say that the liquidator must trace the abstracted funds, but by the time a liquidator has been appointed and found his way through the company's accounts, the abstracted funds will have long since disappeared into the banking system, no doubt laundered through some unscrupulous offshore bank. The creditor thus has to pay the costs of petitioning the courts for the liquidation of the defendant company and of tracing the funds, which are likely to still be under the control of the rogue director, who of course will be taking every advantage of foreign banking secrecy laws and any other methods of avoiding payment. And there may be other creditors who will wish to share in any sums that the liquidator recovers.

If this seems unfair on the plaintiffs, the plaintiffs in this case could have taken more steps to protect themselves. The plaintiffs might have obtained a bond from Rendsburg's bank to make good any loss arising from any breach of the charterparty, or obtained some other form of security against default.

2–21   And finally there is always the commercial point: Yukong was not obliged to deal with Rendsburg, a Liberian company; if you deal with companies registered in flag of convenience countries you must expect from time to time that they will take unfair advantage of their position, and it is up to those who deal with such companies to be on their guard.

Piercing the veil where companies are used in criminal activities

2–22   The courts have little difficulty in piercing the veil when a company is being used as a "façade concealing the true facts" in criminal cases. In a number of cases involving fraud or the evasion of VAT or tax the courts

---

[44] The same principle was applied in *VTB Capital plc v Nutritek International Corpn.* [2013] UKSC 5; [2013] 2 W.L.R. 398 where it was ruled inadmissible to bring a director of the defendant company into the action.

[45] This section does not apply in Scotland, but had the case arisen in Scotland it might have been open to a liquidator to prove that the payment had been a gratuitous alienation under s.242 of the Insolvency Act 1986.

[46] Another option would be for the liquidator to pursue the director personally for his breach of fiduciary duty to the company—though as the director had disappeared anyway this would probably have been a waste of time and effort.

will pierce the veil if they think that the company is the alter ego of the fraudster or tax evader. In *R. v Bassam Omar*[47] a tax evader used an existing and legitimately founded company to hide the proceeds of his tax evasion. The proceeds were used to fund the purchase of property by the company. Richards J. in the Court of Appeal said as follows:

"The important point in the present case is that the company was used by the appellant for the purposes of fraud and that, as the judge[48] found, it was the appellant's alter ego, with the appellant running it and making all the decisions, including decisions on the purchase of the properties. The judge's findings on those matters were all properly open to him on the evidence. They meant that he was fully entitled to lift the corporate veil and to treat the benefit accruing during the period of the company's involvement in the fraud as a benefit of the appellant. Once the corporate veil was lifted ... he was entitled on the facts to treat the properties as assets of the appellant, even though they had been purchased by the company's money."[49]

As a result of this, the court made a compensation order requiring the **2–23** properties in the appellant's company to be sold. In *Kensington International Ltd v Congo*,[50] the Republic of Congo, which had previously defaulted on its debts, set up a network of companies for the express purpose of preventing the proceeds of the sale of valuable oil from Congo being attached by its creditors. Cooke J. had no difficulty in piercing the corporate veil of companies which superficially appeared to be separate companies but were in fact all controlled by one particular official from the Congo for the express purpose of carrying out sham transactions and avoiding pre-existing liabilities. Although there appear to be no recent cases in Scotland covering this particular point, there is no reason to think that the courts in Scotland would be any less willing to pierce the corporate veil in respect of similar criminal matters.

Fraud carried out through a company

In *Standard Chartered Bank v Pakistan National Shipping Corporation* **2–24** (No.2),[51] one of the defendants, Mr Mehra, knowingly gave false information to Standard Chartered Bank in order to receive payment under a letter of credit. This was done by done by persuading officials in the Pakistan National Shipping Corporation to backdate a bill of lading. Mr Mehra tried to avoid liability by saying that he had made the fraudulent misrepresentation on behalf of his company, Oakprime Ltd, and that it, but not he, should be liable. He did this on the basis of a previous case,

---

[47] *R. v Bassam Omar* [2005] 1 Cr. App. R. (S.) 86.
[48] This was the trial judge in the first hearing.
[49] *R. v Bassam Omar* [2005] 1 Cr. App. R. (S.) 86 at [18].
[50] *Kensington International Ltd v Congo* [2006] 2 B.C.L.C. 296.
[51] [2002] UKHL 43; [2003] 1 A.C. 959; [2002] 3 W.L.R. 1547 HL.

Williams v Natural Life Health Foods Ltd[52] where a director had made
negligent misrepresentations but had been negligent through his company
and thus avoided personal liability. The House of Lords was unimpressed
by this argument, in effect saying that negligence is one thing, and fraud
another, but more importantly observing that fraud is a tort (delict) that
an individual commits, whether or not a company is involved as well, and
that when an individual commits a fraud, he remains liable for it, even if
his company is jointly and severally liable with him. As Lord Rodger of
Earlsferry pithily observed, true to his Roman law roots, *culpa tenet suos
auctores*.[53] In these circumstances, no piercing of the veil is necessary, for
the liability for fraud remains with the person who instructed the fraud,
whether or not it is done through the agency of a company. And of
course there is a practical reason for this decision: were it otherwise,
whenever anyone felt like committing a fraud, he would set up a company
to do it for him, and thus avoid liability. The matter here is not veil-
piercing but fraud, and the presence of the company is irrelevant.

The current position on piercing the corporate veil in civil matters

2–25   As indicated earlier, the recent case of *Prest v Petrodel Resources Ltd*[54]
has to some extent clarified the occasions when the corporate veil may be
pierced. This case featured a wealthy Nigerian oil-trader, Michel Prest,
who resisted almost every attempt to pay his ex-wife, Yasmin, a former
model, the maintenance and other sums that she and her children should
have received from him.[55] Exasperated by his reluctance to pay her
money she expected, she sought an order from the courts requiring
various companies, of which he was the controlling shareholder and
director, to transfer various properties to her in settlement of the sums
she was owed. The properties had been owned by the companies for some
time, in some cases predating the marriage. There was no suggestion that
the properties had been placed into the companies fraudulently, but the
properties were at least realisable and tangible assets within the United
Kingdom. An order was made in the lower courts ordering the companies
to transfer the property to Mrs Prest. The companies asserted that the
order was wrongly granted. The matter finally found itself before the
Supreme Court.

The leading judgments were given by Lord Sumption and Lord Neuberger. Lord Sumption clearly had little time for Prest and was

---

[52] [1998] 1 W.L.R. 830.

[53] It is difficult to convey the succinctness of this Latin phrase, for not only does it mean
that no-one should blame his subordinates or delegates for what he has authorised, but
also that the blame for an improper action remains with the person who instigated it even
if others carried it out.

[54] [2013] 4 All E.R. 673; [2013] B.C.C. 571; [2013] 2 A.C. 415; [2013] UKSC 34; [2013] 3
W.L.R. 1.

[55] Prest, a former lawyer who considered training for the priesthood, used to work for the
late Marc Rich, one of the world's most successful and controversial commodities traders, and founder of Glencore Xstrata and Trafigura. Rich was substantially involved in
oil-trading with countries subject to sanctions. Rich fled from the USA to Switzerland to
avoid racketeering and tax evasion charges that could have led to 300 years in prison.

determined to find a way to make Prest treat his ex-wife properly. There are four main strands to the judgment. The first is that Sumption was unable to establish that there was anything inherently improper about the properties being owned by Prest's companies and that there were no grounds to pierce the corporate veils of the companies. The third was that despite some suggestions to the contrary, there was nothing in the Matrimonial Proceeedings Act 1973[56] to suggest that the corporate veil should be pierced in matrimonial disputes in a different way from the occasions when it would be pierced in other commercial disputes. The fourth was that the properties held by the companies were held on a resulting trust for Prest, as a result of which he was deemed to be the beneficial owner of the trusts. As he was the beneficial owner, he was deemed to own them. If so, the properties could indeed be removed from the companies (the nominal owners), and the companies be required to transfer the properties to Mrs Prest. A resulting trust is a term of English law whereby if a settlor transfers an asset of his into a trust of which he is the beneficiary. Unless there is clear evidence of consideration for the transfer or clear benefit to someone else, the presumption is that the asset is not truly held in trust for the settlor and that the property is actually his.[57] The fact that the consideration for the transfer of the properties was in most of the cases only £1, and the fact that the companies had been so obstructive in complying with the courts' demands that the properties be transferred to Mrs Prest, provided the adverse inference that the companies were acting under Prest's direction and that the properties were being held for his benefit. Although the property titles were in the companies' names, Prest was the beneficial owner of the properties. And on these grounds, the properties were required to be transferred to Mrs Prest.

The second strand of the judgment, from a corporate lawyer's point of view, is the most significant. Lord Sumption closely reviewed a number of **2–26** cases where the corporate veil had been pierced in order to ascertain that veil-piercing was not necessary in this particular case. Lord Sumption was keen to set out guidelines when veil-piercing could take place, while making it clear that he was had no wish to extend the occasions when the corporate veil should be pierced. He indicated that in his view veil-piercing should only take place where a company was being used to evade a legal obligation or to frustrate the operation of law. In particular he cited the case of *Gilford Motor Co Ltd v Horne*[58] as being a good example of this. He also said that cases where a director or controlling shareholder uses a company to conceal assets from creditors or others are not cases where the veil should be pierced, since in most of these cases the assets are

---

[56] This is the Act used in English courts to decide the division of assets between spouses.
[57] The resulting trustee has a duty to look after the assets of the trustor for the benefit of the trustor: *Barclays Bank Ltd v Quistclose Investments Ltd* [1970] A.C. 567; *Twinsectra Ltd v Yardley* [2002] UKHL 12; [2002] 2 A.C. 164.
[58] *Gilford Motor Co Ltd v Horne* [1933] Ch. 935.

lurking in the company which is therefore an agent or nominee of the director.[59] Under those circumstances veil-piercing should not take place since there were other remedies to achieve the desired result.

Lord Sumption's decision

2–27   In essence, Lord Sumption's view is that where someone tries to avoid an unwelcome obligation and underhandedly uses a company to get round the obligation, the corporate veil of the company may be pierced. Where a company is being used to hide assets on the concealment principle, agency law may instead be used, since the recipient company is acting as the agent of the person hiding the assets.[60] Where statute may be used, it should be used. Where fraud is taking place, the fraudster remains liable. If an alternative remedy, such as the use of resulting trusts in England, could apply, that should be used too. But veil-piercing, in principle, should be sparingly undertaken.

Lord Neuberger's views

2–28   An interesting aside to Lord Sumption's decision in *Prest* is Lord Neuberger's decision. Lord Neuberger had taken the trouble to see where the corporate veil could be pierced in other English-speaking jurisdictions,[61] but found himself no wiser after the exercise. Initially tempted to abandon any attempt to lay down any rule as to when the veil should be pierced, he finally agreed that Lord Sumption's approach was probably the best solution.[62] However, he did touch on an important point, which is that it is extremely difficult to decide when exactly the corporate veil should be pierced. It is not a question of piercing the veil because it would be the just and proper thing to do: if anything, the scales are weighted against veil-piercing except where there is evasion of obligations, frustration of the operation of law or where statute allows it. Other occasions for making directors or controlling shareholders liable should be carried out by other methods where possible without necessarily piercing the veil. His researches seem to indicate that other countries find this problem just as difficult as we do in the United Kingdom.

There may be a good reason for this. We have constructed an artificial construct, called the veil of incorporation, which under certain circumstances allows companies and limited liability partnerships to behave with impunity in ways that were they human actors would excite dismay. This is never going to sit well with the sense that people who behave improperly ought to be called to account for their misdeeds. Directors or

---

[59] Lord Sumption believes that the case of *Trustor AB v Smallbone* [2001] W.L.R. 1177; [2002] B.C.C. 795, is a good example of concealment, and that while it achieved the correct result, actually it was for the wrong reason.

[60] In England, the doctrine of "knowing receipt" may be invoked, whereby someone holding assets that he knows are not his is obliged to look after them carefully for the true owner and to return them to the true owner. Scotland does not have this doctrine, but the same result may be achieved by the principle of unjust enrichment.

[61] *Prest* per Lord Neuberger at 72–75.

[62] At 81.

shareholders who behave improperly through a company do sometimes "get away with it". This is the nature of company law and it just has to be accepted.

Difficulties with the overall decision

The major problem with the Supreme Court's decision in *Prest* is that **2–29** it only works well in small companies where there are few directors and controlling shareholders, and best with only one director and shareholder who are the same person. In each case it is easy to see what it is going on. When a large company starts evading its legal responsibilities or frustrating the operation of law, it is often much harder to see where this is taking place or who authorises it, and at what level it is being authorised or condoned. The other remedies (instead of veil-piercing) that Lord Sumption suggests should be used wherever possible may not always be feasible, may be too expensive, or too daunting.

What the decision overlooks is the human level. When companies behave improperly, as, for example, encouraging bank staff to sell unsuitable payment protection insurance, it is natural to think that directors ought to bear some responsibility, moral or otherwise, for their companies' actions, and the veil should be pierced to make them liable. So far, this has not happened, and it is unlikely to do so unless legislation is brought in to achieve this or someone with deep pockets is willing to fund a test case. Even if legislation were considered, it would be difficult to draft, and the end result might deter business. So, in the meantime, the reality is that veil-piercing within larger companies, even where evasion of legal responsibilities and frustration of the operation of law are happening, is unlikely to take place, even if it is possible with smaller companies.

THE CRIMINAL RESPONSIBILITY OF COMPANIES

One of the most difficult areas of company law is that of the criminal **2–30** responsibility of companies, and their directors, for certain crimes. There is not normally any difficulty with statutory strict liability crimes, where the prosecution need not prove that anyone within the company actually had the mens rea or wicked intention to commit a crime: it is enough that the crime was committed.[63] Examples of such crimes are pollution and health and safety offences. The company is publicly embarrassed, fined, and sometimes mends its ways.

The situation is more difficult with crimes of recklessness that lead to death.

Parliament resolved this difficulty in the form of the Corporate Man- **2–31** slaughter and Corporate Homicide Act 2007. The name was carefully

---

[63] Much depends on the wording of the strict liability clauses in the legislation. Some strict liability offences have exemptions if it can be proved that the company took all practical steps or exercised all due diligence to prevent the offence occurring.

chosen to reflect the fact that the law was to be in most respects the same in both England and Wales and in Scotland. In essence, where an organisation (not just a company)[64] commits a "gross breach" of a "relevant duty of care" owed by the company to a victim, resulting in death (not merely injury) of the victim, the organisation, at least as far as corporations are concerned, will be guilty of an offence if the way in which its activities are managed or organised by "senior management" is a substantial element in the breach.[65] The words "relevant duty of care" are explained in s.2. A relevant duty of care is one of certain duties owed by an organisation: (i) being that owed under the law of negligence[66] to its employees or other people working for it[67]; (ii) being that of an occupier of premises[68]; and (iii) being that of a supplier of goods and services, or an organisation carrying on any construction or maintenance work, carrying on of any commercial activity, and using or keeping of any plant, vehicle or other thing.[69] It is for the jury to decide if there has been a gross breach (s.8).

The court may make a "remedial order" if the company is convicted, in order to prevent the breach happening again (s.9), and may also order a publicity order to "name and shame" the company in question (s.10). There is no individual liability for directors in terms of being art and part with the actual offence (s.18). Proceedings under this Act may also be conjoined with proceedings arising out of breaches of health and safety (s.19). As with health and safety prosecutions, the penalty that the Act imposes is an unlimited fine.

2–32   *R. v Peter Eaton and Cotswold Geotechnical Holdings Limited*[70] is the first case where a successful prosecution took place. An employee working in a pit was killed when the walls of the pit collapsed on him and it was held that the company had committed a gross breach of its duty of care and that poor management was a substantial element in that breach. This decision was appealed but the Court of Appeal rejected the appeal. The case is important not just for the decision but also because it sets out the level of fine to which the company became subject. Since that first case, there have been others, notably *R v JMW Farms Ltd*[71] and *IR v Lion Steel Equipment Ltd*[72] both of which provide further details about how the fines should be assessed. Although there have, so far as is known,

---

[64] The Corporate Manslaughter and Corporate Homicide Act 2007 uses the word "organisation" to apply to corporations, various Government departments, the police force, and any partnership, trade union or employers' association that employs people (s.1(2)). This text only deals with the Act as it applies to corporations, though it also applies to partnerships employing staff.

[65] See Corporate Manslaughter and Corporate Homicide Act 2007 s.1.

[66] This word was used in preference to "delict" or "tort".

[67] See Corporate Manslaughter and Corporate Homicide Act 2007 s.2(1)(a).

[68] See Corporate Manslaughter and Corporate Homicide Act 2007 s.2(1)(b).

[69] See Corporate Manslaughter and Corporate Homicide Act 2007 s.2(1)(c).

[70] [2011] EWCA Crim 1337; [2012] 1 Cr. App. R. (S.) 26.

[71] 2011 NICC 17.

[72] Unreported Manchester Crown Court, July 20, 2012.

been no prosecutions in Scotland there are more pending for England and Wales.[73] So far the prosecutions have been against small companies, which have sometimes pleaded guilty anyway. The Crown Prosecution Service has shied away from taking on a large well-funded company, perhaps because it may be easier to prosecute such companies for breach of health and safety regulations instead, and perhaps because there may be difficulty in establishing that senior management was responsible for the gross breach of the duty of care to the victim. As is so often the case with companies, it can be very difficult to prove that senior management knew or would have condoned what was going on in the lower reaches of a company.

The Act had been a long time in the making, as it sought to reconcile the desire of the victims' families to see companies punished in a realistic manner with the desire of directors and other managers not to be made scapegoats for unfortunate accidents. The potential for an unlimited fine is no doubt concentrating directors' minds. The publicity order that a court may grant may have some effect amongst more conscientious employers, or, in the case of publicly quoted companies, cause reputational damage which may affect the share price. Remedial orders may ensure that proper attention is paid to safety standards previously ignored.

The Act specifically does not attribute liability for corporate homicide to directors. On the other hand, the Act does sweep away all the difficulties associated with attributing a fatality to any specific persons within a company by instead concentrating on the way that a company is managed generally: is it managed prudently, with proper attention to health and safety matters, and due regard to the wellbeing of employees, or is it managed in a foolhardy and reckless manner, cutting costs and failing to maintain machinery properly?

As regards less contentious and non-fatal matters involving the crim- **2–33** inal liability of companies, probably the leading case in England is *Re Supply of Ready Mixed Concrete (No.2)*.[74] In this case senior management had explicitly undertaken to the Restrictive Practices Court that its middle management, which had been secretly operating a cartel with other middle managers in the concrete business, would no longer operate the cartel. Middle management at RMC was duly told not to operate any more cartels, but nevertheless disobeyed the instructions from senior management. The ensuing cartel was discovered and the company was successfully prosecuted. In vain did senior management explain that middle management had disobeyed express instructions: if the undertaking given to the court was to be meaningful it had to be adhered to, and senior management ought to have monitored middle management properly so that middle management did not repeat its former offences.

There are many sections in the Companies Act 2006[75] and elsewhere

---

[73] Pinsent Masons established that in 2012 the Crown Prosecution Service was examining 63 possible prosecutions in 2012.

[74] *Re Supply of Ready Mixed Concrete (No.2)* [1995] 1 A.C. 456.

[75] See Companies Act 2006 Pt 36 (ss.1121–1133).

which if contravened may result in the conviction of the company or its directors. These sections are mostly regulatory offences where directors may be fined or imprisoned for various failures to lodge the correct documents in time or failure to carry out undertakings required by law. This book does not venture into these criminal matters.

2–34   There are fundamental problems involved in fixing companies and their directors with criminal responsibility. Punishing a company is difficult. A company itself cannot be imprisoned. If instead a company is fined, the ones who suffer are the innocent shareholders or employees, and the fine needs to be enormous to make any difference at all to the profits of a large company. If the fine was very large indeed, the fine might actually put the company out of business, thus hurting innocent employees and inconveniencing its suppliers. Should a director be imprisoned for an unfortunate one-off lapse? Imprisoning the directors could cause a company to collapse, as well as deterring able employees from accepting responsibilities and becoming directors. No director would wish to be the "health and safety" director since he would be the one most likely to be found at fault and most likely to go to prison. Ultimately, the desire to prosecute companies arises from the perception that companies in practice are not often seen to suffer when they act recklessly. From a moral point of view, it is regarded as invidious that a company appears not to feel a sense of opprobrium or humiliation, such as a murderer should feel when he is convicted and sent to prison. Politically, there is a call for "justice to be done" and directors and others to suffer when sloppy practices cause death or injury to a company's employees or customers.

Some legislation is willing to grapple with these difficulties: for example, the Bribery Act 2010 not only forbids bribery generally but section 7 of that Act makes failing to prevent bribery by employees or agents of a company a criminal offence. It is not enough not to know about the bribery; the company should actively try to prevent it happening at all by having proper procedures in place.[76]

One solution adopted in England and Wales is to have Deferred Prosecution Agreements ("DPAs")[77] which are effectively a form of plea bargain. The company agrees to pay fines and compensation and to mend its ways with a certain set time in return for the Crown Prosecution Service not proceeding with charges. If the company defaults, the company will then be prosecuted. This can save a great deal of time and expense, not to mention relieving the prosecution of the burden of proving that there was a directing mind within the company that made the company commit whatever crimes it did commit. Some corporate crimes have significant implications for companies that are found guilty, because they may the bar the companies from being given contracts with the Government or being able to borrow from banks, it being a common

---

[76] David Green of the Serious Fraud Office suggests this broadly American approach should be applied to a wide range of corporate crimes (speech at a conference with Baker Mackenzie, June 6, 2013).

[77] See Crime and Courts Act 2013 Sch.17.

term of loan agreements that the borrowing companies have not been convicted of any crime involving fraud, money-laundering or bribery. At present there are no plans to have DPAs within Scotland.[78]

The Moral Issue and a Company's Involuntary Creditors

Most creditors of a company are in a position to bargain with a company **2–35** and to establish the degree of risk they can absorb from the company. But this is not true of involuntary creditors, these being diffuse creditors such as the environment (in the case of a polluting company) or employees in an area of high unemployment. A further example are victims of torts or delicts perpetrated by the company, particularly when companies that would otherwise be due to pay damages to the victims of their negligence deliberately or otherwise go out of business, thus avoiding paying any negligence claims. As an example of this, during 2001, 600 or so former employees of a South African subsidiary of a well-known British asbestos-manufacturing company, Cape Industries Plc ("Cape"), tried to sue Cape for their asbestos-induced work-related ailments, mostly cancer and lung disease. The subsidiary had been closed down on Cape's orders as the demand for asbestos had diminished following recognition of its dangers, and as the subsidiary was defunct there was no point in suing it. The subsidiary's management had abandoned its factory, leaving clouds of powdery carcinogenic asbestos swirling around to be inhaled by the former employees and their families, most of whom were too poor or ill to leave the area to look for a healthier place to live. After an immense struggle, leaving aside the question of the liability of Cape for its subsidiary, the House of Lords held that the victims were able to have their case heard in the United Kingdom instead of South Africa.[79] The next battle was to establish whether Cape could be held liable for its subsidiary's actions. The point was never established because the case was settled by Cape's insurers. This suggests the following:

- that the victims thought they had better accept a good offer while it still was available and before their money ran out;
- that Cape may have thought that the victims had such a good moral case against them that it was better to settle quickly than attract bad publicity;[80] and
- that the insurers for Cape may have considered that the House of Lords might have ruled in favour of the victims in the light of Cape's lack of concern for the victims.

---

[78] For a good analysis of DPAs and the Scottish position, see Stocker and Keith "DPAs: cross border confusion", 2013 J.L.S.S. 32–33.

[79] *Lubbe v Cape Industries Plc (No.2)* [2000] 1 W.L.R. 1545; [2000] 4 All E.R. 268.

[80] The share price of Cape plc during the court case collapsed dramatically, suggesting that the market thought the case might well go against Cape plc.

This case shows up very clearly the major problem with the idea of the corporate veil. There is little doubt that the dying black workers of the South African subsidiary were only marginally in a position to bargain with their employers, that the factories were not properly looked after and that environmental breaches took place. Although Cape was legally entitled to close down its subsidiary, and although normally a holding company is not liable for the debts of its subsidiaries,[81] it is arguable that Cape had a moral duty towards its subsidiary's employees, having enjoyed the fruits of their labours in the past; and many would think that it would have been unjust to refuse the employees a remedy and abandon them to bleak deaths from asbestos-related illnesses. However, had the House of Lords ruled in favour of the employees, the United Kingdom would overnight have become a less attractive place in which to do business as holding companies became liable for their subsidiaries; furthermore, liability indemnity premiums would have gone up, prices would have gone up and business might have fled abroad to more business-friendly regimes.

Although the recent case of *Prest v Petrodel Resources Ltd*[82] seems to suggest that were a similar case to take place now, it is likely that the pursuers' case would not be successful, on the grounds that the corporate veil was not being used to evade a responsibility or to frustrate the operation of law, it would still be a difficult decision at a human level for the judges to take. No doubt in the *Lubbe* case the House of Lords was very relieved not to have had to make it.

Further Reading

Dignam and Lowry, *Company Law*, 7th edn (OUP, 2012), Ch.3.

Brenda Hannigan, "Wedded to Salomon: evasion, concealment and confusion on piercing the veil of the one-man company" (2013) 50 Irish Jurist 11.

Elisabeth Roxburgh, "*Prest v Petrodel Resources Ltd*: cold comfort for Mrs Prest in Scotland", 2013 S.L.T. 223.

---

[81] *Re Southard and Co Ltd* [1979] 1 W.L.R. 1198; [1979] 3 All E.R. 556.
[82] [2013] UKSC 34.

CHAPTER 3

COMPANY INCORPORATION

THE PRACTICALITIES OF INCORPORATION

The initial documentation

Part of the purpose of the Companies Act 2006 was to make it easier **3–01** and less complex to set up and run a company in the interests of making the United Kingdom an attractive place in which to do business. The rules for setting up a company are therefore handily shown at the beginning of the Act, and they have deliberately been written in a manner that is relatively easy to follow. With effect from October 1, 2009, to set up a company all that is required is the following:

- the completion of the memorandum of association[1]; and
- an application for registration.[2]

The application for registration must contain the following:

- the company's proposed name[3];
- its country of registration within the United Kingdom[4];
- the liability of the members[5];
- a statement indicating that the company is either private or public[6];
- a statement of capital[7] or a statement of guarantee[8];
- a statement of the proposed officers of the company[9];
- a set of articles of association if the standard default model has not been used[10];
- a statement of compliance[11]; and

---

[1] CA 2006 s.8.
[2] CA 2006 s.9.
[3] CA 2006 s.9(2)(a).
[4] CA 2006 s.9(2)(b).
[5] CA 2006 s.9(2)(c).
[6] CA 2006 s.9(2)(d).
[7] CA 2006 s.10.
[8] CA 2006 s.11.
[9] CA 2006 s.9(4)(c).
[10] CA 2006 s.5(b).
[11] CA 2006 s.13.

- the fee.[12]

These forms for all these items and many other forms are available on the Companies House website. They may be printed off and sent in or completed online[13] by those setting up the company or by their agents.[14] The numbers on the forms correspond with the relevant section in the Companies Act 2006.

3–02 The *memorandum of association* merely indicates that the subscribers[15] (or subscriber if the company is a single member company) wish to form a company under the Companies Act 2006, and that they agree to become members of the company, and if the company has a share capital, that they agree to take at least one share each. The memorandum must be signed by each subscriber.[16] This memorandum has in practice very little use: it merely serves as a historical record of the wish of the first subscribers to set up the company. It is very different from the previous memorandum under the Companies Act 1985, which commonly consisted of four pages of close-typed and largely unread documentation about all the things the company was able to do, as well as containing more useful information such as the company's name, authorised share capital, the limited liability of the members and the company's country of registration. None of this is required in the new memorandum under the Companies Act 2006.

The *application for registration* (Form IN01) must contain the company's proposed name, the address of its proposed registered office,[17] an

---

[12] Electronic registration is £15 but hard copy registration is £40. Same day delivery may be effected for £100.

[13] Details are available at the Companies House website. Although there are procedures to minimise the opportunity for identity theft, Companies House does not actually, and indeed could not, check to see if the subscribers or officers truly exist.

[14] An agent, such as a lawyer, accountant or company formation agent, may send in the relevant forms on behalf of those wishing to set up the company. If so, the agent must state his own name and address (s.9(3)).

[15] A subscriber is a person who "subscribes" to be a member of the company by signing his name at the bottom of the relevant company incorporation documents. In this particular context the word "subscriber" means the very first members of the company, and "subscriber shares" refer to these first shares issued to the first members. If the company is a guarantee company, these first members are still subscribers, but they do not take shares. Confusingly, there is a secondary, associated, meaning of "subscriber" which is a person who subscribes for new shares in a company that is already up and running and which needs more capital. Such a person may subscribe (i.e. effectively apply) for new shares and may in due course be allotted them. Even though he "subscribed" for those shares, those later shares are not "subscriber" shares, and are just shares along with all the other existing shares.

[16] See the Companies Registration Regulations 2008 (SI 2008/3014) for the wording of the memorandum. For a limited company the wording is as follows: "Each subscriber to this memorandum of association wishes to form a company under the Companies Act 2006 and agrees to become a member of the company and to take at least one share." The name and signature of each subscriber is inserted on the form along with the date.

[17] CA 2006 s.9(5)(a).

indication of the country within the United Kingdom where the company's registered office will be situated,[18] the liability of the members if limited[19] (and if so, whether limited by shares or by guarantee), and whether the company is public or private.[20]

If the company has a share capital, the application for registration **3–03** must also contain a *statement of capital* and the subscribers' initial shareholding.[21] The statement of capital will show how many shares are taken by each subscriber, the aggregate nominal value[22] of those shares, and where there are classes of shares, information about each class of shares (as in "preferred", "deferred", "non-voting", etc.), the number of shares taken within each class, and the extent to which any shares taken by the subscribers are paid up, plus an indication of any premium paid for any share.[23] If the company is to be limited by guarantee, the application must contain a statement of guarantee by each subscriber.[24] This will state that if the company is wound up while he is a member, or within a year after he ceases to be a member, he will pay to the wound-up company a sum of money, up to the guaranteed amount,[25] towards the debts and other expenses of the company.[26]

The registration application must in addition contain a *statement of the* **3–04** *proposed officers of the company.*[27] These will be the first director or directors of the company, and the first secretary or joint secretaries of the company.[28] The statement must be signed by each director and secretary, though in the case where all the partners in a firm are to be joint secretaries, consent by any one partner will suffice to sign on behalf of all of the partners.[29] The directors must give their names,[30] the country of residence, their nationality, their business occupation (if any)[31] and their

---

[18] There are no provisions in the Act for the alteration of the nationality of the company.
[19] If the company is an unlimited company, it will not be necessary to have any statement about the liability for the shares.
[20] CA 2006 s.9(2)(d).
[21] CA 2006 s.9(4)(a).
[22] See Ch.1 at para.1–04 for the explanation of "nominal value".
[23] CA 2006 s.10. The "premium" on a share is the sum paid in excess of the nominal value by a shareholder keen to acquire a share from the issuing company. It reflects the desirability of the share to the shareholder. The premiums are put not into the share capital account but into a designated share premium account where they may only be used for certain restricted purposes.
[24] CA 2006 s.9(4)(b).
[25] Commonly this is only £1.00.
[26] CA 2006 s.11.
[27] CA 2006 s.9(4)(c).
[28] CA 2006 s.12(1). A private company is not required to have a company secretary (s.270) but may do so if it wishes. A public company must have a company secretary (s.271), who must be properly qualified (s.273).
[29] CA 2006 s.12(3). It is not unusual for a firm of lawyers to act as a company secretary for a company.
[30] CA 2006 s.163(2) explains that names includes present names, forenames, former names (unless those former names have not been used for over 20 years or were only used under the age of 16), title (if a peer) and any other name by which the director was known for business purposes.
[31] Many directors unhelpfully give their occupation as "company director".

date of birth.[32] All directors must be over the age of 16,[33] and each company must have at least one director who is a natural person.[34] Directors no longer need to give lists of their other directorships. The director must also indicate his services address and separately his residential address to the Registrar of Companies.[35] The Registrar will not disclose a director's residential addresses to the public; he maintains a protected register of directors' residential addresses and he may only release directors' residential addresses under certain limited circumstances.[36] He may disclose the residential address to certain public authorities authorised by the Secretary of State and to credit reference agencies.[37] He may disclose the address following a court order.[38] He may disclose it himself where the director is refusing to reply to correspondence sent to the service address, subject to due intimation to the director and his company.[39] Where the directors or secretaries are companies or partnerships, the address of the registered office or principal place of business should be indicated.[40]

3–05   The company is expected to tell the Registrar whenever a director changes his residential address.[41] The service address will commonly be the place of business of the company or its registered office and the directors' service addresses will be available from the published particulars of each company at the Register of Companies. Secretaries are not required to give their residential addresses and may just give a service address.[42] Where the directors or secretaries are companies or partnerships, the address of the registered office or principal place of business should be indicated.[43]

The registration application will indicate the *address of the registered office* of the company.[44] It is permissible to use a post office box number as a registered address provided the full postcode is indicated.[45]

---

[32] The date of birth is necessary because there may well be more than one person with the same name at the same address, particularly in family companies.

[33] CA 2006 s.154.

[34] CA 2006 s.155. A "natural person" is a real human being, not another registered company or a Scottish partnership.

[35] CA 2006 s.163. The company itself must keep a register both of its directors and of its directors' residential addresses, though the addresses will not be open to inspection by the public.

[36] CA 2006 ss.242–244 and the Companies (Disclosure of Address) Regulations 2009 (SI 2009/214).

[37] CA 2006 s.243(2). These include the police, Her Majesty's Revenue and Customs, The Financial Services Authority, the Scottish Ministers, etc.

[38] CA 2006 s.244.

[39] CA 2006 ss.245, 246.

[40] CA 2006 ss.164, 278.

[41] CA 2006 s.167.

[42] CA 2006 s.277. There is, unlike directors, no reference to residential addresses for company secretaries. The company itself, if it has a company secretary, is expected to keep a register of company secretaries.

[43] CA 2006 ss.164, 278.

[44] CA 2006 s.9(5)(a). This must be within the country of registration.

[45] The Companies House website under "Frequently Asked Questions" indicates that this is acceptable.

If the company is not using one of the standard default models of *articles of association*[46] and wishes to make its own personalised version (as is very common) this should be included with the registration application.

Finally a *statement of compliance* is required.[47] The statement indicates **3–06** that the person signing the form has complied with the legislation for the setting up of a company. No statutory declaration by the signatory is required, and the statement does not require to be witnessed. It may be made, as may all these other documents, in paper or electronic form. It is hard to see what is achieved by this statement. It is believed that it is a hangover from the days in the nineteenth century when to set up a company was seen as a privilege or concession by the state, and one not to be embarked upon lightly. When the would-be director swore in front of a notary public that he had complied with the legislation, he recognised the gravity of his responsibility. Such sentiments are probably redundant nowadays.

Companies House receives many applications each day. Should the documentation not be satisfactory in some way, the applicant will receive a letter indicating the matters which in the view of Companies House are unsatisfactory. The letter is not a personalised letter: for every point in apparent error Companies House will issue a standard sentence from a bank of previously prepared sentences. While these previously prepared sentences will indicate what was wrong with the application, what they sometimes fail to say is how the error may be amended, Companies House taking the view that in view of the amount of work they have to do, it is not their place to indicate what the applicant should do to correct the error. In addition they probably do not wish to be liable for giving advice that might not be suitable.[48]

Ironically, if the documentation appears on the face of it to be properly completed, Companies House will take it at face value. Errors or mistakes in documents submitted to Companies House may be picked up by the officials there, but there is little quality control or oversight of the contents—which is not surprising given that there are over three million companies in the United Kingdom.[49]

Assuming the incorporation documents have been completed correctly, **3–07** the fee paid, and the company formed for a lawful purpose,[50] the Registrar of Companies will issue a certificate of registration. It may be

---

[46] These may be found at the Companies (Model Articles) Regulations 2008 (SI 2008/3229). There are three models: private, public and guarantee. Articles of association are discussed in Ch.4.

[47] CA 2006 s.13.

[48] In the author's experience, individual officials, when telephoned, may be quite helpful in providing information on how to resolve a difficulty occasioned by an unusual application.

[49] The satirical magazine, *Private Eye*, gleefully reported that three individuals named Bin Laden, Mubarrak and Gaddafi had taken over a funeral company apparently based in a flat in South London, without anyone in Companies House pausing to consider whether this was genuine. The company was wound up in 2012 by the Insolvency Service. See *Private Eye*, No.1349, Oct 3, 2013, p.36.

[50] CA 2006 s.7(2).

wondered for what unlawful purpose a company might be formed. However, in *R. v Registrar of Companies Ex p. Attorney-General*[51] the frolicsome Miss Lindi St Claire[52] was not allowed to set up a company whose object was prostitution, it being contrary to public policy and therefore unlawful to set up a company for such a purpose, notwithstanding that the Registrar of Companies had issued her a certificate of registration. Ironically, given the demise of the "objects clause" under the old legislation, which indicated for what purpose a company might be founded, it will now be difficult to know for what purpose, let alone prostitution, any company will be founded.

The certificate of registration is prima facie conclusive evidence that the company is properly founded,[53] even if in fact the Registrar of Companies has recorded something incorrectly.[54] The certificate will show the company's name, the company's number, the Registrar's signature and the date of registration.[55] A company comes into existence at midnight on the day of registration. The subscribers are deemed to become members (and where appropriate, shareholders) as at that date, and the directors and secretary become directors and secretary of the company as at that date too.[56]

3–08   On incorporating a company it is quite common to send in a Form AA01 as well. This form deals with the accounting reference date. If no accounting reference date is specified by the use of the Form AA01, a new company's first accounting reference date will be deemed to be the anniversary of the end of the month of incorporation, so that a company formed on, say, March 8, 2014 will have to make up its first accounts up to March 31, 2015. However under CA 2006 s.392, it is possible to extend the normal date though not beyond the second anniversary of the date that it otherwise would have had.[57] In the event of a newly formed company it may be extended for a period of up to 18 months after the date of incorporation. It is also permissible to shorten the period, though the company's then shortened financial year must be at least six months in duration.[58] The common reason for doing this is to align the accounting reference date of a new company with that company's holding company or with another subsidiary.[59] There are restrictions to prevent companies altering their accounting reference dates more than once every

---

[51] [1991] B.C.L.C. 476.

[52] Miss St Claire practised as a dominatrix, and was known as Miss Whiplash. Having retired from her former profession, she now lives in rural Herefordshire and keeps ducks.

[53] CA 2006 s.15(4).

[54] In *Re Baby Moon (UK) Ltd* (1985) 1 B.C.C. 99 a company with a registered office in Livingston in West Lothian was nevertheless held to be registered in England as stated in the certificate.

[55] Certified copy certificates (as replacements for lost originals) may be obtained at a price of £15.

[56] CA 2006 s.16.

[57] CA 2006 s.392(2)(b).

[58] CA 2006 s.391(5).

[59] There is an expectation that holding companies and subsidiaries should all have the same accounting reference date unless there are good reasons otherwise (s.390(5)).

five years.[60] It is not permitted to apply for a new accounting reference date after the due date for lodging the accounts has passed.[61]

For the practicalities of operating a newly formed company, see the end of the chapter.

The company's name

A company may not have the same name as any other company name.[62] The difference may only be minimal—one letter or digit—but there must be no duplication of names within the United Kingdom; and it is sensible not to have a name that is too close to an existing company in the same line of business. It is therefore common in practice for people who wish their company to have a particular name to check with company formation agents or with the officials at the Register of Companies to see if their proposed name is already being used, is too similar to an existing name, or is otherwise unsuitable.[63] There is no virtue in having a name that leads to litigation. However, the Register only contains names of limited companies, and does not have a list of trading names or of partnerships. It is therefore possible to choose a name that appears to be acceptable as far as the Register is concerned, but is not acceptable from the point of view of the existing holder of the same or similar name operating under the mantle of a trading name or a partnership.[64] Even if the Register does accept a name, the Secretary of State may direct that the new company's name was "too like" an existing company's name and insist on change.[65]

3–09

The company must indicate in its name if it is limited company,[66] or a public limited company.[67] Unlimited companies do not need to specify that they are unlimited. Certain charities and other companies may dispense with the word "limited" if they are companies limited by shares or guarantee companies and/or founded under certain conditions before

3–10

---

[60] CA 2006 s.392(3).
[61] CA 2006 s.392(4). For further details about lodging accounts, see Ch.7. The Companies House website is also very informative on this matter.
[62] CA 2006 s.66.
[63] The Companies House website provides much helpful and practical advice on choosing names. See *http://www.companieshouse.gov.uk/about/gbhtml/gp1.shtml#ch7* [Accessed April 22, 2014]. Certain characters in lower case, ligatures, accents and other diacritical marks are not permitted. See the Company and Business Names (Miscellaneous Provisions) Regulations 2009 (SI 2009/1085) and the Company, Limited Liability Partnership and Business Names (Miscellaneous Provisions) (Amendment) Regulations 2009 (SI 2009/2404). As part of the "Red Tape challenge" the Government, responding to criticism that the rules relating to company and business names are complex and burdensome, are proposing to merge the names and trading disclosure regulations so that they may be all found together. See the Company and Business Names: Government response, ref: BIS/13/1139, published: October 4, 2013.
[64] These existing businesses may complain to the company names adjudicator (CA 2006 s.69).
[65] CA 2006 s.67. The Secretary of State may direct a company to change its name even if there has been no objection from an existing company (s.67(1)).
[66] CA 2006 s.59.
[67] CA 2006 s.58(1).

1948.[68] The name that a company chooses must not be one that in the opinion of the Secretary of State for Trade and Industry is a criminal offence[69] or offensive.[70] It is also forbidden (except with the approval of the Secretary of State) for a company to have a name (either its company name or its trading name) that suggests that the company is connected in any way with the Government or any local authority[71] or other sensitive words or expressions specified by the Secretary of State.[72] If a company wishes to use a name that suggests a connection with the government or a local authority (in terms of s.54) or is otherwise sensitive (in terms of regulations made under s.55),[73] the person on behalf of the company that wishes to use the name in question, in order to obtain the approval of the Secretary of State, must seek the view of the relevant government department or other body. The person applying for the name must request the department or body to indicate whether, and if so why, the department or body has any objections to the name. The person applying must tell the Secretary of State that he has made the request to the department or body and send in to the Secretary of State a copy of any response.[74] The point of this rule is to make the person applying for the name take the pro-active step of seeking consent to the name, rather than registering the name and waiting for the Secretary of State to notice it. These regulations referred to in s.55 restrict the use of certain words, amongst them words relating to royalty, health, nationality, insurance and higher education, unless their use can be justified.

3–11   A company must make certain trading disclosures about its name,[75] requiring it to be displayed and easily seen at all its business premises, on any bills of exchange, promissory notes, endorsements and order forms, cheques, orders for money, goods or services, its bills of parcels, invoices and other demands for payment, receipts and letters of credit, applications for licences to carry on a trade or activity and all other forms of its

---

[68] CA 2006 ss.60–64.

[69] CA 2006 s.53(a)—as, for example, a name that would incite racial hatred in terms of the Race Relations Act 1976.

[70] CA 2006 s.53(b) There do not appear to be guidelines as to what the Secretary of State will find offensive, but in practice the Registrar of Companies tends to suggest to company promoters that certain proposed names would be unlikely to be acceptable. Most take the hint.

[71] CA 2006 s.54.

[72] CA 2006 s.55.

[73] Company, Limited Liability Partnership and Business Names (Sensitive Words and Expressions) Regulations 2009 (SI 2009/2615). The Companies House website for "incorporation and names", at *http://www.companieshouse.gov.uk/about/gbhtml/ gp1.shtml#ch7* [Accessed April 22, 2014], has at Chapter 7 references to Annexes A–C. These contain a list of all the sensitive words plus an indication of what sort of permission is required to use those words. Even apparently innocuous words like "association" and "group" need permission or explanation, so it is well worth checking the list before choosing a name.

[74] CA 2006 s.56. See the Company, Limited Liability and Business Names (Public Authorities) Regulations 2009 (SI 2009/2982).

[75] CA 2006 s.82, the Companies (Trading Disclosures) Regulations 2008 (SI 2008/495) and the Companies (Trading Disclosures) (Amendment) Regulations 2009 (SI 2009/218).

business correspondence and documentation.[76] It must also be displayed on its website[77] and at any place where its company books (i.e. registers of members, etc.) may be inspected. Every company must also disclose on its business letters, order forms and websites the part of the United Kingdom in which the company is registered, the company's registered number and its registered office. If the company is not obliged to use the word "limited" as part of its name but it nevertheless is limited, the fact that it is in fact limited must be indicated. A community interest company must indicate that it is a limited company, and investment companies must indicate that they are investment companies.[78] If, in the case of a company having a share capital, there is a disclosure as to the amount of share capital on its business letters, its order forms or its websites, there must be a reference to the paid up share capital.[79] A company must disclose the address of its registered office, any place where the company records may be inspected, and the type of company records which are kept at that office or place to anyone who in the course of business makes a written request to the company for that information. The company must reply within five working days of the receipt of that request.[80]

The civil consequence of the failure to display the name correctly is **3–12** that if the company has not displayed its name in accordance with the legislation, but is trying to raise an action against a defender, and if that defender has a claim against a company which he has not been able to pursue because of the company's failure to indicate or display its name correctly, and has suffered loss thereby, the company will not be allowed to continue with its action, unless the court decides that it is just and equitable to permit otherwise.[81] There are also criminal consequences for the failure to use the correct name.[82] In respect of these civil and criminal actions, the courts will not take account of any minor and trivial inaccuracies such as omitted punctuation or the incorrect use of upper or lower case letters.[83]

Change of name

A company may not, without permission, use a name that is the name **3–13** of a previously insolvent company[84]; and indeed the prohibition is not just for a company using a prohibited name, but any form of business using the prohibited name.[85] It is tempting for directors of a company

---

[76] Companies (Trading Disclosures) Regulations 2008 (SI 2008/495) reg.6(1).
[77] Companies (Trading Disclosures) Regulations 2008 (SI 2008/495) reg.6(2).
[78] Companies (Trading Disclosures) Regulations 2008 (SI 2008/495) reg.7(1), (2).
[79] Companies (Trading Disclosures) Regulations 2008 (SI 2008/495) reg.7(3).
[80] Companies (Trading Disclosures) Regulations 2008 (SI 2008/495) reg.9. The name may even be displayed on a scrolling electric screen provided it appears for at least fifteen seconds every three minutes (Companies (Trading Disclosures) Regulations 2008 (SI 2008/495) reg.5).
[81] CA 2006 s.83.
[82] CA 2006 s.84.
[83] CA 2006 s.85.
[84] IA 1986 s.216(3). It is also a criminal offence.
[85] IA 1986 s.216(3)(c).

either in insolvency or approaching insolvency to set up a new company or business with a similar name, usually with the intention of confusing its creditors. This is prohibited under the "phoenix trading" rules for a period of five years from the date of the date of the first company's insolvent liquidation.[86] This is a strict liability offence and there is no need to prove any intention to deceive.[87] A director who does this will be jointly and severally liable along with the company for the debts of the new company or business,[88] unless the new company has taken over all or nearly all of the business of the insolvent company from the liquidator or adminstrator,[89] permission has been sought from the courts[90] or where there was a pre-existing company with the prohibited name which had been using that name for a year beforehand and which was not dormant.[91] However, although the director will be liable, he is only liable for the debts of the company or business using the prohibited name during the period while the company or business was using the prohibited name, not for the whole five year period during which time the company might well have been using other names.[92]

3–14   It is permissible for a company voluntarily to change its name by means of a special resolution[93] but not to a name that is otherwise forbidden. Under section 64 of the Companies Act 2006 the company may be required to change its name by the Secretary of State to change a company's name,[94] the company names adjudicator,[95] by the court[96] or when a company is restored to the register.[97] It is now possible to have a change of name conditional on the occurrence of some event, such as,

---

[86] IA 1986 ss.216 and 217. See *Archer Structures Ltd v Griffiths* [2004] 1 B.C.L.C. 201.

[87] *R. v Cole* [1998] 2 B.C.L.C. 235; *R. v McCredie* [2000] 2 B.C.L.C. 235. In both cases the directors received community service orders.

[88] IA 1986 s.217. This liability applies not only to the director in question but to those involved in the management of the company or acting on the instructions of someone they know is acting at that time in contravention of s.216.

[89] Insolvency (Scotland) Rules 1986 (SI 1986/1915) r.4.80. The successor company must give notice to all the creditors of the insolvent company. If this is done within the required period of 28 days from the date of the taking-over of the insolvent company, the director may be involved in the taking-over company with the leave of the court. See *First Independent Factors & Finance Ltd v Churchill* [2007] Bus. L.R. 676; [2007] B.C.C. 45, heard under the equivalent (English) Insolvency Rules 1986 (SI 1986/1925) r.4.228.

[90] Insolvency (Scotland) Rules 1986 (SI 1986/1915) r.4.81. In *Re Bonus Breaks Ltd* [1990] B.C.C. 491 the courts granted permission for the use of a forbidden name, subject to certain undertakings by the directors.

[91] Insolvency (Scotland) Rules 1986 (SI 1986/1915) r.4.82. See also *ESS Production Ltd v Sully* [2005] EWCA Civ 554, *Ad Valorem Factors Ltd v Ricketts* [2004] 1 All E.R. 894.

[92] *Glasgow City Council v Craig*, 2009 S.L.T. 212.

[93] CA 2006 s.77. Form NM01 must be sent to the Registrar. It would also be possible for a company to state in its articles that the directors (or indeed someone else) could change the company's name, but when the name change is applied for from the Registrar of Companies, the application would need to indicate that the company had followed its own required procedure under the articles for the name change (CA 2006 s.79).

[94] CA 2006 s.77(2)(a).

[95] CA 2006 s.77(2)(b) and see s.73.

[96] CA 2006 s.77(2)(c) following an appeal against the decision of the company names adjudicator (s.74).

[97] CA 2006 s.77(2)(d) and see s.1033.

say, a successful takeover bid: if this is what the company wants, it must inform the Registrar of Companies of the special resolution approving the change and, later on, once the event had occurred, inform the Registrar of the occurrence of the event, whereupon the change of name will come into effect.[98]

The Secretary of State may require a registered company to change its **3–15** name if it gave misleading information in order to register a particular name, or that some undertaking or assurance in connection with the name had been given but not fulfilled.[99] The Secretary of State may also require a company to change its name if the name gives a misleading impression of the nature of the company's activities, such that is "likely to cause harm to the public".[100] If a company chooses a name that is similar to an existing registered company name, or a name should have been on the register, the Secretary of State may direct that the company change its name,[101] normally within a period of twelve months of the company's registration of its choice of name.[102]

The company names tribunal

A person who has, or is associated with, an existing business (whether a **3–16** company, a partnership, a sole trader or any other form of business) with a name in which he has goodwill may object to a company's choice of name if it is the same name as his business's name.[103] He may also object if the company's choice of name is sufficiently similar to his own business's name in the United Kingdom such that it might mislead by suggesting an unwarranted connection between the company and him.[104] He may take such objection to an official tribunal known as the Company Names Tribunal presided over by a "company names adjudicator" whose role will be to decide whether the objector may retain his rights in the name or the company may adopt its chosen name.[105] The onus is on the company to prove that it should be allowed to have its chosen name.[106] If the company can show that it had registered the name before the objector started to use it, or that the company is already operating under the name, is proposing to operate under the name, or formerly operated under the name even if the company is now dormant, it may keep the

---

[98] CA 2006 s.78(2). Use Forms NM02 and NM03.

[99] CA 2006 s.75(1).

[100] CA 2006 s.76. *Association of Certified Public Accountants of Britain v Secretary of State for Trade and Industry* [1997] 2 B.C.L.C. 307.

[101] CA 2006 s.67.

[102] CA 2006 s.68(2). Failure to change the name is a criminal offence (s.68(5), (6)).

[103] CA 2006 s.69(1)(a). This is done by applying to the Company Names Tribunal at the UK Intellectual Property Office from which further advice may be sought.

[104] CA 2006 s.69(1)(b).

[105] CA 2006 s.69(2). Further rules about the company names adjudicator may be found at ss.70 and 71, and within the Company Names Adjudicator Rules 2008 (SI 2008/1738). Details of the Tribunal and its procedures may be found on the website of the Intellectual Property Office at *http://www.ipo.gov.uk/cna.htm* [Accessed April 22, 2014].

[106] CA 2006 s.69(4).

chosen name.[107] Other grounds on which it may keep the chosen name are
that the objector could buy the name from the company on standard
terms,[108] that the name was adopted in good faith and that the interests of
the objector are not prejudiced to any significant extent.[109] The company
names adjudicator must publish his decision on the matter within 90 days
of the hearing on the matter that takes place before him[110] and he may
require the name to be changed.[111] The decision of the company names
adjudicator may be appealed to the court.[112] The intent behind using the
company names adjudicator as an arbiter on this matter is to save the
expense of going to court, as was formerly the case under actions of
"passing off". The very first case heard by a company names adjudicator
was raised by The Coca Cola Company against a company which had
registered itself as Coke Cola Ltd. Coke Cola Ltd was duly ordered to
change its name within one month of the adjudicator's decision and to
pay The Coca Cola Company's costs of £700.[113]

Passing off

3–17   Instead of using the company names adjudicator, it would also be
possible to use the law relating to passing off, particularly where the
problem is not the company name but its trading name. Passing off is the
adoption of the name, or a very similar name, of an existing business.
This may be done deliberately in order to steal some of the existing
business's custom and goodwill, or inadvertently: either way it may lead
to misrepresentation. If the proposed name prejudices the existing business, leads to confusion in the eyes of customers, or affects the existing
business's goodwill or reputation, the existing business is entitled to raise
an action to prevent the new business using the offending name. The
leading case is *Ewing v Buttercup Margarine Co Ltd*[114] where Ewing, who
operated a number of shops selling tea and margarine under the name of
the Buttercup Dairy Co, successfully prevented the defendants from
setting up a wholesaling business with the name "Buttercup Margarine
Co Ltd" on the grounds that it would cause confusion in the minds of
Ewing's customers. By contrast, in Scotland the mighty American
Dunlop tyre company was refused permission to prevent a small car-
repairing garage of the same name in the Borders carrying on its lawful
business on the grounds that there could be no possible confusion

---

[107] CA 2006 s.69(4)(a), (b).
[108] CA 2006 s.69(4)(c).
[109] CA 2006 s.69(4)(d), (e).
[110] CA 2006 s.72.
[111] CA 2006 s.73.
[112] CA 2006 s.74.
[113] Since that first case there have been many more. Details are available at the Patent Office website.
[114] [1917] 2 Ch. 1.

between the two companies.[115] The use of an ordinary word in a company's name does not entitle that company to the exclusive use of that word.[116] It is permissible to use your own name without fear of being liable in an action of passing off,[117] but not your nick-name.[118] Matters that the court will take into consideration in an action of passing off will be the geographical area where the passing off is taking place, the degree of similarity of the pursuer's and defender's businesses, the degree to which the pursuer has suffered loss and the balance of convenience and fairness. Where an action of passing off is successful, the pursuer will be able to prevent the defender using the challenged name, and may also be able to demand an accounting for profits or indemnity for the pursuer's losses occasioned by the defender's use of the challenged name. The same principle applies to domain names (the names by which a business is known on the internet), whereby an existing company may again object to the registration of a domain name too similar to the existing company's name.[119]

A variation of passing off is what is known as "opportunistic incorporation". There are entrepreneurs who like to make it their business to incorporate companies with names of well-known businesses or individuals in the hope that those businesses or individuals will buy the company names from them. This practice is not well regarded by the courts. In *Glaxo plc v Glaxowellcome Ltd*[120] the defendants incorporated a company that featured the two names of Glaxo and Wellcome, companies that were then proposing to merge. The defendants proposed to sell the company, with its name "Glaxowellcome", to the claimants for £100,000. Lightman J. granted an order requiring the defendants to change the name of their company on the grounds that the defendants were abusing the system of registration of companies' names, not least because the defendants had no goodwill in the names anyway. **3–18**

Continuing obligations despite the name change

The fact that a company changes its name makes no difference to its obligations and rights, and existing litigation against or by the company may be continued under its old or its new name.[121] Despite the change of name, the company number never alters, which is why it is prudent in all **3–19**

---

[115] *Dunlop Pneumatic Tyre Co Ltd v Dunlop Motor Co Ltd,* 1907 S.C. (HL) 15. Similarly in London a firm of fast food Chinese restaurants was allowed to carry on trade under the name of McChina, much to the annoyance of McDonalds, the burger retailers (*The Independent,* November 28, 2001).
[116] *Aerators Ltd v Tollit* [1902] 2 Ch. 319. Tollit proposed to use the words "aerator" in his company's name and it was held that the plaintiffs did not have the sole rights to such an ordinary word.
[117] *Wright, Layman and Unmay Ltd v Wright* (1949) 66 R.P.C. 149 CA.
[118] *Biba Group Ltd v Biba Boutique* [1990] R.P.C. 413.
[119] *British Telecommunications plc v One in a Million Ltd* [1998] 4 All ER 476. For the register of UK internet domain names, see Nominet UK and its website *http://www.nominet.org.uk/* [Accessed April 22, 2014].
[120] [1996] F.S.R. 388.
[121] CA 2006 s.81(2), (3).

formal documentation involving a company to include the company's registered number. The new name takes effect from the date of the new certificate.[122]

It should be noted that merely because a business has registered a trade mark with the Trade Mark Register does not mean that that trade mark (if a name) may be registered as a company's name with the Registrar of Companies. Equally, having an existing registered trade mark will be good grounds for preventing someone trying to register a company name the same name as the trade mark name. Further information on trade mark names may be obtained from the Patent Office.[123]

TYPES OF COMPANY

3–20 There are two main types of company. The first is the public limited company (often written as "plc" or "P.L.C.", and often just known as a "public company"). The second is the private company. Any company that is not a public company will be a private company.[124]

The public limited company

3–21   There are many differences between public companies and private companies, but in essence, the law relating to a public company is more demanding and more detailed than that for a private company. This is because any public company could potentially (though most in fact do not do so) offer its securities[125] to the public, and if the public is to be persuaded to invest in such a company (whether or not the company does offer its shares to the public) there must be high standards of accountability by the directors to its members and creditors.

The capital of a public company

3–22   A public company must have a minimum nominal issued share capital of £50,000.[126] Many public companies in fact have a nominal issued share capital far greater than £50,000. The company must as a minimum have allotted 50,000 £1 nominal value shares or 100,000 50 pence nominal value shares (or such other combination of shares and nominal value as equals £50,000) though the shares only have to be paid up to the extent of one quarter.[127] This means that on becoming a public company a plc could in theory have, say, 50,000 shares of £1 nominal value each, all paid

---

[122] CA 2006 s.81(1).

[123] See its website: *http://www.patent.gov.uk* [April 22, 2014].

[124] CA 2006 s.4(1). It is permissible for a plc to have a share capital and be limited by guarantee at the same time, but it is not possible to be a plc while only be limited by guarantee (s.4(2)).

[125] The word securities encompasses shares, debentures, warrants, options, etc.

[126] CA 2006 s.763. It is now permissible to have the company's share capital denominated in other currencies, such as the euro, provided that the value of the capital is nevertheless equivalent to £50,000.

[127] CA 2006 s.761(3).

up to the extent of one quarter each (i.e. 25 pence), thus making a paid up capital of £12,500. The balance (or part thereof) of £37,500 could then be called for at any time by the directors if the company needed further funds, or could be demanded in full by the liquidator in the event of the company's insolvency. Although it is rare nowadays for shares to be partly paid, the point of the legislation is to provide reassurance to creditors that the company either has £50,000 sitting as cash (or assets) in its accounts or at least £12,500 in cash or assets with the promise of the balance to come whenever needed—all of which could be used to pay creditors' bills. In practice, £50,000 provides very little reassurance to anyone, but the theory is that it forms a sizeable fund, from which to pay creditors.

There are also various rules relating to the capital maintenance rule, in particular the net asset rule for dividends, which apply particularly to public companies but not to private companies. These are dealt with in Ch.6.

A plc, incorporated as such, must have a s.761 trading certificate

Nearly all public companies start off their existence as private com- **3–23** panies, the procedure therefor being explained later in this chapter. But a very few are incorporated as public companies from the beginning, and in order to ensure that the company has the minimum capital it ought to have, the directors have to obtain a s.761 trading certificate before commencing to trade. This is done by furnishing the Registrar of Companies with a statement of compliance[128] indicating that the company has the capital the company says it has, together with information about the company's preliminary expenses and any benefits paid to promoters of the company.[129] If the Registrar of Companies is satisfied with the terms of the statement he will issue the certificate. If the directors do start trading in defiance of the statutory requirements, and the company enters into a transaction and fails to obtain the certificate within 21 days of being called upon to do so, the directors who were directors at the time of the transaction will become personally jointly and severally liable for any loss or damage sustained by the other party to the transaction.[130] Under the circumstances, it is much wiser to start trading as a private company and follow the normal rules for conversion to a public company,[131] in which case no s.761 trading certificate is required.

Non-cash consideration for shares in a public company

Because a public company is supposed genuinely to have the capital it **3–24** says it has, shares may only be offered for non-cash consideration where the non-cash consideration has been independently valued before the

---

[128] CA 2006 s.762(2). Use Form SH50.
[129] CA 2006 s.762(1)(b), (c).
[130] CA 2006 s.767. There are also criminal penalties.
[131] CA 2006 ss.90–96.

allotment of the shares. This is to prevent people selling assets to the public company for more shares than the assets are truly worth. This, and shares generally in a public company, are extensively dealt with in Ch.5.

Officers of a public company

3–25   The company secretary of a public company is required to be properly qualified to act as a company secretary.[132] The members should vote for the appointment or re-election of each director separately unless there has been a previous unanimous vote in favour of permitting the voting for a "package" of directors.[133] There are certain extra restrictions on loans to directors of public companies. These are dealt with in greater detail in Chs 8 and 9.

Single member public limited companies

3–26   Until the Companies Act 2006, a plc normally had to have at least two members, but it is now permissible to have only one[134]. However, a single member public limited company still has to have two directors[135] and a qualified company secretary.[136]

Issue of shares to the public

3–27   Despite the confusing use of the word "public" most public companies do not offer their shares to the public. Furthermore, the use of the word "public" does not mean that a public company is owned by the State for the public benefit (as in the term "public utilities"). As far as company law is concerned, the "public" in "public limited company" means that the shares could potentially be offered to the public provided the company has been admitted to a "regulated market" usually within a recognised investment exchange, of which the best known in the United Kingdom is the London Stock Exchange. The main regulated market in the United Kingdom is the Main Market of the London Stock Exchange ("LSE"). Its younger and less regulated brother, the Alternative Investment Market ("AIM") is not a regulated market. In order for a company to be admitted to the Main Market it must comply with the Listing Rules[137] which contains the requirements for any company that wishes to have its shares floated on LSE. Such a company is said to be on the Official List or "listed". Companies that wish to offer their securities to

---

[132] CA 2006 s.273. See also Ch.10.
[133] CA 2006 s.160.
[134] CA 2006 s.7. This is with effect from October 1, 2009.
[135] CA 2006 s.154(2).
[136] CA 2006 ss.271, 273.
[137] To be found within the Financial Conduct Authority handbook.

investors on these markets or elsewhere[138] must comply with the requirements of the Prospectus Regulations.[139] The issue of shares is dealt with in greater detail in Ch.5.

A company whose securities are available for sale to the public is **3–28** sometimes said to be a "quoted" company. This term is confusing. What this means in ordinary speech is that there are market makers (i.e. stockbrokers) willing to offer a price or a price to sell that company's securities. More accurately, "quoted" has a separate restricted technical meaning purely in the context of the accounts of companies[140] and means a listed company (as above), a company whose equity share capital is listed in another EEA State, or admitted to dealing on the New York Stock Exchange or NASDAQ. Nearly all listed companies are therefore quoted companies.[141] A "traded" company generally means any company whose securities are traded on a regulated market.

General meetings

A public company has to have general meetings (AGMs and where **3–29** necessary EGMs) where the directors may be held accountable to the members.[142] Private companies may in practice dispense with meetings and instead carry out their decision-making by written resolution. This is discussed further in Ch.13.

Accounting requirements

Private companies are not obliged (depending on their size) to give **3–30** quite as much information in their accounts as public companies. This is mainly to preserve commercial secrets. But in a public company, greater transparency in accounting is required, and for listed companies and other companies whose shares are being offered to the public on a recognised investment exchange, the degree of transparency is greater still, and with much more information (at least in theory, if not always in practice) being revealed to members and creditors.

Why become a public company?

The advantages of being a public company are that: **3–31**

- The minimum capital requirements give an impression of commercial credibility.
- The greater accounting and company law requirements enable investors and creditors to have a more informed view of the company.

---

[138] There are other markets such as the Icap Securities and Derivatives Exchange.

[139] Prospectus Regulations 2005 (SI 2005/1433) have been amended by the Prospectus Regulations 2011 (SI 2011/1668) and the Prospectus Regulations 2012 (SI 2012/1538).

[140] CA 2006 s.385.

[141] If a company's debt securities are traded it could be listed but not quoted, as quotation requires the sale and purchase of equity share capital.

[142] CA 2006 s.336.

- An ambitious director who wishes ultimately to have company's securities traded on the LSE or any other regulated market will need to take his company from being a private company to a plc as an initial stage before admission to that market.
- Unsuspecting members of the general population misguidedly think that a public company is automatically bigger and more impressive than a private company, so sometimes even quite small companies convert to public companies because they think it good for their image.
- Some directors like the personal status of being a director of a public company.

Is being a public company worth the effort?

3–32   Many private companies choose not to convert to being a public company, even though they could easily do so. This is generally because the main shareholders have no intention of floating the company's securities and thereby possibly losing control of the company, and because the greater accounting and company law requirements of being a public company are seen as onerous and intrusive. Indeed, in last few years many well established high street retailers, which were formerly listed public companies, have been bought over by private equity companies, these being private companies which were able to borrow large sums of money at cheap rates in order to buy out the shares in the retailers. The retailers were then effectively taken into private company ownership, and the directors of those private companies were spared some of the inconveniences of running a public or a listed company. For those who do not wish to reveal any more information about their businesses than they absolutely have to, a private company is certainly more attractive than a public company.

The private limited company

3–33   There are several types of private limited company.

The private company limited by shares

3–34   This is by far the most common type of company in the United Kingdom. There are no minimum capital requirements, no trading certificate is needed and the capital maintenance rules are more relaxed than for public companies, as are the rules relating to the issue of shares. There are fewer rules relating to directors and company secretaries; with a little ingenuity it is possible to avoid having general meetings altogether; and if the company is small enough not too much information need be revealed in the published accounts. All these points will be discussed in later chapters.

The private company limited by guarantee

This is similar to a private company limited by shares except that **3–35** instead of having shares, each of the company's members undertakes to pay a certain amount by way of a guarantee (commonly £1.00)[143] in the event of the insolvency of the company.[144] Guarantee companies by convention are much used by charities, as the HM Revenue and Customs appears to like the use of guarantee companies for such purposes. When a member leaves he does not sign a stock transfer form. He just resigns and his name is deleted from the register of members.

The single member private limited company

A single member private limited company is one where there is only **3–36** one shareholder.[145] There must also be at least one director but there is no requirement for a company secretary.[146] Single member companies are commonly used by "one man bands", sole traders who are prudently incorporating, or are the wholly owned subsidiaries of holding companies. Single member companies also often originally start off with more than one member but eventually the other members leave and transfer their shares to the remaining, single member. If so, the company minutes must record that the company has become a single member company as from the date of the final transfer.[147] Likewise if the single member recruits some more members, that too must be recorded.[148]

Even though there is only one member, that member must fulfil all the requirements of normal company meetings. There must be a proper record of directors' meetings[149] and general meetings may be held,[150] absurd as it may be to have a meeting of one member. There should be minutes recording the approval of any contracts between the company and the sole member who is also a director,[151] unless the contracts are those entered into in the ordinary course of business.[152] If a minute is not kept, it does not necessarily mean that the contracts are invalid,[153] but it does mean that the person founding on them will have difficulty proving that he complied with other requirements of the Companies Act 2006, such as a director declaring his interest in a contract under s.177.[154] Where the single member of a company (and its sole director) injured

---

[143] There is no reason why the figure should not be larger: sometimes the figure is £1,000 if the company wishes to have a greater degree of financial credibility.

[144] CA 2006 s.3(3).

[145] CA 2006 s.123(1).

[146] CA 2006 s.270(1).

[147] CA 2006 s.123(2).

[148] CA 2006 s.123(3).

[149] CA 2006 s.248.

[150] CA 2006 s.357. Being a private company, it is not actually necessary to have a general meeting and the decisions which would otherwise be taken at a general meeting may be made by written resolution.

[151] CA 2006 s.231.

[152] CA 2006 s.213(1)(c).

[153] CA 2006 s.213(6).

[154] *Re Neptune (Vehicle Washing Equipment) Ltd* [1995] B.C.C. 474.

himself in the course of his employment as a result of his own faulty
maintenance of company's premises, he was unable to sue his company
(or rather its insurers) for the damages occasioned by his own
carelessness.[155]

The quorum for a single member company is one member present.[156]

Unlimited companies

3–37   An unlimited company is one where the members are personally liable
for the company's debts,[157] usually but not necessarily once the company's funds are exhausted. Unlimited companies do not have the word
"limited" in their name because the members' liability is not limited.
Unlimited companies are registered in the same manner as other companies; they have shares and all the usual attributes of a private company
limited by shares, save that they do not need to send their accounts to the
Registrar of Companies except in certain limited circumstances.[158]
Unlimited companies therefore have both the benefit of a separate legal
personality and privacy of accounts. They are sometimes used where
someone wants to keep assets at arms' length or wishes to hide the true
financial position of an undertaking.[159]

Other types of company

Dormant companies

3–38   These are companies that exist but undertake no activity at all. They
are sometimes used to hold an asset at arm's length (using the separate
legal personality of the company) or to keep a potentially desirable name
which the owner of the company may be able to sell one day. Such
companies need only provide minimal accounts and need not have their
accounts audited.[160] The Companies House website provides useful notes
on how to provide the required abbreviated accounts and what resolutions are needed to maintain or change the company's dormant status.

Subsidiaries and holding companies

3–39   A subsidiary company is one that is wholly or partly owned or controlled by a holding company. A holding company is one that has all or
most of the shares or the control of a subsidiary. Subsidiaries are commonly used by holding companies as a way of distancing the holding

---

[155] *Brumder v Motornet Services and Repairs Ltd* [2013] 1 W.L.R. 2783; [2013] 3 All E.R.
412.
[156] CA 2006 s.318(1).
[157] CA 2006 s.3(4).
[158] CA 2006 s.448, and see Ch.7.
[159] One use of unlimited companies is for solicitors' partnership pension funds: since a
pension fund is unlikely to become insolvent there is little risk of the partners being
liable for its debts, and the individual partners can disguise from their employees how
much money is being paid into the pension fund as opposed to being applied to the
employees' wages.
[160] CA 2006 s.480.

company from the commercial activities of the subsidiary: if the subsidiary is profitable, the holding company receives dividends and possibly management fees from it; if the subsidiary is unsuccessful, the holding company can walk away from the subsidiary's debts. Subsidiaries may have subsidiaries of their own. Sometimes companies have a complex network of subsidiaries, cross-holdings and holding companies, often in an attempt to bamboozle auditors, creditors and investors. A subsidiary may not be a member of its holding company,[161] but subsidiaries may own shares in their holding companies when acting as a nominee,[162] or when holding the shares in the ordinary course of business as a dealer in securities on a regulated market.[163]

Under s.1159 of CA 2006 a subsidiary is a subsidiary of a holding company if the holding company:

- holds a majority of the voting rights in it[164];
- is a member of and has the right to appoint or remove a majority of its board of directors[165];
- is a member of it and controls alone, pursuant to an agreement with the other shareholders or members,[166] a majority of the voting rights in it[167]; or
- is a subsidiary of a company which is itself a subsidiary of that holding company.[168]

The point of these definitions of subsidiary and holding company is that there are a few occasions when a rule that is applied to a subsidiary affects a holding company. For example, financial assistance is not easily permissible for public companies, so it might be tempting to arrange for a private company subsidiary of that public company to provide the financial assistance. That would be prohibited.[169]

There is a second definition of subsidiary for accounting purposes.[170] In **3-40** this case the holding company is known as a "parent undertaking" and the subsidiary company as a "subsidiary undertaking". The definition is almost the same as the above, but in addition, the legislation refers to the parent undertaking's right to exercise a "dominant influence" over the subsidiary. A dominant influence is a right given under the company's memorandum or articles to influence the management of the company, or a right given under a "control contract". Control contracts are not

---

[161] CA 2006 s.136.
[162] CA 2006 s.660. This might arise where a subsidiary of a bank acquires shares in the bank as security for a loan given by the bank to a shareholder.
[163] CA 2006 s.141.
[164] CA 2006 s.1159(1)(a).
[165] CA 2006 s.1159(1)(b).
[166] This would commonly be known as a "shareholders agreement".
[167] CA 2006 s.1159(1)(c). This matter was discussed in *Enviroco v Farstad Supply A/S* [2011] 1 W.L.R. 921.
[168] CA 2006 s.1159(1).
[169] CA 2006 s.678(3). Private companies are normally permitted to provide financial assistance for the acquisition of their own shares.
[170] CA 2006 s.1162.

common in the United Kingdom, being a feature of German corporate law, whereby a holding company accepts responsibility for its subsidiary. Furthermore, this second definition of subsidiary applies where a parent undertaking in practice exercises a dominant influence which is not caught by the above rules,[171] or where the parent and the subsidiary are operated on a "unified basis",[172] in which cases, the subsidiary undertaking will be deemed to be a subsidiary undertaking.

The word "undertaking" is used because that word includes not only companies, but also partnerships, limited liability partnerships and unincorporated associations.[173]

3–41   The point of the second definition is to ensure that when companies prepare their consolidated accounts, all the accounts of peripheral businesses partly or wholly owned or controlled by the company are included within those consolidated accounts, thus presenting a more accurate picture of the overall enterprise's financial health.[174]

Overseas companies

3–42   A company that wishes to do business in the United Kingdom is much more likely to be viewed favourably if it registers its presence in the United Kingdom. Registration and in particular compliance with UK rules with regard to accounting and audit will give credibility to the company and reassurance to those considering dealing with it. Although one way of dealing with this matter is to set up a UK subsidiary, the overseas company may instead wish to provide much the same information about itself in the United Kingdom as it does in its home country, and register a branch in the United Kingdom. If so, such a company will be expected to provide much the same information as any UK company under the provisions of the Companies Act 2006 Pt 34.[175] Companies House provides useful information as to what information is needed for registration of the required documentation for an overseas company.[176]

European Economic Interest Groupings

3–43   These are special companies that are designed to encourage cross-border trade. They are registered in the normal manner with the Registrar of Companies. They have a legal personality but their members do

---

[171] CA 2006 s.1162(4)(a).

[172] CA 2006 s.1162(4)(b).

[173] CA 2006 s.1161(1).

[174] It is this provision of UK company accounting rules that would have prevented some of the off-balance sheet accounting that featured in the collapse of Enron in USA. At the time USA accounting rules in this respect were laxer than United Kingdom ones.

[175] More details are to be found in the Overseas Companies Regulations 2009 (SI 2009/1801), the Overseas Companies (Execution of Documents and Registration of Charges) Regulations 2009 (SI 2009/1917) and the Overseas Companies (Execution of Documents and Registration of Charges) (Amendment) Regulations 2011 (SI 2011/2194).

[176] See the Companies House website at *http://www.companieshouse.gov.uk/about/gbhtml/gpo1.shtml* [Accessed April 22, 2014].

not have limited liability. They do not make profits, but exist to provide research, training and other benefits. There is no capital and no investment from members of the public. They are little used.

Societas Europea

Following the implementation of the EC Regulation for the European **3–44** Company Statute,[177] its accompanying employee involvement Directive[178] and the implementing regulations in the United Kingdom, it is now possible to set up a *societas europaea* ("SE") which is registered in one country, but able to trade throughout the EU without the need for subsidiaries. A SE will use its own country's SE rules and these will be applicable throughout the EU. There are proposals for a private company version of a *societas europaea*, to be known as a *societas private europaea*.[179]

Community Interest Companies

These were introduced by the Companies (Audit, Investigations and **3–45** Community Enterprise) Act 2004 and are designed for enterprises that provide benefits to the community while having the benefits of limited liability but without some of the strictures of charity law. They are discussed in Ch.1 at para.1–27.

CONVERSION FROM ONE TYPE OF COMPANY TO ANOTHER

There are five methods of conversion which are summarised below. **3–46**
They are:

- from private to public[180];
- from public to private[181];
- from private limited to unlimited[182];
- from unlimited to private limited[183]; and
- from a public limited to unlimited.[184]

For all of the above, there are special prescribed application forms available from the Registrar of Companies. These need to be carefully completed by the directors or company secretary and sent to the Registrar of Companies along with all the other required documentation.

---

[177] EC 2157/2001.
[178] Council Directive 2001/86.
[179] See Ch.1 at para.1–15.
[180] CA 2006 ss.90–96.
[181] CA 2006 ss.97–101.
[182] CA 2006 ss.102–104.
[183] CA 2006 ss.105–108.
[184] CA 2006 ss.109–111.

From private to public—Companies Act 2006 ss.90–96

3–47 This procedure is not available if the company in question has previously been an unlimited company.[185] The procedure requires:

- the passing of a special resolution[186];
- an increase in the issued share capital to at least £50,000[187] if necessary;
- the alteration of the company's name and articles wherever necessary to effect the change to public status[188];
- a recent balance sheet[189] (confirmed by an unqualified[190] report[191] from the company's auditor) confirming that the company has the required minimum allotted share capital of at least £50,000[192] with each share paid up to at least one quarter plus any premium[193];
- that the company's net assets are not less than the aggregate of the called up share capital and its undistributable reserves,[194] taking account of the consideration (properly performed[195] or to be performed within the next five years,[196] or, as the case may be properly valued[197]) for any shares issued before the balance sheet date,[198] and between the balance sheet date and the date of application[199];
- confirmation that the company's net asset position has not deteriorated to below that aggregate figure since the balance sheet date[200];
- the directors' sending in a statement of compliance indicating that the requirements for re-registration have been complied with[201]; and

---

[185] CA 2006 s.90(2)(e).

[186] CA 2006 s.90(1)(a).

[187] CA 2006 s.90(2)(b), in turn referring to s.91(1). The minimum issued share capital for a plc is £50,000 (s.761).

[188] CA 2006 s.90(3). It would be necessary to rewrite the articles of association to take account of its plc status. See Sch.3 to the Companies (Model Articles) Regulations 2008 (SI 2008/3229) for the set of model articles for a plc.

[189] CA 2006 s.92(1)(a). The balance sheet must not have been prepared more than seven months before the application.

[190] CA 2006 s.92(3).

[191] CA 2006 s.92(1)(b).

[192] CA 2006 s.90(2)(b), in turn referring to s.91(1). The minimum issued share capital for a plc is £50,000 (s.761).

[193] CA 2006 s.91(1)(b).

[194] CA 2006 s.92(1)(c). Undistributable reserves are such reserves as any share premium account or capital redemption reserve.

[195] CA 2006 s.91(1)(c).

[196] CA 2006 s.91(1)(d).

[197] CA 2006 s.93.

[198] CA 2006 s.91.

[199] CA 2006 s.93, as evidenced by another valuation report.

[200] CA 2006 s.92(2).

[201] CA 2006 s.94(3).

- the appointment of a company secretary if the company has not had one before.[202]

Assuming these requirements have been fulfilled, the Registrar of Companies will issue a certificate of re-registration of the company as a public company.[203] This is prima facie conclusive evidence of the re-registration.

The main reasons for such conversions are stated above in *Why become a public company?*[204]

From public to private—Companies Act 2006 ss.97–101

This procedure may not be used to convert a public company into an **3–48** unlimited company as there is a separate procedure for that.[205] The members must pass a special resolution[206] which will also make the necessary changes to the name and articles to delete references to being a public company.[207] If shareholders holding five per cent of the nominal value of the company's issued share capital or of any class thereof, or five per cent of the members in a guarantee company, or at least 50 members, object to the conversion, they may, provided they did not previously vote in favour of the conversion, within 28 days apply to the court to object to the conversion.[208] The court may deal with the objection as it sees fit, either cancelling or confirming the order, arranging some settlement, adjourning the proceedings or requiring the objectors' shares to be bought by the company and making such changes to the memorandum and articles as may be required.[209] One reason for objection may be that once the company is private there will be no further opportunity to trade in the company's shares.

Assuming that there are no objectors, or that the objectors are pacified, the applicants may send in to the Registrar of Companies their application, a copy of the special resolution, and the directors' statement of compliance.[210] A certificate of re-registration will be issued in the normal manner.[211]

A company might wish to re-register as private because of the inconvenience and expense of complying with all the extra accounting and company law rules applicable to public companies. In addition certain actions, such as dispensing with unnecessary general meetings, are

---

[202] CA 2006 s.95.
[203] CA 2006 s.96. At the time of writing the fee for re-registration is £20.00 or same-day registration for £50.
[204] See para.3–31.
[205] CA 2006 s.109–111. See also para.3–51.
[206] CA 2006 s.97(1)(a).
[207] CA 2006 s.97(3). It would be necessary to rewrite the articles of association to take account of its private status. See Sch.1 of the Companies (Model Articles) Regulations 2008 (SI 2008/3229) for the set of model articles for a private company limited by shares, and Sch.2 for a private company limited by guarantee.
[208] CA 2006 s.98(1), (2).
[209] CA 2006 s.98(3) to (5).
[210] CA 2006 s.100. Form RR012 needs to be completed.
[211] CA 2006 s.101.

considerably easier for private companies than for public companies, thus making private status desirable.

From private limited company to unlimited—Companies Act 2006 ss.102–104

3–49   A company that has previously been re-registered as limited may not do this.[212] To enable the re-registration to take place, all the members will need to consent to the change.[213] There needs to be a statement of compliance from the directors confirming that all the members have genuinely signed or had someone properly sign on their behalf[214] and a new name and articles[215] to take account of the loss of limited liability. Assuming all is in order a certificate of re-registration in the usual manner as above will be issued.[216]

The reason for conversion is generally to avoid having to publish the company's accounts while retaining the benefit of the separate legal personality of a company.

From unlimited to limited—Companies Act 2006 ss.105–108

3–50   This procedure may not be used when the company has previously been limited.[217] The members need to pass a special resolution,[218] alter the name and the articles of association to reflect the new limited liability status for the company's shares or for the members (if a guarantee company).[219] If the company is to be limited by shares, it will need to state what its new share capital is to be.[220] If the company is to be limited by guarantee, it will need to state what the guaranteed sum is.[221] The directors will need to sign a statement of compliance.[222] Assuming all is in order, a certificate of re-registration will be issued in the normal manner.[223]

The reason for this conversion is normally the desire to take advantage of the benefits of limited liability despite the requirement to disclose accounts.

---

[212] CA 2006 s102(2). This is to prevent companies confusing their creditors by constantly changing their status between unlimited and limited.

[213] CA 2006 s.102(1)(a). Unanimous consent is required because the members are collectively becoming liable for the company's debts.

[214] CA 2006 s.103(4).

[215] CA 2006 s.102(3).

[216] CA 2006 s.104.

[217] CA 2006 s.105(2).

[218] CA 2006 s.105(1)(a).

[219] CA 2006 s.105(4).

[220] CA 2006 s.105(3).

[221] CA 2006 s.106(3).

[222] CA 2006 s.106(4).

[223] CA 2006 s.107.

From public limited to private unlimited—Companies Act 2006 ss.109–111

To do this, the company must not have been previously re-registered as **3–51** a limited or unlimited company.[224] All the members must assent to the change[225] and the company must make the appropriate changes to its name and articles.[226] A statement of compliance must be signed by the directors.[227] Assuming everything is in place, a certificate of re-registration will be issued.[228]

THE PRACTICALITIES OF OPERATING A NEWLY FORMED COMPANY

As indicated earlier, a company is set up by sending the appropriate **3–52** forms to the Registrar of Companies and waiting for the certificate of registration. Once it has been received, the company should hold its first board meeting, on which occasion the new directors should appoint the company's bankers and auditors (if required), issue share certificates, instruct the directors or company secretary to complete the company books and prepare minutes, etc. If the company has been founded for a particular purpose, such as to acquire a property, the directors will record the purchase of the property in the minutes.

Off the shelf companies

Although it is perfectly possible to prepare all one's own paperwork for **3–53** a company and obtain a company very quickly from the Registrar of Companies, it is common for those who need companies in a hurry to approach either lawyers, accountants or company formation agents to ask them to prepare the paperwork to their specification or to buy from them an already prepared "off the shelf" company. This is a company which already exists, with a name, number and shareholders, directors and, where wanted or necessary, company secretary. On receiving the clients' instructions, it is a simple matter to change the name to the clients' choice of name, to transfer the shares from the existing holders to the clients, for the current company officers to resign their directorships and company secretaryship, having appointed the clients as the new directors and company secretary first by means of a board meeting. Such board meetings do not generally actually take place, but are paper exercises to serve as a formal record for the company's books. The new directors and company secretary may then proceed as in the previous paragraph. The Registrar of Companies will need to be informed of the new directors and company secretary by means of Forms AP01 and AP03 respectively. Retiring directors and secretary will need to complete Forms TM01 and TM02.

---

[224] CA 2006 s.109(2).
[225] CA 2006 s.110(2)(a).
[226] CA 2006 s.109(3).
[227] CA 2006 s.110(3).
[228] CA 2006 s.111.

Acquisition of an existing business from the directors in their private capacity

3–54   Assuming a company has been set up and constituted by one of the methods in the above two paragraphs, the directors may decide that their company should acquire the directors' own personal business. This may happen when an existing partnership decides that it wishes to incorporate in order to avoid the risk of personal liability. In this event a contract for the sale of the business, usually known as a sale and purchase agreement or a vending agreement, is drawn up between the company and the partnership and the partners as trustees for the partnership. The directors of the company will sign the contract for the company, and the partners will sign for the partnership, even though in reality they are all the same people. The company then acquires the business[229] from the partnership and as consideration the directors allot themselves (but in their capacity as former partners) shares in the company. Alternatively the company may give the former partners some cash and allot some shares, or some shares and loan notes if the company has insufficient cash to hand. It is common to have the partnership audited and valued first, not least because of capital gains tax consequences later.[230]

   If the directors are going to issue shares to the former partners, directors may need to obtain authority from the members[231] to allot shares under Companies Act 2006 s.549 if such authority is not already in place, as it generally will be. If the company is a private limited company with only one class of shares, the directors will automatically be deemed to have the authority to allot such shares,[232] but in a private company if the directors wish to allot shares of more than one class, or if the company in question is a public one, the directors will need authority to allot shares under s.549.

   If there are shareholders in the company who are not the same people as the former partners selling the business, account will have to be taken of their interest since, unless the company is private, has only one class of shares and directors have been authorised to allot shares without regard to pre-emption rights,[233] existing shareholders may be entitled to their pre-emption rights.[234] These may need to be disapplied or waived first before the former partners receive their shares, unless the articles

---

[229] Usually what is conveyed is the business's entire assets and undertakings, and its liabilities, but is open to the parties to vary this.

[230] When a company acquires a business from its members, it is possible to defer the capital gains tax liability on the value of the assets acquired by means of roll-over relief.

[231] This is still required even if the members, the directors and the former partners are all in practice the same people.

[232] CA 2006 s.550.

[233] CA 2006 s.569. A pre-emption right is the right given to existing shareholders to buy newly issued shares before they are offered to outsiders who do not already own shares in the company. If an existing shareholder owns 20% of the shares in a company, he is entitled to buy 20% of any newly issued shares in the company. He is thus able to maintain his voting power within the company.

[234] CA 2006 s.561.

preclude pre-emption rights[235] or the directors have previously been authorised to allot shares without the need to take account of pre-emption rights[236] or are otherwise authorised by special resolution to disapply pre-emption rights.[237]

If the partners selling the business are also the directors of the company, the members (who in many cases will be the same people as the partners and the directors) may need to give approval by ordinary resolution to the acquisition of the business by the company under Companies Act 2006 s.190.[238] Directors will also need to disclose their interest in the acquisition in terms of s.177. If the sale and purchase agreement includes the transfer from the partnership to the company of heritage or other items that attract stamp duty, the sale and purchase agreement will need to be adjudicated by the Capital Taxes Office and stamp duty land tax paid to the HM Revenue and Customs by the company. Pending adjudication, the directors may cause the company to issue the new shares to the former partners and their names will be entered in the Register of Members[239] and various other registers (depending on whether the former partners are the company's directors) and a return made to the Registrar of Companies[240] indicating the allotment of the new shares. The company secretary will issue share certificates for the new shares.

There are various practical consequences of such a sale and purchase. **3–55** Dispositions of heritage, standard securities and leases of property will need to show the change of ownership from the partnership to the company. Change of tenant may require consent from landlords. As already indicated, stamp duty land tax may need to be paid on such transfers of ownership. Assets formerly insured in the partnership's name will need to show the company's interest instead. Vehicles will need to be registered in the company's name. Employees will have to have their contracts of employment transferred into the company name. Hire purchase agreements may need to be cancelled and new ones started in the company name. Outstanding liabilities[241] may still need to be met by the partnership, but the company may have to indemnify the partners for the costs arising. Equally if the partners receive any payments which should have been made to the company, they will hold those payments in trust for the company and pay them to the company as soon as convenient.

---

[235] As is possible under CA 2006 s.567.
[236] CA 2006 s.570.
[237] CA 2006 s.571.
[238] This is dealt with further in Ch.9, and refers to substantial acquisitions by and from directors and their companies.
[239] CA 2006 s.112.
[240] CA 2006 s.555.
[241] Such as non-transferrable hire-purchase obligations.

EXECUTION OF DOCUMENTS IN SCOTLAND

3–56 In terms of the Requirements of Writing (Scotland) Act 1995, for a company to execute a document there are two options.

The company may execute a document by having a director, the company secretary or someone authorised to sign on its behalf, duly sign on its behalf in the presence of a witness.[242]

Alternatively, the company may execute a document by having either two directors, a director and a secretary, or two persons duly authorised to sign on behalf of the company, duly sign—but no witness is required.[243]

Where a witness is present, he will be required to state his name and address. In each circumstance, the date of execution should be indicated.

3–57 If the company is a private company and the company has dispensed with the services of the company secretary, but its articles still state that the company secretary is needed for the execution of documents, it may be prudent to revise the articles to remove the reference to the signing by the company secretary. Where an authorised signatory is used to execute documents, it is customary to provide evidence of the authority of the signatory by means of a board minute authorising the signatory to execute documents. Companies are no longer required to have a company seal[244] but if a company has one and wishes to use it, or is required to do in terms of its articles of association, it may continue to do so. The impressing of the seal will be in addition to the requirements above.

The rules in England and Wales for the execution of documents and deeds may be found in ss.43–47 of the CA 2006.

If a common seal is used, the company seal should be used only with the authority of the directors, and even where it is used, the document must also be signed by at least one authorised person, being a director, the company secretary (where there is one) or an authorised signatory. The company may vary these provisions if it wishes.[245]

PROMOTERS

3–58 Promoters of companies were much more common at the beginning of the twentieth century than they are now. A promoter was someone who set up a company and then invited others to subscribe for shares in it. He would issue an impressive prospectus, advertising the likely profits of the company and the desirability of investment in it. If the promoter was a rogue, he would talk up the company's likely profits, and then sell his

---

[242] Requirements of Writing (Scotland) Act 1995 Sch.2 para.3(5).
[243] Requirements of Writing (Scotland) Act 1995 Sch.2 para.3(5).
[244] CA 2006 s.48(2).
[245] See the Model Articles for private companies, r.49 in the Companies (Model Articles) Regulations 2008 (SI 2008/3229). Similar rules apply to public and guarantee companies.

own assets to the company at an inflated price, or would hope to make his money persuading the gullible to pay for his own worthless shares by ramping up the share price.

Nowadays, such frauds are harder to carry out. For shares to be offered to the public the company needs to be admitted to the relevant investment exchange or to find a market maker willing to make a market in the shares of the company. Neither of these will welcome a company whose promoters appear to be gulling the public. The Financial Conduct Authority is empowered under the Financial Services and Markets Act 2000 to police such activity. Furthermore the financial press casts a caustic eye on such promoters. Following the case of *Erlanger v New Sombrero Phosphate Co Ltd*[246] promoters are under a fiduciary duty to disclose any personal benefits they may be receiving from the promotion of the company. In this case, enterprising swindlers sold the lease of a West Indian island, allegedly covered in phosphate-producing guano, to a company of which they were promoters. Not only did they fail to disclose the 100 per cent profit they made on the sale, but they kept quiet about the fact that there was no phosphate on the island anyway.

Promoters as they used to exist do not really exist any longer, and the **3–59** law continues to refer to them purely to prevent anyone trying to carry out the more disreputable practices of yesteryear. Most people employ company agents, lawyers and accountants to set up companies for them, rather than promoters; and if a company's shares are to be offered to the public, the company will approach a merchant bank to help the company do this. Investors may be suspicious of a public company trying to issue its own shares without the advice and support of a reputable merchant bank or firm of stockbrokers.[247] Without the backing of a merchant bank or stockbrokers, the company will have little credibility. In any event, any company seeking to have its shares listed will have to ensure that it complies with the listing rules.

Sometimes directors of a company provide their own services to the company before it is founded, and then seek to obtain shares as recompense for their labour in setting the company up. Provided there is an express contract with the company, once the company is in existence, there is no difficulty with this.

PRE-INCORPORATION CONTRACTS

Sometimes a would-be director of an as yet unformed company is so keen **3–60** to get this company to enter a contract that he will make the company enter into a contract even before the company has any legal existence. If

---

[246] (1878) 3 App. Cas. 1218.

[247] This is not to say that this does not take place. One reason for not using a merchant bank is the familiar agency problem: to what extent are the merchant bank's expensive fees really necessary, and how can the company know that the bank is always working in its client's interest? It is also not unusual for the banks to get it wrong: the price of the shares in Royal Mail plc in 2013 on its flotation was far too low.

this happens the would-be director becomes personally liable[248] unless the contract says otherwise.[249] The solution is therefore to persuade directors not to sign anything until their companies are formally in existence.

Further Reading

There is very little academic literature on the contents of this chapter, which, as will have been observed, addressed the practicalities of incorporation. Further details of incorporation and much useful advice on what needs to be done to incorporate a company are best found on the Companies House website. *Palmer's Company Law* (London: Sweet & Maxwell) Chapter 2 also contains much practical information on the topic covered in this chapter.

---

[248] *Phonogram Ltd v Lane* [1982] Q.B. 938; [1981] 3.W.L.R. 736 CA.
[249] CA 2006 s.51.

CHAPTER 4

THE ARTICLES OF ASSOCIATION

THE CONSTITUTION OF THE COMPANY

The founding documents

Just as most partnerships have a partnership agreement, setting out the **4–01** rights and duties of the partners, and just as most august institutions such as universities, colleges and charitable bodies have a charter which sets out the intentions of the founders, their aspirations for the institution's future and its rules for its governance, so do companies have documentation to the same effect. In the United Kingdom this documentation is known as its constitution, and the most significant part of the constitution is the company's articles of association, commonly known as the "articles".

In the past the constitution was divided into two long documents, the **4–02** memorandum of association and the articles of association. The original purpose of the memorandum was to inform potential investors of six matters, being the company's name, the company's country of registration, its objects (being the purpose for which the company was set up), the limited liability of the members of the company (if appropriate), whether the company is private or public and the authorised capital of the company. Old companies may still have long memoranda of association, but since the CA 2006 came into force a new very brief memorandum of association is now used, as described in the previous chapter.[1] Much of the information formerly in the old-style long memorandum is now contained in either the registration application or the company's articles.

The current rules relating to the name of a company are discussed in **4–03** Ch.3.[2] A company's country of registration is included in the registration application and cannot be altered. The company's objects will be addressed shortly. The limit on the liability of the members is stated in the registration application,[3] as is its private or public status.[4] Companies

---

[1] At para.3–02.
[2] At paras 3–09—3–12.
[3] CA 2006 s.9(2)(c).
[4] CA 2006 s.9(2)(d).

no longer need a provision for authorised capital, though a company may choose to have one if it wishes.[5]

The objects clause

4–04   Historically, the objects clause was the clause in the old-style memorandum that stated the purpose for which the company had been set up. The objects clause would indicate that the company was set up, say, to publish books, or to make furniture. The company and its directors were not supposed to carry out activities that were not connected with the purpose for which the company was set up, and the directors were not supposed to act beyond the powers granted to the company to enable that purpose to be carried out. The original idea was to protect investors from unscrupulous directors misusing the company's funds for unauthorised activities.[6] When a company acted beyond the objects given to it in its objects clause, so that the company did something that strictly speaking it should not have done, it was said to have acted ultra vires.[7] If the company acted within its powers it was said to have acted intra vires.[8] The directors should never have made the company act ultra vires and in theory, the directors, by acting beyond the powers given to them, were liable to the company for making the company act ultra vires. One undesirable effect of the ultra vires rule was that companies could in theory enter into contracts which they were technically not supposed to have entered into, and then refuse to honour the contracts on the grounds that their objects clauses did not allow them to enter into such contracts.[9] This was unfair on the other contracting party, even if it was very convenient for the company. To make the situation worse, the contracting party was deemed to know the contents of the objects clause since it was available for inspection at Companies House, or a copy could be supplied by the company itself.

Reform

4–05   This was clearly unsatisfactory both for contracting parties and for the companies themselves, many of which did not wish to be constrained by objects clauses that limited a company's opportunities for undertaking new ventures. Through artful wording of the objects clause, which resulted in very wordy and long-winded pages of documentation, giving the directors multiple powers to carry out the wide objects of the company, the original ability of the objects clause to protect investors gradually diminished. Meanwhile, investors increasingly did not feel the need

---

[5] The authorised capital was a cap on the number of shares that directors could issue. Although many existing pre-CA 2006 companies may still have authorised capital in their constitutions, following the CA 2006 the authorised capital clause in their constitutions may be removed if the members wish to do so. If they do not, the authorised capital clause remains in place.

[6] *Re German Date Coffee Co* (1882) 20 Ch.D. 169; 46 L.T. 327 CA.

[7] Beyond its powers.

[8] Within its powers.

[9] *Ashbury Railway Carriage and Iron Co Ltd v Riche* (1875) L.R. 7 H.L. 653 HL.

to be protected in this way: there were other more effective ways of holding directors to account. Legislation elsewhere reduced the ability of a company to refuse to honour contracts that were ultra vires.[10] The Companies Act 1989 allowed companies to have objects clauses that allowed companies both to indicate what their primary object was—on the principle that it is not a bad idea to have some general statement of the main aims of the company—and also to give companies a great deal of flexibility. This was done by the company adopting a secondary general trading clause[11] that effectively allowed the company to trade in whatever it fancied. If the company had an objects clause and accompanying powers that allowed it to carry on business as a general commercial company, almost everything that a company could do would be intra vires. There would then be no more litigation about the ultra vires rule.

Regrettably this did not lead to the abandonment of long and tedious list of objects and powers in objects clauses, because a bank, when making a loan, generally insisted on an objects clause stating that the borrowing company had the power to grant security for its loans or had the power to grant guarantees, even if those guarantees were not necessarily beneficial to the company. Because no company wished to argue with a bank that was going to give it a loan, companies continued to have long objects clauses just to keep banks happy, even though the clauses were arguably not necessary.

Despite the reluctance of banks to let companies adapt to newer styles **4–06** of objects clause, the new rules in the Companies Act 1989 ensured that there were no significant recent cases on objects clauses. In addition, the Companies Act 2006 gave its blessing to companies being deemed to be able to carry out any activities they wish unless there is some provision in the articles specifically restricting the objects of the company.[12] The effect of this is that many companies may no longer even bother with an objects clause.[13] If a company founded after October 1, 2009 does want to have an objects clause, the objects clause will need to be inserted in the articles.[14] For companies founded before October 1, 2009, and where such a company still wants to have an objects clause, any objects clause expressed in its old-style memorandum will be treated as if it were in the articles.[15] The objects clause may then be altered by means of a special

---

[10] European Communities Act 1972 s.9 implementing art.9 of the First Company Law Directive.

[11] It was also open to the company not to have a primary object but just to be a general trading company.

[12] CA 2006 s.31(1).

[13] One effect of the CA 2006 is that many companies were encouraged to review their constitutions and update their old-style memorandum and articles. In so doing, many companies took the opportunity to remove any objects clause—assuming, that is, that no bank insisted on its continued presence, as some occasionally did.

[14] CA 2006 s.31(1). This is because there is nowhere else to put it, given that the memorandum is now merely a statement of the subscribers' wish to set up a company.

[15] CA 2006 s.28.

resolution unless there is some special provision for entrenchment of the objects clause.[16]

4–07   This is not to say that the objects clause should disappear entirely. There may be companies, particularly charity companies, where those who set up the company believe that the company should be incorporated for a particular purpose and no other. A person who subscribed for shares in a charitable company set up to protect whales, for example, would be unhappy if he found that the money he had put into the company were being used for some other less worthy purpose. As regards trading companies, it is unwise to have a restrictive objects clause, for what may seem a good idea to the founding members of a company one year may seem uncommercial or unrealistic 20 years later. Even for charitable companies, it may be unwise to have too restricted an objects clause lest the purpose for which the company was set up may become redundant: if a charitable company were set up to alleviate the problems arising from a particular disease, for which subsequently a highly effective vaccine becomes available, it would have no further reason for existence unless its objects clause allowed it to address its efforts to other diseases, or to convey all its assets to a similar charity for a still prevalent disease.

Parliament's solution

4–08   There is a balance to be found between a company having the benefit of an objects clause, but at the same time not letting the objects clause disadvantage contracting parties who are unaware of its significance. The Companies Act 1989 introduced three rules to deal with this point, and in a slightly different form they are now to be found in the CA 2006 at ss.39–42.

The first rule might be called the *overriding statute*. This generally allows companies to do whatever they wish irrespective of the objects clause, though members may object to this by means of the *internal policy* rule. Outsiders are still nonetheless protected by means of the third rule, the *external policy* rule.

4–09 **(1) The overriding statute.** A company's capacity to carry out any act is now no longer limited by its constitution. The CA 2006 s.39(1) states:

> "The validity of an act done by a company shall not be called into question on the ground of lack of capacity by reason of anything in the company's constitution."

This means that if a company has a specific objects clause, and carries out an act that is not permitted by that objects clause (or anything else in its constitution), that act is not in itself invalid just because the company should not have carried it out. In other words the company cannot

---

[16] CA 2006 s.22.

renounce its own act. In s.39(1) the word "act" was used advisedly as it covers not only contracts but gifts, guarantees and other activities.

(2) The internal policy rule. Section 39(1) is all very well for outsiders, **4–10** reassured that the company will not renounce its contracts on the grounds of their being ultra vires, but the members themselves may be unhappy that the company has acted ultra vires. The legislation affords the members limited protection.

Section 40(4) states:

> "This section does not affect any right of a member of a company to bring proceedings to restrain the doing of an action that is beyond the power of the directors. But no such proceedings shall lie in respect of an act to be done in fulfilment of a legal obligation arising from a previous act of the company."

This means that any member may apply to the court for an interdict[17] to prevent the directors making the company enter into a new ultra vires act; but no interdict would be granted if the company had already embarked upon the act, or had already incurred some legal obligation to the other party to the act. It would be very unfair to the other party if, half way through the ultra vires act, an objecting member obtained an interdict preventing the company fulfilling its side of the bargain or completing the act—all to the other party's prejudice. So all the objecting member may do is to prevent the repetition of the same ultra vires acts, and prevent the directors making the company enter into any new and similar ultra vires acts.

Nevertheless, the interdict may be successful within those limited cir- **4–11** cumstances. If so, this places the directors in an awkward position, since they have made the company do something it should not have done. Under s.171 of the CA 2006 directors are already supposed to act within the constitution, and only to exercise their powers for the purposes for which they were conferred. If the directors do not do this, they may be liable to the company for breach of their duty as directors.[18] However, although the remedy of the interdict may be gratifying for the objecting member, the other members may be less impressed. The other members may not have such strong feelings about the importance of the objects clause, and consider that the objecting member is making an unnecessary fuss. If the other members pass a special resolution ratifying the ultra vires act against which the interdict was taken,[19] and for good measure, also pass a separate special resolution exonerating the directors personally from any liability for making the company act ultra vires, the effect

---

[17] Injunction in England and Wales.

[18] CA 2006 s.178. It is also possible that they could be liable under a derivative claim (ss.265–269).

[19] CA 2006 s.239. In this event, the directors' own votes in their own interest may not be used to ensure that the vote at a meeting is passed in their favour (s.239(4)), and if the vote is by written resolution, they may not vote at all (s.239(3)).

of the interdict will be nullified. In addition, the members could pass a special resolution altering the objects clause for the future, thereby permitting the former *ultra vires* act against which the interdict was originally taken.

The purpose of the interdict remedy under the CA 2006 s.40(4) is to provide a remedy for those members who do feel strongly about the company's adherence to its objects. However, the interdict will only be useful: (a) where a company has a very specific objects clause and no general commercial objects; (b) where the objecting member is sufficiently well informed of the company's activities (and indeed its objects) to be aware that the company is not adhering to its objects; (c) where the objecting member is able to obtain the interdict before the company starts the ultra vires act (otherwise it will be too late); and (d) where the other members are unlikely subsequently to overturn the interdict by ratifying the ultra vires act or rewriting the objects clause by passing a special resolution to that effect.[20] As these four requirements are hard to meet in practice, it is not surprising that there have been very few cases on this issue. This suggests both that the obstacles are hard to surmount and that on the whole potential objectors are being advised that trying to obtain an interdict on this matter is probably a waste of effort and expense. However, it does mean that a large number of past cases relating to a company's capacity and the ultra vires rule no longer have any applicability—which is no small mercy.

4–12 **(3) The external policy rule.** Before the reform of the ultra vires rule in the Companies Act 1989, a particular area of difficulty was where directors acted beyond the powers given to them in the objects clause. When objects clauses were four pages long, usually somewhere within them would be authority for the directors to carry out all necessary acts for the promotion of the company. In addition, under reg.70 of the then standard articles of association (Table A), directors commonly had the power to do everything conducive to the promotion of the company. But occasionally there were companies with poorly drafted objects clauses or restrictive articles that did not give the directors all the powers they might have wished, or imposed restraints upon the directors so that they had to seek the approval of the members for certain actions, such as loans. What happened when the board of directors ignored those restrictions on their powers or were inquorate when they made their decisions? To add further to these complications sometimes the directors would act beyond the powers given to them by the company, but the other party to the contract was aware of this.[21] It was recognised that the law left much to be desired in this area, and that third parties dealing with directors or the directors' authorisees should be protected even where those directors, or their authorisees, were strictly speaking not entitled to make the company enter into certain transactions. This has resulted in the CA 2006 s.40(1):

---

[20] CA 2006 s.21(1).
[21] *Rolled Steel Products (Holdings) Ltd v British Steel Corporation* [1986] Ch. 246; [1985] 2 W.L.R. 908.

"In favour of a person dealing with a company in good faith, the power of the board of directors to bind the company, or authorise others to do so, shall be deemed to be free of any limitation under the company's constitution."

Although the matter is not absolutely without doubt, it is thought that this subsection protects third parties generally, in that when they deal in good faith with a company's directors, or with other people authorised by the board of directors to act on the company's behalf (generally agents and employees), the third parties can assume that there is nothing in the constitution or articles prohibiting the directors, or those whom they authorise, from entering into transactions[22] with those third parties.[23] Even if there were, say, an express clause in the articles requiring a particular resolution before the directors could enter into a certain contract with a third party, and that resolution had not been passed, the third party acting in good faith (as later defined for the purpose of this section) is automatically entitled to assume that the board of directors were still authorised to make the company enter into the contract despite the absence of the resolution.

Despite this assumption, the CA 2006 s.40(2)(b)(i) needs to be considered. This deals with the question of whether a third party should try to find out whether an act is ultra vires or not. **4–13**

"A party to a transaction with a company is not bound to enquire as to any limitation on the board of directors to bind the company or authorise others to do so."

From this it would appear that a third party no longer is expected to look at the company's constitution, to ask the company if a proposed act is ultra vires the objects clause, or even to ask if there are limits on the powers of the board of directors either to make a company enter into a transaction or authorise others (namely agents and employees) to enter into the transaction on the company's behalf. Quite whether this subsection achieves anything at all is open to question, but despite it, as a matter of prudence, third parties, dealing with a company, who are unsure as to whether or not the company should be entering into a particular transaction with the third party, are well advised to see a copy of a minute of the board of directors authorising the transaction, or authorising someone, such as an agent or employee, to sign on behalf of the company. It would be difficult for a company to gainsay the validity of such a signature to a transaction if there were a board minute approving it. On a wider point, at the best of times it is sometimes difficult for a company to avoid being liable for a proposed transaction set up by the company's agent, if the company's agent had given the

---

[22] CA 2006 s.40(2)(a) refers to "transactions or acts" thereby meaning both contracts and gratuitous acts such as gifts and guarantees.

[23] *Pharmed Medicare Private Ltd v Univar Ltd* [2002] EWCA 1569.

impression either that he had the requisite authority for the transaction or that it was unlikely that his authority would be withdrawn.[24]

4–14   If a third party is not expected to enquire into any limitation on the directors' ability to make the company enter into transactions, it might be possible, if devious, for company directors to take a decision which perhaps should not have been taken and then try to assert that the decision is valid as far as third parties are concerned. In *Smith v Henni-ker-Major & Co*,[25] a director, Smith, took a company decision which he asserted he made at a board meeting and which therefore, he said, should be binding on a third party. The third party had failed to act on that decision and Smith was suing the third party for negligence. The quorum for Smith's company was two and although he was the only one present when the decision was made, he claimed that he was acting as a board. In a sense, he was ingeniously taking advantage of the law in a manner contrary to the purpose of the law. Rimer J. found against him on the grounds that the then s.35A only applied to directors when they were acting as a board and that to act as a board they must be quorate, which Smith on his own was not. His actions were therefore not binding on a third party acting in good faith. Smith's case was not helped by the fact that he was trying to make the third party liable, whereas as a director, and indeed chairman of the company, Smith knew or should have known perfectly well that he should not have been taking an inquorate decision. In a sense, Smith was twisting the purpose of the law. After all, the purpose of this section is to protect third parties acting in good faith, not to allow companies to ignore their proper internal procedures for some ulterior purpose.[26]

4–15   The next point is that "good faith" (in terms of s.40(1)) was given a special meaning for the purposes of this subsection. First, the CA 2006 s.40(2)(b)(iii) states that a person is not to be regarded as acting in bad faith merely because he happens to know that the board of directors has done something that goes beyond the powers given to it in the company's constitution. So if a third party knew that, as in the example above, a particular resolution ought to have been passed before the board of directors entered into a contract with him, and that the board of directors had omitted to obtain the resolution first, he could still be said to be acting in good faith. Secondly, the third party is assumed to be acting in good faith unless the contrary can be proved.[27] So for a third party not to be acting in good faith would require him to do something suitably wicked, but which is not referred to in the company's constitution.[28]

---

[24] *First Energy(UK) Ltd v Hungarian International Bank Ltd* [1993] 1 Lloyd's Rep. 194; *Bank of Middle East v Sun Life Assurance Co of Canada (UK) Ltd* [1983] 2 Lloyd's Rep. 9.

[25] *Smith v Henniker-Major & Co* [2002] B.C.C. 544.

[26] See also the older case of *Royal British Bank v Turquand* (1856) 6 El. Bl. 327; 5 El. Bl. 248. The law protects the third party acting in good faith who is unaware of the absence of certain required internal procedures.

[27] CA 2006 s.40A(2)(b)(ii).

[28] Such as, perhaps, bribing the directors or blackmailing them? See *Hopkins v TL Dallas Group Ltd* [2004] EWHC 1379.

Charitable companies in Scotland

One area, however, where the old ultra vires rule still applies much as **4–16** before[29] is company entered within the Scottish Charity Register, which specifically must act within the terms of their objects.[30] However, this does not apply to acts of a charitable company in favour of a person who either: (a) (i) had paid a proper price in connection with the acts, and (ii) did not know that the charity company was carrying out acts that were not permitted by the company's constitution, or were beyond the powers of the directors; or (b) did not know that the company was a charity.[31]

Anyone acquiring property from a charitable company in such circumstances is deemed to have good title to the property transferred to him.[32] If a charitable company later realises that it should not have carried out the act, or transferred the property in question, it may try to undo the act or recover the property. But in order to do so, it is for the charitable company to prove that the person acquiring the property: (i) knew that the act was not permitted under the constitution, or was beyond the directors' powers; or (ii) knew the company was a charity. This is unlikely to be easy to prove.[33] On the other hand, the charitable company itself is under a duty to make sure that the word "charity" or "charitable" is on all its paperwork, notices, cheques, invoices, etc.[34] so that it becomes harder for someone to say that he was unaware he was dealing with a charity. There are also rules to protect persons who acquire property from a charity company which later ceases to be a charitable company. The subsequent change does not retrospectively affect any rights someone may have previously acquired for full consideration.[35]

Some of the law relating to Scottish charitable companies is to be found in the Companies Act 1989 s.112. It differs from the slightly similar legislation in England and Wales, which is to be found in the CA 2006 s.42.

---

[29] That is, in the manner before the reforms introduced by the Companies Act 1989 ("the CA 1989").

[30] CA 1989 s.112.

[31] CA 1989 s.112(3). Note that ignorance of the fact that the charitable company is a charitable company is enough to validate the unauthorised act.

[32] CA 1989 s.112(4).

[33] CA 1989 s.112(5). It is conceivable that a purchaser might wish to prove that he knew that some act was beyond the capacity of the company in an attempt to avoid being liable for the act. However, his difficulty would be that he had already given consideration for the act, which suggests that he was willing to accept its consequences.

[34] CA 2006 s.112(6).

[35] CA 1989 s.112(2).

Directors acting in their own interests

4–17   A second area where the ultra vires rule still continues is where a company enters into a transaction with a director[36] (or those connected with a director)[37] in his personal capacity. This is because, of all people, a director ought to know what is ultra vires or intra vires. The company has the right under the CA 2006 s.41 to make the transaction voidable at its instance.[38] This means that the company could terminate any such transaction and demand the return of the subject matter of the transaction. It could also make the director account to the company for any benefit,[39] or indemnify the company for any loss,[40] unless restitution of the subject matter is impossible,[41] the company has been indemnified for any loss,[42] the rights of third parties who acquired the subject matter in good faith and for value would be prejudiced[43] or the members ratify the ultra vires act by ordinary or special resolution.[44] A person connected with the director may be absolved from liability if he can prove that he did not know that the director was exceeding his powers.[45]

ARTICLES OF ASSOCIATION

The function of the articles of association

4–18   The articles of association are in essence the constitution of the company. The articles form a standing set of rules for such matters as the procedure for directors' meetings, the right of members to transfer shares, the right of the company to call members to pay the unpaid capital on their shares, the practice (where not covered in statute) of general meetings, and a host of other procedural matters. The articles detail the tripartite relationship of the company to the members, the members to the directors, and the company to the directors.[46] What is unusual about articles is that while there is a contractual element to articles, in that members, the company and the directors agree to certain terms with each other, unlike other contracts, the articles are published at the Register of Companies and available for all to see. This means that if the members wish to keep something secret they will need to draw up a shareholders agreement, whose terms are privy to the members signing up to that

---

[36] This also applies to a director of the company's holding company (CA 2006 s.41(2)(b)(i)).
[37] For the definition of persons connected with a director, see the CA 2006 s.252. In essence they are close members of the director's family, partners in a partnership with the director, trusts associated with a director, or other companies in which the director has a controlling interest.
[38] CA 2006 s.41(2).
[39] CA 2006 s.41(3)(a).
[40] CA 2006 s.41(3)(b).
[41] CA 2006 s.41(4)(a).
[42] CA 2006 s.41(4)(b).
[43] CA 2006 s.41(4)(c).
[44] CA 2006 s.41(4)(d).
[45] CA 2006 s.41(5).
[46] CA 2006 s.33(1).

agreement. Equally, it means that any future investor who wishes to become a member is entitled, to some extent, to rely on the terms of the articles as being the terms on which he will become a member: in a sense, the articles are a form of advertisement for the company. If he does not like those terms, he should not become a member or once he is a member he should seek to have the articles changed by special resolution.

There are three model sets of articles to found in the Companies **4–19** (Model Articles) Regulations 2008.[47] One set is for a private company limited by shares, one for a guarantee company and one for a public limited company. These may be adopted in their entirety, which means that on the incorporation of the company with the model articles, there is no need to send in a special set of articles[48] along with the registration application. The 2008 model articles are much shorter and more intelligible than their predecessors. Many of the complex rules for the rotation of directors have been discarded and instead of dense, closely worded pages of text, the layout is open and the phrasing user-friendly.

It is common for solicitors, company formation agents and accoun- **4–20** tants to make up their own particular in-house versions of each model, usually by stating that the company's articles are as in the relevant model, subject to certain amendments. The amendments are then tailored, usually by deleting certain regulations and inserting new ones, to suit their clients better than the model articles. Amending the model to suit investors' requirements is perfectly acceptable providing the amendments are not contrary to statute. Common amendments to the model articles are the introduction of terms relating to classes of shares, restrictions on the transferability of shares, weighted voting,[49] defined quora,[50] named directors[51] and for listed companies, the adoption of wording acceptable to the London Stock Exchange for the securities being listed. Banks may also well wish to see a clause in the articles stating that the company has the authority to grant security and to grant guarantees for connected companies even when there may be no commercial benefit to the company issuing the guarantees.

It is permissible to change the articles of association at any time provided a special resolution has been passed first.[52] Any change must again not be contrary to statute. If the company is a Scottish charity, any change in the object of the company, as indicated in its articles, must receive the consent of the Office of the Scottish Charity Regulator.[53] It is

---

[47] Companies (Model Articles) Regulations 2008 (SI 2008/3229).

[48] CA 2006 s.20.

[49] As in *Bushell v Faith* [1970] A.C. 1099.

[50] A quorum is the minimum number of persons required to be present to make a decision valid. It is possible to provide that a meeting is inquorate if a named individual is absent.

[51] Although naming directors in the articles is not as common as it was, namely because of the need to rewrite the articles on the death, illness or retirement of the named director, directors are occasionally still named in articles. Sometimes they used to be given certain employment rights in the articles, but the better practice is to have a separate contract of employment.

[52] CA 2006 s.21(1).

[53] CA 2006 s.21(3)(b), referring to s.16 of the Charities and Trustee Investment (Scotland) Act 2005.

a good idea for companies to review and update their articles every few years. If they do not do so, the articles as drafted remain. This means that a company with a 1948 set of articles would still be operating under those articles and people dealing with that company would need to check the 1948 version of the articles to be sure of the terms of that company's constitution. Unless the members change the articles,[54] the members have to live with the wording of the articles and follow that wording[55]: extrinsic evidence as to what the articles are meant to have said, or evidence of what was omitted as a result of error or oversight when drafting the articles, will not be entertained, because the articles are meant to be a public document[56] and existing and potential members, creditors and others are entitled to rely on what is stated in the company's articles of association as a statement of the company's constitution. There is sometimes a contradiction between what the articles say and what is expected under another set of rules, such as the Listing Rules for companies listed on the London Stock Exchange, in which case the articles will prevail.[57] However, although in principle the courts will not rewrite the articles for the shareholders where something has been omitted, they will sometimes in the interest of business common sense construe the articles to give effect to what had been intended if not very well expressed.[58] Directors may not use their rights under the articles to use their discretion in certain matters to vary the company's pre-existing contractual obligations to the disadvantage of those with whom the company had previously contracted.[59] Shareholders may not use the fact that they have a majority (albeit not a majority sufficient to pass a special resolution to change the articles) to override the provisions of the articles.[60] Directors and indeed members must always be alert to the fact that articles are inherently alterable.[61] If anyone wishes to enforce any provisions of the articles, he must do so in his capacity as a member, not in some other capacity such as the company's proposed solicitor.[62]

---

[54] If there are insufficient members to pass a special resolution to change the articles, the unhappy members' only practical option is to sell their shares if they can—not always easy in a small company.

[55] *Hickman v Kent and Romney Marsh Sheepbreeders Association* [1915] 1 Ch. 881; *Quin Axtens Ltd v Salmon* [1909] A.C. 442; the failure to understand and act on the wording can be costly and inconvenient: *Cottrell v King* [2004] B.C.C. 307.

[56] *Bratton Seymour Service Co Ltd v Oxborough* [1992] B.C.L.C. 693.

[57] *Re Astec (BSR) Plc* [1998] 2 B.C.L.C. 556.

[58] *Folkes Group Plc v Alexander* [2002] 2 B.C.L.C. 254; *Cream Holdings Ltd v Davenport* [2011] EWHC 1287; *Thompson v Goblin Hill Hotels Ltd* [2011] UKPC 8; [2011] 1 B.C. L. C. 587.

[59] *Equitable Life Association v Hyman* [2000] 3 W.L.R. 529; [2000] All E.R. 961 HL.

[60] *Breckland Group Holdings Ltd v London and Suffolk Properties* [1989] B.C.L.C. 100.

[61] *Shuttleworth v Cox Bros Co Ltd* [1927] 2 K.B. 9; *Southern Foundries (1926) Ltd v Shirlaw* [1940] A.C. 701.

[62] *Eley v Positive Government Security Life Assurance Co Ltd* (1875) 1 Ex. D. 20. Eley had drafted the company's articles and included a term stating that he was to be the company's lawyer. The company failed to appoint him, but due to poor pleadings in court, he failed to assert his right as a member to have the terms of the articles followed. On a more practical note, he failed to draw up an employment contract between the company and himself. One begins to see why the company did not appoint him.

Classes of shares

Sometimes the price for new shareholders' investment in a company is **4–21** that the new shareholders will insist having for their exclusive benefit a particular class of shares, with certain rights, such as a right to a prior return on capital or a right to appoint a particular director to represent their interests. Those rights attaching to classes of shareholders (commonly known as "class rights") will normally need to be set out in the articles[63] and unless the class of shares is present in the company from its incorporation, the articles as a whole will need to be varied by a special resolution to allow for the creation of the new class of shares.[64]

Historically in a company with a large class and a small class of shares, **4–22** there was sometimes a temptation for the larger class to use its greater voting power to pass special resolutions which would alter the articles to the detriment of the smaller class.[65] This could be held acceptable if the larger class could persuade the courts that the alteration was carried out bona fide for the benefit of the company as a whole, or that the alteration could be advantageous for the smaller class too,[66] but nowadays if the alteration smacked of oppression to the smaller class, the smaller class would use the minority protection provisions of the CA 2006 s.994 to safeguard its own interests.[67] Furthermore, nowadays, the drafting of class rights is more intelligent than it used to be. It is now common to include in the terms relating to the rights of any class of shares, particularly for a venture capitalist investing in a promising company, a right to prevent any other class of shares improving its rights relative to the rights enjoyed by the venture capitalist. Indeed the wording of the rights attaching to classes of shares is generally very careful, common rights being specification of a method of appointing directors to represent the class, a method of calculating dividends, rights to prevent unauthorised capital expenditure, rights to prevent the directors altering the business of the company in any unapproved manner and rights to ensure a fair buy-out procedure.

Provisions for entrenchment

Historically some companies were very anxious to make certain pro- **4–23** visions within the articles or the old-style memorandum effectively immutable, sometimes by deliberately not including any provision for the

---

[63] In *Cumbrian Newspapers Croup Ltd v Cumberland and Westmorland Herald and Printing Co Ltd* [1987] Ch. 1; [1986] 3 W.L.R. 26; [1986] 2 All E.R. 816; [1986] B.C.L.C. 286, the articles failed to spell out the different classes of shares though it was clear from an overall reading that there were meant to be two classes of share, and so by taking an overview it was established that there were indeed two different classes of share.

[64] Business "angels", or Government agencies that invest in new and developing companies, will commonly have a standard wording for the class of shares that they will wish the company's articles to provide for them. Form SH11 will need to be completed to show the new class of shares.

[65] *Brown v British Abrasive Wheel Co Ltd* [1919] 1 Ch. 290.

[66] *Greenhalgh v Arderne Cinemas Ltd* [1951] Ch. 286.

[67] See Ch.11.

variation of those rights. This is no longer seen as desirable, and while it is still possible to entrench[68] provisions in articles, the CA 2006 in effect discourages this, mainly because in the long run it is usually impractical to make articles difficult to alter. If a company wishes to have clauses in its articles which it wishes to entrench, it will need to include in the articles a "provision for entrenchment". This will indicate the process whereby and the conditions under which the entrenched clauses may be amended or repealed, particularly if that process and conditions are more onerous than the normal method of amending articles, namely a special resolution.[69] If there is a provision for entrenchment, it may at any time be overridden if all the members agree to override it, or if the court orders that it be overridden.[70] If there is provision for entrenchment on incorporation, or the company inserts one at a later date, or if the court alters the articles so as to restrict or exclude the power of the company to amend its articles, the Registrar of Companies must be informed.[71] Likewise if the company decides to remove the provision for entrenchment, or the court removes the provision for entrenchment, the Registrar must again be informed.[72]

4–24   If a company does amend its articles in accordance with the provision for entrenchment, or in accordance with any order of the court restricting or excluding the company's power to amend the articles, the company must send a statement of compliance to the Registrar indicating that the amendment to the articles was made in accordance with the company's articles,[73] and send a copy of the amended articles for registration as well.[74] In practice nowadays, it is rare to find such articles that do not provide a simple variation procedure, because commercially it is unwise to make articles difficult to alter.[75] Historically some companies had their own specially drafted complicated variation procedures but these are also rare nowadays.[76] One former method either of entrenching provisions

---

[68] Entrenching a provision means to make it either impossible to alter, or to place considerable restrictions on how it may be altered. A venture capitalist investing in a company might wish to entrench his right to attend all board meetings or to have the final say in some matter.

[69] CA 2006 s.22(1). Section 22(2) appears to provide that a provision for entrenchment may only be made on the incorporation of the company, or, if it be made at a later date, with the agreement of all the members of the company. However, this particular subsection has not yet been brought into force and is still subject to consultation. This is because it might affect pre-existing class rights.

[70] CA 2006 s.22(3).

[71] CA 2006 s.23(1). There are various Forms CC01 to CC06 on which to intimate these matters to the Registrar.

[72] CA 2006 s.23(2).

[73] CA 2006 s.24.

[74] CA 2006 s.26. If the amendment is to alter the articles to one of the model sets of articles, it is not necessary to send in a copy of the new articles (s.26(2)).

[75] If a company's articles provided for very strongly entrenched class rights, the class of shareholders might be well protected, but equally those class rights might deter anyone else from investing in the company since too much control would be handed to the entrenched class.

[76] This is generally because the more complicated the procedure, the more likely it is that it will not be followed correctly—thus leading to litigation.

generally, or of having only limited provision for entrenchment, was to put certain clauses in the old-style memorandum. This is no longer possible, and indeed, any such clause that is still in an old style memorandum will henceforth be treated as it if were in the articles,[77] and thereby always in principle alterable either by unanimous resolution of the members or by the court.[78]

SHAREHOLDERS AGREEMENTS

Enshrining shareholders' rights in the articles suffers from the drawback **4–25** that there is a loss of commercial confidentiality and any variation of the rights requires general meetings or written resolutions. One solution is a shareholders agreement, which is a contractual document signed by all or some of the shareholders. Common terms will include an agreement all to vote in a certain pre-arranged manner,[79] not to sell shares to outsiders, not to vote to alter the articles, or members leaving the company for certain reasons being required to sell their shares to other members at a predetermined price.[80] If a shareholder does act contrary to the terms of the shareholders agreement, by, say, casting his votes for a resolution in a manner contrary to the manner agreed in the shareholders agreement, the votes will still be validly cast, but the other shareholders in the shareholders agreement could sue him for breach of contract. If shareholders contract in a shareholders agreement that they will not seek repayment of their loans to a company while certain arrangements are in place, any shareholder who in defiance of the agreement seeks to sue the company for repayment of his loan may be stopped from doing so by the terms of the shareholders agreement.[81]

The company whose shareholders enter into a shareholders agreement may enter the shareholders agreement if it wishes to do so, but this may not always be helpful. In one such shareholders agreement, the company undertook not to alter its capital. This proved unenforceable, because the company itself cannot undertake not to alter its capital, as it is the members alone who make that decision.[82]

One significant problem with a shareholders agreement is that it is only **4–26** valid amongst the parties to it, and so if one shareholder leaves or dies, the agreement has to be drawn up again. It is a common term of a shareholders agreement that any shareholder leaving the agreement must procure that the incomer undertakes the outgoing shareholder's obligations instead—until which the outgoing shareholder will not be released from his obligations.

---

[77] CA 2006 s.28.
[78] CA 2006 s.22(3).
[79] *Re A BC Chewing Gum Ltd* [1975] 1 All E.R. 1017.
[80] *Re LCM Wealth Management Ltd*, [2013] EWHC 3957 (Ch).
[81] *Snelling v John G Snelling Ltd* [1972] 1 All E.R. 79.
[82] *Russell v Northern Bank Development Corp Ltd* [1992] 3 All E.R. 161.

Further Reading

For company registration, see:

http://www.companies-house.gov.uk [Accessed April 22, 2014].

On articles of association generally:

Palmer's Company Law (London: Sweet & Maxwell), Chapter 2.11, Articles of Association.

For the need for lawyers to check whether companies may grant security for loans, see:

Karen Lester, "Companies Act 2006: checking constitutional documents—business as usual for lenders' advisers?" (2010) 25(5) B.J.I.B. & F.L. 275.

The riposte to this is to be found in this article:

Richard Bethell-Jones, "Checking constitutional documents: business as usual or money for old rope?" (2010) 25(7) B.J.I.B. & F.L. 395.

Chapter 5

SECURITIES

The Definition of a Security

"Security" is a confusing term in company law, as it covers a multitude of **5–01** terms that convey a degree of ownership of a company or indebtedness of a company to a creditor. Unfortunately "security" also means a charge (a right of recourse against an asset of the company) as, for example, a standard security over a company's heritage or a charge over a company's book debts; and indeed in some respects there is common ground between the two meanings. As far as this chapter is concerned, securities means shares, debentures, warrants, options and convertibles. A *share* is a unit of ownership of a company measured in terms of an imaginary or "nominal" value,[1] predominantly for accounting purposes in order to show the liability of the company to repay the shareholder on solvent liquidation. A *debenture* is the written acknowledgment of a debt by a company to a debenture holder, and in effect is a loan.[2] A *warrant* is an entitlement (which usually must be paid for) to subscribe for a new share from the company usually at a certain price ("the exercise price") and at a certain date.[3] At the time the warrant is exercised, the holder of the warrant hopes that the exercise price is less than the actual share price.[4] A slightly similar instrument, "share warrant to bearer", also known as a share warrant[5] is a negotiable instrument entitling the bearer to the number of shares stated therein and relates to shares already in issue and held by a shareholder. The share warrant to bearer is thus effectively an entitlement to have shares transferred to the bearer: for this reason it attracts stamp duty. An *option* is a right to buy, following payment, an existing share at a predetermined price at a predetermined date. The option can then be exercised in the hope that the predetermined price is

---

[1] Not necessarily in pounds sterling: the Companies Act 2006 ("the CA 2006") s.542 permits different currencies and indeed more than one currency.

[2] Strictly speaking, debentures are not known to Scots law, but as many listed companies use them, they are included here. The Scots terms for a loan, particularly a secured or a registered one, is a bond.

[3] Warrants are obtained from the company itself. The warrant is surrendered to the company and the shares issued to the person surrendering the warrant within two months (CA 2006 s.780). There are special rules applicable to Scotland to deal with criminal offences (mostly forgery) in relation to share warrants (CA 2006 s.781).

[4] He could then sell the shares at the current share price, having made a profit on the difference between the exercise price and the share price.

[5] CA 2006 s.779.

less than the actual value of the share in the market at the time of exercise of the option, so that the share, once purchased following the exercise of the option, may be immediately sold at a profit.[6] *Convertibles* are generally shares which will convert into other types of shares or debentures, according to the terms of the conversion. This chapter concentrates primarily on shares.[7]

SHARES

5–02 As far as Scots law is concerned, a share is an item of incorporeal moveable property.[8] As with most items of property, it conveys rights and duties. It gives the owner a right to a proportion of the value of the company's assets relative to the size and number of the shares overall, if those assets were converted into cash or equivalent, and subject to the company's prior repayment of all creditors. It also gives a right to a vote, if the share is a voting share, and to dividends (if declared by the directors and/or provided for in the articles). It gives the owner various other rights as specified in the company's articles (such as the right to transfer the share subject to any qualifications to that right in the articles), rights granted by the board of directors[9] and certain rights under statute, such as the right not to be treated in an unfairly prejudicial manner if in the minority[10] (all of which rights collectively amount to the word "interest" in the next paragraph). Of the duties, the principal duty is to pay up to the nominal value for each share and to pay any premium if asked.[11] In limited circumstances, owning shares may cause the owner to be liable to the company[12] (all of which duties amount to "liability" in the paragraph below). In short, a share is a bundle of rights and obligations, which the shareholder is bound to accept in terms of Companies Act 2006 ("the CA 2006") s.33.

---

[6] Conversely, it is possible to have an option to sell a share at a price higher than the actual market price. Options are commonly used to motivate staff by letting them have options free or at minimal cost as part of their employment package.

[7] The word "stock", sometimes confusingly used for shares themselves, or more accurately a package of shares, is no longer to be used and shares may not be converted into stock (CA 2006 s.540(2)).

[8] CA 2006 s.541. There were in the past various valiant attempts to say what a share is in English law. The general view is that it was a chose in action sui generis. Section 541 states that a share is personal property in England and is not in the nature of real estate.

[9] For example, shareholders in certain banks may obtain reduced rates on insurance, gold cards, etc.

[10] CA 2006 s.994.

[11] The premium attaching to a share is the amount in excess of the nominal value which must be paid to the company in order to obtain the share. All premiums should be paid into a special capital account known as the share premium account. Sums held in the share premium account may be used for limited purposes such as paying for the expenses of issuing the shares that attracted the premium, commission on the issue of shares, or paying up bonus shares (CA 2006 s.610).

[12] For example, the fraudulent trading rules in Insolvency Act 1986 ("the IA 1986") s.213 apply to the members, i.e. shareholders, if they have been making the company trade while insolvent and for a fraudulent purpose.

The traditional description of a share was given by Farwell J. in *Borland's Trustee v Steel Bros & Co Ltd*[13]:

> "A share is the interest of the shareholder in the company measured by a sum of money, for the purpose of liability in the first place, and of interest in the second, but also consisting of a series of mutual covenants entered into by all the shareholders inter se in accordance with s.16 of the Companies Act 1862 [whose nearest equivalent is now CA 2006 s.33]."

Although this definition is not quite on all fours with the CA 2006 s.33, as a definition it still has its uses. The *sum of money* referred to above is the nominal value of a share. This bears no relation to the market value of the share but exists primarily to indicate the extent of the shareholder's liability to the company. Once the nominal value of the share is paid up, no more need be paid to the company, even in the event of the company's insolvency, unless the shareholder agrees to do so. Such is the nature of limited liability.

The *interest* means the benefit to the shareholder.

The *mutual covenants* referred to above are nowadays the rights under **5–03** the articles of association[14] requiring both the company and the members to adhere to the rights given in the constitution.[15] If a member does not like those rights, his options are to band together with enough other members to change the articles (depending on the change required) by means of a special resolution,[16] to sell his shares if he can (which may not always be possible in a small company with no market in the shares) or in extreme circumstances to give his shares away. Alternatively he may just have to live with the articles and endure them until such time as he can persuade enough others to help him change them.

There are many types of shares, although the standard share is the ordinary share. Where a company wishes to have more than one type of share, the company will either need to be created having different types, or more properly "classes" of shares, or have to change its articles to allow for the creation of new classes of share. This will require a special resolution. Once a class of shares is created, any further alteration of the rights attaching to that class of shares must follow the provisions specified in the articles for the change of class rights.[17] If there is no provision in the articles for variation of a class's rights, the rights attached to the class of shares may instead be varied by the holders of the class of shares

---

[13] *Borland's Trustee v Steel Bros & Co Ltd* [1901] 1 Ch. 279.

[14] And indeed any special or unanimous resolutions passed by the company, since special and unanimous resolutions can also be treated as part of the constitution of the company (CA 2006 s.29).

[15] CA 2006 s.33(1) refers to "covenants on the part of the company and each member" which is not quite the same as the definition in *Borland's Trustee* [1901] 1 Ch. 279.

[16] CA 2006 s.21.

[17] CA 2006 s.630(2)(a).

as follows[18]: either the holders of three quarters in nominal value of the issued shares of that class (excluding any treasury shares) must have consented in writing[19]; or the holders of shares within that class must have passed a special resolution at a general meeting of that class.[20] It is open to a company to impose other restrictions on the variation of class rights if it chooses to do so.[21] Any variation of the variation procedure for the alteration of the rights attaching to a class of shares is itself a variation of class rights.[22]

COMMON CLASSES OF SHARES

Ordinary shares

5–04   In the absence of any definitions to the contrary, the "default" share is an ordinary share, with one vote per share and a right to participate in the company's profits and to receive a return of capital on solvent liquidation. A company may nonetheless provide such further rights for ordinary shares as it chooses, such as a right to have extra votes on certain occasions or a right to arbitration in the event of a dispute.

Preference shares

5–05   These are shares that normally offer by way of dividend a fixed return on capital, commonly a percentage of the nominal value (as in "six per cent preference shares"). They receive this dividend, which may also be provided for by means of an arithmetical formula specified in the articles,[23] before the ordinary shareholders receive their dividend. Since the percentage return may sometimes not be very impressive relative to the dividend the ordinary shareholders are receiving, it is possible to have a "participating preference share" which receives not only a fixed return but an additional right to participate, to an agreed extent, in the dividends that the ordinary shareholders are enjoying—thus obtaining a double benefit. Preference shares are commonly said to be cumulative.[24] Preference shares commonly have a right to receive their capital back on solvent liquidation before the ordinary shareholders receive their capital. By convention many companies' preference shares are non-voting except on such occasions as a resolution to wind up the company.

---

[18] CA 2006 s.630(2)(b), (4).

[19] CA 2006 s.630(4)(a).

[20] CA 2006 s.630(4)(b).

[21] CA 2006 s.630(3).

[22] CA 2006 s.630(5).

[23] The formula will commonly refer to the level of profits made by the company and have a method of preventing the company increasing its overheads, in particular directors' salaries, in order to reduce the amount payable by way of the preferential dividend.

[24] This means that they are automatically entitled to any arrears of dividend as a prior claim on any distributable profits.

Redeemable shares

These are shares issued in the knowledge that they will be repurchased **5–06** ("redeemed") by the company at a future date, at a certain price and at the option of either the company or the shareholder as specified in the articles[25]; and when redeemable shares are issued there must be other, non-redeemable, shares in issue.[26] The terms of the redemption will normally be specified in the articles,[27] but may be determined by the directors if the articles permit the directors to do this or the company has passed a resolution to give the directors such permission.[28] Redeemable shares must be fully paid up before redemption can take place.[29] It is permissible for shares to be redeemed at a premium[30]; the financing of this and indeed of redemption of shares generally is discussed in the next chapter.[31] Redeemable shares are a useful way of obtaining short term finance if a company does not wish to have an outside investor involved in a company for too long: on redemption the company will buy back the investor's shares and return him his capital plus any premium if contracted to do so. Redeemable shares are also useful as a method of giving shares to motivate a temporary manager or other employee who wants a stake in his employer's business but wants to know that there will be a market for his shares eventually.

Convertible shares

These are shares that are designed to be converted either into other **5–07** types of shares or to debentures on the fulfilment of certain events. It is not unusual to have a class of shares with specified rights that enable it to convert to an ordinary share on the flotation of the company's shares on the London Stock Exchange: this is because an ordinary share is more marketable than a share with complex and unusual rights. Sometimes a share will be designed to convert into a debenture. This means that the shareholder turns into a creditor and therefore might stand a chance of getting some money back on the company's liquidation. Shareholders are last to be repaid (if at all) in the event of the company's liquidation.

It is possible to have shares that combine several of the features of the above shares.

---

[25] CA 2006 s.684. A public company may only issue redeemable shares if it is authorised to do so under its articles. Private companies do not need such authority in their articles to issue redeemable shares, but they may choose to exclude or restrict, by means of the articles, the use of redeemable shares.

[26] CA 2006 s.684(4).

[27] CA 2006 s.685(4).

[28] CA 2006 s.685(1). Curiously, the resolution does not need to be a special resolution even if it amends the company's articles (s.685(2)).

[29] CA 2006 s.686.

[30] This means that the shareholder gets his money back plus an extra amount of money (the premium) as a reward for his loyalty or confidence in the company. It can also mean that the shareholder is reluctant to pull his money out early lest he forfeit the premium.

[31] At para.6–41.

Employee shares

5–08　　*Employee* share scheme shares are given to employees in order to motivate them to work harder for the common good of the company and to give employees a sense of identification with their employers. There are complex taxation provisions to allow for the setting up of employee share schemes. *Flowering* shares are employee shares which have a low value to begin with but once the company achieves a predetermined value, the flowering shares receive the benefit of the company's actual worth in excess of that value. These shares can be a tax-efficient reward for employees and help lock in key employees to the company. In September 2013 the Government introduced a new type of employee, known as a *shareholder employee*, who in exchange for being given a £2,000 grant of shares in his employer's company agrees to forfeit certain statutory employment rights such as the right to bring an unfair dismissal claim and maternity and paternity benefits.[32] The grant of the shares would attract income tax or national insurance and any capital gain up to £50,000 will be tax-free. Despite almost total lack of interest in the concept by employers and employees alike when the Government was consulting, the Government enacted the legislation anyway.[33]

Other less common classes of share

5–09　　There are many other classes of share to be found. *Deferred* shares are those that will only pay a dividend, or be repaid in the event of solvent liquidation, once everyone else has received a dividend or been repaid their capital. *Non-voting* shares do not attract votes. *Deadlock* shares are commonly found in joint venture companies: the articles will provide that one shareholder in the company has "A" ordinary shares and the other has "B" ordinary shares, whose terms are identical. Each shareholder has the same number of shares and votes as the other, so this means that every decision has to be agreed by both shareholders. If the shareholders cannot agree, there is a pre-set arbitration clause to break the deadlock, there usually being a method of selecting an arbiter if neither shareholder can agree who the arbiter should be. *Weighted voting* shares are shares that carry extra votes if there is an attempt to remove the shareholder from, say, a directorship or an attempt to overrule his views.[34] *Bearer*

---

[32] The Growth and Infrastructure Act 2013 s.31 inserted s.205A into the Employment Rights Act 1996.

[33] The reasons for such indifference are because few employees will wish to give up their rights, and from the employers' point of view there are still residual opportunities for employees to object to unfair dismissal. In addition most responsible employers felt uncomfortable about denying their staff their hard-earned employment rights. At the time of writing, as far as is known, no company has offered its staff this particular opportunity.

[34] *Bushell v Faith* [1970] A.C. 1099; [1970] 1 W.L.R. 272 HL.

shares are ones that do not record the owner's name and the owner's name is not included in the company's register of members.[35] *Treasury* shares are shares in which have been bought back by the company in question out of distributable profits.[36] Normally shares that a company buys back are cancelled but if the shares are held "in treasury" it means that those shares may be reissued at a later date without the inconvenience of having to create them. In the meantime they sit within the company. No votes are attached to treasury shares, and no dividends may be received from them.[37] *Bonus* shares are shares are dealt with in para.5–23.

ALLOTMENT OF SHARES

To borrow or to seek further capital?

When a company needs more cash it has the choice of borrowing more **5–10** money or seeking more share capital. The advantage of borrowing is that the existing shareholders' control of the company is not diluted; but instead the company may be under the thumb of the lender, who may also insist on strict rules for payment of interest on the loan and on security over the company's assets, and indeed the directors' personal assets, as a precondition of the loan. The advantage of seeking more share capital is that it may be cheaper to pay dividends than to pay interest on a loan. It may be possible to persuade investors to accept a lower dividend on their investment than the same amount of money could receive sitting in a deposit account, if those investors believe that there are compensatory opportunities for capital growth in the long run. The investors may also have the attraction of the company's potential flotation of its shares on the Stock Exchange if the company prospers, or of its shares being bought at a premium by someone who wishes to purchase the company. Ultimately it is a commercial decision by the potential investors and the directors.

The disadvantage, from the existing shareholders' point of view, in having further shares issued is that unless the existing shareholders are given and take up the opportunity to acquire further shares in proportion to their current shareholdings (known as the right of pre-emption) they will find that their control of the company diminishes.

"Allotment" and "issue" have similar but different meanings. Allotment is the unconditional right to have the member's name inserted in the

---

[35] As bearer shares do not indicate who the owner of the share is, bearer shares are of considerable interest to fraudsters. The Government is proposing to abolish bearer shares. See *Transparency and trust: enhancing transparency of UK company ownership and increasing trust in UK business—Government response*, BIS/14/672, published April 16, 2014.

[36] CA 2006 s.724.

[37] CA 2006 s.724.

register of members[38]; issue takes place the moment the member's name is inserted in the register of members.[39] The date of issue may occasionally be important for taxation purposes.[40]

The procedure for allotment

5–11   The procedure for allotment of shares in essence has four main steps.[41] These are:

(1) Have the directors authority to issue the shares?
(2) Do the existing members propose to exercise their pre-emption rights?
(3) Has payment been made for the new shares, and has the consideration for the shares taken account of all the relevant rules, particularly where there is non-cash consideration?
(4) Has proper intimation of the allotment of shares been given to the Registrar of Companies and have the new members received their share certificates?

For public companies issuing shares to the public there are further issues to consider in addition to the above. Where a public company[42] offers shares to the public, the offer must in addition to the above comply with the Financial Services and Markets Act 2000 Pt VI, both as to listing (where applicable) and to prospectuses[43] in particular. As regards listed

---

[38] CA 2006 s.558. A person to whom a share is allotted is not obliged to take up the allotment. He may sell that allotment, or more properly, renounce the allotment in favour of someone else.

[39] CA 2006 s.112(2).

[40] *National Westminster Bank Plc v Inland Revenue Commissioners* [1994] 2 B.C.L.C. 239 HL. The point is that any capital gain in the value of the issued shares starts from the date of issue, not allotment.

[41] It used to require five main steps, since there was the requirement to check that the authorised share capital was sufficient for the issue of the new shares. Following the implementation of the CA 2006, authorised share capital is no longer required, though a company may choose to retain the concept if it wishes to do so. If the proposed new shares bring the total number of issued shares to a figure greater than the authorised share capital, the authorised share capital will either need to be increased or removed altogether.

[42] In practice not many public companies do offer their shares to the public, and the most that do so are listed on the Official List of the London Stock Exchange. However, there are public companies whose shares are traded either on other markets such as AIM or for which market makers, i.e. stockbrokers, will "make a market" by agreeing to act as a middleman or broker who will buy and sell securities in the companies concerned. Needless to say, non-listed securities are generally considered very speculative and not for the unwary. Exceptionally, there are companies which do not have market makers offering a market place for the trading of shares, and any shares have to be purchased directly from the company itself, with a recognition all round that there may be difficulties in transferring those shares except by private bargain. One such company is the iconoclastic Scottish beer company, Brewdog.

[43] A prospectus is effectively an invitation to treat issued by the company offering more shares. Prospectuses tend to be weighty documents detailing all the information that a prudent investor could want in order to enable him to decide whether or not to invest in the company. See para.5–26.

companies, the Financial Conduct Authority is the body that draws up the listing rules that are implemented by the London Stock Exchange for the listing of companies.[44] This book does not deal with the process of offering shares in UK companies elsewhere in the EU.

The directors' authority for allotment

Directors' authority for allotment comes either from statute, the arti- **5–12** cles or members' resolutions.[45] If a private company has only one class of shares, the directors may allot shares as they see fit, without the need for members' authority, unless the company's articles positively restrict this.[46]

Where this does not apply, as for example, when the company in question is a public company, or when a private company has more than one class of shares, on incorporation a company, public or private, will commonly authorise its directors to allot shares for a period of no more than five years commencing from the date of incorporation of the company,[47] or will permit its directors, by ordinary resolution, to allot relevant shares for a period of no more than five years from the date of the resolution.[48] The authority may be renewed or indeed revoked where necessary.[49]

The authority (either in the articles or the resolution) must indicate the maximum number of shares that may be issued, and the total figure for the shares already issued and to be issued must not exceed the maximum number of shares that may be issued.[50]

No private company may issue securities to the public,[51] and any **5–13** attempt to do so places the person (or the company itself) who is behind the issue at risk of receiving a remedial order. This may mean that he has to offer to buy the securities on offer himself.[52] To avoid this directors of a private company must approach potential investors by means other than public advertisements or notices.

---

[44] For further details about the precise requirements for listing and prospectuses, see the website for the Financial Conduct Authority at *http://www.fca.org.uk/firms/markets/ukla* [Accessed April 22, 2014].

[45] CA 2006 ss.549–551.

[46] CA 2006 s.550.

[47] CA 2006 s.551(3)(b)(i).

[48] CA 1985 s.551(3)(b)(ii).

[49] CA 2006 s.551(4).

[50] CA 2006 s.551(3)(a), (6).

[51] CA 2006 s.755. There are provisions to allow a company to allot shares to the public if the company is just about to become a public company (s.755(3), (4)) and where the shares were not intended to be offered to the public and were meant to be a purely private offering (s.756). It is possible for a private company to seek outside investors, but it may only do so provided it does not contravene the terms of the Financial Services and Markets Act 2000 s.86. So, for example, an offer to a restricted circle of investors, or to employees, or to a group of no more than 150 persons, does not count as "an offer to the public".

[52] CA 2006 ss.757–759.

Members' pre-emption rights

5–14   Pre-emption rights are the rights of existing shareholders to subscribe for new shares in their company whenever the company is issuing new shares. Normally this right is proportionate,[53] so, for example, if a shareholder owns 20 per cent of the company's ordinary shares, the pre-emption right would give him a prior right to acquire up to 20 per cent of any further ordinary shares that the company is about to issue. A shareholder is wise to exercise his pre-emption right because if he does not do so, he might find that where formerly he had a considerable influence on the company by virtue of, say, his 26 per cent shareholding, which would enable him to block special resolutions, he no longer could do so once more shares were in existence and he no longer had 26 per cent of the company.[54]

The principle is simple and sensible but the expression of that principle in legal terms leads to considerable complexity. The CA 2006 s.561(1) predicates that existing members will wish to be offered the right to an allotment of their proportion of "equity securities"[55] (effectively, shares) and that the company should continue to offer those equity securities to existing holders of "ordinary shares"[56] until that offer has expired, the duration of the offer at the time of writing being 14 days.[57] For ease of understanding, it will be assumed for the rest of this paragraph that ordinary shares are being discussed. The directors must both make and communicate the pre-emption offer to the existing shareholders, and deliberate failure to do so, except where the directors have received permission not to do so, renders the directors jointly and severally personally liable, along with the company, for any loss occasioned to the shareholders deprived of this offer.[58] If the shareholders have not objected to this failure within two years of the allotment, they are precluded from bringing any proceedings against the directors on this matter.[59]

Even if the directors have written to the shareholders explaining their pre-emption rights and inviting the shareholders to subscribe for the

---

[53] CA 2006 s.561(1)(a).

[54] Phrases to describe this are, "the reduction of the shareholder's equity in the company" or, more colloquially, "stock-watering".

[55] The legislation refers to "equity securities" which under CA 2006 s.560(1) means ordinary shares or the rights to subscribe for or to convert securities into ordinary shares, i.e. warrants or convertibles, but excluding the following: preference shares (these are referred to in s.560(1) as "shares that as respects dividends and capital carry a right to participate only up to a specified amount in a distribution"); initial subscriber shares (s.577); bonus shares (s.564); and shares in an employee share scheme (s.566).

[56] Ordinary shares under CA 2006 s.560(1) are shares in a company excluding preference shares.

[57] CA 2006 s.562(5). Formerly 21 days. Regulation 2 of the Companies (Share Capital and Acquisition by a Company of its Own Shares) Regulations 2009 (SI 2009/2022), amended s.562(5) (communication of pre-emption offers to shareholders) of the 2006 Act to reduce the minimum period of notice for pre-emption rights from 21 days to 14 days in line with art.29(3) of the Second Company Law Directive 77/91.

[58] CA 2006 s.563(2).

[59] CA 2006 s.563(3).

shares in proportion to their existing shareholdings, shareholders are not obliged to take up their pre-emption rights in full (unless the articles say otherwise) and may transfer or sell their entitlement to the new shares if they wish,[60] or may elect not to exercise their rights. Such election may take place either by inertia (by not responding within the 14 days or such greater period as may be permitted by the directors)[61] or in writing, known as a "waiver of pre-emption rights", again within the required time period.

Private companies, if they wish, may in their articles of association **5–15** disapply the rules relating both to the pre-emption right offer and to the communication of the pre-emption right offer either generally, or specifically for particular allotments.[62] In addition, the directors of private companies with only one class of shares may be given power by the articles or by a special resolution of the company to allot equity securities as if the pre-emption rights under s.561 did not apply, or are applied in such a way as the directors may decide.[63]

It was mentioned earlier that the directors may be authorised for a period of five years to allot shares under s.551.[64] Assuming this authority has already been given to the directors, under s.570 the directors may be given power under the articles, or by a special resolution, to allot equity shares as if the pre-emption rights under s.561 did not apply to the directors' allotting of shares over the five year term, or would apply subject to such modifications as the directors choose.[65] However, on the expiry of the five year term, and unless the authority were renewed, the power (unless renewed in its own right by a special resolution) to allot shares on a non-pre-emptive basis would lapse.[66]

Alternatively, where directors already have authority to allot shares under s.551, either generally or otherwise, under s.571 the company may by special resolution resolve that pre-emption rights under s.561 do not apply in respect of a particular allotment of equity securities to be made following the grant of the directors' authority, or would apply subject to such modifications as the directors choose.[67]

The rather arcane distinction between s.570 and s.571 is that s.570 gives power to the directors to allot the shares over the five year period

---

[60] CA 2006 s.561(2).

[61] CA 2006 s.562(5).

[62] CA 2006 s.567. In practice, private companies either accept the statutory rules or impose similar ones of their own, sometimes with different periods of notice. In that event, effectively the same rules as in the normal pre-emption provisions apply. It is also not uncommon for small family companies to have "offer-round" provisions, which allow existing shareholders the right to take up their pre-emption rights, and then any shares in respect of which pre-emption rights are not exercised by some shareholders are then offered round again to the remaining shareholders until all the new shares are taken up.

[63] CA 2006 s.569.

[64] The five year authorisation requirement does not apply in the case of private companies with only one class of share.

[65] CA 2006 s.570(1).

[66] CA 2006 s.570(3).

[67] CA 2006 s.571.

without pre-emption rights applying, whereas s.571 applies to a particular "one-off" allotment.

However, any special resolution for the non-applicability of the pre-
emption rights under s.571 must first have been proposed by the directors
to the shareholders in a written statement, indicating their reasons for
this recommendation.[68] These reasons must be intimated to every member before the meeting at which the special resolution is to be passed, or
before or at the time that the resolution is sent to the members if the
resolution is to be passed as a written resolution.[69]

The pre-emption rights do not apply, however, on all occasions. Shares
held in treasury do not attract pre-emption rights,[70] nor do preference
shares.[71] Under the CA 2006 s.565 pre-emption rights do not apply where
the equity securities are to be wholly or partly paid up otherwise than in
cash.[72] Neither do they apply to an issue of bonus shares,[73] nor to shares
held under an employee share scheme.[74] The pre-emption rights also do
not initially apply to the whole company in respect of a class of shares:
when a class of shares is issued with further shares specific to that class,
the members of the class get the first right to the shares.

Since the loss of pre-emption rights, even where preference shares or
employee share scheme shares are concerned, may be a significant matter
for all the investors generally, it is possible to word the articles so that
pre-emption rights apply even for preference shares or employee share
scheme shares.[75]

Payment for the shares

5–16   Shares may not be issued at a discount.[76] The only permissible form of
discount is where a company pays a commission, usually to an under-
writer, for subscribing for shares, or for arranging for others to subscribe
for shares, providing that no more than 10 per cent of the price for the
subscribed shares is used by way of commission, and providing the
articles permit the payment of the commission.[77]

Although the consideration for shares will normally reflect the true
value of the consideration, and be paid in cash, in private companies it
would appear that provided there is no fraud a company may accept non-

---

[68] CA 2006 s.571(6).
[69] CA 2006 s.571(7). Private companies cannot use the written resolution procedure.
[70] CA 2006 s.573.
[71] CA 2006 s.560(1).
[72] That is, if an asset of some sort is transferred or services supplied to the company as
consideration for the shares. Presumably even a small element of non-cash consideration
would be sufficient to disapply the pre-emption rules.
[73] CA 2006 s.564.
[74] CA 2006 s.566.
[75] CA 2006 s.575.
[76] CA 2006 s.580. This means that if a share has a nominal value of £1.00, it may not be
issued to shareholders on the basis that the cost will be, say, 60p per share, and that the
balance of 40p per share will never be payable to the company.
[77] CA 2006 s.553.

cash consideration even if it does not truly reflect the value of the shares[78] but provided there is genuine and present consideration.[79]

However, in public companies the position is different. In order to **5–17** maintain the impression that public companies are relatively safe to invest in or to trade with, public companies are required to ensure that the consideration they receive for their issues is justified. The shares for the subscribers to the memorandum of a public company must be paid up in cash.[80] A public company may not in exchange for shares accept an undertaking from a would-be shareholder (the "allottee") to carry out work or perform services for any other person,[81] and if it does so, the allottee has to pay the nominal value of the shares concerned, plus any premium on the shares and any exigible interest.[82] A person who acquires shares from an allottee who has been allotted shares in contravention of the above rules is also liable[83] unless he can prove that he acquired the shares for value and without notice of the contravention.[84]

In a public company, shares must be paid up at least to the extent of one-quarter of each share's nominal value, together with payment of the premium in full.[85]

In a public company, if the consideration for the shares is an undertaking to be performed for the public company more than five years after the date of the allotment, and the undertaking is not carried out within that period, the allottee must pay the full amount plus the premium and any interest.[86] If the contract for the undertaking is for a lesser period than five years and the undertaking is still not completed by the expiry of the period, the same penalty applies.[87] Either way the allottee is penalised in order, quite deliberately, to make him think twice about accepting such terms.

In a public company, where non-cash consideration is given for the allotment, the non-cash consideration must be independently valued to ensure that the company truly receives its money's worth.[88] The reason for this is that the company one day might potentially offer its shares to the public. Future investors would wish to be reassured that the existing share capital of the company was truly represented by valuable assets, and that whoever had supplied the non-cash consideration to the company in exchange for shares had not received far too good a bargain at the expense of the company. The non-cash consideration will be valued by the company's auditor, or someone qualified to be an auditor[89] or

---

[78] *Re Wragg Ltd* [1897] 1 Ch. 795 CA.
[79] *Hong Kong and China Gas Co Ltd v Glen* [1914] 1 Ch. 527.
[80] CA 2006 s.584.
[81] CA 2006 s.585(1). Any other person means any person other than the public company itself.
[82] CA 2006 s.585(2). At present the interest rate is 5 per cent, CA 2006 s.592.
[83] CA 2006 s.588(1).
[84] CA 2006 s.588(2).
[85] CA 2006 s.586. There are exemptions for shares in employee share schemes.
[86] CA 2006 s.587(1), (2).
[87] CA 2006 s.587(4).
[88] CA 2006 s.593.
[89] CA 2006 s.1150(1).

someone appointed by him as a specialist valuer[90] and who must be provided with all relevant information about the non-cash consideration.[91] The auditor or valuer must be completely independent of the company.[92] The valuer's report must state whether or not the value ascribed to the non-cash consideration is proper,[93] that the method of valuation was reasonable, that since the valuation there has been no material change in the value of the non-cash consideration as well as detailing the method by which the valuation was carried out[94] and must state that the valuation was carried out within six months prior to the allotment.[95] The allottee is entitled to see the valuation report.[96] A copy of the report must be sent to the Registrar of Companies.[97]

In the event of contravention of the above rules, the allottee will be required to pay the proper price that should have been paid, together with any premium and interest, thus putting the burden on the allottee to ensure that the procedure is properly carried out.[98] A person who acquires shares from an allottee who has been allotted shares in contravention of the above rules is also liable[99] unless he can prove that he acquired the shares for value and without notice of the contravention.[100]

5–18   A further issue connected with the allotment of shares for non-cash consideration arises when either: (i) a public company incorporated as such, within two years of the issue of its s.761 trading certificate, or (ii) a private company which has re-registered as a public company, within two years of the date of re-registration, as the case may be, allots shares for non-cash consideration.[101] Under such circumstances, if the allottee is a subscriber to the memorandum in the case of a public company incorporated as such, or a member of the (formerly private) company at the time of re- registration, and the consideration is equal to one-tenth of the company's nominal share capital at the time, the consideration will need to be independently valued in the same manner as above.[102] In addition the terms of the agreement for the non-cash consideration must be approved by the members by ordinary resolution[103] having been circulated (along with a copy of the valuer's report) to the members beforehand.[104] This rule does not apply, however, where the company in the

---

[90] CA 2006 s.1150(2).
[91] CA 2006 s.1153.
[92] CA 2006 s.1151.
[93] CA 2006 s.596(3)(d).
[94] CA 2006 s.596(2).
[95] CA 2006 s.593(1)(b).
[96] CA 2006 s.593(1)(c).
[97] CA 2006 s.597.
[98] CA 2006 s.593(3).
[99] CA 2006 s.605(1), (2).
[100] CA 2006 s.605(3).
[101] CA 2006 s.598.
[102] CA 2006 s.598, referring to ss.599, 600.
[103] CA 2006 s.601(1)(a). The person providing the non-cash consideration needs to see a copy of the resolution (s.601(1)(c)). The Registrar of Companies receives a certified copy of the resolution (s.602).
[104] CA 2006 s.601(1), (3).

ordinary course of business acquires assets of a particular description in exchange for shares.[105]

In a public company, where the non-cash consideration being provided is all or some of the shares in another company, the shares in that other company will not need to be independently valued, provided that the public company offers its own shares in exchange for the shares in the other company or in a class of shares in the other company[106] and provided the offer is made to all of the members of the other company (irrespective of whether or not they take up the offer) or all of the members of the class[107] of that other company. In addition there is no requirement for independent valuation of non-cash consideration in the form of all the assets and liabilities of another company which will merge with the public company which is offering its own shares as consideration for those assets and liabilities.[108]

Intimation of allotment and registration of the new shares

Assuming all the above has been dealt with, the directors will normally **5–19** convene a meeting at which the payments for the shares are approved and the company secretary or company registrar instructed to allot the shares. The Form SH01 is used to intimate the allotment and the new allottees to the Registrar of Companies within a month of the allotment. If the company whose shares are being allotted is a listed company, and if the allottee is a director of a listed company, or a member of his family, the allotment also must be intimated to the London Stock Exchange within four days following the allotment.[109]

When the company secretary, director or registrar inserts the details of the new allotment against the new (or as the case may be, existing) shareholder's name in the company's own register of members, the shares are said to be issued to the shareholder.[110] Although the register of members is prima facie evidence of the ownership of shares,[111] if there is an inaccuracy in the issue of shares or the register of members, it is open to an aggrieved shareholder to apply to the courts for rectification of the register if the company is unwilling to rectify it itself.[112] The register of members is normally kept at the company's registered office but may be maintained by a professional registrar.[113] If the company is a single member company, that fact must be noted on the register, along with the

---

[105] CA 2006 s.598(4).
[106] CA 2006 s.594(2). This is effectively a takeover, and in a takeover, at least in theory, the shares should be at market value anyway.
[107] CA 2006 s.594(4).
[108] CA 2006 s.595.
[109] See the *FCA Handbook*, DTR 3.1.2.
[110] CA 2006 s.112(1).
[111] CA 2006 s.127.
[112] CA 2006 s.125. See also *Re Thundercrest Ltd* [1994] B.C.C. 855; *Cadbury Schweppes Plc v Halifax Share Dealing Ltd* [2006] B.C.C. 707; [2007] 1 B.C.L.C. 497.
[113] CA 2006 s.114. Section 1136 details the documents and records that should be kept either at the company's own registered office or at the professional registrar's office. See also, para.5–30.

date of sole membership, and any subsequent increase in membership must also be recorded.[114] In England a trust may not be noted in the register[115] but a trust may be registered in Scotland. In England it is possible to have a stop order or a stop notice placed by a creditor (or other interested party) against a member's entry in the register of members. This effectively prevents the transfer of the shares or payment of a dividend without intimation to the creditor or other party. There is no such mechanism in Scotland, though it is possible to arrest dividends in the hands of the company, or the proceeds of a sale of shares in the hands of the debtor's stockbrokers.

5–20   Within two months the company or its registrar must issue the share certificates for the new shares.[116] These were traditionally paper based and were signed by a director or the company secretary or their authorisee. Paper certificates are nowadays usually only applicable for private and non-quoted companies. A share certificate is sufficient evidence of share ownership.[117] When a company issues a share certificate it is personally barred from denying the validity of the share certificate,[118] and while this may be onerous for the company, most companies will insure against the risk of being tricked into issuing a share certificate when they should not have done. Wise registrars should take indemnities from those asking for replacement share certificates.[119]

5–21   Some private investors like the reassurance of a paper certificate, but many investors now increasingly use CREST, which is an electronic log of investors' shareholdings. CREST is used extensively as a computerised record of each investor's holding. This can be held directly by the investor or more commonly, stockbrokers', accountants' and lawyers' firms set up nominee companies which are CREST members. These nominee companies hold the shares on behalf of those firms' clients who are investors and are thus able to deal swiftly and cheaply with allotments to their clients and transfers of shares by and to their clients.

A particular issue arising out of CREST nominee companies is the fact that the client is one step removed from the company in which he is investing and so sometimes information about his investments does not always percolate down to him as effectively as it might. To counter this it is possible for the nominee company to indicate who should be receiving the documentation—namely the client—by telling the company that the client has "information rights" under the CA 2006 s.146. This should encourage the client to tell the nominee company how he, for example,

---

[114] CA 2006 s.123.

[115] CA 2006 s.126. This is a quirk of English law. What usually happens instead is that the first-named trustee is held to be the nominee for the trust.

[116] CA 2006 s.769.

[117] CA 2006 s.768. Owning the certificate does not necessarily mean that the certificate-owner is entitled to all the benefits of the underlying shares: *Re Baku Consolidated Oilfields Ltd* [1993] B.C.C. 653.

[118] *Re Bahia and San Francisco Railway Co Ltd* (1868) L.R. 3 Q.B. 584; *Bloomenthal v Ford* [1897] A.C. 156; *Sheffield Corp v Barclay* [1905] A.C. 392. See para.5–28.

[119] *Royal Bank of Scotland v Sandstone Properties Ltd* [1998] 2 B.C.L.C. 429.

wishes the votes pertaining to his shares to be cast.[120] If any nominee company exercises clients' rights in a particular holding of shares for more than one client, it may exercise those rights in different ways for each client.[121] Quoted companies are now all expected to have websites and to publish their reports and accounts on those websites.[122] Members are being encouraged to look at the report and accounts of quoted companies on the web to save the unnecessary sending out of reams of paper which often are unread anyway. If members wish to receive hard copy of the report and accounts, they have positively to tell the company that they wish to do so.[123] Unquoted companies are not expected to have a website but they are expected to provide members with copies of the report and accounts.[124]

RIGHTS, BONUS AND SCRIP ISSUES

Rights issue

A rights issue is an offer on a pre-emptive basis to existing shareholders **5–22** to subscribe for further shares in proportion to their existing holdings. It is generally done when a company needs more cash and wishes to tap its shareholder loyalty first and to enable existing shareholders to maintain their equity in the company. Rights issues are usually issued at a discount to the existing share price to take account of the dilution of the value of each share once further shares are in existence. It is also possible to sell one's entitlement to a rights issue. Rights issues for listed companies generally are underwritten by major financial institutions which undertake to buy the shares if the company's existing investors will not do so. The exercise of the rights issue must be carried out by the shareholder within 14 days.[125]

Bonus issue

A bonus issue is when retained profits, or sums held in the share **5–23** premium account or capital redemption reserve, are converted into share capital. If, for example, a company had £100 by way of retained profits, it could, instead of paying that £100 to the members by way of dividends, use the £100 to create a further 100 shares of one pound nominal value each and issue these to the existing members in proportion to their existing holdings. This procedure, which only requires an ordinary resolution, enables members to gain more shares without paying stockbrokers' fees. Following a bonus issue the value of each share may go

---

[120] CA 2006 s.149.
[121] CA 2006 s.152.
[122] CA 2006 s.430.
[123] CA 2006 s.432.
[124] CA 2006 ss.423, 431.
[125] CA 2006 s.562(5).

down to reflect the greater number of shares in existence, but having shares of a lower price may make them more marketable. If members wish to sell their bonus shares they may do so.

Scrip issue

5–24 A scrip issue is a method of paying dividends in the form of shares. The sums that would normally be paid in cash are paid in shares instead. The articles must permit this. This practice is particularly advantageous for investors who wish to build up capital and do not need the dividends for income. It also saves stockbrokers' fees.

CONVERSION OF SHARE CAPITAL

5–25 A company may increase its share capital or indeed reduce it, but in addition it may subdivide or consolidate its shares. Subdivision is when shares with a large nominal value are divided up in a larger number of shares with a small nominal value. So a company with 100 ordinary shares of £1.00 nominal value each could subdivide them into 400 ordinary shares of 25 pence each. Consolidation is the opposite process, of making a large number of shares with a small nominal value into a lesser number of shares with a larger nominal value. In each case, the members must have passed an ordinary resolution approving this, unless the articles exclude or restrict this power.[126] Having duly converted the share capital, a statement of capital must be sent to the Registrar of Companies within one month of the conversion.[127] There are complex provisions to allow for the conversion of shares in one currency to convert to shares denominated in another currency.[128]

PROSPECTUSES

5–26 A prospectus is a document either inviting potential investors amongst the general public to subscribe for shares in a company seeking capital, or to buy shares from an existing shareholder. A prospectus is not an offer to the shareholder: it is an invitation to treat and when the potential shareholder completes the documentation in the prospectus and sends it to the company or its agent with his cheque, he is making an offer which the company may accept or reject as it chooses. Prospectuses are predominantly used in public companies. As over many years potential investors have been gulled into subscribing for shares on what turned out subsequently to be erroneous or misleading information in prospectuses, prospectuses are now expected to be as honest as possible. For public but non-listed companies offering their securities to the public, the Financial

---

[126] CA 2006 s.618.
[127] CA 2006 s.619. See Form SH02.
[128] As from, say, pounds sterling to euros. See CA 2006 ss.622–628.

Services and Markets Act 2000 ("the FSMA 2000") Pt VI applies, but does not apply when the offer of shares via a prospectus is made to small well-informed groups of investors, family members related to the founder members of the company, employees, etc. all as specified in s.86. The information that is supplied in the prospectus must be easily analysable and as comprehensible as possible.[129] There must be disclosure of all information that an investor could reasonably want in order to make an informed assessment of the present and future financial state of the company and the rights attaching to the securities offered in the prospectus.[130]

Where a company's financial situation changes during the time of the offer, the company must issue a supplementary prospectus.[131] In any prospectus, information for which the disclosure might be contrary to public policy need not be disclosed.[132] Those who prepare the prospectus may be required to pay compensation to any person who has acquired securities to which the prospectus relates and who suffered loss as a result of inaccurate or misleading statements or omitted information in the prospectus.[133] There are exemptions from liability for compensation where the person who provided the inaccurate or misleading statement, or who omitted the omitted information, did all he could to bring the error or omission to the attention of investors, reasonably believed that the statements were true or properly omitted, reasonably relied on an expert's opinion or otherwise reasonably ought to be excused.[134]

For listed companies, very similar rules apply. Under the FSMA 2000, **5–27** when a listed company issues a prospectus, that prospectus must comply with what are effectively the same rules applicable to non-listed companies in terms of the requirement for transparency, compensation for erroneous, misleading or omitted information,[135] all to be found in Pt VI of the FSMA 2000.[136] For a company to be listed, it must be first admitted to the London Stock Exchange by complying with the terms of the Financial Services Authority handbook. This is the rule book for listed companies, and while there are no direct sanctions against companies that fail to adhere to it, other than suspension of trading in the shares, failure to adhere to the practice recommended without good cause will cause doubts to arise about the company—doubts which will

---

[129] FSMA 2000 s.87A.
[130] FSMA 2000 ss.80, 87A.
[131] FSMA 2000 s.87G.
[132] FSMA 2000 ss.82, 87B.
[133] FSMA 2000 s.90.
[134] FSMA 2000 Sch.10.
[135] See, in particular the FSMA 2000 ss.84, 90.
[136] Even after publication of the listing particulars or the prospectus there is still a requirement that issuers should be liable to pay compensation to those who suffer loss as a result of relying on dishonest information coming from an issuer. In order for the issuer to pay compensation the information in question must have promulgated by a manager working for the issuer who knew that that information was untrue or misleading or who was reckless as to whether it was untrue or misleading. Similar rules apply when the manager deliberately or recklessly conceals information from the person who suffers loss. (FASM 2000 s.90A and Sch.10A Pt 2).

generally affect the company's share price negatively. The handbook operates on the principle that listed companies should adhere to the spirit of its rules, rather than its letter: such an approach sometimes goes counter to the grain of the more buccaneering financiers to be found in the City.

Although there are also common law rules to the same end, it is more than likely nowadays that investors would use the above statutory rules to claim compensation where they have been misled. The effect of the rules has been salutary in ensuring that transparency and fair and open practices are increasingly required in the financial industry. Although there will always be some companies tempted to beguile investors if they can possibly do so, the common practice in prospectuses and listing particulars of noting who is responsible for every single statement in those documents ensures that sharp practice is a questionable activity. No merchant bank, market maker or stockbroker will wish, in the long run, to attract a reputation for lack of integrity.

TRANSFER AND TRANSMISSION OF SHARES

5–28 Subject to the terms of the company's articles,[137] a shareholder may normally transfer his shares to whomever he pleases. However, many small family companies' articles impose restrictions on the transfer of shares away from the founder members, impose certain pre-emption requirements in favour of existing members or reserve to directors an unfettered right not to register the transfer of any shares to those of whom they disapprove. If the wording in the articles allows directors such discretion, then provided the directors have not acted in bad faith they will be entitled to refuse to register such transfers.[138] When a transferee asks to have his shares registered, the company (through the directors) should either register the transfer or, as soon as possible, give the transferee notice of the refusal, and explain the reasons for the refusal.[139] If the transferee is unhappy with this, he is entitled to ask for such additional information about the reasons for the refusal as he may reasonably request.[140] Such additional information does not extend to the provision to the transferee of copies of minutes of directors.[141] It is therefore prudent, from a directors' point of view, to follow very closely the rules relating to transfer as laid down in the articles. If they are not followed, the transferee is entitled to apply to the court for rectification of

---

[137] See the model articles for private companies, reg.26 for standard wording: Companies (Model Articles) Regulations 2008 (SI 2008/3229).
[138] *Re Smith and Fawcett Ltd* [1942] Ch. 304 CA.
[139] CA 2006 s.771(1). These rules do not apply to a transfer of shares in connection with the issue of a share warrant under s.779 nor to the transmission of shares by operation of law, as in, for example, a trustee in sequestration taking over a bankrupt's shares (s.771(5)).
[140] CA 2006 s.771(2).
[141] CA 2006 s.771(2).

the register to have his shares duly transferred.[142] Listed companies generally do not impose restrictions on transfers since that would affect the liquidity of the shares, thus negating the point of having the shares in the market in the first place. Most share transfers attract stamp duty at the rate of half a per cent and stock transfer forms are used for this purpose. Gifts of shares do not attract stamp duty. The seller or donor signs the stock transfer form and the transferee need only sign it if the shares are partly paid, thereby acknowledging his liability for the unpaid part of the shares. The transferee will exhibit the stamped stock transfer form to the company in order to have his name entered into the register of members.

As stated earlier, if a company is wrongfully induced to issue a share certificate following a purported transfer, the new share certificate is still prima facie valid[143] and an innocent third party buying in good faith from the transferee the shares represented by the share certificate is entitled to rely on it[144]; and likewise the person who is wrongfully apparently deprived of the shares by, say, the forging of his signature on a stock transfer form, is entitled to be restored to the company's register of members since he never actually loses the shares anyway, and a forged transfer is a nullity.[145] Where the issue of the share certificate has followed representations made to the company (or its registrar) and the representor then sells the shares to a third party (who then obtains the share certificate), the representor may be liable to the company or its registrar as having induced the company or its registrar to issue the share certificate, even if he acts in good faith.[146]

Transmission arises when a share moves from its original owner to **5–29** someone who is looking after it but does not have true ownership. For example, a bankrupt does not transfer his shares to his trustee in sequestration: the shares are said to be transmitted to the trustee. The trustee may transfer the shares to somebody else.

Register and index of members

The company is obliged to keep a register of its members.[147] On that **5–30** register will be indicated the name and address of each member, the date of his becoming a member, and the date of his cessation of membership.[148] Where the company has a share capital, the register must indicate

---

[142] CA 2006 s.125. See also *Re New Cedos Engineering Co* [1994] 1 B.C.L.C. 797; *Popely v Planarrive Ltd* [1997] 1 B.C.L.C. 8; *Lloyd v Popely* [2000] B.C.C. 338; [2000] 1 B.C.L.C. 19; [2007] 1 B.C.L.C. 497; *Romer-Ormiston v Claygreen Ltd* [2006] B.C.C. 440; [2006] 1 B.C.L.C. 715; *Mactra Properties Ltd v Morshead Mansions Ltd* [2008] EWHC 2843 (Ch); *Re Dunstans Publishing Ltd* [2010] EWCH 3850 (Ch); [2012] B.C.C. 515.

[143] Even when the company makes a mistake, as when shares were stated to be fully paid when in fact they were not: *Bloomenthal v Ford* [1897] A.C. 156.

[144] *Re Bahia and San Francisco Railway Co Ltd* [1868] L.R. 3 Q.B. 584.

[145] *Sheffield Corporation v Barclay* [1905] A.C. 392.

[146] *Sheffield Corporation v Barclay* [1905] A.C. 392; *Royal Bank of Scotland v Sandstone Properties Ltd* [1998] 2 B.C.L.C. 429.

[147] CA 2006 s.113(1).

[148] CA 2006 s.113(2).

the number of shares, and the different classes of shares (if applicable) the member has.[149] The register must be available for inspection either at the company's registered office or at the place where its registers are kept.[150] If the company has more than 50 members there must be an index of the members and any alteration to the information in the index must be carried out within 14 days of the alteration.[151] The index must be open to inspection, free to members and for a fee for others.[152]

Access to the company's register of members

5–31   The CA 2006 brought in rules to restrict access to the register of members. The rules were introduced to protect shareholders from harassment. For example, animal rights protestors accessed the register of members for GlaxoSmithKline and wrote tendentious letters to each shareholder, accusing the shareholder of complicity in animal torture. Sometimes shareholders have also been targeted by boiler room scams, which is where a fraudster, nearly always based abroad, but who has access to a register of members, writes to or telephones a member encouraging the member to invest in some sure-fire new enterprise. The fraudster gulls the naive member into investing his money in the new enterprise; the money is never seen again.[153] Other forms of harassment may be unwanted commercial mailings, or agencies pretending to be specialists in recovering unclaimed dividends.

The new rules, to be found in the CA 2006 ss.116–119, require that any person who wishes to access the register of members must request the company to be allowed to access the register or be supplied with a copy of the register of members.[154] To do so he must indicate his name and address,[155] the purpose for which the information is sought, whether the information will be disclosed to anyone else, and if so who that person is, his address, any organisation he represents and the purpose for which that person or organisation will use that information.[156] The company, on receiving the request, must, within five working days, either comply with the request or apply to the court[157] for permission not to let the applicant access the register on the grounds that the purpose for which the request is sought is not a proper purpose. If the court is satisfied that the purpose

---

[149] CA 2006 s.113(3).
[150] CA 2006 s.114(1). Under s.1136 the registers may be kept at an address other than the registered office. If so, this address must be clearly indicated on company documentation and intimated to the Registrar of Companies (s.114(2)). Many listed companies use professional registrars to maintain their registers. For the precise terms of access to the registers, see the Companies (Company Records) Regulations 2008 (SI 2008/3006). For the fees that may be charged for copying, see the Companies (Fees for Inspection and Copying of Company Records) Regulations 2007 (SI 2007/2612).
[151] CA 2006 s.115.
[152] CA 2006 s.116.
[153] This is the subject-matter of the 2013 film, *The Wolf of Wall Street*.
[154] CA 2006 s.116(2).
[155] CA 2006 s.117(4)(a). If an organisation wishes to access the register, it needs to name an individual responsible for making the request on its behalf (s.116(4)(b)).
[156] CA 2006 s.116(4)(d).
[157] CA 2006 s.117(1).

is indeed not a proper purpose, the court may direct the company not to comply with the request and direct that the company's expenses be paid by the applicant. If the person making the request attempts to deceive the company when making the request, by pretending to need the information for an innocent purpose, they may be penalised.[158]

Much then depends on what is meant by the term "proper purpose". This has been deliberately been left open so that the courts may interpret it. But there has been some guidance. The Department for Business, Information and Skills ("BIS") has let it be known that it is a proper purpose if a credit reference agency wishes to access the register in order to comply with anti-money laundering regulations or "know your customer" requirements. Other BIS approved purposes are to allow trustees in sequestration or liquidators to see what shares are held by debtors or companies. The Institute of Chartered Secretaries and Administrators ("ICSA") has also come up with various purposes likely to be proper ones, such as a member checking that his details are correct, members trying to requisition a general meeting, requests from regulators such as the Financial Conduct Authority or HM Revenue and Customs, requests concerning a potential takeover, register analysis for statistical reasons, stockbrokers checking the register before rights issues and the like, or creditors of shareholders trying to arrest the payment of dividends.[159]

The corollary of companies' right to refuse access to the register of members is that if the court sees no reason to refuse the request for access, access must be granted immediately.[160] Even where there has been no referral of the request to court, refusal or delay by the company in letting the person making the request access the register or obtain the copy of the register is a criminal offence[161] and the court can compel the access or the copy to be provided.[162] When providing the information, the company must provide the person making the request with the most recent copy of the register, including the date the register was last made up to, and indicating if there are any further alterations to the register not yet included in the register. Information about a past member may be removed after 10 years from his ceasing to be a member.[163] Someone who believes he ought to have his name entered on the register but finds that it is not there may apply to the court to have the register rectified to show his correct membership and, where necessary, his correct shareholding.[164]

---

[158] CA 2006 s.119.

[159] ICSA's guidance is available at *http://www.icsa.org.uk* [Accessed April 22, 2014], ref 090114.

[160] CA 2006 s.117(5). One reason for seeking a list of members would be for a takeover bidder to write to all the members inviting them to sell their shares to the takeover bidder. Directors, being likely to lose their jobs on a takeover, might then have every incentive to delay providing the list, or to provide an inaccurate or out-of-date list.

[161] CA 2006 s.118(1).

[162] CA 2006 s.118(3).

[163] CA 2006 s.121.

[164] CA 2006 s.125. See also, paras 5–19 and 5–28.

Concert parties and disclosure of interests

5–32   A "concert party" is when a shareholder in a listed public company buys a substantial number of shares, but does it through various subsidiaries and other interests in order to disguise his true identity. When the shareholder and those connected with him are in a strong position to do so, they will unexpectedly make a bid for at least a controlling shareholding (30 per cent) in the company. Although this is improper, such things happen. Since ingenious investors, seeking to build up a commanding position in a company prior to launching a takeover bid, will generally wish to disguise their actions, a common practice is to acquire shares in the name of nominees or associates. The rules in the CA 2006 ss.793–825 are designed to see who is building up shares in a public company as a way of flushing a predatory takeover bidder out of the bushes. Furthermore, sometimes a company may wish to know the true identity of someone who owns shares in the company (whether a takeover bidder or not). The directors may give notice under the CA 2006 s.793 to the named shareholder to divulge what his interest[165] in the shares is, or has been over the last three years, and if he is a representative or nominee for another person, who that representative or nominee is, together with any other matters which may be of relevance. If the shareholder is unwilling to provide the requested information within a reasonable time, the company may apply to the court for an order under s.794 to make the shareholder divulge that information—for if he does not, the company may prohibit the shareholder from transferring any of his shares, receiving any of his dividends, voting, receiving any bonus issues or obtaining rights under a rights issue.[166] The shares may even be sold.[167] This order effectively renders the shares useless, except on a solvent liquidation, so there is considerable incentive to comply with the request.[168]

It is not just the directors who may choose to make the shareholder disclose his interest in the shares. The members may do so[169] and the company is under a duty to comply with that requirement.[170] The company will need to report back to the members on the success of the attempt to make the shareholder disclose his interest. The company will also need to keep a register of interests that have been disclosed.[171] There is no need to verify the information that is put on the register, though under s.817 someone wrongly put on the register may apply to the company, or if necessary the court, to get the wrong information

---

[165] The word "interest" is exhaustively defined in ss.820–825 and covers the shareholder's own interest, that of any trust he is involved in, any control rights he have in the shares, his family's interests in the shares, his connection with any company holding the shares, or any agreements in connection with a potential takeover.

[166] CA 2006 s.797. There are also criminal penalties for the shareholder (s.795).

[167] CA 2006 ss.801–802.

[168] Artful concert-party goers, however, merely have a further nominee or nominees as the beneficial owners of the shares.

[169] CA 2006 s.803.

[170] CA 2006 s.804.

[171] CA 2006 s.808.

removed. At the time of writing there are moves afoot for the Government to see up a central registry of company beneficial ownership. It will contain information on individuals with an interest in more than 25 per cent of a company's shares, voting rights or control.[172]

Charges over shares

Sometimes shareholders wish to borrow against the security of their **5–33** shares. As a practical matter this is only worthwhile, from the lender's point of view, when the shares are in a well-known listed company.[173] A lender is unlikely to seek security over the relatively illiquid shares of a small private company. The borrower/shareholder may deposit the share certificates with the lender by way of semi-security for a loan,[174] but there is then a danger that the shareholder might fraudulently persuade the company to issue him with a duplicate share certificate and then attempt to sell his shares without repaying the loan. The proper method of obtaining a charge in Scotland is for the borrower to transfer his shares to the lender by means of a stock transfer form. The lender then apparently owns the shares, but issues the borrower with a back letter whereby the lender undertakes to re-transfer the shares to the borrower on the expiry of the loan and full payment of all sums due. The back letter will also indicate what may be done with the votes, dividends and other rights attaching to the shares for the duration of the loan. If the borrower defaults, the lender merely sells the shares which are already in its name.[175]

If a company grants a floating charge over its assets, technically the charge would cover any shares the company owns.

Lien and forfeiture

It is now rare to have a lien[176] over shares, but the model articles for **5–34** public (but not private) companies provide that a company may have a lien over a partly paid share.[177] If the share is not paid up as requested, the company may then arrange for lien enforcement procedure to take place, this being the transfer of the shares to a purchaser, with the purchase price being used to defray the unpaid part of the share. Some companies may have articles that allow them a lien over a member's share if the member owes any money for any reason to the company.

---

[172] Department for Business Innovation & Skills, *Transparency and trust: enhancing the transparency of UK company ownership and increasing trust in UK business—Government response*, BIS/14/672, published April 16, 2014. It is thought that the register may reduce tax evasion and provide a clearer picture of share ownership and company control.

[173] There are mechanisms within CREST to take account of the charging/mortgaging of uncertificated shares.

[174] This is not a proper security under Scots law, since the shares still remain in the ownership of the borrower and delivery has not therefore taken place.

[175] *Enviroco v Farstad Supply A/S* [2011] 1 W.L.R. 921.

[176] A lien over shares is the right of the company to prevent the shareholder transferring the shares or receiving dividends.

[177] Regulation 52 of the model articles for public companies: the Companies (Model Articles) Regulations 2008 (SI 2008/3229).

Forfeiture is the right of the company to insist that if a member does not pay the unpaid amount on a share the company may arrange that the shareholder forfeits his share.[178] He then loses all sums that he may already have paid on the shares and any sums, such as dividends, that he may be due. He loses all rights in the shares and the company will normally cancel the shares.[179] Both lien and forfeiture are rare nowadays, mainly because shares are now generally fully paid.

DEBENTURES

5–35 A debenture is the written acknowledgement of a loan, whose nearest equivalent in Scots law is a bond. The law relating to debentures is to be found in the CA 2006 ss.738–754. When a company borrows money, it may either borrow in terms of one large loan from one or a few lenders, each of whom receives a debenture in similar terms, or may borrow from many lenders all lending similar sums of money to the company and receiving what is commonly known as debenture stock or loan stock within one larger debenture. Where a company borrows from one or only a few lenders, each lender is usually in a good position to monitor the loan and its repayment, but where a company borrows from many thousands of lenders, there will need to be a system for the registration of debenture-holders, a procedure for the transfer of debentures, and a method of ensuring that debenture-holders' interests are properly looked after. The common solution to the latter problem is that the debenture-holders collectively join a trust, in terms of a debenture trust deed, supervised by a debenture trust deed trustee. It is his job to look after the interests of the debenture-holders collectively, to ensure that the debenture-holders receive their interest on their loans regularly and to ensure, on the debenture-holders' behalf, that the company complies with the terms of the debentures by, say, ensuring that the company's assets are properly insured and by insisting that there will always be funds available to repay the debentures.

5–36 Where this particular method of dealing with debenture-holders is not followed, and a company has a number of debenture-holders without using a debenture trust deed, companies will need to keep a register of debenture-holders themselves.[180] The rights of access to the register of debenture-holders is similar to that of the access to the register of shareholders, requiring an applicant to write in explaining why he wants the list of debenture-holders and the purpose for obtaining a list of or other information about the debenture-holders.[181] If the purpose is in the company's eyes unsatisfactory, the company may apply within five days

---

[178] Companies (Model Articles) Regulations 2008 (SI 2008/3229) regs 54–61. The procedure indicated in the articles must be closely followed.
[179] A public company must reissue or cancel the shares in three years (CA 2006 s.662). A private company is not required to do this.
[180] CA 2006 s.743.
[181] CA 2006 s.744.

to court to refuse the application, failing which the application must be honoured.[182] Debentures in quoted companies may be traded in the same manner as shares and attract the same stamp duty on transfer. A listed debenture issued by a company will undertake to repay the borrowed sum on a date (or choice of dates, usually at the company's option) several years in the future, with repayment sometimes being at a premium, depending on the terms of the debenture itself.[183] The debenture will also specify the interest (or "coupon") being paid on the loan. If the interest rate is high relative to market rates for interest generally, the price of the debenture will rise in the market to reflect the desirability of the high interest rate being paid. The price of the debenture also reflects the degree of risk of non-repayment of the loan or default on the interest payments.

Debentures may be secured, so that when the company receives the **5–37** loan it grants in favour of the debenture-holder a charge over the company's assets. This charge must be registered in the normal manner.[184] Where there are many debenture-holders and a debenture trust deed, the company issues a charge in favour of the debenture trust,[185] so that the trustee can monitor the company's adherence to the terms of the charge, and if necessary appoint a receiver (in the case of a pre-Enterprise Act floating charge) or an administrator (in the case of a post-Enterprise Act qualifying floating charge) or enter into possession of the secured subjects (in the case of a standard security or, in England, legal mortgage) if the company defaults on its obligations. A secured debenture is generally a safer investment than an unsecured one, but equally may attract a lesser interest rate for the lender. Unsecured debentures which attract a high interest rate but have a high risk of non-repayment are sometimes known as a "junk bonds". They are sometimes used to fund takeover bids.

Further Reading

Paul L. Davis, *Gower and Davies' Principles of Modern Company Law*, 9th edn (London: Sweet and Maxwell, 2012), Chs 23–25, 27.

---

[182] CA 2006 s.745.
[183] This means that, say, loan stock of £100 repayable in 2010 might be repaid at a premium of 20 per cent, making a payment of £120.
[184] See Ch.15.
[185] In England the charge would have to be in favour of the trustee as the representative of the trust.

CHAPTER 6

CAPITAL MAINTENANCE

THE CAPITAL OF A COMPANY

The theory behind capital maintenance

6–01   The theory behind capital maintenance is that shareholders' capital is paid to the company to serve as a fund of last resort for the benefit of creditors. For that reason, the share capital is sometimes known as the "creditors' buffer", in that once the rest of the company's resources have been used up in settling creditors' bills, the creditors can then evacuate the fund containing the share capital.

Given that the share capital exists for the creditors' benefit, the law has deliberately made it difficult for shareholders to withdraw their capital from the company. If there were no restrictions on withdrawal, the moment there was anything untoward with the company, astute members would promptly withdraw their capital, thus depriving the creditors of much chance of getting their money back, and leaving the less well informed investors to carry the burden of the company's losses. Accordingly if a member wishes to get his capital back from a company in which has invested, he must either sell his shares, if there is a market for those shares, persuade the company to buy back his shares using the particular procedures outlined in the Companies Act 1985 ("the CA 1985"), or if the worst comes to the worst, put the company into liquidation.

6–02   The theory of capital maintenance is also extended to prevent the reduction of capital being carried out without proper checks on what is happening to the company's capital, to restrict companies from providing financial assistance to enable potential shareholders to acquire shares in their company[1] and to prevent companies paying dividends out of anything other than distributable profits.[2]

The reality of capital maintenance

6–03   While the theory is admirable, it is easily undermined. Many private companies have an issued share capital of £100, and in theory a company could have an issued share capital of one penny. Furthermore, there is nothing to prevent a company spending all its capital reserves so that there is little left in the capital accounts with which to satisfy creditors.

---

[1] Except for private companies, as will be explained shortly.
[2] Dividends are dealt with in the next chapter.

The former rules relating to capital maintenance, with the exception of the rules relating to dividends, are widely seen as complex and lacking commercial justification. The involvement of the court in reductions of capital, which is still required for public limited companies, is arguably an unnecessary expense, and does not significantly protect creditors. The rules relating to financial assistance are seen as bewildering. The rules relating to capital maintenance stem from a time when creditors looked much more than they do now to a company's capital for reassurance as to the company's solvency. Nowadays creditors are more interested in net assets, cash flow and interest cover than in share capital. The whole concept of capital maintenance is of slender benefit, at least to private companies, because with twenty first century standards of transparency and accountability in accounting there are fewer opportunities than there were in the past of hiding a company's true financial state.[3] The CA 2006 has, therefore, abolished some of the former capital maintenance rules applicable to private companies but these rules still remain in place for public companies.[4]

Types of capital account

There are various types of capital account to which the capital main- **6–04** tenance regime applies. The collective nominal value of all the issued shares in a company comprises the *issued share capital*. If subscribers paid premiums to acquire newly allotted shares, the collected premiums are paid into a *share premium account* (discussed later). A company's *capital redemption reserve* (or *fund*) comprises a sum of money equal in value to the nominal value of shares that are redeemed or repurchased by a company. It may be used for paying up bonus shares.[5] A company's *revaluation reserve* comprises a sum of money representing the difference between the historic cost of any particular asset or assets and its or their estimated current value (assuming the value is higher). Although it is not normally considered part of a company's capital (since it represents paper or unrealised gains) it too may be used for bonus shares.[6] A company may have other capital reserves if its articles permit. Some companies used in the past to have *reserve capital*, which was a capital fund that would be touched only in dire financial emergency. It is little used now.

---

[3] In certain other jurisdictions the whole concept of capital maintenance is removed entirely by having no-par value shares. A no-par value share is only worth what it will fetch in the marketplace, and there is no creditors' buffer. Creditors assess the risk of dealing with the company purely on the basis of its solvency and its projected cash flow, not on the basis of a fund retained for their benefit. UK and EU accounting systems are not designed to cope with this approach to company finance.

[4] The UK rules on capital maintenance are very close to the European Union Directive 2012/30/EU. This imposes certain on Member States safeguards for the protection of the interests of members and others within companies (within the meaning of the second paragraph of art.54 of the Treaty on the Functioning of the European Union), in respect of the formation of public limited liability companies and the maintenance and alteration of their capital.

[5] CA 2006 s.733(5).

[6] Small Companies and Groups (Accounts and Directors' Reports) Regulations 2008 (SI 2008/409) reg.35, and Large and Medium-sized Companies and Groups (Accounts and Reports) Regulations 2008 (SI 2008/410) reg.35.

Together these various capital accounts (with the exception of the share capital) amount to the "undistributable reserves" referred to from time to time through the Act.[7]

Alteration of capital

6–05   The issued share capital may be consolidated or subdivided[8] or converted into other currencies.[9]

REDUCTION OF CAPITAL

6–06   A company may reduce its capital. This means that the company writes off some of the money stated to be in the company's capital accounts,[10] or decides not to seek payment of a sum to a capital account.[11] As this potentially means that there is less money available for its creditors, the following procedure has to be followed (at least for public companies) so that no creditors or investors have grounds for complaint. The main method of reduction of capital is to be found in the CA 2006 ss.641–657, but a company may also reduce its capital when a private company buys or redeems its own shares out of capital,[12] when a company is ordered by the court to buy back a minority shareholder's shares under the minority protection provisions of the CA 2006 s.994 or when a member surrenders or forfeits his shares to the company.

Reasons for reduction of capital under the Companies Act 2006 ss.641–657

6–07   The main reasons why a company might wish to reduce its capital are:

(1) the nominal value of the company's share capital is greater than the value of its assets;

(2) the company may wish to be rid of a class of shareholders;

(3) the company may have more capital than it knows what to do with, and wishes to return some to the members; or

(4) the company may wish to use unused funds held in a capital account for some other purpose.

Of these reasons, the first is the most common, particularly in property companies or shipping companies, when an economic downturn means

---

[7] For example, CA 2006 s.831(1)(a).

[8] CA 2006 s.618.

[9] CA 2006 ss.622–628. See para.5–25.

[10] For example, a company could reduce its share capital account from £1million to £600,000 and write off £400,000 if it is no longer represented by assets. In this case each shareholder has 40 per cent of his shareholding cancelled. Another option would be to close a share premium account or capital redemption reserve.

[11] A company could have partly paid shares. The company could decide to renounce its claim to payment of the remaining amount required to pay the shares up in full. It could do this if the company decided it did not need the extra capital.

[12] CA 2006 ss.709–723.

that the value of the company's assets are far less than had previously been the case. This type of reduction of capital may also be useful when the company's assets have in practice depreciated more than had been anticipated. It is also useful for public companies, where the full net worth rule applicable to dividends[13] prevents public companies paying dividends where the net asset value of the company after payment of the dividend would be less than the aggregate of the company's share capital and undistributable reserves. By reducing the company's capital (i.e. effectively writing off the loss in value of some its assets) the company may pay dividends again.[14] The loss must be permanent[15]; and where there is doubt as to whether it will be permanent, the court in one instance in England insisted that there be an undertaking that if the loss were made good, the recovered sums should be placed in an undistributable capital reserve,[16] but in another instance suggested that such recovered sums would not necessarily need to be placed in such a reserve provided adequate arrangements had been already made for the benefit of any creditors.[17] In *Quayle Munro Ltd, Petitioners*[18] the court permitted the petitioners to cancel the share premium account and use the funds therefrom to write off a deficit on the profit and loss account. In addition, the company undertook to place any remaining funds from the share premium account into a special reserve which would not be distributed while the company had outstanding creditors, but which could be used to repay certain preference shareholders and to write off future losses.

The second reason is less common nowadays, because of greater skill in **6–08** drafting the rights attaching to classes of shares. If the company follows the required procedure and pays the members of a class of shares exactly what they would have received in a solvent liquidation, the repaid members have no grounds for complaint, except to the extent that the shares have not provided their expected dividends for as long as might have been anticipated.

House of Fraser v AGCE Investments Ltd[19]
House of Fraser attempted to reduce the company's capital and repay AGCE, which had a class of shares which attracted a high preferential dividend. AGCE claimed that the reduction could not be done without their consent, but it was held that reduction of capital had not been stated in their class rights as an alteration of their class rights,[20]

---

[13] CA 2006 s.831. See also paras 7–23—7–24.
[14] This makes the company more attractive to new investors, even if existing investors have had to suffer a reduction in the value of their shareholdings in the company.
[15] *Re Haematite Steel Co Ltd* [1901] 2 Ch. 746, per Romer L.J. at 749.
[16] *Re Jupiter House Investments (Cambridge) Ltd* [1985] 1 W.L.R. 975.
[17] *Re Grosvenor Press Plc* [1985] 1 W.L.R. 980.
[18] *Quayle Munro Ltd, Petitioners*, 1992 S.C. 24; 1993 S.L.T. 723; [1994] 1 B.C.L.C. 410.
[19] *House of Fraser v AGCE Investments Ltd* [1987] A.C. 387.
[20] One presumes that this was an oversight of the part of AGCE or their advisors; alternatively it may never have occurred to anyone that reduction of capital was a possible means of removing AGCE.

that AGCE was receiving exactly what it would have received in a solvent liquidation and that any shareholder stood the risk at any time of his investment being curtailed by the company's liquidation or reduction of capital; House of Fraser was therefore entitled to take advantage of the omission in the drafting of the class rights in order to reduce its capital by paying back AGCE its share capital.

Following the decision in that case, classes of shareholders normally include in the terms attaching to their class rights a provision that there is to be no reduction of capital as it affects their shares without their consent.[21]

The third reason is also uncommon though still valid. Where a company has more funds than it knows what to do with, i.e. over-capitalisation, it may choose to return its capital to its members. Provided the creditors, members and potential creditors or investors are content with this, and the repayment is in accordance with the articles, there should be no difficulties with this.[22]

6–09   As for the fourth reason, it is possible to reduce a capital account and use the released funds to pay for some newly acquired asset, such as the goodwill of a company the petitioner had purchased.[23]

The main types of reduction of capital

6–10   Under the CA 2006 s.641(4) there are three main types of reduction:

(1) the extinction or reduction of liability on any of the company's shares in respect of capital not paid up (for example, if a company had £1.00 nominal value shares each paid up to the extent of 60 pence only, the company might extinguish the liability for the remaining 40 pence per share, thus making the former £1.00 nominal value shares into 60 pence nominal value shares);

(2) the cancellation of any paid up capital which is lost or no longer represented by assets (for example, if a company's issued share capital is £1 million, but its net assets are only £400,000 due to various trading losses, the company could write off £600,000 of share capital); and

(3) the repayment of share capital in excess of the company's wants.

The legislation does not exclude other types of reduction[24] but the above are the common ones, and in practice the second is the one most used.

---

[21] Such a provision was upheld in *Re Northern Engineering Industrial Plc* [1993] B.C.C. 267.

[22] *Wilson and Clyde Coal Co Ltd v Scottish Insurance Corporation Ltd*, 1949 S.C. (HL) 90.

[23] In *Re Ratners Group Plc* [1988] B.C.L.C. 685, the share premium account was reduced. The released funds were used to help acquire the goodwill of a company Ratners had taken over.

[24] The wording of s.641(1) states that a company "may", having followed the required procedure, reduce its capital "in any way". For example, it is possible to return capital at a premium (*Re Saltdean Estate Co Ltd* [1968] 1 W.L.R. 1844), or to use the released funds to pay for the conversion of ordinary shares into redeemable deferred shares (*Forth Wines Ltd, Petitioners*, 1993 S.L.T. 170).

The procedure for reduction of capital in a public company

Under the CA 2006 s.641(1) it is permissible to reduce a company's **6–11** capital provided that:

(1) the company's articles permit it (the model articles for private and public companies do not prohibit it);
(2) the members pass a special resolution approving the reduction[25]; and
(3) the court approves the reduction.

The role of the court is to ensure that creditors are aware of and content with the reduction. Accordingly, where the reduction involves:

(1) the diminution of liability in respect of unpaid share capital, i.e. writing off the unpaid part of each share;
(2) the payment to a shareholder of any paid-up share capital; or
(3) in any other case where the court so directs,

creditors must be given the opportunity to object to the reduction unless the court directs otherwise.[26] This is done by making a list of creditors and contacting them by newspaper advertisement, or better, by writing to each creditor or potential creditor intimating the proposed reduction to him and indicating the date by which any objection must be received.[27] Although creditors are entitled under s.646 to object to the reduction[28] where the reduction concerns the diminution of liability in respect of paid up share capital, or the payment to any shareholder of paid up share capital, the courts may agree to dispense with the requirements of s.646 if they can be persuaded to do so.[29] This would generally be done by ensuring all known creditors have been paid off and that those creditors whose claims are contingent or disputed can have their claims met by sums or bonds paid into court for the creditors' benefit.[30] When the reduction is by means of cancelling paid up share capital unrepresented

---

[25] CA 2006 s.641(1)(b). When there is a vote in a class of shares in respect of the resolution, the members of the class are expected to vote with "detached altruism" as members of that class, as opposed to voting according to any other more selfish interests arising out of their ownership of any other shares in the company and not part of that class of shares: *Re Holders Investment Trust Ltd* [1971] 1 W.L.R. 583; [1971] 2 All E.R. 289 Ch.Div.
[26] CA 2006 s.645.
[27] CA 2006 s.646(3).
[28] CA 2006 s.646(1) as amended by the proposed Companies (Share Capital and Acquisition by a Company of its Own Shares) Regulations 2009 (SI 2009/2022) para.3. If creditors wish to object to the reduction, creditors will have to prove that their claims are at risk and that the company has not provided safeguards for those claims. In *Royal Scottish Assurance plc* [2011] CSOH 2 it was held that creditors should only be allowed to object if there were a "real likelihood of risk" which, in the circumstances of the case, was not apparent.
[29] CA 2006 s.645(2).
[30] CA 2005 s.646(5)(a).

by assets, s.646 will not apply,[31] unless the court directs otherwise.[32] The court can compel the company to set aside funds for such claims if necessary.[33] If a creditor on the list does not have his claim discharged and does not consent to the reduction, the court will dispense with his consent if his claim is met.[34] It has been to known for members to object to the reduction of capital, but provided their interests have already been properly taken care of[35] and there is scrupulous adherence to their rights under the articles, it will be difficult for them to prevent the reduction taking place.[36] If there are difficulties with a class of shareholders, a better solution may be to petition the court for approval of a scheme of arrangement under the CA 2006 ss.895–901.[37] In practice it is rare for a reduction of capital petition to be opposed. The court will need to be satisfied that every creditor has consented to the reduction or that every claim has been discharged or security granted for it.[38] What does take place, however, as part of the court hearing, is that the court will normally remit the petition to a court-appointed Reporter, usually a solicitor or advocate with an expertise in corporate law, who will check the documentation for any procedural or other irregularities.[39] The Reporter will commonly draw the attention of the petitioner's agents or the court to any defects to allow the petitioner the opportunity to correct them. Once the Reporter has received the documentation to his satisfaction his approval will be communicated to the court, which will then grant the petition.

6–12   Once the court has ordered the reduction, a minute confirming the

---

[31] CA 2006 s.646(2). The problem with s.646 is that inserting a newspaper advertisement about a company's reduction of capital may confuse those creditors who are unaware of the distinction between reduction of capital and the winding up of the company. To the ill-informed, reduction is as alarming as winding up. It is therefore sometimes in a company's interest to avoid having a newspaper advertisement. If the court is satisfied that no creditor will object to the reduction because they have already been repaid, there should be no need for advertisement in the newspapers.

[32] CA 2006 s.646(4).

[33] CA 2006 s.646(5)(b).

[34] CA 2006 s.646(4).

[35] *Re Northern Engineering Industries Plc* [1993] B.C.C. 267; [1993] B.C.L.C. 1151. On this occasion a class of shareholders were able successfully to object because the proposed reduction was actually a variation of one of the rights attaching to the class, and approval should have been sought from that class. However, in *Fife Coal Co Ltd, Petitioners; Arniston Coal Co Ltd, Petitioners*, 1948 S.C. 505; 1948 S.L.T. 421; 1948 S.L.T. (Notes) 39, no separate meeting of preference shareholders was needed because even after the reduction of capital there were assets sufficient to repay the preference shareholders.

[36] *Re Ransomes Plc* [1999] 4 B.C.L.C. 591.

[37] *Re Stephen Robert Holdings* [1968] 1 W.L.R. 522; [1968] 1 All E.R. 195 (Note).

[38] CA 2006 s.648(2). There are also penalties for misrepresenting creditors' consent or concealing the existence of affected creditors (s.647) and members who were members at the time of the reduction may potentially be personally liable to any creditor who was omitted from the list of creditors (s.653(2)).

[39] For example, there might be some provision in the articles which had been overlooked and prevented certain aspects of the reduction taking place, or there might be inaccuracies in the financial figures. A reporter is not always necessary: in *Fowlers (Aberdeen) Ltd, Petitioners*, 1928 S.C. 186, no creditors were affected at all, and all the members had consented to the reduction; under these circumstances there was no need for a Reporter.

reduction is sent to the Registrar of Companies who registers it and certifies it.[40] The court may also, if it chooses, demand that the company publish its reasons for the reduction of capital and/or change its name to include, bizarrely, the words "and reduced" after the word "limited" in its name.[41] If in the process of reduction a public company finds that its capital is less than £50,000, it must re-register as a private company[42] unless that matter has already been dealt with in the court's inter-locutor,[43] or the period of time when the capital is below that figure is momentary.[44] There is no stamp duty to be paid on the cancellation of the shares that are written off.

The procedure for reduction for a private company

The above procedure has long been recognised as costly and time **6–13** consuming, and not even of particular use to creditors, many of whom are not particularly interested in a company's reduction of capital but are interested in getting their bills paid. So the above procedure has been abolished for private companies. Instead, the CA 2006 ss.642–644 impose a new, simpler method for private companies, though it is not without its own difficulties.

If a private company wishes to reduce its share capital or any other **6–14** capital fund, every single director must sign a "solvency statement" not more than 15 days before a special resolution[45] is passed authorising the reduction.[46] The solvency statement is a declaration by each director that he has "formed the opinion" that as at the date of the statement, "there is no ground on which the company could then be found to be unable to pay (or otherwise discharge) its debts."[47] Furthermore, each director must also have been of the opinion that either, if it is intended to wind up the company within a year of making the statement, the company could pay all its debts within a year of the winding-up[48]; or that the company could pay all its debts within a year of the making of the statement.[49]

In order to make this statement, the directors should take account of **6–15** all prospective and contingent liabilities[50] of the company. If the directors make the solvency statement without good grounds for doing so, they can

---

[40] CA 2006 s.649.
[41] CA 2006 s.648(3), (4). Although this never happens nowadays, it was not unheard of in the 1920s. It is baffling that officials in BIS felt that it was still worth preserving in the CA 2006.
[42] CA 2006 s.650.
[43] *Re Thompson Clive Investment Plc* Unreported June 8, 2005 Ch.D. Companies Court.
[44] *Re MB Group Plc* (1989) 5 B.C.C. 684; [1989] B.C.L.C. 672.
[45] If the resolution is passed as a written resolution, as it usually will be, a copy of the solvency statement must be sent to each member along with the proposed resolution (s.642(2)).
[46] CA 2006 s.642(1).
[47] CA 2006 s.643(1)(a).
[48] CA 2006 s.643(2)(b)(i).
[49] CA 2006 s.643(2)(b)(ii).
[50] In other words, both the known debts likely to become due, and the debts that may become due depending on the fulfilment of uncertain other events, such as losing a court case.

be sentenced to prison for up to two years on indictment or six months on summary conviction. In each event the directors may also be fined. The solvency statement and the special resolution must both be filed with the Registrar of Companies within 15 days of the special resolution,[51] along with a statement of capital indicating what shares are being reduced,[52] and a further statement by the directors confirming that the solvency statement was both shown to the members before they voted on the special resolution and that the solvency statement was made not more than 15 days before the resolution was passed. This further statement must be sent to the Registrar within 15 days of the passing of the resolution.[53]

6–16   As may be seen, the procedure for a private company may be less onerous and cheaper than for a public company, but it is not without its perils. The first is that the directors will have to be very sure of their company's finances for them all to sign the solvency statement. If even one director breaks rank, unless he resigns first, the only options are to persuade him to sign the statement, or to follow the public company method of going to court—which is still permissible for a private company as the court procedure under ss.645–653 is not exclusive to public companies. The worry for directors is the word "contingent". For example, it is a common term of a lease of property in England, where a lease is broken, that the outgoing tenant has to guarantee the rent of an incoming term. While this term does not apply in every case, it is by no means unusual. A director of a Scottish company which leased premises in England would have to be very confident that if it terminated the lease the next tenant would be a reliable tenant.

Distribution of reserve arising out of a reduction of share capital

6–17   If a limited or unlimited company reduces its share capital, whether by solvency statement (if a private company) or by going to court (whether public or private), and as a result a reserve arises out of the reduction of the capital, that reserve is to treated as a realised profit (and therefore available for distribution), unless there is any contrary provision contained in a court order, the wording of the special resolution for the reduction of capital, any undertaking given previously to the court, or in the company's articles.[54] Note that this rule only applies to reduction of share capital, not any other fund such as the capital redemption reserve, unless the court says otherwise.[55]

---

[51] CA 2006 s.644(1)

[52] CA 2006 s.644(2). The statement of capital is Form SH19.

[53] CA 2006 s.644(5).

[54] CA 2006 s.654 and the Companies (Reduction of Share Capital) Order 2008 (SI 2008/1915) art.3(2).

[55] CA 2005 s.654(1).

FINANCIAL ASSISTANCE

Financial assistance arises where a company (or one of its subsidiaries) **6–18** provides a potential or existing shareholder with some form of financial help[56] (by gift,[57] guarantee, security, indemnity,[58] loan[59] or any other means causing the company's net assets to be reduced to a material extent[60]) in order to enable that shareholder to buy shares in that company.[61]

The law relating to financial assistance is one of the more unhappy aspects of the capital maintenance rule. On the one hand it is prohibited for the good reason that it is not necessarily a good use of the company's assets for them to be applied to enable a shareholder to acquire shares in the company itself; but on the other hand, if the members of a company are content that the company's assets should be used in this way, and if creditors are aware of what is happening, is there any reason why it should not be permitted? As can be imagined, this dichotomy makes the drafting of the legislation problematic, and it is widely acknowledged that the current wording of the Act leaves much to be desired. The original theory behind the prohibition was that it prevented the paying away of the company's funds to favoured shareholders, but in more recent years, a more commercial feature of the prohibition is to limit the opportunities for market manipulation and to prevent directors or takeover bidders misusing the company's assets generally.

Evils that the prohibition is designed to prevent are the practice of **6–19** using the company's funds (which could be better used to pay dividends) to help certain investors acquire shares,[62] with the risk that the investors might sell their shares without repaying their company the borrowed funds, or asset-strip the company using the company's funds. An asset-stripper borrows from the bank to raise enough funds to take over a listed company. Once he has the majority of the company's shares in his pocket, he arranges for the company to grant a charge over the company's assets as security for his own personal borrowings from the bank.[63]

---

[56] The words "financial assistance" are apparently to be given their normal commercial meaning: *Charterhouse Investment Trust Ltd v Tempest Diesels Ltd* [1986] B.C.L.C. 1, per Hoffman J. at 10; and *Barclays Bank Plc v British and Commonwealth Holdings Ltd* [1996] 1 B.C.L.C. 1, per Aldous L.J. at 40.

[57] CA 2006 s.677(1)(a).

[58] CA 2006 s.677(1)(b).

[59] CA 2006 s.677(1)(c)(i).

[60] CA 2006 s.677(1)(d)(i). There is no clear indication as to what is meant by "material" in these circumstances though in practice one per cent would be considered material. See also *Parlett v Guppys (Bridport) Ltd (No.1)* [1996] 2 B.C.L.C. 34.

[61] CA 2006 s.678(1).

[62] *Chaston v SWP Group Plc* [2003] B.C.C. 140 CA. In this case accountants' fees for carrying out a report on a target company for the benefit of those wishing to take over the company were charged to the target company. The target company had effectively subsidised the takeover bidders.

[63] Alternatively he makes the company lend him enough money which he uses to repay the bank. If he were a director he would in so doing contravene the rules at s.197 against giving loans to directors, though if he owned all the shares he could then vote in his own interest to approve the loan.

He then proceeds to break up the company, the value of the separately sold off parts in total being greater than his loan, and the parts he cannot he sell he puts into liquidation. Out of the proceeds of the break-up he repays his loan. After repayment of the loan, he should have made a profit out of the demise of the company.[64] A third evil is the practice of giving favoured shareholders or would-be shareholders the opportunity to acquire shares in the company with minimal risk. This can be done by the company offering an indemnity to those shareholders. The company could undertake to reimburse any losses that the shareholders might suffer if the share price dipped below the acquisition price. In the scandal relating to the Guinness takeover of Distillers in the 1980s certain shareholders were given such indemnities as part of a concerted plan to keep the Guinness share price high (also known as a "share support scheme") so that the Guinness shares would be seen to be desirable to Distillers shareholders—a classic example of market manipulation and arguably a breach of fiduciary duty by the Guinness directors giving the indemnities.[65]

6–20   Some of the private equity deals carried out before the economic collapse of 2009 involved financial assistance. The private equity firm would borrow large sums of money while interest rates were low. Using the borrowed money, it would then acquire most of the shares in the target company, such as a large listed retail company, and having done so, using its majority share-ownership would delist the company and convert its status to that of a private company. Private companies could provide financial assistance under the then whitewash procedure, and the target company would then grant a security over its assets in favour of the bank that had originally lent the money to the private equity firm. The private equity firm would then take over the management of the retailer, perhaps more efficiently[66] than the previous management, and the company's profits would be used to repay the loan to the bank. The firm would often sell on the retailing company, and having repaid the bank in the process, would make a substantial profit.

A similar, perhaps more benign, use of financial assistance involves management buy-outs, whereby the managers of a subsidiary buy the shares in the subsidiary from its holding company using money borrowed by the managers personally from a bank. Once the subsidiary has been acquired, the managers make the former subsidiary grant a charge over its assets to the bank as security for the managers' loans. As the former subsidiary prospers, dividends are paid to the managers, and the bank loans are repaid out of the dividends. If the managers fail to make the

---

[64] What some consider objectionable about this practice is that he is risking not his own money (which might be fair enough) but instead using the company's assets to carry out the destruction of the company. He also is likely to cause employees to lose their jobs.

[65] *Report of the Inspectors into the affairs of Guinness plc, Investigation under ss.432 and 442 of the Companies Act 1985*, HMSO, 1997.

[66] This usually involved removing unnecessary layers of management or divesting the company of less profitable parts of the business.

subsidiary prosper, the bank at least has the security of being able to realise the subsidiary's assets.[67] Another benign use is where a company lends money to someone who wants to be a member of the company in order to show his commitment to the company but is short of cash. If that potential member has commercial benefits he can bring to the company, the price for his membership of the company may be a loan by the company to enable him to buy some shares.

All financial assistance is in principle unlawful,[68] but that rule is subject **6–21** to various exceptions, of which the main one is that the prohibition does not apply to private companies[69] unless: (i) those private companies are subsidiaries of public companies[70]; or (ii) the person receiving the assistance is receiving it in order to obtain shares in a private company with funds borrowed from a public company subsidiary of that private company.[71] If assistance is given at a time when the company is public, even if it later becomes private, the assistance is still unlawful.[72] Significant exceptions may be found in ss.678 and 681, these being the "principal purpose" exception[73] (to be discussed shortly), the payment of lawful dividends,[74] the allotment of bonus shares,[75] the redemption or purchase of shares under the CA 2006 ss.684–737,[76] a scheme of arrangement under the CA 2006 s.895,[77] anything connected with a winding up in terms of the Insolvency Act 1986 ("the IA 1986") s.110[78] and a company voluntary arrangement under the IA 1986 ss.1–7.[79]

Further exceptions include the lending of money by a commercial **6–22** lender to a shareholder in the ordinary course of business,[80] the provision of financial assistance for an employees' share scheme,[81] the provision of financial assistance to help employees and their families acquire shares in their employers' companies[82] and the making of loans to employees other than directors in order to enable those employees to buy shares in their companies or those companies' holding companies.[83]

---

[67] This is the same principle as asset-stripping as described above but seen as more socially acceptable as at least the managers are trying to be entrepreneurial.
[68] CA 2006 s.680. There are criminal penalties.
[69] CA 2006 s.682(1)(a).
[70] CA 2006 s.678(1).
[71] CA 2006 s.679.
[72] CA 2006 s.678(3)—that is, unless one of the permitted exceptions applies.
[73] CA 2006 s.678(1), (2).
[74] CA 2006 s.681(2)(a).
[75] CA 2006 s.681(2)(b).
[76] CA 2006 s.681(2)(d).
[77] CA 2006 s.681(2)(e).
[78] CA 2006 s.681(2)(f).
[79] CA 2006 s.681(2)(g).
[80] CA 1985 s.682(2)(a): this is designed to cover the situation where a bank lends money to a debtor who then chooses to use his loan to buy shares in the bank.
[81] CA 2006 s.682(2)(b).
[82] CA 2006 s.682(2)(c).
[83] CA 2006 s.682(2)(d).

In respect of these further exceptions, where a public company provides the relevant financial assistance, the company may only provide such assistance if the company has net assets[84] which will not be reduced, or if the net assets are reduced by the assistance, the assistance is to be provided out of distributable profits.[85] Both assets and liabilities in this context should be determined by reference to the company's most recent accounting records prior to the financial assistance.[86]

A foreign subsidiary is not prohibited from providing financial assistance to individuals purchasing shares in its UK holding company.[87]

6–23   If unlawful financial assistance takes place, the company is liable to a fine and the officers of the company may be imprisoned or fined.[88] It is curious that the company could be fined, thus penalising shareholders who may well have known nothing about the financial assistance anyway. As unlawful financial assistance is criminal, it means that transactions "downstream" of the financial assistance may be unenforceable even if the parties involved were unaware of the original assistance.[89] This too is often seen as unsatisfactory.

The principal purpose

6–24   If a company is not a private company, and thus free to provide financial assistance,[90] or if the assistance does not come within the list of exemptions mentioned above, how may financial assistance to buy shares in a public company legitimately be provided? How feasible is it for a public company to provide financial assistance?

The answer to these questions is that s.678(2) states that any company may give financial assistance for the purpose of buying shares in a company or its holding company if, "(a) the company's principal purpose in giving that assistance is not to give it for the purpose of any such

---

[84] CA 2006 s.682(3). For the purposes of this part, net assets means aggregate assets less aggregate liabilities, including reasonably anticipated contingent and prospective liabilities, as indicated by the company's accounting records immediately before the financial assistance is given: s.154(2).

[85] CA 2006 s.682(1)(b). If the company provides a gift by way of assistance, there would be a reduction of net assets and so the assistance would have to be provided out of distributable profits; if the company grants a charge over its assets in favour of someone lending to the purchaser of the shares, the net assets are not reduced unless the purchaser defaults on the loan.

[86] CA 2006 s.682(4)(a). "Liabilities" are also further defined to include what effectively are prospective and contingent liabilities such as any prudent accountant would provide for.

[87] *Arab Bank Plc v Mercantile Holdings Ltd* [1994] 1 B.C.L.C. 330. It is on one view strange that the rules are so strict to forbid many forms of financial assistance, but so easily circumvented by the ruse of using a foreign subsidiary.

[88] CA 2006 s.680.

[89] *Heald v Connor* [1971] 1 W.L.R. 479; [1971] 2 All E.R. 1105 QBD.

[90] Historically it was not unknown for public companies to become private again to take advantage of the previous rules, known as the whitewash rules, which if carefully followed, allowed for the provision of financial assistance by private companies.

acquisition, or (b) the giving of the assistance for that purpose is only an incidental part of some larger purpose of the company, and (c) the assistance is given in good faith". A similar provision applies in s.678(4) applicable to the provision of assistance by way of reducing or discharging any liability incurred by the purchaser for the purpose of the acquisition.

The words "principal purpose" and "incidental part of some larger **6–25** purpose" have given rise to much doubt.[91] They were considered in the case of *Brady v Brady*[92] where two brothers whose group of companies were involved in the drinks and haulage trade engineered a complex reorganisation and break-up of their own and their companies' debts and shareholdings. The point of the reorganisation was to prevent the companies collapsing into deadlock while the brothers bickered. The reorganisation proceeded relatively smoothly until one brother decided that the terms were unsatisfactory for him and sought an excuse for withdrawing from the deal. The prohibition against financial assistance provided that excuse, but the other brother insisted on specific performance and the case eventually went to the House of Lords. The House of Lords specifically addressed the issue of "principal purpose". In order to give meaning to the opaque legislation, Lord Oliver drew a distinction between the "purpose" of the financial assistance, which was to reduce a liability incurred by the purchaser of shares, and the "reason" why a purpose is formed, in this case to enable the break-up of the business to take place. He stated that the saving of the business from collapse was a by-product of the financial assistance, but would not accept that the avoidance of the collapse of the business was a principal or larger purpose of which the financial assistance was but an incidental part. As far as Lord Oliver was concerned, the purpose of the financial assistance was to make it easier for someone to buy the shares because the company was helping that person. It is evident that Lord Oliver found the wording of the then s.153[93] very difficult, and had trouble making sense of it[94]; but if it comes to that, many people have found trouble making commercial sense of Lord Oliver's decision.[95] His fine distinction between the meanings of the words "reason" and "purpose" may be all very well for lawyers, but do not make life for businessmen any easier. Despite hopes that the CA 2006 would clarify matters, the wording in essence is little

---

[91] These words, and the good faith requirement, were introduced into the CA 1985 as they were omitted in the Companies Act 1948 which forbad any form of financial assistance. *Belmont Finance Corp v Williams Furniture Ltd (No. 2)* [1980] 1 All E.R. 393 and *Armour Hick Northern Ltd v Whitehouse* [1980] 3 All E.R. 833 both raised issues as to the purpose of the assistance and the good faith of those involved and it was deemed necessary therefore to insert the principal purpose and the good faith rule into the CA 1985.

[92] *Brady v Brady* [1989] A.C. 755 HL; [1988] B.C.L.C. 20 CA.

[93] Section 153 was the equivalent of ss.678, 679.

[94] In fairness to Lord Oliver, he was also trying to prevent any future company from asserting any form of motivation or reason as counting towards a "greater purpose", thus making the prohibition in the legislation effectively pointless.

[95] This has not prevented it being followed: *Plaut v Steiner* (1989) 5 B.C.C. 352.

different in 2006 Act from the 1985 Act.[96] An ironic feature of the *Brady* case was that Lord Oliver finally granted an order for specific performance on the grounds that as the company involved was a private company, it could have used the whitewash procedure anyway—and indeed was directed to do so.

6–26   So when may financial assistance be lawful for a public company or one of its subsidiaries? The answer is by no means clear, but it is suggested that the best approach, following the *Brady* case, is to take a very commercial approach, which is that any form of benefiting a purchasing shareholder at the company's expense will be unlawful,[97] unless it really can be shown that the benefit was a tiny or incidental part of some larger purpose, or unless it comes within one of the recognised exceptions. For example, where the assistance actually provides a benefit for the company,[98] as opposed to benefiting a particular shareholder, the financial assistance may be acceptable, or perhaps where the financial assistance is an insignificant matter within a more complex strategy, the assistance may be acceptable. But broadly speaking anything that benefits a favoured shareholder who is trying to buy shares in the company at the expense of the company will effectively be prejudicing other shareholders, as the favour will be coming out of funds that could otherwise be used for their dividends, or will be effectively prejudicing creditors, since the funds available to satisfy their claims will be reduced as well. For those two reasons, in principle financial assistance will be prohibited, at least in public companies, even if the assistance is provided in good faith. It is no surprise that the common practical solutions to the matter are to convert the public company into a private one, whereupon it may provide as much financial assistance as it likes, or to provide the assistance from a foreign subsidiary, that not being illegal.[99]

6–27   In other jurisdictions, such as the United States, financial assistance is legitimate provided it is approved by the members and entirely transparent. But in the United Kingdom, because of the uncertainty arising from the *Brady* case, it is still not known whether certain forms of activity are potentially criminal—these including the payment of a venture capitalist's legal fees by a company in which he has just invested[100]; the payment by a company to a stockbroker or other agent who has found an new investor for the company; the granting of floating charges by newly acquired subsidiaries as part of a continuing obligation under a loan whereby a company undertakes to grant floating charges over itself and all its present and future subsidiaries, irrespective of whether or not the

---

[96] It is very telling that the Government's own Explanatory Notes to the legislation on the internet at *http://www.legislation.gov.uk/ukpga/2006/46/notes/contents* [Accessed April 22, 2014] glide over these matters, as if the draftsman of the notes did not quite know what safely to say about them.

[97] *Chaston v SWP Group Plc* [2002] EWCA Civ 1999; [2003] B.C.C. 140.

[98] *Re Uniq plc* [2011] EWHC 749 (Ch); [2012] 1 B.C.L.C. 783.

[99] *Arab Bank Plc v Mercantile Holdings Ltd* [1994] 1 B.C.L.C. 330.

[100] By contrast, the payment by the target company of a success fee was not seen as an infringement of the financial assistance rules: *Corporate Development Partners LLC v E-Relationship Marketing Ltd* [2007] All E.R. 162.

subsidiary was acquired using the lender's funds; and "piggybacking", which is where illegal financial assistance is taking place, causing market manipulation, but astute investors follow the market anyway—are their trades all illegal too? To these questions there are no satisfactory answers, but it is noticeable that the relative lack of litigation recently on this point suggests that other solutions—such as schemes of arrangement—are being found for the difficulties which might otherwise be resolved by recourse to financial assistance.

Private companies

A private company is allowed to provide financial assistance[101] unless **6–28** those private companies are subsidiaries of public companies,[102] or the person receiving the assistance is doing so to obtain shares in a private company with funds borrowed from a public company subsidiary of that private company.[103] There is no requirement to go through any formal procedure or send in any returns to the Registrar of Companies. The company may provide as much assistance as it likes, subject to the terms of the articles. The former "whitewash" procedure is abolished.

However, if banks are lending to individuals who are securing or **6–29** propose to secure their loans over the assets of the private company that they are about to take over, or whose shares they are about to buy, banks may sometimes impose requirements very similar to the former whitewash rules. Banks may insist on directors' minutes approving the loan and the granting of a charge over the company's assets; they may want the company's articles specifically to allow for the granting of financial assistance, they may want audited accounts, confirming that in the auditors' view the company can pay all its bills and in particular could repay all or some of the loan within a requisite period; and the banks may want personal guarantees from the directors.

Purchase and Redemption of Shares

Historically companies could not buy back their own shares. This was to **6–30** prevent a simple fraud whereby the directors used the company's money to buy shares in the market, thus driving up the price. When the price was high enough, the directors sold their own shares and disappeared, and the remaining company members would then find the company had plenty of its own shares but no funds. Such a fraud was easier where the stock exchange could not monitor transactions as effectively as can be done nowadays, and where the accounting rules were less closely followed than they are now.

The rules have now been changed, as will be seen shortly. Although a

---

[101] CA 2006 s.682(1)(a).
[102] CA 2006 s.678(1).
[103] CA 2006 s.676.

company may not own its own shares,[104] and nor may a subsidiary own its holding company's shares (except as nominee for some other interest),[105] a company may now acquire its own shares,[106] create redeemable shares intended to be repurchased by the company, receive a gift of its own shares,[107] accept surrendered and forfeited shares[108] or be required by the court to acquire its members' shares.[109]

6–31   If a public company acquires shares in which it has a beneficial interest, or a member's shares are surrendered or forfeited to the company, those shares must be cancelled within three years[110] unless the company provided financial assistance to a person to enable him to buy shares in the company and the company has a beneficial interest in the shares. In that case the time limit is 12 months.[111] If in the process the cancellation of the shares causes the company's issued share capital to fall below £50,000, the company must re-register as a private company.[112] While the company is holding the shares in the period up to their cancellation, no voting rights may be exercised in respect of the held shares.[113] These rules are also extended to shares in a private company which re-registers as a public company.[114]

Treasury shares

6–32   The cancellation rules may be disapplied in respect of treasury shares. Formerly only available to companies whose shares were publicly traded, now any limited company may retain shares in treasury for subsequent resale rather than cancelling them. The shares may only be bought out of distributable profits or in the case of a private company out of capital,[115] no votes may be exercised in respect of them,[116] no dividends may be paid on them[117] but there is no maximum amount of a company's share capital that may be held in this way.[118] The advantage of holding treasury shares is that there is no need to go through the entire allotment procedure to sell them again, and in particular after the shares have ben "warehoused"

---

[104] CA 2006 s.658.
[105] CA 2006 s.660(3)(b). See also *Acatos and Hutcheson Plc v Watson* [1995] 1 B.C.L.C. 218.
[106] See CA 2006 ss.690–737.
[107] CA 2006 s.659(1).
[108] CA 2006 s.659(3).
[109] CA 2006 s.659(2)(b).
[110] CA 2006 s.662(3)(a).
[111] CA 2006 s.662(3)(b).
[112] CA 2006 s.664.
[113] CA 2006 s.662(5), (6).
[114] CA 2006 s.668.
[115] CA 2006 s.724(1)(b). The payments out of capital are restricted to the lower of £15,000 or the value of 5% of the company's share capital, and there must be authority under the articles to do this. See the Companies (Share Capital and Acquisition by Company of its own Shares) Regulations 2009 (SI 2009/2022).
[116] CA 2006 s.726(2).
[117] CA 2006 s.726(3).
[118] The previous limit of 10% (in what was then s.725) was disapplied by the Companies (Share Capital and Acquisition by Company of its own Shares) Regulations 2009 (SI 2009/2022).

(as it is known) in treasury, on their re-issue there is no need to take account of any pre-emption rights. This could be useful if the shares in treasury were to be offered to a manager as part of his employment package.

Reasons for a company's purchase of its own shares

A company may wish or agree to purchase its shares for the following **6-33** reasons:

- a member may be unable to find any other purchaser for his shares;
- the remaining members may be glad to "pay off" an unwelcome member but lack the funds to do so; instead the company may do so;
- purchasing shares drives up the share price, thus possibly deterring takeover bidders (though it may also signal that the company has cash to spare and that the shares are undervalued);
- buying back the shares will normally increase the net asset value per share for the remaining shares, even when taking account of the cost of re-purchase;
- buying back the shares may increase the earnings per share for the remaining shares if the company continues to make the same level of profit notwithstanding the loss of capital;
- investors may be able to shelter their capital profits within the capital gains tax exemption threshold;
- companies that are over-capitalised do not necessarily use their capital efficiently and there is not the same urgency to maximise profits. Investors may prefer a company to return excess capital to the investors and thus be forced to use its remaining capital more effectively, thus generating a better return for the investors;
- employees' shares may be purchased by the company;
- it may be cheaper for the company to operate through borrowed funds (especially if interest rates are low) than to pay high dividends to preference shareholders, in which case it makes sense to buy back the preference shares;
- directors' remuneration packages may allow a director to obtain a bonus if the share price achieves a certain target. By buying back the company's shares, the remaining shares in the company should be worth more (if the company makes the same level of profits as before, even taking account of the cost of buying back the shares) and the director can then obtain his bonus without having made the company any more productive or efficient.

Redemption of shares

6–34   A company, as stated in Ch.5,[119] may issue shares in the knowledge
that those shares will be bought back by the company at a predetermined
price and a predetermined time, normally as determined in the articles.
These are known as redeemable shares. A public company may only issue
redeemable shares if its articles permit it,[120] while private companies are
deemed able to issue redeemable shares unless their articles restrict or
forbid this.[121] It is not permissible to issue redeemable shares when the
only other type of share in the company are also redeemable shares.[122]
Directors may be given the right to determine the terms and conditions of
redemption if they are so authorised by the articles[123] or by ordinary
resolution.[124] If they do this, they must do so before the allotment of the
shares and they must indicate the terms and conditions of redemption on
the statement of capital sent to the Registrar of Companies.[125] Redeemable shares may not be redeemed unless they are fully paid[126] although it
is now permissible to redeem the shares on a date later than the original
redemption date if both the company and the redemption shareholders
agree.[127] The rules that relate to the funding of the redemption of shares
are exactly the same as the rules that relate to the funding of the purchase
of shares and will be dealt with at paras 6–41—6–50. If the company is
private, it may in addition redeem its redeemable shares out of capital in
accordance with the provisions of ss.709–723.[128] Redeemable shares must
be fully paid up on redemption.[129] Once redeemable shares have been
redeemed, the shares must be cancelled[130] and a statement of capital to
indicate the redemption sent to the Registrar of Companies.[131]

The process of purchasing shares

6–35   If a company wishes to purchase its shares, no longer does there need
to be the requisite power under the articles. If as a result of the repurchase
there would be no other shares other than redeemable shares or treasury
shares in existence, the purchase may not take place.[132] On repurchase the

---

[119] See para.5–06.
[120] CA 2006 s.684(3).
[121] CA 2006 s.684(2).
[122] CA 2006 s.684(4). This is because on redemption there would then be no shares left.
[123] CA 2006 s.685(1)(a).
[124] CA 2006 s.685(1)(b).
[125] See Form SH01.
[126] CA 2006 s.686(1).
[127] CA 2006 s.687(2).
[128] See paras 6–48, 6–49.
[129] CA 2006 s.686(1).
[130] CA 2006 s.688. Note that if shares are repurchased, they may be held as treasury shares
(s.724) but if the shares were redeemable shares, this is not possible as s.724 makes no
reference to redeemable shares.
[131] CA 2006 s.689. Form SH02 will need to be completed.
[132] CA 2006 s.690(2).

shares must be fully paid,[133] and when a limited company repurchases its shares, the shares must be paid for on purchase.[134]

There are two methods of purchasing shares: the off-market purchase[135] and the market purchase.[136]

Off-market purchase

This is designed for shares either in a private company, in a non-quoted **6–36** public company or occasionally in a quoted public company where the company has been allowed to have private arrangements or dealings with permission from the relevant investment exchange where the company's securities are normally traded.[137] The last of these is rare, since investment exchanges are not in general keen on private arrangements which may distort the market. An off-market purchase is basically a private transaction between the shareholder who wishes to sell his shares and the company in question.

In order for the off-market purchase to take place, there must first be a contract[138] drawn up between the company and the shareholder, whose terms must be approved by an ordinary resolution of the members,[139] thus giving authority to the directors to make the company enter into the contract.

As at the time of writing, the authority in the case of a public company may not endure more than five years from the date of the resolution.[140] The contract must be available for inspection by the members for a period of 15 days before the meeting for the passing of the resolution.[141] In voting on the resolution,[142] the member whose shares are to be repurchased is entitled to vote, but if the votes attaching to those shares

---

[133] CA 2006 s.691(1).

[134] CA 2006 s.691(2). In this respect it differs from redeemable shares which do not need to be paid for on the date of redemption by the company (s.686(2), (3)).

[135] CA 2006 ss.694–700.

[136] CA 2006 ss.701–708. There are also extensive arrangements for the purchase of shares for employee share schemes, not discussed here, but introduced by the Companies Act 2006 (Amendment of Part 18) Regulations 2013 (SI 2013/999).

[137] CA 2006 s.693(2). The words "marketing arrangement" are explained in more detail in s.693(3).

[138] CA 2006 s.694(1).

[139] CA 2006 s.694(2). The resolution may be passed at a meeting, or if the company is private, it may be passed by a written resolution. It is also possible to vary, revoke or renew the terms of the authority given to the directors to make the company enter into the contract: CA 2006 s.694(4).

[140] CA 2006 s.694(5).

[141] CA 2006 s.696(2). The legislation says that the contract (if in writing) must be exhibited but if there is no contract in writing, a memorandum setting out its terms must be exhibited instead. Given that s.694 seems to require a contract, and that it is probably as much effort to prepare a written memorandum as it is to write down a contract, it is hard to see the value of a memorandum. If there is a memorandum there must be a list of the names of the members to whom the contract relates (s.696(3)), and if there is a contract, there must be a written memorandum specifying such of the names as do not appear to be on the contract itself (s.696(4)).

[142] This refers to not just the resolution to confer authority; it also refers to the variation, revocation or renewal of authority (s.698(1)).

that are to be purchased are the ones that cause the vote to reach the required approval level of 50 per cent, those particular votes are to be ignored and the vote should be taken again without the member voting in respect of the votes attaching to the shares that are about to be purchased.[143] The member is however perfectly at liberty to vote in respect of those of his shares that are not to be purchased. If the vote is by written resolution, the members whose shares are being purchased may not vote at all.[144] There are special provisions for variation of the contract[145] or the release of the company from the contract.[146]

Market purchase

6–37   This takes place where the company's shares are traded on a recognised investment exchange, such as the London Stock Exchange, and approval for the purchase only requires an ordinary resolution.[147] The authority for the purchase endures for five years,[148] and may be revoked, varied or renewed within that period by ordinary resolution.[149] The authority for which approval is given must specify the maximum number of shares to be acquired and the maximum and minimum prices which may be paid for the shares, together with the date of expiry of the authority.[150] It is also possible to specify the maximum sum that the directors may spend in acquiring the shares, or to draw up an arithmetical formula for calculating how much may be spent acquiring the shares.[151] Where the company in question is listed, the London Stock Exchange must be informed of the transaction.[152] Form SH03 needs to be completed and sent to the Registrar of Companies.

Assignment of the right to purchase

6–38   Only the company has the right to purchase the shares, and that right may not be assigned.[153]

Contingent purchases

6–39   A company may not enter into an option to purchase its own shares.[154]

---

[143] CA 2006 s.698(3).
[144] CA 2006 s.698(2).
[145] CA 2006 s.699.
[146] CA 2006 s.700.
[147] CA 2006 s.701(1). There is no need for a contract, since shares are being bought in the marketplace and it would be impossible to make separate contracts with every person selling his shares to the company.
[148] CA 2006 s.701(5).
[149] CA 2006 s.701(4).
[150] CA 2006 s.701(3). There is no virtue in specifying one price for the shares, since the company's purchase of the shares in the market will probably cause the price to fluctuate anyway.
[151] CA 2006 s.701(7).
[152] See the London Stock Exchange Listing Rules, Ch.15.
[153] CA 2006 s.704.
[154] CA 2006 s.694(3). Without this prohibition, listed companies could purchase traded options and speculate against the value of their own share price movements.

Disclosure

If the purchase takes place under either method, within 28 days the **6–40** company must inform the Registrar of Companies of the repurchase of the shares[155] and provide a statement of capital to indicate the cancelled shares.[156] A copy of the contract is required to be kept at the company's registered office,[157] no doubt getting in the way and covered in dust, for ten years.[158] The purchased shares must be cancelled unless they are being kept in treasury.[159]

Payment for the purchase or redemption

The method of payment for the purchase or the redemption is the **6–41** same.[160] The funds for the purchase of the shares, or redemption of redeemable shares, should be provided either out of distributable profits, out of the proceeds of a fresh issue of shares made for the purposes of the redemption[161] or by cash, (if authorised by the articles) with a limit of £15,000 or 5 per cent of the company's issued capital.[162] It may also be provided out of a combination of the first two provisions. The point of the first two provisions is to ensure that the company does not use any capital in buying back its shares and thereby deprive the creditors of potential funds, even though the third method, at a small scale, is effectively payment for the redemption or the purchase out of capital.[163] Payments apart from the purchase price must be made out of distributable profits.[164]

If the purchased or redeemed shares are to be purchased or redeemed at a premium,[165] that premium will normally be paid out of the company's distributable profits.[166] However, if the company issued the original shares (later to be purchased or redeemed) at a premium, it is also permissible for the company to pay for the premium on purchase or redemption out of the proceeds of a fresh issue of shares made for the

---

[155] CA 2006 s.707(1). See Form SH03.

[156] CA 2006 s.708. See Forms SH06, SH07.

[157] It may also be kept at the place where the company's other records are kept (s.702(4)(b)) in terms of s.1196.

[158] CA 2006 s.702(3).

[159] CA 2006 s.706.

[160] The financing of the purchase of shares is to be found at the CA 2006 s.692 and that for redeemable shares at the CA 2006 s.687. The wording is almost identical.

[161] For purchase, the CA 2006 s.692(2)(a)(i), (ii); for redemption s.687(2)(a), (b).

[162] CA 2006 s.692(1). The point of this is that the company can fund the buy-back from cash even though it has no distributable reserves. This means the funds are coming from capital but this method avoids the normal complex procedure required for paying for shares out of capital (see para.6–45). It is only available to private companies.

[163] Leaving aside the £15,000 or 5 per cent rule, it is also possible to pay for redemption or repurchase out of capital using CA 2006 ss.709–723 if the company is a private company.

[164] CA 2006 s.705. This is not applicable to redeemable shares.

[165] The company pays back not only the nominal value of the share but an extra sum (the premium) as agreed in the original allotment documentation.

[166] For purchase, the CA 2006 s.692(1)(b); for redemption s.687(3).

purposes of the purchase or redemption.[167] However, this right is tempered by the requirement that the premium payable on purchase or redemption may only be paid out of the funds arising out of the proceeds of a fresh issue of shares up to an amount equal to whichever is the lesser of:

(a) the total premiums received on the original issue of the shares about to be purchased or redeemed[168]; or

(b) whatever happens to be in the share premium account at the time of the purchase or redemption, which amount includes any premiums paid on the issue of the new shares issued for the purpose of paying for the purchase or redemption.[169]

6–42 For example, if on the original issue five years ago of 10,000 ordinary shares of £1.00 nominal value shares the total premium paid for the shares was, say, £2,000: (a) would amount to £2,000. But if since the £2,000 was paid into the share premium account, £1,000 worth of that share premium account had been used to fund the creation of 1,000 bonus shares, £400 had been used to pay for some expenses arising on the allotment of some other shares, and £200 had been paid into the account as being premiums on the fresh issue of shares made for the purposes of the purchase; (b) would only amount to £800.[170] The amount that could be taken out of the proceeds of the fresh issue of shares in order to pay for the premium on redemption will be the lesser of (a) or (b), in this case (b). Since this could potentially lead to a diminution of the share capital, the share premium account is reduced by the amount that is taken out of the proceeds of the fresh issue of shares[171] so that although the share premium account goes down the share capital still reflects the true number of shares in issue.

The point of this provision, which is really an accounting exercise designed to maintain a company's share capital, is that it is possible to evacuate the share premium account if there is not much in it, but it is not possible to have a negative share premium account.

Stamp duty is payable on the value of the repurchased shares.

The capital redemption reserve

6–43 When a company purchases or redeems its own shares out of distributable profits, the company is treated as having cancelled the shares and thereby the company's issued share capital is reduced.[172] As this potentially means an overall reduction of the creditors' buffer, it is

---

[167] For purchase, the CA 2006 s.692(3); for redemption s.687(4).

[168] For purchase, the CA 2006 s.692(3)(a); for redemption s.687(4)(a).

[169] For purchase, the CA 2006 s.692(3)(b); for redemption s.687(4)(b). In paying for the premium, a company might choose to use a combination of distributable profits and the proceeds of a fresh issue of shares.

[170] This is £2,000 less £1,000, less £400, plus £200.

[171] For purchase, CA 2006 s.692(4); for redemption s.687(5).

[172] For purchase, CA 2006 s.706(b), unless they are treasury shares; for redemption s.688.

necessary to create a new capital fund, equal in value to the nominal value of the purchased or redeemed shares.[173] This is called the capital redemption reserve.[174] The new funds in the capital redemption reserve, plus the funds in the now reduced share capital account, together will be equal in value to the company's issued share capital position before the purchase or redemption. Thus is the overall capital position maintained at its previous level and the capital maintenance rule not offended.

So if a company with issued share capital of £10,000 repurchased 1,000 £1.00 nominal value ordinary shares at a price of £1,000, the repurchase payment of £1,000 would have been provided out of distributable profits. In addition, as the shares have been repurchased, they no longer exist and are cancelled, which means that the issued share capital of £10,000 is decreased by £1,000 to £9,000. Since that could potentially mean that the creditors' buffer is less able to meet creditors' claims, the sum of £1,000 is credited to the capital redemption reserve, having been taken out of, say, cash sitting on deposit in the bank. The total of the now diminished share capital (£9,000) plus the new figure in the capital redemption reserve (£1,000) is equal to the previous share capital figure of £10,000.

If the company already has a capital redemption reserve, each time the company purchases or redeems its own shares out of distributable profits, the company should transfer to the capital redemption reserve a sum equal in value to the nominal value of the purchased or redeemed shares.

Where the purchase or redemption is funded wholly or partly out of **6–44** the proceeds of a fresh issue of shares, and those proceeds are less than the aggregate nominal value of the purchased or redeemed shares, the balance of the funding of the repurchase price will have to be out of distributable profits[175] in which case the difference between the proceeds of the fresh issue and the nominal value of the purchased or redeemed shares is transferred to the capital redemption reserve.[176] There is no requirement to transfer sums to a capital redemption reserve where the funding of the purchase is wholly through the proceeds of a new issue of shares.

So if the same company as above is repurchasing £1,000 £1.00 nominal value ordinary shares at a price of £1,000, and if part of the payment for this is coming from the proceeds of an issue of preference shares designed to help pay for the purchase of shares, and if the proceeds only amounted to £400, the balance of £600 would have to come from distributable profits. In that case the sum credited to the capital redemption reserve would be £600. The overall capital position would still be £10,000, constituted by £9,000 of share capital, £400 of preference shares and a capital redemption reserve of £600.

The capital redemption reserve may be used for the creation of bonus

---

[173] CA 2006 s.733(2).
[174] Occasionally known as the capital redemption fund.
[175] CA 2006 s.733(3) unless it is a private company, in which case it may be able to use a payment out of capital.
[176] CA 2006 s.733(2).

shares,[177] and the rules relating to reduction of capital, as explained above, apply to this reserve.[178] One effect of the capital redemption reserve is that where a company pays for the purchase or redemption out of distributable profits, not only does the company have to hand over some of its distributable profits to its former shareholder, but it needs also to set aside funds which might otherwise be available for distribution (such as retained profits) to be transferred into the capital redemption reserve. There is therefore less overall available for distribution to shareholders by way of dividend.

Purchase or redemption of own shares out of capital in private companies

The funding arrangements

6–45   Private companies are permitted to pay for the purchase or redemption of their shares out of capital, instead of out of distributable profits or the proceeds of a new issue of shares.[179] The rules are the same for both purchase of a company's own shares or the redemption of its shares. This is a derogation of the normal capital maintenance rule, and is only permissible because of the strict rules attaching to the procedure.

The company must not have any restriction or prohibition against making such a payment in its articles.[180] The amount that may be taken from capital is known as the permissible capital payment[181] ("PCP") and may be stated as follows:

PCP = the repurchase or redemption price
        less any "available profits" of the company and
        less the proceeds (if any) of a fresh issue of shares made for the
        purposes of the purchase or redemption.

For example:

PCP = £100 (the purchase or redemption price)
        less available profits of £30 and
        less the proceeds of a not very successful fresh issue of shares,
        £60
        = £10.

The term "purchase or redemption price" means the total of the nominal value of the purchased or redeemed shares plus any premium payable on purchase or redemption.

6–46   The point of the PCP is to ensure that the company uses up such distributable profits as it has, followed by the proceeds of any new issue of shares, before it dips into capital. The "available profits" are the

---

[177] CA 2006 s.733(5).
[178] CA 2006 s.733(6).
[179] CA 2006 s.709.
[180] CA 2006 s.709(1).
[181] CA 2006 s.710(2).

company's normal distributable profits as shown in the accounts in the period of up to three months before the directors' solvency statement under s.720A[182] or the statutory declaration referred to later,[183] but excluding from those profits any sums used by way of financial assistance or the purchase or redemption of shares.[184]

If the PCP plus the proceeds of any fresh issue, if any, amount to *less* than the *nominal* value of the shares purchased or redeemed, the amount equivalent to the difference is transferred to the capital redemption reserve.[185]

> For example, ABC Ltd agrees to redeem 120 £1.00 nominal value ordinary shares at par, making a total price of £120. The company has available profits of £35. The company has a fresh issue of shares to pay for the redemption, which brings in only £30. The PCP is £120 − £35 − £30 = £55.
>
> Following s.734(2),[186] as the PCP (£55) plus the proceeds of the fresh issue (£30), making £85, is less than the nominal value of the redeemed shares (£120), the difference of £35 is transferred to the company's capital redemption reserve. The redeeming shareholder receives his £120 and the company's issued share capital is reduced by £55. Overall the company's capital position is reduced by £20.
>
> The position could be complicated by the situation where the redemption price includes an element of premium. So in the above example, if ABC Ltd agrees to redeem 120 £1.00 nominal value ordinary shares at a premium of 10p per share, the redemption price will be £132.00. The PCP is calculated on the purchase price (£132) less available profits (£35) and the proceeds of a new issue of shares (£30) = £67.
>
> Following s.734(2),[187] the PCP (£67) plus the proceeds of the fresh issue (£30) make £97 which is less than the *nominal* value of the redeemed shares (£120). The difference of £23 is thus transferred to the capital redemption reserve. The redeeming shareholder receives his £132, and the issued share capital is reduced by £67. Overall the company's capital position is reduced by £32.

---

[182] This refers to the required solvency statement before a payment into an employees' share scheme.

[183] CA 2006 s.712(7).

[184] CA 2006 s.712(4). Remember that this does not include the figure that may be put in treasury (s.724(1)(b)), being the lower of £15,000 or the value of 5% of the company's share capital, and there must be authority under the articles to do this. See the Companies (Share Capital and Acquisition by Company of its own Shares) Regulations 2009 (SI 2009/2022).

[185] CA 2006 s.734(2). This will normally mean that it has to be taken from some reserve of the company's, such as money sitting in a deposit account.

[186] Taking account of s.734(4), whereby one adds back into the PCP the proceeds of a fresh issue of shares if there are any.

[187] Again taking account of s.734(4), whereby one adds back into the PCP the proceeds of a fresh issue of shares if there are any.

6–47   However, if the PCP plus the proceeds of any fresh issue amount to *more* than the *nominal* value of the shares purchased or redeemed, it is permissible to reduce the company's share premium account, capital redemption reserve, fully paid share capital or revaluation reserve share capital by the amount by which the PCP exceeds the nominal value of the shares.[188]

> For example, DEF Ltd agrees to redeem 100 £1.00 nominal value ordinary shares at a premium of 40 pence per share, making a total price of £140. There is a share premium account containing £10. The company has available profits of £15. There was an unsatisfactory fresh issue of shares that brought in £8.
> The PCP is £140 - £15 - £8 = £117.
> Following s.734(3),[189] as the PCP of £117 is greater than the nominal value of the redeemed shares (£100), the company's share capital account and the share premium account may be reduced by £17 in addition to the cancellation of the 100 shares, and there is no need to transfer any sums to the capital redemption reserve.

As will be seen, the effect of each of these methods ensures that the capital is reduced. Since this makes a mockery of the capital maintenance rule, it is worth noting that apparently originally it was intended that the shortfall in capital in each case was supposed to be made good in subsequent years by the company, but the legislation to that effect was omitted and never seen as sufficiently important since to be worthy of amendment.

Conditions for payment out of capital

6–48   There must be a special resolution of the company[190] which must be passed within one week[191] of the day the directors make a directors' statement confirming that they have made full enquiry of the affairs and prospects of the company and believe that the company can pay its debts on the proposed day of the payment,[192] and that it will continue as a going concern, and able to pay its debts as they fall due,[193] for a further 12 months.[194] Lest the directors' opinion be misjudged, the company's

---

[188] CA 2006 s.734(3).
[189] Taking account of s.734(4), whereby one adds back into the PCP the proceeds of a fresh issue of shares if there are any.
[190] CA 2006 s.716(1). As with the special resolution for approving the purchase of shares by the company under s.695(3), the votes attaching to the shares that are to be purchased must not be what causes the resolution to be passed. At the meeting the members must be allowed to inspect the directors' statement and the auditors' report: s.718. However, if the resolution is to be passed by written resolution, the selling or redeeming shareholder may not vote at all (s.717(2)) and the remaining shareholders must see the statutory statement and auditors' report before or at the time of the signing of the resolution.
[191] CA 2006 s.713(1).
[192] CA 2006 s.714(3)(a).
[193] CA 2006 s.714(3)(b).
[194] CA 2006 s.173(3)(b).

auditors are required to produce a report confirming that they too have inquired into the company's state of affairs, that the PCP is properly calculated, and that they are not aware of anything to indicate that the directors' statutory declaration is unreasonable under the circumstances.[195] If the directors make their statement without reasonable grounds for the opinion stated in it, there are criminal sanctions against them,[196] and under the IA 1986 s.76(1)(a) the directors will be required to make good to the company any loss occasioned to their company by their misplaced views.

Within a week of the resolution, the company must publish a note in the *Edinburgh Gazette* and an appropriate national newspaper stating that the company will be using capital to pay for the purchase or redemption of its shares, specifying the amount of the PCP and the date of the resolution, indicating the availability of the directors' declaration and auditors' report[197] for inspection and intimating that any creditor may within five weeks of the resolution apply to the court for an order prohibiting the payment.[198]

If there is an objection under s.721 by either a member or a creditor to **6–49** the proposed payment out of capital, the court must consider the objection but is free to make such order as it sees fit in order to protect the dissentient members or dissentient creditors.[199] The person applying to the court is required to give notice to the Registrar of Companies of the application,[200] and when the company is served the notice of the application, it too must tell the Registrar.[201] Within 15 days of the court's order on the application, the company must tell the Registrar of the order.[202] But if there is no such objection, the payment may take place no sooner than five weeks after the passing of the special resolution under s.716 and no later than within seven weeks of the original special resolution.[203]

Failure to purchase or redeem

If a company does not purchase or redeem its shares when it said it **6–50** would, the company will not be liable in damages for its failure to purchase or redeem its shares,[204] and the court will not grant an order for specific implement if the company does not have the distributable profits

---

[195] CA 2006 s.714(6).
[196] CA 2006 s.715(1).
[197] Under CA 2006 s.720 these must available at the company's registered office or the place where its other records are kept in terms of s.1136.
[198] CA 2006 s.719.
[199] CA 2006 s.721(3)–(7).
[200] CA 2006 s.722(1). See Form SH16.
[201] CA 2006 s.722(2). See Form SH17.
[202] CA 2006 s.722(4).
[203] CA 2006 s.723(1). If the court allows extra or indeed shorter time as part of its order under s.721(5), the company would need to make the payment at such time as the court directs.
[204] CA 2006 s.735(2).

with which to meet its obligation.[205] If the company is wound up and the purchase or redemption is incomplete by the time of the commencement of the winding up, the selling or redeeming member's rights in respect of the purchase or redemption will be postponed to all other debts of the company but is higher than the right to repayment of shareholders' capital, subject to any overriding terms in the articles relating to other shares' rights.[206]

SERIOUS LOSS OF CAPITAL

6–51 If the net asset value of a public company drops to below half or less than the company's issued share capital, the directors must within 28 days of their first awareness of the loss of capital convene an extraordinary general meeting ("EGM") of the company to take place within 56 days of that first awareness.[207] Somewhat unhelpfully the legislation does not state what the company is supposed to do at the meeting. One option might be to put the company into voluntary liquidation before things get any worse.

SHARE PREMIUM ACCOUNT

6–52 A share premium account is the account where the premiums paid by subscribers for their newly issued shares are kept. The premium on a share (the difference between its nominal value and the market price paid to acquire it from the company) reflects the desirability of the share to the subscriber. The share premium account may be used to create bonus shares, pay the cost of any expenses (including commission) arising from the issue of shares.[208] In addition, as already indicated sums in the share premium account may be used under limited circumstances to pay the premium on the re-purchase or redemption of shares.[209] There is no obligation on a company to seek the maximum premium.[210]

Special relief rules apply to share premium accounts. Where company A acquires company B, and B's shareholders are offered shares in A as consideration for selling A their shares, and where the total assets in B turn out to be greater in value overall than the value of the A shares offered to the B shareholders in exchange for selling A their shares, that difference in value would in theory normally be credited to the share premium account and would then be undistributable. Since this would then deny A any use of B's excess assets there would be little incentive to

---

[205] CA 2006 s.735(3).

[206] CA 2006 s.735(5), (6).

[207] CA 2006 s.656.

[208] CA 2006 s.130(2). Note the absence of any reference to the use of the share premium account to write off the expenses of incorporation, or to pay the premium on redemption of debentures.

[209] CA 2006 s.687(4).

[210] *Cameron v Glenmorangie Distillery Co Ltd* (1896) 23 R. 1092.

carry out takeovers. Accordingly merger relief under the CA 2006 ss.612–613 is permitted, whereby if A acquires 90 per cent[211] or more of B's shares and allots B's shareholders shares in A as consideration, the difference between the nominal value of newly allotted A shares (after the takeover) and the actual value of the B shares need not be credited to the share premium account.[212] The same relief applies where the consideration provided by A is a cancellation of any shares in B not already held by A. This means that the funds not credited to the share premium account could be used to pay dividends.

Group reconstruction relief applies where a wholly owned subsidiary **6–53** ("C") allots its holding company or another subsidiary shares in C in exchange for non-cash assets (including shares) from any company ("D") within a group comprising the holding company and C; and where those new C shares are issued at a premium, that premium in excess of the lower of cost or book value of the assets in D need not be credited to the share premium account.[213]

Further Reading

Paul L. Davis, *Gower and Davies' Principles of Modern Company Law*, 9th edn (London: Sweet and Maxwell, 2012), Chs 12, 21.

David Ereira, "Financial assistance for the acquisition of shares in private companies: finally laying the undead to rest" (2008) 6 B.J.I.B & F.L. 289.

Pieter Leyte, "The Regime of Capital Maintenance pertaining to Public Companies: its Reforms and Alternatives" (2004) 25 B.L.R. 84.

Shivani Singhal, "Financing of leveraged buy-outs" (2009) 29 (12) Comp. Law. 355.

Habib Ullah, "Financial assistance and the EU's second Company Law Directive: here we go again?" (2007) 5 B.J.I.B & F.L. 251.

---

[211] This applies whether company A is acquiring all 90% at once or if it is merely acquiring, say, 40% of B's shares, having purchased 50% of the shares on some previous occasion.
[212] CA 2006 s.612(2).
[213] CA 2006 s.611.

CHAPTER 7

DIVIDENDS AND ACCOUNTS

7–01 In the previous chapter we discussed the important principle of maintenance of capital. Part of this principle is that dividends may only be paid out of distributable profits and not out of capital. It is therefore necessary to define what is meant by "distributable profits". Distributable profits as a term is defined in the Companies Act 2006 ("the CA 2006") at the CA 2006 s.830(2):

> "A company's profits available for **distribution** are its accumulated, **realised profits**, so far as not previously utilised by distribution or **capitalisation**, less its accumulated, **realised losses**, so far as not previously written off in a **reduction** or **reorganisation** of capital duly made."

These terms may be taken in order.

Distribution

7–02 Under the CA 2006 s.829, distribution means any method of handing back the company's assets to the members, whether in cash or in the form of any other assets of the company, with the exception of the following:

- an issue of partly or fully paid bonus shares[1];
- the reduction of share capital (extinction or reduction of shareholders' liability in respect of share capital not fully paid up, or the repayment to shareholders of paid-up share capital)[2];
- the redemption or purchase of any of the company's own shares out of capital (including the proceeds of any new issue of shares) or out of unrealised profits[3] in terms of ss.684–723[4]; and
- a distribution of assets on winding up.[5]

---

[1] CA 2006 s.829(2)(a).
[2] CA 2006 s.829(2)(b).
[3] CA 2006 s.263(2)(c).
[4] This will include shares put into treasury.
[5] CA 2006 s.263(2)(d).

Accumulated

"Accumulated" means that previous years' profits, if they have not **7–03** been used for any other purpose, are amalgamated with the current year's profits and create an overall figure, known as the accumulated profits. The same principle applies to losses. Although historically if a company had suffered losses for several years and then made a profit, it was allowed to distribute that profit in the form of dividend, this is not now possible because of the use of the word "accumulated" in s.830(2) in respect of both profits and losses. In other words, a company must make good its accumulated losses out of subsequent profits before it starts to pay dividends.

Realised profits and realised losses

"Realised profits" and "realised losses" are defined in the CA 2006 **7–04** s.853(4) and (5). They are such profits and losses as:

> (4) ... fall to be treated as realised in accordance with principles generally accepted, at the time when the accounts are prepared, with respect to the determination for accounting purposes of realised profits or losses.
>
> (5) This is without prejudice to—
>
> > (a) the construction of any other expression (where appropriate) by reference to accepted accounting principles or practice, or
> > (b) any specific provision for the treatment of profits or losses of any description as realised.

Profits must actually have arisen by the balance sheet date.[6] When an asset is sold at a profit, the profit will be recorded as a profit on the day of sale. However, if the asset is sold on credit, the profit is not treated as realised until payment has been made. Even if an asset has been upwardly revalued, the increase in value is not treated as a realised profit until the day of sale. Any interim increase in value prior to sale may instead be credited to a revaluation reserve.[7]

If a limited or unlimited company reduces its share capital, whether by solvency statement (if a private company) or by going to court (whether public or private), and as a result a reserve arises out of the reduction of the capital, that reserve is to be treated as a realised profit (and therefore available for distribution), unless there is any contrary provision contained in a court order, the wording of the special resolution for the

---

[6] Small Companies and Groups (Accounts and Directors' Reports) Regulations 2008 (SI 2008/409) Sch.1 Pt 2 Section A para.13(a). There are similar provisions for larger companies known as the Large and Medium-sized Companies and Groups (Accounts and Reports) Regulations 2008 (SI 2008/410). They operate to the same effect but are not included here.

[7] Small Companies and Groups (Accounts and Directors' Reports) Regulations 2008 (SI 2008/409) Sch.1 Pt 2 Section C para.35(1).

reduction of capital, any undertaking given previously to the court, or in the company's articles.[8]

7–05   "Principles generally accepted" is a deliberately vague term which covers the idea that accounting principles change over time and that it would be an impossible task to state exactly what principles would currently be applying. Without such a term there would need to be endless updating of the legislation to take account of new accounting principles as they are gradually adopted. Generally the phrase "principles generally accepted" puts the onus on companies to explain why they are using principles other than those generally agreed to be best practice. By way of limited help, there are two main sets of guidelines, these being Statements of Standard Accounting Practice ("SSAPs"), issued by the Accounting Standards Committee, and Financial Reporting Standards ("FRSs"), issued by the Financial Reporting Council. The FRSs have mostly replaced the SSAPs. When directors are preparing their companies' accounts, they have to state that the accounts have been prepared in accordance with applicable accounting standards (i.e. SSAPs and FRSs) and any departures from those standards must be explained.[9] In *Lloyd Cheyham Co Ltd v Littlejohn Co*[10] the judge stated that SSAPs are "very strong evidence as to what is the proper standard which should be adopted and unless there is some justification, a departure from this will be regarded as constituting a breach of duty."[11] Alternatively, the CA 2006 ss.395(1)(b) and 397 allows individual companies to adopt the accounting principles recommended by the International Accounting Standards Board.[12]

Although a realised profit must genuinely have arisen, unrealised losses do not always require to have arisen at the time of the preparation of the accounts but as a matter of prudent accounting the accounts should take the potential losses into consideration even if the actual losses do not take place for some time, if ever. Or to put it another way, although unrealised profits are not treated as realised profits, unrealised losses will sometimes be treated as realised losses. For example, under the CA 2006 s.841(2) a provision,[13] such as a claim for damages following a negligence claim against the company, is treated as a realised loss. Although the company might ultimately win the case, the company's accounts should in the meantime be drawn up on the assumption that the claim against the company will be successful.

---

[8] CA 2006 s.654 and the Companies (Reduction of Share Capital) Order 2008 (SI 2008/1915) art.3(2).

[9] Small Companies and Groups (Accounts and Directors' Reports) Regulations 2008 (SI 2008/409) Sch.1 Pt 2 Section A para.10(1), (2). Similar provisions apply for larger companies.

[10] *Lloyd Cheyham Co Ltd v Littlejohn Co* [1987] B.C.L.C. 303, per Woolf, J. at 313, d.

[11] This case actually dealt with the liability of auditors, but it nonetheless established the principle of judicial approval of SSAPs.

[12] The same principle applies to group accounts: ss.403(2)(b), 406. Listed companies are expected to comply with IAS board accounts.

[13] A future liability uncertain as to the amount or the date on which it may be due: Small Companies and Groups (Accounts and Directors' Reports) Regulations 2008 (SI 2008/409) Sch.7 Pt 1 reg.12. Similar provisions apply for larger companies.

There is a proviso to the above rule concerning the unrealised losses **7–06** provisions in the CA 2006 s.841(2), namely, that if:

(a) there is a revaluation of all the fixed assets of the company, or all the fixed assets save goodwill, and
(b) the revaluation indicates that an unrealised profit overall in respect of all the revalued fixed assets (with or without goodwill) has been made,
(c) any one fixed asset which—

(i) has in fact diminished in value, and
(ii) whose diminution in value would normally be treated therefore as a provision,

need not have its diminution in value treated as a provision or as a realised loss.

It can therefore be set against the unrealised profits of the rest of the revalued assets.[14] This takes account of the realistic view that if all but one of a company's assets have gone up in value it is not unreasonable for the directors to set off the apparently diminished value of the one fixed asset against the general upwards revaluation.

However, before the directors do this (unless the fixed asset or assets **7–07** have actually been properly revalued by an independent valuer) the directors must have satisfied themselves that even without independent valuation, in their consideration the value of some or all of the current fixed assets is greater than the value that is stated for those assets then stated in the company's accounts.[15] If the directors are satisfied that on their own consideration that the total current value for all the fixed assets at the time of their consideration is greater than the original historic-cost values stated in the accounts, they must say so in a note to the accounts.[16] They must also state that they did genuinely consider the value of the assets in question and that their consideration is treated as a revaluation as at that time.[17] The purpose of this subsection is to ensure that the directors do genuinely apply their mind to the revaluation of the fixed assets if they are to be allowed to offset the realised loss on one fixed asset against the upwards revaluation of some or all of the other fixed assets. As the directors' consideration of their company's assets will no doubt be viewed with a certain scepticism, in practice it may nevertheless be wise to have the company's assets independently valued.

As a further part of the rules on revaluation the CA 2006 s.841(5) states that if:

(i) any fixed asset is revalued, and
(ii) thereby makes an unrealised profit, and

---

[14] CA 2006 s.841(4).
[15] CA 2006 s.841(4)(a), (b)(i).
[16] CA 2006 s.841(4)(b).
[17] CA 2006 s.841(4)(b)(iii).

(iii) on or after the revaluation a sum ("A") is taken off the value of the asset in respect of depreciation for each year (or such other period), and

(vi) prior to the revaluation a sum ("B") is taken off the value of the asset in respect of depreciation,

the difference between A and B is treated as a realised profit.

7–08 The reason for this is that if the depreciation is done on a percentage basis, an asset that was worth, say, £50,000 and was depreciated at a straight line rate of 10 per cent a year would suffer a realised loss of £5,000 each year until such time as it was written off. The figure of £5,000 represents B. If that asset was revalued and now found to be worth £200,000, the annual depreciation charge at 10 per cent would be £20,000. The figure of £20,000 would represent A in the above paragraph. The company might have been able to bear £5,000 a year as part of its losses, but £20,000 might impose an intolerable strain on its profits, and its profits might all be eaten up by the depreciation charge. What the CA 2006 s.841(5) allows the company to do is to treat £20,000 − £5,000 (i.e. A - B) = £15,000 as realised profit. Effectively the company may, if it wishes, continue to use the pre-revaluation depreciation charge.

Following this procedure may in practice suggest an unrealistic view of the company's accounts. Therefore, although the directors are permitted to treat the depreciation charge in this way, there must be a note in the accounts stating why the more usual statutory depreciation method has not been followed.[18]

If for some reason the original value of a fixed asset is not known, the earliest available recorded figure after the asset's acquisition will be deemed to be its acquisition value.[19]

Capitalisation

7–09 This means the conversion of retained and current net profits into bonus shares.

Written off

7–10 This means treated as no longer present in the accounts either as an asset or a liability.

Reduction

7–11 This means reduction in terms of the CA 2006 s.641 or any other permitted reduction such as the redemption or repurchase of a private company's own shares out of capital.

---

[18] Small Companies and Groups (Accounts and Directors' Reports) Regulations 2008 (SI 2008/409) Sch.1 Pt 3 reg.44.
[19] CA 2006 s.842.

Reorganisation

Reorganisation means any valid form of rearrangement of capital such **7–12** as a scheme of arrangement under the CA 2006 s.895 (see Ch.19), or a reorganisation following, for example, a successful minority petition under the CA 2006 s.994.

DISTRIBUTABLE PROFITS

Distributable profits are the net profits (i.e. profits after deduction of all **7–13** overheads) available for the payment of dividends to the members, either in cash or assets of the company (known as "specie"). The dividend is the amount of profit per share that the directors consider appropriate or is required (depending on the articles) to pay out of the company's distributable profits to the shareholders. Not all the profits of a company are usually paid out in dividends: what is not paid out is known as "retained profit" or "undistributed reserves". A prudent company always keeps enough retained profit to meet any unexpected liabilities, but not so much that the members claim that there is a poor income arising from their investment.

Furthermore, no distribution may be made except out of profits available for the purpose.[20] A company may not use the proceeds of an issue of new shares[21] nor use its existing capital to pay dividends, as that offends the principle of capital maintenance. The capital exists for the benefit of those who trade with the company. Directors who knowingly permit the payment of capital as dividend will be personally liable for the loss to the company and potentially to the company's creditors.[22]

Distribution in kind: determination of amount

Special accounting difficulties arise from the decision in *Aveling Bar-* **7–14** *ford Ltd v Perion Ltd*.[23] In this case a company ("A") with no distributable profits sold at an undervalue assets to another company ("B") controlled by A's sole beneficial shareholder. In effect this was an unauthorised return of capital by A and therefore void, though it would have been acceptable if there had been some available distributable profits. Section 845 of the CA 2006 preserves this rule, but it was considered important to deal with the situation where a company with distributable profits makes an intra-group transfer of assets at book

---

[20] CA 2006 s.830(1).
[21] Paying dividends out of capital contributed by new shareholders is known as a "Ponzi" fraud, after an infamous American fraudster of that name who carried out this simple but effective fraud. This was the same type of fraud that the American financier Madoff admitted to carrying out until his arrest in early 2009.
[22] See para.7–27.
[23] *Aveling Barford Ltd v Perion Ltd* [1989] B.C.L.C. 626.

value.[24] As a transfer of an asset at book value may in some circumstances have an element of undervalue, the transaction could possibly constitute an improper distribution of capital. The company would therefore have to have sufficient distributable profits sufficient to cover any potential undervalue. This would mean that the company might simply not carry out the transfer, or the company would need to carry out a revaluation of the assets followed by a sale or a distribution under s.846 of the CA 2006 (described in the next paragraph) so that there could be either a true or a deemed "realised profit" which could be distributed to the relevant group member. The revaluation of the assets could be burdensome and expensive. The way that this matter has been resolved is as follows.

First, the decision in *Aveling Barford* remains in place, so that when a company without distributable profits makes a distribution by way of a transfer of assets at an undervalue, this company will have made an unlawful disposition contrary to s.830(1) or s.831 of the CA 2006.

Secondly, when a company does have distributable profits, the amount of any distribution consisting of or arising from the sale, transfer or other disposition by a company of a non-cash asset to a member of the company is calculated by reference to the value at which that asset is stated in the company's accounts, that being its book value.

Thirdly, if an asset is transferred for consideration not less than its book value, the amount of the distribution is zero,[25] but if the asset is transferred for consideration less than its book value, the amount of the distribution is the difference between the consideration and the book value. There will therefore need to be distributable profits to cover that difference. Those profits must be available for distribution in terms of ss.830 and 831.

Fourthly, s.845(3) indicates that, when assessing whether the company has profits available for distribution, the company may treat any profit that would arise on the disposition of the non-cash asset (in other words, the amount by which the consideration received for the asset exceeds the book value of the asset) as increasing its distributable profits.

Non-cash dividends and revaluations

7-15   Under s.846, if any company is making a distribution of a non-cash asset, or sells or otherwise transfers a non-cash asset thereby generating funds to be used for a distribution, and that non-cash asset has been revalued so that its book value contains an element of unrealised profit (being the difference between its original value and its revalued value),

---

[24] "Book value" is stated at s.845(4)(a) to be the value at which the asset is stated in the accounts, or where it is not stated in the accounts at any amount, as zero. Book value is the historic cost of the asset less any depreciation that has been applied to the value of the asset over time. The book value may therefore be less than the market value. A shareholder who receives a non-cash asset at book value may be receiving assets at an undervalue to their true worth.

[25] CA 2006 s.845(2)(a).

that element of unrealised profit is deemed to be a realised profit[26] and the distribution itself is deemed to be legal—which it might not otherwise be, since normally one cannot distribute any part of an unrealised profit.

Treatment of development expenditure

Research and development expenditure may be dealt with by three **7–16** methods:

(1) The costs may be paid for as they are incurred.

(2) The company may choose to carry forward all the development costs together, and charge them all against the first year of sales. This would mean that:

    (a) the profits for the years while development was taking place would not show the extent of the development costs;

    (b) the first year of production would be unlikely to show much profit for the new product, but (assuming it was successful); and

    (c) subsequent years might show very good profits.

(3) The company may save up all the costs until such time as the product is ready, and then set the costs off over a period of years during the time that the product is selling (also known as "amortisation").

Method (1)

Method (1) would require the development costs to be treated as a **7–17** realised loss as they arose.[27]

Method (2)

Under method (2) the development costs are still treated as a realised **7–18** loss,[28] except where there is an unrealised profit arising out of any revaluation of those costs. The unrealised profit can be set against the realised loss of all the other development costs.[29]

Method (3)

Method (3) is also possible, but there must be special circumstances **7–19** which justify the directors using this method.[30] Those circumstances must be explained in the notes to the accounts.[31]

---

[26] CA 2006 s.846.
[27] CA 2006 s.844(1).
[28] CA 2006 s.844(1)(a), (b).
[29] CA 2006 s.844(2).
[30] CA 2006 s.844(3)(a).
[31] CA 2006 s.844(3)(c).

Relevant accounts

7–20   Dividends may only be paid out of distributable profits, and distributable profits may only be calculated by reference to the company's accounts as prepared by the directors. The Small Companies and Groups (Accounts and Directors' Reports) Regulations 2008 (SI 2008/409) and the Large and Medium-sized Companies and Groups (Accounts and Reports) Regulations 2008 (SI 2008/410) set out extensive rules for the layout of accounts, the notes to the accounts and many other details. In order to calculate the distributable profits, one must refer to the last annual accounts made up to the most recent accounting reference date in respect of which the accounts were prepared[32] and in the case of a public company, tabled at a general meeting,[33] or, in the case of private companies, sent to the members.[34] Except where the company is exempt from the auditing requirements because of its small size[35] the accounts must be audited, and the auditors must indicate that the accounts give a true and fair view of the balance sheet and the profit and loss account.[36]

The auditors must also indicate in their report on the accounts whether the report is "qualified" or not, and must include a reference to any matters to which the auditors wish to draw attention by way of emphasis without qualifying the report, and in particular for determining whether a distribution could be made without contravening the 2006 Act.[37]

Initial accounts

7–21   If the directors wish to declare a final dividend before the end of the company's first accounting reference period, they may refer to its initial accounts,[38] prepared in the same manner as ordinary accounts.[39] If the company is a public company, an auditors' report is required.[40] This must state any material qualification which affects the company's ability to make a distribution and which would make the distribution unlawful as above.[41]

---

[32] CA 2006 ss.836(2), 837(1).
[33] CA 2006 s.437.
[34] CA 2006 s.423.
[35] CA 2006 s.477.
[36] CA 2006 s.495(3).
[37] CA 2006 ss.495(4), 837(4)(a).
[38] CA 2006 s.836(2)(b).
[39] CA 2006 s.839(4).
[40] CA 2006 s.839(2). By exclusion, an auditors' report is not required by a private company.
[41] CA 2006 s.839(5).

Interim accounts

A company may pay a dividend on the basis of interim accounts.[42] **7–22** These do not need to be audited even in the case of public companies as there is no subsection specifically stating the need for auditing. Initial and interim accounts for public companies must be filed with the Registrar of Companies.[43]

DISTRIBUTION RULES FOR PUBLIC LIMITED COMPANIES

Although a private company may not pay a dividend unless its accu- **7–23** mulated realised profits are greater than its accumulated realised losses, there is a further rule for the payment of dividends that applies to public companies, known as the "net assets rule"[44]:

A public company may only make a distribution at any time:

   (a) if at that time the amount of its net assets is not less than the aggregate of its called up share capital and undistributable reserves; and
   (b) if, and to the extent that, the distribution does not reduce the amount of those assets to less than that aggregate.[45]

What this means in practice is that before any distribution is made:

   (a) the net assets must be greater in value than the total of the called-up share capital and the undistributable reserves; and
   (b) the payment of the proposed distribution must not cause the value of the net assets to fall to less than that total of the called-up share capital and the undistributable reserves.

So, for example, if a company has net assets of £100,000, share capital of £50,000 and a share premium account of £10,000, the maximum distributable profits that could be distributed by way of dividend is £100,000 − £50,000 − £10,000 = £40,000. Any payment in excess of £40,000 would cause the net assets to fall below the required aggregate figure of £60,000. The term "undistributable reserves" is defined in the CA 2006 s.831(4) as **7–24** any of the following:

   ● share premium account;
   ● capital redemption reserve;
   ● the amount by which the company's accumulated unrealised profits, less any unrealised profits capitalised into bonus shares,

---

[42] CA 2006 s.838.
[43] CA 2006 ss.838(6), 839(7).
[44] It is also sometimes known as the "full net worth" rule.
[45] CA 2006 s.830(1).

exceed its accumulated unrealised losses, insofar as these have not been written off in a reduction of capital[46]; or

- any other reserve which the company is prohibited from distributing either under statute or under the terms of the company's articles.

A public company may not treat any uncalled share capital as an asset in terms of the net asset rule.[47] There are special distribution rules for investment companies.[48]

Payment of dividends

7–25   It is common for companies to pay final dividends and interim dividends, interim usually being half-yearly. A few companies pay dividends quarterly. How dividends are to be paid is normally stated in the articles, but commonly:

- a full dividend is only payable on a fully paid-up share, partly paid shares attracting only a proportion of the dividend;
- unless the articles say otherwise, there is no automatic right of the members to a dividend. The directors recommend the amount of the dividend to the members at a general meeting. The members then pass an ordinary resolution to approve the level of dividend or reduce it, but not increase it[49];
- if the members insist on there being a dividend which is unjustified, the proper course of action is for the directors to resign[50];
- dividends are payable in cash or in assets of the company[51];
- a dividend is a debt due to the members only once it has been declared. It is a deferred debt in a liquidation, and shareholders will only receive their outstanding dividends once preferential and ordinary creditors have been paid[52];
- dividends may be paid in the form of further shares of the company provided there are sufficient distributable profits to do so, and provided the company's articles permit it[53];
- dividends suffer tax before payment, so that the investor receives his dividend less the tax paid on it, on the investor's behalf, by the company. If he has a high income he may have to pay additional tax later;

---

[46] This effectively is the revaluation reserve.
[47] CA 2006 s.831(5).
[48] CA 2006 ss.832–833.
[49] Private company model articles reg.30(2). There are equivalent provisions for public companies too.
[50] *Re AG (Manchester) Ltd (formerly The Accident Group Ltd) (In Liquidation)*; sub nom. *Official Receiver v Langford, Official Receiver v Watson* [2008] B.C.C. 497; [2008] 1 B.C.L.C. 321.
[51] Private company model articles reg.34.
[52] Insolvency Act 1986 ("the IA 1986") s.74(2)(f).
[53] Private company model articles reg.36.

- interim dividends do not need the approval of the members in general meeting;
- dividends are normally paid by cheque or paid straight into the shareholder's bank account. In the case of joint ownership of a share, the dividend is normally paid to the first-named holder unless there is written notice otherwise[54];
- a shareholder loses the right to his unclaimed dividends after a period of time. For a private company, the model articles state that the period is 12 years[55];
- in order to pay the dividends, companies may close their shareholders' registers for a period of time prior to the payment in order to send out the dividend cheques. Alternatively, dividends will be payable to all those registered as members on the date selected by the directors as the date of payment. The purchase price of the share will reflect whether the share is sold with a due dividend (known as cum) or if it is sold without (ex);
- an investor has a period of up to five years[56] in which to sue for non-payment of a declared dividend.[57]

Members' liability for an improper distribution

Under the CA 2006 s.847(1), any member of a company who receives a **7-26** distribution knowing, or having reasonable grounds for believing, that the payment of the distribution was in contravention of the CA 2006 ss.830–832 is liable to repay it, or in the event of the dividend being of a non-cash asset, is liable to repay the value of the asset.[58] This does not preclude any other liability to repay the distribution which might arise, say, through being a company officer.[59]

A member who receives an improper dividend, even if he does not know or has no reason to believe that the dividend is improper, may still be liable if there is a clause in the articles specifying this, or he has otherwise accepted liability. The CA 2006 ss.847(3) and 852 also catch members who knowingly receive distributions (or other payments that were in essence distributions even if disguised as something else) that are illegal.[60] A purported ratifying resolution in general meeting by the recipients of the dividend cannot validate a payment that is illegal.[61]

---

[54] Private company model articles reg.31.
[55] Private company model articles reg.33.
[56] Prescription and Limitation (Scotland) Act 1973 s.6.
[57] In England the position is six years: Limitation Act 1980 s.5.
[58] CA 2006 s.847(2).
[59] CA 2006 s.847(3).
[60] *Aveling Barford Ltd v Perion Ltd* [1989] B.C.L.C. 626. In this case Aveling Barford Ltd arranged for one of its assets to be transferred at a considerable undervalue to a Perion Ltd, a company wholly owned by the owner of Aveling, thus effectively making an illegal return of capital. See also *It's A Wrap (UK) Ltd (In Liquidation) v Gula* [2006] EWCA Civ 544; [2006] 2 B.C.L.C. 634 for a discussion of the extent to which members must know that their dividend is improper.
[61] *Precisions Dippings Ltd v Precisions Dippings (Marketing) Ltd* [1986] Ch. 447.

Directors' liability for an improper dividend

7–27   Directors who negligently authorise a payment of a dividend which is improper are under common law jointly and severally liable for the sums paid on the grounds of the breach of their fiduciary duty[62] unless they can convince the court under the CA 2006 s.1157 that they acted reasonably and honestly with regard to all the circumstances.[63] Directors who cause the company to be wound up because of unjustified distributions might also find that the liquidator could ask the court under the Insolvency Act 1986 ("the IA 1986") s.218 to refer the matter to the authorities. The directors might then also be disqualified under the Company Directors Disqualification Act 1986.[64]

ACCOUNTING RECORDS

7–28   Under the CA 2006 s.386 every company must keep accounting records that are sufficient to show and explain the company's transactions, that disclose with reasonable accuracy, at any time, the financial position of the company at that time, and that enable the directors to ensure that any balance sheet and profit and loss account complies with the requirements of the CA 2006.

The accounts should record all receipts and expenditure and contain a record of the company's assets and liabilities.[65] Failure by the directors, without good excuse, to keep such records may well interest the HM Revenue and Customs, be potential grounds for disqualification as a company director[66] or be grounds for prosecution.[67] Accounting records must be kept for three years for private companies and for six years for public companies.[68] The records will normally be kept at the company's registered office and are open to inspection by the company's officers at any time.[69] For reasons of commercial confidentiality members normally do not have access to the accounting records except as permitted by the company's articles.[70]

---

[62] *Re Exchange Banking Co (Flitcroft's Case)* (1882) 21 Ch. D. 519 CA; *Bairstow v Queens Moat Houses Plc* [2002] B.C.C. 91; [2001] 2 B.C.L.C. 531; *Allied Carpets Group Plc v Nethercott* [2001] B.C.C. 81.

[63] *Re D'Jan of London Ltd* [1994] B.C.L.C. 561: this case concerns relief under s.1157, and it is not a case dealing with the wrongful payment of dividends.

[64] *Re AG (Manchester) Ltd (formerly The Accident Group Ltd) (In Liquidation)*; sub nom. *Official Receiver v Langford, Official Receiver v Watson* [2008] B.C.C. 497; [2008] 1 B.C.L.C. 321.

[65] CA 2006 s.386(2).

[66] Company Directors Disqualification Act 1986 Sch.1.

[67] CA 2006 s.387.

[68] CA 2006 s.388(4).

[69] CA 2006 s.388(1).

[70] Private company model articles, reg.50, permits access under statute or where authorised by the directors or members following an ordinary resolution.

Preparation and publication of accounts, directors' reports and auditors' reports

The accounts[71] will normally include a balance sheet, made up to the **7–29** end of the company's financial year, and a profit and loss account for the same period.[72] These accounts must give a true and fair view of the company's financial position[73] and the form and content must comply with the provisions of the CA 2006 s.396. Section 396 in turn refers to the Small Companies and Groups (Accounts and Directors' Reports) Regulations 2008[74] and the Large and Medium-sized Companies and Groups (Accounts and Reports) Regulations 2008.[75] It is open to companies to present their accounts in conformity with the International Accounting Standards conventions.[76] It is a requirement of companies whose shares are traded on the Main Market (i.e. listed companies) that their group accounts conform with IAS conventions.[77]

Notes to the accounts may be used to explain any deviations from standard accounting practice. There are extensive provisions requiring the disclosure of information about related undertakings,[78] off-balance sheet arrangements,[79] employee numbers and costs,[80] directors' remuneration[81] and directors' advances, credits and guarantees.[82] There are also extensive provisions for the preparation of group accounts.[83] Listed companies are expected to provide a great deal more by way of explanatory notes than non-listed companies, and listed companies also need to provide cash-flow statements. The details of these provisions are beyond the scope of this book.

The true and fair view

Under the EC Fourth Directive[84] annual accounts are required to give **7–30** a "true and fair view" of the company's assets, liabilities, financial position and profit or loss.[85] Although there is no satisfactory definition of "true and fair view", the consensus seems to be that a true and fair view is that which accountants versed in company accounts consider in

---

[71] CA 2006 s.394 refers to "individual accounts". This means that each company has to prepare its own individual set of accounts. These individual accounts may later be combined as consolidated accounts or group accounts (s.405).

[72] CA 2006 s.396(1).

[73] Companies Act 1985 ("CA 1985") s.226(2).

[74] Small Companies and Groups (Accounts and Directors' Reports) Regulations 2008 (SI 2008/409).

[75] Large and Medium-sized Companies and Groups (Accounts and Reports) Regulations 2008 (SI 2008/410).

[76] CA 2006 s.397.

[77] CA 2006 s.403.

[78] CA 2006 ss.409, 410.

[79] CA 2006 s.410A.

[80] CA 2006 s.411.

[81] CA 2006 s.412.

[82] CA 2006 s.413.

[83] CA 2006 ss.398–408.

[84] Directive 78/855.

[85] CA 2006 s.393(1).

the context of company law to be a true and fair view: some might call this a circular definition. SSAPs[86] and FRSs[87] promulgated by the Accounting Standards Board and its successor the Financial Reporting Council try to maintain common standards in accounting so that accounts should present true and fair views of companies' financial positions.

Accounting reference date

7-31   The accounts are made up to the end of the company's financial year. A company's first financial year is from the date of its incorporation until its accounting reference date—or up to seven days before or after, at the directors' discretion,[88] provided that the period between those two dates may not be less than six months nor greater than 18 months.[89] Although a company may change its accounting reference date, in the absence of any change, a company will have an accounting reference date which ends on the last day of the month in which the anniversary of its incorporation falls.[90] If this date is unsuitable, the company may alter its accounting reference date by sending the Registrar of Companies a Form AA01 altering the date.[91] One reason for altering the date is to make a newly created subsidiary company have the same accounting reference date as its parent company.[92]

A company's subsequent financial years

7-32   A company's subsequent financial year begins with the day that immediately follows the company's last financial year and ends with the last day of its next accounting period (or up to seven days before or after, at the directors' discretion).[93] Normally, an accounting reference period will be 12 months after the end of the previous one, unless altered by using the requisite form, though it may be lessened or increased according to circumstances.[94] No change in the accounting reference date is possible if it means that an accounting reference period will be longer than 18 months[95] or if the company has already extended the accounting reference period within the previous five years (unless the Secretary of State grants a special exemption).[96] This five-year rule will not, however, apply

---

[86] Statements of Standard Accounting Practice.
[87] Financial Reporting Standards.
[88] CA 2006 s.390(2).
[89] CA 2006 s.391(5).
[90] CA 2006 s.391(4).
[91] CA 2006 s.392.
[92] CA 2006 s.390(5). There is an expectation that subsidiaries should have the same accounting reference date as their holding companies, but directors are not obliged to follow this rule if there are good reasons otherwise.
[93] CA 2006 s.390(3).
[94] CA 2006 s.392.
[95] CA 2006 s.392(5).
[96] CA 2006 s.392(3).

if the purpose of the extension is to make the accounting reference dates of parents and subsidiary companies or undertakings coincide[97] or if an administration order under Pt 2 of the IA 1986 is in force.[98]

Auditors

Auditors are required to check that the directors' assessment of the **7–33** accounts is correct. The auditors' report must state whether, in the auditors' opinion, the accounts have been properly prepared in accordance with the relevant accounting framework and the requirements of the CA 2006,[99] and whether a true and fair view has been given of the balance sheet, profit and loss account,[100] and also of the consolidated accounts in the case of a group.[101] The auditors' report must be signed by the auditors[102] and a copy (usually the one signed by the directors) must be lodged with the Registrar of Companies.[103] When the auditors are preparing their report, they are required to investigate:

- whether proper accounting records have been kept[104];
- whether proper returns for the purposes of the audit have been sent from branches of the company which the auditors have not been able to visit[105];
- whether the company's individual accounts are in agreement with the accounting records and returns.[106]

If the auditors form the view that proper accounts and returns have not **7–34** been kept or made, or if the auditors fail to obtain the information and explanations necessary for the preparation of the audit, they must say so in their report on the accounts.[107] They are allowed access to any information about the company and nothing should be withheld from them.[108] They should also disclose in their report any information about directors' earnings, pensions, compensation or loans which might not otherwise be shown in the accounts.[109] If the company is required to prepare a corporate governance statement, the auditors must indicate whether or not it has been prepared.[110] They need to confirm that the information in the directors' report and strategic report is conform with the information in

---

[97] CA 2006 s.392(3)(a).
[98] CA 2006 s.392(3)(b).
[99] CA 2006 s.495(3)(b), (c).
[100] CA 2006 s.495(3)(a)(i), (ii), (b).
[101] CA 2006 s.495(3)(a)(iii).
[102] CA 2006 s.503(1).
[103] CA 2006 ss.444–447.
[104] CA 2006 s.498(1)(a).
[105] CA 2006 s.498(1)(a).
[106] CA 2006 s.498(1)(b).
[107] CA 2006 s.498(2), (3).
[108] CA 2006 ss.499–501.
[109] CA 2006 s.498(4).
[110] CA 2006 s.498A.

the accounts.[111] Auditors are also required to qualify[112] their report if there are matters which might materially affect the ability of the company to make distributions.[113] These matters are stated in the CA 2006 s.836(1), being:

- profits;
- losses;
- assets and liabilities;
- provisions (i.e. depreciation, diminution in value of assets, retentions for liabilities);
- share capital; and
- reserves.[114]

Since August 11, 1994 certain small companies have been exempt from supplying audited accounts. This will be discussed in the context of small companies later in this chapter.

Directors' report

7–35   The directors' report[115] states who the directors are and have been during the financial year,[116] the principal activities of the company and its subsidiaries,[117] and any significant changes from previous years. The directors' report should provide inter alia:

- any changes in the value of the company's assets, directors' shareholdings, political and charitable contributions;
- information concerning the company's acquisition of its own shares or any charges on the company's shares;
- information about the training, employment and advancement of disabled people;
- information about the health, safety and welfare at work of the employees; and
- information about the involvement of employees in the "affairs, policy and performance" of the company.

These provisions may now be found in the Small Companies and Groups (Accounts and Directors' Report) Regulations 2008 (SI 2008/409) Sch.5 or in the Large and Medium-sized Companies and Groups (Accounts and Reports) Regulations 2008 (SI 2008/410) Sch.7.

7–36   A feature of the directors' report not present to the same extent

---

[111] CA 2006 s.496.
[112] "Qualify" in this context means indicate by means of clause or statement in the report that the accounts are unsatisfactory or inadequate for some specified reason. Ideally a company will always wish to have an "unqualified" auditors' report.
[113] CA 2006 s.837(4).
[114] CA 2006 s.836(1).
[115] CA 2006 s.415.
[116] CA 2006 s.216(1)(a).
[117] CA 2006 s.216(1)(b).

previously is the "strategic report".[118] Although no strategic report is needed for small companies[119] it is needed for all other companies with enhanced provisions for quoted companies.[120] The point of the strategic report is to make the company's activities more intelligible to the company's shareholders and creditors. The strategic report is also intended to make members better able to decide if the directors are promoting the success of the company, as is their duty under s.172.[121] Amongst other things, the business review must contain a fair review of the company's business and a description of the principal risks and uncertainties facing the company.[122] The review requires a "balanced and comprehensive" analysis of the development and performance of the company over the financial years, the position of the company at the end of the year, all consistent with the size of the company.[123] Quoted companies are expected also to provide information about the main trends and factors likely to affect the future of the business and information about environmental matters, greenhouse gas emissions, the company's employees, and social and community issues, including information about the company's policies on these matters.[124] Corporate governance matters must be addressed as well.[125]

Although the strategic report only applies to companies other than **7–37** small companies, directors are made potentially liable to the company (and only the company) to compensate it for any loss under s.463 if the directors' report, and within it the strategic report, the directors' remuneration report, and any summary financial statement derived from those reports, are untrue, misleading, or dishonestly concealing a material fact. The director will only be liable if he knew anything in those documents was untrue, misleading or omitted material facts. This so-called "safe harbour", while not universally welcomed, at least restricts the liability of the director only to the company, and not to individual or prospective shareholders, creditors or other third parties. Those people may sue the company itself, but not the director personally.

A requirement for directors of companies other than small companies **7–38** is that in the directors' report there must be a statement that as far as

---

[118] CA 2006 s.414A. This replaces the previous business review and was introduced by the Companies Act 2006 (Strategic Report and Directors' Report) Regulations 2013 (SI 2013/1970).

[119] CA 2006 s.414B.

[120] CA 2006 s.414A. The companies required to do this are indicated at s.385. They comprise companies on the Official List, companies officially listed in an EEA State, companies admitted to dealing on the New York Stock Exchange or Nasdaq. Note that this does not include companies on the Alternative Investment Market. The extra requirements for quoted companies are that the report must provide a description of the company's strategy and business model; to the extent necessary for an understanding of the development, performance and position of the company's business, information on human rights issues, including the company's policy and the effectiveness of that policy; and quantitative information on gender diversity.

[121] CA 2006 s.417(2). See para.9–11 for the effect of s.172.

[122] CA 2006 s.417(3).

[123] CA 2006 s.417(4).

[124] CA 2006 s.417(5)(a), (b).

[125] CA 2006 s.419A.

each director is concerned, he has not held back from the auditor any information of which the auditor ought to be aware, and that he has taken "all the steps" that he ought to have taken as a director to make himself aware of any information of which the auditor ought to be aware and to have ensured that the auditor is aware of that information.[126] The term "all the steps" is explained as requiring the director to make such enquiries of his fellow directors and of the auditors for the purpose of making himself aware of the information the auditor ought to be aware of, such as would be expected of his duty as a director of the company to act with reasonable care, skill and diligence.[127] There are criminal sanctions for the director's failure to do this.[128]

7–39   This provision signalled a profound shift in the law relating to the relationship between directors and auditors. In the past, it was not necessarily seen as unacceptable business practice for a director not to volunteer unwelcome information to an auditor, and if an auditor failed to spot something significant in the accounts, and the company's accounts passed muster, the directors would breathe a sigh of relief. No longer is this acceptable. There is now a positive duty to draw the auditor's attention to problems within the accounts, and a director must positively ask his fellow directors if there is any information that ought to be passed to the auditors, however reluctant the directors might be to do so.

7–40   The directors' report is approved by the board of directors and signed on its behalf by a director or the company secretary.[129] The directors' report, the accounts, the strategic report where needed, the remuneration report if necessary, and the auditors' report (unless the company has taken advantage of any exemption from audit) are sent to all the members, debenture-holders and anyone else entitled to see a copy of the accounts[130] and a signed copy of each document, signed by a director or secretary as far as the directors' report and accounts are concerned and by the auditors for their report, must be sent to the Registrar of Companies.[131] It is common as regards public companies for the directors' report, the accounts and the other reports to be considered at a forthcoming annual general meeting, but in fact they may be tabled and approved at any general meeting.[132] The accounts and reports must be sent out to the members at least 21 days before the meeting.[133] In the case of a private company there is no need to lay the accounts and reports before a general meeting at all, but the copies must have been sent to

---

[126] CA 2006 s.418(2).
[127] CA 2006 s.418.
[128] CA 2006 s.418(5), (6).
[129] CA 2006 s.419(1).
[130] CA 2006 s.423(1). For companies subject to the UK Corporate Governance Code there are further disclosures by audit committees and confirmation by the directors that the annual report and accounts are fair, balanced and intelligible.
[131] CA 2006 ss.441–450. Failure to do so attracts criminal and civil penalties (ss.451–453).
[132] CA 2006 s.437. There are criminal penalties for failure to do so. The accounts and reports must be sent out to the members at least 21 days before the meeting.
[133] CA 2006 s.424(3).

those entitled to receive them no later than the end of the period for filing the accounts and reports with the Registrar or, if earlier, the date on which the company actually delivers the accounts and reports to the Registrar.[134]

The directors of quoted companies must also prepare a directors' **7–41** remuneration report[135] (with both a policy section and an implementation section) duly approved by the board and signed by a director or the company secretary.[136] The members must be given notice of the intention to move the resolution approving the directors' remuneration report at the meeting where the accounts and directors' reports are approved.[137] However, although the directors are obliged to put the remuneration report to the members for their approval[138] the vote has no bearing on the payment of the remuneration to the directors.[139] The directors still get paid. All the members can do is show by their vote how disgruntled they are (or not, as the case may be) with the level of the directors' remuneration.

A quoted company must publish its accounts on its website.[140]

Time for lodging of accounts and reports

As indicated above, all public companies are required to lay the **7–42** accounts and reports before a general meeting.[141] Private companies are not obliged to do so. Neither do dormant companies. Nevertheless, all companies must deliver a signed copy of their accounts and reports to the Registrar of Companies.[142] The time limits for laying and delivering are as follows:

(a) for a private company, nine months after the end of its accounting reference period[143]; and
(b) for a public company, six months after the end of its accounting reference period.[144]

If a company's first accounting reference period is greater than 12 months, the maximum period before laying and delivery is nine (for a private company) or six (for a public) months from the first anniversary of the incorporation of the company[145]; or three months from the end of the accounting reference period,[146] whichever is the later.

---

[134] CA 2006 s.424(2).
[135] CA 2006 s.420. This is discussed in the next chapter at para.8–16.
[136] CA 2006 s.422.
[137] CA 2006 s.439(1).
[138] CA 2006 s.439(4). This is colloquially known as "say on pay".
[139] CA 2006 s.439(5).
[140] CA 2006 s.430.
[141] CA 2006 s.437.
[142] CA 2006 s.441.
[143] CA 2006 s.442(2)(a).
[144] CA 2006 s.442(2)(b).
[145] CA 2006 s.442(3)(a).
[146] CA 2006 s.442(3)(b).

7-43   This means that a private company could have up to 21 months before its first accounts had to be laid and delivered, and a public company could have up to 18 months. Listed companies require the accounts and reports to be laid and delivered within six months of the end of the company's financial year.[147] Failure to lay and deliver the accounts is treated very seriously by the Registrar of Companies and incurs substantial penalties.[148] The directors can also be personally prosecuted for failure to lodge the accounts in time.[149]

Unlimited companies

7-44   In general, unlimited companies do not need to deliver accounts to the Registrar of Companies[150] though the accounts still need to be sent to the members. However, if an unlimited company at any stage during its accounting reference period was:

(a) ... a banking or insurance company or the parent company of a banking or insurance group, or

(b) each of the members of the company is—

(i) a limited company,

(ii) another unlimited company each of whose members is a limited company,

(iii) a Scottish partnership which is not a limited partnership, each of whose members is a limited company, or

(iv) a Scottish partnership which is a limited partnership, each of whose general partners is a limited company.[151]

This is to prevent the potential fraud of liabilities being hidden in unlimited companies which are subsidiaries of larger companies, thus disguising the true extent of the group's liabilities or solvency.

Summary accounts

7-45   Any company may send a summary of its accounts to those members who wish to receive a summary financial statement as opposed to the full accounts and reports.[152] Full accounts are still available to those who wish to have them. As regards quoted companies, the accounts must be available on its website.[153]

---

[147] Admission of Securities to Listing, Ch.12 s.42(e).

[148] CA 2006 ss.451–453.

[149] CA 2006 s.451(1).

[150] CA 2006 s.448(1).

[151] CA 2006 s.448(2), (3).

[152] CA 2006 s.426. This takes account of the considerable expense of sending out full accounts to members, many of whom neither read nor understand the reports and accounts anyway.

[153] CA 2006 s.430.

Small and medium-sized private companies

Private companies that fall into the above two categories must present **7–46** their members with their full accounts in the normal way. However, if the companies are small they do not need to publish at the Registrar of Companies all their accounts: they need only present their accounts in terms of the formats outlined in the Small Companies and Groups (Accounts and Directors' Report) Regulations 2008.[154]

A small company is one that under the CA 2006 s.382(3) in relation to a financial year comes within two or more of the following specifications:

- turnover: not more than £6.5 million;
- balance sheet total: not more than £3.26 million; or
- average number of employees per week: not more than 50.

A small company may publish accounts without any:

- profit and loss account[155];
- business review[156]; or
- remuneration report.[157]

Micro-entity companies

With effect from December 1, 2013 a new type of small company, **7–47** known as a micro-entity, or more colloquially a very small company, is permitted to prepare and published simplified financial statements (profit & loss account; and balance sheet) provided it meets at least two of the following conditions:

- turnover must be not more than £632,000;
- the balance sheet total must be not more than £316,000;
- the average number of employees must be not more than 10.[158]

The micro-entity is only obliged to publish its balance sheet and there is no requirement to publish a directors' report or profit and loss. The advantages of being a micro-entity are that the accounting and disclosure requirements are less onerous than those of a small company and even the accounts for the members require very little by way of detail.[159]

The point of these provisions is to enable companies to retain some **7–48** degree of commercial confidentiality and to save paperwork for the directors.

---

[154] Small Companies and Groups (Accounts and Directors' Report) Regulations 2008 (SI 2008/409).

[155] Small Companies and Groups (Accounts and Directors' Report) Regulations 2008 (SI 2008/409) reg.3.

[156] CA 2007 s.417.

[157] This is because only quoted companies need to produce a remuneration report.

[158] For more details of eligibility see CA 2006 ss.384A and 384B.

[159] For further details see the Small Companies (Micro-Entities' Accounts) Regulations 2013 (SI 2013/3008).

The small company and micro-entity exemption from preparing full accounts is not available to the following if at any stage the company is or was during the financial year to which the accounts relate:

- a public company;
- a banking or insurance company, or a company that is an e-money issuer, a MiFID investment firm or a UCITS management company;
- a company that carries on insurance market activity, or
- or a member of an ineligible group.[160]

An ineligible group is a group of companies with at least one of its members a member of the above list or a body corporate other than a company whose shares are admitted to trading on a regulated market in an EEA State.[161]

Although many companies do take advantage of the opportunity to produce abbreviated accounts, HM Revenue and Customs and any prospective lender or investor may still wish to see full accounts. However, abbreviated accounts do provide some degree of commercial secrecy which some companies may find advantageous.

Small companies exemption from audit

7–49   In addition to the above dispensation for providing full accounts, certain small companies (as defined above) may be exempted from having their accounts audited, although under the CA 2006 s.478 the exemption does not apply to the following types of company:

- public companies;
- banks, insurance companies or a company that is an e-money issuer, a MiFID investment firm or a UCITS management company;
- a company that carries on insurance market activity, or
- special register bodies and employers' associations under the Trade Union and Labour Relations (Consolidation) Act 1992; or
- parent companies or subsidiary undertakings, unless part of a small group and within the terms of the financial limits for small groups at the CA 2006 s.383.

The exemption is also not available to companies whose articles require or whose members demand an audit.[162]

7–50   For a small company[163] to be exempt from audit:

---

[160] CA 2006 s.384(1).
[161] CA 2006 s.384(2).
[162] CA 2006 s.476.
[163] In terms of s.382.

- its turnover must be less than £6.5 million[164];
- its balance sheet total must be more than £3.26 million[165];
- there must be a statement by the directors on the company's balance sheet indicating that the company is exempt from audit[166];
- there must be a statement by the directors on the company's balance sheet confirming that the members have not lodged a notice demanding an audit in terms of the CA 2006 s.476.[167] This subsection states that holders of 10 per cent of the company's issued share capital, or 10 per cent of any class of shares, or in a guarantee company, 10 per cent of the members, may require the company to have the accounts audited. If the members wish to demand an audit, they must give written notice to the company at its registered office at least one month before the end of the company's current financial year[168]; or
- there must be a statement by the directors acknowledging that they are responsible for ensuring that the company keeps proper accounting records and prepares proper accounts.[169]

The purpose of audit exemption is to save cost and inconvenience. However, lenders and investors may still require audited accounts before lending or investing, and investors and creditors in general may be somewhat sceptical of the value of unaudited accounts.

Medium-sized companies

Under the CA 2006 s.465 a company qualifies as medium-sized as **7–51** follows:

- turnover: not more than £25.9 million;
- balance sheet total: not more than £12.9 million; or
- average number of employees per week: not more than 250.

A company does not qualify as a medium-sized company if it is:

- a public company;
- a company that has permission under Part 4 of the Financial Services and Markets Act 2000 to carry on a regulated activity;
- carries on insurance market activity; or
- a member of an ineligible group.[170]

A group is ineligible if any of its members is:

---

[164] CA 2006 s.477(2)(a).
[165] CA 2006 s.477(2)(b).
[166] CA 2006 s.475(1), (2).
[167] CA 2006 s.475(3)(a).
[168] CA 2006 s.476.
[169] CA 2006 s.475(3)(b).
[170] CA 2006 s.467(1).

- a public company;
- a body corporate other than a company whose shares are admitted to trading on a regulated market;
- a person (other than a small company) who has permission under Part 4 of the Financial Services and Markets Act 2000 to carry on a regulated activity;
- a small company that is a bank, an authorised insurance company or a company that is an e-money issuer, a MiFID investment firm or a UCITS management company; or
- a company that carries on insurance market activity.[171]

The Large and Medium-sized Companies and Groups (Accounts and Reports) Regulations 2008[172] apply to the preparation of medium-sized companies' accounts.

Group companies, and small and medium-sized groups

7–52   For the distinction between and the significance of group companies and subsidiaries see Ch.3. The directors of a parent company are obliged to prepare group accounts.[173] Group accounts combine the accounts of a parent company with its subsidiary undertakings' accounts and are known as consolidated accounts. These effectively ignore inter-company transfers which might be used to disguise the unsatisfactory financial position of some of the companies or undertakings within the group. Under the CA 2006 s.400, a parent company is exempt from preparing consolidated accounts in the United Kingdom if the parent company itself is part of a group elsewhere in the European Community and that group's consolidated accounts are drawn up and audited in terms of the provisions of the EC Seventh Directive (83/349).[174] This does not apply, however, if the parent company is listed on a stock exchange anywhere in the European Community.[175] Each subsidiary undertaking's accounts must be included within the consolidated accounts unless the subsidiary undertaking comes within the terms of the exemptions specified in the CA 2006 s.405:

- the inclusion of the subsidiary undertaking's accounts would not be material for the purpose of giving a true and fair view of the consolidated accounts[176];
- the parent company is severely restricted from exercising any rights to the assets or management of the subsidiary

---

[171] CA 2006 s.467(2).
[172] Large and Medium-sized Companies and Groups (Accounts and Reports) Regulations 2008 (SI 2008/410).
[173] CA 2006 s.399.
[174] CA 2006 s.400.
[175] CA 2006 s.400(4).
[176] CA 2006 s.405(2).

undertaking, perhaps because of the terms of a shareholders' agreement[177];

- the information necessary for the preparation of the group accounts could not be obtained from the subsidiary undertaking without excessive time, trouble and expense[178]; and
- the parent company's interest in the subsidiary undertaking is restricted purely to a subsequent resale and at no previous stage have the subsidiary undertaking's accounts been included within the group accounts.[179]

Just as companies can claim exemptions from some of the normal accounts rules requirements if they are small, so small groups may do this as well.

A small group is one that under the CA 2006 s.383(4) in relation to a **7–53** financial year comes within the following specifications:

- aggregate turnover: not more than £6.5 million net or £7.8 million gross;
- aggregate balance sheet total: not more than £3.26 million net or £3.9 million gross; and
- aggregate number of employees: not more than 50.

The Small Companies and Groups (Accounts and Directors' Report) Regulations 2008 apply to the preparation of the accounts of small groups.[180]

A medium-sized group is one that under the CA 2006 s.466(4) in relation to a financial year comes within the following specifications:

- aggregate turnover: not more than £25.9 million net or £31.1 million gross;
- aggregate balance sheet total: not more than £12.9 million net or £15.5 million gross; and
- aggregate number of employees: not more than 250.

The rules that apply to the ineligibility of certain small companies[181] and **7–54** medium-sized companies[182] applies to a small group and a medium-sized group respectively.

The Large and Medium-sized Companies and Groups (Accounts and Reports) Regulations 2008[183] apply to the preparation of medium-sized group accounts.

---

[177] CA 2006 s.405(3)(a).
[178] CA 2006 s.405(3)(b).
[179] CA 2006 s.405(3)(c).
[180] Small Companies and Groups (Accounts and Directors' Report) Regulations 2008 (SI 2008/409).
[181] CA 2006 s.383.
[182] CA 2006 s.467.
[183] Large and Medium-sized Companies and Groups (Accounts and Reports) Regulations 2008 (SI 2008/410).

Dormant companies

7–55   Dormant companies are also referred to in Ch.3. Providing there has been no accounting transaction in the company records a company may be treated as dormant and is not required to have an audit.[184] For each year that the company is dormant the directors will prepare their own accounts showing the company's assets (commonly the capital value of just one or two shares) and stating that there has been no change in the company's financial position.[185] The dormant state of the company stops the moment there is a significant accounting transaction,[186] and thereafter accounts will need to be prepared in the normal manner.

Revision of defective accounts or reports

7–56   If the directors consider that the published accounts or reports are defective, they may voluntarily prepare revised ones, as permitted by the CA 2006 s.454. If, however, the accounts come to the notice of the Secretary of State as to whether the accounts have been properly prepared within the terms of the Companies Acts, he may ask the directors to explain any non-compliance with the terms of the Companies Acts[187] and if necessary apply to court to insist that the accounts be revised.[188] At present the Secretary of State delegates his authority in this matter to the Monitoring Committee of the Financial Reporting Review Panel which, in turn, is part of the Financial Reporting Council which advises on Financial Reporting Standards (FRSs). Understandably companies are sometimes reluctant to revise their accounts, but refusal to do so when asked may invite more attention from the financial press than compliance.

Further Reading

Jennifer Payne, "Recipient liability for unlawful dividends" (2007) 1(Feb) L.M.C.L.Q. 7.

Robins, "Knowledge, ignorance, and unlawful dividends" (2007) 20(3) Insolv. Int. 33.

Rod Edmunds and John Lowry, "The continuing value of relief for directors' breach of duty" (2003) 66(2) M.L.R. 195.

---

[184] CA 1985 s.480.
[185] CA 2006 s.448A.
[186] Accounting transactions that are not significant are such matters as payment of the annual registration fee to the Registrar of Companies, etc. See the CA 2006 s.1169.
[187] CA 2006 s.455.
[188] CA 2006 s.456.

CHAPTER 8

DIRECTORS I: APPOINTMENT, DISMISSAL AND DISQUALIFICATION

THE DEFINITION OF A DIRECTOR

What is a director? A director is a person, either authorised under the **8–01** company's constitution and appointed by one of the methods of appointment outlined under the company's constitution[1] or other legal method, to whom the members have delegated the task of managing the company, usually in terms of the company model articles, reg.3 (or variants thereof) but subject to any special resolutions passed by the members; or a person who is deemed in law to be a director, either because the company has willingly held him out to be a director and/or he is treated as a director by the company even if not formally appointed as such (known as a de facto director); or a shadow director,[2] who causes the company to act according to his instructions, but who does not generally wish to be seen to be managing the company; both of which latter types of director are treated in law as directors, irrespective of their wishes in the matter.[3] Although every company must have at least one director who is a "natural person"[4] (i.e. a human being), any other director does not need to be human, but must have a legal persona: consequently any registered company may be a director; a Scottish partnership may be a director; and a limited liability partnership may be a director. A director need not have any educational or other qualifications. There is now a lower age limit on being a director,[5] in that all directors must be over the age of 16.[6] There is no upper age limit for directors though some companies' articles may impose one. Directors may simultaneously be shareholders and may also be company secretaries. As will be indicated later, certain persons may be forbidden to be

---

[1] See model articles reg.17 (for private companies) and reg.20 for public companies.

[2] Companies Act 2006 ("the CA 2006") s.251.

[3] See also CA 2006 s.250(1): "In the Companies Acts, 'director' includes any person occupying the position of a director, by whatever name called."

[4] CA 2006 s.155(1).

[5] In 2005 there were apparently 431 directors under the age of 16 in England and about 200 under the age of 10. There were no child directors in Scotland.

[6] CA 2006 s.157. It is permissible to appoint a director before the age of 16, but the appointment may not take effect until the appointed person attains that age. If an underage director purports to act as a director without having attained that age, he is potentially liable for any of the penalties for which directors may be liable elsewhere in the Companies Act (s.157(5)).

directors either under the terms of the company's own articles or because they are banned under the Company Directors Disqualification Act 1986 ("the CDDA 1986").

The director's primary task is to manage the company, but a director does not generally have a completely free hand.[7] The members own the company and so retain residual rights in the management: for example, although directors may wish to change the company's name, change of name is a matter normally reserved to members alone,[8] and while the directors may recommend the change, ultimately the decision belongs to the members, though those directors who are members are entitled to vote for their own proposals at general meetings. Generally speaking, the directors deal with the commercial and administrative matters of the company, and the members are content to let them do so, on the grounds of the directors' probable greater expertise, and because members may not themselves wish to bother with the management of the company as long as they receive a reasonable return on their investment. The directors carry out the management usually through meetings of the board of directors, and a well-run company will have monthly board meetings and keep accurate records of all its decisions.[9] Meetings require reasonable notice.[10] Minutes must be kept of those meetings[11]: board minutes may be examined by the auditors or the courts and in the event of impropriety by the directors, minutes indicating who approved which decisions may prove influential in apportioning liability for problems attaching to the company. The minutes are also prima facie evidence of what was decided at the meetings.[12] The absence of minutes may also impugn the credibility of directors' statements of what they assert the board decided.[13] The company's own articles will generally indicate the extent of any delegation of authority extended to directors (subject to any overriding statutory requirements) and where the directors transgress that authority, the directors will be liable.[14]

---

[7] Even in a single member private limited company, where the director has in his capacity as shareholder all the shares, the artificial division between director and shareholder must be maintained and reflected in the company's minutes. Some decisions may still only be taken by that person in his capacity as shareholder and not in his capacity as director—for example, changing the company's articles of association.

[8] CA 2006 s.77.

[9] Directors are expected to keep minutes of their meetings for up to 10 years. See model articles for private companies, reg.15 and the CA 2006 s.248(2).

[10] Board meetings require reasonable notice: a chance encounter at Paddington station does not constitute a proper board meeting: *Barron v Potter* [1914] 1 Ch. 895; 83 L.J. Ch. 646. For the notice for meetings, see the private company model articles reg.9, and for the conduct of directors' meetings generally, see regs 7–16.

[11] CA 2006 s.248.

[12] CA 2006 s.249.

[13] This is particularly true of single member private limited companies: *Re Neptune (Vehicle Washing Equipment) Ltd* [1995] 3 W.L.R. 108; [1995] 3 All E.R. 811.

[14] See also *Mitchell and Hobbs (UK) Ltd v Mill* [1996] 2 B.C.L.C. 102, where a director raised an action without seeking the approval of the board first.

Guinness Plc v Ward and Saunders [1990] All E.R. 652
Three Guinness directors, to whom had been delegated the business of the takeover of Distillers Plc, secretly agreed between themselves that in the event of the successful takeover of Distillers Plc, one of them, Ward, should receive a success fee of 0.2 per cent of the purchase price of Distillers Plc, being £5.2 million. Although this matter should have been referred back for approval to the main board of directors of Guinness, as indicated in Guinness's articles, no such reference was made, and when the takeover duly took place, Ward received his funds. He was held liable as constructive trustee for the money purloined from the company.[15]

As far as outsiders are concerned, where the directors carry out the management of the company, it is on the whole expected that directors will have the authority to carry out the acts that they are doing. Even if that is not the case, under the Companies Act 2006 ("the CA 2006") ss.40 and 41, it is generally safe to assume that even if directors do not have the requisite authority to carry out certain acts, outsiders may still expect that the company will have to accept responsibility for the directors' actions, even if those actions are technically ultra vires the directors' powers under the company's constitution.[16] **8–02**

Directors of listed companies are expected to adhere to the UK Corporate Governance Code, which is issued by the Financial Reporting Council.[17] The UK Corporate Governance Code is the agreed best practice for directors as recommended in the Cadbury, Greenbury, Hampel and other reports. There is no statutory obligation to follow the UK Corporate Governance Code and no penalties—apart from obloquy—for transgression. Directors of companies on AIM are not obliged to adhere to the UK Corporate Governance Code, but directors' willingness to do so is generally observed favourably by the markets.

Apart from attending board meetings and managing the company, directors have various other tasks. They are required to sign the directors' report and accounts,[18] sign various statements about the capital of the company from time to time,[19] consider the interests of the company's **8–03**

---

[15] The managing director, Ernest Saunders, arranged for the conduit of Ward's payment through Switzerland to the USA. As a result of the ensuing Guinness scandal, Ernest Saunders was imprisoned in Ford open prison in Sussex. Once there, he successfully persuaded the Court of Appeal that he was suffering from pre-senile dementia and should be released on compassionate grounds. Following his release he has enjoyed excellent health and made the only known recorded recovery from this sad ailment.

[16] See Ch.4.

[17] Available at the FRC website: *http://www.frc.org.uk* [Accessed April 22, 2014].

[18] CA 2006 s.414.

[19] Such as, for example, purchasing a company's own shares out of capital (CA 2006 s.714) or indicating the likely continued solvency of a company in a members' voluntary winding-up (Insolvency Act 1986 ("the IA 1986") s.89).

employees,[20] return various forms to the Registrar of Companies,[21] convene meetings when required to do so following a requisition by the members to do so[22] or following a serious loss of capital in a public company,[23] produce proposals for approval of creditors in a company voluntary winding up,[24] and many other duties under health and safety legislation, tax and Customs and Excise legislation, etc.[25] Directors also have certain statutory and common law duties to follow which will be examined in detail in the next chapter.

The significance of being a director

8–04   While on the one hand it is normally quite an achievement to become a director of a major listed company, on the other it is surprisingly undemanding to set up a new private company and appoint oneself a director. However, in either situation, a director, once appointed, or, as the case may be, deemed in law to be a director, is potentially liable to the company for any breach of any statutory or common law duty (as discussed in the next chapter). In addition, in the event of the company's insolvency, a liquidator or administrator may apply to the court to make a director compensate the company for any loss occasioned to the company (and thereby its creditors) for misfeasance,[26] fraudulent trading,[27] wrongful trading[28] or phoenix trading.[29] There are also numerous criminal penalties under company law, revenue law, health and safety law, etc. for directors who fail to carry out prescribed tasks. There are extensive disclosure requirements for directors and various prohibitions on loans to directors[30] from the company. For public companies and listed companies there are extra requirements of disclosure, not all of which are welcome to directors. As indicated above, directors of listed companies are expected to follow the UK Corporate Governance Code, and to adhere to the standards expected of good corporate governance. Most trying of all for directors, or putative directors, is that they may be disqualified from acting as a director for up to 15 years if they fall foul of the CDDA 1986.

These collective inconveniences are often palliated by the fact that

---

[20] CA 2006 s.172(1). This is discussed further in the next chapter.

[21] Such as the annual return under the CA 2006 s.854; though in practice this is often a task carried out by company secretaries.

[22] CA 2006 s.303.

[23] CA 2006 s.656.

[24] IA 1986 s.1.

[25] Health and safety regulations are not dealt with in this book. For information on directors' duties in this respect, see *http://www.hse.gov.uk* [Accessed April 22, 2014]. The Institute of Directors also provides much useful information on this area: see *http://www.iod.com/hsguide* [Accessed April 22, 2014].

[26] Misfeasance is a general term for any breach of duty to the company: the IA 1986 s.212.

[27] IA 1986 s.213.

[28] IA 1986 s.214.

[29] IA 1986 s.216.

[30] CA 1985 s.330.

directors of successful companies are on the whole well rewarded for their activities.

Types of directors

There are various different types of director. These are definitions by **8–05** convention, as opposed to definitions with legal status. They are as follows:

- managing director;
- executive director;
- non-executive director;
- chairman of the board of directors;
- nominee directors;
- alternate directors;
- de facto directors;
- shadow directors; and
- "directors" by title but not directors recognised as such in terms of company law.

Managing director

The managing director is sometime known as the CEO (chief executive **8–06** officer). His task is to implement the policies of the company. It is not obligatory to have a managing director. As regards listed companies, the UK Corporate Governance Code A.2.1 disapproves of the managing director also being the chairman. A managing director will normally be an employee of the company. If a company does not have a managing director, but the company holds out a person to be its managing director, even if that person was not actually appointed as such, that person will nevertheless be deemed to be its managing director.[31] A managing director has no specific role in law: in each case it is a question of what powers the company chooses to grant him.[32]

Executive director

An executive director is generally a director who is an employee of the **8–07** company, or even if not actually an employee, fulfils an executive role within the company.

---

[31] *Freeman Lockyer v Buckhurst Park Properties (Mangal) Ltd* [1964] 2 Q.B. 480; [1964] 2 W.L.R. 618.
[32] *Harold Holdsworth Co (Wakefield) Ltd v Caddies* [1955] 1 W.L.R. 352; [1955] 1 All E.R. 725; *Mitchell Hobbs (UK) Ltd v Mill* [1996] 2 B.C.L.C. 102.

Non-executive director

8–08   A non-executive director is generally a director who is not an employee
of the company, but who is appointed for other skills or connections that
he may have.[33] Sometimes a non-executive director is a substantial
shareholder whose interests in the company the other directors would be
wise to consider. The idea behind non-executives is that at least some of
them should bring to the director's role an independence of mind that
allows them to ask questions about the company that otherwise might
not be asked.[34] Although good non-executives are a considerable asset to
a company, sadly it is not unknown for non-executives merely to be the
managing directors' placemen, content to pick up directors' fees[35] for
rubber-stamping the managing director's opinion, contributing little to
the efficacy of the company,[36] and reluctant to prejudice their non-
executives' salary by asking awkward questions. At the same time, some
people who might otherwise be suitable to be non-executives are choosing
not to put themselves forward because of the potential for personal liability in their capacity as directors, as the law makes no distinction in
terms of liability between those working for the company as executives
and those non-executives merely occasionally adding their wisdom to the
board's decisions.

In a large listed company the non-executives should comprise at least
one-half of the board.[37] Non-executives should sit on the remuneration
committees.[38]

It is not unusual for large private companies, or small public companies, to have non-executives on the board, but they cannot avoid
responsibility for their actions on the grounds that they had little idea of
what was going on in their company.[39] Small private companies rarely
have non-executive directors.

Chairman of the board

8–09   Not all companies need a chairman, in smaller companies the more
usual practice being for the managing director to take the chair at any
meeting. But in larger companies it is common for there to be a chairman,
ideally an independent and respected person, who commands the

---

[33] For an interesting article on the role of the NED, see Sharon Constançon, "Independent
Thought", Governance and Compliance, ICSA magazine, May 1, 2013.

[34] The UK Corporate Governance Code A.3.1. requires the board to consider carefully how
independent each non-executive director may be.

[35] At the time of writing, the average fee for a non-executive's services for a listed company
is between £60,000–£80,000 a year.

[36] The late twentieth century corporate buccaneer Tiny Rowland, a famous and feared
tycoon in his time, contemptuously described non-executives as "decorations on the
Christmas tree". More recently, the presence of non-executives on the board of the Royal
Bank of Scotland signally failed to restrain some of the more excitable decisions of its
then managing director, Sir Fred Goodwin.

[37] UK Corporate Governance Code A.3.2. In a listed company there is no sanction for
failure to adhere to this practice.

[38] UK Corporate Governance Code B.2.1.

[39] *Lexi Holdings (In Administration) v Luqman* [2009] EWCA Civ 117.

authority of the members and the other directors, who is able to provide an overview of the company's progress and who ideally is able to stand up to the managing director. His task is to chair meetings, to ensure that meetings are properly run and to ensure that decisions are validly reached.

Under the UK Corporate Governance Code it is recommended that the chairman and managing director should not be the same person. Where they are the same person there will be no-one to call the managing director to account apart from a few intrepid shareholders, and this is not necessarily good for a company. The City has noticed over many years that, with a few notable exceptions, companies tend not to prosper in the long run where too much power is concentrated in the hands of one person. The UK Corporate Governance Code states as follows, in words that should be engraved on every director's heart:

> "There should be a clear division of responsibilities at the head of the company between the running of the board and the executive responsibility for the running of the company's business. No one individual should have unfettered powers of decision."[40]

Nominee director

A nominee director is a director who represents a particular interest in **8–10** the company, such as a bank, a class of shareholders, a trades union representative or some other stakeholder in the company. The difficulty for a nominee director is that strictly speaking he should always consider the interests of the company as a whole as opposed to the interests of the body he represents; and if he strongly dissents with what the company is doing, he may have to resign, thereby further limiting his opportunity for bringing his guidance to the company. Furthermore, being a director, if he is not careful he may be liable for some of the penalties attaching to being a director.

Sometimes a nominee director exists purely for the purpose of establishing residency or as a front for other interests. This will not necessarily protect the nominee director from disqualification proceedings.[41]

De facto director

A de facto[42] director is a person who is treated as a director even **8–11** though he has not been formally appointed as a director, and his name is not on the company's documentation as being a director, or his appointment has not been forwarded to the Registrar of Companies.[43]

---

[40] UK Corporate Governance Code A.2. Chairman and chief executive—Main principle.

[41] *Official Receiver v Vass and Croshaw* [1999] B.C.C. 516. Croshaw was a director of nearly 4,000 companies from his residence in Sark. He took no part in the management of the companies for which he was a director and merely enabled the companies to keep out of the way of the prying eyes of the then DTI.

[42] i.e. "from his deeds".

[43] *Secretary of State for Trade and Industry v Hollier* [2006] EWHC 1804 (Ch.); *Re Mumtaz Properties Ltd* [2011] EWCA Civ 610.

Generally speaking, a de facto director is someone whom the law treats as being a director,[44] because of the way he is treated by the company and by the fact that the company does not do anything to counter the impression that he is authorised to act as a director[45] even if he holds some other title. A dutiful spouse, carrying out a secretarial role within a company, who had not been appointed a director but merely tried to help her director husband, was not held to be a de facto director,[46] but an investor who did take an active role in a company but without being appointed as a director was held to be a de facto director.[47] De facto directors are liable for all the same penalties as ordinary directors if they fail to adhere to the duties expected of directors generally.[48] A person who was a director of a company which was a corporate director of another company was not considered a de facto director of the second company.[49]

8–12   By contrast a shadow director is one, "in accordance with whose directions or instructions the directors of the company are accustomed to act"[50] but who generally does not wish to be seen as a director. The familiar example of this is the person who for nefarious purposes does not wish to be seen to be associated with the company[51] but whose orders the other directors follow. A matter of some concern for banks[52] and "company doctors" who are sent in by banks to sort out companies in difficulties is the extent to which the banks or company doctors could be held to be shadow directors and thus liable for the penalties attaching to directors of companies in liquidation. A prudent bank, or important creditor, however tempted, should present options to a company that is one of its customers without insisting that the company follow its suggestions: any decisions should be taken by the company's directors and not by the bank or creditor.[53] In the important case of *Re Hydroban (Corby) Ltd*[54] the court stated that for a person to be a shadow director that person should have directed the existing directors of the company,[55] that the directors followed that person's directions, and that they were used to following that person's directions. This case also established that the directors of a parent company were not themselves shadow directors, merely the agents of the parent company. Having the right to appoint

---

[44] CA 2006 s.250(1).
[45] In this respect there is an element of holding out under agency law or personal bar under contract. See *Freeman Lockyer v Buckhurst Park Properties (Mangal) Ltd* [1964] 2 Q.B. 480; [1964] 2 W.L.R. 618.
[46] *Re Red Label Fashions Ltd* [1999] B.C.L.C. 308.
[47] *Secretary of State for Trade and Industry v Jones* [1999] B.C.C. 336.
[48] *Primlake Ltd v Matthews Associates* [2006] EWHC 1227 (Ch.).
[49] *Revenue and Customs Commissioners v Holland* [2010] 1 W.L.R. 2793. This case contains a detailed analysis of what is meant by a de facto director.
[50] CA 2006 s.250(2).
[51] Perhaps because he is disqualified or because his professional reputation leaves something to be desired.
[52] For the potential position of banks, see *Re A Company (No.005009 of 1987) Ex p Copp* [1989] B.C.L.C. 13.
[53] See *Re A Company* (1988) 4 B.C.C. 424; *Re Tasbian (No.3) Ltd* [1992] B.C.L.C. 358 CA.
[54] *Re Hydroban (Corby) Ltd* [1994] 2 B.C.L.C. 180.
[55] The case of *Ultraframe (UK) Ltd v Fielding* [2005] EWCH 1638 Ch seems to suggest that by "directors" what is meant is the majority of the directors.

some directors does not necessarily make a person a shadow director.[56] Further views on establishing whether or not someone is a shadow director may be seen in *Secretary of State for Trade and Industry v Deverell*.[57] An additional statutory definition of shadow director may be seen at the CDDA 1986 s.22(5).

The provision of professional advice by, say, an accountant advising the company, will not normally make the accountant a shadow director; but equally advice not given by a professional could still make that person a shadow director.[58]

"Directors" by title but not recognised as such under company law

Sometimes companies will give their senior executives important titles, **8–13** such as "marketing director" or "sales division director" without actually having such executives on the board of directors. In this case the titles carry no significance in terms of company law, and the executives will not be treated as directors in law unless they happen to be de facto or shadow directors as above.

Persons who may not be directors

The following persons may not be directors: **8–14**

- those who have been sequestrated[59];
- those who have been disqualified under the CDDA 1986[60];
- those not permitted to be directors under the terms of the company's articles[61];
- the company's auditor.[62]

Formal appointment as a director

Formal appointment as a director is generally publicised by means of **8–15** signing the registration application, if one of the original directors, or the requisite appointment of director form, if a subsequent director, and insertion in the company's own register of directors.[63] It is common for directors to sign service contracts, but not obligatory to do so. The actual method of appointment will vary from company to company, depending

---

[56] *Kuwait Asia Bank E.C. v National Mutual Life Nominees Ltd* [1990] B.C.L.C. 868.
[57] *Secretary of State for Trade and Industry v Deverell* [2001] Ch. 340.
[58] *Secretary of State for Trade and Industry v Deverell* [2000] Ch. 340; [2000] 2 All E.R. 365; [2000] 2 W.L.R. 907.
[59] CDDA 1986 s.11.
[60] CDDA 1986 s.1.
[61] See the model articles for private companies at reg.18 and for public companies, regs 21, 22.
[62] CA 2006 s.1214.
[63] However, having one's name registered as a director does not necessarily mean that one is a director: *Pow Services Ltd v Clare* [1995] 2 B.C.L.C. 435. A degree of intention to be a director is required, even if (as will be seen later) no great commitment to the post once appointed is necessary. New directors must complete Form AP01 and send it to the Registrar of Companies.

on the company's articles, and may even be by being named as a director
in the company's articles. It is however common that new directors are
appointed at AGMs, or appointed by existing directors but ratified by the
members at the next available AGM. Some companies' articles require
that one third of the directors should be retired and seek reappointment
every three years (as under the old Table A) or such lesser period. There
are less complex procedures within the model articles for public companies.[64] Nonetheless, strictly speaking all such provisions should be
followed to the letter unless the members choose to rewrite them—as
many do. Some companies will specify a minimum or maximum number
of directors. In a public company, directors must be voted for separately
unless there has been a unanimous resolution to the contrary passed
beforehand.[65]

The remuneration of directors

8–16   Directors are entitled to be remunerated[66] and to be reimbursed their
expenses.[67] Although the normal method of remuneration will be through
a salary, salaries attract income tax and national insurance, and sometimes it is therefore more tax-efficient for a director to receive less by way
of salary and more by way of dividend on his shares (particularly if he has
most of the shares in his company) since he does not have to pay national
insurance on dividends. Other methods of rewarding directors are by
means of share option schemes, the exercise price of which is sometimes
geared to the profitability of the company. Further methods of rewarding
directors include the use of employee shares and by issuing redeemable
shares which will be purchased by the company on the fulfilment of
certain criteria. Whatever methods are involved, they must be displayed
in the director's service contract which is available for the members'
inspection[68] and which, if in excess of two years in duration without being
easily terminable by the company, will need to be voted upon before the
company enters into the service contract.[69] Likewise any payments in
consideration of loss of office must be disclosed to and voted upon by the
members.[70] Information about the directors' remuneration must be disclosed in the company's accounts in a separate report attached to the
directors' report and accounts.[71] Under s.439A of CA 2006 the members
of a quoted company are permitted to vote on the directors' remuneration policy indicated in the report. The remuneration policy itself must be
approved by ordinary resolution every three years (known as "say on
pay"); payments for loss of office may only be made if they conform with

---

[64] See the model articles for public companies, regs 21, 22.
[65] CA 2006 s.160. This is to prevent "packages" of directors where the price of some good
directors is the simultaneous appointment of some weaker directors.
[66] Model articles for private companies, reg.19, and for public companies, reg.23.
[67] Model articles for private companies, reg.20, and for public companies, reg.24.
[68] CA 2006 s.228.
[69] CA 2006 s.188.
[70] CA 2006 s.215.
[71] CA 2006 s.439.

that policy or have been specifically approved by the members; any payment not made in accordance with these rules should be held on trust by the director for the company and may be recovered from him or from any other directors who authorised the payments unless they can demonstrate that they were acting honestly and reasonably.[72]

Disclosure of information by directors

Disclosure to the Registrar of Companies

Each company must keep at its own registered office a register of **8–17** directors[73] and as far as directors are concerned, the register will contain details of each director's full name,[74] his business occupation (if any)[75] service address,[76] business occupation, nationality, and date of birth.[77] Any changes must be notified to the Registrar of Companies within 14 days.[78] All directors must be over the age of 16,[79] and each company must have at least one director who is a natural person.[80] Directors no longer need to give lists of their other directorships. The company will maintain a register of directors' residential addresses[81] but this is not available to the public, unlike the other information.[82] On the appointment of a new director, the director must complete the requisite form as provided by the Registrar of Companies and provide the same information as above.[83] The director must also indicate his services address and separately his residential address to the Registrar of Companies.[84] The Registrar will not disclose a director's residential address to the public; he too maintains a protected register of directors' residential addresses and he may only

---

[72] See CA 2006 ss.226A–F. In addition see the Large and Medium-sized Companies and Groups (Accounts and Reports) (Amendment) Regulations 2013 (SI 2013/1981). This amends the Large and Medium-sized Companies and Groups (Accounts and Reports) Regulations 2008 (SI 2008/410) and inserts a new Sch.8 which details the above information and other important changes to remuneration procedure in quoted companies.

[73] CA 2006 s.162(1).

[74] CA 2006 s.163(2) explains that names includes present names, forenames, former names (unless those former names have not been used for over 20 years or were only used under the age of 16), title (if a peer) and any other name by which the director was known for business purposes.

[75] Many directors unhelpfully give their occupation as "company director".

[76] Note that this need not be his residential address: it is acceptable to use his service address, commonly the company's registered office. For the rules relating to disclosure of directors' addresses, see ss.240–246. The director may disclose his residential address if he wishes to do so.

[77] The date of birth is necessary because there may well be more than one person with the same name at the same address, particularly in family companies.

[78] CA 2006 s.167. Use Form CH01.

[79] CA 2006 s.154.

[80] CA 2006 s.155. A "natural person" is a real human being, not another registered company or a Scottish partnership.

[81] CA 2006 s.165.

[82] CA 2006 s.162(2).

[83] Forms AP01 or AP02 (for a corporate director) should be used.

[84] CA 2006 s.163. The company itself must keep a register both of its directors and of its directors' residential addresses, though the addresses will not be open to inspection by the public.

release directors' residential addresses under certain limited circumstances.[85] He may disclose the residential address to certain public authorities authorised by the Secretary of State and to credit reference agencies.[86] He may disclose the address following a court order.[87] He may disclose it himself where the director is refusing to reply to correspondence sent to the service address, subject to due intimation to the director and his company.[88] Where the directors are companies or partnerships, the address of the registered office or principal place of business should be indicated.[89]

Disclosure to the company of any interest in securities

8–18   If a company's securities are traded on a regulated market, and a director or those connected with him buy or sell securities in that company, this fact must be communicated to the relevant investment exchange within four days.[90] The company itself must then make an announcement of the fact via a Regulated Information Service by the end of the following day. Clearly if a director is buying or selling securities in his own company, he probably knows something that others do not. The Model Code for directors restricts directors' opportunities for dealing in their companies' securities to certain specified occasions.[91]

Disclosure of interests of the directors in any contracts entered into by the company

8–19   This matter is dealt with in greater detail in the next chapter. Under the Companies Act 2006 ("the CA 2006") ss.175 and 177 a director is supposed to declare his interest, or proposed interest, in any contract with the company at the next available meeting of the board of directors.

Termination of directorship

The unsatisfactory director

8–20   What may the members do if one or more of their directors is unsatisfactory? If a director loses the confidence of the members, the members have a number of options:

- they may dismiss him by ordinary resolution with special notice under the CA 2006 s.168;

---

[85] CA 2006 ss.242–244 and the Companies (Disclosure of Address) Regulations 2009 (SI 2009/214).
[86] CA 2006 s.243(2). Other people to whom he may disclose the address are such bodies as the Police, the Scottish Ministers, the Financial Services Agency, etc.
[87] CA 2006 s.244.
[88] CA 2006 ss.245, 246.
[89] CA 2006 ss.164, 278.
[90] *FCA Handbook*, Disclosure and transparency rules, 3.1.1–3.1.8.
[91] These are to be found in the Financial Conduct Authority Handbook, Admission of Securities to Listing, Listing Rule 9, Annex 1.

- they may rewrite the company's articles or pass a special resolution to impose controls on that director (assuming the disgruntled members have the votes to command a special resolution)—though this does not of itself terminate his directorship;
- they could "encourage" him to resign;
- they could refuse to re-elect the director when he next stands for re-election as a director; or
- as a last resort the company could be wound up on the just and equitable grounds of Insolvency Act 1986 ("the IA 1986") s.122(1)(g)—though the company would have to be solvent and no better remedy should be available.[92]

Other methods of termination of directorship

These include the following: **8–21**

- death;
- dissolution and striking from the register (if the director is a limited company or a limited liability partnership);
- sequestration (if the director is a Scottish partnership);
- sequestration (if the director is a person);
- expiry of his service contract;
- breach of his service contract by the director himself;
- failure to obtain qualification shares[93];
- mental or physical incapacity[94];
- retirement[95]; and
- disqualification under the CDDA 1986.

The company is required to intimate to the Registrar of Companies the termination of the directorship.[96] Any director forced to leave office before he is contractually due to do so may be entitled to damages for breach of contract by the company—usually amounting to the value of the unexpired portion of his contract. Alternatively they may be able to negotiate a substantial sum if they "promise to go quietly" without speaking to the financial press about the circumstances of their termination. Members are allowed to vote on a pay-off for loss of office,[97] unless the sum involved is less than £200.[98] An artful way to avoid a

---

[92] IA 1986 s.125(2).

[93] This would have to be indicated in the articles. Qualification shares are rare nowadays, but it used to be common for directors to have to buy a minimum number of shares in the company of which they were proposing to become a director, such shares being known as qualification shares. If the director did not buy the shares, he was not supposed to practise as a director of that company.

[94] Model articles for private companies, reg.18(d) (for public companies, see reg.22(d)).

[95] Model articles for private companies, reg.18(f) (for public companies, see reg.22(f)).

[96] CA 2006 s.167(1)(a). Companies should also tell the Registrar of any changes to the particulars relating to their directors. See Form TH01.

[97] CA 2006 ss.215–217.

[98] CA 2006 s.221.

potentially embarrassing vote is to provide in advance for the director's compensation by specifying it in his service contract, because payments which are made in order to discharge some legal obligation do not require members' approval.[99] For the directors of quoted companies, there are special rules to be found in CA 2006 ss.226A–226F which cover payments for loss of office in connection with a takeover, such payments only to be made within the terms of the directors' remuneration policy or separately approved by the members.

Dismissal of a director under Companies Act 2006 s.168

8–22   Under the CA 2006 s.168 a director may be dismissed by means of an ordinary resolution provided special notice of 28 days has been given to the company of the intention that the resolution be moved at the forth-coming meeting where the resolution will be moved. The idea behind the 28 days is to allow the insertion within the notice of the next general meeting of the words "special notice"[100] in front of the wording of the resolution for dismissal. The words "special notice" are supposed to draw members' attention to the significance of the matter.[101] The 28 days notice also allows the director in question time to prepare a statement con-cerning his dismissal. This statement must be of reasonable length and the director may insist that it be circulated to the members before the meeting[102] (unless it is received too late to be so) and if it is not sent out as it should be, it may be read out at the meeting itself.[103] The director may in any event insist on speaking at the meeting.[104] This process is some-times known as the director's right of protest. Copies of the statement need not be circulated nor read out at the meeting if the company, or any person referred to in the statement, persuades the court that the director's rights conferred by s.169 are being abused.[105] The intention behind the legislation is to allow a director to bring to members' attention any matters which the director feels they ought to know about and for which he may be being dismissed. It is arguable how beneficial a solution it is to have this protection, since if the members are determined to remove the director, his protests may carry little weight.

Even though private companies may pass nearly all their resolutions by written resolution, it is not permissible to dismiss a director by means of a written resolution.[106]

---

[99] CA 2006 s.220.

[100] Alternatively, the notice of the general meeting may say, "Special notice has been received by the company of the following resolution", followed by the wording of the s.168 resolution.

[101] Given that most private shareholders rarely even read any notices of general meetings and even more rarely vote, it is debatable how useful this provision is.

[102] CA 2006 s.169(3).

[103] CA 2006 s.169(4).

[104] CA 2006 s.169(2).

[105] CA 2006 s.169(5).

[106] CA 2006 s.288(2)(a).

DISQUALIFICATION OF DIRECTORS UNDER THE COMPANY DIRECTORS DISQUALIFICATION ACT 1986

The law relating to disqualification of directors was consolidated in 1986 **8–23**
as part of the various reforms to company law which were designed to
encourage more responsible behaviour by directors. Not only could
directors be found liable to their insolvent companies in terms of the IA
1986 ss.212–216, but they could also be banned from being directors for
up to 15 years. The purpose of this was primarily to protect the public as
opposed to punishing the directors, although it undoubtedly has that
effect as well. The Registrar of Companies has a register of disqualified
directors and the Insolvency Service even has a hotline for those who
wish to phone in to complain that a disqualified director is still conducting business through a company. In 2012–13 a total of 1,039 directors were disqualified. Of these disqualifications the greater proportion
were of directors who had provided a disqualification undertaking,
(explained shortly) the next most common being those who were convicted of some offence in connection with their company or its
insolvency.

Disqualifying directors has thrown up some difficulties: the disqualification of a director who controls many businesses, and who was
himself the victim of unfortunate circumstances, may result in substantial
job losses for his employees as his businesses collapse without him to
manage them. Unscrupulous directors who have been disqualified merely
get their spouses to run their businesses for them, and if ultimately found
to be shadow directors commonly ensure that they are bankrupt anyway,
so that the law holds few terrors for them. Directors, who were directors
in name only, who took no part in management and received no remuneration for their directorships, have sometimes been disqualified, on the
grounds that by accepting the position of director, they have to accept the
responsibilities that come with directorship, even if they have not exercised any directorial role and never sought to do so.[107] It was no excuse
for a director, least of all a chairman, to claim ignorance of accounting
and to have relied on fellow directors, more versed in accounting matters
than he, to deal with financial matters, when it would have been apparent
to the director, a man of some business experience, that those financial
matters were not being properly handled.[108]

Disqualification orders in general

There is a common misconception that members of a company may **8–24**
disqualify directors: this is not the case.[109] Only the courts may disqualify
directors, and they will do this on a discretionary basis unless they are

---

[107] *Re Park House Properties Ltd* [1997] 2 B.C.L.C. 530.
[108] *Secretary of State for Trade and Industry v Bairstow* [2004] All E.R. (D.) 333 (Jul) Ch.D.
See also *Re Barings Plc (No.5)* [1999] 1 B.C.L.C. 433.
[109] Only the court may disqualify a director, but under s.16 the Secretary of State, a
liquidator, a member or creditor may apply to the court for the director to be disqualified because of his transgression of the CDDA 1986 ss.2–4.

obliged to do this in terms of s.6 (unfitness of directors of insolvent companies) of the Company Directors Disqualification Act 1986 ("the CDDA 1986"). Furthermore, just because a director of a solvent company breaches some duty or acts negligently does not mean that he will be disqualified. In order to give some degree of protection to directors, and not to have the converse effect of driving entrepreneurs from the United Kingdom, directors will only be disqualified by the courts under the restricted circumstances indicated in the CDDA 1986.

The legislation applies both to company directors and to insolvency practitioners, (for the purposes of the rest of this chapter known collectively as "directors") and prohibits such persons from being involved in any company in any way as directors, promoters, managers or founders of a company except with leave of the court.[110] The maximum period of disqualification is 15 years, but if a director is disqualified in respect of more than one company, the period of disqualification is concurrent. It is common for a director to give an undertaking to the Secretary of State, known as a disqualification undertaking, whereby as a form of fast-track procedure a director undertakes to accept his disqualification on agreed terms. This saves unnecessary dispute and expense in the courts, may cause the period of disqualification to be lessened, and lets it both start and finish earlier.[111] The court has power to vary the disqualification undertaking if necessary.[112] Even companies which are directors may be disqualified.[113]

The grounds for a disqualification order

8–25   Under the CDDA 1986 s.2 a disqualification order may (as opposed to "shall") be made on the application of the Secretary of State[114] where the director has been convicted of an indictable offence in connection with the promotion, formation, management, liquidation, striking off or

---

[110] CDDA 1986 s.1. "Directors" includes bodies corporate (CDDA 1986 s.14; and see *Official Receiver v Brady* [1999] B.C.C. 258). "Director" includes de facto directors and shadow directors. For de facto directors, see *Secretary of State for Trade and Industry v Hall* [2009] B.C.C. 190. For shadow directors, see *Secretary of State for Trade and Industry v Deverell* [2001] Ch. 340; [2000] 2 W.L.R. 907; [2000] 2 All E.R. 365; [2000] 2 B.C.L.C. 133; [2000] B.C.C. 1057.

[111] CDDA 1986 s.1A.

[112] CDDA 1986 s.8A. This is generally only when circumstances have arisen since the undertaking was given which were either unforeseen or not intended to be covered by the undertaking: *Secretary of State for Trade and Industry v Jonkler* [2006] 2 All E.R. 902 at [39]–[40].

[113] *Official Receiver v Brady* [1999] B.C.C. 258.

[114] CDDA 1986 s.8. Note that a director of a Scottish company should have the disqualification proceedings raised against him in Scotland, but that his conduct as regards his Scottish company could nevertheless be mentioned in respect of any concurrent proceedings against him as regards any English companies of which he might be a director because of ss.6, 7 (*Secretary of State for Trade and Industry v Forsyth*; sub nom. *Helene Plc (In Liquidation), Re Barry Artist Ltd, Re Secretary of State for Trade and Industry v Forsyth* [2000] 2 B.C.L.C. 249.

receivership[115] of a company. This section has been used for such matters as insider dealing,[116] fraud,[117] or carrying on a business for which the director lacked the appropriate authority.[118]

Under s.3 a director may be disqualified for persistent breaches of companies legislation with regard to the delivery of documents or accounts to the Registrar of Companies, such as repeated failure to send in proper returns.[119] "Persistent" here means at least three defaults in the previous five years.[120]

Under s.4 a director may be disqualified for fraud in winding up[121] or of a breach of duty to a company in liquidation or receivership.[122]

Under s.5 a director may be disqualified on summary conviction for **8–26** any failure to make proper returns of company documentation (such as sending in certain documentation to the Registrar of Companies), such failure being established by at least three defaults in the previous five years.[123] The differences between s.3 and s.5 are that under s.5 the judge may impose a disqualification order at the same time as convicting the director for his failure whereas under s.3 a judge may impose a disqualification order without an accompanying conviction. The maximum duration of the disqualification under both sections is five years.[124]

Under s.9A, which was introduced by the Enterprise Act 2002, where a director has committed a breach of competition law, and is also unfit (as defined in terms of s.6 to be discussed below, but excepting therefrom consideration of Sch.1 to the CDDA 1986 in order that the grounds for unfitness should be specifically related to the breach of competition law) to be a director, he may be disqualified as a director and receive a "competition disqualification order". He may alternatively give an undertaking to be disqualified under s.9B. Breach of competition law involves such matters as preventing, restricting or distorting competition or abusing a dominant economic position.[125]

Under s.10 where a director has been found liable by the court to make a contribution to his insolvent company's assets in terms of the IA 1986 s.213 (fraudulent trading) or s.214 (wrongful trading), the court may, at the same time, disqualify the director.

---

[115] And in England and Wales, administrative receivership.

[116] *R. v Goodman* [1994] 1 B.C.L.C. 349.

[117] *R. v Creggy* [2008] Bus. L.R. 1556; [2008] 3 All E.R. 91; [2008] B.C.C. 323; [2008] 1 B.C.L.C. 625.

[118] *R. v Georgiou* (1988) 4 B.C.C. 322. Georgiou carried out an insurance business through a company without having complied with the requirements of the Insurance Companies Act 1982.

[119] *Re Arctic Engineering Ltd* [1986] 1 W.L.R. 686; [1986] 2 All E.R. 346; [1986] B.C.L.C. 253.

[120] CDDA 1986 s.3(2). The defaults in question relate to default orders under the CA 2006 ss.442, 1113 and IA 1986 ss.41, 170.

[121] Following his guilt if liable for the crime of fraudulent trading under CA 2006 s.993 (and applies whether or not he has been convicted).

[122] CDDA 1986 s.4(1)(b).

[123] CDDA 1986 s.5.

[124] CDDA 1986 ss.3(5), 5(5).

[125] CDDA 1986 s.9A(4).

Bankrupts are not permitted to be directors, or directly or indirectly involved in the promotion, formation or management of a company except with leave of the court.[126] If they do so, they are liable to prosecution,[127] and indeed to further disqualification.

The unfit director of an insolvent company

8-27   Section 6 obliges the court to disqualify a director for "unfitness" of a company which has become insolvent.[128] This is possibly the most problematic of the disqualification criteria and has led to a great deal of case law. The word "insolvent" in this context means not only insolvent liquidation and administration, as might be expected, but also receivership.[129] In order to catch shadow directors the legislation specifically applies to them as well.[130] The minimum period of disqualification is two years and the maximum 15.[131]

Who may apply for a disqualification order for an unfit director?

8-28   The Secretary of State may apply for a disqualification order for an unfit director of an insolvent company[132] if it appears to him, on the basis of information received by him from the company's liquidator, administrator, receiver or in England the Official Receiver[133] where it is "expedient in the public interest"[134] to do so.[135] This must be done within two years of the date of the director's company's insolvency[136] unless leave has been granted by the court otherwise. Leave is less likely to be granted where the delay is not the fault of the director or where there is a risk of prejudice to the director, although in each case the public interest will still have to be taken into account.[137] Even if the action for disqualification has been raised in time, the Secretary of State must still be seen to prosecute the case with some degree of urgency, since in the intervening period until the decision on disqualification the director cannot practise as a director. A total delay of four and a half years was

---

[126] CDDA 1986 s.11.
[127] CDDA 1986 s.12. *R. v Brockley* [1994] 1 B.C.L.C. 606.
[128] The previous sections apply to both solvent and insolvent companies.
[129] CDDA 1986 s.6(2).
[130] CDDA 1986 s.6(3C). See also s.22(5).
[131] CDDA 1986 s.6(4). This is the case even if the director's behaviour has improved in the meantime: *Re Grayan Building Services Ltd* [1995] Ch. 241; *Re Migration Services International Ltd* [2000] 1 B.C.L.C. 666.
[132] CDDA 1986 s.8.
[133] CDDA 1986 s.7(3).
[134] CDDA 1986 s.7(1). *Secretary of State for Trade and Industry v Lovat*, 1996 S.C. 32; 1997 S.L.T. 124.
[135] For the process of obtaining the information, see the Insolvent Companies (Reports on Conduct of Directors) (Scotland) Rules 1996 (SI 1996/1909). The Deregulation Bill cl.588 and Pt 4 Sch.5, propose to allow the Secretary of State to make enquiries of third parties (perhaps affected by the directors' conduct) and indeed from the directors themselves. This has led to possible concerns that a director might incriminate himself.
[136] CDDA 1986 s.7(2).
[137] *Re New Technology Systems Ltd* [1997] B.C.C. 810; *Re Polly Peck International Plc (No.2)* [1994] 1 B.C.L.C. 574; [1993] B.C.C. 890.

held to be unacceptable under human rights legislation.[138] Members and creditors may also apply for a director's disqualification for this misconduct under the terms of ss.2–4. Such applications are available under s.16 and the director must be given 10 days' notice of the application.[139]

The Secretary of State may accept an undertaking[140] by the director to be disqualified if the Secretary of State believes this to be in the public interest.[141] As an undertaking involves an admission of guilt, and saves valuable court time, since the director's behaviour does not need to be rehearsed in court, the period of disqualification may reflect the director's acknowledgment of his behaviour.[142]

The Secretary of State may also apply for a disqualification order on the strength of a report or other documentation following a BIS inspection.[143] The two year rule does not apply in this case, generally because BIS reports take so long to prepare. The Secretary of State may also accept a disqualification undertaking by a director who is featured in the report or other documentation.[144]

How unfit is "unfit"?

As a guide to the degree of unfitness required for disqualification, s.9 **8–29** refers to Sch.1 Pt I for general unfitness as regards the directorship of any company and Pt II for unfitness as a director of an insolvent company. The reason for the two matters is that while unfitness primarily refers to the directorship of insolvent companies, a director might simultaneously be a director of an insolvent company and of a solvent company and might need to be disqualified from the solvent company too. Part 1 refers primarily to breaches of duty to the company, failure to keep proper records and the failure to send in returns to the Registrar of Companies. Part II refers to the extent of the director's responsibility for the company's insolvency, his responsibility for his company's failure to provide services or goods which have been paid for, his responsibility for any unfair preferences or gratuitous alienations made by the company, his failure to call creditors' meetings in a creditors' voluntary winding up and various failures to co-operate or provide information to liquidators, administrators, receivers, etc.

As all this gives wide scope for argument, the courts have tried to lay down guidelines as to the degree of unfitness which qualifies as worthy of disqualification. In principle, unfitness contains some degree of lack of

---

[138] *EDC v United Kingdom* [1998] B.C.C. 370 ECHR.

[139] For the 10-day period of notice required therein, which is directory rather than mandatory, see *Secretary of State for Trade and Industry v Langridge*; sub nom. *Re Cedac Ltd, R. v Secretary of State for Trade and Industry Ex p Langridge* [1991] Ch. 402; [1991] 2 W.L.R. 1343; [1991] 3 All E.R. 591; [1991] B.C.C. 148; [1991] B.C.L.C. 543; *Secretary of State for Trade and Industry v Lovat*, 1996 S.C. 32; 1997 S.L.T. 124.

[140] These are available under the CDDA 1986 s.1A.

[141] CDDA 1986 s.7(2A).

[142] *R. v Randhawa and Randhawa* [2008] EWCA Crim 2599.

[143] CDDA 1986 s.8(1); *Secretary of State for Business Enterprise and Regulatory Reform v Sullman* [2008] EWHC 3179 (Ch).

[144] CDDA 1986 s.8(2A).

probity or negligence. The courts appear unwilling to condemn mere commercial misjudgement or minor incompetence,[145] but a breach of commercial morality or gross incompetence, such that the director would be a danger to the public, would be unacceptable.[146] In *Secretary of State for Trade and Industry v Griffiths*[147] the Court of Appeal recommended the use of common sense combined with a practical and flexible approach to case management in ascertaining the degree of unfitness. Matters that the court should take into consideration are the fact that the purpose of disqualification is to protect the public, to serve as a deterrent to other directors and to ensure that directors generally recognise that being a director brings inescapable personal responsibilities.

8–30   Examples where disqualification orders have been granted on the grounds of unfitness (and there are many) include the following:

- causing the company to trade while insolvent, and in particular, not paying some creditors (such as the Inland Revenue) and using the money for those creditors to pay other less pressing creditors[148];

- drawing excessive salaries at a time when the company could not afford it[149];

- paying no attention to a company's activities and in particular not ensuring that it properly paid its taxes[150];

- aggressive sales techniques which deprived consumers of their normal rights[151];

- paying unjustified dividends in the period leading to the insolvency of the company[152];

- failure on the part of a director of a major company to monitor his undermanagers[153];

- not standing up to dominant directors[154]; and

- lack of co-operation with the insolvency practitioner.[155]

---

[145] Browne-Wilkinson V.C. in *Re Lo-Line Electric Motors Ltd* [1988] Ch. 477 at 479.

[146] Hoffmann J. (as he then was) in *Re Dawson Print Group Ltd* (1987) 3 B.C.C. 322 at 324; *Re Barings Plc (Secretary of State v Baker (No.5))* [1999] 1 B.C.L.C. 433, affirmed [2000] 1 B.C.L.C. 523 CA.

[147] *Secretary of State for Trade and Industry v Griffiths* [1998] 2 B.C.L.C. 646 CA.

[148] *Secretary of State v Laing* [1996] 2 B.C.L.C. 324; *Secretary of State for Trade and Industry v Creegan* [2002] 1 B.C.L.C. 99.

[149] *Secretary of State v Lubrani* [1997] 2 B.C.L.C. 115.

[150] *Secretary of State v Reza* [2013] CSOH 86.

[151] *Official Receiver v Wild* [2012] EWHC 4279 (Ch).

[152] *Re AG (Manchester) Ltd (formerly The Accident Group Ltd) (In Liquidation)*; sub nom. *Official Receiver v Langford, Official Receiver v Watson* [2008] B.C.C. 497; [2008] 1 B.C.L.C. 321.

[153] *Secretary of State v Baker (No.6)* [2001] B.C.C. 273; [2000] 1 B.C.L.C. 523. The undermanager in question was Nick Leeson, whose unwise trading led to the collapse of Barings Bank.

[154] *Re Westmid Packing Services Ltd* [1998] 2 All E.R. 124.

[155] *Secretary of State for Trade and Industry v Gerard*, 2008 S.C. 409.

For how long should the director be disqualified?

Broadly speaking the courts have adopted the guidelines set out in *Re* **8–31**
Sevenoaks Stationers (Retail) Ltd[156] whereby an order of two to five years
is appropriate for first cases involving negligence and incompetence,[157] six
to 10 years is for cases involving misappropriating assets and prejudicing
creditors,[158] and 11 to 15 years is for very serious cases and repeat offences.

Application for leave

It is possible for the courts to exercise their discretion under CDDA **8–32**
1986 s.17 to lift the disqualification order or disqualification undertaking
in respect of one or more particular companies, usually because the
company might collapse without the director present[159] or because there
is no danger to the public.[160] The courts may impose a condition: for
example in *Secretary of State for Trade and Industry v Rosenfield*[161] the
courts permitted Rosenfield to act as a director provided the company
produced quarterly accounts and that someone with financial expertise
was appointed to the board of directors. In general leave is not lightly
given, particularly where fraud is concerned.[162]

Consequences of breach of disqualification order

If a disqualified director continues to act as a director, or as a de facto **8–33**
or shadow director, in addition to any criminal consequences under the
CDDA 1986 s.13 he may be held jointly and severally personally liable,
along with the company and with anyone who is involved with him in the
company while knowing that the disqualified director is disqualified.[163]
Any person acting on the disqualified director's instructions is presumed
to have been aware that he knew that the director was disqualified. This
provision is designed to catch, in particular, spouses or other business
partners who act at the disqualified director's bidding.

It would be pleasant to think that disqualification acts as a deterrent.
Sadly the incidence of cases such as *Re Moorgate Metals Ltd*[164] suggests
that it does not. In this case, a former bankrupt teamed up with a thrice
bankrupted and undischarged scrap metal merchant to run a scrap metal

---

[156] *Re Sevenoaks Stationers (Retail) Ltd* [1991] B.C.L.C. 325 CA.
[157] *Secretary of State for Trade and Industry v McTighe (No.2)* [1997] B.C.C. 224.
[158] *Secretary of State for Business, Innovation and Skills v Bloch* [2013] CSOH 57; 2013
G.W.D. 13-275; *Secretary of State for Business Innovation and Skills v Din* [2013] CSOH
98; 2013 G.W.D. 22-429.
[159] *Re Chartmore Ltd* [1990] B.C.L.C. 673; *Re Cargo Agency Ltd* [1992] B.C.L.C. 686; *Re
Gibson Davies Ltd* [1995] B.C.C. 11.
[160] *Re Portland Place (Historic House) Ltd* [2012] EWHC 4199 (Ch); [2013] W.T.L.R. 1049.
[161] *Secretary of State for Trade and Industry v Rosenfield* [1999] B.C.C. 413.
[162] *Re Morija Plc*; sub nom. *Kluk v Secretary of State for Business Enterprise and Regulatory
Reform* [2008] 2 B.C.L.C. 313. For the occasions when leave should be given, see *Re
Barings Plc (No.3)* [2000] 1 W.L.R 634 per Scott VC.
[163] CDDA 1986 s.15. *Inland Revenue Commissioners v McEntaggart* [2006] 1 B.C.L.C. 476,
Re Prestige Grindings Ltd, Sharma v Yardley [2006] 1 B.C.L.C. 440.
[164] *Re Moorgate Metals Ltd* [1995] B.C.L.C. 503; [1995] B.C.C. 143.

business. The scrap metal merchant persuaded his wife to act as a director but to his order, and they all ran a completely hopeless business with bogus accounts. What little money the business made in its short existence was spent on large salaries, bigger cars and expensive holidays in France. Both directors were disqualified for further periods. A similarly depressing case is *Wirecard Bank AG v Scott*,[165] a company set up for the express purpose of swindling innocent customers into buying non-existent tickets online for the Beijing Olympics in 2008. It featured at least one director who had been previously disqualified.

8–34 If an honest director realises that the company with which he is involved may collapse and that he may be disqualified, he should resign where possible, and he should also ensure that his opposition to any improper or foolish decisions is noted in the board minutes. By such means in *Re CS Holidays Ltd*[166] a prudent director was able to protect himself while all his fellow directors were disqualified.

Further Reading

Chris Noonan and Susan Watson, "Examining company directors through the lens of de facto directorship" (2008) J.B.L. 587.

Chris Noonan and Susan Watson, "The nature of shadow directorship: ad hoc statutory intervention or core company law principle?" (2006) J.B.L. 763.

Donna McKenzie Skene, "Director disqualification" (2008) 94(Jun) Bus. L.B. 4.

Directors' Disqualification & Insolvency Restrictions 3rd edn (London: Sweet & Maxwell, 2009).

Palmer's Company Law, Ch.8, Directors Disqualification Orders and Undertakings.

---

[165] [2010] EWHC 451 (QB).
[166] Also known as *Re A Company (No.004803 of 1996)* [1997] 1 W.L.R. 407.

CHAPTER 9

DIRECTORS II: POWERS, RIGHTS, DUTIES, LIABILITIES AND OTHER OBLIGATIONS

DIRECTORS' POWERS AND RIGHTS

The model articles for a private company, reg.3 states as follows: **9–01**

> "Subject to the articles, the directors are responsible for the management of the company's business, for which purpose they may exercise all the powers of the company."

This wide authority is constrained by reg.4 which states:

> "(1) The shareholders may, by special resolution, direct the directors to take, or refrain from taking, specified action.
> (2) No such special resolution invalidates anything which the directors have done before the passing of the resolution."[1]

Within these parameters, directors have a free hand as regards their powers.[2] This is convenient for the members, who often are not interested in managing the company and merely seek a return on their investment, and handy for the directors, who would find it inconvenient to obtain members' approval for everything of a commercial, administrative or otherwise managerial nature that the directors wish to do. Some companies' articles may be more restrictive than the above regulations allow. For example, many companies will have a regulation in their articles stating that before the directors make the company borrow more than a certain amount the directors must seek the members' approval. In addition, statute imposes limitation on directors, such as preventing them altering the articles or the company's name or capital, these being matters reserved to the members. The members may choose to impose restrictions on directors by special resolution in an attempt to limit directors' exercise of their powers, but any director who finds himself in this position should

---

[1] The same rules are replicated for a public company and a guarantee company.
[2] There is one specific power stated in the CA 2006: the power to make provision for the employees on the cessation or transfer of business (s.247). This is permissible even if doing so does not necessarily promote the success of the company. The members will need to vote to approve the exercise of this power unless the directors are permitted to exercise this power under their company's articles (s.247(4)–(6)).

consider resigning, since any such resolution would be a criticism of the director's behaviour.

Directors may have rights under their service contracts. They generally (depending on the articles) have the right to keep the minutes of the board meetings confidential. Their predominant right is the right to manage the company as they see fit. But with rights come duties, and the failure to carry out those duties brings sanctions.

DIRECTORS' DUTIES

9–02 Traditionally there were three main types of duty that a director owed to his company:

- the fiduciary duty;
- the duty of skill and care; and
- statutory duties.

There were other duties that arose under certain circumstances:

- duties to creditors;
- duties to employees;
- duties to members; and
- duties to auditors.

Certain other duties arise on insolvency:

- the duty to co-operate with insolvency practitioners; and
- the duty to contribute to the company's assets on insolvency under certain circumstances (this is dealt with under "directors' liabilities" later).

As will be seen later, the company itself has certain duties regarding directors, such as making copies of directors' service contracts available to the members at AGMs and the like. These duties concern directors, but are mainly for the benefit of the members.

Directors' duties under the Companies Act 2006

9–03 Until the implementation of the Companies Act 2006 ("the CA 2006"), apart from certain duties that were clearly laid down in statute (mostly as a result of previous corporate scandals), directors' duties were part of the common law. Directors were supposed, somehow, to know what their common law duties were, although in practice, at least as regards smaller or new companies, many directors had little idea what their duties were and received little guidance from either the then DTI[3] or the Registrar of Companies.

---

[3] The DTI was the Department of Trade and Industry, now replaced by the Department for Business, Information and Skills.

This ignorance of the common law was not wasted on the Company Law Review Steering Group, appointed by the then DTI, for the purpose of updating, simplifying and codifying the common law in order to make and keep the United Kingdom an entrepreneurial country, sympathetic to people wishing to set up and run businesses. The Group's recommendations[4] led to the White Paper[5] that underpinned much of the CA 2006. The intention behind the CA 2006 was that it would be an Act that would codify the common law on directors' duties, and would do away with pointless rules[6] which contributed nothing towards directors' setting up and running businesses. In addition the CA 2006 was to be written in such a way that the director of a small company could find all the rules for his business quickly and easily. This would be because the rules applicable to him would always be in the first part of the relevant section of the Act.[7] The rules for larger companies and public companies would follow next, and finally there would be the rules for quoted companies. This approach was known as the "Think small first" approach.

The CA 2006 was also, at least as far as some parts of the Act (and in particular directors' duties) were concerned, to be written in a way intended to be readable and intelligible. The parliamentary draftsmen set out the legislation in an open and uncomplicated way, with short sentences, open texture, and with cross-referencing so that readers could not only be directed to an important section, but obtain some indication of what that other section was about. The legislation, unusually, was written for the benefit of the people who would be using it, as opposed to those who drafted it.

In addition, there was a further intention which was to rewrite company law so that directors of companies, when running their companies, should have to take account of various other interests in the company, as opposed to merely making money for the shareholders. This proved a contentious issue which ultimately became quite politicised. The end result is to be seen in the CA 2006 s.172, to be discussed shortly.

There are two main theoretical approaches to how companies should **9–04** be run. The first is the hardline approach that the directors' sole responsibility should be the maximisation of the returns to the shareholders, an approach sometimes known in the United States as "ROI", otherwise "return on investment"; any activity by the directors that does not benefit the shareholders by means of ROI should not be encouraged.[8]

---

[4] The Group produced various documents culminating in *Modern Company Law for a Competitive Economy—the Final Report*, published by the then DTI in July 2001.

[5] *Company Law Reform White Paper*. DTI, 2005. Cm. 6456. Available on *http://www.berr.gov.uk/files/file13958.pdf* [Accessed April 22, 2014].

[6] For example, under the Companies Act 1985 s.311 there used to be a rule that stated that directors were not to receive tax-free payments—something that could not happen under tax law anyway.

[7] Even finding the legislation should be easy, because it is now available on the internet.

[8] This view was memorably espoused by the eminent Chicago School economist, Milton Friedman, who stated in an article for the New York Times on September 13, 1970: "There is one and only one social responsibility of business—to use its resources and engage in activities designed to increase its profits so long as it stays within the rules of the game, which is to say, engages in open and free competition without deception or fraud."

Then there is the more inclusive and generally European approach, which suggests that companies (through their agents, the directors) have responsibilities to more than just the shareholders: companies have responsibilities to the communities in which they are situated, to their employees, to the environment, to their customers and to the wider world, these bodies being known as "stakeholders". This approach asserts that a company is more effective, productive and profitable if it takes accounts of these stakeholders. The Company Law Steering Group backed this approach and s.172 of CA 2006 was drafted in such a way to force directors to take account of stakeholders. This, it was thought, would lead to what was termed "enlightened shareholder value", to better labour relations, greater prosperity for companies and share-holders alike, and perhaps to a happier world.

There is something to be said for both approaches. If the directors do not keep members happy by delivering good returns, members, at least in publicly quoted companies, will invest elsewhere and the company will suffer a shortage of capital or be at risk of takeover. On the other hand, a company that concentrates solely on delivering profits and takes no account of wider interests may lose the support of the community where it works (thus making planning permission difficult for expansion), attracts bad publicity (which may affect the share price), and has trouble retaining effective staff. If the staff are not valued, product quality will decline. At the same time, companies cannot be expected to solve all the world's ills, and while they may have a part to play in local communities, it is not necessarily a company's responsibility to keep communities going, nor to be a social or employment network. Directors of companies may be good at making products, managing people, and making money, but are not necessarily good politicians or social workers.

Enlightened shareholder value requires shareholders to exhibit self-restraint in terms of expectations of dividends, to exercise altruism, to forgo high short-term yield for long term profits, and to temper their self-interest. However, not all shareholders are so self-denying or so high-minded, and some do not care much about the long-term existence of the companies in which they are investing.[9] Amongst the major shareholders in UK companies are employee pension funds: the price of altruism could be reduced pensions.

9–05   Those who promote enlightened shareholder value place faith in the perfectibility of mankind, and appear to believe that if legislation is drafted in the right way, directors will behave in a high-minded and thoughtful manner, and in a manner considerably better than, say, the late Robert Maxwell, or over in North America, the directors of Enron and Worldcom. Sceptics assert that despite the introduction of the new rules in the CA 2006, directors of certain well-known UK companies did not noticeably demonstrate the enlightened shareholder value envisaged by those who passed the legislation. For example, from the period from

---

[9] If the shareholders (particularly pension funds) did care more about the companies in which they were investing, they would presumably not lend shares to hedge funds to take short positions in companies whose share price was likely to fall.

2006 until the economic collapse of 2009–12, many UK banks indulged in a number of sharp practices including money-laundering of drug cartel cash (HSBC[10]) and mis-selling of unsuitable products (particularly payment protection insurance) to trusting and naive borrowers.[11] Meanwhile energy companies such as SSE missold energy packages to bamboozled customers[12] and GlaxoSmithKlein was less than candid about the failings of some of its pharmaceutical products.[13] Enlightened shareholder value would not appear to have made much impression on the directors of those major UK companies.

As far as smaller private companies' directors were concerned, there was similarly little enthusiasm for enlightened shareholder value. While most directors did what was necessary to be on the right side of the law, to "tick the boxes" as it were, they did so while grumbling that it would help if more politicians had actually run businesses themselves before telling other people how to do so. The new rules required more paperwork than had hitherto been the case, contrary to the intention that the CA 2006 should make life easier for directors.

The counterview is that some well-run companies already aimed for enlightened shareholder value, by practising good corporate governance, active involvement in the local community, employee engagement and straightforward business practices. The retail store, John Lewis, encompassing Waitrose, is commonly seen as a good example of this. Such companies did not require legislation to make them behave in the manner indicated in the legislation, because for them it made good commercial sense to behave well anyway. One effect of the financial crash is that there has been a realisation that customer goodwill and trust had been substantially eroded. The focus is now on running a business not purely to benefit the employees and shareholders in the short term but satisfying customer and other requirements in the long run. This is seen as a more sustainable business model. In short, enlightened shareholder value may well after all be desirable. Whether it needs to be enshrined in legislation is another matter.

So what were the new rules introduced in 2006? How were the common law rules codified?

---

[10] "US Vulnerability to Money-laundering, drugs, and terrorist financing: HSBC case history", Permanent Sub-committee on Investigations, US Senate, December 2012 available at *http://www.hsgac.senate.gov/subcommittees/investigations/media/levin-statement-on-hsbc-settlement* [Accessed April 22, 2014].

[11] Nearly all the UK banks have had to repay substantial sums to borrowers as a result of mis-selling.

[12] In March 2013 SSE was fined £10.3 million by Ofgem for mis-selling of its products. The management of SSE was specifically criticised for its inadequate supervision of its sales teams.

[13] In July 2012 the US branch of the UK company was fined $3bn for falsifying information about its new heart drug, Avandia.

The scope and nature of the general duties: Ch.2 ss.171–177

9–06   The Companies Act 2006 s.171 states that the general duties are owed by a director *to his company*.[14] The "general duties" are specifically the duties outlined in ss.171–177 and they are the statutory codification of the former common law duties known as the fiduciary duty and the duty of skill and care. The fiduciary duty is the duty to act in good faith in the best interests of the company. Part of the fiduciary duty includes the "no conflict of interest" rule, whereby a director must not act in such a way as to permit a conflict of interest between what might benefit him and what might benefit the company. Since in running a company there are bound to be occasions when a director may have a conflict of interest between his personal benefit and the company's benefit, as, for example, when a company wants to enter a contract with a partnership, and one of the partners is a director of the company, the law permits such conflicts provided the other directors, or the members, as the case may be, have been previously told about the conflict and permitted it. What is required is disclosure plus approval. The duty of skill and care is the duty to run the company competently and with, as a minimum, the care and attention that a normal person would exercise when running his own business. If a director fails to exercise his fiduciary duty, if he breaches the no-conflict rule, or if he manages the company negligently, the company may sue him for his breach of his duty to it.

The basis and interpretation of the general duties

9–07   According to s.170, the general duties are:

> "... based on certain common law rules and equitable principles as they apply in relation to directors and have effect in place of those rules and principles as regards the duties owed to a company by a director."[15]

The next subsection continues:

> "The general duties shall be interpreted and applied in the same way as common law rules or equitable principles, and regard shall be had to the corresponding common law rules and equitable principles in interpreting and applying the general duties."[16]

---

[14] This formula was used in the CA 1985 s.309 with regard to employees. When the UK joined the EU it was required to have a provision in its company law stating that directors had to have regard to the interests of their companies' employees. With artful wording, each director was put under a duty, owed to the company, "and to the company alone" to consider the interests of the employees. The addition of the words, "and to the company alone", effectively ensured that no director was ever sued by the collective body of shareholders for not taking enough account of the employees' interests—just as intended.

[15] CA 2006 s.170(3).

[16] CA 2006 s.170(4).

What is meant by this is that the duties to be found in the following sections are based both on the existing common law and equitable principles. In Scotland we do not have "equitable principles" as a term of law: what it means by this term is those principles arising out of the English legal concept of equity (the 15 badges of equity) which broadly in the interest of fairness or natural justice are designed to ameliorate the harsher effects of existing law, statutory or common. For example, one of the best known badges of equity is "he who comes to equity must come with clean hands". So if a claimant seeks an order from the court to make a defendant carry out an act the defendant has failed to carry out, the claimant must be acting in good faith and have done whatever he ought to have done first before he starts complaining about the defendant. A claim under equity may be made where damages would not be the most satisfactory remedy, as would more often be the case under common law or statute. A claim under equity would allow an order to be granted that something be done (or not done). Although "equitable principles" are not a term of Scots law, a court in Scotland can still take account of the intent behind the principles, since in Scotland it is perfectly permissible to petition the court for a particular remedy, as opposed to seeking damages.

Both the virtue and the difficulty with common law and equity alike is **9–08** that, unlike statute, they change according to recent judicial decisions which may in turn reflect wider social or other changes within society. What the common law and equity lack in certainty (subject to the constraints of judicial precedent) they gain in flexibility and adaptability. This flexibility is what s.170(3) and (4) are trying to retain, by saying that the general duties are to be based on and have the flexibility of common law and equity. In effect what is happening is that the common law and equity have been temporarily adopted into statute for the purposes of ascertaining directors' duties. So if a director breached one of his duties in ss.171–177, he would technically have breached the terms of the statute, but to assess the extent of his breach, or the remedy, or even his liability, if any, one would have to look at the continuing stream of common law and equity. This is, depending on one's point of view, either a very ingenious method of getting the flexibility of the common law and equity into statute and thereby the best of both worlds, or a very dangerous precedent that should not be countenanced by legal purists. Whether it is the one or the other now hardly matters, since it is already in operation.

However, what this ingenious solution lacks is accessibility. The whole point of the codification of directors' duties in the CA 2006 was to make the duties accessible and intelligible, even to those who may not have known much about the law, and especially to company directors. It is difficult to access the common law and equitable principles relating to the subject matter of ss.171–177 unless one is already a lawyer, particularly well advised or willing to read a book on the matter. Many a director must think that by finding the law relating to his duties codified in statute, he will neither need to seek further legal advice nor refer to any law books. If so, he is mistaken.

Section 179 states that there may be occasions when more than one of **9–09** the general duties may apply to any particular case, so that, for example, not only is a director expected to have acted within the powers granted to him under the constitution under s.171 but he is also expected to have no conflicts of interest. His failure to abide by the general duties could therefore render him liable to the company on more than one count. The general duties may well also apply to directors in respect of any of the matters explained later on, such as loans to directors or payments to directors: not only will members need to approve the matters in question, but the directors individually and collectively should have been exercising their general duties, when considering whether their company (or the director in question) should be involved in those loans or payments.

The general duties not only apply to properly appointed directors but to shadow directors to the extent that common law or, equitable principles so apply.[17] A shadow director is not always under a fiduciary duty: it depends on what the shadow director was doing.[18] Each general duty will now be examined.

The duty to act within powers: s.171

9–10   A director is expected to act within the powers under the company's constitution. The company's constitution comprises the articles and any special resolutions that have been passed to constrain or otherwise limit (or indeed enhance) the directors' powers, plus any resolutions under s.29.[19] If a company has an objects clause,[20] the directors are expected to act within its terms, even though the company would be required, as indicated in Ch.4, to honour any ultra vires acts undertaken by the directors[21] unless they were personal transactions involving the directors themselves.[22] The director must only exercise such powers as he is given under the constitution for the purposes for which those powers were conferred. The model articles (art.3) merely state that the directors may exercise all the powers of the company as part of their management of the company. The purposes for which the powers are conferred will generally be the promotion of the success of the company.[23] A difficulty arises when

---

[17] CA 2006 s.170(5).

[18] *Ultraframe UK Ltd v Fielding* [2005] EWHC 1638 Ch at 1268. Lewison J. explains that while it is possible for a creditor to be a shadow director because of the degree of influence he has over the company, in the same way as an important customer might have some influence over a company, it would be not be right to expect that type of shadow director to have a fiduciary duty to the company.

[19] CA 2006 s.17.

[20] Increasingly it is unlikely that companies will have restrictive objects clauses. See CA 2006 s.31.

[21] CA 2006 s.40.

[22] If the director was making the company enter into an improper transaction (i.e. contrary to the objects clause or beyond the director's authority) involving the director himself, the transaction is voidable at the instance of the company (CA 2006 s.41(2)). *Re Torvale Group Ltd* [1999] 2 B.C.L.C. 605.

[23] CA 2006 s.172.

directors in practice exercise their powers for questionable ends, even if they claim that they are acting in good faith. This can be exemplified by three cases.

In *Howard Smith Ltd v Ampol Petroleum Ltd*[24] directors claimed that it was desirable for their company to be taken over by a particular bidder for the company. Using their authority under the articles to allot shares on a discretionary basis the directors used that authority to allot shares to their preferred takeover bidder, so that the combination of the directors' shares and the bidder's shares outweighed the other shareholders who had hitherto been in a majority and who had opposed the proposed takeover by the bidder. The former majority shareholders objected to the directors' misuse of their undoubted authority to allot shares, and it was held that while the directors were entitled to use their authority to allot shares, they were not entitled to use that authority for the purpose of wrecking an existing majority—and so they were not using their powers for a proper purpose. A slightly similar issue arose in the case of *Hogg v Cramphorn*[25] where directors allotted shares to the employees' pension scheme as part of an attempt to prevent a takeover bid and thus keep the directors in their jobs. The directors genuinely believed that this was in the best interests of the company, but notwithstanding the directors' good faith in the matter, it was held that this too was an improper use of their power.[26] The moral of both these cases is that directors should direct their minds to act within the powers given to them for the promotion of the success of the company (as in the next section) and not for some ulterior motive.[27] In *West Coast Capital (LIOS) Ltd*[28] the entrepreneur Tom Hunter was unable to demonstrate that a rights issue ordered by the board of Dobbies plc was a stratagem by Tesco (which owned most of the shares in Dobbies plc) in order to marginalise his own investment company's interest in Dobbies. The Tesco-appointed directors in Dobbies had carefully recused themselves from any decision-making on this matter and so the remaining board was acting within its powers when it ordered the rights issue.

The duty to promote the success of the company: s.172

This section has attracted much attention. It reads as follows: **9–11**

(1) A director of a company must act in the way he considers, in good faith, would be most likely to promote the success of the company for the benefit of its members as a whole, and in doing to so have regard (amongst other matters) to—

---

[24] *Howard Smith Ltd v Ampol Petroleum Ltd* [1974] A.C. 821; [1974] 2 W.L.R. 689.

[25] *Hogg v Cramphorn* [1967] Ch. 254; [1966] 3 W.L.R. 995.

[26] As it happened, the judge in this instance allowed the matter to be put to the vote, with the interested parties not being allowed to vote. The vote in the end was duly passed.

[27] This particularly applies to nominee directors who should consider the interests of the company, and not just the interests of their nominators: *Meyer v Scottish Co-operative Wholesale Society (No.3)*, 1958 S.C. (HL) 40.

[28] [2008] CSOH 72.

    (a) the likely consequences of any decision in the long term,
    (b) the interests of the company's employees,
    (c) the need to foster the company's business relationships with suppliers, customers and others,
    (d) the impact of the company's operations on the community and the environment,
    (e) the desirability of the company maintaining a reputation for high standards of business conduct, and
    (f) the need to act fairly as between members of the company.

This section has been carefully worded to be a modern exposition of the previous law on directors' duties. In *Cobden Investments Ltd v RWM Langport Ltd* Warren J. said that: "The perhaps old-fashioned phrase acting 'bona fide in the interests of the company' is reflected in the statutory words acting 'in good faith in a way most likely to promote the success of the company for the benefit of its members as a whole'. They come to the same thing with the modern formulation giving a more readily understood definition of the scope of the duty."[29]

It is worth analysing some of the wording.

"He considers ... would be most likely" indicates that the director must exercise his own judgement thoughtfully.

The words "good faith" are problematic. Those two innocent words are words that are well understood but hard to define. The general view seems to be that good faith is predominantly a subjective matter for directors. In *Regentcrest Ltd v Cohen*[30] Jonathan Parker J. indicated that the question is whether the director honestly believed that his act or omission was in the interests of the company. The issue is as to the director's state of mind. In this case the director failed to claw back a sum of money due to his company but he made his decision for what he genuinely believed were sensible commercial reasons that would benefit the company. If the director honestly believes what he is doing is for the good of the company, and has taken the trouble to satisfy himself as to the correctness of his decision, even if it not one with which other directors (or a subsequently appointed liquidator) might agree, it is not for the court to gainsay that.[31]

However, there may be occasions when it strains credulity to believe that a director could reasonably believe that he was acting in good faith. One such occasion arose in *Item Software (UK) Ltd v Fassihi*,[32] where Fassihi, a director and employee of Item, tried to persuade his managing director to impose terms on a supplier, Isograph, that would be so onerous that Isograph would take its business elsewhere, namely into the hands of a company Fassihi had secretly set up, named RAMS. RAMS would then take over the distribution of Isograph's products. Item duly

---

[29] [2008] EWHC 2810 (Ch) at 52.
[30] [2002] 2 B.C.L.C. 80 at 105B.
[31] *Madoff Securities International Limited (In Liquidation) v Stephen Raven* [2013] EWHC 3147 (Comm.)
[32] [2004] B.C.C. 944.

lost the contract, though not necessarily as a result of Fassihi's machinations. Item discovered Fassihi's underhandedness and dismissed Fassihi. Item then sued Fassihi for damages for his breach of duty in failing to disclose his own wrongdoing. Fassihi counterclaimed for unfair dismissal and maintained that there was no duty requiring him to disclose his own wrongdoing. The Court of Appeal held that Fassihi was indeed in breach of his duty as a director in this respect. In particular, Arden L.J. approvingly referring to the "time-honoured rule", a rule that would apply to Fassihi, "the duty to act in what he in good faith considers to be the best interests of his company",[33] stated, "Furthermore, on the facts of this case, there is no basis on which Mr Fassihi could reasonably have come to the conclusion that it was not in the interests of Item to know of his breach of duty. In my judgment, he could not fulfil his duty of loyalty in this case except by telling Item about his setting up of RAMS, and his plan to acquire the Isograph contract for himself."[34]

"Good faith" therefore appears to be at heart a subjective matter, a **9–12** belief that what the director is doing will benefit the company, but when there are doubts as to how reasonable or plausible that belief is, the courts may take a robust view of the validity of that belief.[35]

The verb "promote" conveys a sense that the directors should try to achieve the required success (about to be discussed) even if they fail to do so. As for "success", the word appears to have been chosen as a wider word than the phrase previously much used in company law, "best interests". "Success" appears to be a word that can cover a host of desirable outcomes, from an increased share price to contented customers and staff. "Success" appears to mean whatever the members want it to mean, as indicated in the company's objects clause or any other indication of its objectives. Subsection (2) allows for the possibility that companies may be set up for purposes other than benefiting the members, such as charitable companies, in which case satisfying the charitable intent is deemed to be equivalent to promoting the success of the company.

The director has to act for the members as a whole, not any one part of it, nor purely for his own benefit. This ties in later with the rules relating to minority protection and derivative claims, explored in Chapter 11.

Next, the director has to "have regard" to a list of various matters. To "have regard" is an uncertain term: it seems to be less demanding than to

---

[33] At 41.

[34] At 44. Interestingly, the Scots courts do not appear to share Arden L.J.'s view on the requirement to disclose one's own wrongdoing, slightly drawing away from it in *Commonwealth Oil & Gas Co. Ltd v Baxter* (2010) S.C. 156. Perhaps the real point in *Fassihi* was not so much Fassihi's failure to disclose his own wrongdoing, as the fact that Fassihi's underhand behaviour, in trying to mislead his fellow director and to gain the contract for himself, could not, by any standard, be seen as acting in good faith.

[35] In Chapter 4 of his book, *The Enlightened Shareholder Value Principle and Corporate Governance* (Routledge, 2012), Professor Keay undertakes an extensive review of the views of the major contemporary legal authors' views on "good faith" in this context, indicating the difficulties both judges and academics share in establishing exactly what is meant by these two words.

"consider" or "take account of", but it is probably more demanding than having a passing mild concern.

The list has attracted a degree of criticism. The list has been said to be a statement of fashion rather than the law, in that it covers many concerns dear to politicians' hearts, but gives no guidance on the practicalities of how a director is supposed to run a company, having regard to all these matters at once. The list does not explain what to do if attending to any one matter is at the expense of another. There is no requirement to consider, say, health and safety matters or competition matters. It fails to take account of the fact that a large company, with plenty of staff, may well be able to devote time, energy and funds to considering these matters and bringing them to the attention of the board of directors, but that it is unrealistic for a small company to do so.

Despite these criticisms, a large, well-run company will have directors who would in any event want to take account of these matters whether they were obliged to or not under statute: it would make commercial sense to do so. A company that respects its employees, treats its customers properly, and thinks to the future is more likely to prosper than one than does not.

As it is not apparent to what extent all the various matters on the list should be considered—and there was little guidance from the Government, other than suggestions that the requirement to "have regard" should not be seen as a mere box-ticking exercise—it is now common for directors to be seen to have board minutes that show that when they make their decisions, they take due account of the matters to which they should address their minds under s.172. For a particularly contentious decision that appears to run counter to the spirit of s.172 more detail will need to be recorded in the minutes, or the board papers need to be fuller than otherwise, to prove that the directors really did address their minds to the decision. There is no requirement in the legislation be the right or best decision, but merely that when the directors were making their decision they had regard to s.172.

9–13   The final part of s.172 states that the duty to consider the various matters imposed by s.172 is subject to any enactment or rule of law requiring directors to act in the interests of creditors of the company. This refers to the case of *West Mercia Safetywear Ltd v Dodd*[36] which stated that there was a duty of care owed by directors to creditors not to make the creditors' situation any worse if the directors could see insolvency looming for their company.[37]

The major difficulty with s.172 from a practical point of view is that the right to enforce the duty of the director to have regard to the various items in s.172(1)(a)–(f) is given under s.171 to the collective body of members, and not to the interest groups represented in s.172(1)(a)–(f). So in s.172(1)(d), where the director, in promoting the success of the

---

[36] *West Mercia Safetywear Ltd v Dodd* (1988) 4 B.C.C 30. This case predated the Insolvency Act 1986 s.214 and is authority under common law for the duty of directors to consider creditors' interests in these circumstances.

[37] *Re HLC Environmental Projects Ltd* [2013] EWHC 2876 (Ch).

company, is expected to have regard to the community and the environment, the community and the environment cannot gang up together and sue him, for his duty is not owed to the community and the environment per se, but owed to the company. Only in the unlikely event of the members of the company being very public-spirited would the members decide that the director of their company should be sued for breach of his duty to have regard to the community and the environment.[38] In practice it would be uncommon for the members of the company collectively to sue the directors for such breach. It is, however, possible that a liquidator could raise an action against the directors for such a breach, or new shareholders, following a successful takeover, and discovering what the previous directors had been up to, might do so as well.[39]

The effect of this is to render much of s.172 a fond wish rather than useful. It leaves s.172 as having some slight moral force, but few teeth. It is hard to know whether many of the Members of Parliament who voted to approve it understood its limitations. It is possible that the legalistic point about the duty being owed to a company escaped some politicians. Others, better informed, probably reckoned that a duty to the company was better than no duty. However, before dismissing s.172 as futile, it should be remembered that even if the company, to which the duty is owed, is unlikely to raise an action against a director, under restrictive conditions any individual shareholder may bring a derivative claim on behalf of the company against the director.[40] And to that extent, s.172 appears to be working well, particularly when directors are not treating all the members of the company fairly. This is discussed in greater depth in Chapter 11.

On the other hand, if, say, the community and the environment, or any of the other interest groups in s.172 had been given the power to sue the director directly, it would have been a signal for astute directors to close down their businesses in the United Kingdom—and move elsewhere to a corporate law regime more director-friendly, with considerable consequences for employment and the nation's wealth.

Has s.172 overall make a historic change in attitudes in directors' management of companies, as the promoters of the CA 2006 presumably hoped? Or has it made remarkably little difference? The legislation gives the impression that its promoters thought that business in the United Kingdom would be more thoughtful and considered as a result of s.172, and it would lead to fewer examples of cavalier management of companies. In one sense, s.172 is trying to make businessmen nicer people. Whether this is a function for company law is a question worth asking. The general view is that while s.172 was undoubtedly well-intentioned, the legislation for the benefit of the stakeholders was ineffective and flawed because most shareholders had better things to do than use the law

---

[38] This could perhaps be done by means of the derivative action at s.265. Any wise director in this position would have resigned by then anyway. This is discussed in Chapter 11.

[39] *Gencor ACP Ltd v Dalby* [2000] 2 B.C.L.C. 734. Even so, a director who had acted honestly and reasonably might be able to advance the "get out of gaol" defence of s.1157.

[40] See Ch.11 and s.265.

to hold the directors to account. The sanction of collective shareholder action against the directors is not realistic. Of the few cases on s.172, s.172(1)(f) seems to be reasonably effective,[41] but the rest of s.172(1) seems to have been a kindly but futile failure.[42] If s.172 were effective, other countries would have adopted it. At the time of writing, no other country, at least within the Commonwealth, appears to have done so, and it is noticeable that at the time of writing, Ireland, which is revising her own company legislation, has carefully not followed the British wording of s.172, merely requiring directors to act "honestly and responsibly".

The duty to exercise independent judgement: s.173

9–14   A director is expected to exercise independent judgment. This means he is expected to apply his own mind to the company's circumstances and not merely rely on others' words or instructions.[43] This does not mean that he can ignore any agreement that his company may have entered into which would restrict the exercise of his discretion,[44] or ignore any directions contained within the company's constitution.[45] Sometimes the directors are put in a difficult position in that they may have undertaken to commit themselves to a course of action which at the time was in their view in the best interests of the company. Does this decision fetter their future discretion? May they change their minds in the best interests of the company as a whole? It would appear that in principle they can,[46] provided there is no breach of any contract[47]—much therefore depending on the extent to which the directors have actually made their company form a contract with the other party, and if there has been any consideration.

The duty to exercise reasonable skill, care and diligence: s.174

9–15   The duty to exercise reasonable skill and care is not a fiduciary duty. It is a duty in its own right and breach of it entitles the company to claim from the director the loss that his incompetence or negligence has caused the company to suffer.

---

[41] For example, *Hughes v Weiss* [2012] EWHC 2363 (Ch).

[42] Professor Keay of Leeds University has written extensively on this area (see *http://www.law.leeds.ac.uk/assets/files/research/events/directors-duties/keay-the-duty-to-promote-the-success.pdf* [Accessed April 22, 2014] and "Moving towards stakeholderism? Constituency statutes, enlightened shareholder value, and more: much ado about little?" 2011, 22(1) E.B.L. Rev. 1-49, in particular) and his view is that s.172 has, frankly, not worked. He is not alone in this view: see D. Fisher, "The Enlightened Shareholder—Leaving Stakeholders in the Dark: Will Section 172 (1) of the Companies Act 2006 make Directors Consider the Impact of their Decisions on Third Parties?" [2009] I.C.C.L.R. 10.

[43] *Re Westmid Packing Services Ltd; Secretary of State for Trade & Industry v Griffiths (No 3)* [1998] B.C.C. 836; *Re Barings Plc (No 5)* [1999] 1 B.C.L.C. 433; *Lexi Holdings Plc v Luqman No.2* [2008] 2 B.C.L.C. 725. For a recent case relating to the Cayman Islands, but covering the same point, see *Weavering Capital (UK) Limited (In Liquidation) v Peterson* [2012] EWHC 1480 (Ch).

[44] CA 2006 s.173(2)(a).

[45] CA 2006 s.173(2)(b).

[46] *Dawson International Plc v Coats Paton Plc* [1989] 5 B.C.C. 405; [1990] B.C.L.C. 560; 1989 S.L.T. 655.

[47] *Fulham Football Ltd v Cabra Estates Plc* [1994] 1 B.C.L.C. 363.

Historically the standard of care that a director was expected to exercise in the management of his company was, by modern standards, very low. It was even possible to provide in a company's articles that the directors would not be personally liable for any actions carried out by them in the course of their directorship of the company, and the courts' view, to justify this, was that no-one was obliged to be a member of a company, and anyone who did was bound to accept that the company's articles might allow directors such freedom.[48] The rationale behind this was that directors should not be trammelled by anything that would interfere with the free market.

Such laxity is not available now,[49] except to the extent of permitted indemnities under ss.233–235, which provided that the only protection the company may supply is insurance for its officers' liabilities in the event of actions being raised against them, though such insurance would only cover officers' expenses in successfully defending any actions against them. This is discussed further below. Furthermore the climate of opinion has also changed in the light of the recent banking scandals. Although there may not have been any recent actions raised against negligent bank directors, a number of senior bank directors were required to resign.[50] Where a company has become insolvent, the Company Directors Disqualification Act 1986 interacts with the Insolvency Act 1986 ("the IA 1986") to provide for the disqualification of directors who have allowed their subsequently insolvent companies to trade fraudulently[51] or wrongfully[52]; and even if the company is solvent, as indicated in the previous chapter, a director may be disqualified. The UK Corporate Governance Code for directors of listed companies requires high standards of disclosure and probity. Non-executive directors are expected to keep an eye on their fellow directors. The financial press has grown more sceptical of directors' behaviour in the light of the increase in directors' salaries irrespective of the success of their companies. Furthermore, it is increasingly becoming evident that unprofessional behaviour by directors leads to a lower share price[53]: it is thus in everyone's interests that directors behave properly.

From a legal, as opposed to a commercial, point of view, the standard of care that is now expected of a director is both objective—that of a person in a similar position to the director—and personal to the director

---

[48] *Re City Equitable Fire Insurance Co Ltd* [1925] Ch. 407. In this case the chairman himself was a "daring and unprincipled scoundrel" but as the articles provided that directors would not be liable even for their own "wilful neglect or default" the directors escaped scot-free. For a discussion on how this case was nevertheless an advance on previous cases, see Adrian Walters, "Directors' duties: the impact of the Company Directors Disqualification Act 1986" (2000) 21(4) Comp. Law. 110.

[49] CA 2006 s.232.

[50] For example, Bob Diamond of Barclays Bank and Fred Goodwin of Royal Bank of Scotland.

[51] IA 1986 s.213.

[52] IA 1986 s.214.

[53] The shares in Robert Maxwell's Mirror Group, while he was at the helm, consistently traded at a discount to the underlying value of the business, because of the "Max" factor which reflected his general unreliability and questionable integrity.

in that if a director is experienced or professionally qualified, expected of him.[54] Lord Hoffmann stated in *Re D'Jan of London* at the standard of care to be exercised by a director was as d in the IA 1986 s.214(4), being that of:

a reasonable diligent person having both—

    (a) the general knowledge, skill and experience that may reasonably be expected of a person carrying out the same functions as are carried out by that director in relation to the company, and

    (b) the general knowledge, skill and experience that that director has.

Lord Hoffmann's view has the merit of matching the standard expected of a competent director of a company with the standard expected of a director trying to avoid being found liable for wrongful trading where a company has gone into insolvent liquidation. It is no accident that s.174 echoes that of the IA 1986 s.214(4), and it is closely based on s.1 of the Trusts Act 2000.

It is important to recognise that even though the company for which directors are working may be controlled by a fraudster, it is does not mean that the directors themselves are liable under s.214 if they were genuinely unaware of what the controlling shareholder was doing and were acting properly in accordance with their duties.[56]

The duty to avoid conflicts of interest: s.175

9–16   A director's fiduciary duty is the common law duty to act in good faith in the best interests of the company as a whole with a proper purpose in mind. It is the same duty that an agent owes to a principal, a partner to his partnership and co-partners, and a solicitor to his client. There should be no conflict of interest between the director and his company. Given such a duty, if the director wishes to take any advantage whatsoever from his position, or to benefit any other person, or to do anything other than what he is supposed or already authorised to do, he may only do so provided he has told the company about it, received approval or authority from the company to do so, either in advance, or after the company has ratified it, and provided the proposed action is within the proper exercise of his powers. If he receives any benefit from his position, he may only keep that benefit if he discloses it and seeks approval or authority to keep it. He must also act in good faith throughout.

In its purest form, this is a very strict duty. In *Aberdeen Railway Co v Blaikie Bros*[57] the chairman of a railway company was a partner in a firm

---

[54] *Dorchester Finance Co Ltd v Stebbing* [1989] B.C.L.C. 498.

[55] *Re D'Jan of London Ltd* [1994] 1 B.C.L.C. 561.

[56] *Madoff Securities International Limited (In Liquidation) v Stephen Raven* [2013] EWHC 3147 (Comm.)

[57] *Aberdeen Railway Co v Blaikie Bros* (1854) 1 MacQ. 416 HL.

that made iron chairs[58] on which the railway lines for the railway company were set. There was no suggestion that the chairman, Blaikie, had actually behaved dishonestly, but nevertheless the point at law was that as chairman of the board of directors of the railway company it was his responsibility to obtain the lowest terms he could for the railway company, while in his personal capacity as a partner in a firm supplying goods to that railway company he would be tempted to obtain the best terms he could for the partnership. The two roles were incompatible. He should not have been involved in the negotiations, or if he were to be involved, he should have received approval from the company for his involvement and for permission to keep any benefit that accrued to him as a result. As he did not have this approval, he had breached his fiduciary duty.[59]

With such a breach, the director would usually be required either to **9–17** hand over the profit he had improperly made or otherwise return to the company what he had improperly gained or obtained from the company. In *Regal Cinemas (Hastings) Ltd v Gulliver*[60] the directors of a cinema company had the opportunity (which came to them in their position as directors) of buying certain cinemas in Hastings. They personally formed a company to acquire the cinemas and then sold the company to the plaintiff company of which they were directors, thereby making a profit. Had they sought approval from the members of the plaintiff company— which would have been easily achieved, since the directors in their personal capacity were at that time the majority of shareholders—they could perfectly well have kept the profit; but they failed to obtain such approval. When in due course they sold the company, the new owner of the company's shares realised what the by now former directors had done and was able to recover the profit from those directors.

Although this duty is both strict and in its way sensible, it fails to take account of the practicalities of being a company director: sometimes it is not unreasonable to allow a director to set up a business which in practice would not cause any problems for the director's existing company. In particular, what caused concern to the Government was the fact that the conflict of interest rule could, in the Government's view, actively deter directors from setting up businesses in their own personal capacity, lest there be even a hint of a conflict of interest with the companies of which those directors were already directors.

The Government felt that this was an entrepreneurial opportunity lost, **9–18** and that directors, while not exactly being encouraged to have conflicts of interests, should not be barred from having conflicts of interests where no harm would result, and where the other directors were aware of what was

---

[58] The chairs are actually the brackets or sockets that are bolted to the railway sleepers and hold the railway lines in place.

[59] A more recent case on the same basic point is *Commonwealth Oil & Gas Co. Ltd v Baxter* (2010) S.C. 156.

[60] *Regal Cinemas (Hastings) Ltd v Gulliver* [1967] 2 A.C. 134; [1942] 1 All E.R. 378.

going on and were willing to permit the conflict of interest. Historically it had not been always been clear whether members could authorise such conflicts, and if so, whether the directors, in their capacity as members, could vote in their own interest. Some companies' articles had delegated the authority to rule on directors' interests to the directors, but again, depending on the company's articles, some allowed the director in question to vote in his own interest and some did not. The Companies Act 2006 s.175 tries to resolve these difficulties by clarifying the rules.

Accordingly, under the new rules, a director is not in principle supposed to have a conflict of interest with the interests of his company,[61] the conflict of interest being an exploitation of property, information or opportunity, even if the company itself was unable to exploit that property, information or opportunity.[62]

The duty not to have a conflict of interest is not infringed if the situation cannot reasonably be regarded as likely to give rise to a conflict of interest[63] or authorisation for the conflict has been given by the directors.[64] If for some reason the directors do not vote on the matter, but all the shareholders approve anyway, or in the absence of express approval, acquiesce in the decision, the conflict of interest is permissible.[65] A "transaction or arrangement" with the company, which is dealt with under s.177, is not seen as a conflict of interest either.[66] As an example of the former one might have the situation where the company wishes to borrow money from a bank in which the director has a tiny shareholding. This would probably be considered perfectly acceptable. But what if a director saw a plot of land near his company's premises and he decided to buy it for his own use, knowing that at the time the company had no intention of expanding?[67] Is that a conflict of interest? The proper and prudent course of action would be declaration to and approval from the directors, assuming the directors have the authority to receive such a

---

[61] CA 2006 s.175(1).

[62] CA 2006 s.175(2). Previously there was doubt as to whether or not a conflict of interest was acceptable if the company itself could not have exploited the opportunity. This section makes it clear that the company's inability to exploit the opportunity is not the point: it is the director's lack of authority for exploiting the opportunity that constitutes a conflict of interest.

[63] CA 2006 s.175(4)(a). As an example of a director misguidedly thinking that the benefits accruing to him were unlikely to give rise to a conflict of interest, see *Towers v Premier Waste Management Ltd*, 2011 EWCA Civ. 923. This was decided under the previous common law but there was extensive reference to the legislation in the CA 2006.

[64] CA 2006 s.175(4)(b).

[65] In *Sharma v Sharma* [2013] EWCA Civ 1287; [2014] W.T.L.R. 111, permission for a conflict of interest was duly obtained for the benefit of the sole director. The remaining shareholders, who subsequently objected to the conflict of interest, and who knew all about it, were held to have acquiesced in the decision, following the principle of *Re Duomatic Ltd* [1969] 2 Ch. 365. In this case, although no formal meeting had taken place to approve a particular matter, all the available shareholders had known of the matter and were therefore deemed to have consented to it.

[66] CA 2006 s.175(3). See para.9–23 for explanations of the terms "transaction" and "arrangement".

[67] *Bhullar v Bhullar* [2003] 2 B.C.L.C. 421; [2003] B.C.C. 711. Just because at the time the company has no intention of expanding does not mean it might not do so at a later date.

declaration and to grant such approval. If the company is a private one, the assumption, under s.175(5)(a), is that the directors will have that authority[68] (unless the articles say otherwise), and therefore the members will not need to grant the authority[69]; but if the company is a public one, the directors will not automatically have that authority, and if they wish to have the authority to grant such approval, it will need to be inserted in the articles.[70] In addition, the director in question, or any other interested director, should not be counted as part of any quorum when voting on the matter, and when there is a vote by the directors to decide on the matter, the director with the conflicted interest (and those connected with him) either should not cast his votes,[71] or the vote should be in his favour even without counting his votes.[72]

In practice, many private companies had provisions to this effect **9–19** already in their articles, so s.175 merely puts common practice on a statutory basis. If companies wish to have something different in their articles, perhaps permitting the director to vote in his own interest, there is nothing to say that a company may not have such an article if it wishes.[73] For example, a director who is a director of many companies, some of which may be connected with each other, might wish his companies' articles to state that he may have an interest in his other companies. If the articles say that directors may decide on conflicts of interest, the members may not overturn the directors' decision,[74] but if directors for some reason do not decide on a conflict of interest, the members will retain a residual right to do so.[75] Members may also at a later date ratify the director's conflict, provided that they are not attempting to authorise a conflict inherently unauthorisable, such as a fraud on the company,[76] an illegal act[77] or where the director's own votes in the ratification cause the vote to be passed in his favour, which otherwise it may not have been.[78] However, if the vote is unanimous in the director's favour (including the director's own votes, which would be the case in a single member

---

[68] It is already inserted in the model articles for private companies at reg.14. The articles provide for conflict where the matter cannot reasonably be regarded as giving rise to a conflict of interest, or where there are certain "permitted causes". The causes (granting of guarantees, subscription for shares, employee benefits) are explained in that regulation.

[69] As stated in the CA 2006 s.180(1), unless the articles say otherwise. There are also special provisions for charitable companies (s.181).

[70] CA 2006 s.175(5)(b). The model articles for public companies at art.16 specifically allow the director to vote at the directors' meeting granting approval for his conflict of interest but only if the members by ordinary resolution agree that he may do so or where the matter cannot reasonably be regarded as giving rise to a conflict of interest, or where there are certain "permitted causes".

[71] *West Coast Capital (LIOS) Ltd v Dobbies plc* [2008] CSOH 72.

[72] CA 2006 s.175(6). This overrules the previous rule that the directors could vote in their own interest, as in *Beattie v E & F Beattie Ltd* [1938] Ch.708; [1938] 3 All ER 214 CA.

[73] CA 2006 s.234(4).

[74] CA 2006 s.180(1).

[75] CA 2006 s.180(4).

[76] *Cook v Deeks* [1916] 1 A.C. 554.

[77] *Aveling Barford Ltd v Perion Ltd* [1989] B.C.L.C. 626.

[78] CA 2006 s.239. It is not just the director's own votes that should not cause the vote to be passed in his favour but also the votes of those connected to him (s.239(3)).

company of which the director was the sole shareholder) the ratification vote is still validly passed.[79]

9–20 The no-conflicts rule continues in force even after the director has resigned his directorship.[80] Although the following case took place before the enactment of the CA 2006, it is a good example of the retrospective effect of the rule. In *Industrial Developments Consultants Ltd v Cooley*,[81] Cooley, in his capacity as a director of the plaintiffs, had been approached by Gas Board officials to see if his company would carry out some work for them. The officials at the Gas Board then indicated that they were interested in his particular skills rather than the skills of his company, and that they were willing to give him, personally, the contract for the required work. Assenting to this arrangement, Cooley persuaded his company that he should take early retirement on health grounds. Once he had retired, he took up the contract from the Gas Board as arranged. When his former company heard what he had done, it successfully sued him to make him return to the company the contract (or the value thereof) that he had been able to obtain through his position as a director of the company.[82]

9–21 Although these new rules have much to commend them, it is probable that there will always be occasions when a dominant director, commonly the managing director or chairman, handpicks stooges to act as his fellow directors so that they always vote at board meetings the way he wants them to, whether or not he personally votes in his own interest. One way of dealing with this, at least at the level of listed companies, is by having non-executive directors and another is to improve standards of corporate governance.

What the new rules may also do is ensure that directors are more careful in how they behave. In *Gencor ACP Ltd v Dalby*[83] the managing director of a road-building company used to divert business opportunities that came to his company to his son's business in which he had an interest, and used the company's funds for the redecoration of his home and the payment of his credit card bills. When he sold the company, the incoming owner, by inspecting the company's paperwork, was able to see the former managing director's conflicts of interest. The incoming owner was able to make the former director reimburse the company (now in the possession of the incoming owner) what had been abstracted from it without authority. Had the former director taken the trouble to receive authorisation for his actions by whatever means was permitted under the company's articles, he might not have been caught out.

A director need not comply with s.175 if he has already obtained shareholders' approval for any of the matters covered in ss.188–226, or

---

[79] CA 2006 s.239(6)(a).
[80] CA 2006 s.170(2).
[81] *Industrial Developments Consultants Ltd v Cooley* [1972] 1 All E.R. 443.
[82] *Kingsley IT Consulting Ltd v McIntosh* [2006] B.C.C. 875.
[83] *Gencor ACP Ltd v Dalby* [2000] 2 B.C.L.C. 734.

where shareholder approval is not necessary because the matter is one that is already provided for by means of an exemption.[84]

The duty not to accept benefits from third parties: s.176

Although it might seem self-evident that a director should not let **9–22** benefits from third parties cloud his judgment as to whether some action would be good for his company, the fact remains that it happens, as with *Boston Deep Sea Fishing Co Ltd v Ansell*.[85] In this case, the defendant, the managing director of the plaintiffs, was given a commission for placing an order for a new trawler with a firm of shipwrights, and secretly kept the commission instead of declaring it to his company and seeking permission to keep it. Had he received permission he might have been allowed to retain it: as it was, his company, whose interests he as managing director was supposed to uphold, had effectively overpaid the cost of the trawler to the extent of the commission and he had to repay it. His interest was in getting the commission, not necessarily in getting the best deal for the company of which he was managing director. The difference between ss.175 and 176 is that s.176 specifically deals with benefits from third parties, as opposed to s.175 which deals with benefits deriving from the director's own actions. The benefits from third parties could be secret profits or commission, bribes or other inducements.

The duty not to accept the benefits from third parties is strict: a director must not accept any such benefits. However, there are a few exceptions. Section 176(4) states that the duty is not infringed if the acceptance of the benefit cannot reasonably be regarded as likely to give rise to a conflict of interest. A dinner with the directors of a company's suppliers might not be seen as heinous: a holiday for the director and his wife in the Seychelles paid for by those same suppliers might be another matter. Because there is no reference to directors' approval in s.176, it is not possible to have a benefit from a third party approved by the other directors, but it would still be possible to have the benefit approved by the members.[86] This duty continues even after the director has left the employment of the company of which he was a director.[87] A director may accept a benefit from a third party in respect of the matters covered in ss.188–226 if he has already obtained shareholders' approval, or where shareholder approval is not necessary because the matter is one that is already provided for by means of an exemption.[88]

---

[84] CA 2006 s.180(2). Note the exceptions in ss.204–209, such as expenditure on company business, etc.
[85] *Boston Deep Sea Fishing Co Ltd v Ansell* (1888) 39 Ch. D. 339.
[86] CA 2006 s.180(4)(a).
[87] CA 2006 s.170(2)(b).
[88] CA 2006 s.180(2). Note again the exceptions in ss.204–209.

Duty to declare interest in proposed transaction or arrangement: s.177

9–23   If a director is in any way, directly or indirectly,[89] interested in a proposed transaction or arrangement with the company, he must declare the nature and extent of that interest to the other directors.[90] The essential points about this provision are the words "proposed", "transaction or arrangement" and the words "nature and extent". The significance of the word "proposed" is that the director is supposed to tell his fellow directors of his interest before the company enters into the transaction or arrangement—not afterwards. For the situation where the company is already involved in an *existing* transaction or arrangement with the director[91] (so that the matter cannot be said to be "proposed") the matter must be dealt with under s.182.[92] A "transaction or arrangement" is both any contract or other transaction with the company that obviously and directly involves the director, such as a contract of employment, or a contract to sell some asset to the company, as well as any transaction which not so obviously involves the director, such as the loan of money from a bank in which the director owns shares. These transactions or arrangements may be called into question if the director has not followed the requirement of declaration to the other directors of the interest and, separately, the "nature and extent" of his interest. It is not enough to tell the directors about the existence of the interest: the nature of the interest, and how substantial that interest is, must also be separately disclosed.

9–24   Although the meaning of the words "transaction or arrangement" may be apparent to the parliamentary draftsman, it may be open to question how much the average director is able to distinguish between a conflict of interest under s.175 and a transaction or arrangement. The distinction is that a conflict of interest involves some suggestion of exploitation of information or opportunity arising from the director's work with the company, and which may possibly be to the detriment of the company, and a transaction or arrangement which is more innocent and is more usually the sale of the directors' goods or services to the company. Nevertheless there may be some occasions when a transaction that is apparently innocent, such as the grant (on perfectly normal commercial terms) by the director to his company of a licence to use some technology that he has developed, slides into a conflict of interest, when the director

---

[89] The use of the word "indirectly" catches those connected with the director in terms of ss.252–257.

[90] CA 2006 s.177(1).

[91] For example, a person with an interest in an existing transaction or arrangement with the company might be appointed a director. Under the previous rules there would have been no reason to declare the matter to the other directors since the transaction was extant, as opposed to "proposed".

[92] The procedure for disclosure is the same as in s.177, but the board minutes would need to refer to s.182 rather than s.177. In addition there are criminal penalties (not applicable under s.177) and there is a provision that where there is a single director company, he is not obliged to make the disclosure, but in the case of a company where there ought to be more than one director, but in fact there is only one director, the director must make the disclosure in writing and the matter should be discussed at the next meeting of the directors (s.186(1)). These rules also apply to shadow directors (s.187).

is more concerned about the royalties due to him under his licence than the advantage to the company of having the grant.

In order for the proposed transaction or arrangement to be acceptable, **9–25** the director must declare the interest and the nature and extent of his interest in the transaction or arrangement to the other directors at a directors' meeting, by notice in writing (in terms of s.184) or by general notice (in terms of s.185). Section 184 requires the director to tell the other directors in writing (in hard copy or electronically); it is then deemed to be part of the proceedings for the next directors' meeting and minutes should be kept of that meeting. Section 185 (general notice) does not require the matter to put in writing, but the director must tell his fellow directors of his interest, its nature and extent, and the directors must either be told of it at a meeting of the directors or the matter must be brought up and read out at the next board meeting.[93]

A director does not need to declare an interest in the transaction or **9–26** arrangement if the matter is not reasonably to be regarded as likely to give rise to a conflict of interest.[94] Likewise no declaration need be made if the directors are already aware of the matter,[95] or if it concerns terms of his service contract that either have been or will be considered by a meeting of the directors or a committee of the directors for that purpose (all in terms of the company's constitution).[96] If the company has only one director, there is no provision in the Act that says the director has to declare an interest to himself, although in such circumstances the director should be aware of s.231 which requires a director involved in a contract with a single member company (of which he is the single member), and where the contract is not in the ordinary course of business, to have the contract in writing or set out in a memorandum approved at the next meeting of the company's directors.

Remedies for breach of the general duties: s.178

If a director breaches any of the general duties outlined in ss.171–177, **9–27** the company may call upon him to reimburse the company for any loss it has suffered, indemnify the company for any expenses, hand over any profit which he has obtained and which rightfully should be the company's, and return to the company any assets which he has misappropriated. The company could go to court to reduce any contract where the director failed to declare his interest.[97] If any misappropriated assets are in the hands of a third party who has acquired them in good faith for a fair price from the director, it is unreasonable to expect the third party to hand them back, but the director can still be required to account to the company for the value of the assets themselves. The company might also take out an interdict to prevent the repetition of the breach. For good measure, the members could also vote to dismiss the

---

[93] CA 2006 s.186(1).
[94] CA 2006 s.177(6)(a).
[95] CA 2006 s.177(6)(b).
[96] CA 2006 s.177(6)(b), (c).
[97] CA 2006 s.178.

director under the CA 2006 s.168. All these would amount to the "consequences of breach ... if the corresponding common law or equitable principle applied".[98]

Forgiveness for the breach—ratification

9–28   Although it is possible, retrospectively, to ratify a breach, to what extent may a director, proposing to breach one of his general duties, seek approval from the members in advance for doing so? Historically, depending on the articles, approval could be obtained by the members, with the director voting in his own interest,[99] unless there was a question of a fraud on the minority[100] or an inherently unapprovable contravention of some other rule of law, such as improper return of capital.[101] Members' approval is still permissible,[102] but in practice: (a) directors should not be intending to breach their duty anyway; (b) the private company model articles provide for directors' authorisation of what otherwise might be breaches; and (c) most members do not wish to be bothered by having to vote on resolutions about directors, are content to let directors get on with their jobs and are willing to trust the directors to act sensibly. This trust may not always be repaid, but if it is not, the directors may lay themselves open to a derivative action for failure to promote the success of the company.[103]

9–29   Forgiveness, or more properly "ratification" of the breach, after the event, must be done by the members in general meeting by ordinary resolution, following full disclosure of the entire matter.[104] However, the significant change under the CA 2006 s.239 is that in order to ratify some transgression by the director, if the company is a private company, and the vote is by means of a written resolution, the director, and those who are connected with him in terms of s.252, are not eligible to vote on the matter.[105] If the vote on ratification takes place at a general meeting, the resolution may only be passed if the necessary majority voted in favour, disregarding the votes of the director and the votes of those connected with him. The director may still be counted as part of any quorum and

---

[98] This section implicitly refers back to s.170(4), (5). In essence, although the breach of a rule may be an infringement of statute, the nature and extent of the breach will be ascertained by looking at the continued parallel stream of common law on these matters.

[99] *North-West Transportation Co v Beatty* (1887) 12 App. Cas. 589 PC.

[100] *Cook v Deeks* [1916] 1 A.C. 554 PC.

[101] *Aveling Barford Ltd v Perion Ltd* [1989] B.C.L.C. 626. In this case a holding company engineered the disposal of a subsidiary's asset to the holding company for much less than its true value. The subsidiary then went into insolvent liquidation. The holding company claimed that as shareholders of the subsidiary it was entitled to ratify the disposal, but the liquidator successfully argued that the disposal had been an improper return of capital and that the company had failed to follow the proper procedures required for a return of capital; a return of capital was inherently unratifiable and could only be carried out by the required procedures.

[102] CA 2006 s.180(1).

[103] CA 2006 ss.265–269.

[104] *Bamford v Bamford* [1970] Ch. 212 CA.

[105] CA 2006 s.239(3).

speak at the meeting.[106] If the overall vote, including the votes of the director and the votes of those connected with the director, is unanimously in favour of ratifying the director's transgression, the resolution is validly passed, for without this provision a single member company, when the director was the sole shareholder, would never be able to ratify anything.[107] However, it is not possible to have a clause in the articles or in any contract with the company pre-emptively absolving the directors from any liability for any breach of their fiduciary (or indeed any other) duty.[108] Despite this, the courts may forgive a breach where in their opinion the director has acted honestly and reasonably.[109]

The wider picture

Every year there are reported cases of conflicts of interest and breach of **9–30** fiduciary duty by directors towards their companies. Leaving aside the commonest reason, which is fraud, one reason that these breaches are so common is because in many of the companies involved, the director in question has built up the business himself or been so long in control that he sees the company as an extension of his own personality. Although a director is always supposed to remember that he and the company are separate, in practice, the boundaries in some directors' minds are blurred, and it does not occur to some directors that what they are doing is improper. Commonly the breach only comes to light when the company's shares are sold and the incoming owners, going through the past paperwork, discover what has been taking place, as in *Gencor ACP Ltd v Dalby*.[110] Sometimes the breach comes to light when disgruntled employees tip off the non-executives or alert an influential shareholder to what has been taking place. Auditors may also notice what has been taking place and draw the attention of the body of shareholders to the director's behaviour. Some directors attempt to justify their behaviour by saying that the other directors had approved their actions: while this sometimes may be true, this could mean that the other directors could also become liable to the company for failing to promote the interests of the company by allowing the offending director to receive so many benefits at the company's expense.

The prudent course of action is for the director to seek legal advice ahead of his proposed action. His failure to take such advice may show a lack of ability as a director, which, were the company subsequently to be wound up, might be of matter of interest to the liquidator in terms of the IA 1986 ss.212 and 214. In addition, if the advice he received were poor advice, he could sue the solicitor who provided it.

---

[106] CA 2006 s.239(4).

[107] CA 2006 s.239(6)(a). This would also apply in a husband and wife company where some breach has occurred and the two shareholders vote to ratify their own transgression perpetrated in their position as directors.

[108] CA 2006 s.232(1).

[109] CA 2006 s.1157. See para.9–59.

[110] *Gencor ACP Ltd v Dalby* [2000] 2 B.C.L.C. 734. See para.9–21.

Statutory duties that require disclosure to and approval from the members: Ch.4 ss.188–226

9–31   The general duties mentioned hitherto sometimes required disclosure to or approval from the directors. The following duties require disclosure to and approval from the members, on the principle that they are sufficiently important matters not merely to be delegated to the directors, although directors should consider them too, since each matter should be considered by the directors against the requirement to promote the success of the company. There therefore will need to be prior board approval before members' approval. Obtaining members' approval may be laborious, but at least in a private company the matter may be dealt with by written resolution. Because the duties are statutory, the company's articles cannot be written to exclude the need for the members' approval.

Directors' service contracts

9–32   Directors obtain rights from their service contracts. Directors' service contracts or a memorandum of its terms are available for inspection at the company's registered office or at a place specified under the regulations under s.1136[111] and each member may be entitled to inspect or obtain a copy of the contract or a memorandum of its terms.[112] Even the contracts of directors who have retired must have their former contracts available for inspection.[113] Although it is highly unlikely that a shadow director would have a service contract, the above rules apply to shadow directors as well.[114] The CA 2006 s.188 states that any provision of a director's contract which states that the contract is to continue for a period in excess of two years[115] and which may be terminated at the director's instance, but not the company's, or may be terminated by the company under specified circumstances, will only be valid if the contract with the offending term has been approved by the members first. Without such approval any such provision will be void and the company will then be able to terminate the contract by giving reasonable notice.[116] There are further rules to prevent the overlapping of directors' service contracts in an attempt to avoid the rules stated above.[117] The purpose of this provision is to prevent a director imposing upon his company a one-sided service contract in his favour and in excess of two years, this making it very difficult for the company to remove a director without significant expense. A sensible company accordingly provides its directors with contracts that are fair to both the company and the director and would

---

[111] CA 2006 s.228. This now includes the contracts of directors outside the UK.
[112] CA 2006 s.229.
[113] CA 2006 s.228(3).
[114] CA 2006 s.230. The purpose of the application of the rule to shadow directors is not to spawn the production of service contracts for shadow directors, but to be able to penalise the other directors who have permitted the shadow director to practise as a director without complying with the required rules.
[115] Under CA 1985, the period was five years.
[116] CA 2006 s.189; *Bain v The Rangers Football Club plc* [2011] CSOH 158.
[117] CA 2006 s.188(4).

not need shareholder approval. Common provisions that are to be found in most directors' contracts will deal with the following matters: appointment, term, duties and responsibilities, remuneration, expenses, holiday entitlement, motor car, pension, sickness absence, restrictions on other employment, intellectual property (inventions clause), confidentiality, termination and restrictions after termination.

Substantial property transactions

In order to prevent directors selling a non-cash asset to their companies for an excessive value, or buying assets from their companies for less than proper value, s.190 requires that members must give approval to the directors[118] for the sale or purchase of such an asset, if that asset is either worth more than £100,000 or more than 10 per cent of the company's net asset value, subject to a de minimis exception where the asset is less than £5,000 in value.[119] Where the directors fail to obtain such approval, the transaction is voidable at the instance of the company,[120] and the asset, where it is feasible to do so, and provided it is not in the hands of a third party who has acquired it in good faith and for value, or its value, must be returned to the company unless the members have affirmed the transaction within a reasonable period of time.[121] In the absence of such affirmation, the directors in question are liable to account to the company for any gain they have made, or must indemnify the company for any loss.[122] It is acceptable to take a subjective valuation of the asset since Parliament did not state that the value should be market value.[123] This particular set of provisions is of particular importance when a partnership sells its assets to a newly set up company, where the partners are the same people as the directors of the company buying the partnership assets. The directors, in their capacity as members, must be seen to have passed the s.190 resolution approving the sale to the company. There are exceptions to this requirement when the transaction in question is with a member (rather than a director) or another company in a group,[124] when the company is being wound up (unless it is a members' voluntary winding up) or in administration[125] or when the transaction takes place on a recognised investment exchange (i.e. the London Stock Exchange or

9–33

---

[118] This includes shadow directors (s.223(1)(b)).

[119] CA 2006 s.191(2). It is permissible to have conditional approval from the members (s.190(1)). There are also provisions for the aggregation of transactions involving non-cash assets so that if the aggregate value is greater than the figures indicated, the requirement for members' approval applies (s.190(5)).

[120] CA 2006 s.195(2). See also *Re Duckwari Plc (No.1)* [1997] 2 B.C.L.C. 713.

[121] CA 2006 s.196.

[122] CA 2006 s.195(3). *Re Duckwari Plc (No.2)* [1999] Ch. 253; [1998] 3 W.L.R. 913; [1999] B.C.C. 11; [1998] 2 B.C.L.C. 315.

[123] *Micro Leisure Ltd v County Properties and Developments Ltd*, 1999 S.L.T. 1428; [2000] B.C.C. 872.

[124] CA 2006 s.192.

[125] CA 2006 s.193.

one of the other recognised exchanges) since the transaction would be at market price anyway.[126] Service contracts and payments for loss of office are also excepted.[127]

Loans, quasi-loans, and credit transactions: ss.197–214

9–34   Subject to certain exceptions, a company may not lend money (or provide a guarantee or security) to a director unless the loan has been approved by the members. The reason for this prohibition is that if a director is reduced to borrowing money from his own company, or having to get the company to guarantee his loans, it suggests his own personal credit is poor and he is therefore a potentially risky borrower from the company. It is not generally a sensible use of company money. In practice unauthorised loans happen a great deal, particularly in small companies, and so the law takes account of the fact that however much legislation is in place they will still occur, which is why there is a de minimis exception for loans of less than £10,000.[128] The reasons it happens arise from the practical availability of the money to the director, a lack of awareness of the prohibition, and, despite the apparent intention of Parliament to make the CA 2006 user-friendly, the sheer length and complexity of the 17 sections of the CA 2006 applicable to loans. There are different rules for private companies, public companies, and private companies associated with public companies. Three different types of loan (loans, quasi-loans and credit transactions)[129] are prohibited. The rules for directors and those connected with directors are not entirely the same. However, at least these loans are no longer a criminal matter, as was the case under the CA 1985, and otherwise prohibited loans are permissible if the members allow the loans to take place.

Loan

9–35   In essence, a private or a public company may make an ordinary loan of any amount to its director or to a director of its holding company, or give a guarantee, or provide any form of security for a loan made by someone to such a director, provided the transaction[130] has been approved by the members.[131] If the director is a director of the company's holding company, the holding company's members must also approve the loan. Approval is obtained by providing the members with a

---

[126] CA 2006 s.194.
[127] CA 2006 s.190(6).
[128] CA 2006 s.207.
[129] Intelligibility is not helped by the fact that the two latter terms are not terms that are used in common parlance anyway.
[130] The legislation uses the word "transaction" to avoid having to repeat the words "loan", "guarantee" and "security".
[132] CA 2006 s.197(2).

memorandum outlining the terms of the transaction and the members voting on the matter.[132] If the company is a private company, the resolution may be passed by written resolution. However, if the transaction is less than £10,000, shareholders' approval is not needed.[133] If the company is a public company, and the loan is to a person connected[134] with the director, members' approval is necessary.[135]

Quasi-loan

A private company, but not a public company nor a private company **9–36** associated[136] with a public company,[137] may make a quasi-loan of any amount to its director or to a director of its holding company, or give a guarantee, or provide any form of security for a quasi-loan made by someone to such a director, and no members' approval is needed.[138]

By contrast, a public company, or a private company associated with a **9–37** public company, may let a director have such a quasi-loan, or give a guarantee, or provide any form of security for a quasi-loan, without members' approval provided it is under £10,000[139]; but where the quasi-loan is greater than £10,000, the members must approve it in the manner previously indicated in para.9–35.[140] If the director is a director of the company's holding company, the holding company's members must also approve the loan.[141] If the recipient of the quasi-loan is connected[142] with the director, the above rules apply as they do to directors.[143] A quasi-loan is laboriously explained in s.199 in very technical terms. What it actually means is an indirect loan, such as the use by a director of his company's Mastercard or other company credit facility to obtain funds, goods or services for his own benefit, in the expectation that in due course the director will reimburse his company.

---

[132] CA 2006 s.197(3), (4). No vote is needed if the lending company is not a UK registered company or if the company is a wholly owned subsidiary of some other registered company (s.197(5)).

[133] CA 2006 s.207(1).

[134] "Connected" is now explained in ss.252–255. In essence it means the director's close family, companies in which he has a considerable interest, trusts (or fellow trustees) and partners (in a commercial partnership).

[135] CA 2006 s.200. This rule also applies to companies associated with public companies, but not to free-standing private companies.

[136] See CA 2006 s.256. "Associated" in essence means a holding company, subsidiary company, or another company that is also a subsidiary of the same holding company.

[137] CA 2006 s.198(1).

[138] No section of the Act positively permits this: it is merely that it is not excluded by the other provisions.

[139] CA 2006 s.207(1).

[140] CA 2006 s.198(4)–(6).

[141] CA 2006 s.198(3).

[142] As defined in CA 2006 ss.252–255. In essence it means the director's close family, companies in which he has a considerable interest, trusts (or fellow trustees) and partners (in a commercial partnership).

[143] CA 2006 s.200.

Credit transaction

9–38   A private company, but not a public company nor a private company associated[144] with a public company,[145] may enter into a credit transaction of any amount with its director or with a director of its holding company, or with anyone connected[146] either with its director or with a director of its holding company, or give a guarantee, or provide any form of security for the credit transaction entered into by someone for the benefit of such a director or person connected with the director, and no members' approval is needed.[147]

9–39   By contrast, a public company, or a private company associated with a public company, may enter into a credit transaction, or give a guarantee, or provide any form of security for the credit transaction, with such a director, or person connected[148] with such director, without members' approval provided the credit transaction is under £15,000[149]; but where the credit transaction is greater than £15,000, the members must approve it in the manner previously indicated in para.9–44.[150] If the recipient of the credit transaction is a director of the company's holding company, or a person connected with him, the holding company's members must also approve the credit transaction.[151]

9–40   The words "credit transaction" are explained in s.202. In essence a credit transaction is one which enables the director (or person connected with him) to defer payment for goods or land because the company, on a hire purchase agreement or a conditional sale agreement, acquires the goods for him on the understanding that he will ultimately repay the company.[152] It also applies where the company leases or hires any land or goods for the benefit of the director (or person connected with the director).[153] However if the credit transaction is in the ordinary course of business and the terms of the credit transaction are no different from the terms that would be offered to anyone who was not involved in the company, no approval is required.[154]

---

[144] See CA 2006 s.256.

[145] CA 2006 s.198(1).

[146] As defined in CA 2006 ss.252–255.

[147] No section of the Act positively permits this: it is merely that it is not excluded by the other provisions.

[148] As defined in the CA 2006 ss.252–255.

[149] CA 2006 s.207(2).

[150] CA 2006 ss.201(4)–(6).

[151] CA 2006 s.198(3).

[152] CA 2006 s.202. A company, for example, could buy a car on hire purchase for the director, with the company making all the payments in the interim, even if the director is required ultimately to reimburse the company. The director has the advantage of not having to spend his own money in the interim.

[153] CA 2006 s.202(1)(b). Effectively the company is paying the rent for the director.

[154] CA 2006 s.207(3).

Prevention of evasion of the rules

In addition to the above restrictions on loans, quasi-loans and credit **9–41** transactions, there is a further provision to prevent the potential evasion of the rules, whereby a company provides a benefit to a person, in the expectation that that person would then provide a loan or quasi-loan to the director or enter into a credit transaction for his benefit.[155] In this event, the same rules as above relating to directors of holding companies, persons connected with the director, and members' approval apply as before.

Other exemptions

Notwithstanding the general restriction on loans, quasi-loans and **9–42** credit transactions, there are other exemptions from the overall rule. A company may give a loan or a quasi-loan, or guarantees for their loans or quasi-loans, to associated companies[156] or enter into a credit transaction for associated companies.[157] Companies may lend money to their directors to enable them to meet expenditure on behalf of the company or to carry out their duties[158] provided the transactions[159] involved no expenditure greater than £50,000.[160]

Yet further exemptions apply in respect of money-lending compa- **9–43** nies.[161] This is because traditionally one of the perquisites of working for banks and similar institutions is a cheap mortgage or low rates of interest on loans. Accordingly a money-lending company may give a director a loan or a quasi-loan, or guarantee a loan or a quasi-loan, provided the loan or quasi-loan is in the ordinary course of business, is for a home loan[162] and is on no more favourable terms than would be offered to anyone not connected with the money-lending company[163] but subject to the further provision that if the money-lending company provides subsidised home loans for its employees, the home loans for the directors are on terms no more favourable than those for the employees.[164]

Connected persons: ss.252–255

All the above rules relating to loans, quasi-loans and credit transac- **9–44** tions apply not only to directors but to those connected with them, these being:

---

[155] CA 2006 s.203.
[156] CA 2006 s.208(1).
[157] CA 2006 s.208(2).
[158] CA 2006 s.204(1).
[159] "Transactions" here includes loans, quasi-loans and credit transactions. There are further provisions to ensure that the aggregate figure of £50,000 covers previous transactions made for the benefit of the director or those connected with him. See ss.210–212.
[160] CA 2006 s.204(2).
[161] As defined in the CA 2006 s.209(2).
[162] CA 2006 s.209(4). This effectively means a mortgage over the director's own home.
[163] CA 2006 s.209(1)(b).
[164] CA 2006 s.209(3).

- a director's family[165] (i.e. spouse, civil partner, person (of either sex) with whom the director has an enduring family relationship,[166] children, stepchildren, children (up to the age of 18) of the person with whom he has the enduring family relationship, and parents);
- bodies corporate with which the director is connected[167];
- trustees of any trust for the benefit of the directors and their family (as defined above) or any bodies corporate connected with the director;
- the trust itself;
- partners (in terms of partnership law) of the director or the members of his family (as defined above) or bodies corporate with which the director is connected; and
- the partnership itself.

Curiously the word "connected" does not include employees or siblings.

Consequences of an unauthorised loan

9–45   If a company makes an unauthorised[168] loan or quasi-loan or enters into an unauthorised credit transaction, the loan, quasi-loan or credit transaction is voidable at the instance of the company and the director or connected person is required to account to the company for any gain made directly or indirectly, and jointly and severally with anyone else involved,[169] to indemnify the company for any loss.[170] The loan, quasi-loan or credit transaction will not be voidable if restitution is impossible, if the company has already been indemnified for any loss, or rights in the subject matter of the loan, quasi-loan or credit transaction have been acquired by a third party for value in good faith and without notice of the lack of authorisation.[171] A director will not be liable if he took all reasonable steps to obtain authorisation,[172] and neither a connected person nor a director who authorised the loan, quasi-loan or credit transaction will be liable if he did not know all the relevant circumstances.[173] All the provisions relating to these matters also apply to shadow directors.[174]

---

[165] As defined in s.253.

[166] This excludes the director's grandparent, grandchild, sister, brother, aunt, uncle, nephew or niece (s.253(3)).

[167] This effectively means that the director has at least a 20 per cent interest either in share capital or voting power in a company, limited liability partnership or limited partnership (ss.254, 255).

[168] "Unauthorised" here means that the members did not approve the loan and the loan was not exempt from disclosure.

[169] This also includes any director who authorised the improper loan.

[170] CA 2006 s.213. *McGregor Glazing Ltd v McGregor*, 2013 G.W.D. 19-379.

[171] CA 2006 s.213(2).

[172] CA 2006 s.213(6).

[173] CA 2006 s.213(7).

[174] CA 2006 s.223(1)(c).

Affirmation of an unauthorised transaction

If a loan, quasi-loan or credit transaction is unauthorised, but the **9–46** members of the company (and, as the case may be, the members of the holding company) affirm it within a reasonable time, it will no longer be voidable.[175] A "reasonable time" is not defined in the legislation.

Payments on loss of office, transfer of property or transfer of shares

Should a director[176] receive a payment for loss of office or retirement,[177] **9–47** on takeover or on any other occasion, that payment should be disclosed to and approved by the members first, without which the company may demand it back from the director.[178] If a director receives payment on the occasion of the transfer of some or all of the company's property or undertaking,[179] that payment should be declared to and approved by the members[180]; and if the director receives such payment without approval he is to hold it in trust for the company.[181] The rationale of this is if the director is in effect receiving an inducement to leave the company, or to sell some or part of the company's property, he is personally benefiting from a payment that really ought to be shared out amongst all the shareholders. A similar provision applies under s.219 where the director receives payment for loss of office following the sale of all or part of the company's shares on a takeover,[182] with similar consequences for unapproved payments.[183] In each event any unauthorised benefit must be returned to the members. This again is designed to prevent directors receiving bribes to persuade the shareholders to sell their shares to a bidder. How such bribes could in practice be detected is not explained. There is an exception for small payments of up to £200,[184] and if the payments are being made in good faith as a discharge of some legal obligation, damages for breach of that obligation, a settlement of a claim or pension, members' approval is not required.[185] Astute directors therefore arrange that their contracts of employment contain suitable provisions for lucrative pay-offs or pension contributions in the event of

---

[175] CA 2006 s.214.

[176] This includes a shadow director (s.223(1)(d)).

[177] As defined in CA 2006 s.215. This includes any form of employment with the company, not just loss of office as a director.

[178] *Lander v Premier Pict Petroleum Ltd*, 1997 S.L.T. 1361. This case concerned the viability of a "golden handshake" on a director's departure.

[179] CA 2006 s.218. This effectively means the sale of all or part of the company's business. The provision also covers the sale of a subsidiary or its business (s.218(2)) in which case the subsidiary's members would need to vote as well.

[180] CA 2006 s.217. If the payment is to a director of a holding company, the approval of the holding company's members is necessary as well. The approval is in the same manner as the approval for loans indicated above.

[181] CA 2006 s.222.

[182] However, in this case, the person making the takeover, and anyone associated with him, may not vote to approve the resolution (s.219(4)).

[183] CA 2006 s.222.

[184] CA 2006 s.221.

[185] CA 2006 s.220.

early termination of the contract: this will suit the other directors who will not relish defending to outraged shareholders at the next annual general meeting their former colleague's payment.

There are special provisions for payment to directors of quoted companies. The remuneration policy itself must be approved by ordinary resolution every three years (known as "say on pay"); payments for loss of office may only be made if they conform with that policy or have been specifically approved by the members; any payment not made in accordance with these rules should be held on trust by the director for the company and may be recovered from him or from any other directors who authorised the payments unless they can demonstrate that they were acting honestly and reasonably.[186] These were introduced by the Enterprise and Regulatory Reform Act 2013.

Contracts with sole members who are also directors

9–48　　Where a company is a single member company, any contracts between the company and its single member who is also a director of the company must either be in writing, set out in a memorandum or recorded in the minutes of the first meeting of the company after making the contract.[187]

Clauses protecting directors from liability

9–49　　It is not permissible for a company to have articles or any other contract that relieves a director from liability to his company for any negligence, default, breach of duty or breach of trust in relation to his company. A provision that attempted to do this would be void,[188] as would be the provision of any indemnity to a director for any of the above.[189] However, it is permissible for a company to provide for the director insurance, certain types of third party indemnity and certain types of pension scheme provision indemnity.[190] A company may pay the premiums for an insurance policy to cover any claim by the company against the director personally.[191] It may also pay the premiums for an insurance policy to cover any claim by third parties,[192] such as creditors, against the director personally, but in this case, unlike the previous one, the policy must not cover any liability suffered by the director where he has to pay a fine following criminal proceedings, pay a penalty to a regulatory authority, or pay his court costs for his unsuccessful defence in a criminal prosecution, his unsuccessful defence in any civil proceedings against him, or any unsuccessful application for relief either under

---

[186] CA 2006 ss.226A–F. See also para.8–16.
[187] CA 2006 s.231. See also *Re Neptune (Vehicle Washing Equipment) Ltd (No.2)* [1995] B.C.C. 1000. This section applies to shadow directors (s.231(5)).
[188] CA 2006 s.232(1).
[189] CA 2006 s.232(2).
[190] CA 2006 s.232(2).
[191] CA 2006 s.233.
[192] CA 2006 s.234.

s.661[193] or s.1157.[194] If the director wins the case, the insurer will pay his legal expenses. If he loses, the policy does not pay out and he has to bear his own costs. This type of insurance is colloquially known as "D & O insurance"[195] and is available through chambers of commerce, banks and specialist brokers.[196] The company may also pay the premiums for an insurance policy to cover any claim by the company's pension scheme against the director personally when acting as a trustee for the company's pension scheme.[197] This policy may also not pay out should the director be convicted of any crime in connection with the company, but will cover civil actions. This is because it is so difficult to get anyone to be a trustee anyway that unless insurance was provided, no-one would do the job at all.[198] The terms of all these policies need to be disclosed in the directors' report[199] and available for inspection by the members.[200]

Derivative proceedings

This topic, which is the right of a shareholder to bring an action against a director for his failure to promote the success of his company, is dealt with in Ch.11. **9–50**

Restriction on political donations

Directors can instruct their companies to make donations to political parties[201] of up to £5,000[202] a year without the need for prior authority from the members, but for sums greater than this, the directors must seek the prior approval of the members by means of an ordinary resolution.[203] If this approval is not obtained, the directors will become jointly and severally personally liable for the donation and for any damages for loss suffered by the company arising out of the donation, together with interest.[204] **9–51**

---

[193] This deals with the power of court to grant relief in the case of acquisition of shares by an innocent nominee.
[194] This deals with the power of court to grant relief where a director has acted honestly and reasonably in all the circumstances.
[195] Directors and officers.
[196] Prudent directors can also take out their own personal "run-off" insurance to cover their expenses should their companies' insurance cover be inadequate.
[197] CA 2006 s.235.
[198] The trustees of pension schemes have great responsibilities, the law is complex and bewildering, the labour is considerable and gratitude is slender.
[199] CA 2006 s.236.
[200] CA 2006 ss.237, 238.
[201] CA 2006 ss.362–379. There are certain exemptions, such as to certain trades unions and employers' organisations.
[202] CA 2006 s.378.
[203] CA 2006 s.366.
[204] CA 2006 s.185.

' duties to creditors

ıciple, directors owe no duty of care to creditors,[205] at least while
ɔany is solvent. The whole point of the limited liability company
ılate the directors and members from the claims of the company's
ᴄⁱᵤ....‾ s provided, that is, that the company is not being run as a sham
or façade, or provided that some other occasion for the lifting of the
corporate veil has not taken place.[206] Creditors are not normally obliged
to deal with limited companies,[207] and if a creditor chooses to deal with a
limited company, he must take the risk that the company may be run
badly or without any consideration for creditors' interests. If the creditor
is anxious about the trustworthiness of directors of a company, he should
take adequate precautions such as obtaining personal guarantees from
them, inspecting the company's accounts in the Register of Companies,
seeking performance bonds or finding some other method of safe-
guarding his position. If the company is heading towards insolvency, the
position may be different.[208] But otherwise, the Scottish case of *Nordic Oil
Services Ltd v Berman*[209] suggests that directors are not responsible for
economic loss suffered by a creditor as a result of the directors' actions,
and the English case of *Williams v Natural Life Health Foods Ltd*[210] also
bears this out. In the latter case, a director provided negligent advice to
clients seeking to buy a health food shop. The advice was undoubtedly
negligent but because the advice had been provided by the director in his
capacity as a director of his company, and not in a personal capacity, he
personally was not liable.[211]

9–53   Although a director acting negligently towards his creditors through
his company may be free from liability, carrying out a fraud on his
creditors through his company will not serve to protect him from liability.
If a fraudster carries out a fraud through his company, he still remains
liable for his liable fraud, even if the company is liable with him.[212] In the
case of *Standard Chartered Bank v Pakistan National Shipping Corporation (No.2)*[213] the claimants were obliged to honour a bill of lading that
had been falsely dated on behalf of his company by the director of the

---

[205] *Multinational Gas and Petrochemical Co Ltd v Multinational Gas and Petrochemical Services Ltd* [1983] Ch. 283; [1983] 2 All E.R. 563, per Dillon L.J. One rare case where directors were liable, under exceptional circumstances, to creditors arose in *Winkworth v Edward Baron Development Co Ltd* [1986] 1 W.L.R. 1512; [1987] 1 All E.R. 114.

[206] See Ch.2.

[207] That is, if one excludes involuntary creditors such as victims of the company's delicts.

[208] *Liquidator of West Mercia Safetywear Ltd v Dodd* [1988] B.C.L.C. 250 CA.

[209] *Nordic Oil Services Ltd v Berman*, 1993 S.L.T. 1168 OH.

[210] *Williams v Natural Life Health Foods Ltd* [1998] 1 W.L.R. 830; [1998] 2 All E.R. 577.

[211] The clients wished to sue the directors personally because his company was not worth suing and he was, but also because there was some doubt as to whether or not he had provided the advice personally. The House of Lords decided that he had provided the advice through the company.

[212] This particularly applies to copyright infringements: *C Evans and Sons Ltd v Spitebrand Ltd* [1985] 1 W.L.R. 31; *Naxos v Project Management (Borders) Ltd & K.J. Salmon,* 2012 CSOH 158.

[213] *Standard Chartered Bank v Pakistan National Shipping Corporation (No.2)* [2002] 3 W.L.R. 1547; [2003] 1 All E.R. 173.

fourth defendant, Mr Mehra, who was one of four directors of his company, Oakprime Ltd, as part of a fraud on the Vietnamese Government. The claimants sought to recover from Mr Mehra. Mr Mehra's argument was that he should not be liable because it was his company, Oakprime Ltd, that had carried out the fraud. By this stage Oakprime Ltd was in liquidation. The House of Lords held that a fraudster was subject to the maxim *culpa tenet suos auctores*[214] whether or not his company was involved. Indeed the House of Lords was deeply unimpressed by Mehra's argument, not least because had it succeeded it would have allowed any future fraudster to carry out any fraud scot-free through his company.[215]

As was discussed in Ch.2, in the context of *Prest v Petrodel Resources Ltd*,[216] there is an overlap with the issue of "piercing the veil". In small companies in particular, the controlling (and often sole) shareholder is also the director, and may be using his company to evade a legal responsibility or frustrate the operation of law, as in *Gilford Motor Co Ltd v Horne*.[217] In that event, so Lord Sumption said in *Prest*—the corporate veil may be lifted to make the director/controlling shareholder liable, or as the case may be, comply with the legal responsibility or cease to frustrate the operation of law. In cases where a company is being used to conceal assets, as in *Trustor AB v Smallbone*,[218] the company is merely acting as the agent or nominee of the director/controlling shareholder, and the director/controlling shareholder remains liable.

There have not been at the time of writing any major recent cases in **9-54** Scotland on these points, but it is submitted that the principle in Scotland would be the same as in England—and in the interests of commercial certainty it would be wise for it to be consistent—that a director is not in general personally liable for the delicts committed by his company, unless: (i) he has assumed personal responsibility; (ii) he has committed a fraud through the company, in which case he has to accept responsibility for what he has done; (iii) that he is using his company to evade his legal responsibility or to frustrate the operation of law.

Duty to employees

Under the CA 2006 s.172(1)(b) the directors are required to have **9-55** regard to the interests of their companies' employees. The duty to "have regard" is owed by the directors not to the employees directly, but to the company, and is enforceable in the same manner as any other fiduciary duty owed by the directors. This means that only if the members collectively decide that the employees' interests are not being regarded may they exert pressure on the directors to have some regard for the

---

[214] Those who carried out a wicked act are liable for its consequences. Per Lord Rodger at [40].

[215] See also *Contex Drouzhba Ltd v Wiseman* [2008] B.C.C. 301; [2008] 1 B.C.L.C. 63.

[216] [2013] 4 All E.R. 673; [2013] B.C.C. 571; [2013] 2 A.C. 415; [2013] UKSC 34; [2013] 3 W.L.R. 1.

[217] [1933] Ch. 935.

[218] [2001] W.L.R. 1177; [2002] B.C.C. 795.

employees. As in many cases, except perhaps companies where the employees have a large shareholding in the company, the members' interests will be antithetical to the employees' interests, this sub-section is likely to be of little practical benefit to employees.[219] The directors also have extensive duties to employees under health and safety legislation which may not be avoided by the exercise of the corporate veil. This book does not address these large issues and reference should be made to other literature on the subject.

The duty to members

9–56   Historically, while directors might be expected to owe various duties[220] to the collective body of shareholders (in other words the company as a whole) there was no specific duty of care to individual members.[221] This is understandable in one sense, in that directors could not be expected to be concerned about every single member in his company, and it would be a deterrent to people becoming directors if they could be sued by any disgruntled member of their company. At the same time, it is clearly not desirable to let directors think they can walk roughshod over certain members or to treat one set of members better than another, except when members know where they stand before they become members. For example, a company might have two sets of shares: voting shares held by the directors and non-voting shares. Anyone buying a non-voting share in that company will know in advance that the voting shareholders/ directors will always be in an advantageous position relative to the non-voting shareholders. CA 2006 s.172(1)(f) now requires directors to act fairly as between members of the company, but the duty to act fairly is owed to the company. If the company is not able or willing to raise an action against the directors, the members who feel that they have not been treated fairly by the directors may bring a derivative claim against the director. Derivative claims are discussed more fully in Ch.11, but they allow the unhappy members the right to claim on behalf of the company against the directors. If the claim is established, any damages or restitution of assets taken by the directors is for the benefit of the company, out of which, indirectly, the petitioner may benefit. In *Hughes v Weiss*[222] both claimant and defendant had one share in the company[223] and were both directors. Hughes was given permission to continue her derivative claim against Weiss who had misappropriated much of the company's money. Another option for members who feel that they have been treated unfairly is to petition on the grounds of CA 2006 s.994 (unfairly

---

[219]   The reason this section was originally inserted was that one of the terms of entry to the European Union was a greater regard for employees' interests; the wording was ingeniously drafted apparently to satisfy this requirement but without it actually being of any use to employees.

[220]   The fiduciary duty and the duty of skill and care, now part of the general duties in CA 2006 s.171–178.

[221]   *Percival v Wright* [1902] 2 Ch. 421.

[222]   [2012] EWHC 2363 (Ch).

[223]   With each member only having one share, there was no majority mandate for the company to bring a claim against Weiss.

prejudicial conduct by the majority shareholders). This strictly speaking is not a claim against the directors as directors, but it is common for the directors in smaller companies to have a majority of the shares and thus, whether in their capacity as majority shareholders or as directors, not to be acting fairly as between the members.

Duty to auditors

A requirement for directors of companies other than small companies **9-57** is that in the directors' report there must be a statement that as far as each director is concerned, he has not held back from the auditor any information of which the auditor ought to be aware, and that he has taken "all the steps" that he ought to have taken as a director to make himself aware of any information of which the auditor ought to be aware and to have ensured that the auditor is aware of that information.[224] The term "all the steps" is explained as requiring the director to make such enquiries of his fellow directors and of the auditors for the purpose of making himself aware of the information the auditor ought to be aware of, such as would be expected of his duty as a director of the company to act with reasonable care, skill and diligence.[225] There are criminal sanctions for the director's failure to do this.[226]

Duty to co-operate with insolvency practitioners and others

When a company goes into administration, receivership or liquidation **9-58** the directors and any other officers of the company are expected to supply such information as those persons may require. Failure to do so is a criminal offence.[227] Where a company is in liquidation and the directors have carried out a fraud or other deception, such as destruction of or failure to maintain the company's records, false representations to creditors and so on, further criminal sanctions will be applied.[228]

Where the company is undergoing a BIS inspection, there is a duty on the directors to co-operate to the fullest extent with the BIS inspectorate[229] at the risk of being liable for contempt of court.[230]

Directors free from liability under Companies Act 2006 s.1157

It is true that if a director has failed to exercise a duty of care towards **9-59** his company, it is open to the members to forgive him, and ratify his breach of duty of care under the CA 2006 s.239. The director in question may no longer use his own shareholding to absolve himself of any breach unless the vote was unanimously in his own favour. However, even if the

---

[224] CA 2006 s.418(2).
[225] CA 2006 s.418.
[226] CA 2006 s.418(5), (6).
[227] IA 1986 ss.22, 66, 157, 208.
[228] IA 1986 ss.206–211, 218–219.
[229] CA 1985 s.434. These provisions (within Pt 14 of the CA 1985) are not repealed by CA 2006 and reference will still need to be made to the CA 1985.
[230] CA 1985 s.436.

members do not forgive the director, the courts may possibly do so, under the CA 2006 s.1157. This section acts as complete or partial relief (at the court's discretion) for directors who have acted honestly and reasonably under the circumstances. For example, in *Re D'Jan of London Ltd*,[231] D'Jan had relied on his insurance broker to complete a fire insurance application for his company. D'Jan signed the application without checking the details, one of which was a question about previous fires associated with his company. Later his company had a fire on its premises and the insurance company refused to pay out because there has been no disclosure of a previous fire suffered by his company. The company then went into liquidation and the liquidator tried to recover from D'Jan on the grounds of his carelessness in not checking the insurance application. Although the court found that D'Jan had been careless, D'Jan was relieved of part of his liability on the grounds that, whether or not he had acted reasonably in relying on the insurance broker and not checking the application, there was no question about his honesty. By way of contrast, in *Cohen v Selby*,[232] Mr Selby took uninsured diamonds belonging to his company, but paid for by post-dated cheques, from the south of England in a canvas hold-all on to a cross-channel ferry. At some stage on the rough ferry crossing, seasick or possibly drugged, he apparently lost the bag with the diamonds, which meant that he could not sell them as intended in Germany. The company was consequently unable to honour the post-dated cheques, causing the company to be put into liquidation. When the liquidator raised proceedings against him, Selby tried to avail himself of the benefits of the then equivalent of s.1157, but was unable to persuade the courts that his actions had been "honest and reasonable in all the circumstances".[233]

DIRECTORS' LIABILITY ON INSOLVENCY

9–60 When a company is solvent, a director will be liable to his company where he has breached his various duties, all to the extent indicated earlier in the chapter, and liable to its creditors only in limited circumstances. When a company becomes insolvent, the position changes.

Directors' liability on winding-up

9–61 When a company is wound up, the court on the application of the liquidator[234] may under ss.212–217 of the Insolvency Act 1986 ("IA 1986") make the directors compensate the company for its losses. If a company is not wound up, mainly because there are no funds available to

---

[231] [1994] 1 B.C.L.C. 561.

[232] *Cohen v Selby*; sub nom. *Re Simmon Box (Diamonds) Ltd* [2000] B.C.C. 275, upheld on appeal [2001] 1 B.C.L.C. 176 CA.

[233] The unkind might suggest that the uninsured jewels never actually left England.

[234] Strictly speaking, the liquidator, Official Receiver in England, any creditor or contributory may apply to the court in respect of s.212, but as regards ss.213, 214 only the liquidator may apply.

pay for a liquidator, the directors, at least in Scotland, may, regrettably, be able to avoid such penalties.[235] If the directors have committed any criminal offences in the period leading up to winding up, such as fraud, concealment of assets, removing or destroying the company's assets, making or keeping false records, falsifying the company's books, defrauding creditors or failing to provide proper information to the liquidator, etc. the directors may be imprisoned or fined.[236] Again, if the company is not wound up, these sanctions may not be applied.

The civil sanctions outlined in the IA 1986 ss.212–217 were introduced **9–62** in order to concentrate directors' minds as a result of various scandals in the 1970s and 1980s. There was great alarm at their introduction on the grounds that the provisions were eroding the sanctity of limited liability, but the Government's view was that honest directors had nothing to fear and that there had been too many instances of directors abusing the privileges of limited liability. There are some difficulties in using these sanctions, mainly because of the cost of having the liquidator apply to the court for a compensation order (unless some of the creditors are willing to fund the action, liquidators in general being unwilling to fund the actions themselves), the uncertainty of obtaining the order and the fact that many directors are not in practice worth suing anyway once their companies are insolvent. In addition, any creditor who feels sufficiently strongly to persuade the liquidator to take action against the errant directors may well find that such sums as the directors provide by way of compensation are distributed amongst the creditors generally rather than to the aggrieved creditor himself. As a further complication, the approval of the court or the creditors is needed before raising any actions against directors under the fraudulent trading or wrongful trading provisions.[237]

Nonetheless the sanctions are some deterrent to misbehaving directors. There are also extensive criminal sanctions against fraudulent practices by directors and officers of wound-up companies.[238]

Breach of duty to the company under Insolvency Act 1986 s.212

Where an officer of the company,[239] or promoter, manager or someone **9–63** otherwise involved in the formation of the company, has misapplied or retained the company's assets, or been guilty of misfeasance or breach of

---

[235] In England and Wales, under such circumstances, the Official Receiver would be appointed as the liquidator and might take action against errant directors. There are moves to make the Accountant in Bankruptcy the equivalent of the Official Receiver in Scotland. In the absence of the equivalent of the Official Receiver in Scotland, some insolvent companies are not wound up, creditors are repaid nothing, eventually the company is struck off and no action is taken against the directors.

[236] IA 1986 ss.206–211.

[237] IA 1986 ss.165, 167 and Sch.4 Pt 1 para.3A, as inserted by the Enterprise Act 2002 s.253.

[238] IA 1986 ss.206–211.

[239] In the context of a company in liquidation, "officer" means not only a director, the company secretary and the auditor, but also any receiver, administrator, administrative receiver (in England) or liquidator.

any fiduciary or statutory duty[240] to his company, including being negligent, any creditor, the Official Receiver in England, the liquidator or a
contributory,[241] but not an administrator,[242] may apply to court in order
to have the court examine the person alleged to be liable. If necessary the
court can compel that person to repay any sums or return any assets due
to the company and to contribute to the company by way of compensation such sums as the court sees just.[243] Note that the company does not
require to be in insolvent liquidation.

9–64   Misfeasance means using the company's assets for the director's own
benefit without permission, or in any other way breaching his duties to
the company. In many respects it is a "catch-all" provision and whereas
the IA 1986 ss.213 and 214 have their difficulties, s.212 is relatively easy
to operate. It is not unknown for an application to be made both under
s.212 and s.214.[244] The important issue concerning s.212 is that the
liquidator or other applicant is claiming sums back from the director as a
result of the breach of the director's duties to the *company* as a whole, as
opposed to ss.213 and 214 which involves claims by the liquidator arising
out of the director's failure to consider properly the interests of *creditors*.
The relief afforded by the CA 2006 s.1157 therefore does apply to s.212
orders,[245] but not to ss.213 or 214 orders.[246]. It is not possible to use an
application under s.212 to obtain information about the directors'
activities, an application under s.236 being the proper means of achieving
this objective.[247]

9–65   In the event of a company being put into liquidation and a successful
claim being made against the director under s.212, a receiver operating
under the terms of a crystallised old style floating charge[248] would be able
to seize the recovered funds at the expense of the liquidator on the
grounds that what the director returned to the company was originally
funds of the company's and therefore covered by the terms of the floating

---

[240] This would include the general rules and the statutory duties referred earlier in this
chapter.

[241] A contributory is a person who has a partly paid share and is still due to repay the
unpaid amount on his share. The rights and definition of contributory are more fully
explained in Ch.16.

[242] Except in respect of those few companies to which the former rules on administrative
receivership in England (receivership in Scotland) still apply as they are exempt from the
administration provisions under the Enterprise Act 2002. For those companies, see
para.15–32. It is also arguable that an administrator exercising his rights under the IA
1986 Sch.1 para.5 could still sue a director for misfeasance (i.e. breach of the director's
duty to promote the success of the company under the CA 2006 s.172) generally but not
under s.212 of the IA 1986 since that section makes no provision for the administrator to
do this.

[243] *Bairstow v Queens Moat Houses Plc* [2000] 1 B.C.L.C. 549.

[244] *Re DKG Contractors Ltd* [1990] B.C.C. 903; *Re Brian D Pierson (Contractors) Ltd*
[1999] B.C.C. 26.

[245] As happened in *Re D'Jan of London Ltd* [1994] 1 B.C.L.C. 561.

[246] *Re Produce Marketing Consortium Ltd* [1989] B.C.L.C. 513.

[247] *Gray v Davidson*, 1991 S.L.T. (Sh. Ct.) 61.

[248] That is, a floating charge that was in place before the commencement of the relevant
provisions of the Enterprise Act 2002.

charge.[249] Given that most companies nowadays go into administration this is less significant than it once was.

Fraudulent trading under Insolvency Act 1986 s.213

Only a liquidator (and not a receiver or administrator) may apply to **9–66** court[250] for an order that anyone,[251] knowingly party to the carrying on of a business through a company (whether solvent or not) with the intent to defraud creditors of the company, creditors of any other person, or for any fraudulent purpose, will be liable to make such contributions to the company's assets as the court thinks proper. The difficulty with fraudulent trading is having to prove the deliberate intent to defraud,[252] and since the effort of doing so may not be worth the return, liquidators rarely use this provision. But from time to time it is still used, generally where the evidence of fraud is unequivocal.[253] Note that the wording of s.213 does not require that the company be in insolvent liquidation.

There is also a separate criminal offence of fraudulent trading which applies to directors, irrespective of the company's solvency.[254]

Wrongful trading under Insolvency Act 1986 s.214

A liquidator (but not a receiver nor an administrator) may apply to the **9–67** court for an order to make a director, or past director, of a company that has gone into insolvent liquidation liable to make such contribution to the company's assets as the court thinks proper.[255] The director will be liable for this if:

- the company is in insolvent liquidation;
- at some time before the commencement of the winding up, that director knew or ought to have concluded that there was no reasonable prospect that the company would avoid going into insolvent liquidation; and
- that person was a director of the company at the time.[256]

---

[249] *Re Anglo-Austrian Printing and Publishing Union* [1895] 2 Ch. 981.

[250] The court or the creditors must approve this course of action: IA 1986 ss.165, 167 and Sch.4 Pt 1 para.3A, as inserted by the Enterprise Act 2002 s.253.

[251] The word "anyone" covers not only directors and officers of the company, but also members who are aware of what is taking place (*Morris v Banque Arabe Internationale d'Investissement SA (No.2)* [2001] B.C.L.C. 263), and recipients of the proceeds of fraud (*Morris v Bank of India* [2003] B.C.C. 735; [2004] B.C.L.C. 236).

[252] *Galoo Ltd v Bright Grahame Murray* [1994] 1 W.L.R. 1360.

[253] *Morphites v Bernasconi* [2001] 2 B.C.L.C. 1; *Morris v Bank of America* [2000] B.P.I.R. 83 C; *Alpha Sim Communications Ltd v Caz Distribution Services Ltd* [2014] EWHC 207 (Ch).

[254] CA 1985 s.458.

[255] IA 1986 s.214(1). The court or the creditors must approve the action against the director (Enterprise Act 2002 s.253). The money provided by the director is for the benefit of the unsecured creditors; *Re Oasis Merchandising Services Ltd* [1998] 1 Ch.170.

[256] IA 1986 s.214(2).

The courts will not make such an order if they are satisfied that the director took:

> "... every step with a view to minimising the potential loss to the company's creditors as (assuming he knew there was no reasonable prospect that the company would avoid insolvent liquidation) he ought to have taken".[257]

9–68 As to the facts the director ought to have known or found out, the conclusion he ought to have reached and the steps he ought to have taken, are those which should be known, found out, reached and taken by a reasonably diligent person, having:

- the general knowledge, skill and experience as may be expected of a person carrying out the same functions as are carried out by that director in relation to the company; and
- the general knowledge, skill and experience that that director has.[258]

This test is a demanding one, and the point of the above wording is deliberately to encourage directors to seek professional advice before the company's financial position deteriorates any further, in order to protect the interests of creditors. There has been concern with the wording of this section in that it imposes a standard that is easy to deliver in hindsight, especially by a judge who himself has probably never entered the commercial arena, and concern that it may drive companies into administration or liquidation (erring on the side of prudence) when in fact the company could in fact continue perfectly viably. As indicated earlier, the standard that is expected of a director is the dual standard both of any director in the same position as the director in question and, where applicable, a higher level if the director has extra skill or experience, such as a professional qualification or many years' practice. Directors are expected to be realistic in their expectations of the company's fortunes and not to be blind to the obvious facts.[259] At the same time, there seems simultaneously to be a more generous approach, which allows the directors to continue if they genuinely, and with some good reason, believe that matters will improve (sometimes known as the sunshine test). This is apparent from the words of an unreported decision of Buckley J. in *Re White & Osmond (Parkstone) Ltd*,[260] in the course of which he said:

> "In my judgment, there is nothing wrong in the fact that directors incur credit at a time when, to their knowledge, the company is not able to meet all its liabilities as they fall due. What is manifestly wrong is if directors allow a company to incur credit at a time when

---

[257] IA 1986 s.214(3).
[258] IA 1986 s.214(4).
[259] *Re Rod Gunner Organisation Ltd* [2004] B.C.C. 684; [2004] 2 B.C.L.C. 110.
[260] *Re White & Osmond (Parkstone) Ltd* Unreported June 30, 1960.

the business is being carried on in such circumstances that it is clear the company will never be able to satisfy its creditors. However, there is nothing to say that directors who genuinely believe that the clouds will roll away and the sunshine of prosperity will shine upon them again and disperse the fog of their depression are not entitled to incur credit to help them to get over the bad time."

Indeed, in *Re Hawkes Hill Publishing Co Ltd*[261] Lewison J. went as far as to reject a liquidator's application for a contribution under s.214 on the grounds that the liquidator had not established that the directors of that company had no reasonable grounds for believing it would not survive. Each case must very much be taken on its facts.

As an example of the operation of s.214, in *Re Produce Marketing* **9–69** *Consortium Ltd (No.2)*[262] the directors deliberately ignored auditors' advice and overstated the value of stock in their refrigerated warehouse in order to present a more viable impression of the company's solvency. They were consequently found liable. Another case suggests that poor judgment by one director when he could have taken advice rendered him liable. His wife, who was also a director, hoped to avoid liability because she had played no part in the management of the company was also held liable on the grounds that ignorance and inactivity are no excuse.[263]

If a director is found liable under s.214, the courts may in addition disqualify the director under the Company Directors Disqualification Act 1986.

"Phoenix trading"

Phoenix trading is the loose term[264] for the re-use of an insolvent **9–70** company's name by the directors who were involved in the insolvent company. Sometimes companies collapse, leaving creditors empty-handed, whereupon the former directors quickly re-establish themselves as directors or promoters of a new enterprise with a similar name in the same line of business. When the director, or person who had been a director in the last 12 months, of an insolvent company does this within five years of the insolvent company's liquidation, he commits a criminal offence by having the new enterprise's name identical or very similar to the insolvent company's name,[265] unless the courts have expressly

---

[261] *Re Hawkes Hill Publishing Co Ltd* (2007) 151 S.J.L.B. 743.

[262] *Re Produce Marketing Consortium Ltd (No.2)* [1989] B.C.L.C. 520.

[263] *Re Brian D. Pierson (Contractors) Ltd* [1999] B.C.C. 26.

[264] A phoenix is a mythical Arabian bird, the only one of its kind, which after many years makes itself a nest of spices, sings a melancholy song, and flaps its wings to set its nest on fire. In the process it is burnt to ashes, but an egg is found in the embers, out of which the phoenix is born anew. In the same manner the phoenix company rises out of the ashes of its own immolation.

[265] *R. v Cole* [1998] 2 B.C.L.C. 234.

permitted such a name.[266] Although the Registrar of Companies would probably detect the re-use of a name or the use of a similar name if a new company were formed, the Registrar would not be aware of a partnership with such a name, but the legislation still prevents the use of the forbidden name by any enterprise unless permission has been granted.[267]

In addition if the new enterprise becomes insolvent and is a company, the directors involved in the new company will be jointly and severally liable along with the company and anyone else who knew of the contravention and ignored it and who was involved with the management of the company.[268]

NON-STATUTORY DUTIES

9–71 There are some duties that perhaps do not count as "duties"—more as expectations. The directors of premium listed companies are expected to adhere to the UK Corporate Governance Code, which is a voluntary non-binding code managed by the Financial Reporting Council.[269] Being only a code and therefore "soft law", there are no minimal sanctions against failure to adhere to its requirements, other than public disapproval and possible criticism at general meetings and in the financial press. At the worst, the company could be fined by the Financial Conduct Authority or delisted. The UK Corporate Governance Code is promulgated by the Financial Services Authority and it is a condition of listing that companies and their directors adhere to it.[270] If directors choose not to adhere to the provisions of the UK Corporate Governance Code, they are expected to explain why they are not doing so. The UK Corporate Governance Code promulgates the virtues of accountability, integrity and transparency in corporate transactions by the directors. On the whole, most listed companies comply with the UK Corporate Governance Code—some more grudgingly than others—but it is difficult for listed companies' directors to complain too vociferously about the UK Corporate Governance Code's requirements without the directors being

---

[266] IA 1986 s.216(3). The courts permitted the re-use of a name in *Re Bonus Breaks Ltd* [1991] B.C.C. 491, subject to certain undertakings by the directors. In this case the creditors of the original insolvent company were willing to allow the new company to be set up. For the procedure on how a name may be re-used, see the Insolvency (Scotland) Rules 1986 (SI 1986/1915) rr.4.78–4.82.

[267] IA 1986 s.216(3)(c).

[268] IA 1986 s.217(2). *Glasgow City Council v Craig*, 2009 S.L.T. 212. In *Ricketts v Ad Valorem Factors Ltd* [2004] 1 All E.R. 894; [2004] B.C.C. 164; [2004] 1 B.C.L.C. 1, the phoenix company's name "Air Equipment Company Ltd" was found to be too close to the defunct "Air Components Company Ltd" and the directors became personally liable for the phoenix company's debts.

[269] There is another, less demanding, code for quoted companies, mostly standard listed companies on the Stock Exchange or companies on the AIM or ICAP Securities and Derivatives Exchange. It is known as the Corporate Governance Code for Small and Mid-Size Quoted Companies.

[270] It was originally hoped that it would be extended to all quoted companies but this proved difficult to enforce. AIM companies are not required to adhere to all parts of it, though some may choose to do so.

asked what they have to hide. Only if a company is conspicuously successful can it afford to ignore the UK Corporate Governance Code's requirements.[271] Amongst the main requirements of the Combined Code are that the managing director and chairman should be separate, one half of the board should be independent non-executive directors, non-executive directors should be the majority on the audit, remuneration and appointment committees, the non-executives should meet independently of the other board members and once a year without the chairman being present, and there should be a senior independent director whom shareholders may approach if they have concerns.

Although this has not been universally well received, it is arguably a **9–72** more flexible arrangement than what is required in the United States where the Sarbanes Oxley Act introduced, as ever with these matters, as a result of various scandals,[272] very strict rules on corporate governance. These have been costly to introduce but are gradually forcing corporate America to change its culture to one of greater transparency and integrity. The main effect of current corporate governance in the United Kingdom is to force listed companies to adhere to the UK Corporate Governance Code, which, broadly speaking, is common sense writ large, in that it encourages best practice, transparency, fair dealing and open communication between a company and its shareholders. However, for individual companies not every aspect may suit that company's individual culture, in which case it is open to that company to explain in report and notes to the accounts why the company has not adhered to the UK Corporate Governance Code. This process is known as "comply or explain". Where the shareholders are content with the explanation, the share price will be unaffected and the directors' actions approved; but where the explanation is found wanting, the lack of compliance will affect the share price and the directors may be criticised. Although there was initial reluctance to the "comply or explain" regime, it becomes difficult for a company to object to it too loudly on the grounds that the company must have something to hide.

A more cynical method of dealing with corporate governance has **9–73** begun to arise recently. Having to comply with the UK Corporate Governance Code is seen by some as more trouble than it is worth, as so much has to be revealed to competitors, creditors and investors. Canny entrepreneurs in the private equity field are therefore buying listed companies and turning them private, making them more profitable (usually having cut costs and staff) and then selling them back into the market. Once private, the companies are not required to waste (as the directors see it) time and money on corporate governance, the financial press takes less interest in them, the directors have a freer hand to do as

---

[271] Back in 2005, Monsoon, the high street clothes shop, as an AIM company was not required to adhere to the Combined Code (the predecessor to the UK Corporate Governance Code), but had been extremely successful, possibly, some would say, as a result of not having to adhere to the Code. Its managing director, Peter Simon, memorably described the Code as "a load of bollocks" (*The Independent*, April 9, 2005).

[272] Enron, Worldcom and others.

they wish. It is arguable that the opportunities for wealth creation are greater in non-listed companies, but equally, companies where there is good corporate governance are likely to find that the worst excesses of directorial greed or incompetence are mitigated so that investors' money is safer. Where there is corporate governance, the financial returns are broadly speaking safe but unlikely to be huge; where there is no corporate governance, the financial returns are possibly greater but so too are the losses. A pension fund should invest in a company where there is good corporate governance: a speculative entrepreneur with money he can afford to lose should invest in a company without corporate governance.

Further Reading

Deirdre Ahern, "Directors' duties, dry ink and the accessibility agenda" (2012) 128(Jan) L.Q.R. 114.

Parker Hood, "Directors' duties under the Companies Act 2006: clarity or confusion?" (2013) 13(1) J.C.L.S. 1.

Elaine Lynch, "Section 172: a ground-breaking reform of director's duties, or the emperor's new clothes?" (2012) 33(7) Comp. Law 196.

Andrew Keay, "The authorising of directors' conflicts of interest: getting a balance?" (2012) 12(1) J.C.L.S. 129.

Andrew Keay and Hao Zhang, "An analysis of enlightened shareholder value in light of ex post opportunism and incomplete law" (2011) 8(4) E.C.F.R. 445.

Robin McDonald, "The Companies Act 2006 and the directors' duty to disclose" (2011) 22(3) I.C.C.L.R. 96.

Peter Yeoh, "Who'd be a director?" (2012) 33(7) Bus. L.R. 174.

CHAPTER 10

COMPANY SECRETARY AND AUDITOR

THE COMPANY SECRETARY

The company secretary is treated as an officer of the company, which **10–01** means that where statute specifically refers to "officers" as opposed merely to directors, the legislation applies to company secretaries as well.[1] Under the Companies Act 2006 ("the CA 2006"), every public company must have a company secretary[2] but company secretaries are optional for private companies.[3] Many companies, whether or not they are obliged to have company secretaries, continue to retain them in the interests both of credibility and efficiency.

The company secretary was historically a person of little importance, **10–02** whose role was a mere minute-taker and organiser of meetings, but increasingly he is seen as a useful and professional member of the senior management of the company. Company secretaries have their own professional body, the Institute of Chartered Secretaries and Administrators,[4] and most company secretaries have either a legal or an accounting qualification. Although it is possible simultaneously to be a director and secretary,[5] and in many small family companies the practice is that one spouse is the managing director while the other spouse is the other director and company secretary, it is also possible to have a professional company secretary[6] who carries out the necessary work. Sometimes a firm of solicitors, or a partner in a firm of solicitors or accountants, acts as a company secretary.[7]

In a public company, the company secretary must either be a chartered

---

[1] See the CA 2006 s.1121(2).
[2] CA 2006 s.271. If a public company lacks a company secretary, there are procedures to enable the Secretary of State to give a direction to the company to obtain one (s.272).
[3] CA 2006 s.270.
[4] Based at 16 Park Crescent, London. Their website contains much useful information on the practicalities of company secretarial practices.
[5] Unless there is only one director in a public company or a private company which still requires a company secretary under its articles—under which circumstances that one director may not be company secretary as well (CA 2006 s.280).
[6] A professional company secretary can be a limited company or a Scottish partnership providing company secretarial facilities.
[7] This is increasingly less common, because of the potential risk of liability. Most large solicitors' practices have in-house limited companies to act as company secretaries if clients wish the firm to provide company secretarial facilities.

secretary, a lawyer, an accountant,[8] a person who has held the office of a company secretary of a public company within three of the previous five years, or someone who by virtue of his holding any office or position or being a member of some professional body appears to the directors to be capable of holding the office of company secretary of a public company.[9] A sole director of a public company may not be that company's company secretary.[10] The purpose of this rule is to ensure that two separate human beings are involved in every public company.

10–03   A company secretary is an employee of the company and the company is vicariously liable for his acts in the course of his duty.[11] Unlike a director or auditor he has no right of protest on dismissal. There is usually a provision in a company's articles providing for the appointment of a company secretary and providing that he may sign documents on behalf of the company—sometimes without the need for a director to sign as well. Normally most company documents will be signed by both a director and the secretary but it is open to a company to permit either one of these to execute documents in the presence of a witness. A company's articles may also authorise a deputy company secretary to sign documents in the absence of the company secretary, and if there is no such appointment someone within the company may be authorised by the directors to act in place of the secretary.[12] Even where there is no such specific authority to permit company secretaries to enter into contracts on behalf of the company, it is likely that the CA 2006 s.40(2) would protect third parties dealing with the company secretary in good faith.[13]

The first company secretary indicates his willingness to take up office on the registration application and thereafter new ones will sign the required form to be sent to the Registrar of Companies.[14] If a company has a company secretary, it must keep a register of its company secretaries[15] and give the prescribed particulars of those company secretaries.[16] Company secretaries do not need to give information about themselves other than their name and address, and the address may be the company's registered office.[17] Company secretaries are under no obligation to disclose to the directors or members any personal contracts they may have with their companies, and while they may owe duties of allegiance and good faith to their employers, the fiduciary duty, so highly developed for directors, does not directly apply to company secretaries. A company secretary who took too great an involvement in a company's

---

[8] Qualified under any of the various professional accountancy bodies such as ACCA, CIMA, ICAS, etc.

[9] CA 2006 s.273(1).

[10] CA 2006 s.280.

[11] *Panorama Developments Ltd v Fidelis Furnishing Fabrics Ltd* [1971] 2 Q.B. 711; [1971] 3 W.L.R. 440.

[12] CA 2006 s.274.

[13] *Panorama Developments Ltd v Fidelis Furnishing Fabrics Ltd* [1971] 2 Q.B. 711; [1971] 3 W.L.R. 440.

[14] CA 2006 s.276. See Forms AP03 and AP04 (for corporate secretaries).

[15] CA 2006 s.275.

[16] CA 2006 ss.277, 278.

[17] CA 2006 s.277(5).

management could in theory be a shadow director, though there are no cases on this point. As has been indicated, private companies are not obliged to have company secretaries, but if the articles of an existing company refer to a company secretary, and if the company declines to re-appoint a retiring company secretary, the articles may need to be amended to delete any reference to the company secretary and any of his duties. This is especially important if one of the company secretary's tasks was signing important documents.

Although the Government believed that the lack of requirement to **10–04** have a company secretary for private companies would make life easier for private companies, in practice it makes very little difference at all. The work previously carried out by a company secretary still needs to be done either by a director himself, or more commonly by solicitors or company formation agents in the name of one of the directors.

The duties of a company secretary

There are very few duties laid down in statute concerning the duties of **10–05** a company secretary, and many of the tasks they traditionally fulfil may equally well be carried out by a director. However, by convention, the following tasks are commonly carried out by company secretaries:

- taking the minutes of general and board meetings;
- organising and preparing the paperwork for general and board meetings;
- signing of company documents and contracts;
- keeping the company's statutory registers, such as the register of shareholdings, etc.; and
- sending registrable documents to the Registrar of Companies.

In addition, the following duties are often carried out by company secretaries:

- any legal work or work connected with such matters as employment, banking, tax, pensions, insurance and office administration;
- ensuring compliance with health and safety legislation;
- in finance companies, acting as compliance officer[18]; and
- any other reactive tasks the directors cannot face dealing with themselves.

A company secretary's tasks at meetings were once described thus:

> "*After the board has gone to its dinner,*
> *The secretary stays and gets thinner and thinner:*
> *Racking his brains to record and report*
> *What he thinks they think they ought to have thought.*"

---

[18] A compliance officer has the unenviable task of monitoring his company's employees' personal shareholdings in order to deter insider dealing.

10–06 The Institute of Chartered Secretaries and Administrators is trying to raise the profile of company secretaries, and in this respect they were helped by the UK Corporate Governance Code which indicated that company secretaries of listed companies were to act as the conscience of the company, there to provide best advice on how to comply with the requirements both of corporate law and also of current best practice in terms of corporate governance.

AUDITORS

10–07 As indicated in Ch.7, every company, with the exception of dormant companies[19] and certain small companies,[20] together with certain non-profit-making companies subject to public sector audit,[21] needs auditors.[22] If it is not to have an auditor, its balance sheet must have a statement by the directors to that effect,[23] an indication that the members have not requested an audit under s.476, and an acknowledgment by the directors that they recognise their responsibilities for complying with the CA 2006 with respect to accounting records and the preparation of accounts.[24] To be allowed to audit a company, and to ensure the maintenance of standards, an auditor must be a "statutory" auditor in terms of s.1210. To be a statutory auditor the individual auditor or firm of auditors must be a member of a recognised supervisory body[25] and eligible for appointment under the rules of that body.[26] An auditor may be either an individual, a partnership, a limited liability partnership or a registered company but under whatever form the auditor is operating, the auditor must be independent of the company.[27]

Appointment of auditors in a private company

10–08 A private company's first auditors are appointed by the directors,[28] and, apart from the company's first financial year, their appointment must be made before the end of the period of 28 days beginning with either: (i) the end of the time allowed for the sending out of the

---

[19] As explained in the CA 2006 s.479.

[20] Small companies are explained at paras 7–46—7–50 and see the CA 2006 ss.477, 479. Section 478 explains the small companies that may not take advantage of the exclusion from audit, including in particular public companies, banks and insurance companies.

[21] As explained in the CA 2006 ss.482, 483.

[22] CA 2006 s.475(1).

[23] CA 2006 s.475(2).

[24] CA 2006 s.475(3).

[25] This is defined in the CA 2006 s.1217. The main bodies are ICAS, ICAEW, ACCA and AAPA. The auditor needs to be appropriately qualified in terms of those bodies (ss.1219–1222).

[26] CA 2006 s.1212.

[27] CA 2006 s.1214.

[28] CA 2006 s.485(3)—though if the directors do not get round to appointing them, the members may do so by ordinary resolution (s.485(4)), as may the Secretary of State (s.486). The company is supposed to tell the Secretary of State within one week of the expiry of the time for appointing auditors, with criminal sanctions for failure to do so.

company's annual accounts and reports for the previous financial year under s.424[29]; or (ii) if earlier, the day the annual accounts and reports are actually sent to the Registrar of Companies. In a private company the current auditors will be deemed to be re-appointed for the following financial year unless a new auditor has been appointed. Automatic re-appointment will not apply if the auditor was appointed by the directors, the company's articles require actual re-appointment, the members object under s.488[30] to his re-appointment, the members resolve that he not be re-appointed, or the directors have resolved that no auditors should be appointed.[31]

Where there is a casual vacancy in the office of auditor, the directors[32] or the members by ordinary resolution may appoint another auditor to fill the post.[33]

Appointment of auditors in a public company

Auditors must be appointed for each financial year, unless the directors **10–09** reasonably resolve otherwise on the grounds that audited accounts are unlikely to be necessary.[34] Other than for the first financial year, during which the directors may appoint the auditors,[35] the appointment must be made before the end of the accounts meeting at which the company's annual reports and accounts for the previous financial year are laid.[36] In practice this means that the appointment is made at the AGM or an EGM for the consideration of the accounts. The directors retain the right to appoint directors to fill a vacancy[37] as do the members if there is no auditor appointed.[38] As with a private company, the Secretary of State may appoint an auditor if necessary.[39]

The rights of auditors

In order to carry out their task of auditing a company's accounts, **10–10** auditors have the right of access to all the company's books and accounts, and are entitled to obtain such information and explanation from the company's officers as they need.[40] Misleading the auditors is a

---

[29] This refers to the time by which the accounts and reports must be sent out. For a private company these must be sent to the Registrar of Companies within nine months of the end of the company's accounting period (CA 2006 s.442(2)(a)).

[30] This provides if 5 per cent of the members (or such lower percentage as is indicated in the articles) object, the deemed re-appointment will not take place, and the members would then need to vote on his re-appointment.

[31] CA 2006 s.487(2).

[32] CA 2006 s.485(3)(c).

[33] CA 2006 s.485(4). This would apply where the directors had failed to obtain an auditor.

[34] As, for example, if the company was going to be converted into a dormant private company.

[35] CA 2006 s.489(3)(a).

[36] CA 2006 s.489(2).

[37] CA 2006 s.489(3)(c).

[38] CA 2006 s.489(4).

[39] CA 2006 s.490.

[40] CA 2006 s.499.

criminal offence.[41] Directors and other officials of overseas subsidiaries are required to give the auditors of holding companies all the information that the auditors of the holding company may reasonably require.[42] Directors should be aware of this duty because in the directors' reports of all companies other than small companies there must be a statement that as far as each director is concerned, he has not held back from the auditor any information of which the auditor ought to be aware, and that he has taken "all the steps" that he ought to have taken as a director, including making enquiries of his fellow directors, to make himself aware of any information of which the auditor ought to be aware and to have ensured that the auditor is aware of that information.[43]

Auditors have the right to receive notices of and attend all general meetings and to speak at such meetings. Auditors should also receive copies of resolutions which are proposed to be passed by means of written resolution (in the case of private companies only) before the resolutions are passed.[44] This is an attempt to prevent private companies passing either inappropriate resolutions or resolutions that require a particular procedure. For example, a private company could attempt to reduce its capital by written resolution, but as the procedure also requires a solvency statement from the directors, the auditor should in practice (though there is no statutory duty to do so) warn the members that reduction of capital is more complicated than a mere resolution. In a public company the auditor would be able to warn the members by speaking at the general meeting.

10–11 Auditors are entitled to be paid for their services but their fee must be approved by the members or fixed by such other method as the members determine.[45] Their remuneration must be indicated in the annual accounts.[46] Furthermore, the auditors and their associates must also disclose what other benefits the auditors carrying out the audit receive from the audited company.[47] This is because auditing is not particularly remunerative for accountants compared to more lucrative consultancy work, the preservation of which might, in some cases, cause auditors' independence to be compromised.

---

[41] CA 2006 s.501.
[42] CA 2006 s.500.
[43] CA 2006 s.418.
[44] CA 2006 s.502.
[45] CA 2006 s.492.
[46] CA 2006 s.493.
[47] CA 2006 s.494.

Removal and resignation of auditors

Under s.511, a company may at any time by ordinary resolution,[48] of **10–12**
which special notice[49] has been given,[50] at a general meeting remove an
auditor from office, notwithstanding any contract between the company
and the auditor.[51] If this takes place, the company must tell the Registrar
of Companies of the removal within 14 days.[52] The removed auditor may
still be notified of and attend any general meeting which had he not been
removed he would still otherwise have been entitled to be notified of or
attend had his term of office expired at it, or at which the vacancy caused
by his removal would have been filled.[53]

Because of the special notice provisions for the removal of an auditor
before the expiry of his term of office,[54] or appointing someone other than
the retiring auditor as auditor,[55] the members should, at least in theory,
be aware of the significance of the removal or the non-reappointment of
the existing auditor. If the directors or a body of members wish to remove
an auditor, there is inevitably a suspicion that the auditor may have
uncovered something untoward that either the directors or some of the
members may not wish revealed. Accordingly the special notice provisions require that the auditor in question be informed of the resolution,[56]
in which case he may make representations in writing of a reasonable
length which should then be notified to the members of the company.[57]
Unless the representations arrive too late to make it possible, the company must tell the members in the notice of the general meeting (at which
the resolution is to be moved) of the receipt of the representations, and
send a copy of them to each member entitled to receive notice of the
meeting.[58] If the representations do arrive late, or the company fails to
send them out, the auditor may insist that they be read out at the
meeting.[59] However, if the right to make representations is being abused
in order to, "secure needless publicity for defamatory matter" (as the
statute pompously puts it) the court may rule that the representations
should not be sent out or read out.[60] It will be noticed that a private

---

[48] CA 2006 s.510(1).
[49] Special notice means that the company has to be given notice by those moving the
resolution at least 28 days prior to the meeting where the resolution is to be moved (CA
2006 s.312). The words "special notice" are normally printed above the wording of the
resolution in the optimistic belief that the members will appreciate the significance of the
resolution.
[50] CA 2006 s.511.
[51] Removal before the expiry of his term of office may entitle the auditor to compensation
for breach of contract (CA 2006 s.510(3)).
[52] CA 2006 s.512.
[53] CA 2006 s.513.
[54] CA 2006 s.511.
[55] CA 2006 s.514.
[56] CA 2006 s.511(2).
[57] CA 2006 s.511(3).
[58] CA 2006 s.511(4).
[59] CA 2006 s.511(5). This is in addition to his normal right to be heard at a general meeting
anyway.
[60] CA 2006 s.511(6).

company cannot remove an auditor by written resolution: the removal has to be by the above method.[61]

10–13　　The above rules relate to the removal of an existing auditor. If there is a resolution to appoint an auditor in place of an auditor whose term of office has expired, or is about to expire, and the company is a private one, so that the resolution is to take place by written resolution rather than by voting at a general meeting, under s.514 there are procedures similar to s.511 to be followed, save that members are allowed 28 days in which to cast their vote[62] and any failure precisely to follow the required rules of s.514 render the resolution ineffective.[63] In the case of a public company, when there is a resolution to appoint an auditor in place of an auditor whose term of office has expired, or is about to expire, rules similar to those above s.511 apply, and because with a public company a general meeting would have to be held, special notice is, as in s.511, required. If, however, an auditor resigns, he may do so by leaving a notice to that effect at the company's office,[64] but such notice will not be effective unless it is accompanied by the s.519 statement referred to below. A copy of the notice of resignation must be sent to the Registrar of Companies within 14 days.[65] On resignation, an auditor has various rights. In addition to the deposit with the company of the s.519 statement, which as will be seen will normally be sent to every member,[66] on the occasion of the deposit he may sign a requisition requiring the directors to convene a general meeting for the purpose of receiving and considering any explanation of the circumstances in connection with his resignation which he considers should be brought to the attention of the members at a meeting.[67] He may supply a statement in writing of those circumstances[68] which must be circulated in the same manner as the representations above.[69] The directors must, within 21 days of the deposit of the requisition, send out a notice convening a general meeting, and the general meeting itself must take place within 28 days of that notice.[70] If the directors do not do this, the directors commit a criminal offence.[71] The auditor may speak at the meeting even if by that stage he has resigned.[72]

10–14　　The s.519 statement referred to above is a statement required to be deposited at the company's registered office by the auditor if for any

---

[61] CA 2006 s.510(1).

[62] CA 2006 s.514(6)(a).

[63] CA 2006 s.514(8).

[64] CA 2006 s.516.

[65] CA 2006 s.517. Use Form AA03.

[66] CA 2006 s.520.

[67] CA 2006 s.518(2).

[68] CA 2006 s.518(3).

[69] CA 2006 s.518(4). As with ss.511 and 514, the same rules apply to late arrival of the statement (s.518(8)), and to the right of the company to refuse to send out the statement (s.518(9)).

[70] CA 2006 s.518(5). If the directors do not do this, the directors commit a criminal offence (s.518(6), (7)).

[71] CA 2006 s.518(6), (7).

[72] CA 2006 s.518(10).

reason (including the above methods) that auditor ceases to hold office. In the case of an unquoted[73] company, the statement must disclose any circumstances in connection with the auditor's ceasing to hold office and which he considers should be brought to the attention of the members or creditors of the company.[74] Equally, if he considers that there are no such circumstances that need to be brought to the attention of the members and creditors, the auditor must still deposit the statement, but need not disclose any of the circumstances if he considers there are none to be disclosed—though his statement should positively indicate that he considers there are none.[75] In the case of a quoted company[76] he must deposit a note of the circumstances, whatever they may be, irrespective of whether they might need to be brought to the attention of the members and creditors.[77] This statement must be deposited within 14 days of the notice of resignation, within 14 days before the end of the time allowed for next appointing auditors or, in any other case, within 14 days of the date when the auditor ceases to hold office.[78]

The statement, if it does contain circumstances which the auditor considers should be brought to the attention of the members and creditors, must then either within 14 days be sent by the company to all those entitled to receive copies of the accounts[79] or, in the event of the statement containing needlessly defamatory matter (as above) there must be an application to the court to obtain an order allowing the company not to send out the statement.[80] If, however, the application to the court is rejected, the company must within 14 days of the court's decision send out the statement to those entitled to receive it.[81] Provided there has been no application to the court, the auditor must send in his statement to the Registrar of Companies within 28 days of the date of the original statement[82] or, where the court has rejected the application, within seven days of receiving notification of the court's rejection of the application.[83]

In addition to the above procedure, where the company in question is a

---

[73] As defined in CA 2006 s.385(3).

[74] CA 2006 s.519(1).

[75] CA 2006 s.519(2).

[76] As defined in CA 2006 s.385. Broadly speaking as far as the United Kingdom is concerned, this means a company on the Main Market of the London Stock Exchange (otherwise known as a listed company). AIM companies are not quoted companies in terms of this definition.

[77] CA 2006 s.519(3).

[78] CA 2006 s.519(4).

[79] CA 2006 s.520(1), (2)(a).This does not just include members: it may include certain creditors such as debenture-holders.

[80] CA 2006 s.520(4). The auditor may also be liable for the expenses of the application to court.

[81] CA 2006 s.520(5).

[82] CA 2006 s.521(1).

[83] CA 2006 s.521(2).

listed company or any company in which there is a major public interest (the audit for which is known as a "major audit")[84] the s.519 statement must be sent, on resignation or retirement before the end of his term of office, to the appropriate audit authority,[85] which, if it has concerns about the auditor and the circumstances of his leaving office, must inform the Professional Oversight Board of the Financial Reporting Council.[86]

It should be noted that the Deregulation Bill, going through Parliament in 2014, is likely to amend the entire process of dealing with the termination of an auditor's appointment and the informing the relevant bodies of the reasons for ceasing to hold office. This is because the existing rules are complex, burdensome and arguably not very useful for smaller companies. Slightly less complicated rules than at present will be retained for auditors of listed companies.

10–15 The purpose of this procedure, which is backed up by criminal sanctions for failing to comply with it,[87] is to prevent auditors from sitting on their hands if they discover something unpleasant in the accounts. In the past auditors who were scared by the directors of the company they were auditing, and who were worried by the prospect of being sued for not approving the accounts,[88] could resign in mid-office without having to give any reason for doing so.[89] Nowadays, auditors must either indicate what there is that causes them concern, or state unequivocally that there is nothing that does give them concern. While this practice does mean that auditors have to state whatever the matter of concern is, auditors are nevertheless still very cautious in what they say lest they be sued by the company. If an auditor indicated that there were matters of concern which on investigation turned out to be unjustified, the auditor could be sued for damages equivalent to the loss of reputation and goodwill arising out of the querying of the accounts. The net result of this is auditors' statements on these matters of concern are very carefully worded.

---

[84] CA 2006 s.525(2). This covers companies on the LSE Main Market, PLUS, AIM, unquoted companies with group turnover above £500 million, unquoted companies or groups (being subsidiaries of foreign parent companies) where the turnover of the UK company or group is greater than £1,000 million, charitable companies with income over £100 million, or any subsidiary of the above. See *https://www.frc.org.uk/Our-Work/ Conduct/Professional-Oversight/Audit/Notification-of-change-of-auditor/Flow-chart-for-audit-firms.aspx* [Accessed April 22, 2014].

[85] CA 2006 s.522. This at present is the Conduct Committee of the Financial Reporting Council, which is the body with which the audit firm is registered and is responsible for its regulation, usually one of ICAS, ICAEW, ACCA or ICAI.

[86] CA 2006 s.524.

[87] CA 2006 s.522(5)–(8).

[88] Qualifying the accounts might call the directors' integrity in question, giving rise to the possibility of an action for defamation.

[89] As happened during the audit for the late Robert Maxwell's Mirror Group. The law was changed to ensure that resignation without explanation was no longer possible.

The role of the auditor

Auditors have various tasks, of which the primary one is the scrutiny of **10–16** the company's accounts. Auditors normally draw up a terms of engage- ment for the company for which they are working, indicating how they will carry out the audit and what they expect the company and its officials to do. Notwithstanding the common misconception to the contrary, auditors have never held themselves out as checking that a company's accounts are all perfect. They could not possibly inspect every single entry in the company's books. They merely provide some degree of reassurance as to the accuracy of the company's finances,[90] but are not there to track down every transgression. As was stated in the vivid phrase of Lopes L.J. in *Re Kingston Cotton Mill (No.2)*,[91] "the auditors are watchdogs not bloodhounds". It is the directors' duty to prepare the accounts, even if the directors have accountants to do the work for them, and it is the directors who are responsible for the accounts. Once the accounts have been pre- pared, the auditors add a report to the accounts confirming that the accounts, as stated above, present a true and fair view[92] of the company's finances, and are consistent with the information given in the directors' report,[93] but if there is something in the accounts with which the auditors are not satisfied, a "qualification" will be added to the report,[94] which will indicate in what respects the accounts fall short of the requirements of normal accounting practice and the requirements of the Companies Acts. The report should also indicate any other accounting failings within the company.[95] Having a qualification to the accounts is not in itself fatal for the company, for the members may be sufficiently close-knit not to mind. However, creditors and potential investors will be concerned, and a company that has the report to its accounts qualified may have trouble maintaining its credibility in the long run.

The auditor's report needs to be signed and dated by the individual auditor who carried out the audit, or, in the event of an audit being carried out by a firm, by the "senior statutory auditor".[96] This means that someone, usually a senior partner in the accountancy firm carrying out the audit, is required to put his own signature on the audit report. The point of this exercise is to concentrate the auditor's mind on the reliability of the auditor's report, since it will be his name that is shown to all the world. No reputable auditor would wish to put his signature against a negligent or fraudulent audit. This is not to say that the auditor is per- sonally liable,[97] for he is signing on behalf of his firm (which in his place may be liable should the audit be improperly carried out).

---

[90] CA 2006 s.498.
[91] *Re Kingston Cotton Mill (No.2)* [1896] 2 Ch. 279 at 288.
[92] CA 2006 s.496(3).
[93] CA 2006 s.496.
[94] CA 2006 s.495(4). The word "qualification" in this context means that the accounts are less than perfect in the areas indicated by the auditors in the report.
[95] CA 2006 s.498.
[96] CA 2006 s.503.
[97] CA 2006 s.504(3).

It is permissible to omit an auditor's name if: (i) there is a risk that the auditor might be subject to violence or intimidation if his name were published; (ii) the members have approved the omission of his name on the auditor's report; and (iii) the Secretary of State has been informed of the company in question, the financial year to which the auditor's report relates, and the name, and firm where applicable, of the auditor in question.[98]

If the auditor knowingly or recklessly causes a report on the company's annual accounts[99] to include anything that is misleading, false or deceptive in a material matter, he commits a criminal offence.[100]

There are various other occasions under company law when auditors' reports or certificates are needed. For example, a private company converting itself into a public company will need an unqualified report on the company's balance sheet,[101] and a private company paying for the repurchase of shares out of capital requires a report by the auditors confirming that the directors' belief that the company could pay all its debts within the following year is not unreasonable in all the circumstances.[102]

The liability of auditors

10–17 Although there may be contractual arrangements to the contrary, the primary duty of care that auditors owe is to the company that hires them to carry out the audit. This was established in the case of *Caparo Industries Plc v Dickman Touche Ross*[103] where the plaintiffs, who had been shareholders in a company they had taken over, sued the defendant auditors for their failure to carry out the audit of the target company properly, thus misleading the plaintiffs into believing that the target company was more viable than it was and therefore worth taking over. While the audit was undoubtedly inaccurate, the important issue in law was whether individual members themselves had a right to sue the auditors. It was held that while the company itself had the right to sue the auditors, that right did not extend to individual members. Were individual members given that right, there might be no end of litigation, and the auditors could not possibly be expected to have such an indeterminate duty of care to such an indeterminate group of people. It would be impossible to insure against such risk, and carried to its logical extension accountants would then all pull out of auditing. The only way the auditors could have a responsibility to individual members or bodies other than the company which commissioned the audit was if they were

---

[98] CA 2006 s.506.

[99] In terms of CA 2006 s.495.

[100] CA 2006 s.507. The criminal provisions are extended to inaccurate statements under s.498(2)(b), (3) and (5). At the time the legislation was being considered in Parliament, these particular provisions excited much interest from MPs who were practising accountants.

[101] CA 2006 s.92(1)(b).

[102] CA 2006 s.714.

[103] *Caparo Industries Plc v Dickman Touche Ross* [1990] 2 W.L.R. 358; [1990] 1 All E.R. 568.

put on notice that a particular member or body was relying on the audit,[104] or where it could be reasonably anticipated that a particular member[105] or body would be relying on the audit even if there were no contractual relationship.[106] Auditors of subsidiaries can reasonably expect that a holding company will have an interest in its subsidiaries' accounts and auditors may then be liable to the holding company.[107]

The *Caparo* decision, much beloved by auditors, is still the current law, but increasingly the duty of care that is to be expected of auditors in each case will be specified in the terms under which the audit is carried out. Auditors are becoming very cautious as to the terms of engagement under which they will do their audit and generally make it quite clear that only the commissioners of the audit (generally the company) will have the legal standing to sue on the audit if it is inaccurate.

Auditors may be liable to their companies for other breaches of their **10–18** duties: for example, auditors may be liable where they fail to give advice that a proposed action by the directors would breach the requirements of company law[108] or fail to spot that a company was insolvent and therefore should not be paying a dividend.[109] Auditors will not in general be liable if they had been misled by fraudulent directors[110] but if they uncover fraud they are expected to report it to the relevant authorities and will be liable for any loss to the company arising out of their failure to do so.[111] Auditors are allowed to obtain indemnities for their legal costs from the companies for which they work in the event of their successfully defending any action raised against them,[112] and in the event of a claim against them from the company which they are auditing, or indeed anyone else, the auditors may be able to obtain the benefit of the court's protection if they have acted fairly and reasonably in terms of the CA 2006 s.1157. The Companies Act 2006 ss.534–536 allows companies and their auditors to negotiate "liability limitation agreements" which serve to cap the auditors' liability to the companies which they are auditing. The agreement must be approved by the members and must limit the potential liability to such amount as is fair and reasonable under all the circumstances.[113] The agreement must also be disclosed in the annual accounts and directors' report.[114] It may only last for one year at a

---

[104] *ADT Ltd v Binder Hamlyn* [1996] B.C.C. 808.
[105] *Electra Private Equity Partners v KPMG Peat Marwick* [2000] B.C.C. 368.
[106] *Royal Bank of Scotland v Bannerman Johnstone Maclay*, 2003 S.C. 125; 2003 S.L.T. 181; [2005] B.C.C. 235; *Precis (521) Plc v William M Mercer Ltd* [2004] EWHC 838 Ch.D.
[107] *Barings Plc v Coopers and Lybrand* [1997] 1 B.C.L.C. 427; [1997] B.C.C. 498.
[108] *Coulthard v Neville Russell* [1998] 1 B.C.L.C. 143.
[109] *Sasea Finance Ltd v KPMG* [2000] 1 B.C.L.C. 236; [2000] B.C.C. 989. In this case the auditors were liable to the extent of the improper dividend.
[110] *Galoo Ltd v Bright Graham Murray* [1994] B.C.L.C. 319; *Barings Plc (In Liquidation) v Coopers and Lybrand (No.5)* [2002] EWHC 461 Ch.D.
[111] *Sasea Finance Ltd v KPMG* [2000] 1 B.C.L.C. 236; [2000] B.C.C. 989.
[112] CA 2006 s.533.
[113] CA 2006 s.537.
[114] CA 2006 s.538.

time.[115] The Financial Reporting Council has various recommendations for the terms of such agreements and observations on the implications of having such agreements.[116] The purpose of these agreements, which until the CA 2006 was implemented were not permitted, is to permit auditors to undertake audits which they might otherwise be reluctant to consider because of the risk.[117] Only the major auditing firms could afford the insurance cover to carry out audits and the Government felt that the top four firms were in practice acting as a cartel. The Government believed that other firms of auditors ought to have the chance to carry out audits of major listed companies and would be able to offer cheaper audits if the auditors knew that their liability was capped. A few companies have been willing to have liability limitation agreements with their auditors, but most auditors rely on their carefully worded terms of engagement. Overall, liability limitation agreements have not been a great success.

Contemporary issues involving auditing

10–19   The scandals in the USA involving the destruction of Enron's financial records by Andersens, the firm of accountants that was supposed to be auditing Enron, has focused minds on some of the intrinsic problems surrounding auditing, including an unhealthy lack of distance between auditor and auditee and a reluctance on the part of the auditor to queer the pitch of a high-paying client. There are occasional suggestions that major companies should have new auditors every five years, and it is likely that the role of the auditor will be increased to take account of today's ever greater requirements for transparency and accountability. Until recently, auditing was sometimes seen as the poor relation of accountancy practice, lacking glamour and perceived as lacking in creativity, but the recession, as at the time of writing, has re-established the importance of accurate and informed auditing.

Further Reading

Company Secretaries

See the website for the Institute of Chartered Secretaries and Administrators: *http://www.icsa.org.uk* [Accessed April 22, 2014].

Auditors

See the website for the Financial Reporting Council: *https://www.frc.org.uk/Home.aspx* [Accessed April 22, 2014].

---

[115] CA 2006 s.535(1).

[116] See their website: *https://www.frc.org.uk/FRC-Documents/FRC/Guidance-on-Auditor-Liability-Limitation-Agreement.aspx* [Accessed April 22, 2014].

[117] An inaccurate audit can be extremely expensive for the auditors, and there have been occasions when the entire insurance cover was used up and each partner in the firm had personally to contribute to his partnership's debts—all arising from a negligent audit. This happened to the firm, Binder Hamlyn, after the case *ADT Ltd v Binder Hamlyn* [1996] B.C.C. 808.

CHAPTER 11

MINORITY PROTECTION, DERIVATIVE CLAIMS AND BIS INVESTIGATIONS

MINORITY PROTECTION

Those who have the most shares in a company generally have the most to **11–01** gain and most to lose from the company. It is therefore only fair that they should have the most say in the management of the company. Unfortunately, over the years it has sometimes been found true that those who have most shares in the company see the company's interests purely as an extension of their own interests, at the expense of those with fewer shares. If the minority shareholders dislike this, they may:

- sell their shares, if they are able to;
- accept the fact that they are outvoted;
- in limited circumstances raise an action to protect their own interests;
- under certain circumstances ask the BIS to investigate the company;
- petition to have the company wound up; or
- (in Scotland only) have a judicial factor appointed to run the company.

This at least is the current position. But for many years, the courts found it very difficult to cope with the idea of a minority of shareholders having a justified grievance against a majority. There were various reasons for this:

(1) When you become a member of a company, under the Companies Act 2006 ("the CA 2006") s.33 (and its predecessors) you become a member on the terms and conditions of the company's constitution, one of which is that in general the majority rule prevails.

(2) It was not always clear whether a minority shareholder treated badly by the majority was seeking redress for himself, or the company or for both. Whom or what should the minority shareholder sue? Should he properly be suing the majority shareholders, the company or the directors?

(3) If every disgruntled minority shareholder were entitled to rush to the courts to complain every time the company made a decision with which the minority disagreed, the courts might be full of pointless and expensive actions.

(4) The courts are very reluctant to question commercial decisions.

When is a resolution passed by the company a commercial decision which is entirely the company's business, and when is it mistreating a minority?

11–02 At the same time, there are occasions when it is clear that a minority is being mistreated by the majority:

(1) Majority shareholders may use their strong voting position to change the company's articles in such a way as to disadvantage a minority.

(2) If the majority shareholders are also directors, they may award themselves high salaries and pension contributions as directors while giving the minority shareholders little or nothing by way of dividends.

(3) Directors are not obliged to discuss all business and financial matters with the shareholders. If the directors are also the majority shareholders, they may be tempted deliberately to keep the minority in the dark to prevent the minority asking awkward questions.

(4) If the directors in their personal capacity comprise the majority of the members, or have most of the control of the company, it becomes impossible for the minority shareholders to dismiss the directors under the CA 2006 s.168, however badly the directors might behave.

(5) The minority shareholders may find the cost of raising an action against the majority expensive, and the majority may take advantage of the minority's reluctance to incur expenses.

(6) Although it is easy to say to a disgruntled minority shareholder that he should sell his shares, in practice in any but a quoted company (and sometimes not even then) it may be difficult to find purchasers for the shares.

(7) If the directors are doing something which they should not be doing, the company should raise an action against them. But if those directors are also the majority shareholders, they are not going to vote to make the company raise an action which might ultimately be to their personal detriment.

(8) The majority shareholders in company A Ltd might be shareholders in company B Ltd, with which A Ltd is in dispute. Even if A Ltd had a good claim against B Ltd, the majority shareholders in A Ltd might be unwilling to raise an action against B Ltd because of their personal interest in B Ltd.

11–03 Historically the progress of legal protection for minority shareholders has proceeded as follows:

(1) Following the rule in *Foss v Harbottle*[1] (to be discussed below) minority shareholders could not obtain redress against a

---

[1] *Foss v Harbottle* (1843) 2 Hare 461.

majority of shareholders unless the company in general meeting authorised action against the majority. Only the company had title to sue the majority shareholders—clearly an unlikely prospect.

(2) It was soon realised that this was unduly oppressive to minority shareholders who had been treated unfairly. Under the common law a few categories of unfairness were established, and these acted as permitted exceptions to the rule in *Foss v Harbottle*.[2]

(3) Despite having admitted those categories, the courts were extremely reluctant to use them or to expand them, though the position of directors (who often were the same people as the majority shareholders) was increasingly brought under control by statute and the common law.

(4) After an unsatisfactory statutory attempt in the Companies Act 1948 s.210 to protect minority shareholders, Companies Acts 1980, 1985 and 1989 all improved the position of the minority shareholder significantly, at least as far as personal remedies for the minority shareholder himself. The Companies Act 1985 s.459 (as amended by the Companies Act 1989) advanced the current statutory remedy for the minority shareholder, which is now to be found at s.994 of the CA 2006. However, as the use of what was then s.459 developed, it was noticed that the scales were increasingly tipping in favour of the minority shareholder. As most companies did not wish to be tied up in litigation, and because the courts appeared to be becoming ever more sympathetic to minority shareholders, it became easier to pay the aggrieved minority shareholders to go away even if their case was not very strong. However, the case of *O'Neill v Phillips*,[3] and Lord Hoffmann's pronouncements therein, restored the scales to a more balanced position.

(5) CA 2006 introduced a statutory derivative procedure (to be found in the CA 2006 ss.265–269) to allow shareholders redress against directors (but not majority shareholders) who have failed to promote the success of the company under CA 2006 s.172 or in some other way breached their duty to the company.

The common law rule in *Foss v Harbottle* and the exceptions thereto

The case of *Foss v Harbottle* predates the first Companies Acts but **11–04** deals with a fundamental problem in company law.

Foss and Turton were minority shareholders in a company of which Harbottle and his associates were directors and majority shareholders. In their personal capacities Harbottle and his associates sold

---

[2] These still exist to cope with the situation (at least in England) where statute does not provide a remedy, as in multiple derivative claims—see *Universal Management Services Ltd v Fort Gilkicker Ltd* [2013] EWHC 348.

[3] *O'Neill v Phillips*; also known as *Re A Company (No.00709 of 1992)* [1999] 1 W.L.R. 1092.

a plot of land to the company at an inflated price. At that time the present rules on fiduciary duties of directors were undeveloped and there was little judicial control over companies. Foss claimed that Harbottle and his associates had made the company pay too much for the land, thus unduly benefitting the majority shareholders, and indeed diminishing the value of his own shares. Harbottle replied that as directors they were entitled to decide what price the company should pay for its acquisitions, and as they also constituted the majority shareholders, they could do as they liked, including approving the directors' decisions. Foss and the other minority shareholders sued Harbottle and his associates. It was held that it was not for Foss and his fellow minority shareholders to raise an action against the directors for making the company overpay on expensive purchases. The proper plaintiff was the company itself, as it was the company as a whole that was buying the land. As the plaintiffs (Foss and Turton) were not the company, the issue of overpayment did not need to be decided upon.

This case is renowned both for its logic and its unfairness. The decision is logical because it is true that the company was the direct victim of the overpriced sale. The company had suffered: Foss personally had not suffered, except indirectly as his shares were now under-represented by assets. If the company had suffered, it was for the company to raise proceedings. To do this would need the approval of the shareholders, and Foss and Turton had not obtained shareholders' approval for an action against the directors. They therefore could not speak for the company.

11–05 The decision is unfair because of the requirement of shareholders' approval for action against the directors. The decision in *Foss v Harbottle* took no account of the fact that the majority shareholders, whose approval would have been needed for any action, were the perpetrators of the overpayment. They would have been most unlikely to vote for an action to be raised against themselves. A subsidiary point was that the purchase of the land was a commercial decision and the courts do not judge the merits of commercial decisions, not least because a judge's decision on a commercial matter might then in its own right be open to question.

The exceptions to the rule in *Foss v Harbottle*

11–06 Gradually the courts realised that the "proper plaintiff"[4] rule, although not without its merits, did lead to injustice. Four exceptions were permitted to the rules:

(1) ultra vires transactions;
(2) failure to follow proper procedure[5];

---

[4] A "plaintiff" would nowadays be called a "claimant".
[5] *Quinn and Axtens Ltd v Salmon* [1909] A.C. 442; *Edwards v Halliwell* [1950] 2 All E.R. 1064.

(3) infringement of the personal rights of the shareholders[6]; or

(4) fraud on the minority by the majority.[7]

Although at the time these four exceptions were seen as very important, in view of the current existence of the unfair prejudice rules of the CA 2006, much of this old law in practice will be of historical interest only, although it may perhaps serve as a marker towards interpretation of the current statutory provisions. The fact that there are no significant recent cases on the ultra vires rule anyway suggests that it is not the issue it once was[8]; failure by the directors to follow proper procedure or infringement of personal rights would be a personal matter for the affected shareholders who could use s.994 to obtain a remedy; and the codified directors' duties in ss.170–222, plus the creation of the derivative proceedings to be found in ss.265–269, deal with the fact that fraud on the minority, in practice, is commonly a breach of duty by the directors.

Although the common law above is not defunct, in practice there are **11–07** now two clear paths, one for a minority shareholder, seeking a remedy for himself, as a result of being prejudiced by the actions of the majority shareholders, and another for a shareholder (minority or otherwise), seeking a remedy for his company, and believing that his company is being prejudiced by the failure of the directors (who in many cases, particularly in private companies, are the majority shareholders anyway) to promote the success of the company. The former is dealt with by s.994, and the latter by the derivative proceedings at ss.265–269.

If the shareholder cannot seek a remedy under either the minority **11–08** protection measures or derivative proceedings, he may sell his shares, and if those are not possible, he may apply to court for the winding up of the company on just and equitable grounds.[9]

STATUTORY PROTECTION UNDER THE COMPANIES ACT 2006 SECTION 994—THE UNFAIR PREJUDICE REMEDY

The CA 2006 s.994 reads as follows: **11–09**

"(1) A member of a company may apply to the court by petition for an order under this Part on the ground—

(a) that the company's affairs are being or have been conducted in a manner which is unfairly prejudicial to the interests of its members generally or of some part of its members (including at least himself), or

---

[6] *Pender v Lushington* (1877) 6 Ch.D. 70.

[7] *Cook v Deeks* [1916] 1 A.C. 554 PC.

[8] And if someone did care enough to do something about it, s.40 provides a remedy for the shareholder.

[9] Insolvency Act 1986 ("the IA 1986") s.122(1)(g).

(b) that any actual or proposed act or omission of the company (including an act or omission on its behalf) is or would be so prejudicial."

The wording of this section is very careful and as a result there is a number of points to note from this.

A member

11–10   Any member, however small his interest, may apply, provided he applies in his capacity as a member, and not as an employee or a director. "Member" is also deemed to mean those who have shares transferred or transmitted to them by operation of law, such as trustees in bankruptcy or executors under a will.[10] A former member may not apply even though the prejudicial conduct occurred while he was still a member.[11]

Order

11–11   Under the CA 2006 s.996 the courts have wide discretion as to the type of order that they may grant in response to the petition, and may impose any order that they see fit. The commonest order is that the company or the majority shareholders buy out the petitioner's shares at a fair price reflecting the value of his shares prior to the behaviour to which the petitioner is objecting took place.

Are being or have been conducted

11–12   The use of the present and past tense enables the petitioner to petition in respect of current mistreatment or of past mistreatment, providing, it would seem, that he was a member at the time of the past mistreatment. However, once the member has left the company there is no provision for him to petition the court on this matter.

A manner that is unfairly prejudicial

11–13   This phrase means what it says: there is a requirement both of unfairness and of prejudice. For example, in the case of *R.A. Noble (Clothing) Ltd*[12] (to be discussed later) the petitioner had indeed suffered some prejudice, in the sense that he had suffered loss, but in view of his own behaviour it could not be said that he was treated unfairly.

---

[10] CA 2006 s.994(2).
[11] *Re A Company* [1986] 2 All E.R. 253.
[12] *Re R.A. Noble & Sons (Clothing) Ltd* [1983] B.C.L.C. 273.

To the interests of the members generally or of some part of the members

The word "generally" allows a claim to be made, not just if some of the **11-14** members suffered prejudice, but even if the entire body of shareholders was unfairly prejudiced in their capacity as share-holders.[13] The word "interests" is used, rather than "rights", specifically to widen the range of matters which might be the subject of unfairly prejudicial conduct.

Actual or proposed act or omission

The conduct being complained of need not already have taken place or **11-15** the omission need not have occurred; it is sufficient if the majority are going to do it or are thinking of doing it.

The court's remedies

The CA 2006 s.996 states that: "If the court is satisfied that a petition **11-16** under this Part is well founded, it may make such order as it thinks fit for giving relief in respect of the matters complained of". This gives the court wide discretion, provided that the court agrees that the complaint is justified.[14] The rest of s.996 gives various specific examples of remedies that the court could grant if it saw fit. In essence they are:

- regulating the affairs of the company in the future[15];
- preventing the company doing something the majority wished it to do, or making the company do something the majority did not wish it to do,[16] or convening an extraordinary general meeting;
- authorising the commencement of civil proceedings in the name of the company[17];
- requiring that the articles should not be altered without the leave of the court[18]; and
- ordering the company or the majority shareholders to buy out the minority.[19]

When the court orders shares to be bought back by the company, it may **11-17** be necessary for the company's capital to be reduced as well. This is usually taken account of in the court's interlocutor. The price that at

---

[13] For example, a company could be paying very large sums of money to the directors, so that the dividends are very small. The directors themselves might be shareholders but they would not be distressed if the dividends were low as they were receiving good salaries anyway.

[14] It even permits payments from the respondents to be made on an interim basis if necessary: *Ferguson v MacLennan Salmon Co Ltd*, 1990 S.L.T. 658.

[15] CA 2006 s.996(2)(a).

[16] CA 2006 s.996(2)(b).

[17] CA 2006 s.996(2)(c).

[18] CA 2006 s.996(2)(d).

[19] CA 2006 s.996(2)(e). There are cases where the minority has been allowed to buy the majority instead—see *Re A Company Ex p Shooter* [1990] B.C.L.C. 384 and *Re Brenfield Squash Racquets Club Ltd* [1996] 2 B.C.L.C. 384.

which the shares are bought back is generally the price most favourable to the petitioner with regard to all the circumstances. This might be the value at the date of the petition, the value at the date of the court's decision or the value at the date when the prejudicial conduct took place, depending on what would be fairest or what the company's documentation has already provided for.

Sections 994–996 have been productive of much case law, much of it illustrating the remarkable high-handedness of majority shareholders. Below are examples of various remedies or decisions that have been given over the years, many under the predecessor to s.994, which was Companies Act 1985 s.459.

Purchase of the minority shareholding by the majority at a fair value

11–18   *Re Bird Precision Bellows Ltd*[20]

The petitioner was unhappy with the way the majority shareholder was running the company. The petitioner believed that the majority shareholder in his position as managing director was paying bribes to obtain business opportunities. The minority shareholder asked the then Department of Trade and Industry[21] to investigate. The DTI declined to do so. By way of retaliation the majority shareholder convened a general meeting at which he was able to use his majority shareholding to dismiss the petitioner from the directorship. The judge held that the petitioner should have his shares bought by the majority shareholder at a price that ignored the discount in value normally attributable to a minority shareholding because of a minority's minimal voting power.

The minority shareholder need not come to the court with clean hands

11–19   *Re London School of Electronics Ltd*[22]

"Coming to the court with clean hands" is a term in English law, meaning that if the claimant seeks an equitable remedy against someone, the claimant must not have himself behaved dishonourably. In this case, neither party had behaved particularly honourably. The petitioner, Lytton, was a teacher at the London School of Electronics, and was a director and shareholder in the company that ran the school. The majority shareholder was a company run by two Greek brothers, who were also directors of the school. The Greek brothers considered Lytton's work unsatisfactory and diverted some students to another school they had set up, thus depriving Lytton of his work. Lytton then set up a school himself and diverted some other of the school's students to it. The Greek brothers then convened a meeting at which they dismissed Lytton from his directorship. When the matter came to court the respondents argued that Lytton was no better than they were and that he had not come to the

---

[20] *Re Bird Precision Bellows Ltd* [1986] 2 W.L.R. 158.
[21] The predecessor to the Department of Business, Information and Skills.
[22] *Re London School of Electronics Ltd* [1986] Ch. 211.

court with clean hands. However, Nourse J. held that having "dirty hands" was not of itself a barrier to seeking redress under s.459 of the Companies Act 1985, though it might affect the extent and type of the remedy granted. Lytton was duly entitled to his redress.

The petitioner must look after his own interests, and must not act unreasonably

Re R.A. Noble Ltd [23]   **11–20**

The petitioner was a director of the above company, but had taken little interest in its affairs. He later complained that he had been excluded from management of the company. It was held that if he had taken the trouble to attend board meetings he would have been able to remedy the situation without recourse to court. He was not therefore able to seek redress under s.459 of the Companies Act 1985. When a shareholder could have used his own votes at general meetings to remedy his situation, his failure to do so prevented him obtaining his desired remedy.[24]

Even if the majority shareholder disposes of his shares, he may still have a complaint raised against him

Re a Company (No.005287 of 1985) [25]   **11–21**

The majority shareholder took all the profits out of the company in the form of management fees and then transferred all his shares to a Gibraltar registered company. He was made to account for the abstracted money even though he was no longer a shareholder.

The court may give a remedy appropriate to the facts of the case

Re H.R. Harmer Ltd [26]   **11–22**

This case was decided under much earlier legislation but is still a good example. At the age of 82, H.R. Harmer set up a company to acquire and manage his stamp-selling business. He and his wife were the majority shareholders with 78.6 per cent of the votes, but had contributed only about 10 per cent of the capital, the rest being contributed by Harmer's sons. Harmer and his wife were thus able to direct the management of the company as they pleased, notwithstanding that he and his two sons were stated in the articles to be directors for life. He also had a casting vote as chairman of the board of directors. Harmer did not trouble himself with other people's views and ran the company as if it were his own private fiefdom. In the process he made several unwise investment and personnel decisions. He even hired a private detective agency to spy on the staff. His sons became so vexed by the father's conduct that they

---

[23] *Re R.A. Noble & Sons (Clothing) Ltd* [1983] B.C.L.C. 273.
[24] *Re Baltic Real Estate Ltd (No.2)* [1993] B.C.L.C. 503; *Re Legal Costs Negotiators Ltd* [1999] 2 B.C.L.C. 171.
[25] *Re A Company (No.005287 of 1985)* [1986] 1 W.L.R. 281.
[26] *Re H.R. Harmer Ltd* [1989] 1 W.L.R. 62; [1958] 3 All E.R. 689.

petitioned for relief. By the time of the court case Harmer was deaf, confused and had trouble understanding what the case was about. The judge ordered that Harmer be made a consultant to the company, that the articles be amended so that he could no longer be a director for life with a casting vote, that he was not to interfere in the management of the company and that he was to be appointed president of the company but without any duties or rights whatsoever.

The majority may not use its controlling position to further weaken the position of the minority

11–23   *Re Cumana Ltd*[27]
The majority and minority shareholder agreed that the company's profits should be divided in three, with the majority shareholder receiving two-thirds. The majority shareholder then diverted some of the company's business to another company which he controlled, and convened a general meeting at which he ensured that a resolution giving himself a large bonus and large pension contributions was passed. When the minority shareholder started proceedings under the then s.459 of the Companies Act 1985 the majority shareholder convened a meeting to pass a resolution for a rights issue which he knew the minority shareholder could not afford to take up—or if the minority shareholder had taken it up, it would have deprived him of funds with which to continue the s.459 petition. The minority shareholder successfully obtained an order preventing the implementation of the large bonus, the pension contributions and the rights issue.[28]

However, the minority shareholders do not always triumph.
11–24   In a publicly quoted public company, any informal arrangements between certain shareholders will be ignored by the courts in the context of a s.994 petition.

Re Tottenham Hotspur Plc[29]
As part of the dispute between Terry Venables (the minority shareholder) and the then Sir Alan Sugar, Venables petitioned for relief under s.459 of the Companies Act 1985 on the grounds that there had been an understanding between him and Sugar that they would share control and that Venables would be chief executive of the football club. It was held that even if there had been some understanding between Venables and Sugar, this was a private matter between the two of them which was not specifically about Venables's rights as a shareholder and did not affect any other shareholders' rights. Furthermore it would be a misuse of the

---

[27] *Re Cumana Ltd* [1986] B.C.L.C. 430.
[28] For a Scottish example of a majority allotting shares in an improper manner see *Pettie v Thomson Pettie Tube Products Ltd*, 2001 S.L.T. 473.
[29] *Re Tottenham Hotspur Plc* [1994] B.C.L.C. 655.

company's money to have it involved in what was essentially a private dispute. Relief was not therefore available. The court was clearly reluctant to use s.459 as a remedy for all private disputes between shareholders in publicly quoted companies—which should not be entertaining such private arrangements anyway.

Shareholders cannot necessarily use s.994 petitions to force the hand of **11–25** the majority shareholders if they have not actually suffered any unfairly prejudicial conduct.

Re Astec BSR Plc[30]

Astec BSR Plc was listed on the London Stock Exchange but its registered office was in Hong Kong. Most of the shares in the company were held by a large shareholder, Emerson, and the minority shareholders hoped that in accordance with the normal listing rules Emerson would buy out them out, preferably at a substantial premium. However, it is not obligatory or a legal requirement to follow the listing rules, although failure to do so may attract criticism from the London Stock Exchange.

When Emerson failed to buy the minority as expected, the minority claimed that they had suffered unfairly prejudicial conduct as a result of being denied what they had thought should take place. However it was held that desirable as adherence to the listing rules might be, the rules were not binding on the company. The company's articles in Hong Kong did not require that buy-outs should take place merely because the majority were expected to do so or because the minority would like them to do so, and the listing rules were not part of the articles. The minority shareholders had been aware of this (or at least should have been) when they became shareholders. A s.459 petition (as it was then) was not a method for forcing majority shareholders to buy out minority shareholders who perfectly well knew the risks of being minority shareholders.

Over time, a s.994 petition began to be used as a bargaining tool against directors and/or majority shareholders in the knowledge that it would be expensive[31] and time-consuming for them to defend the action—better to settle the matter on the petitioner's terms, however outrageous, than waste time in court. But with the number of cases growing, and particularly because of the costs and time involved,[32] the courts became anxious not to widen the gates of litigation to litigants unless s.994 genuinely was the appropriate remedy, and there had genuinely been unfairly prejudicial conduct. Unfairly prejudicial conduct now requires

---

[30] *Re Astec BSR Plc* [1998] 2 B.C.L.C. 556.
[31] As in *Re Elgindata Ltd* [1991] B.C.L.C. 959 where £320,000 was spent arguing over shares which finally were decided to be worth £24,600.
[32] One of the issues the courts felt was a particular waste of time and effort was the rehearsal at length of all the instances of alleged prejudicial conduct.

the intention to make life difficult for the minority, and in the absence of such difficulty, a s.994 petition may fail.

11–26   *Re Saul Harrison Sons Plc*[33]

The petitioner held special shares which did not permit her any votes but which did instead enable her to receive high dividends and a capital distribution on a winding-up. The company had run at a loss for some time but had substantial assets. The directors, who were also the majority shareholders, having taken professional advice, moved their business premises, paid themselves greater (though not unreasonably so) salaries, and attempted to improve the business generally. By contrast the petitioner believed that the directors should have had the company wound up and a return of capital made to all the members. She sought a petition under the then s.459 to obtain redress for what she saw as unfairly prejudicial conduct towards her. In the light of the evidence it became apparent that the directors' actions were unexceptionable. They had taken commercial decisions which the petitioner might not have liked, but were still properly arrived at. It was true that there had been some trivial and technical breaches of their duties under the articles, but none of those breaches was serious enough to constitute unfairly prejudicial conduct towards the petitioner. The important issue was that the directors had not breached their fiduciary duties in the management of the company, and that they had overall conducted themselves in accordance with the articles of association. There was no element of "self-serving" by the directors/majority shareholders as is found in other minority protection cases, such as *Re Bird Precision Bellows Ltd*, nor any suggestion of ill-will towards the petitioner. Lord Hoffmann in his judgment introduced the term "legitimate expectations" to describe what the shareholder might have hoped to receive in her capacity as a shareholder. She was not entitled to expect more than that the directors had abided by their fiduciary duties and managed the company within the rights and powers given to them under the company's memorandum and articles. Furthermore, as a shareholder she had known what she was entitled to in terms of the rights attaching to her shares, and she had consented to their management of the company within those parameters. She could not have legitimately expected that the other shareholders/ directors should have taken any further consideration of her particular wishes. It was apparent that the majority shareholders/directors had not breached their duties and they had acted lawfully. They were entitled to take such commercial decisions as they saw fit; whether or not the majority shareholders' actions had prejudiced her, it was clear that their actions were not unfair as she had

---

[33] *Re Saul Harrison Sons Plc* [1994] B.C.L.C. 475.

voluntarily renounced any powers of management when she had accepted her high-yielding non-voting shares; and her petition was refused.[34]

The concept of "legitimate expectation" was reviewed in the first **11–27** important House of Lords case on minority protection for many years, *O'Neill v Phillips*.[35]

> O'Neill, the petitioner, had been given 25 per cent of the shares of a company for which he worked as a foreman. The majority share-holder in the company, and therefore the effective controller of the company, Phillips, indicated that in due course a further 25 per cent of the company's shares would be made available to O'Neill, in the expectation that O'Neill would permanently take over the manage-ment of the company. O'Neill was also to receive 50 per cent of the company's profits. Phillips did not, however, put this indication in writing, and subsequently decided in the light of a turn-down in the company's business neither to give O'Neill any more shares nor let him take over the management of the company. O'Neill, feeling treated hardly, asserted that he had been prejudiced as a minority shareholder. When the case reached the House of Lords, Lord Hoffmann held that O'Neill had not been treated unfairly. This was mainly because there had never been any binding agreement on Phillips to grant O'Neill the extra shares. Both O'Neill and Phillips had taken professional advice and had agreed that the shares would not be transferred until a formal document had been signed, and no formal document ever was signed. At no stage did Phillips give O'Neill any formal entitlement to the shares, although O'Neill may well have believed that his own actings were sufficient to be equivalent to an entitlement to the transfer of the shares. However unhappy O'Neill may have been with Phillips's actions, it was dif-ficult for him to deny that Phillips had at all times reserved to himself the right to take back the management of the company and not to transfer the shares. O'Neill's real problem was that from his point of view there had been a breach of contract, but as it was impossible to establish that there had been a contract, he used a s.459 petition as his fall-back position to claim unfairness to him as a shareholder. But any prejudice he suffered, such as it was, was not ultimately related to the fact that he was a shareholder.

In the course of the judgment, Lord Hoffmann took the opportunity to lay down various guidelines which should be used in connection with unfairly prejudicial conduct petitions. The first of these is that fairness

---

[34] This case particularly well demonstrates the need for unfairness if a petitioner is to be successful. It is arguable that her interests had been prejudiced, but the requirement for unfairness under s.459 had not been demonstrated.

[35] *O'Neill v Phillips*; sub nom. *Re A Company (No.00709 of 1992)* [1999] 1 W.L.R. 1092; [1999] 2 All E.R. 961 HL.

alone is not a matter for the judge at first instance to decide upon at his own discretion[36]; there must be "rational principles"[37] on which to make any decision as to fairness, and these rational principles should establish a degree of certainty which will enable professional advisers to tell their clients whether or not their petition is likely to succeed.[38] One of these principles is that the constitution of the company is paramount (as suggested in *Re Astec BSR Plc*).[39] This is because members of a company must be assumed to be aware of the contents of the constitution of the company of which they are members,[40] and are free to take legal advice as to the implications of the terms of those documents. Having become a member of a company on such terms, the member must live with those terms (as in *Re Saul Harrison and Sons Plc*)[41] or seek to have them changed by special resolution. Shareholders' agreements or other contractual agreements are equally important; and in either case rights or expectations clearly contracted for and subsequently ignored by a majority might give rise to a claim for breach of contract or possibly a petition under s.994. However, there may be occasions where the majority shareholders might not be technically transgressing the terms of the constitution or other contractual agreement but still not be treating the minority fairly, as for example, where the majority is exercising its rights in bad faith. On such an occasion there would be an equitable restraint[42] on the strict application of the terms of the memorandum, articles or shareholders' agreement. As an example of an equitable restraint, Lord Hoffmann referred to the case of *Ebrahimi v Westbourne Galleries Ltd*[43] where the petitioner was given the remedy he sought (winding-up) because the respondents, although apparently acting within the letter of the law, had used their rights under the law in bad faith. As further examples he referred to promises which it would be unjust not to enforce because the majority and minority shareholders had actually agreed them at the time of making them (in which case it would be unjust of the majority to break them) or to the situation where both the majority and minority shareholders had agreed to a course of action which

---

[36] Lord Hoffmann was at pains to point out that fairness is a concept that varies according to its context, and that what might be seen as unfair in, say, a family or a game of cricket, is not necessarily unfair in business.

[37] *O'Neill v Phillips*; sub nom. *Re A Company (No.00709 of 1992)* [1999] 1 W.L.R. 1092 at 1098.

[38] Effectively what he was saying was that there should be an objective view of "fairness".

[39] *Re Astec BSR Plc* [1998] 2 B.C.L.C. 556.

[40] As in the terms of CA 1985 s.14.

[41] *Re Saul Harrison and Sons Plc* [1995] 1 B.C.L.C. 14.

[42] An equitable remedy is one given by the courts when although the strict letter of the law denies a claimant his remedy, it would be contrary to justice and fairness to deny him it, usually because the respondent has acted in bad faith or taken unfair advantage of some rule of law. An equitable restraint is therefore an occasion when some legal rule is not followed because of the dubious conduct of the party seeking to enforce the rule.

[43] *Ebrahimi v Westbourne Galleries Ltd* [1973] A.C. 360; [1972] 2 All E.R. 492. In this case the petitioner was forced out of his directorship by the majority shareholders and the majority shareholders also refused to buy his shares, both actions being technically permissible under the articles, though not quite in the spirit under which the company had originally been set up by the petitioner and his former partner.

subsequently could not be carried out because of an unforeseen change in circumstances. If the majority insisted that the course of action should still take place notwithstanding the change of circumstances, despite the fact that it would be prejudicial to the minority shareholders, an equitable restraint would apply.

Lord Hoffmann, clearly unhappy at the potential direction of his **11–28** former idea of "legitimate expectation", also indicated that a legitimate expectation could only arise out of an equitable restraint, and that he was anxious not to let the concept of a "legitimate expectation" have a life of its own,[44] thereby widening the opportunities for minority protection. Indeed, Lord Hoffmann indicated a restrictive view of s.994 by saying that merely because a member is dismissed as a director or otherwise excluded from management, and/or has difficulty withdrawing his capital, he is not automatically entitled to a remedy under s.994. Just because the minority has lost trust or confidence in the majority it cannot demand that its shares be bought by the majority or the company; or as Lord Hoffmann put it, there is no system of "no-fault divorce" operating. "Unfairly prejudicial conduct" thus becomes something more demanding than mere dissatisfaction with the majority.

Lord Hoffmann also suggested how a majority shareholder may protect himself from petulant actions by minority shareholders. The normal order granted following a s.994 petition is for the majority (or the company) to buy the petitioner's shares. If the majority offers:

- to buy the minority's shares;
- at a fair value;
- with no discount for being a minority shareholding;
- with the value if necessary being established by independent valuers acting as experts not as arbiters; and
- with both parties being entitled to equal access to all relevant financial information

it will be difficult for the minority to complain that he is the victim of unfairly prejudicial conduct. Prudent company directors, who also happen to be majority shareholders in companies with minority shareholders that might at a later stage prove troublesome, should therefore consider building into their companies' articles or shareholders' agreements provisions that echo Lord Hoffmann's pronouncements. By doing so, and by following the terms specified to the letter, it will be very difficult for a minority shareholder to claim that he has been unfairly treated. This practice protects majority shareholders from unnecessary litigation from minority shareholders, and gives a clear and fair exit route for minority shareholders who may indeed be the victim of unfairly prejudicial conduct by the majority.

Although this may seem harsh for minority shareholders, Lord Hoff- **11–29** mann was in effect (albeit in a part of his judgment that is obiter) reining

---

[44] *O'Neill v Phillips*; sub nom. *Re A Company (No.00709 of 1992)* [1999] 1 W.L.R. 1092 at 1104.

in the rights of the minority shareholders who, in some quarters at least, had been seen to be making life unreasonably difficult for majority shareholders.

Lord Hoffmann's decision was followed in *Re Guidezone Ltd*[45] and *Anderson v Hogg*.[46] In this latter case, Anderson had objected to the fact that Hogg, a majority shareholder and director, had taken it upon himself to pay himself out of their company's slender funds a sum of money, described as a redundancy payment, but which might more properly be described as non-statutory payment for termination of office. Hogg had not received approval of this payment from the company. Hogg agreed that the payment was unlawful, but maintained that it was not unfair and that therefore, ingeniously, the then s.459 did not apply and he was therefore entitled to keep the money. Before the Lord Ordinary, Anderson's petition was rejected on precisely these grounds. However, on appeal, applying the *O'Neill v Phillips* approach, it was clear that unfairness is to be established by established equitable principles, such as seeing whether or not the majority has acted in good faith. This was a hurdle too high for Hogg to leap, and Hogg was not entitled to award himself the payment.

Section 994 undoubtedly fills a need. Some majority shareholders do behave in a blatantly oppressive way, and the virtue of s.994 is that provides a remedy for minority shareholders when the majority shareholders ought to have behaved better.[47] Minority protection problems remain a rich source of income for corporate lawyers as majority shareholders, frequently doubling as directors, try to take advantage of their position and minority shareholders in turn make themselves as awkward as possible to that they have to be bought out at a premium. With minimal effort, the disputes may continue for many months. But when the majority shareholders are directors, and are acting improperly, the derivative claim serves to bring them to heel.

STATUTORY PROTECTION UNDER THE COMPANIES ACT 2006 SECTIONS 265–269—THE DERIVATIVE PROCEDURE

11–30 One of the past difficulties in the law relating to minority protection was how to deal with the situation where the member who was making a fuss was doing so not on his own behalf, but on behalf of his company. The member was not the company and therefore had no standing to sue either the majority shareholders or the directors. As with *Foss v Harbottle*, the majority could say that they had voted to approve their own actions, and a minority shareholder must respect a majority decision. His second problem was that suing either the majority shareholders or the directors was an expensive activity, with no guarantee that his expenses would be met. A third problem was that if every minority shareholder made a fuss

---

[45] *Re Guidezone Ltd*; sub nom. *Kaneria v Patel* [2001] B.C.C. 692; [2000] 2 B.C.L.C. 321.
[46] *Anderson v Hogg*, 2002 S.C. 190; 2002 S.L.T. 354; [2002] B.C.C. 923.
[47] *O'Donnell v Shanahan* [2009] EWCA Civ 751.

about any decisions made within his company, there would be no end to petty disputes, nor to actions raised by attention-seeking troublemakers. English courts dealt with this by allowing for the concept of the derivative action, whereby the member's right to sue on behalf of the company is derived from his concern for the welfare of the collective interests of the members. The derivative action was a two stage process. The first is that the member applied to court for permission to raise an action on behalf of his company; and if having made out a good case, permission was granted, the second stage was the action itself against the majority shareholders or the directors as the case may be. Unfortunately the English rules of court had no set procedure for this, and as a result much of the case law was tangled up in procedural issues of how such cases should be managed. In addition, traditionally many judges, at least until the 1970s, did not readily entertain the idea of minority protection cases, but once the idea of unfair prejudice remedy became better known, judges generally favoured s.459 of the Companies Act 1985 (now the CA 2006 s.994) over the two stage derivative process. The derivative process was not barred, but it was certainly not made welcome. In Scotland, there were fewer hurdles under Scottish court procedure and there was no intrinsic reason why an equivalent procedure to a derivative action could not take place,[48] but there were few cases, and as may be seen in the overruled decision of the Lord Ordinary in *Anderson v Hogg*, those that existed were not always well understood.

Fortunately, as part of the reforms under the CA 2006, we now have a **11–31** proper derivative procedure, set out on a statutory basis. The Scottish procedure is to be found at the CA 2006 ss.265–269.[49] Section 265 of the CA 2006 gives the right to a member to raise proceedings against a director or "another person"[50] in circumstances where there is an actual or proposed act or omission, involving negligence, default, breach of duty or breach of trust by a director of the company.[51] "Breach of duty" is wide enough to cover a breach of the director's duties to his company in terms of the duties to be found in ss.170–187 of the CA 2006. The member will raise the proceedings in order to protect the interests of the company and to obtain a remedy, not on his own behalf, but on behalf of the company.[52] The term "director" covers present and past directors and shadow directors, and the term "member" covers those to whom shares have passed by operation of law.[53] There is no requirement in the statute

---

[48] See *Wilson v Inverness Retail and Business Park*, 2003 S.L.T. 301.
[49] The equivalent sections for England, Wales and Northern Ireland are at ss.260–264.
[50] CA 2006 s.265(4). Any other person could be someone involved with the director, or who knowingly had benefited from the director's actions to the detriment of the company. The "another person" could presumably include a majority shareholder who was not a director.
[51] CA 2006 s.265(1)–(3). Note that the detrimental behaviour must be carried out by the director.
[52] If the member wishes to raise proceedings for his own benefit, s.994 would generally be the better remedy.
[53] CA 2006 s.265(7).

that the director should have personally benefited in order to be caught by these provisions.

The most important Scottish decision to date on derivative proceedings is Lord Reed's decision in the Inner House in *Wishart v Castlecroft Securities Ltd.*[54] Lord Reed closely spells out the practicalities of the legislation.

Requirement for leave to raise derivative proceedings

11–32   Under s.266 the member may only bring the derivative proceedings with the leave of the court,[55] and in applying for leave, must specify the cause of the action and the facts of the matter.[56] There is effectively a three-fold process: initial application; first order hearing if granted; final hearing on the merits of the case once leave has been granted to the member to represent the company.[57]

The initial application requires the member to apply to court on an ex parte[58] basis to be given leave to bring his proceedings on behalf of the company.

If the initial application and the evidence in its support at this first stage clearly do not disclose a prima facie case for granting such leave, the court must reject the application and make any necessary consequential order.[59] It would appear, at least from *Wishart v Castlecroft Securities Ltd*,[60] that the applicant does not positively have to make a prima facie case; all the applicant has to do is the lesser task of not producing an application and/or evidence that do not "disclose" a prima facie case.[61] A "prima facie case" is where the applicant has to demonstrate to the court

---

[54] 2010 S.C. 16; 2009 S.L.T. 812; [2010] B.C.C. 161.

[55] Note that the equivalent English provisions at s.261 refer to an applicant bringing a derivative claim and seeking permission to continue it, as opposed to obtaining leave to raise derivative proceedings in Scotland. The English procedural rules slightly differ from the Scots ones. In England there is still the initial prima facie hearing but if the application is not immediately dismissed the company is invited to join in the application to see if leave should be granted to continue the derivative claim. These two stages are normally separate but occasionally they are "telescoped" and heard together, as in *Mission Capital plc v Sinclair* [2008] B.C.C. 866 and *Frambar Holdings Ltd v Patel* [2008] B.C.C. 885. Note that in England there is a "claim" but in Scotland there are "proceedings".

[56] CA 2006 s.266(2). Rule of Court 14.5 deals with the proper procedure in the Court of Session. For the Sheriff Court see Act of Sederunt (Sheriff Court Rules) (Miscellaneous Amendments) 2011 (SSI 2010/279).

[57] This third stage proceeds as an action in the usual way. In *Wishart v Castlecroft Securities Ltd* the applicant had a summons ready to serve on the defenders if the derivative proceedings went in the applicant's favour (which they did).

[58] This means that the applicant applies to the court for his order, but the respondent is not represented and indeed may be unaware of the application.

[59] CA 2006 s.266(3). Implicit within this is the requirement that the applicant is a member of the company, and that he seeks to raise a derivative claim—as opposed to, say, a judicial review or a personal claim for damages.

[60] 2010 S.C. 16; 2009 S.L.T. 812; [2010] B.C.C. 161.

[61] At 31.

that "on the face of it" he has a case which has enough substance to it to deserve a hearing by the court.[62] Just because a prima facie case has been disclosed does not necessarily mean that ultimately the case will succeed. The purpose of this first stage in the proceedings is to weed out the applications that clearly are frivolous, vexatious or otherwise without merit.

In making its decision, the court will apply the provisions of s.268, to be discussed shortly. By implication, any application that is not rejected there and then as obviously hopeless is acceptable, so if it is acceptable the court will make a first order requiring the applicant to serve the application on the company.[63] The company may also be required to produce its own evidence on the matter and the court may adjourn the proceedings for the obtaining of this evidence.[64] The company (but not the director alleged to have committed the breach which is the subject of the litigation) will then be entitled to take part in any further proceedings. On the basis of any further evidence produced by the company (if so required), at this second stage the court will then decide whether or not leave should be granted to the applicant to raise derivative proceedings on behalf of the company. How it will make that decision is once more predicated by s.268. The application may be granted, if necessary on such terms as the court sees fit, or the proceedings may be adjourned,[65] perhaps for a meeting of the shareholders to consider the position. Equally, the court having heard the evidence, the application may be refused.

Application for continuation of proceedings as derivative proceedings

Under s.267, if a company has already raised proceedings against a **11–33** director, and those proceedings are in respect of an act or omission by the director and which could be the basis for derivative proceedings, a member may apply to the court to be substituted for the company, and for the proceedings to continue as derivative proceedings. The important words here are "continue as". The company may well have raised proceedings against a director, but not be making much headway. The member will then seek to continue the proceedings, but as derivative proceedings, as opposed to proceedings pursued by the company itself. The member steps into the shoes of the company, and continues the case on its behalf. The reasons for doing this would be: (i) the way in which the company has been conducting its own proceedings amounts to an abuse of the process of court; (ii) the company has not been diligent in prosecuting its own proceedings; or (iii) it is appropriate for the member

---

[62] Although the case was not discussed in Lord Reed's judgment, it is generally accepted that *Gillespie v Toondale Ltd*, 2006 S.C. 304 is the leading case on what is meant by a prima facie case.

[63] CA 2006 s.266(4)(a).

[64] CA 2006 s.366(4)(b). It is thought that during the adjournment the company may take the opportunity to convene a meeting to ratify the director's acts or omissions, or alternatively disown those acts or omissions.

[65] CA 2006 s.266(4).

to take over the proceedings instead.[66] Section 267 is designed to cover situations such as when the directors of Company A are not making much effort to sue one of Company A's directors, B, who may have breached his duty to the company. This may be because the other directors of Company A are friends or relations of B and see no reason to make difficulties for him. The member may then apply to take over the proceedings against B on behalf of Company A in order to ensure proper redress for Company A.

Again, as in s.266, if it appears to the court that the application and the evidence in support of the member's application, taking account of s.268, do not disclose a prima facie case, the court must refuse the application; but if the application is not rejected, the court will make a first order, requiring the applicant to serve the application on the company, thus entitling the company to take part in the further proceedings and to produce further evidence if necessary.[67] The court will then decide, at this second stage, once more on the basis of s.268, whether leave should be granted.

Grounds on which the granting of leave to raise derivative proceedings under s.266 or an application under s.267 will be refused

11–34   The courts are given guidance at s.268 as to what to consider during the ex parte application or the first stage hearing with the company present when deciding whether or not a prima facie case has been made out under either s.266 or s.267. Under s.268(1) the court *must* refuse leave to raise derivative proceedings under s.266 or refuse the application under s.267 if it is satisfied that:

   (a) a person (generally a director) acting in accordance with s.172 of the CA 2006[68] would not seek to raise or continue the proceedings[69];
   (b) the future act or omission which is the matter of the dispute has already been authorised[70]; or
   (c) where the matter in question is an act or omission which has already occurred, the act or omission has already been authorised or ratified.[71]

Under these circumstances, the application is rejected.

But if those circumstances do not apply, so that the application is not automatically rejected, under s.268(2) the court must take into account, in particular,[72] the following matters:

---

[66] CA 2006 s.267(2).
[67] CA 2006 s.267(4).
[68] This is the duty to promote the success of the company.
[69] CA 2006 s.268(1)(a).
[70] CA 2006 s.268(1)(b).
[71] CA 2006 s.268(1)(c).
[72] The words "in particular" suggest, at last according to Lord Reed's pronouncements in *Wishart v Castlecroft Securities Ltd* at 36 that the list is non-exhaustive.

(a) whether or not the member was acting in good faith;
(b) the importance that a person acting in accordance with s.172 would attach to the raising or continuing of the action or the application;
(c) the likelihood of authorisation by the members of the future or past act or omission before it occurs or ratification after it occurs;
(d) where an act or omission has already occurred, whether the act or omission would be likely to be ratified;
(e) whether the company has decided not to raise proceedings or to persist in the proceedings; or
(f) whether the member would be better pursuing the matter in his own right, preferably by using the minority protection provisions of s.994.[73]

When considering whether or not to grant leave for derivative proceedings or a s.267 application, the court should pay particular regard to the views of the members who have no personal interest, direct or indirect, in the matter.[74] There may well be a temptation to go through the entire evidence to establish whether or not a prima facie case has been made out, and certainly in England there is a concern that the prima facie hearing may become a mini-trial in its own right.[75] In Scotland there is a similar concern to prevent there being a long hearing to establish whether or not there may be a later long hearing.[76]

It should be noted that there is a distinction between s.268(1)(a) and **11–35** s.268(2)(b). Section 268(1)(a) is concerned with the question as to whether a hypothetical director trying to promote the success of the company would raise or continue the proceedings. Section 268(2)(b) concerns the degree of the importance that that director would attach to the raising or continuing of the proceedings. There might be a situation where a hypothetical director would, in theory, support the raising of proceedings since there would be a benefit to the company if the proceedings were successful, but the importance of the proceedings might not be great since the value of the claim within the proceedings might in practice be small, or the time and effort involved would be disproportionate to the outcome. Although there are no cases at present in Scotland on s.268(1)(a), under equivalent English legislation (s.263(2)(a)) potential grounds for a hypothetical director acting under s.172 not proceeding with a derivative claim were: (a) the unlikely prospects of success; (b) the questionable ability of the company to make a recovery; (c) the disruption that would be caused to the company by the commencement or continuation of proceedings; and (d) the cost of such proceedings.[77] In another case, the

---

[73] See *Mission Capital Plc v Sinclair* [2008] B.C.C. 866. This English case refers to s.263(3) which is equivalent to s.268(2).
[74] CA 2006 s.268(3).
[75] Per L.J. Vos, in *Sukhpaul Singh v Satpaul Singh, Singh Bros Contractors (Northwest) Limited* [2014] EWCA Civ 103 at 15.
[76] Per Lord Reed, in *Wishart*, at 39.
[77] *Franbar Holdings Ltd v Patel* [2008] EWHC 1534 (Ch); [2008] B.C.C. 885.

acts complained of had taken place long ago, and had since been ratified, so no director acting in accordance with s.172 would bother about them.[78]

There are no reported decisions in Scotland other than *Wishart* on s.268(2)(b), but the equivalent in England is s.263(3)(b). In *Phillips v Fryer*[79] a derivative claim was indeed seen as very important and something for a hypothetical director to take account of, as it would be considerably quicker than the alternative of a minority protection petition under s.994.

As for the requirement to act in good faith, the court would make an assessment of the applicant's good faith, partly on the evidence produced by the applicant but also possibly on the evidence produced by the company. For an example of good faith, see *Hughes v Weiss*,[80] for something approaching lack of good faith (though not explicitly stated as such in the judgement) see *Abouraya v Sigmund*,[81] where the claimant was trying to position himself as an applicant member when actually he stood to gain as a creditor.

11–36   The remaining parts of s.268(2) are self-evident save for s.268(2)(f). Under the equivalent legislation in England (s.263(3)(f)) there have been a number of applications which the courts have decided would be better dealt with under the minority protection provisions of CA 2006 s.994. This is particularly when the remedy is really being sought for the benefit of the applicant rather than for the benefit of the company as a whole. Where the company stands to benefit, the derivative claim is more appropriate, but when the individual applicant stands to benefit, a s.994 is more appropriate, though as *Philips* above indicates, the two alternatives are not necessarily mutually exclusive; nevertheless there may be good reasons for preferring one to the other depending on the circumstances.[82]

As regards the expenses of derivative proceedings the latter part of Lord Reed's decision in the Inner House in *Wishart v Castlecroft Securities Ltd*[83] indicates that in principle the applicant's expenses (if the proceedings are successful) should be met by the company, since the company is the one to benefit from the applicant's zeal.

Assuming leave is given, the proceedings may then proceed as normal, with the member either raising the proceedings in place of the company, or, as the case may be, continuing the proceedings on behalf of the company.[84] In practice, if leave has been granted by the courts to allow the derivative proceedings to proceed, it suggests that the applicant probably has a good case against the errant director of the applicant's company. Under such circumstances it would probably be wise for the

---

[78] *Sukhpaul Singh v Satpaul Singh, Singh Bros Contractors (Northwest) Limited* at 26.
[79] [2013] B.C.C. 176.
[80] [2012] EWHC 2363 (Ch).
[81] [2014] EWHC 277 (Ch).
[82] This point is also made in *Wishart* at 46.
[83] 2010 S.C. 16; 2009 S.L.T. 812; [2010] B.C.C. 161.
[84] For example, *Hughes v Weiss* [2012] EWHC 2363 (Ch).

director to settle quickly rather than incur the expenses of an unsuccessful defence.

It is also possible for a different member to seek the court's leave to stand in place of the member pursuing the derivative action or continuing a s.267 application.[85]

The wider purpose and effect of derivative proceedings

It will be recalled that the grounds for derivative proceedings are "any **11–37** actual or proposed act or omission involving negligence, default, breach of duty or breach of trust by a director of the company."[86] The underlying point of these provisions is to allow a member the right to challenge a director's behaviour if the director has been abusing his position within the company. It is important to remember that when this legislation went through Parliament, there were MPs whose constituents had died in poverty, waiting in vain for payment of their pensions, because Robert Maxwell had stolen their pension fund's assets.[87] While not every Maxwell pensioner would necessarily have been a shareholder in Mirror Group pension fund, it is thought that had there been more opportunities for employee-shareholders or even ordinary, if altruistic, shareholders to use the equivalent of derivative proceedings, something might have been done, were the shareholder brave enough, to hold Maxwell to account at an earlier stage. The idea is that the provisions of ss.265–269 will allow a shareholder, who has a genuine grievance about the director's behaviour, the opportunity to call an errant director to stop. The words "breach of trust" have a moral ring about them that while not necessarily causing a director to desist from any questionable behaviour at the expense of his company or fellow shareholders may cause his professional advisers to warn him that if what he is doing on the face of it looks dubious, the courts will be likely to allow derivative proceedings to begin against him.

Other minority rights

Certain other rights are conferred by the CA 2006 on a minority of the **11–38** members, and may be exercised despite the wishes of the majority. These include the right of the minority of not less than 10 per cent of the paid-up capital to requisition the holding of an extraordinary general meeting,[88] of a specified minority to demand a poll,[89] and of 15 per cent of the holders of special classes of shares to object to a variation of the rights

---

[85] CA 2006 s.269.
[86] CA 2006 s.265(3).
[87] Robert Maxwell, the mercurial and unscrupulous former proprietor of the *Daily Mirror* newspaper, arranged for the abstraction from the Mirror Group employees' pension fund of many valuable assets, which he then used in a futile attempt to shore up his own personal business losses.
[88] CA 2006 s.303.
[89] CA 2006 s.321(2).

attached to that class.[90] Ten per cent of members, or members with 10 per cent of the control of the company, may insist on the majority buying out their shares by an offeror following a takeover.[91]

WINDING UP ON THE "JUST AND EQUITABLE GROUNDS"

11–39 Before the existence of the CA 1985 s.459 and the later version in the CA 2006 s.994, an unhappy minority shareholder had either to obtain redress through the limited exceptions to *Foss v Harbottle* or, in desperation, have the company wound up. Having the company wound up might ensure the return of the shareholder's capital, but in many cases was a drastic remedy for a particular problem. It could also be unfair on other shareholders who were not involved in the unfairly prejudicial conduct, either as perpetrators or as victims.

11–40   The remedy of winding up where there has been prejudice to a minority is nevertheless available under the Insolvency Act 1986 ("the IA 1986") s.122(1)(g) where it is stated that the court may wind up the company if the court is of the opinion that it is just and equitable that the company should be wound up. Windings-up are not lightly entered upon, and the courts will need to be satisfied that no better remedy (such as the use of a s.994 petition) is available and that the petitioner is acting reasonably in seeking a winding up order.[92] Winding up generally is dealt with in Ch.17.

JUDICIAL FACTORS IN SCOTLAND

11–41 This remedy for an aggrieved minority is only available in Scotland. If the directors are at loggerheads or have all resigned, or for any other good reason which is acceptable to the court, it is possible for any shareholder to petition the court for the appointment of a judicial factor to the company. A judicial factor is a court-appointed accountant (usually) or lawyer who in these circumstances is given the task of acting as a temporary company caretaker and protecting the interests of the shareholders while the wreck of the company is sorted out.[93] At the time of writing, the position of judicial factors is being reviewed by the Law Commission of Scotland, with a view to modernising their role and function.

---

[90] CA 2006 s.633.
[91] CA 2006 ss.983–985.
[92] IA 1986 s.125(2).
[93] *Weir v Rees*, 1991 S.L.T. 345.

Department of Business, Informaton and Skills Investigations

The BIS has extensive powers to investigate the affairs of a company. **11–42**
This can be one more weapon in the minority shareholders' armoury
although in practice the use of inspectors by the BIS for minority protection purposes appears to be slender. Investigations are carried out by
one or more inspectors, usually a lawyer and an accountant working
together, and are appointed by the Secretary of State. BIS-appointed
inspectors can be asked specifically to investigate majority shareholders'
abuse of their majority voting power. BIS investigations are also sometimes used to investigate alleged insider dealing or other nefarious activity
within a company. Although most of the final reports from the investigations make fascinating reading, they frequently take many years to be
written and cost a great deal. In the meantime, the perpetrators and
victims of the frauds or company collapses (for these are often what the
investigations are looking into) may well have died, or have spent many
years waiting for the investigation to be finished. This is one reason why
there have been very few investigations recently.

The present law on BIS investigations is contained in the CA 1985 Pt
XIV, although the CA 2006 adds to the existing provisions by adding new
sections (see ss.1035–1038) to the CA 1985 and keeping the existing
provisions of CA 1985 relating to BIS investigations extant.

Who may apply to have a company investigated?

A company with a share capital, 200 or more members, or members **11–43**
holding in total more than one-tenth of the shares issued, may apply,[94] or
the company itself may apply,[95] for a BIS investigation.

In a company without a share capital, a minimum of one-fifth of the
members on the company's register of members can apply.[96] The application must be supported by evidence showing that there is good reason
for requiring the investigation.[97] In order to deter frivolous applications,
the Secretary of State may require the applicant to provide security for
the costs of the investigation.[98]

If a court by order declares that its affairs ought to be investigated, the
Secretary of State must appoint inspectors for the investigation.[99]

When may a company be investigated?

In addition to investigation following an application by the company **11–44**
or the members as detailed above, the Secretary of State may appoint
inspectors on the following grounds under the CA 1985 s.432(2), if it
appears to him that:

---

[94] CA 1985 s.431(2)(a).
[95] CA 1985 s.341(2)(c).
[96] CA 1985 s.421(2)(b).
[97] CA 1985 s.431(3).
[98] CA 1985 s.431(4).
[99] CA 1985 s.432(1).

"(a) the company's affairs are being or have been conducted with intent to defraud its creditors or the creditors of any other person, or otherwise for a fraudulent or unlawful purpose, or in a manner which is unfairly prejudicial to some part of its members;

(b) any actual or proposed act or omission of the company (including an act or omission on its behalf) is or would be so prejudicial, or that the company was formed for any fraudulent or unlawful purpose;

(c) persons concerned with the company's formation or the management of its affairs have in connection therewith been guilty of fraud, misfeasance or other misconduct towards it or towards its members; or

(d) the company's members have not been given all the information with respect to its affairs which they might reasonably expect."

While normally the inspectors publish a report on their investigations, if the inspectors are appointed on any of the above four grounds they may be appointed on the basis that any report they prepare is not for publication.[100]

11-45   Even if a company is in voluntary liquidation, under the CA 1985 s.432(3) inspectors may be appointed if the court requires it under the CA 1985 s.432(1) or if the Secretary of State considers it appropriate under s.432(2). Where the Secretary of State has ordered the appointment of inspectors, he is not obliged to give his reasons for the appointment provided he has not ordered the investigation for an improper purpose or in the absence of good faith.[101]

The inspectors have wide powers to interview directors and employees and anyone else connected with the company—including its solicitors, bankers and auditors—under investigation. All such persons have to provide such assistance as they reasonably can, and to produce any relevant documents in their care[102] except where in the case of solicitors they can justifiably claim that they hold privileged information which they would be entitled to refuse to disclose in the Court of Session or the High Court.[103]

11-46   Bankers have a similar privilege except where the bankers' client is the company being investigated, where the company itself consents to disclosure or where the Secretary of State orders the privilege to be overruled.[104] The inspectors can demand that the interviewees can be put on oath,[105] and refusal by the interviewees to comply with the inspectors' requests may result in the matter being reported to the court. Any statements thus obtained may be used in civil matters, as for example,

---

[100] CA 1985 s.432(2A).
[101] *Norwest Holst Ltd v Secretary of State for Trade* [1978] Ch. 201.
[102] CA 1985 s.434(1), (2).
[103] CA 1985 s.452(1).
[104] CA 1985 s.452(1A).
[105] CA 1985 s.434(3).

disqualifying a person from being a director[106] but it was held that it was a breach of art.6(1) of the European Convention on Human Rights to use those statements in criminal matters.[107] As a result there are now statutory limits on the use to which the statements may be put in criminal trials in order to prevent self-incrimination.[108]

The inspectors are required to act fairly while remembering that they are not a court of law. This was established by the cases raised by the late Robert Maxwell in *Re Pergamon Press Ltd*[109] and *Maxwell v Department of Trade and Industry*,[110] where he attempted to deter or delay the publication of the report into his questionable business practices.

The inspectors' report

The inspectors compile a report within the terms of the remit given to **11–47** them by the Secretary of State. If the court had ordered the report to be produced, the courts must be given a copy.[111] If it appears from the report that in the public interest civil proceedings ought to be instituted on the company's behalf, perhaps against errant directors or majority shareholders, the Secretary of State has power to order this to be done.[112] The report is itself admissible evidence to be used if necessary against any director under the Company Directors Disqualification Act 1986[113] or in any criminal proceedings.[114] The report may also be used as evidence in any petition brought by the Secretary of State to have the company wound up under the IA 1986 s.124A, or to obtain a remedy for conduct unfairly prejudicial to the company's members.[115]

Other powers of investigation

The inspectors may be appointed to report on the membership of the **11–48** company, and in particular the ownership of its shares and debentures, and to ascertain who truly controls the company.[116] Under the CA 1985 s.442(3) the Secretary of State must appoint inspectors to ascertain the true ownership where requested to do so by the minorities referred to in the CA 1985 s.431(2)(a) and (b), unless he considers that the members' application is vexatious or where it is unreasonable that any or part of the matters to which the minorities are objecting should be investigated.[117]

If the Secretary of State wishes he may investigate the ownership of

---

[106] *R. v Secretary of State for Trade and Industry Ex p. McCormick* [1998] 2 B.C.L.C. 18.
[107] *Saunders v United Kingdom* [1998] 1 B.C.L.C. 362. It was not disputed that Ernest Saunders committed criminal acts, but the use of statements of his, obtained from the inspectors, was held to be unjust.
[108] CA 1985 s.434(5A), (5B).
[109] *Re Pergamon Press Ltd* [1971] Ch. 388.
[110] *Maxwell v Department of Trade and Industry* [1974] Q.B. 523.
[111] CA 1985 s.437(2).
[112] CA 1985 s.438.
[113] CA 1985 s.441.
[114] CA 1985 s.441.
[115] CA 1985 s.460.
[116] CA 1985 s.442.
[117] CA 1985 s.442(3A).

shares or debentures in the company or its members using inspectors.[118]
To refuse to give information or to give false information is an offence.

11–49   If members are being obstructive about providing the information to
the inspectors or to the Secretary of State, the Secretary of State, under
the CA 1985 ss.454–457, may prohibit all or any of the following:

- the transfer of any shares;
- the transfer of the right to be issued with new shares and any
  subsequent issue of those new shares;
- the exercise of any voting rights in respect of shares whose
  ownership is being investigated;
- the issue of any further shares arising out of the existing ownership of shares (i.e. a bonus issue or the exercise of pre-emption
  rights); or
- the repayment of capital or payment of dividends, except in the
  case of a liquidation.

Requisition and seizure of books and papers

11–50   Appointing inspectors is a public process and may do the company and
innocent shareholders more harm than good. There is a more discreet
option available to the Secretary of State in order to establish whether or
not a full-scale investigation is necessary. This is the requisition and
seizure of the company's books by personnel within the BIS. Compared
to a full-scale investigation, this type of investigation is cheap, and is by
far the commonest response by the BIS to any requests for an investigation. Any statements obtained in the process may again be used in civil
matters,[119] but in criminal matters there are restrictions on the use of
these statements without evidence.[120]

The Secretary of State may require documents to be brought to him.[121]
He may obtain warrants to permit the police to search premises to prevent the destruction or concealment of such documents.[122] He is only
allowed to disclose what information he finds within certain defined
circumstances, these being mostly in connection with criminal matters,
disciplinary proceedings, or disqualification of company directors.

Further Reading

David Cabrelli, "Statutory derivative proceedings: the view from the
Inner House" (2010) 14(1) Edin. L.R. 116.

Brenda Hannigan, "Derivative claims; Reflective loss; Unfairly prejudicial conduct" (2009) 6 J.B.L. 606.

---

[118] CA 1985 s.444.
[119] CA 1985 s.447(8).
[120] CA 1985 s.447(8A), (8B).
[121] CA 1985 s.447.
[122] CA 1985 s.448.

Andrew Keay and Joan Loughrey, "Derivative proceedings in a brave new world for company management and shareholders" (2010) 3 J.B.L. 151.

Edwin C. Mujih, "The new statutory derivative claim: a delicate balancing act: Part 1" (2012) 33(3) Comp. Law. 76.

CHAPTER 12

INSIDER DEALING

12–01 Insider dealing is the use for gain of secret information about publicly traded securities by those who are privy to that information and who should not be taking advantage of their knowledge of that information.

The victimless crime

12–02   Insider dealing is described sometimes as a victimless crime, because, while it is easy to see who benefits from it, it is harder to see who loses by the crime. Nevertheless the victims are those investors who are denied the same opportunities as the insider dealers to make profits or avoid losses because they do not have access to the information which the insider dealers have.

The need for immediate access to information

12–03   In order to minimise the opportunities for insider dealing or misleading the financial markets, the Financial Conduct Authority requires that in the United Kingdom all relevant information about securities is made public as soon as possible.[1] In the gap between a price-sensitive event taking place and the release of the information about the event to the market, the opportunity for insider dealing arises: the smaller the gap, the less opportunity for insider dealing. When insider dealing takes place, it causes investors to lose confidence in the stock market because those "not in the know" feel that not all investors are being treated equally. They feel that the market is rigged in favour of the insider dealer. The market will not be seen to be running smoothly and fairly. "Clean" investors may then go to another stock market abroad, where the market is seen to operate more fairly and share prices more truly reflect the value of stock.

Arguments in favour of insider dealing

12–04   Although few would now openly approve of insider dealing, there are those who claim that as it has always existed, and always will, it is as well to accept the fact of its existence.[2] Some see insider dealing as a reward for managers for their entrepreneurial ability.[3] However, there are other

---

[1] *FCA Handbook*, DTR 2, Disclosure and control of inside information by issuers (available at the FCA website).
[2] Harry McVea, "What's wrong with Insider Dealing?" (1995) 15(3) L.S. 390.
[3] Manne, "In Defense of Insider Dealing" (1996) 44(6) Harv. L.R. 113.

fairer and more accountable methods of ensuring that managers are rewarded for their entrepreneurial skills. Managers allowed to reward themselves by means of insider dealing will forget their wider duties to act for the overall body of shareholders, let alone impress the employees. Insider dealing may also be a breach of the fiduciary duty of the managers to act in the best interests of the company as a whole, and at least in the United Kingdom it would be a breach of London Stock Exchange rules for directors of listed companies for directors to acquire or sell securities without full disclosure of the fact.[4]

Those who support the argument that insider dealing is a fair return for managers' entrepreneurial ability struggle to justify managers' sales of securities in advance of price-sensitive bad news about the company. It is one thing to reward managers by letting them take advantage of good results arising from their hard work or good ideas when the share price rises: it is another to let those same managers be rewarded for knowing about bad news sooner than anyone else—and making a profit out of the fall in their company's share price.

Insider dealing helps relay information into the market and thereby makes it efficient

It is said that insider dealers, by their moving before anyone else, **12–05** ensure that price-sensitive information about the company is not withheld by the company. If a company had poor end of year results, it might wish to delay publishing them for as long as it could get away with. But the insider dealer would sell his shares while he could. Because he would sell them, other investors would wonder what was behind the inside dealer's move, and raise questions about the company's finances—thus flushing out the unwelcome news about the accounts. Thus to a certain extent, this argument is valid. However, even if it is valid, it does not mean that it serves as a justification for unfair treatment of shareholders not "in the know".

CRIMINAL JUSTICE ACT 1993 SECTIONS 52–64

The above legislation contains most of the current law on insider dealing **12–06** because insider dealing is a criminal offence, not a civil offence. The offence of insider dealing is defined in terms of the actual dealing by insider dealers within the context of a regulated market. Any act within those parameters is an offence unless it comes within the various permitted defences. What is meant by insider dealing, insider dealers, and regulated markets is carefully explained. Insider dealing, depending on the severity of the offence, can be prosecuted either at summary level (i.e. before one judge with a maximum penalty of two years' imprisonment

---

[4] FCA Handbook, DTRS, Transactions by persons discharging managerial responsibilities and their connected persons (available at the FCA website).

and/or a fine)[5] or on indictment (i.e. before a judge and jury, with a maximum penalty of seven years' imprisonment and/or a much greater fine). As an additional penalty, a company director may be disqualified from being a director under the Company Directors Disqualification Act 1986.[6]

The offence of insider dealing

12–07   The offence of insider dealing takes place when an individual (but not a corporate entity)[7] who has insider information (from an inside source) as an insider deals in securities whose price will be affected by that information if and when the information is made public. The dealing must take place on a regulated market, and must be done by the insider or through a professional intermediary or by an insider acting in his capacity as a professional intermediary.[8] In addition, the legislation catches an insider who encourages some other person to deal in securities which are price-affected—irrespective of whether or not the other person knows they are price-affected—while knowing or expecting that dealing would take place on a regulated market, through a professional intermediary, or through the insider acting as a professional intermediary.[9]

It is also insider dealing to disclose information which a person has as an insider to any other person except in the proper performance of his employment, office, or profession.[10]

Inside information

12–08   This is information about particular securities, or a particular issuer of securities, which is specific to the securities in question. The information must not have been made public, but if it were to be made public it would have a "significant" effect on the price or value of the securities.[11] "Significant" is not defined in the Criminal Justice Act 1993 ("the CJA 1993"), but presumably means non-marginal. "Public" is discussed shortly.

---

[5] In the case, *R. v McQuoid* [2009] EWCA Crim 1301, an in-house solicitor (McQuoid) with an IT firm, aware that his employers were going to be taken over by Motorola, tipped off his father-in-law to buy shares in his employer. The father-in-law made nearly £49,000 profit and handed half of it to McQuoid. McQuoid had £35,000 confiscated, had to pay £30,000 in prosecution costs and was sentenced to eight months in prison. The elderly father-in-law received a suspended sentence of the same length.

[6] *R. v Goodman* [1993] 2 All E.R. 789.

[7] This is because it would be difficult to establish who in a company had the relevant mens rea to carry out the act, and also because in, say, a merchant bank, there might be one department innocently dealing in the shares without knowing that another department was privy to inside information about the shares.

[8] Criminal Justice Act 1993 ("CJA 1993") s.52(1), (3).

[9] CJA 1993 s.52(2)(a). This is designed to prevent insider dealers either using unsuspecting friends or relations to do their insider dealing for them or trying to give their friends and relatives the benefit of secret "tips" even if the original insider dealer himself does not benefit.

[10] CJA 1993 s.52(2)(b).

[11] CJA 1993 s.56(1).

Insider

Under the CJA 1993 s.57(1) an insider is someone who: **12–09**

"(1) has inside information (as opposed to information which he thinks is inside information but actually is public knowledge);
(2) knows that the information he has is inside information;
(3) has information which he has obtained from an inside source (as opposed to obtaining it from some other method, such as an intelligent guess or by deduction from observing the previous business practice of the company and its directors); and
(4) knows that it came from an inside source (as opposed to obtaining it from someone who he did not realise was an inside source)."

So if an accused can prove that he genuinely did not know his information was inside information and that he did not know it came from an inside source (neither of which would be easy to prove unless the accused was very naïve) he should be able to raise a defence.

Inside source

Under the CJA 1993 s.57(2) a person has information from an inside **12–10**
source if he has that information:

(1) because he is a director, employee or shareholder of an issuer of securities; or
(2) because he has access to the information through his employment, office or profession; or
(3) because the direct or indirect source of his information was from someone in (1) or (2) above.

This provision is designed to widen the range of persons to whom the legislation applies, and in particular to professional and others persons not just in the employment of the company but also working for the company as consultants, as professional advisers or by having the company as a client.

Securities

The word "securities" is defined in Sch.2 to Pt V of the CJA 1993 and **12–11**
covers:

- shares;
- debt securities, being debentures, bonds, deposit certificates, local authority bonds, and treasury bonds ("gilts");
- warrants to subscribe for shares or debt securities;
- depositary receipts[12];

---

[12] Depositary receipts are a form of investment comprising a package of securities issued by a particular issuer, commonly based in a foreign country, and deposited with that country's branch of a UK bank. The UK head office of the bank then issues further securities which can be traded on the UK markets but whose underlying value is secured by the deposited securities held abroad.

- options to acquire any of the items in Sch.2;
- futures[13] in respect of shares, debt securities, or depository receipts; and
- contracts for differences[14] in respect of the same items as futures.

For the definition of shares, debentures, warrants and options, see Ch.6.

Public

12–12   The CJA 1993 clearly did not wish to limit the many potential ways by which information can be made public. It therefore stated that information is made public under the CJA 1993 s.58(2) if:

- it is published in accordance with the rules of the market in which the securities are being traded for the purpose of informing investors and their professional advisers;
- it is to be found in records which under statute are open to the public;
- it can be readily acquired by those likely to deal either in the securities to which the information relates or of an issuer to which the information relates; and
- it derived from information which has been made public.

Information is still deemed to be public even if it can only be acquired by persons exercising "diligence or expertise", is limited to a few recipients, can only be obtained by observation or requires to be paid for, or is published outside the United Kingdom.[15] This particular exemption is designed to protect investment analysts who study company results and happen to be very well informed relative to other investors. It would be iniquitous if perspicacious analysts were to be classed as insider dealers just because they happened to be more perceptive or astute than others. These rules are not exhaustive,[16] and other methods of becoming public, such as publication in a newspaper, will be deemed to be public.

Dealing

12–13   Dealing is any buying or selling, or agreeing to buy or sell, securities as principal or as agent, or the procuring of any buying or selling of any securities by an agent or nominee or someone acting under the dealer's directions.[17] Holding shares without buying or selling, even if the price

---

[13] A future is a contract which provides for securities to be bought or sold and delivered at a future date at a predetermined price.

[14] A contract for differences is where an investor makes a contract with a broker whereby the broker pays the investor the difference between the price at which he buys shares on the investor's behalf and the price at which the investor tells the broker to sell them. If there is a loss, the investor pays the broker the difference. An investor generally needs only to put up 10 per cent of the value of the shares being speculated on.

[15] CJA 1993 s.58(3).

[16] CJA 1993 s.58(1).

[17] CJA 1993 s.55.

rises as a result of insider information that the insider knows about, is not insider dealing.

Regulated market

A regulated market (for the purposes of insider dealing) at present **12–14** means the London Stock Exchange (both the Main Market and the Alternative Investment Market) and such other markets as the Treasury approves from time to time,[18] but it also includes investment exchanges elsewhere within the European Economic Area.[19]

Professional intermediary

A professional intermediary means, in effect, a stockbroker or other **12–15** broker of securities acting in the course of his regular business. Occasional broking transactions are not deemed to be carrying on a business.[20]

Price-affected and price-sensitive

In relation to securities and information respectively, the information **12–16** about the securities must be likely to have an effect on the price of the securities if the inside information about the securities were made public.[21]

Issuer

An issuer is a company, public sector body or individual which or who **12–17** issues securities. A public sector body includes the Government, local authorities, international organisations which include the United Kingdom or other EU members, the Bank of England or the central bank of any sovereign state.[22]

To whom does the Criminal Justice Act 1993 apply?

Clearly the CJA 1993 applies to insider dealers, but as a matter of **12–18** practice certain people are more likely to have to be aware of the reach of the CJA 1993 than others. These include:

- directors and employees of quoted companies;
- professionals, such as lawyers and accountants, acting for such companies;
- those providing services to such companies, such as analysts, bankers or stockbrokers;
- those working in certain government departments which have access to confidential matters in connection with such

---

[18] CJA 1993 s.60(1).
[19] Insider Dealing (Securities and Regulated Markets) Order 1994 (SI 1994/187).
[20] CJA 1993 s.59.
[21] CJA 1993 s.56(2).
[22] CJA 1993 s.60.

companies, such as the HM Revenue and Customs, the BIS and the Monopolies Commission; and
- those working for the Stock Exchange itself.

This list is not exhaustive. Bank employees and other persons working in the financial industry to have to report their personal dealings in any investments to an official known as a compliance officer (frequently the same person as the company secretary) whose task is to monitor those dealings and thereby to ensure that no employee is taking advantage of any inside information.

Investigations into insider dealing

12–19   In order to prosecute an insider dealer, it is necessary to detect instances of insider dealing and, if necessary, to investigate those instances. The Financial Conduct Authority has a dedicated enforcement division to deal with insider dealing and market abuse. In particular they monitor unusual share price movements whose successful timing seems a little too good to be true.

Under the Financial Services and Markets Act 2000 ("the FSMA 2000") Pt XI[23] the Financial Conduct Authority may appoint inspectors to investigate various frauds including any insider dealing and make a report.[24] The team of investigators, who usually comprise an accountant and lawyer, can require anyone who knows about the insider dealing to hand over documents (whether in written or computer form) to them, to be examined by them, on oath if necessary, and to assist in the investigation.[25] It is the duty of that person to comply with these requirements. Any evidence supplied by that person may later be used in evidence against him[26] in criminal or civil proceedings subject to provisions to prevent self-incrimination.[27] Exemptions to this also arise where banking confidentiality arises[28] though legal privilege still applies, except to the extent that a lawyer must provide the name and address of his client.[29]

Since anyone involved in insider dealing would be understandably reluctant to volunteer information to the investigators, the FSMA 2000 s.177 provides means of enforcing compliance. If someone refuses to co-operate or answer questions put to him, the matter can be referred to court. If there is no reasonable excuse for his lack of co-operation or refusal to answer questions he can be punished as if for contempt of court even though he is not technically before a court of law when he is being questioned by the investigators.[30]

---

[23] FSMA 2000 ss.168, 169.
[24] FSMA 2000 ss.167, 168.
[25] FSMA 2000 s.171.
[26] FSMA 2000 s.174.
[27] FSMA 2000 s.174.
[28] FSMA 2000 s.175(5).
[29] FSMA 2000 s.175(4).
[30] FSMA 2000 s.177.

The permitted defences

Normally in a criminal trial, the burden of proving that the accused **12–20** committed a crime lies upon the prosecution. If the prosecution cannot prove beyond reasonable doubt that the accused committed the crime, the accused is acquitted. However, in a trial for insider dealing, the burden of proof lies upon the accused to show that his defence comes within the terms of one or more of the permitted defences stated in the CJA 1993 s.53 and Sch.1. But because the wording of the CJA 1993 s.53 and Sch.1 specifically uses "shows", as opposed to "proves", the accused does not have to prove beyond all reasonable doubt that his actions fell within the terms of the permitted defences.

Specific defences

Some of the defences involve the lack of a deliberate intention to **12–21** commit an insider deal. So if someone was unaware that certain information was inside information, although in reality it was, and he made a profit because the information turned out to be price-sensitive, he would not be committing a crime.[31] Likewise if someone had reasonable grounds for believing that his information was sufficiently well known to ensure that no other investors were prejudiced, although in reality it was inside information, he would have committed no crime.[32] If someone would have dealt anyway even if he had not had the information, again no crime is committed[33] as might happen when someone is forced to sell all his securities to pay a debt.

There are similar defences for those who encourage others to deal in securities.[34] In each case it will be quite difficult for the panel[35] to demonstrate his innocence, because the mere fact that someone is selling the shares and making a profit ahead of the release of price-sensitive information suggests, at least on the face of it, that the seller has been tipped off and knew it.

For those who disclose inside information, and would normally be guilty of insider dealing under the CJA 1993 s.52(2)(b) (disclosing information other than in the proper course of their business), there are two defences. The first is that they did not expect those who received the

---

[31] CJA 1993 s.53(1)(a).

[32] CJA 1993 s.53(1)(b). In *R. v Holyoak, Hill and Morl* (Unreported, but referred to in a speech by Margaret Cole, Director of Enforcement, Financial Services Authority (the predecessor to the Financial Conduct Authority), at the London School of Economics on March 17, 2007) the prosecution failed to establish that the three accused, who dealt in a takeover target's shares seven minutes before a takeover deal was announced, knew the information to be unpublished price-sensitive information at the time of dealing. The day after the announcement they sold the shares making a profit of £13,000. They were employed by the accountancy firm advising the bidders, and claimed that they thought the takeover was public knowledge when they dealt. Internet discussion sites are also a common source of gossip and market tips, some of which are genuine, thus allowing an insider dealer to claim that apparently secret information was in the public domain.

[33] CJA 1993 s.53(1)(c).

[34] CJA 1993 s.53(2).

[35] The accused.

information to use it to deal in securities on a regulated market,[36] and the second is that while they did expect the recipients of the information to deal on a regulated market, they did not expect that dealing to result in profit because the information turned out to be price-sensitive.[37]

In all these defences, making a profit means both making a profit and avoiding making a loss.[38]

12–22   In addition to the above defences, there is another set of defences, known as "Special Defences", to which the same shifting of the burden of proof applies as above. The special defences are to be found in Sch.1.

The first of them protects market-makers who are acting in good faith in the course of business.[39] The second defence is that the insider dealer (or the person encouraged to deal on his behalf) was using "market information" and that it was reasonable for him to have used it as he did. "Market information" is information about the buying or selling of securities, their prices and the identity of the buyers and sellers[40] and the sort of person who might be in possession of it without being categorised as an insider dealer might be, for example, a liquidator winding up the assets of a company which happens to have investments in another company which that liquidator, in another capacity, might happen to have inside information about, or someone, say, working in a merchant bank, involved on his client's behalf in mounting a takeover bid, and being instructed to acquire more securities in the target company. The third defence is that the accused was acting in conformity with the price stabilisation rules under the Financial Services and Markets Act 2000 s.144(1). These are rules which an authorised body can draw up for the purpose of preventing the price of investments fluctuating wildly. Acting in accordance with the regulations will be a valid defence.[41]

12–23   There are further possible defences. Under the CJA 1993 s.62 the legislation only applies within the United Kingdom, so insider dealing carried out from abroad will be difficult to prosecute. To prosecute an insider dealer, the dealer or the professional intermediary needs to have been within the United Kingdom at the time of the insider dealing or the market itself on which the dealing was taking place was a market regulated in the United Kingdom.[42]

A further defence arose in the Scottish case of *HM Advocate v Mackie*,[43] where the accused was acquitted because of the failure on the

---

[36] CJA 1993 s.53(3)(a).

[37] CJA 1993 s.53(3)(b).

[38] CJA 1993 s.53(6).

[39] CJA 1993 Sch.1 para.1.

[40] CJA 1993 Sch.1 para.2.4.

[41] CJA 1993 Sch.1 para.5.

[42] CJA 1993 s.62(1)(b).

[43] *HM Advocate v Mackie*, 1994 S.C.C.R. 277. Mackie, a well-known Edinburgh stockbroker, was held in Edinburgh's Gayfield Square police station after his arrest. A fellow inmate in the cells asked him what he was in for. Mackie replied that he was accused of insider dealing. The other inmate apparently then asked if insider dealing was some form of sexual offence.

part of the prosecution to establish corroboration of the evidence from two independent sources.[44]

Should insider dealing give rise to civil penalties?

At present insider dealing does not gives rise to civil penalties **12–24** (although market abuse, as defined later, does). Some would say that it should, on the grounds that having to repay, by way of damages, the amount that others have lost, or failed to gain, might, it is thought, concentrate the insider dealer's mind towards honesty. On the other hand there are various practical difficulties with the idea of having to pay damages to such victims. This is because it is difficult to establish who suffered loss as a result of the insider deal, how great the loss was, and sometimes, who the victim actually was. The insider dealer who buys in the stock market does not generally know who held the shares before he did, and any former shareholder might have been quite happy to sell anyway irrespective of the fact that the purchaser had the benefit of insider information. The insider dealer who sells shares while they are still high before the announcement of bad news will not generally know who buys his shares once he sells them. A purchaser might have been quite happy to buy at the insider dealer's price anyway. It is thus difficult precisely to identify the aggrieved shareholders who could be the pursuers in any action for civil damages against an insider dealer.[45]

It is also difficult to devise a scheme whereby compensation was payable to those who were truly the victims of an insider deal (which might be hard to establish), but not to those who would have been dealing anyway. In any event for some smaller shareholders the amount of compensation might be minimal—far less than the administrative cost of giving each shareholder his proportional share of the compensation.

If it is difficult to identify the pursuer, it can be difficult to identify the **12–25** defender. Although the Financial Conduct Authority Markets Division may notice insider dealing, the astute inside dealer spreads his insider deals through a number of different brokers, through different pseudonyms or nominee companies, and makes sure that as much as possible of his activity is based offshore. Ingenious use of online spread-betting on shares makes it harder to prove who is carrying out the insider dealing. Spreading rumours on the internet, some of which may actually be true, allows insider dealers to claim that information is in the public domain.

The quantification of loss is also a difficult issue: it is not easy to establish how much a victim of insider dealing lost as a result of insider deals taking place.

---

[44] At the time of writing, consideration is being given to the dropping of corroboration as a normal requirement of Scots criminal evidence.

[45] This leaves aside the further vexed issue of jurisdiction, and the fact that an offshore company carrying out insider deals might apparently have no assets. Enforcement of any decree might be pointless.

Market abuse

12–26   This is a term introduced by Part VIII of the Financial Services and
Markets Act 2000 ("FSMA"). Market abuse is a wide term that covers a
number of activities relating to a person's behaviour relating to qualifying
investments admitted to trading on certain markets, such as the London
Stock Exchange.[46] There is a considerable overlap with insider dealing,
except that market abuse does not lead to criminal penalties, is not subject
to the same evidential rules as criminal matters, and attracts fines rather
than the possibility of imprisonment. Market abuse is also a wider term
than insider dealing. The word "behaviour" is carefully used and s.118 of
FSMA indicates seven types of behaviour deemed to be market abuse.

Market abuse covers the following types of behaviour:

- an insider dealing in qualifying investments on the basis of inside
  information[47];
- an insider disclosing inside information other than in the proper
  course of employment, profession or duties[48];
- behaviour based on information about qualifying investments
  not generally available to those using the market, but which, if it
  were available, would be relevant to any transactions involving
  those investments, such behaviour being likely to be regarded by
  a regular user of the market as a failure to observe the standard
  of behaviour expected of a person in his position in relation to
  the market[49];
- effecting transactions, other than for legitimate reasons or in
  conformity with accepted market practices, which give a false or
  misleading impression as to the supply or price of qualifying
  investments or secure the price of such investments at an
  abnormal or artificial level[50];

---

[46] FSMA s.118(1).

[47] FSMA s.118(2). As an example of s.118(2) in operation, an IT technician at Body Shop
International, John Shevlin, had access to the secret passwords of various executives at
Body Shop. He accessed their emails and knew that the company had made a loss. He
therefore, with borrowed money, bought a contract for difference in Body Shop antici-
pating the publication of the loss. Although he made a profit of £38,472, he was caught,
and in July 2008 fined £85,000 as well as being sacked by Body Shop. His case was heard
by the Financial Services Tribunal.

[48] FSMA s.118(3).

[49] FSMA s.118(4).

[50] FSMA s.118(5). An example of this arose in *7722656 Canada Inc and Beck v Financial
Conduct Authority* [2013] EWCA Civ 1662, heard by the Court of Appeal. A Canadian
company used two direct market access providers to place orders to trade on the London
Stock Exchange. The orders were for contracts for differences in relation to certain
quoted shares. Once the orders were placed, the direct market access providers automatically hedged the contracts for differences by placing their own orders to buy or sell
an equivalent number of shares. Shortly after the contracts for differences were placed,
the orders were cancelled and the hedging orders also cancelled. But in the meantime,
there had been a movement in the share price of shares relating to the contracts for
differences both after the order was placed and after it was cancelled. The Canadian
company was trying to take advantage of these movements in the share prices. This
process is known as "spoofing" or "layering" and was very definitely market abuse.

- effecting transactions while employing fictitious devices or any form or contrivance or deception[51];
- the dissemination of information which gives a false or misleading impression of a qualifying investment by a person who knew or reasonably could be expected to know that the information was false or misleading[52];
- behaviour (not caught by any of the above categories) which is likely to give a regular user of the market a false or misleading impression as to the supply of, demand for or price or value of, qualifying investments, or would be regarded by a regular user of the market as behaviour that would distort or be likely to distort the market in such an investment—and behaviour was such that it would be likely to be regarded by a regular user of the market as a failure to observe the standard of behaviour expected of a person in his position in relation to the market.[53]

To make it clearer as to what sort of behaviour is not considered acceptable in terms of market abuse, the Financial Conduct Authority has produced a Code of Market Conduct, available on its website. The Code takes account of the EU Market Abuse Directive 2005. Most similar codes (such as the Highway Code) are not statutory though they may be referred to, but the Code of Market Conduct has a higher standing than that and may be relied upon in courts.[54] The Code itself is therefore closely studied within the financial services industry and it gives "safe havens" whereby normal and innocent business practices, which under certain conditions might be seen as market abuse, may be maintained without risk of sanction from the FSA, and provides "reasonable belief" and "reasonable care" defences for anyone breaching the Code.[55]

The market abuse legislation only applies in the United Kingdom and to qualifying investments on a market within the United Kingdom.[56] There are also special exemptions for journalists acting within their professional codes and not taking any personal advantage from their information, and various technical exemptions concerning price-stabilisation of financial instruments, approved buy-back programmes and people acting on behalf of local authorities in respect of exchange rates, management of public debt and foreign exchange reserves.[57] An "insider" is defined in s.118B and "inside information" is defined in s.118C: in each case the definition is broader than the insider dealing provisions and consequently harder to evade, from the market abuser's point of view.

If the market abuser is found indeed to have carried out market abuse,

---

[51] FSMA s.118(6).
[52] FSMA s.118(7). For example, in 2004 Shell was fined £17 million for having lied about the extent of its reserves, pretending that they were greater than they actually were in order to maintain the apparent value of its business.
[53] FSMA s.118(8).
[54] FSMA 2000 s.122(2).
[55] FSMA 2000 s.123(2).
[56] FSMA s.118A(1).
[57] FSMA s.118A(4), (5).

the Financial Conduct Authority may impose a penalty upon the market abuser.[58] The Financial Conduct Authority may also make an order for restitution.[59] The Financial Conduct Authority may then pay the restitutory sums to those who have suffered loss as a result of the breach or are those to whom the profit should be attributable. An equivalent of an appeal may be made to the Financial Services and Markets Tribunal[60] and appeals on points of law may be made to the courts.[61] If necessary the matter may be remitted to the court anyway in order to obtain an interdict,[62] or an order for restitution.[63] There are criminal penalties available under s.397, with a maximum sentence of seven years in prison and a fine.

Is the criminalisation of insider dealing and market abuse an effective sanction?

12–27   It is unlikely that insider dealing and market abuse will ever be eradicated. Although most banks and other financial organisations are scrupulous about ensuring that their employees do not carry out any forms of insider dealing, the fact remains that inside dealing is still rife. It is not unusual to see waves of selling of shares ahead of bad news, and purchases ahead of takeover announcements. The insider dealers who get caught tend to be inept, careless or greedy[64]: the more astute cover their tracks, operate in rings, operate infrequently in order not to excite suspicion, and quit before they get caught. In some financial organisations, particularly when there are many highly competitive dealers on the trading floors, the employees almost consider it a sport to run rings round the compliance officers. As with other forms of crime detection, the resources of the criminal are always greater than the resources of the authorities. Nevertheless, as was stated earlier, it is important that the UK's markets should be seen to be clean markets, well regulated and policed, for if they are not, good business will go elsewhere. Although there is a certain amount of identification of suspected insider dealing and market abuse, the prosecution rate has not been high. Nonetheless, the legislation has been effective in that:

(1) it serves as a deterrent to insider dealing and market abuse; and
(2) it changes people's attitudes to something which to a certain extent had formerly been seen as one of the perquisites of working in the City of London or in a stockbroker's office;

---

[58] FSMA s.123.
[59] FSMA s.384.
[60] FSMA 2000 ss.132–136.
[61] FSMA 2000 s.137.
[62] FSMA s.381.
[63] FSMA s.383.
[64] The Financial Conduct Authority maintains a list of its successful convictions, detailing how the insider deals and market abuse was carried out in each case.

(3) it has encouraged reputable businesses to have compliance officers and to set up systems to limit the opportunities for self-seeking behaviour; and

(4) it has forced businesses in the financial sector to remember that they should consider the interests of their clients as paramount.

On the other hand, the criminalisation of insider dealing and market **12–28** abuse has made those who work in the financial services industry a great deal more cautious and professional in their research. It is no longer widely acceptable to be taking advantage of investors by being cavalier with facts about investments, and the management of a merchant bank or a firm of stockbrokers whose employees have a reputation for insider dealing or market abuse will in the long run suffer a loss of credibility. Despite this, insider dealing and market abuse will inevitably always take place sometimes,[65] and the best the legislation can do is to minimise the opportunities for them taking place and to ensure that the sanctions for those who are caught serve as a deterrent for others.

Further Reading

Insider Dealing

Barry Rider, Kern Alexander and Lisa Linklater, *Market Abuse and Insider Dealing*, 2nd edn (Haywards Heath: Tottel, 2009).

Hector L. MacQueen, *Insider Dealing*, Hume Occasional Paper No.41 (Edinburgh: David Hume Institute, 1993).

Market Abuse

Andrew Haynes, "Market abuse, an analysis of its nature and regulation" (2007) 28(11) Comp. Law. 323.

Jonathan Marsh and Brian McDonnell, "Handling price sensitive information: a guide to the legal and regulatory obligations" (2005) 23(Feb) C.O.B. 1.

---

[65] The editor of the *Daily Mirror*, Piers Morgan, was alleged to have carried out an insider deal when he bought shares in Viglen the day before his own newspaper tipped the stock.

CHAPTER 13

MEETINGS AND RESOLUTIONS

13–01 There are two main reasons that meetings are held. The first is that meetings are an opportunity to hold the directors accountable to the members for the directors' use of the members' funds. On the whole, members will be content to let the directors carry on the management of the company in terms of the powers delegated to them under the articles, but from time to time members like to be reassured that the directors are making the best use of the funds entrusted to them. Directors must justify to the members their use of the company's resources, and on the basis of what the directors tell the members about the company's past performance and future prospects the members will decide whether or not to continue investing in the company. If the members, who after all are the ones who actually own the company and so should have some say in how their investment is spent, are not happy with what the directors are doing, they may impose restrictions upon the directors' behaviour and actions by means of a special resolution (which is tantamount to rewriting the articles of association) or in extremis dismiss the directors under Companies Act 2006 ("the CA 2006") s.168.

13–02 There is a human side to this issue. Few people like to be exposed to public criticism, and a general meeting, when the directors have made a poor return on their investors' funds and when the members are baying for the directors' blood, can be a humiliating experience for conscientious directors. On the other hand, there are high-handed directors whose hides are so thick that only the public scrutiny of a general meeting, sometimes with journalists present, will cause the directors to reconsider their actions. Directors tend to associate with their own kind, and may from time to time lose sight of the impact of their decisions on ordinary members—and a general meeting is an opportunity to remedy this.

13–03 Furthermore, an indifferent performance by the directors at a general meeting, where it can be assumed that the directors ought to be primed on all aspects of the company's activities, says much about the quality of the management—a view that may swiftly be reflected in the share price.

13–04 The second reason that meetings are necessary is that (with certain exceptions for private companies) company law and companies' articles of association require that certain acts may only be performed following the members' approval obtained in general meeting, or for private companies, written resolutions.

13–05 Although general meetings are designed primarily for these two purposes, they have one further significant feature. This is that meetings are a form of democracy within the microcosm of the company, save that (except in companies limited by guarantee) instead of each member having only one vote, each member has the number of votes represented by the number of shares that he owns.[1] Those who have most shares have most votes. Even so, every shareholder is entitled to a copy of the accounts and directors' report, and entitled to attend and speak at general meetings: it is for that reason that sometimes environmental protestors and other lobby groups will buy one share in a company, thus entitling them to attend general meetings and protest at the company's policies—often to the directors' and other shareholders' irritation. However, it is possible to subvert the effects of shareholder democracy by such means as having shares with weighted voting rights,[2] having articles that require a named individual to be present to make the meeting quorate, having articles that permit classes of shares to have a veto on certain actions, or having a shareholders' agreement.

Types of Meeting

There are four main types of meeting: **13–06**

- annual general meeting ("AGM");
- extraordinary general meeting ("EGM");
- class meeting; and
- board meeting.

Annual general meetings

By convention at an AGM it is common to discuss the following: **13–07**

- tabling and approval of the accounts and directors' report on the company's activities for the year;
- declaration of a dividend;
- re-appointment of auditors;
- directing the directors to fix the auditors' remuneration; and
- (sometimes) appointment of directors.

There is no requirement that a company has to deal with these matters at an AGM unless the articles say so: these matters could equally well be dealt with at an EGM. Although public companies are obliged to have annual general meetings once a year,[3] private companies are not required to have annual general meetings at all unless they choose to do so. This is because private companies, as will be seen later, may pass all their resolutions, except the dismissal of auditors or of directors, by written resolution.[4] On the grounds that private companies are more common

---

[1] Unless the shares are non-voting shares, or the shares have weighted voting rights.
[2] *Bushell v Faith* [1970] A.C. 1099.
[3] CA 2006 s.336.
[4] CA 2006 ss.288–300.

than public companies, the law relating to private company AGMs will be dealt with first.

AGMs for private companies

13–08   An AGM (where one is held) for a private company requires 14 days' notice,[5] but shorter notice is permissible.[6] In a private company, where a general meeting is actually being held, the required percentage majority to approve short notice is 90 per cent or such higher percentage (not exceeding 95 per cent) as is specified in the articles.[7] Normally directors convene any general meeting.[8] The rules about notices of meetings are given in para.13–14.

Members' demand for a private company AGM

13–09   If the directors will not convene an AGM, under s.303 the members may require the directors to call a general meeting.[9] In order to do so, there must be requests to do so from at least 10 per cent of the members whose shares carry voting rights or, in the case of companies without shares, who have 10 per cent of the voting rights.[10] If it is at least 12 months since the last general meeting, the required percentage is five per cent.[11] The members should include within their request an indication of the general nature of the business to be discussed at the meeting[12] and if there is a particular resolution that the members wish to have discussed,[13] that may be included within the request. It is permissible to move such a resolution at the meeting unless it is ineffective,[14] defamatory, frivolous or vexatious.[15] The directors are then expected, within 21 days of the members' request, to call a meeting, and the meeting itself should take place within 28 days of the date of the notice convening the meeting.[16] The notice of the meeting must include a notice about the resolution.[17] If the directors, for some reason, will not call the meeting they are required to call under s.303, the members may do so,[18] within three months, on

---

[5] CA 2006 s.307(1). It is permissible to use electronic communications to call meetings and to post notices of meetings on a website (s.308).

[6] CA 2006 s.307(4).

[7] CA 2006 s.307(6)(a).

[8] CA 2006 s.302.

[9] CA 2006 s.303(1).

[10] CA 2006 s.303(2).

[11] CA 2006 s.303(3).

[12] CA 2006 s.303(4)(a).

[13] This is the nearest continuing equivalent to the former requisitioned resolution.

[14] It might be inconsistent with some provision of company law generally, or some provision of the articles.

[15] CA 2006 s.303(5).

[16] The reason for this was that in the past, the members would force the directors to convene a meeting, but arrange for the meeting itself to be held in, say, three or four months time, in the hope that the members would have calmed down by then.

[17] CA 2006 s.304(4). If the resolution itself is a special resolution, the wording of the special resolution must be included in the notice itself and it must be clearly indicated that it is to be passed as a special resolution in terms of s.283(6).

[18] CA 2006 s.305(1).

terms as near as possible as those that would have applied had the directors called the meeting properly.[19] The members' expenses in calling the meeting will be met by the company[20] and the company will be reimbursed out of the directors' remuneration.[21]

AGMs for public companies

For a public company the notice of an AGM is 21 days.[22] The notice of **13–10** an AGM of a public company has to make it clear that it is an AGM.[23] AGMs of public companies may be held at short notice.[24] For a public company, unanimous consent is required for short notice of an AGM.[25] A public company must hold its general meeting within six months after its accounting reference date.[26] Where this does not happen because of bringing forward the company's accounting reference date, the AGM must be within three months of the date of notice of the change of accounting reference date.[27] AGMs are usually called by the company secretary on the instruction of the board of directors, on the application of a member, or by the court on the application of a director, a member or by the court itself.[28] If the directors will not call an AGM when they should, the members may demand that the directors call a general meeting, on exactly the same terms as for the convening of an AGM of a private company in the preceding paragraph.

Extraordinary general meetings

An EGM is any general meeting that is not an AGM. An EGM for a **13–11** private company requires 14 days notice.[29] For a public company the period of notice is the same.[30] EGMs may be held at short notice if sufficient members agree.[31] In the case of a private company, the required majorities for short notice are 90 per cent of the members, or such higher percentage (not exceeding 95 per cent) as may be specified in the articles.[32] For a public company, the required majority is 95 per cent.[33]

---

[19] CA 2006 s.305(3), (4).
[20] CA 2006 s.305(6).
[21] CA 2006 s.305(7).
[22] CA 2006 s.307(2)(a).
[23] CA 2006 s.337(1).
[24] CA 2006 s.307(4).
[25] CA 2006 s.337(2). This means that provided each member has signed a paper indicating his consent to holding the meeting without the normal 21-day period of notice, the meeting could take place immediately.
[26] CA 2006 s.336(1).
[27] For change of accounting reference date, see s.392.
[28] CA 2006 s.306.
[29] CA 2006 s.307(1).
[30] CA 2006 s.307(2).
[31] CA 2006 s.307(4).
[32] CA 2006 s.307(6)(a).
[33] CA 2006 s.307(6)(b).

Auditors' demand for an EGM

13–12   If the auditors believe there is something that should be brought to the attention of the members they too may demand a meeting in the same manner as the members demand above, with the meeting being held within 28 days of the date of the notice convening the meeting.[34]

EGM for a public company suffering a fall in net asset value

13–13   Under CA 2006 s.656 the directors must convene an EGM for a public company if the net asset value of the company falls to half or less than the value of the paid up share capital. However, the legislation is silent as to what should be done at that EGM other than consider what steps the directors should take to deal with the loss of assets. Two sensible solutions would be to reduce the capital, or, if the company is in serious difficulties, resolve to put the company into voluntary liquidation. A third, perhaps less useful, might be to convert the company into a private company.

The information contained in notices of general meetings

13–14   Notice of any general meeting is given normally in hard copy, but it may be given electronically or on a website.[35] Subject to the articles, a copy of the notice is sent to every member and every director,[36] and also to the auditor.[37] The notice must state the time, date and place of the meeting, and the general nature of the business of the meeting.[38] Normally a director or the company secretary will sign and date the notice, and indicate that he signs it by order of the board of directors and writes from the company's head office or registered office. Accidental failure to give the notice to a member will not generally invalidate the meeting.[39] The notice will also give the full text of any special resolution,[40] together with instructions on how to arrange for a proxy[41] to vote on the member's behalf. On every notice calling a general meeting there must be a statement informing the member of his rights under s.324 to appoint a proxy

---

[34] CA 2006 s.518.
[35] CA 2006 ss.308, 309.
[36] CA 2006 s.310. "Member" here includes an executor of a deceased shareholder or a trustee in sequestration of a bankrupt shareholder (s.310(2), (3)).
[37] CA 2006 s.502.
[38] CA 2006 s.311.
[39] CA 2006 s.313.
[40] CA 2006 s.283(6). Curiously there is no requirement to provide the text of ordinary resolutions, but in practice most notices of AGMs and EGMs do so.
[41] CA 2006 s.324. A proxy is a person (already a member) who is asked by the member to vote on his behalf, either in accordance with the member's instructions, or in accordance with the proxy's own views. Proxy forms normally allow the member to select his own proxy, or if he cannot think of anyone to be his proxy, to select the chairman to be his proxy, again either voting according to the member's direction or at the chairman's discretion. See model articles for private companies, arts 38, 39. A company is not allowed to make life difficult for members by insisting that proxy forms will be deemed to be invalid unless they are lodged more than 48 hours before the actual meeting, not taking account of any day that is not a working day (CA 2006 s.327).

on his behalf, who may attend, speak and vote for him at his direction.[42] If the company itself invites a member to suggest a particular person as his proxy, that person being, typically, the chairman, that invitation must be extended to all members.[43]

Resolutions requiring special notice

"Special notice" means that in the notice of the general meeting there **13–15** will be a statement that the company has received special notice of a particular resolution, such special notice being required to be given to the company at least 28 days before the meeting at which the resolution is to be moved.[44] This is because the matters that require special notice, being:

- the dismissal of a director at a general meeting[45];
- the removal of an auditor before the expiry of his term of office[46];
- the appointment of an auditor other than the retiring auditor in a private company[47]; and
- the appointment of an auditor other than the retiring auditor in a public company[48]

all are matters which the legislation deems to be sufficiently important that members should be told that the matter is "special"—though of the few members who actually bother to read the notice of a general meeting even fewer probably will be aware of the significance of the words "special notice". As all of these require a general meeting to be held, the written resolution procedure for private companies does not apply.

Companies may, if they wish, provide in their articles that certain other matters will need special notice too.

Members' statements

The members are entitled to insist that the company circulate a **13–16** statement[49] of not more than 1,000 words in connection with any resolution (whether one proposed by the directors or one proposed by the members) or with any other business at the meeting.[50] In order for a statement to be circulated at least 5 per cent of the members with voting rights, or not less than 100 members holding shares in the company, on

---

[42] A proxy may now demand a poll to be taken (s.329) and may even be elected chairman (s.328).
[43] CA 2006 s.326.
[44] CA 2006 s.312. Where this is not practicable, there may be at least 14 days notice, following advertisement or any method specified in the articles (s.312(3)).
[45] CA 2006 s.168.
[46] CA 2006 s.511.
[47] CA 2006 s.514.
[48] CA 2006 s.515.
[49] These sections replace the sections in Companies Act 1985 ss.376, 377 dealing with members' resolutions.
[50] CA 2006 s.314.

which there has been paid up an average sum per member of not less than £100, must have signed the request that the statement be circulated.[51] The company must then circulate the statement in the same manner as the notice of the meeting.[52] The expenses of the statement will be borne by the company if the statement relates to the AGM of a public company and sufficient approval for the request for the circulation of the statement arrives before the end of the financial year preceding the meeting.[53] In all other circumstances, the expenses may be borne by those requesting the statement.[54] The company is not obliged to circulate the statement following a successful application to court not to have the statement circulated.[55]

The practice of the meeting

13–17   Assuming the meeting has been properly summoned, and is taking place with sufficient notice or consent to short notice, the meeting, if quorate,[56] will be duly convened. Part 4 of the model articles provides standard rules for the conduct of the meeting. The chairman chairs the meeting,[57] and if there is a company secretary, the company secretary commonly sits beside him, guiding the chairman on any points of order. The other directors will normally be beside him. Normally there will be a note of those present (i.e. members), those attending (such as auditors or other experts in a professional capacity) and apologies from those who are absent. After the approval of minutes of the previous meeting, and the insertion of any corrections (or instructions to rewrite the minutes as necessary) and the discussion of any business arising from those minutes and not already on the agenda for later in the meeting, the chairman will go through each item on the agenda, taking the mood of the meeting and allowing some discussion of each item before proceeding to a vote, unless the item is one merely to be noted for the record, adjourned pending further information or withdrawn, perhaps because of a change of circumstances. It is customary to discuss the exciting business first, such as

---

[51] CA 2006 s.314(2).
[52] CA 2006 s.315. For the notice of a meeting, see para.13–14.
[53] CA 2006 s.316(1).
[54] CA 2006 s.316(2).
[55] CA 2006 s.317.
[56] CA 2006 s.318. The point of a quorum is to show that decisions have been considered by at least a modicum of members rather than the sole dictat of one member. The quorum for companies other than single member companies is two, though companies' articles may provide for more to be present if necessary. If a meeting is inquorate, technically no resolutions may be passed, though resolutions may be taken on an interim basis and ratified at a later quorate meeting. If a company takes a decision at an inquorate meeting and acts upon it in a transaction with a third party, unless the third party is aware of the inquoracy, he will normally be protected by the operation of the CA 2006 s.40. Under certain circumstances the company might also be personally barred from founding on its own inquorate decisions.
[57] The chairman will normally be the chairman of the board of directors, but the members may if they wish (and provided the articles do not say otherwise) elect some other member to be chairman (CA 2006 s.319).

the accounts and the directors' report, before the less glamorous company law resolutions such as votes on repurchase of shares or other administrative matters.

Voting

Voting is normally done on a show of hands with the result declared by **13–18** the chairman,[58] but if necessary, a poll may be demanded by the chairman, by two voting members, by a member or members representing one-tenth of the voting rights, or by voting members whose paid-up capital in the company collectively is equal to one-tenth of the company's issued share capital.[59] It is not possible to build in provisions in the articles that effectively make it difficult for members to demand a poll by insisting on at least five members asking for a poll, or insisting that members have more than the above voting rights or capital in the company[60] except on the matter of the election of the chairman or the adjournment of the meeting.[61] A proxy is entitled to demand a poll[62] and a proxy in a public company may now speak at a general meeting.[63] A proxy may now vote on a show of hands[64] and should do so on a poll.[65] Companies and other corporations, which are physically unable to represent themselves, may send "corporate representatives" to speak and vote on their behalf.[66] Many companies' articles provide that the chairman will have a casting vote.

There are extensive provisions to cover the extremely rare situation where there is a suggestion of miscounting or fraud in the counting of votes at a poll.[67] Quoted companies must put the results of any polls on their websites.[68]

---

[58] CA 2006 s.320.
[59] See Pt 4 model articles for private companies, art.44. The distinction between a vote on a show of hands is that each person present may only raise one hand, but on a poll, each person present or represented by a proxy votes according to the number of shares he represents (s.284). Some shares in some companies also may attract multiple votes in which case those extra votes will need to be taken into account as well. It is not permissible to have articles that say a member has different votes on a written resolution from votes cast at a general meeting (s.285).
[60] CA 2006 s.321(2).
[61] CA 2006 s.321(1).
[62] CA 2006 s.329.
[63] CA 2006 s.324(1).
[64] CA 2006 ss.284(2), 285.
[65] CA 2006 s.324(1). This is because the whole point of a proxy is to vote when the member cannot do so in person, or when he is happy that his votes be cast for him by someone whose judgment he respects.
[66] CA 2006 s.323.
[67] CA 2006 ss.342–354. In listed companies, nearly all voting scrutiny is carried out by the Electoral Reform Society. There have been no instances of fraud or deceit in any recent polls.
[68] CA 2006 s.341.

Any other business

13–19   After each item on the agenda has been duly considered, voted on, adjourned or otherwise dealt with, the chairman will commonly invite questions from the audience (sometimes known as "any other business"). This is the opportunity for the members to put the directors "on the spot" on any matters on which the directors or their company may not have fared well. Some directors are known to be so alarmed by this process that they arrange for stooges in the audience to set up gentle questions for them to answer, or insist that they will only answer questions of which they have had prior notice—thereby confirming other members' worst suspicions. As it is well known that chairmen only will ask for questions from respectable-looking people, environmental or other protestors have been known to go to Oxfam beforehand to buy second hand shirts, suits and ties in order to pass themselves off as investment analysts or chartered accountants before asking awkward questions on environmental or ethical matters.[69] Most questions need not be asked at all, since a careful reading of well drafted accounts and directors' reports will generally contain all the information investors could want.

After dealing with any other business, the meeting is drawn to a close and the company secretary goes off to write up the minutes.

Class meetings

13–20   Class meetings are run as a smaller version of general meetings, save that only the members of the class are entitled to be present at the meeting. If a class of shareholders wishes to change certain matters relating to its own class of shares, it will need to pass a resolution itself.[70] As a matter of practice, a class of shares is unlikely to be allowed to change any rights attaching to its own class of shares without consent from the other classes of shares beforehand.

Board meetings

13–21   How the directors run their board meetings is a matter for the directors alone unless the articles say otherwise, or unless the board members devise their own standing orders. The model articles lay down standard rules which many companies will adopt. It is common for larger companies to have board meetings every month, where the board deals with the commercial and administrative matters of the company and any business of the company that does not require shareholders' approval. The company secretary will normally take the minutes of the meetings. Members are not entitled to see board minutes, though auditors are. Companies are expected to give board members reasonable notice and there is normally a quorum of two directors. If they wish, directors may

---

[69] As happened to Robert Wilson, chairman of the controversial mining group, Rio Tinto Zinc, at its AGM on May 12, 1999.
[70] Normally this will be a special resolution of the class's own members.

delegate certain matters to a committee, and that committee may have such powers as the articles provide or as the directors may decide. The model articles, Pt 2 supply a set of intelligible and sensible rules for directors' meetings generally.

TYPES OF RESOLUTION

There are three main types of resolution. They are: **13–22**

- ordinary resolutions;
- special resolutions; and
- written resolutions.

In addition some ordinary resolutions require special notice, as discussed earlier at para.13–15.

Ordinary resolutions

Ordinary resolutions need a simple majority of those voting and **13–23** entitled to vote in person or by proxy. Ordinary resolutions are used for less contentious matters, though dismissing a director, which one might well consider contentious, only requires an ordinary resolution, albeit with special notice. Most ordinary resolutions do not need to be registered with the Registrar of Companies, but for those that do, the company has a month in which to do so.[71] When CA 2006 does not state what type of resolution is required to approve a certain action, it is deemed to be an ordinary resolution unless there is some other requirement in the articles, such as unanimity or a higher majority.[72]

Special resolutions

Special resolutions need a 75 per cent majority of those voting and **13–24** entitled to vote in person or in proxy.[73] Special resolutions are generally used for contentious and significant matters, such as the alteration of the company's constitution or its capital. The high percentage approval is to ensure that a significant number of the members genuinely approve of the resolution. Whenever a special resolution is indicated in the CA 2006, there is always a requirement that it be registered with the Registrar of Companies within 15 days.[74]

---

[71] For example, see the CA 2006 ss.618, 619.
[72] CA 2006 s.281(3).
[73] CA 2006 s.283.
[74] For example, see CA 2006 s.30.

Written resolutions

13–25 Written resolutions were introduced as part of an attempt to make life easier for private companies. It was also to legitimise a practice that had been unofficially going on for some years of members all signing a resolution and claiming that that was equivalent to a passed resolution.

Written resolutions have the following features:

- they are only available to private companies;
- they can be used for any type of resolution[75] except dismissal of auditors[76] and directors,[77] because of those officers' right of protest;
- they must be signed by the required percentage of members entitled to vote and voting in person or in proxy; and
- they must be intimated to the auditors beforehand.[78]

The point of the intimation to the auditors is that the auditors will, it is hoped, warn the company if it is about to pass by way of written resolution something that cannot be done by written resolution, such as dismissing a director, or something that actually requires more procedure than the directors might be aware of, such as a company reducing its capital by written resolution alone.

13–26 Written resolutions need to be registered within 15 days in the normal manner provided that the resolution itself was one that if it were passed at a general meeting would need to be registered.

Although in the past written resolutions required unanimity of assent, what is necessary now is that within 28 days (or such lesser period as may be specified within the articles)[79] of the date of issue of the resolution (the "circulation date"),[80] enough members will have indicated their assent to the resolution to have it passed. For an ordinary resolution, the date that the resolution is passed is the date that at least 50 per cent of those members eligible to vote do so in favour of the resolution. For a special resolution, the date the resolution is passed is the date that 75 per cent of the members eligible to vote do so in favour of the resolution. Although most resolutions will in practice be proposed by the directors,[81] members may propose their own resolutions and insist that the company circulates them for approval,[82] unless the resolutions are ineffective, defamatory, frivolous or vexatious.[83] Providing at least 5 per cent of the members so desire, the company will be obliged to circulate an accompanying

---

[75] CA 2006 s.288.
[76] CA 2006 s.510.
[77] CA 2006 s.168.
[78] CA 2006 s.502. There appears to be no sanction for failure to do this.
[79] CA 2006 s.297.
[80] CA 2006 s.290.
[81] CA 2006 s.291.
[82] CA 2006 s.292(1).
[83] CA 2006 s.292(2).

statement of not less than 1,000 words to accompany the text of the resolution.[84] There are provisions to deal with the expenses of the circulation[85] and to deal with the situation where the company or another person is able to persuade the court that the requirement to circulate the statement is being abused.[86]

Written resolutions have been very successful and have saved many unnecessary meetings and much unnecessary travel. It is not necessary that all the members' signatures be on the one sheet of paper attached to the resolution: it is possible to send a copy of the resolution to each member who may then sign it. It is acceptable that email or other electronic means be used to send out the resolution and the statement.[87]

A well organised private company, provided nothing contentious arises, can effectively avoid having general meetings at all by the judicious use of written resolutions.

SHAREHOLDER DEMOCRACY

Although meetings are ostensibly about the democratic right of members **13–27** to vote on matters that affect their shareholdings, it is well recognised that they are often failing to do what they are supposed to do. This is for various reasons, amongst them being:

- the fact that in larger companies, the major investors will be reluctant to air grievances with the company's management in open forum when quieter, more effective results can be obtained round the boardroom table;
- the major investors in larger companies are usually insurance companies and pension fund companies (the "institutions") who can command far more clout than private investors;
- most private investors cannot be bothered to read the directors' report, cannot understand the accounts, only look at the dividend figure, don't fill in the voting forms and certainly cannot be bothered to turn up to an AGM;
- AGMs are quite stage-managed to be over as soon as possible before anyone asks any awkward questions;
- AGMs are often held at a time when most working people are at work anyway, so those who attend are often corporate representatives of major investors appearing for form's sake, the retired or pensioners, employees' representatives, and those with axes to grind;
- there is little point in having meetings for small companies where all the members are related or see and work with each other every day; and

---

[84] CA 2006 s.292(4), (5).
[85] CA 2006 s.294.
[86] CA 2006 ss.295, 296.
[87] CA 2006 ss.291, 293.

- the perception that many companies' managements are not very interested in shareholders' views anyway, though with the rise in shareholder activism, directors are having to pay more attention to shareholders' views before, particularly on such matters as "say on pay", otherwise known as directors' remuneration.

It is noticeable that the most popular AGMs are those of companies, particularly food and drinks companies, that provide free samples of their products after the meeting is over.

CHAPTER 14

TAKEOVERS AND MERGERS

TAKEOVERS

Strictly speaking a takeover of a company occurs when one company, **14–01** whose shares are publicly traded, buys either all or the greater part of the share capital of the other. The company carrying out the takeover is sometimes called the acquiring company, the bidder, the offeror, or in the case of an unwelcome takeover bid, the "predator". The company whose shares are being bought by the acquiring company is sometimes known as the "target" company, or in extreme cases, the "victim". In the circumstances of a takeover bid, the acquiring company will wish to buy sufficient of the share capital of the target to be able to control its board of directors and to pass ordinary resolutions. The acquiring company will give the shareholders of the target company either cash, assets, shares or other securities[1] in the acquiring company in exchange for their shares in the target company. Takeovers may be agreed between the directors of the two companies, who will draw up a large contract outlining the terms on which the acquisition will proceed. With an agreed takeover, there should be plenty of warranties[2] available should the target company turn out not to be all that it appears.

It is also possible to have a hostile takeover, particular when one listed company takes over another. Often the target company resists the approach of the predator company, on the grounds that the offer being made to the target company shareholders is not high enough, or that the predators are unprincipled rogues who will destroy a good business. With a hostile takeover there is no contract: the predator merely has to acquire a majority of shares in the target, and having done so is in control and may do with it, up to a point, as it pleases. At the same time, because there is no contract, the predator may not necessarily know exactly what the target company's assets and liabilities are until it is in possession of the shares and in a position to find out. With a hostile takeover, both predator directors and target directors are appealing directly to the

---

[1] Bonds may be advantageous for the sellers of the shares, because there may be capital gains tax reliefs available, in particular roll-over relief.

[2] A warranty is an undertaking, usually by the target company's directors, that if the accounts or turnover or some other important matter turn out to be inaccurate, the directors will indemnify the purchasing company for any loss. Commonly warranties endure for two years and the directors' liability is restricted to a predetermined sum.

shareholders of the target in a bid to convince the shareholders either to sell or to hang on to their shares.

Sometimes, in what is known as the Pacman[3] defence, the target turns round and starts bidding for the predator.

A takeover can be contrasted with a merger, also sometimes known as an amalgamation. In a merger two companies happily unite to become one company, which may be a brand new company designed to absorb both businesses. The controllers of both original businesses become controllers of the new combined business and are given shares in the new merged company in exchange for their shares in the two old companies. One way of doing this is by a scheme of arrangement under the Companies Act 2006 ("CA 2006") s.895 (described later).

The law relating to takeovers

14–02   There is very little law relating to the above, though sometimes there are legal implications arising out of the practice of the takeover: for example, a company fearing a takeover might try to buy back its own shares to drive the predator away by the rising share price; takeover bids attract furtive insider dealers; or there might be illegal financial assistance, as arose in the Guinness takeover of Distillers. Another area where there is also difficulty relates to directors: the directors should above all consider the interests of the company as a whole, and if the directors receive an offer that in their view is the best price the members are likely to get for their shares, they should be mindful of their fiduciary duty to their members collectively and recommend it—but by so doing, the directors may well be doing themselves out of their jobs. The CA 2006 ss.175–177 and 215–219 are designed to prevent directors receiving secret blandishments to encourage their shareholders to accept takeover offers.

The bid documentation inviting the target company's shareholders to sell their shares to the bidder must be accurate and informative in conformity with the requirements of the Financial Services and Markets Act 2000 and the FSA requirements.

For smaller takeovers (such as one private company taking over another, or a private company taking over a listed company and thereafter delisting the company), takeovers are essentially a matter of contract as indicated above. After much negotiating and arm-twisting, the buyers and sellers will agree the basic outline of the terms. Once agreed, the buyer's agent presents a draft sale and purchase agreement to the seller's agent and instruct their lawyers and accountants to do due diligence on the seller's company. Due diligence is the practice of checking that everything the seller claims to be saying about his business is true. All the seller's documentation is (or ought to be) made over to the checking lawyers and accountants, and if it turns out, at the end of the day, that the seller has misled the purchaser or some other breach has

---

[3] Pacman was one of the first computer games, featuring a small bloblike mouth which scurried about in a labyrinth while trying to avoid being gobbled by various monsters. From time to time it would turn round and gobble its attackers.

taken place,[4] the purchaser usually has the option of suing the seller for misrepresentation or of suing the checking lawyers and accountants for negligence, depending on the terms on which the due diligence is carried out.

Most large firms of solicitors will have a standard style sale and pur- **14–03** chase agreement[5] plus other documentation which will deal inter alia with the following:

- the corporeal moveable assets to be transferred (stock, products, machinery);
- the incorporeal moveable assets to be transferred (intellectual property, shares, etc.);
- the heritage to be transferred plus evidence of good title, valid standard security documentation, planning permission and all other matters relating to land;
- earn-out clauses
- insurance documentation;
- lists of employees and the effect of any TUPE regulations;
- lists of clients;
- known and quantified liabilities;
- outstanding litigation and other contingent and prospective liabilities;
- pension matters;
- balance sheet as at the date of transfer;
- provisions for dealing with sums that come in after transfer;
- appointment of new directors and company secretary on transfer;
- resignation of outgoing directors and company secretary after transfer;
- indemnities from directors of the selling company;
- restrictive covenants from the outgoing directors;
- warranties from the directors;
- tax indemnities; and
- auditors' confirmation of the value of the company.

There are various well known sticking points, one of which is the duration and extent of the warranties for the selling directors, normally two years, and another is how long the sellers must stay within the purchasing company if the sellers' expertise is sought by the purchasing company.[6] These are matters for negotiation. If the purchase is being funded through bank borrowing by the purchaser, there will also need to be security documentation, such as floating charges and standard security

---

[4] *Parks of Hamilton (Holdings) Ltd v Colin Campbell* [2013] CSOH 67.

[5] If they do not have a standard style, the common practice is discreetly to make a copy of some other firm's contract and steal the best clauses out of it. Alternatively, there are excellent styles such as the ones on the PLC website.

[6] As an example of claims being made under warranties, see *Lonedale Ltd v Scottish Motor Auctions (Holdings) Ltd* [2011] CSOH 4.

documentation over the selling company's assets (once purchased) and evidence of the discharge of any previous securities over the selling company's assets. There will also be stamp duty land tax to be paid on the transfer of any heritage unless the company's shares are being sold, in which case stamp duty will be paid on the transfer of the selling company shareholders' shares, since the heritage will remain throughout in the ownership of the selling company. Another form of takeover is a management buy-out, where is where the managers of a subsidiary buy the shares of that subsidiary from the subsidiary's holding company, quite commonly with the assistance of the holding company, on the grounds that motivated managers, with a personal stake in the company because of owning the majority of shares in the subsidiary, might actually make more money for the holding company than leaving the holding company in charge.

14–04   One of the advantages of buying all or most of the sellers' shares in a company is that the company's assets remain in the ownership of the company. There is therefore no need to tell the DVLA of the new owners of any vehicles, no need to tell hire purchase companies who the new owners are, and no need to alter the terms of employment of the staff. In theory the company may continue as before, just with new shareholders and new directors. In practice some lenders and landlords may not always be so willing to accept new shareholders and directors, and may impose their own requirements should there be a change in share-ownership or directors.

Share for assets offers

14–05   Although most company purchases involve the purchasers buying all or most of the share capital of the sellers' company, so that the sellers hand over their shares to the purchasing company and receive shares, cash, loan notes or some other form of consideration in return, there are other forms of buy out: a company may sometimes sell all its assets and undertaking to a purchasing company, so that after sale and purchase has been effected, the selling company has a large amount of shares in the purchasing company, or cash which the selling company's shareholders can either pay out as dividends, use to invest in other businesses or use to repay outstanding debts. The procedure should follow the terms of the CA 2006 ss.904–918 relating to mergers. This, broadly speaking, requires there to be disclosure of all relevant information to the members of both companies, together with experts' reports and draft documentation for the members' approval prior to the court's approval. In effect, as much information is presented to the members as would be presented in a prospectus. The above set of rules, enacting the terms of the Sixth Company Law Directive[7] is not in practice much used in the United Kingdom, partly because of its complexity, but mainly because it is more usual in the United Kingdom to effect takeovers and mergers by way of purchases and sales of shares rather than of assets. One reason for this is

---

[7] Directive 1978/855.

that a transfer of assets and undertaking will result in a change of ownership. This may trigger capital gains tax charges and stamp duty land tax charges as well as possibly triggering renegotiation of loan agreements and leases.

A similar set of rules also applies when public companies split off and transfer their assets and undertaking to another company by means of a demerger and a scheme of arrangement.[8]

The commercial significance of the takeover market

Takeovers and mergers matter not just to companies and their share- **14–06** holders themselves, but also to the public generally, because of the dangers of industrial giants "cornering the market" in particular products, which is why the Competition Commission may have an interest in the matter (see para.14–13). Takeovers and mergers also matter to the economy of the United Kingdom as a whole, because of the enormous sums of money involved, most of it being dealt with in the City of London. The City of London, with all its financial markets and resources, generates enormous invisible earnings for the United Kingdom, but it can only do so while the City is seen to be a place where honest businessmen can practise. Should the conduct of takeovers and mergers in Britain attract a reputation for dishonesty and sharp practice, the City would cease to attract foreign capital, resulting in diminished opportunities for all who work there. It is therefore in the City's interest that takeovers and mergers are properly policed to ensure that shareholders are treated properly and that there is a fair and established set of rules for takeovers and mergers. This set of rules is known as the City Code on Takeovers and Mergers ("the City Code").

THE CITY CODE

The City Code is administered by the Takeover Panel.[9] The Panel was **14–07** designated as the supervisory authority to carry out certain regulatory functions in relation to takeovers under the EC Thirteenth Company Law Directive on Takeover Bids (2004/25). Its new statutory functions are narrated in Ch.1 of Pt 28 of the CA 2006. Previously it was a non-statutory self-regulating body and in nearly all respects it remains much as it was, regulated and controlled by members of the leading accountancy and legal bodies and representatives from banking, insurance, stockbroking, industry and various financial regulatory authorities. The Panel promotes the City Code which applies to all those involved in takeovers and mergers of major publicly quoted companies, whether as directors or in any other capacity in connection with the company, such as its corporate advisers, lawyers, bankers or accountants. Companies mounting takeovers and mergers, and those connected with such

---

[8] CA 2006 ss.919–934.
[9] The Takeover Panel has a helpful and informative website.

companies, are expected to abide by the regulations promulgated by the Panel. The precept behind the general principles and the regulations of the City Code is that the spirit rather than the letter of the regulations should be followed, and furthermore the regulations are deemed to apply even in circumstances not specifically mentioned in the regulations. The regulations are in effect a set of best commercial practices which directors and their advisers in the context of takeovers and mergers are expected to follow. The advantage of having regulations drafted in this way is their commendable flexibility and adaptability, as well as their appeal to the integrity of the participants. Although there are some legal sanctions for non-compliance,[10] the non-legal sanctions are not without effect[11]: delisting and the denial of access to the securities markets would have a serious effect on a company, and those working in the financial services industry might find that they ceased to be authorised by their appropriate self-regulatory authority to carry on their business.

The City Code is drawn up on the basis of:

- providing all shareholders with equal, sufficient and accurate and independent information to enable them to decide whether or not to accept the bid;
- treating all shareholders fairly, so that none receives a better price for his shares than others, and each shareholder is offered an equal chance to sell his shares;
- treating all shareholders within a class of shareholders equally;
- making directors of the target company obtain approval of the members before disposing of any assets that could prejudice the desirability of the takeover bid;
- making directors, when advising the members on the terms of any takeover, disregard their own personal interest in the company,[12] and concentrate on what in their view would be best for the members generally;
- daily disclosure of any dealings in securities of the companies involved by anyone connected with the takeover;
- preserving the strictest confidentiality in relation to price-sensitive information (to prevent insider dealing and market abuse);
- preventing the operation of a false market in shares on the basis of inadequate or inaccurate information;
- ensuring that offers for takeovers should only be made when the acquiring company believes it can indeed implement the takeover;
- "testing the water" being unacceptable;

---

[10] The Panel may require companies to produce documents (s.947), and where companies or others flout the Panel's rules, there are sanctions under ss.952–956 which include criminal and civil consequences.

[11] See cl.11 of the City Code.

[12] This in particular means that self-seeking defensive tactics are unacceptable. This is in contrast to what is permitted elsewhere in other jurisdictions, where sometimes local legislation or local politics intrude on the otherwise free market approach to takeovers.

- making it difficult for takeover bids to be withdrawn without the consent of the Panel; and
- making all parties conform to strict guidelines and time limits, failing which the bid will lapse unless it has been withdrawn.

Those involved in takeovers and mergers are expected to consult the executive of the Panel where they are unsure of their proposed course of conduct. Where there has been a breach of the City Code there is a disciplinary hearing which may be appealed if necessary. Where decisions have not been well received by the protagonists, the Panel's decisions have from time to time been challenged in the courts by means of judicial review, though not always to the satisfaction of the challengers.[13]

The City Code is well regarded because every honest businessman **14–08** stands to gain by adhering to sensible common standards of integrity and fair play. In addition, the City Code tells foreign investors that the British capital markets are well regulated and reasonably free from market manipulation. The City Code and the Panel to a certain extent was the original model for the Thirteenth Company Law Directive on Takeovers promulgated by the EC Commission which finally adopted in March 2004.

Mandatory bids

Where a shareholder has, either on his own account or in conjunction **14–09** with others, acquired 30 per cent or more of the voting rights of the company, and subsequently acquires more than 1 per cent more of the voting rights within a 12 month period, he is obliged to make a mandatory bid for the company. This must be addressed to all the members, and must be for cash or for a cash alternative such as shares. Any shares issued for this purpose will need to comply with the normal rules for allotment of shares and the rules relating to the issue of shares following a prospectus.[14]

Buying out the minority ("squeeze out" and "sell out" provisions)

Once an acquiring company has obtained acceptances from over 50 per **14–10** cent of the members it has effective control of the company as it can then control the board of directors. However, although the acquiring company could state that its offer was binding even with a bare majority shareholding, it is common for the acquiring company to state that the offer will only be unconditional and binding once it has acceptances from 90 per cent of the target company's shareholders or from those who have 90 per cent of the control of the company. From the point of view of the acquiring company, it may wish to have at least 90 per cent or complete

---

[13] *R. v Panel on Takeovers and Mergers Ex p. Guinness Plc* [1990] Q.B. 147 CA; *R. v Panel on Takeovers and Mergers Ex p. Datafin* [1987] Q.B. 815; *R. v Panel on Takeovers and Mergers Ex p. Fayed* [1992] B.C.L.C. 938.
[14] See City Code s.F, r.9.

control of the company if it is going to invest substantial sums in the company. Furthermore, the acquiring company may not wish to trouble itself with the problem of possibly dissentient minorities.

If the acquiring company is able to obtain 90 per cent of the target company's shares or 90 per cent of the control of the company, there are statutory provisions to enable it to acquire the remaining shares or remaining degree of control. In order to obtain the benefit of the provisions under statute, the acquiring company must have made a takeover offer under the CA 2006 s.974. A takeover offer is one where the acquiring company undertakes to buy all the shares of a target company, or all the shares of a class of shares in the target company, other than those already held by the acquiring company, on terms that apply equally to all the shares to which the offer relates.

14–11   Where the offer is accepted by 90 per cent of the shareholders, or from those who have 90 per cent of the voting rights, within three months from the beginning of the offer, the acquiring company can serve a notice on the remaining shareholders stating that it proposes to buy their shares.[15] A copy must also be sent to the company along with a statutory declaration confirming that the grounds under which the notice can be given have been satisfied.[16]

The notice will state that the acquiring company can buy the remaining shares at a price the same as that offered to all the other shareholders. If the remaining shareholders are dissatisfied with this for a valid reason they may apply within six weeks of the date of the notice to the courts for an order[17] that the acquiring company may not buy their shares or may only do so on different terms. If the complaint is that the offer is not high enough, it is for the complainers to explain why it was clearly good enough for 90 per cent of the other shareholders to accept it. The complaint may succeed when, as in *Re Bugle Press Ltd*[18]:

(1) those 90 per cent shareholders were the instigators of the offer; and

(2) there were very few or no other shareholders available to provide a different view as to the fairness of the price the majority shareholders were offering.

14–12 Assuming there is no objection, the purchase of the outstanding shares may take place after the expiry of the six-week period.[19] The acquiring company sends the target company the consideration for the purchased shares and the target company holds the consideration monies (or shares, as the case may be) in trust for the target company's shareholders.[20] If

---

[15] CA 2006 s.979(2).
[16] CA 2006 s.980(4).
[17] CA 2006 s.986(2).
[18] *Re Bugle Press Ltd* [1961] Ch. 270.
[19] CA 2006 s.981(2).
[20] CA 2006 s.981(6).

after 12 years some untraced shareholders have still not emerged, the funds held to their account are paid into court.[21]

Just as the acquiring company may buy out a 10 per cent minority, so may the 10 per cent minority ask to be bought out. A minority shareholder may write to the acquiring company requiring it to purchase his shares.[22] It then has one month in which to tell the shareholder of his rights under the takeover offer, and it must give the shareholder a period of at least three months after the expiry of the takeover offer in which to take up the offer[23] after which the offer may lapse. If the acquiring company chooses to buy the minority shareholder's shares, he may do so in terms of the offer or under any other terms as may be agreed.[24]

It should be pointed out that the above methods of buying out the 10 per cent minority apply in respect both of public and private companies.

The Competition Commission and the Office of Fair Trading

It is not usually in the public interest to have companies operating **14–13** cartels or monopolies, and accordingly there is extensive legislation, both at a national and at a European level, to limit the opportunity for cartels or monopolies to arise. Inevitably some cartels and monopolies do arise, either because without them the business in question may disappear or may lower its standards to a level injurious to the common good, or because the Government has given the cartel or monopoly its blessing— as initially happened with the privatised utilities. In such circumstances the cartel or monopoly may be allowed to continue in existence.

If, however, there is a possibility of a cartel or monopoly arising through a takeover or a merger, and where such a cartel or monopoly might adversely affect the public interest,[25] under the Fair Trading Act 1973 and the Enterprise Act 2002 Pt III, the Office of Fair Trading may refer a takeover or merger to the Competition Commission, part of the Competition and Markets Authority, which will then decide whether or not it is permissible for the takeover or merger to proceed. Formerly the Competition Commission would then make a recommendation to the Secretary of State for Trade and Industry. The Secretary of State would then make the ultimate decision, which in most cases led to a political rather than an economic decision. Since the passing of the Enterprise Act, the role of the Secretary of State is much diminished and only applies to such matters as companies with an interest in national security.

Large mergers within Europe that exceed certain jurisdictional thresholds of the European Community Merger Regulation[26] will be

---

[21] CA 2006 s.982(7).

[22] CA 2006 s.983.

[23] CA 2006 s.984(2).

[24] CA 2006 s.985(2).

[25] Particularly when the target company has an annual turnover of over £70 million or has 25% of the market.

[26] Council Regulation No.139/2004.

investigated by the European Commission.[27] Mergers where more than two-thirds of the Community-wide turnover of each enterprise concerned arises within the one Member State are not caught by the EC Merger Regulation.

SCHEMES OF ARRANGEMENT

14–14 The problems with an Insolvency Act 1986 s.110 reconstruction as a method of one company taking over or merging with another company as later described in Ch.16 are that the company has to be in liquidation, shareholders' rights have to be strictly adhered to, creditors' rights cannot be altered and its only options are sales or amalgamations. A more flexible method had to be found which could accommodate such matters as the continuation of the company's trade, and variations to shareholders' and creditors' rights. Indeed so inflexible is the s.110 method that it is not much used nowadays. A more satisfactory method is to be found in what is known as a s.895 compromise or, more commonly, s.895 scheme of arrangement.

The word "compromise" is, however, apt. The essence of a scheme of arrangement is that all interested parties are fully aware of what is being suggested. The court gives approval to various rearrangements of a company's or companies' debts and shareholdings which reconcile various differing interests and effect a compromise between those interests. There must be an element of give and take for a compromise, and without some give and take between all or most of the interests the courts will not sanction the arrangement. Once the courts have given their approval to the scheme of arrangement it is binding on all the parties, even though there may be some objectors. Unlike a s.110 voluntary arrangement neither the objecting shareholders nor creditors can prevent the scheme of arrangement taking place once the court has given its approval.

The procedure for a s.895 scheme of arrangement is as follows:

14–15 If a company is proposing to have a s.895 scheme of arrangement, the company, a member, a creditor, the administrator or the liquidator may apply to the court for an order for meetings of the creditors, classes of creditors, members, or any classes of members to be called.[28] At each meeting the terms of the arrangement are explained and those present can vote on it. In order for the scheme of arrangement to take place, at each meeting those in favour of the scheme of arrangement must:

- in each meeting be at least a majority in number; and
- in the case of a creditors' meeting, hold at least 75 per cent of the debt due to all the creditors collectively; or

---

[27] Mergers of enterprises with an aggregate world-wide turnover of more than €5 billion, and where the aggregate EU-wide turnover of each of at least two of the enterprises concerned is more than €250 million, will be investigated by the European Commission, having taken into account the views of Member States.

[28] CA 2006 s.896(1).

- in the case of a meeting of a class of creditors, hold 75 per cent of the debt due to the collective debt of that class of creditors; or
- in the case of members, hold 75 per cent in value of the issued share capital; or
- for a class of members, have 75 per cent of the capital relating to that class of shares.[29]

The notice calling the various meetings must be accompanied by an **14–16** explanatory note detailing what the scheme of arrangement proposes and in particular how it may affect the material interests of the directors, either in their capacity as directors or in their capacity as members or in any other capacity such as a lender to the company.[30] In the case of debenture-holders, a similar disclosure must be made.[31] However, shareholders or creditors who are not actually affected by the scheme of arrangements are not given the right to object to it,[32] and neither are beneficiaries under a trust.[33]

Assuming the meetings approve the scheme of arrangement, the scheme of arrangement and confirmation of the approval from the relevant meetings are sent to the court. The court can then sanction the arrangement[34] and the scheme of arrangement becomes binding on the company, the members and the creditors.[35] A copy of the scheme of arrangement must be sent to the Registrar of Companies and the court's order is ineffective until this has been done.[36]

The court has wide powers under the CA 2006 s.900, to implement **14–17** whatever the scheme of arrangement proposes, to transfer property, to allot shares, debentures or other interests, to institute legal proceedings, to dissolve any unwanted companies, to deal with dissentient members or creditors or to carry out whatever else needs to be done.

The main advantage of a scheme or arrangement is that only a majority in number and 75 per cent in value of the members and creditors need approve the scheme. This can be compared with the requirement that 90 per cent of the shares (or voting rights) in a takeover or merger be acquired before the remaining 10 per cent can be compulsorily bought out. This means that it is easier to overrule objecting creditors or shareholders. The main disadvantage is that the whole procedure is extremely expensive, as there have to be two applications to court, meetings need to be convened, and extensive negotiations between all the interested parties have to take place before the meetings take place. On the other hand, once the court's sanction has been given, the scheme of arrangement can be fully implemented without reference to any other authority.

---

[29] CA 2006 s.899(1).
[30] CA 2006 s.897(2).
[31] CA 2006 s.897(3).
[32] *Bluebrook Ltd* [2009] EWCH 2114.
[33] *Lehman Bros. International (Europe) Ltd* [2009] EWCA Civ 1161.
[34] CA 2006 s.899(1).
[35] CA 2006 s.899(3).
[36] CA 2006 s.899(4).

IMPEDIMENTS TO TAKEOVERS

14–18 A distinctive feature of the British and American approach to takeovers has been that, in principle, the interest of the shareholders is paramount and there should be few barriers to one company taking over another company if that is what the shareholders want. The rationale for this is that where companies are artificially protected by the state imposing barriers to takeovers (and in particular takeovers by foreign companies of nationally important companies), or by shareholding structures that limit the transferability of shares, in the long run they will become complacent and uncompetitive. Such companies will, it is suggested, become sleepy and exist more to protect the interests of favoured investors, employees and politicians than because they are contributing to the company's shareholders collectively or the nation's economy. Conversely, the knowledge that a company may be taken over by a competitor keeps the company on its toes, ensures that capital is used effectively and that the company continues to produce products that the market wants. The Anglo-American approach is that there should be a level playing field for takeovers, and that the state should not insert impediments to a free and open market.

14–19 In certain other jurisdictions in Europe, and even in the United Kingdom, there is considerable scepticism about this approach to takeovers. This is for the very good reason that takeovers often result in job losses for the ordinary employees, dismissal and replacement of senior management by the takeover company's management, and foreign ownership of national businesses. It can mean the loss of perfectly viable businesses and the loss of many communities' livelihoods. For that reason, some jurisdictions permit their major companies the right to take protectionist measures that make it difficult for takeover bidders, and often in particular foreign takeover bidders, to take those companies over.[37] This preserves, so it is thought, jobs, votes for local politicians, businesses dependent on the target companies, and prevents unwelcome foreigners[38] owning important national assets. The sort of protectionist methods that may be used are sometimes known as "poison pills", the general effect of which is to make it very expensive for a company to be taken over. One example is a "golden parachute" which states that in the event of a takeover, the directors of the company that is about to be taken over have to be paid phenomenal amounts of money as the price for their leaving the company. Another method is the "golden share", which can mean that the state will take 51 per cent of the shares in an important company, so that it may always have the final say in the appointment of directors.

---

[37] For example, it was not difficult for Nestle to take over Rowntree Macintosh some years ago, but at the time, Swiss law would have prevented Rowntree Macintosh taking over Nestle.

[38] This is not merely xenophobia: it is always easier for a foreign company at a later date to close down a distant subsidiary than it is to close a factory near its main base of operations.

The Thirteenth European Company Law Directive on Takeovers[39] **14–20** ("the Takeover Directive") in principle supported the idea of the level playing field as regards takeovers within Europe. The intention behind the original version of the Takeover Directive was to allow any company in Europe to take over any other company elsewhere in Europe, with limited exceptions for a few businesses (such as those working in the defence industry). This proved too deep a draught for the MEPs to swallow, mainly because there was so little protection for employees. The draft Directive was then amended to provide greater protection for employees and rights of consultation with employees, but, in an important concession to those countries that were still very suspicious of a level playing field, allowed countries not to take part in the level playing field. This was considered more acceptable and was duly adopted on April 21, 2004.

More specifically, what the Takeover Directive art.9(1) required **14–21** directors of a company, in a level-playing country, at the receiving end of a takeover bid (the "target company") to do was to seek the prior authorisation of the shareholders before inserting any defensive measures (other than seeking other bids) which might result in the frustration of the bid. Secondly, under art.11(2) (known as "breakthrough") any restrictions in the articles, or in other contractual agreements between the target company and its security-holders, should not apply when seeking this authorisation; restrictions on members' voting rights should not apply when the members are casting their votes for the authorisation under art.9(1); and where, following a bid the bidder holds 75 per cent of the voting capital, no restrictions (under the articles or in contracts) on members' voting rights should apply as regards the appointment or removal of board members. Furthermore, members with multiple voting rights should only have one vote per share when that bidder wishes to amend the articles or to appoint or remove board members. In effect, this removes any existing barriers to takeovers. Since this could place some members, who had perhaps been relying on the restrictions for some reason, at a disadvantage, there are provisions to allow them compensation for their loss of opportunity to prevent these restrictions being used.[40]

Although the hope of Commissioner Bolkstein, the prime mover **14–22** behind the Takeover Directive, was that countries would sign up to a level playing field, in practice few countries did, mainly for protectionist reasons or to keep jobs secure and voters happy, at least in the short term. Article 12 allows countries to reserve the right not to require companies in their countries to sign up to art.9(2) and (3) and art.11. In other words, the countries could opt out of these provisions of arts 9 and 11. However, individual companies within those countries may still, even if their countries have opted out, opt into those provisions, if that is what

---

[39] Directive 2004/25.
[40] Directive 2004/25 art.11(5). This is replicated in CA 2006 s.968(6). The amount of compensation would be such amount as a court considers just and equitable. There is no guidance as to how a court is supposed to carry out this task.

the shareholders wish to do at a general meeting. So if the hypothetical country of Ruritania opts out of these provisions on protectionist grounds, it is still permissible for the members of a particular target company within Ruritania to agree that they are happy to opt into the provisions,[41] and that existing provisions in their company's articles preventing takeovers should not apply.[42]

14–23   The United Kingdom has opted out of art.11, so that it is, unusually, a level-playing field country, except to the extent that individual UK companies may opt in to art.11 if they wish. This was no great difficulty, for the good reason that in the United Kingdom there are very few listed companies where there are any restrictions on the easy transferability of shares. This is because the market is highly suspicious of such companies. Where there are restrictions in place, there is always the danger that there could be a self-perpetuating clique of the founder's family running the company and keeping out new blood, or it might become difficult to get rid of unsatisfactory directors. Anything that smacks of less than satisfactory corporate governance or restricting the voting rights of shareholders is ill received unless the financial returns are enough to overcome shareholders' misgivings. So when the United Kingdom put on a statutory basis in ss.966–971 the above rules, it did so in the knowledge that the rules would be very unlikely to be needed. In any event, the rules are so complex it is unlikely that any company would wish to have to deal with them.

14–24   Following the recent credit crisis, there have been many fewer mergers and acquisitions. Private equity companies are, at the time of writing, still buying businesses, but there is little takeover of one listed company by another. In retrospect, some takeovers and mergers, which had seemed the right idea at the time, are now, in the cold and unfair light of retrospect, seen as ambitious or ill judged, and lost money and lost jobs. As a further issue, it is also now well recognised that many takeovers do not in practice work nearly as well as the takeover bidders thinks they are going to. Commonly there is a clash of cultures, the target company employees fear for their jobs and have low morale, the best of middle management leaves taking with it experience and goodwill, and consumers sometimes do not like the style of the new owners. Sometimes takeovers appear to be more to do with gratifying the egos of the directors who successfully carry out the takeovers than in creating genuine value for shareholders.

Three important features, however, remain constant: takeover activity is extremely exciting for those who take part in it; it is immensely profitable for the banks, lawyers and other financial advisers involved; and a large number of innocent employees, generally through no fault of their own, lose their jobs.

---

[41] The company may opt back out again later if it wishes.

[42] It should be explained that there are specific provisions which may prevent this, such as Ruritania having a golden share in the target company or some other valid reason (art.11(7)). This is replicated in the CA 2006 s.966(4).

Further Reading

A. Johnston, "Takeover regulations; historical and theoretical perspectives on the City Code" (2007) 66 Cambridge L.J. 422.

George O. Barboutis, "Takeover Defence Tactics: Part 1: The general legal framework on takeovers" (1999) 20(1) Comp. Law. 14.

George O. Barboutis, "Takeover Defence Tactics: Part 2: The general legal framework on takeovers" (1999) 20(2) Comp. Law. 40.

The Takeover Panel, *The City Code on Takeovers and Mergers*, available at *http://www.thetakeoverpanel.org.uk/* [Accessed April 22, 2014].

CHAPTER 15

CHARGES AND RECEIVERSHIP

CHARGES

The concept of the charge

15–01   The concept of a charge[1] is simple. If a borrower borrows money, there is always the risk that he will not repay it. If the borrower physically deposits one of his assets with the lender as security for the loan, he must repay the loan and any interest if he wants the asset back. If the borrower never reclaims the asset, the lender has the right under the charge either to sell the asset or keep it.

The practice of a charge is not so simple. In the example above, the asset is moveable and so can be placed in the lender's hands, but while the lender has it the borrower cannot use it.[2] This means that he cannot use the asset to generate the funds to repay the lender. The lender also has to look after it, which may be inconvenient for the lender if it is large.[3]

15–02   Suppose the lender agrees that he will lend against the value of an asset, but that the borrower, whom he trusts to some extent, may continue to use the asset in the meantime. What would prevent the borrower selling the asset and disappearing with the borrowed money, or charging the asset to some other lender who might insist on the asset being lodged with him? As far as companies are concerned, some of those concerns are dealt with by having a registration system, whereby a charge is not valid to confer rights on the secured creditor unless the charge is properly registered in accordance with the required methods.

Registration, to a limited extent, also alerts other creditors and potential investors to the extent to which the company's assets are secured in favour of the secured creditor, and it provides a degree of reassurance to the creditor that the charge is valid. Registration is performed by lodging the required form and a copy of the charging

---

[1] The words "charge" and "security" do not mean the same thing but there is considerable overlap. A charge, strictly speaking a term of English law, is a right in security, and in practice involves some form of legal documentation that acknowledges a security-holder's interest in an asset. A "chargeholder" is a person who has security over a debtor's asset, but such a person may also be known as a "security holder". Because of the huge influence of English law on Scots corporate law, the word "charge" is used for convenience sake in this book.

[2] This form of charge is known as a pledge.

[3] So if a farmer borrowed money against the value of a tractor, the lender in theory would have to keep the tractor in the lender's back yard and the farmer could not use the tractor to plough his fields and raise the money to repay the loan.

document with the Registrar of Companies. If the procedure is correctly carried out, the Registrar issues a certificate of registration which is evidence, not as to the actual viability of every aspect of the charge, but as to the fact that the charge was properly registered. It is not a perfect system, but it suffices.

The Enterprise Act 2002 made significant changes to the law on **15–03** charges and receivership, such that with effect from September 15, 2003 a new type of floating charge, known as a qualifying floating charge, became the standard type of floating charge that must be used, except for certain specific exemptions. A qualifying floating charge entitles the floating charge holder to appoint, not a receiver, but an administrator. This is discussed in the next chapter. Floating charges registered before September 15, 2003 will still be governed by the pre-Enterprise Act rules, so that there are likely to be for many years both floating charges and qualifying floating charges in existence, each with their different set of rules. This chapter deals with charges and the pre-Enterprise Act rights granted under old style floating charges, since there are still a few of them extant, even if lenders do not always exercise their rights under old style floating charges.

A possible change—and at the time of writing it seems unlikely that anything will come of it—is the creation of a dedicated Scottish Register of Floating Charges covering assets in Scotland. The Bankruptcy and Diligence etc. (Scotland) Act 2007 Pt 2 allows for this. The difficulty lies in the practicalities of making it operational.[4]

Fixed charges

There are two main categories of company charges: fixed charges and **15–04** floating charges. A fixed charge is one that is secured over an asset itself, and which prevents the disposal of the asset by the owner without the consent of the charge holder. The easiest example is the standard security.[5] The owner of heritage[6] may not sell a house subject to a standard security without the consent of the standard security holder. The standard security holder will only give his consent to sale following repayment of the loan. If a purchaser bought the seller's house without the standard security being discharged, apart from the fact that this would be impossible in terms of conveyancing practice, the standard security holder could still enforce his right to repossess the house and sell it despite the purchaser's interest in the house. A fixed charge is the best charge there is from the security holder's point of view, because the security holder has the right if necessary to enter in possession of the asset, and the charge runs with the asset,[7] not with the person who

---

[4] The banks are not keen, and have not been persuaded that the new proposals would be markedly better than the current system. For this reason the proposals are not discussed further in this book.

[5] The equivalent of a land mortgage in England. A more formal definition is given at s.486(1) of the Companies Act 1985.

[6] "Heritage" is the Scots law term for land and buildings.

[7] This is known as a jus in rem (a right in the asset).

granted it.[8] So if the grantor of a fixed charge becomes insolvent, the charge is still valid over the asset, the asset can be sold by the fixed chargeholder, thus getting his money back, plus interest and expenses. A fixed chargeholder does not have to worry about preferential creditors or other imposts.

In return for accepting a fixed charge, a fixed chargeholder may charge a lower interest rate for the loan than he might otherwise do.

15–05 As indicated above, the problem with the fixed charge over a moveable asset is that the lender normally has to look after the asset, and the borrower cannot (usually) use the asset, or sell it, without the lender's consent. In addition, Scots law cannot cope with the idea of a fixed charge over an asset which is not in the hands of the lender.[9] This is because of Roman law origins of Scots law, and is summed up in the Latin maxim, *Traditionibus, non nudis pactis, dominia rerum transferuntur.*[10] This leads to ingenious practices. Casks of whisky used as security for a loan have to be stored in a special part of a bonded warehouse, carefully partitioned off, with the key being under the control of a stock-keeper who reports to the lender and not to the actual owner of the whisky.

The floating charge

15–06 These difficulties are not unique to Scots law, but in England commerce proved more willing to entertain the idea of a charge, whether fixed or not, over moveable assets, even if those assets were still in the hands of the borrower. Mercantile law in England was willing to accept this risky notion on the principle that if that is what a lender wanted to do, that was his choice, and he would probably charge the borrower a higher rate of interest to compensate him for the danger of default. In due course, this led to the invention of the floating charge. A floating charge can be likened to an imaginary net suspended from the lender's hand over the assets of a company.[11] In return for the loan of money by the lender to the borrowing company, the borrower agrees to the charging of the company's assets to the lender, to repay the loan on a predetermined date, to pay the interest on the loan and to fulfil all other necessary requirements of the loan. The loan, however, is not generally secured on any one

---

[8] This is known as a jus in personam (a right against the person). A jus in personam is less useful than a jus in rem because a person could disappear or become bankrupt, in which case the right is worthless, whereas a thing, particularly if it is a house, is more likely to remain in existence.

[9] In England to get round this problem, bills of sale were invented. A charge over a person's moveable assets can be registered in a special registry. The procedure is little used.

[10] By physical delivery, rather than by mere agreement, is the ownership of assets transferred. This rule makes sense in a rural economy. Under Roman law, although a seller could agree to sell, say, a cow to a purchaser, the purchaser only could get ownership of the cow once it was in his hands. With physical delivery everyone knows where they stand, and there should be no disputes over ownership.

[11] Floating charges are in general only available to companies and limited liability partnerships though they do also exist for farming businesses under the Agricultural Credits Act 1928.

particular asset belonging to the company: it is secured collectively over all or most of the assets of the company, whatever they may happen to be from time to time, usually provided that the total value of the assets is no less than the loan. While the interest on the loan continues to be paid on time, the net/charge remains suspended over the assets of the company, and the company may change those assets in the course of business. If the company defaults on the loan, the charge is said to "crystallise" or "attach" to the assets of the company, or to adapt the simile, the net is released by the charge holder and traps all the assets of the company not already subject to a prior-ranking security (or otherwise unavailable). At that point a receiver, at least under the pre-Enterprise Act rules, is appointed, as will be discussed shortly. The receiver then exercises the powers open to him to recover the sums due to the charge holder.

A particular issue with regards to floating charges is the extent to which the company can exercise its rights to use the assets that are subject to the floating charge. It is not such an issue in Scotland, where, because of the requirement of delivery, an asset is either subject to a fixed charge or it is not, but in England, in their quest for ever more ingenious wording to allow maximum flexibility for both lender and borrower alike,[12] there is a long line of cases trying to establish whether or not a particular charge is fixed or floating, irrespective of the label given to the charge. The best-known definition of a floating charge was given by Romer L.J. in *Re Yorkshire Woolcombers Association Ltd*[13]:

> "I certainly think that if a charge has the three characteristics that I am about to mention it is a floating charge. (1.) If it is a charge on a class of assets of a company present and future; (2.) if that class is one, which, in the ordinary course of business, would be changing from time to time; and (3.) if you find that by the charge it is contemplated that, until some future step is taken by or on behalf of those interested in the charge, the company may carry on its business in the ordinary way as far as concerns the particular class of assets I am dealing with."

Despite some bizarre decisions on the way,[14] the current position in England as regards the distinction between a fixed and a floating charge, particularly in connection with book debts, is encapsulated within the case of *Re Spectrum Plus Ltd*.[15] This case restated the previous view that where assets are under the control of the borrower, the assets are subject to the floating charge; but if the assets are under the control of the lender, **15–07**

---

[12] It is theoretically possible to have a charge that is both fixed and floating under English law, so that it can convert from being a floating charge to a fixed charge (though there might be difficulty in appointing an administrative receiver because of the operation of the Insolvency Act 1986 ("IA 1986") s.29(2)(a)), or a fixed charge to a floating charge, and despite the possible adverse effect on creditors, there is no requirement for the conversion to be made apparent to those creditors.

[13] *Re Yorkshire Woolcombers Association Ltd* [1903] 2 Ch. 284 at 295.

[14] For example, *Re New Bullas Trading Ltd* [1994] 1 B.C.L.C. 485 CA.

[15] *Re Spectrum Plus Ltd* [2005] All E.R. (D) 368.

they are subject to a fixed charge. The important issue is that of control: if the borrowing company controls the asset, it is a floating charge; if the company is not at liberty to deal with the assets, the lender controls the asset, and it is a fixed charge. There is always an incentive for a charge holder to seek a fixed charge rather than a floating charge from the company, since a fixed charge gives almost total control over the charged asset, takes priority over a floating charge (and therefore is repaid first) and needs take no account of such preferential creditors as there are.[16]

In terms of priority, a fixed charge always ranks ahead of a floating charge unless there is some agreement to the contrary.[17] If a company grants a floating charge, the floating charge holder must be aware that unless there is a term in the charging documentation to the contrary (as there usually will be, such a term being known as a negative pledge clause), it is open to the company to grant a fixed charge which will take priority over the floating charge.[18] This is discussed later at para.15–17.

Floating charges in Scotland

15–08   A particular difficulty for floating charges in Scotland is that floating charges do not sit easily with the way that Scots law sees property. Floating charges were only introduced into Scotland with the Companies (Floating Charges) (Scotland) Act 1961 and receivers were introduced by the Companies (Floating Charges and Receivers) (Scotland) Act 1972. Most floating charges are over the entire assets and undertaking of the company but it is permissible for the floating charge only to be over some of the company's assets, provided this is made clear in the charging documentation.[19]

An advantage of being such a late admission to the law was that it was introduced by statute. The entire procedure is at least accessible and relatively public. The legislation also sets out the receiver's duties. It should be noted that what in Scotland is called a receiver is called in England an administrative receiver. A receiver in English law is sort of manager or factor appointed by a creditor (particularly in respect of collecting rent from a debtor's tenants and then paying the rent directly to the creditor).

15–09   One disadvantage of the Scots law relating to floating charges is that when a company grants a floating charge over all its assets, it will not be apparent from the Scottish property registers, being the Land Register and the Register of Sasines, that a floating charge is in existence,[20] and

---

[16] As will be seen later, a post-Enterprise Act floating charge gives less control to the lender than a pre-Enterprise Act floating charge, and there is consequently since the passing of the Enterprise Act an even greater incentive for a lender to take a fixed charge if he can.

[17] Companies Act 1985 ("CA 1985") s.464(4)(a). The lenders to a company may agree to this between themselves by means of a ranking agreement.

[18] CA 2006 s.859D(2)(c). The Form MR01 has a tickbox to indicate if a negative pledge clause is in existence in the charging documentation. If a charge does not have a negative pledge, but the parties wish to alter it so that it does, the Form MR07 is used. Where the charge was created before April 6, 2013 a different form, Form 466, should be used.

[19] CA 2006 s.859D(2)(b).

[20] CA 1985 s.462(5).

that it might affect heritage owned by the company. One might have thought that the whole point of a property registration system is to show the world at large who has what rights in the property but this does not happen with a floating charge.[21] The current practice is that when it is apparent that a seller of heritage is a company it should also be ascertained from Companies House or the seller's agent whether or not that company has granted a floating charge. The seller will then show to the purchaser a letter of non-crystallisation from the company's floating charge holder confirming that the company will not be put into receivership, or as the case may be, administration within a designated number of days and permitting the transaction to take place. In return the purchaser's agent must register/record the disposition and any other documents within a specified period of days.

A second disadvantage of floating charges involved the case of *Sharp v Thomson*[22] which highlighted difficulties with the law of receivership, whereby a new category of ownership, known as beneficial ownership, which can defeat a receiver, was introduced to the law of Scotland. This is discussed later.

For many years there were questions as to whether or not a retention of title clause was a registrable charge, but following the case of *Armour v Thyssen Edelstahlwerke*[23] it was established that such a clause was neither a charge nor registrable.

The practice of registering charges

Historically there was only a specified number of charges that could be **15–10** registered, but with effect from April 6, 2013, any charge is now registrable except for charges in rent deposit deeds (not common in Scotland), charges created by a member of Lloyds in connection with underwriting business, pledges[24] and any charge excluded by virtue of some other legislation.[25] All charges must be registered within a period of 21 days beginning with the day after the date of creation of the charge,[26] unless that period has been extended under CA 2006 s.859(F)(3). CA 2006 s.859D indicates what information needs to be sent to the Registrar of Companies to enable the charge to be registered. This includes the

---

[21] The fact that the property registers do not show the interests of floating charge holders is probably: (a) because statute does not require it at present; (b) because when the legislation was drafted, it would have been physically very difficult to note on every property title that the company that owned it had granted a floating charge, since someone would physically have had to check all properties owned by UK companies. Before computers this would not have been feasible.

[22] *Sharp v Thomson*; sub nom. *Sharp v Woolwich Building Society*, 1997 S.C. (HL) 66; 1997 S.L.T. 636; 1997 S.C.L.R. 328 HL; [1997] 1 B.C.L.C. 603; [1998] B.C.C. 115.

[23] *Armour v Thyssen Edelstahlwerke* [1991] 2 A.C. 339; [1990] 3 W.L.R. 810; [1990] 3 All E.R. 481; 1990 S.L.T. 891; [1991] B.C.L.C. 28; [1990] B.C.C. 925.

[24] A pledge is when a debtor hands an asset to a lender in exchange for a loan or some other benefit. A common example would be the pledge of an asset at a pawnbroker's.

[25] CA 2006 s.659A(6). Examples of such legislation are the Banking Act 2009 or the Financial Collateral Arrangements (No.2) Regulations 2003 (SI 2003/3226).

[26] CA 2006 s.859A(4).

name and registered number of the company, the type of charge, the charging documentation, the name of the chargeholder, a short description of what is being charged (if the asset being charged is land, a ship, an aircraft or intellectual property) and if the charged assets are not those items, there needs to be an indication that the charge is over corporeal or incorporeal property.

In practice the most common types of charge that are registered are standard securities and floating charges.

15–11   As regards standard securities, the company executes the standard security[27] and sends the top copy to the Keeper of the Land Register or the Register of Sasines, while retaining a certified copy in the office. On confirmation from the Keeper of the date of registration or recording of the standard security,[28] which is what gives the company a real right in the heritage, and when the charge is deemed to be created,[29] the company, or the standard security holder, must send the certified copy standard security, the Keeper's confirmation and the Form MR01 to the Registrar of Companies within 21 days of the date of registration or recording of the standard security.[30] Assuming everything is in order, the Registrar of Companies will then issue a certificate of registration of the charge. A copy of that certificate will need to be sent to the Keeper, thus proving that the standard security was properly registered with the Registrar of Companies, as otherwise it will not be a valid standard security. There will also need to be confirmation from the company's lawyers that the standard security that has been registered with the Registrar is the same standard security as the one that the Keeper registered.

If the charge to be registered is a floating charge, the date of the charge's creation is the date that it is executed by the company.[31] The 21-day period runs from day after the date of execution of the floating charge. A certified copy of the floating charge is sent to the Registrar along with the Form MR01 and the fee.[32]

Other common charges that may require to be registered will include assignation of intellectual property rights, bank accounts, rental payments, royalties etc. When the charge is over, say, rent from tenants, there will need to be intimation to the tenant to tell him that his payments will no longer be made to the landlord but to the chargeholder. The Registrar of Companies will need to see the evidence of the intimation, the intimation itself usually being done by recorded delivery. If a

---

[27] Execution of a document such as a standard security is normally done by having a director, the company secretary or someone authorised to sign on its behalf, duly sign on its behalf in the presence of a witness. Alternatively, the company may execute a document by having either two directors, a director and a secretary, or two persons duly authorised to sign on behalf of the company, duly sign, but no witness is required. A seal may be used if the articles so require.

[28] CA 2006 s.859D(1)(b).

[29] CA 2006 s.859E(1).

[30] CA 2006 s.859A(4). The fee at present is for paper registration is £13 or £10 for electronic registration.

[31] CA 2006 s.859E(1).

[32] The fee is the same as for standard securities.

company acquires property which is subject to a registrable charge, the Form MR02 would apply.[33] Not every charge will necessarily have a charging document attached, but form MR08 requires sufficient information to be disclosed to indicate the existence of the charge.

The entire process of registering the charge with the Registrar of **15–12** Companies may be done electronically, with the certified copies being sent in in PDF form.[34] If a Scottish company is granting a charge over English property it too must now use the Form MR01 while complying with the English mortgage registration requirements. Securities over a ship or aircraft need also to be registered in specialist shipping[35] and aircraft mortgage[36] registries. Since October 2011 there is no longer any mechanism for enabling an overseas company to register charges over property in the United Kingdom.

Although s.859A(2) says that that the Registrar of Companies must register a charge, subs.(2) says that it may be registered by anyone who is interested in the registration of the charge: this may be the chargeholder, the company, the chargeholder's agents or the company's agents. It will be noted that the certified copy charging document is sent to the Registrar of Companies and once there it will be published in the company's records.[37] For confidentiality reasons it is now permissible to redact personal information relating to an individual, signatures and account numbers,[38] but that is the limit of permitted confidentiality. It is therefore prudent for charging documentation not to contain any commercially sensitive information.

The certificate of registration

Once the charge is registered, the Registrar of Companies returns the **15–13** documentation together with a certificate of registration of charge and a special unique reference code.[39] The certificate is only evidence of the lodging of the documents within the correct period to enable the registration of the charge. It is not a guarantee that any of the information within the charge is accurate. The code will enable the subsequent discharge or variation of the charge to be more easily effected and ensure that the right charge is discharged or varied as the case may be.

---

[33] This covers the situation where a company acquires, say, a ship subject to a charge. The Form MR02 will indicate both the new owner and the fact that the ship remains subject to the original charge.

[34] If the charge is being submitted electronically by a lender, as opposed to the company itself, the lender will need to apply to Companies House for a lender authentication code on a one-off basis. Companies may use their normal electronic authentication code.

[35] The Shipping Register is expressly designed to keep a record of ships and mortgages granted over ships. See the Merchant Shipping Act 1995 and the Merchant Shipping (Registration of Ships) Regulations 1993 (SI 1993/3138).

[36] Mortgaging of Aircraft Order 1972 (SI 1972/1268).

[37] It is possible to register a charge without the charging document being attached (CA 2006 s.859D(1)(d)) but the relevant particulars must be shown on the Form MR08.

[38] CA 2006 s.859G.

[39] CA 2006 s.859I.

Failure to register in time

15–14   The charging documentation must be submitted to the Registrar of Companies within a period of 21 days starting with the day after the day of execution. If this is not done, the only remedies are to apply, expensively and embarrassingly, to the court for late registration,[40] or to start again. Failure to register in time renders the charge void against a liquidator, creditor or administrator[41] and while the debt still stands and is immediately repayable, the priority relative to other creditors is lost. This means that when a bank advances funds to a company in the expectation that it will be placed at the top of the list of creditors as a secured creditor with a registered charge, it could find that it was merely an unsecured creditor with no registered charge to its name. Any loss it suffered would have to be recovered from the agents who were supposed to be lodging the charge in time.

The company's own copies of charges

15–15   Each company is supposed to keep copies of every instrument or document capable of being registered as a charge plus any variations or amendments to those documents.[42] They should be available for inspection.[43] Apparently very few creditors or members ever take advantage of this opportunity.

Entries of satisfaction and relief

15–16   It is best practice whenever all or part of a charge is discharged to send in the required form[44] proving that the charge is discharged.[45] This clears the searches as well as putting paid to any arguments as to whether or not a charge is still in existence.

Ranking agreements

15–17   Ranking agreements are complex and frequently confusing documents that are used when a company borrows funds from a number of different lenders, secured over heritage by standard securities and over the rest of the company's assets by floating charges. In the absence of a ranking agreement, fixed charges rank in date order of registration to each other, fixed charges rank in priority to floating charges,[46] floating charges rank

---

[40] CA 2006 s.859F. Late registration will only be permitted where the delay was inadvertent or accidental, the courts consider it just and equitable and no creditors or shareholders would be prejudiced thereby.

[41] CA 2006 s.859H.

[42] CA 2006 s.859P.

[43] CA 2006 s.859Q. This is normally at the registered office but if the company's records are elsewhere, as is sometimes the case, they may be inspected there instead.

[44] The form required would be a MR04 for satisfaction and repayment of a charge and MR05 for release of partial release of property from a charge or from a company.

[45] CA 2006 s.859L.

[46] CA 1985 s.464(4)(a). Note that as stated before, this part of CA 1985 has not been repealed at the time of writing.

in date order of registration[47] and where floating charges arrive in the same post they are deemed to rank with each other equally.[48] With a ranking agreement it is possible to re-arrange the pecking order of the charges, so that in the event of the liquidation of the company it is possible to ascertain who gets what and in what order, usually so that the company's assets are divided up proportionally instead of the first lender getting all the assets.[49] But in the absence of a ranking agreement, if there is an existing registered floating charge and the company grants a second floating charge, the first charge holder is only entitled to his present advances, any future advances which he had contracted to make, interest due on all such advances, expenses reasonably incurred by the holder, and the value of any contingent liability for the charge that had been granted.[50]

A floating charge may, and indeed commonly does, on creation contain provisions restricting the grant of any charge ranking in priority to the floating charge (the "negative pledge"), or may contain provisions allowing another charge to rank ahead of it.[51] These will normally be indicated on the required form, and it is generally agreed that this is useful, as no later creditor can claim he was unaware of these provisions. However, whenever an existing floating charge, predating April 6, 2013 is varied, a Form 466 needs to be completed and sent to the Registrar of Companies in respect of each floating charge to be varied.[52] This can mean that for a complex transaction with several lenders, each of whose advance is secured by a floating charge, there will need to be a Form 466 in respect of each floating charge. The Form 466 will normally be accompanied by and refer to the ranking agreement, although this will not be shown on the register.[53]After April 6, 2013 the Form MR07 is used.[54]

---

[47] CA 1985 s.464(4)(b).

[48] CA 1985 s.464(4)(c).

[49] If the first lender stood to get everything, the company would never be able to get further loans, and the lender would have no opportunities to limit its exposure short of causing the company to collapse.

[50] CA 1985 s.464(5). These rules could be disapplied, if necessary, by a ranking agreement.

[51] Technically a fixed charge, whenever created, ranks ahead of a floating charge anyway. But a lender who had secured his loan by means of a floating charge would be most unhappy if he found that some other lender had put a fixed charge on one of the debtor company's assets, thus giving the fixed charge holder priority as regards that asset. For that reason, floating charge holders commonly insist on negative pledges.

[52] Alternatively an existing charge could be discharged and a new one lodged, but there might then be a hiatus during which a lender's advance might be at risk.

[53] This results in a plethora of registered documents filed with the Registrar of Companies, making it even more confusing for any outside creditor researching the company to work out the extent of its indebtedness.

[54] See CA 2006 s.859O.

Invalidity of charges generally

15–18 Provided the charge is registered properly within the time-limit, a charge is likely to be valid, but there may be occasions when a charge is not valid. For example, a charge may be invalid if it is held to be an unfair preference[55] in an insolvent winding up.

The following only arises in the context of a liquidation, but if a company has granted a charge to a creditor within six months of the company's winding up or administration, the floating charge may be reduced by the courts on the application of a creditor, the liquidator or the administrator under the Insolvency Act 1986 ("the IA 1986") s.243(5) unless it was:

(1) a transaction in the ordinary course of business[56];

(2) a payment in cash for a debt which was due and payable, unless the payment had been collusively set up between the company and the creditor in order to prejudice other creditors[57];

(3) part of some reciprocal obligations (not necessarily contemporaneous) between the company and the preferred creditor, unless it was collusive as in (2)[58];

(4) the grant of instructions or mandate to a third party to pay out arrested funds to an arrester.[59]

15–19 The point of this provision is that it might be tempting for a company to arrange for a favoured creditor to receive a charge which allows him rights over the company's assets at the expense of all the other creditors— especially if the creditor had not supplied full consideration to the company in exchange for the charge.

Invalidity of floating charges under Insolvency Act 1986 s.245

15–20 A floating charge will be invalid if:

(a) it is granted to a connected person within two years of the onset of the company's insolvency[60]; or

(b) it is granted to any person at any time between the presentation of a petition for the making of an administration order and the making of that order.[61]

---

[55] IA 1986 s.243. Fraudulent preferences exist at common law as well, but they are very rarely used nowadays.

[56] IA 1986 s.243(2)(a).

[57] IA 1986 s.243(2)(b). *R Gaffney and Son Ltd v Davidson*, 1996 S.L.T. (Sh Ct) 36.

[58] IA 1986 s.243(2)(c). *Nicoll v Steel Press (Supplies) Ltd*, 1992 S.C. 119.

[59] IA 1986 s.243(2)(d).

[60] IA 1986 s.245(3)(a). The "onset of insolvency" means the commencement of the winding up or the date of the presentation of the petition on which an administration order was made (IA 1986 s.245(5)).

[61] IA 1986 s.245(3)(c).

A "connected" person is a director or shadow director of the company, an associate of the company, or an associate of a director or shadow director.[62] An associate is extensively defined in the IA 1986 s.435, but in essence is a close relative or spouse of a director, a partner of the director, an employer or employee either of the director or the company.

When the charge is granted within 12 months to someone not connected with the company, the charge will be invalid if:

(c) at the time of granting the security the company was unable to pay its debts in terms of the IA 1986 s.123[63]; or

(d) the company became unable to pay its debts because of the transaction for which the charge was granted.[64]

Despite the above, a charge in favour of either a connected person or an **15-21** unconnected person will still be valid if the charge was granted in respect of:

(e) monies paid, or good or services supplied at the same time or after the creation of the charge[65];

(f) the value of any reduction or discharge of debt of the company in exchange for which the charge was granted[66]; or

(g) any interest payable in respect of (e) or (f) above.[67]

The point of the legislation is to prevent the granting of a retrospective charge to one creditor at the expense of other creditors when a company is heading towards insolvency, in order to put that creditor in a good position in the event of the company going down. If a creditor wants the benefit of a charge, he should obtain the charge at the time he, say, makes a loan to the company, not a later date. However, it does not necessarily mean that the charge is completely invalid.

In more detail what it means is that if the company is insolvent at the time an *unconnected* person gets the floating charge (or becomes so as a result of the transaction involving the floating charge) (and provided the charge was granted within the 12 month period prior to the onset of insolvency) the unconnected person does not get the benefit of the floating charge except to the extent of (e), (f) and (g) above. If the company was solvent at the time of granting the floating charge, even if it was within the 12 month period, an unconnected person can have the entire benefit of the floating charge, including money lent before the granting of the charge, as well as the sums under (e), (f) and (g).

On the other hand, it makes no difference whether the company is **15-22** solvent or not as far as the granting of a floating charge to a *connected*

---

[62] IA 1986 s.249.
[63] IA 1986 s.245(4)(a).
[64] IA 1986 s.245(4)(b).
[65] IA 1986 s.245(2)(a).
[66] IA 1986 s.245(2)(b).
[67] IA 1986 s.245(2)(c).

person is concerned: within the two year period the connected person can only get the benefit of the floating charge to the extent of (e), (f) or (g).

Outside the time periods above the charges will be valid.

RECEIVERSHIP (PRE-ENTERPRISE ACT)

15–23 A receiver is an insolvency practitioner appointed under the terms of a floating charge granted by a company to a floating charge holder. It is the receiver's task to ingather the assets caught by the attached floating charge and to use the proceeds thereof to repay the loan from the floating charge holder. In the past, this was quite often done by the receiver taking over the management of the company until such time as the debt to the floating charge holder was repaid. In the past, this was an easier task than it is nowadays, because it was more common for businesses to own their own premises, and not to borrow against the value of their own stock or book debts. Now that many businesses lease their premises, companies are much smarter than they used to be about factoring their debts, and plant and machinery is often acquired on hire purchase, there tends to be less with which a receiver can operate, and it is generally much easier for the receiver to conduct a fire sale and sell as much as he can as quickly as he can in order to repay the loan to the lender. It is now very rare for a receiver to take over the management of the company, restore it to health, pay off the lender's debt, and return the management to the directors.

The rules relating to receivership in Scotland are to be found in the IA 1986 ss.50–71 and the Insolvency (Scotland) Rules 1986.[68] The rules on receivership continue to apply to all floating charges registered before the date of implementation of the Enterprise Act 2002,[69] but since that date, with eight exceptions[70] (to be discussed shortly) all new floating charges must be qualifying floating charges which entitle the floating charge holder to appoint an administrator, rather than a receiver. It is likely that it will be 15 or so years before the last old-style floating charge is finally discharged or the last receiver put in place, and it is therefore necessary both to explain the law relating to pre-Enterprise Act receivership and, later, Enterprise Act administration.

15–24   The eight exceptions which retain (with a slight modification) the old pre-Enterprise Act rules relating to receivership, and which may continue to use old-style floating charges, are as follows:

- capital markets;
- public-private partnerships;
- utilities companies;
- urban regeneration projects;
- project finance;

---

[68] Insolvency (Scotland) Rules 1986 (SI 1986/1915).
[69] September 15, 2003.
[70] Enterprise Act 2002 s.250(1), inserting the IA 1986 ss.72B–72GA.

- financial markets;
- registered social landlords; and
- protected railway companies.

The capital market exception: Insolvency Act 1986 s.72B

This arises where there are capital market investments (loosely, these **15–25** are listed or otherwise traded bonds, debentures and other debt instruments (including for the purposes of the legislation options, futures and contracts for differences) to the value of at least £50m issued by a company to investors, who have their interests looked after for them by means of a trustee (as in a debenture trust deed trustee) or other nominee. That trustee or nominee will arrange that the company's obligations to the bondholders are guaranteed by another party, or security will be given to the trustee by the company or some other party to ensure due performance.

This exception also covers a bond or other commercial paper issued to an investment professional, a certified "high net worth individual", a "high net worth company", a certified "sophisticated investor" (all within the terms of Financial Services and Markets Act 2000 (Financial Promotion) Order 2001)[71] or to a person in a state other than the United Kingdom and who is not prohibited by the laws of that state from investing in bonds or commercial paper.[72]

It would appear that the £50m does not continually have to be outstanding: even if a lesser sum is outstanding, provided at some stage the debt has been at least £50m, an administrative receiver may still be appointed.[73]

Public-Private Partnership ("PPP"): Insolvency Act 1986 s.72C

A PPP is body whose resources are provided by one or more public **15–26** bodies but some of whose finance is provided privately and which is set up to enable a public body to fulfil some function (commonly the building of schools and hospitals). Such PPPs are used in PPP projects and commonly provide that the finance provider to the project has "step-in rights" which would enable the finance provider to take over sole or principal contractual responsibility for the carrying-out of the project.

Utilities: Insolvency Act 1986 s.72D

A utility project company which has step-in rights as above and both **15–27** involves a project and one of the regulated utilities companies (gas, electricity, etc.) may grant old-style floating charges.

---

[71] Financial Services and Markets Act 2000 (Financial Promotion) Order 2001 (SI 2001/1335).
[72] IA 1986 Sch.2A paras 1–3.
[73] IA 1986 s.72B(1)(a).

Urban regeneration projects: Insolvency Act 1986 s.72DA

15–28   In order to encourage the redevelopment of disadvantaged land, and where there is a project company with step-in rights for the finance provider, old-style floating charges may be granted by the project company.

Project finance: Insolvency Act 1986 s.72E

15–29   This category is supposed to cover projects that are neither PPP projects, utilities projects nor urban regeneration projects, and where the project company incurs or is expected to incur a debt of at least £50m with step-in rights for the project creditor.

Financial market exception: Insolvency Act 1986 s.72F

15–30   This permits the use of old-style floating charges for market charges, system-charges and collateral security charges. These are granted in favour of the Stock Exchange by stockbrokers, issuing houses and others to cover the due payments for market contracts for the transfer and allotment of securities of various sorts.

Registered social landlords: Insolvency Act 1986 s.72G

15–31   These housing associations may grant old-style floating charges.

Protected railway companies: Insolvency Act 1986 s.72GA

15–32   Certain railway companies and water companies may grant old-style floating charges.

Where a receiver is appointed in any of the above exceptions after September 15, 2003,[74] it should be noted that of the sums the receiver gathers in, he must retain a certain amount for the few remaining preferential creditors[75] and another amount for any unsecured creditors, this being known as the "prescribed part".[76] The "prescribed part", referred to in the IA 1986 s.176A(3)(a), is to be found in the Insolvency Act 1986 (Prescribed Part) Order 2003,[77] and is as follows:

- where the company's net property is less than £10,000, the prescribed part is 50 per cent of that property;
- where the company's net property is more than £10,000, the prescribed part is 50 per cent of the first £10,000's worth of property; plus
- 20 per cent of the remainder in excess of that first £10,000's worth of property, all subject to a maximum overall prescribed part of £600,000.

---

[74] IA 1986 s.176A(9).
[75] IA 1986 Sch.6.
[76] IA 1986 s.176A, as inserted by Enterprise Act 2002 s.252.
[77] Insolvency Act 1986 (Prescribed Part) Order 2003 (SI 2003/2097).

If the company's net property is less than £10,000, and the person who will be distributing the company's monies (liquidator, receiver, or administrator as the case may be) believes that the cost of making a distribution to the unsecured creditors would be greater than its benefits, the payment to the unsecured creditors need not be made.[78] The person distributing the funds may also apply to the court if necessary to seek approval for non-payment on those grounds.[79] Net property in these circumstances means all the property that would otherwise be available to a floating charge holder if the prescribed part did not exist.[80]

The idea is that the prescribed part will go some way to redeeming the position for unsecured creditors who hitherto often received nothing on a company's receivership. It is discussed further in the next chapter.

APPOINTMENT OF A RECEIVER IN SCOTLAND

As far as Scots law is concerned, under the IA 1986 s.52 a receiver is **15–33** appointed on the occurrence of any of the following events:

(1) the expiry of a period of 21 days after a demand for payment of the whole of part of the principal sum secured by a charge without payment having been made[81];
(2) the expiry of a period of two months during which interest has been unpaid and is in arrears[82];
(3) the making of an order or the passing of a resolution to wind up the company[83];
(4) the appointment of a receiver by virtue of any other floating charge created by the company.[84]

A floating charge may specify other grounds as well, such as the failure to keep the assets insured up to a certain level, or a failure to adhere to certain covenants in a debenture.

Normally there is some prior warning to the debtor company by the **15–34** floating charge holder of imminent receivership, but this is not necessary unless the charging documentation provides for it.

Although it is possible to appoint a receiver by application to the court[85] this would normally only be used where there was some defect in the floating charge documentation which precluded the normal method of appointment by the charge holder, or where assets were situated abroad and would only be released to a court-appointed receiver.

The charge holder completes an instrument of appointment which is

---

[78] IA 1986 s.176A(3)(a), (b).
[79] IA 1986 s.176A(5).
[80] IA 1986 s.176A(6).
[81] IA 1986 s.52(1)(a).
[82] IA 1986 s.52(1)(b).
[83] IA 1986 s.52(1)(c).
[84] IA 1986 s.52(1)(d).
[85] IA 1986 ss.52(2), 54. Receivership by application to court would be expensive.

sent to the nominated receiver. The receiver must accept his appointment the day after appointment[86] and the Registrar of Companies and Accountant in Bankruptcy must be informed of his appointment within seven days[87] and an entry made in the company's register of charges.[88] On the appointment of the receiver the floating charge attaches to the company's assets and becomes a fixed charge over those assets.[89] All creditors must be informed of the receivership by post[90] and by publication.[91] A Registrar of Companies booklet (available on its website) details all the forms that the receiver (and indeed administrator and liquidator) will need to complete.[92]

15–35   Following appointment the receiver:

   (1) ascertains what assets are caught by the floating charge;
   (2) tries to realise them as advantageously as possible from the point of view of the charge holder[93];
   (3) uses the proceeds to pay the preferential debts exigible under IA 1986 s.59;
   (4) remits the sums due to the charge holder; and
   (5) if there is anything left over (which is unlikely), returns it to the company.

The receiver has extensive powers under the IA 1986 Sch.2 to carry out the above and he may apply to the courts for further powers if necessary. As part of this process he requires the officers and employees to supply to him affidavits which will make up a statement of affairs about the company's assets, debts, liabilities and the grant of any securities.[94] Within three months of appointment the receiver must prepare a report for the benefit of the floating charge holder and the creditors about the events leading up to his appointment, about his disposal of the company's assets or his continuation of the company's business, the amounts due to the floating charge holder and preferential creditors and the amount likely to be left over for the unsecured creditors.[95] The report will contain a summary of the statement of affairs.[96] If the company has gone

---

[86]   As evidenced by a docquet which the receiver completes (IA 1986 s.53(6)(a), (b)).

[87]   IA 1986 s.53(1). The seven-day gap is a problem for unsecured creditors who may unwittingly be supplying goods to the company in receivership without knowing of the receivership.

[88]   IA 1986 s.53(5).

[89]   IA 1986 s.53(7). This means that the directors may not deal with the company's property from that moment.

[90]   IA 1986 s.65(1)(b).

[91]   IA 1986 s.65(1)(a). This is normally done in the newspapers. The Accountant in Bankruptcy, who maintains the Register of Insolvencies, would also need to be informed.

[92]   The booklet is entitled "Liquidation and Insolvency (Scotland) - GPO8s Feb 2014".

[93]   This can be done either by holding a sale of the assets, by hiving off the better assets to a subsidiary which is then sold, or by continuing to trade the company out of difficulty until the debt, interest and expenses are repaid and the company can be handed back to the directors.

[94]   IA 1986 s.66.

[95]   IA 1986 s.67.

[96]   IA 1986 s.67(5).

into liquidation, the liquidator will need to receive a copy too.[97] A committee of unsecured creditors may be set up,[98] consisting of between three to five persons, in order to advise the receiver of the concerns of the unsecured creditors.

During the receivership the directors lose their management rights in **15-36** respect of the assets caught by the receivership, though if the floating charge is only partial, they may maintain their management roles in respect of the unsecured parts of the company. There is conflicting case law on the extent to which directors may exercise rights over the company's assets.[99] However, where the receiver is failing in his duties, it is open to the directors to act against him if they think he is not overall acting in the best interests of the company,[100] or if the receiver has either failed to make a claim for assets which he should have claimed or been involved in a conflict of interest between him and the company.[101] There is English authority to the effect that a receiver may be liable for his incompetence in running the business which has been handed over to him[102] but this was in the context of a farming receivership and it will not necessarily apply in respect of company law.

The receiver as agent

The receiver acts as agent for the company in relation to such property **15-37** of the company as is attached by the floating charge.[103] In general, unless he is acting on his own account and/or breaching his fiduciary duty to the company,[104] he will not be at risk personally in respect of that property. If he were not an agent, he would be liable for whatever he did, which would serve as little incentive to act as receiver. However, he is personally liable for any contract entered into by him, except to the extent that the contract provides otherwise.[105] Not surprisingly, a receiver, wherever possible, will state in the terms of any new contract with a third party that he will not personally be liable under the terms of that contract. The third party may resist this, but even so, where the receiver is personally liable, he is still entitled to be indemnified out of the company's assets to the

---

[97] IA 1986 s.67(4).

[98] IA 1986 ss.67(2), 68 and Insolvency (Scotland) Rules 1986 (SI 1986/1915) Pt 3 Ch.3.

[99] *Imperial Hotel (Aberdeen) Ltd v Vaux Breweries Ltd*, 1978 S.L.T. 113, suggests that directors have no rights, while *Shanks v Central Regional Council*, 1987 S.L.T. 113 allows directors very limited rights. For the English position, see *Newhart Developments Ltd v Co-operative Commercial Bank Ltd* [1978] 1 Q.B. 814 (which did allow the directors some rights) and *Tudor Grange Holdings Ltd v Citibank NA* [1991] B.C.L.C. 1009 (which did not).

[100] *Standard Chartered Bank v Walker* [1982] 3 All E.R. 938.

[101] *Independent Pension Trustee Ltd v Law Construction Co Ltd* 1996 G.W.D. 33–1956.

[102] *Medforth v Blake* [1999] B.C.C. 771.

[103] IA 1986 s.57(1). For an explanation of the theory behind this, see *Gaskell v Gosling* [1896] 1 Q.B. 669, per Rigby L.J. at 692–693, and subsequently approved by the House of Lords ([1897] A.C. 575).

[104] Technically he would also be liable if he acted ultra vires the company's objects clause, but this is not likely to be an issue nowadays.

[105] IA 1986 s.57(2).

extent of his liability.[106] If the company's funds are unlikely to cover this indemnity, the receiver may request an indemnity from the floating charge holder before he enters into the contract.

As regards contracts in existence before the receiver was appointed, they may continue in existence[107] but the receiver will not be liable in respect of those contracts.[108] This means that if the receiver chooses to make the company break those contracts he will not be liable, and it will probably not be worthwhile for the other party to the contract to sue the company in receivership. However, there have been cases in England where the other party to the contract has attempted to take out an injunction to prevent the receiver making the company dishonour a contract.[109] The general view is that if honouring the contract would not make any difference to the receiver's ability to realise the company's assets at the best price, the contract should be allowed to continue. In one Scottish case, what the other party wanted the company in receivership to do was an impossibility, and so no interdict could force the company to do it.[110]

15–38   There are special provisions with regard to the employees of a company in receivership. Following the Insolvency Act 1994, a receiver is only the agent of the company in relation to the adoption of any employment contracts in the carrying out of his functions as a receiver and is therefore not personally liable for the employment contracts of employees whose contracts were in existence prior to the receivership,[111] but he does become personally liable to the extent of a "qualifying liability" for the employment contracts of those employees whose contracts he adopts after the onset of receivership either formally or after a period of 14 days, during which time the receiver can make up his mind whether or not to adopt the contracts.[112] A qualifying liability is a liability to pay wages, salary or contributions to a pension scheme, is incurred while the receiver is in office, and is in respect of services rendered wholly or partly after (but not before) the adoption of the contract by the receiver.[113] In

---

[106] IA 1986 s.57(3).

[107] In practice many contracts will have a clause that automatically terminates the contract in the event of the appointment of a receiver.

[108] IA 1986 s.57(4).

[109] *Airline Airspares Ltd v Handley Page Ltd* [1970] 1 All E.R. 29; *Freevale Ltd v Metrostore Ltd* [1984] 1 All E.R. 495; *Ash Newman Ltd v Creative Devices Research Ltd* [1991] B.C.L.C. 403.

[110] *Macleod v Alexander Sutherland Ltd*, 1977 S.L.T. (Notes) 44.

[111] IA 1986 s.57(1A).

[112] IA 1986 s.57(2), (5). The point of the legislation was that if receivers became liable for all employment claims from the original date of commencement of the employee's employment, as opposed to those claims with effect from the dates that receivers adopted the employee's contract, receivers would not be in a position to rescue companies as all their efforts would end up being diverted into satisfying employees' claims. Accordingly the 14 day rule was adopted, which is perhaps unfortunate for some employees, but equally gives a chance for the rest of the business (and its employees) to survive.

[113] IA 1986 s.57(2A).

Lindop v Stewart Noble & Sons Ltd,[114] Lindop, the former managing director of a company in receivership, was dismissed despite having had his contract adopted. He claimed that the damages for his dismissal should entitle him to a higher claim than his mere qualifying liability, but it was held that though he was entitled to his qualifying liability, he was not entitled to any more except as an unsecured creditor.

When the receiver does become personally liable for an employment contract, he is able to indemnify himself out of the company's assets.[115]

The receiver as collector of preferential debts

Out of the assets gathered in by the receiver in satisfaction of the **15–39** floating charge, he must pay himself and his expenses, and the preferential creditors, thus giving himself and them a prior right to funds before the floating charge holder. Preferential debts can be found at the IA 1986 s.386(1) and Sch.6. The main ones, until September 15, 2003, used to be PAYE on employees' wages for the last six months, VAT for the last six months, various other taxes, social security and pension contributions, and wages to employees of up to £800 for the last four months. Since that date, the date of coming into force of the Enterprise Act 2002, the taxes, customs duty and national insurance contributions and other sums due to the Government no longer are preferential debts. This effectively means that the main preferential creditors are the employees, up to £800 per head.[116] If there are insufficient funds to go round, the preferential creditors abate their claims proportionally, though the receiver gets his fees and expenses first—otherwise he would not do the work.[117]

The disbursal of the sums gathered in by the receiver

Of the sums the receiver gathers in, he must first pay his own creditors' **15–40** fees and expenses, and then his own fees and expenses. After that he pays the preferential creditors as above. Once these have all been paid, the floating charge holder gets what he is due.[118] If there are other postponed receivers, they have what is left over,[119] in accordance with any ranking agreement, if there is one, or if not, in date order of priority. If there is a surplus, it is handed back to the company so that it may keep on trading with it if the company is still solvent and not in liquidation. If the company is in liquidation, it is handed to the liquidator. If there is a shortfall in the sums due to the floating charge holder, the floating charge holder is an unsecured creditor to that extent in the liquidation.

The receiver will not generally have any dealing with assets secured by

---

[114] *Lindop v Stewart Noble & Sons Ltd*, 1999 S.C.L.R. 889. See also Lewis, "Lindop is back" (1999) 7 Insolv. L. 303.
[115] IA 1986 s.57(3).
[116] If a bank lends money for the employees' wages, that too counts as a preferential debt. See IA 1986 Sch.6.
[117] Unless the charge holder guaranteed his fees.
[118] IA 1986 s.60.
[119] IA 1986 s.60(2).

prior-ranking fixed securities and so will not receive any sums in respect of those assets, unless those fixed securities have been ranked behind the floating charge in a ranking agreement or otherwise. When a company goes into receivership, the fixed security holders are entitled to enter into possession and sell their secured assets, usually with the co-operation of the receiver.[120] The receiver will receive any surplus on the sale of the assets.

15-41   As regards the unsecured, non-preferential creditors, they are usually unable to obtain much satisfaction from a receivership and have to write off their losses. The receiver may not needlessly dissipate the company's assets, but he is not obliged to do much more than keep the unsecured creditors informed[121] though as indicated above a failure to exercise a duty of care may be actionable.[122] Unsecured creditors should therefore, wherever possible, try to protect their position by means of retention of title clauses, hire purchase agreements and other mechanisms whereby title does not pass to the company.[123] Unsecured creditors can always try to put the company into liquidation, which may well wreck the receiver's ability to trade the company out of any difficulties. No prescribed part needs to be set aside by the receiver in respect of unsecured creditors, because the prescribed part only applies to qualifying floating charges (i.e. floating charges created after September 15, 2003)[124] and the eight exemptions mentioned earlier.

A receiver is entitled to any assets recovered from directors by a liquidator under the IA 1986 s.212 (the misfeasance provision) since the assets were originally part of the company's assets and thus subject to the floating charge[125] assuming the charge was properly drafted to that effect.

Cross-border receiverships

15-42   A Scottish receiver can exercise his powers over English property and an English one over Scottish property, subject to the requirement that *lex situs* will apply to the disposal of any property.[126] In *Norfolk House Plc (In Receivership) v Repsol Petroleum Ltd*[127] the company had granted a fixed and floating charge which duly converted to a fixed charge, such conversion not being recognised in Scotland. The question arose as to whether the conversion amounted to a fixed charge over heritage in Scotland. It did not, but it was also held that the appointment of a receiver did cause the floating charge to attach to heritage, and by that

---

[120] Commonly the fixed charge holder and the floating charge holder will be the same lender anyway.

[121] IA 1986 ss.66, 67.

[122] *Standard Chartered Bank v Walker* [1982] 3 All E.R. 938.

[123] This is particularly unfortunate for unsecured creditors supplying services to the company—such as electricians, plumbers, and so on—who by the nature of their work are not able to impose retention of title clauses.

[124] IA 1986 s.176A(9); Insolvency Act (Prescribed Part) Order 2003 (SI 2003/2097) art.1.

[125] *Re Anglo-Austrian Printing and Publishing Union* [1895] 2 Ch. 891.

[126] IA 1986 s.72.

[127] *Norfolk House Plc (In Receivership) v Repsol Petroleum Ltd*, 1992 S.L.T. 235.

method the receiver was able to sell heritage in Scotland. A holder of a floating charge created outside the United Kingdom may appoint through the courts a receiver to deal with assets within Scotland.[128]

Methods of defeating receivership

Apart from the invalid charges referred to above, there are some **15–43** methods of defeating a receivership.

Retention of title

A supplier may be able to rely on a retention of title clause,[129] which **15–44** ensures that goods never leave the supplier's ownership until the purchasing company pays the full price. As the goods are not part of the purchasing company's assets, the receiver has no rights in the goods. Provided the goods are significantly the same, the retention of title will still apply.[130]

Goods subject to hire-purchase agreements and other conditional sale agreements, where title does not pass to the user of the goods, also cannot be caught by the receiver.

Effectually executed diligence

Subject to the overriding proviso that a receiver could apply to the **15–45** court for permission to sell or dispose of an asset over which some other creditor has a right,[131] a receiver has no power, either under the wording of the floating charge documentation or Sch.2 to the IA 1986, to deal with assets of the company that are subject to "effectually executed diligence prior to the appointment of the receiver".[132] Two cases may help elucidate this phrase. In the case of *Iona Hotels Ltd*,[133] a creditor arrested on the dependence of an action an item of a company's property but did not have the opportunity to proceed to an action of furthcoming. The company subsequently granted a floating charge. A receiver later appointed by the floating charge holder was unable to seize the arrested item since it was litigious. Whether or not this was an effectually executed diligence even though no action of furthcoming had taken place, the arresting creditor was protected as it was held that the arrested item was not encompassed within the range of assets that could be seized by the subsequent attachment of the floating charge. In the earlier case of *Lord Advocate v Royal Bank of Scotland*[134] a company had granted a floating charge. A creditor later arrested in the hands of a third party an asset of that company's, but failed to carry out an action of furthcoming before

---

[128] IA 1986 s.51, incorporating Insolvency Act 1986 Amendment (Appointment of Receivers) (Scotland) Regulations 2011 (SSI 2011/140).
[129] Sale of Goods Act 1979 s.19.
[130] *Kinloch Damph Ltd v Nordvik Salmon Farms Ltd*, 1999 S.L.T. 106; 1998 S.C.L.R. 496.
[131] IA 1986 s.61(1).
[132] IA 1986 s.55(3)(a).
[133] *Iona Hotels Ltd (In Receivership), Petitioners*, 1991 S.L.T. 11.
[134] *Lord Advocate v Royal Bank of Scotland*, 1977 S.C. 155.

the appointment of a receiver under the floating charge. The receiver successfully took possession of the asset on the grounds that an arrestment not followed up by an action of furthcoming was not effectually executed diligence. These two cases would seem to suggest that arrestment *before* the creation of a floating charge puts the arrested item out of the reach of the floating charge holder, but arrestment *after* the creation of a floating charge is only valid providing the arresting creditor has completed the action of furthcoming. This suggests that the words "effectually executed diligence" require the completion of the entire procedure for diligence for each type of diligence taking place after the creation of the floating charge.[135]

Confusingly, Sch.5 para.14 to the Bankruptcy and Diligence etc. (Scotland) Act inserts a new subs.(1B) into s.61 of the IA 1986. Its wording is as follows:

> "For the purposes of subsection (1) above, an arrestment is an effectual diligence only where it is executed before the floating charge, by virtue of which the receiver was appointed, attached to the property comprised in the company's property and undertaking."

Is there meant to be a difference between an "effectually executed diligence" and an "effectual diligence" that is executed? Does the service of an arrestment on a bank account, leading to automatic furthcoming in 14 weeks count as "effectually executed diligence"? One presumes so, but it would be good to have the matter clarified.

As regards inhibitions, an inhibition obtained over the company's property *before* the attachment of the charge will defeat the receiver.[136] This would appear to be similar to *Iona Hotels Ltd* in that the property becomes litigious. However, an inhibition taking effect after the creation[137] of a floating charge by virtue of which a receiver is appointed is not an effectual diligence.[138] The inhibitor's claim is postponed to the receiver's.

---

[135] Whether or not this is a correct interpretation of the words has been open to doubt for some time, and there is a powerful argument adumbrated by Scott Wortley in "Squaring the circle: revisiting the receiver and 'effectually executed diligence' " (2000) 5 Jur. Rev. 325, that the courts were completely mistaken in what was properly meant by "effectually executed diligence", when deciding *Lord Advocate v Royal Bank of Scotland*, 1977 S.C. 155.

[136] *Armour and Mycroft, Petitioners*, 1983 S.L.T. 453.

[137] For a pre-Enterprise Act floating charge and a qualifying floating charge, the date of creation will be the date of execution. If the (Scottish) Register of Floating Charges is ever set up, the date of creation will be the date of registration.

[138] IA 1986 s.61(1A), as inserted by the Bankruptcy and Diligence etc. (Scotland) Act 2007 s.155, with effect from April 22, 2009 (Bankruptcy and Diligence etc. (Scotland) Act 2007 (Commencement No.4, Savings and Transitionals) Order 2009 (SSI 2009/67) art.3(a)). This leaves aside the question of what is meant by "effectual diligence".

Of the other forms of diligence, such as attachment, or the proposed new forms of diligence, residual attachment, and land attachment,[139] it is also not clear at what stage in the attachment process the attachment is "effectually executed" or "effectual". All these matters may need to be reviewed, although given that there are very few receiverships now anyway, administrations increasingly being used instead, the problem in practice may not be very significant.

Prior-ranking fixed charges arising by operation of law

Apart from various possessory liens and pledge, the best known prior **15–46** ranking fixed charge arising by operation of law is the landlord's hypothec, which in the event of the debtor company's insolvency (by which term receivership is expressly included) entitles the landlord to a right in security over the tenant's *invecta et illata*[140] in respect of the current year's rent. It ranks ahead of the unsecured creditors and the receiver.[141]

The new form of "beneficial interest"

The case of *Sharp v Thomson*[142] introduced a controversial form of **15–47** ownership to Scots property law, this being beneficial interest. Due to incompetent conveyancing practice on the part of the Thomsons' lawyers, the Thomsons were allowed into a new house on the missives alone, without a recorded title, but having paid the purchase price. There has been no satisfactory explanation of why the disposition was not properly recorded in the normal manner, but before it should have been recorded, the selling company went into receivership, and the Thomsons found themselves in the unhappy position of having paid for and living in a house that now apparently belonged to the receiver. In the normal course of events the Thomsons would have been thrown out of the house and sued their solicitors. The House of Lords, taking pity on the innocent Thomsons, and possibly mindful of the potential for a roar of abuse from consumer rights organisations, said that the Thomsons had a "beneficial interest" in their home by virtue of having paid for it, and that equally the company no longer had their former interest in the house by virtue of having received payment for it. This decision effectively destroyed the integrity of the property registers,[143] since the whole point of the property registers is to provide confirmation by registration of ownership. It also reduced the scope of the receivership. The Scottish Law Commission

---

[139] It would appear at the time of writing that residual attachment and land attachment are unlikely to proceed. As regards money attachment, debtors have grown wise to this diligence and tend not to keep large quantities of cash in places where sheriff officers may be able to uplift it.

[140] This means effectively furniture and equipment, stock and other items belonging to the tenant.

[141] Bankruptcy and Diligence etc. (Scotland) Act 2007 s.208(2), (12).

[142] *Sharp v Thomson*; sub nom. *Sharp v Woolwich Building Society*, 1997 S.C. (HL) 66; 1997 S.L.T. 636; 1997 S.C.L.R. 328 HL; [1997] 1 B.C.L.C. 603; [1998] B.C.C. 115.

[143] See George L. Gretton, "The integrity of the property law and the property registers", 2001 S.L.T. (News) 135.

came up with various sensible proposals to deal with this, not just in the context of receivership but also of administration and liquidation, though at the time of writing none has been implemented.[144] These would involve greater publicity to a company's insolvency proceedings, measures to ensure that attachment could not take place unless there had been public registration of the attachment, and the abolition of the rule in s.25 of the Title to Land (Consolidation) (Scotland) Act 1868 which allows a liquidator swiftly to complete title thus depriving an innocent purchaser of the opportunity to record title. The Law Society of Scotland has also issued practice notes which effectively make the failure to register the disposition timeously a breach of professional practice. In addition, receiverships are so rare nowadays it is probably not worth changing the law for the very few people who might be affected.

Problems with receivership

15-48   The major problem with receivership is that it was unduly unfavourable for unsecured creditors, and too easily led to the death of a company and employment losses. The United Kingdom, at least until the passing of the Enterprise Act 2002, was a very secured-creditor-friendly environment, and was out of step with most other European countries where more is done to save the company if possible. The next chapter will address the law on administration which, under the Enterprise Act, is designed, amongst other things, to help unsecured creditors of a financially troubled company.

Further Reading

Donna Mckenzie Skene, *Insolvency Law in Scotland* (Edinburgh: T & T Clark, 1999).

Greene and Fletcher on The Law and Practice of Receivership in Scotland, edited by I.M. Fletcher and Roy Roxburgh, 3rd edn (Haywards Heath: Tottel, 2005).

Kerr and Hunter on Receivers and Administrators, edited by Frisby and ors, 19th edn (London: Sweet & Maxwell, 2009).

John St Clair and the Hon. Lord Drummond Young, *The Law of Corporate Insolvency in Scotland*, 4th edn. (Edinburgh: W. Green, 2011).

---

[144] Scottish Law Commission, *Report on Sharp v Thomson*. The Stationery Office, 2007. Scot. Law Com. No.208.

CHAPTER 16

ADMINISTRATION AND COMPANY VOLUNTARY ARRANGEMENTS

ADMINISTRATION

The need for administration

Companies in financial difficulties often need some skilled management **16–01** to take over from directors who may not have been up to the task. A "company doctor", parachuted in, can take an overview of what needs to be done, and can restore a company to health or at least keep it going as a viable enterprise with minimal loss to its custom and employees. Alternatively, under what used to be sometimes called the "London approach", when a large company got into difficulties, its main banker would summon a meeting of all the creditors, landlords, suppliers and anyone else significantly involved in the company, and discreetly arrange a restructuring of the company. This operated on a consensual basis and the "deal" normally was that the main banker would arrange some form of priority funding to keep the company going for the benefit of all the creditors, employees, customers and so on, but no creditor would break ranks and put the company into liquidation. If liquidation took place, everyone would stand to lose, but a restructuring might benefit most people. Independent consultants were brought in to take charge of the company and return it to health, and typically they would suggest the following:

- re-writing of contracts of key staff to persuade them to stay;
- reducing headcount;
- sale of under-performing assets or subsidiary businesses;
- outsourcing of things that could be done more cheaply or efficiently elsewhere, such as payroll, debt collection;
- moving manufacturing to lower cost areas;
- reorganisation of such areas as sales, marketing, distribution, advertising;
- sale and leaseback of premises;
- refinancing of corporate debt, perhaps turning debt into share capital; and
- improving the company's PR to get it more in the public eye.

None of this procedure had any formal basis and there was no reporting to court or need to follow complex legislation. It was effective, but it required all those involved to co-operate with each other.

Sadly, sometimes this type of arrangement is not possible, and more formal and legalistic methods of resolving a company's financial difficulties are required. The difficulty with receivership as one of these methods is that it is very advantageous for the secured creditor, but of little help to employees and unsecured creditors. In any case, since the Enterprise Act 2002 came into force, receivership is broadly only available to companies with floating charges created before September 15, 2003. Liquidation often kills the company, leaves unsecured creditors stranded, members empty-handed, and allows the defunct company to dump all its responsibilities on those least able to cope with them or on those who never anticipated having to deal with them—such as the environment, local councils or the taxpayer.

Company voluntary arrangements are a solution, but they too require considerable goodwill and are little used in Scotland.

Administration fills the gap in terms of giving a company a breathing space during which it can sort itself out. It insulates the company from its creditors temporarily while preserving the creditors' entitlements though denying the creditors, for the time being, the opportunity to enforce their rights. Administration is designed to produce a better return for everybody than the alternatives. Administrators, like receivers and liquidators, must be insolvency practitioners.[1]

The process of administration requires the completion of a number of forms for the Registrar of Companies. The requirements are indicated in its helpful booklet, "*Liquidation and Insolvency (Scotland)—GPO8s*" which is available on its website.

Old style administration retained for certain companies

16–02   Administration has been available since the Insolvency Act 1986 ("the IA 1986"), but with the advent of the Enterprise Act 2002, administration was reviewed and a new type of administration was introduced, both to replace current administration practice and to serve as the replacement for receivership under a qualifying floating charge. Confusingly, however, under the Enterprise Act 2002 s.249 old-style administration, using the former Pt II of the IA 1986,[2] has been retained for the following:

- water companies under the Water Industry Act 1991;
- railway companies under the Railways Act 1993 and Channel Tunnel Rail Link Act 1996 s.19;
- air traffic controlling companies under the Transport Act 2000;
- London Underground private public partnership companies under the Greater London Authority Act 1999; and
- building societies under the Building Societies Act 1986.

---

[1] IA 1986 Sch.B1 para.6.

[2] The rules relating to new-style administration are to be found in Sch.B1 to the IA 1986 and came into force on September 15, 2003, but the rules relating to old-style administration are to be found in what was then Pt II of the IA 1986 up until September 15, 2003.

Old-style administration is a court-based procedure, so unlike receivership it is recognised abroad.[3] One major difficulty with old-style administration was that once an old-style administration order is in place, it could defeat all other creditors, but until it was in place, a receiver and/or floating charge holder had a right of veto over an administration, thus giving floating chargeholders, generally banks, a considerable advantage and preventing what otherwise might have been a viable administration taking place. A bank holding a floating charge could veto the appointment of an administrator and appoint his own receiver instead. While this may have been acceptable when administration was first introduced, it became less so as the business climate shifted more towards a "rescue culture" which receivership did not encourage, but which administration did.

The process of old-style administration

Because old-style administration is only available for the few compa- **16–03** nies referred to in the previous paragraph, it is not dealt with here at length. Assuming a company in financial difficulty is not already in receivership or liquidation,[4] the court, on the application by petition of the company, the directors, any creditor or creditors, or any combination of the above, may apply for an administration order.[5] The court will grant an administration order if the court is satisfied that the company is not or is unlikely to be able to pay its debts and considers that the making of the order will be likely to achieve one or more of the following[6]:

(1) the survival of the company as a going concern;
(2) the approval of a voluntary arrangement;
(3) the sanctioning of a scheme of arrangement under the Companies Act 2006 ("the CA 2006") s.895; and
(4) a more advantageous realisation of the company's assets than would be effected by a company's winding up.

Applying for an old-style administration order

Before an administration order may be granted, floating charge holders **16–04** must be told of the possible administration,[7] in which event those floating charge holders may appoint a receiver,[8] thus frustrating the appointment of an administrator. Only if the court is satisfied that notwithstanding the floating charge holder's right to appoint a receiver, he is not going to do

---

[3] It is true that it is possible to have a court-based receivership, but this is rare.
[4] IA 1986 s.8(4).
[5] IA 1986 s.9.
[6] IA 1986 s.8(3).
[7] IA 1986 s.9(2).
[8] Assuming, that is, that those floating charge holders have floating charges that were created before September 15, 2003, or the company in question is within one of the eight categories of company to which old-style receivership still applies in terms of the IA 1986 ss.72B–72GA, as indeed some of them are.

so, or that the charge which might have allowed the floating charge holder to appoint a receiver would in any event have been struck down as an unfair preference,[9] gratuitous alienation[10] or an avoidable floating charge,[11] will the order be granted or the court make such other decision as it sees fit.[12]

From the moment of the presentation of the petition, creditors lose their rights to enforce any securities they may have or any other rights, such as retention of title, which they may have.[13] A creditor may still present a petition to have the company wound up, but the petition will not be granted unless the administration order petition is refused, whereupon the creditor's petition will be entertained.[14]

16–05   Once an administration order has been granted, the company may not be put into liquidation or receivership and any existing receiver demits office.[15] Creditors lose their rights of enforcement of any decrees or rights against the company though not their rights to what they are owed. Any documentation coming from the company must make it clear that it is in administration[16] and the utilities are not allowed to use administration as an excuse to cut off supplies.[17]

The administrator has extensive powers under Sch.1 to the IA 1986 to deal with the company's assets and he may seek court advice on his powers if necessary.[18] He may override existing securities or retention of title clauses[19] and sell assets otherwise subject to a charge—though the charge holder's entitlement to the value of the charged asset remains protected. He must prepare a statement of the company's assets and liabilities and order a meeting of the company's creditors if 10 per cent of the company's creditors request it or the court so orders.[20] He has extensive duties as well and must adhere to them, and so must look after the company's assets properly.[21] Within three months of his appointment he must present to the Registrar of Companies, all creditors and in due course all members of the company a statement of proposals for achieving the purposes of the administration.[22] The creditors may then vote on his proposals according to the value of their claims against the company.[23] If the creditors suggest modifications to his plan he is not

---

[9] IA 1986 s.242.
[10] IA 1986 s.243.
[11] IA 1986 s.245.
[12] IA 1986 s.9(4).
[13] IA 1986 s.10.
[14] IA 1986 s.10.
[15] IA 1986 s.11.
[16] IA 1986 s.12.
[17] IA 1986 s.233.
[18] IA 1986 s.14.
[19] IA 1986 s.15.
[20] IA 1986 s.17(3).
[21] IA 1986 s.17(2).
[22] IA 1986 s.23(1), (2).
[23] IA 1986 s.23.

obliged to accept them.[24] The administrator must make a report to the court[25] and indicate if the proposals were accepted, on which occasion the courts may if necessary discharge or otherwise vary that administration order.[26]

If the creditors or members have good grounds for complaining about the management of the administration, they may apply to court for relief.[27]

As with a receiver, an administrator is only liable to the extent of a **16–06** qualifying liability in respect of employees' wages with effect from his adoption of their contracts, and he has 14 days from the date of his appointment during which to decide whether or not to adopt their contracts without incurring liability.[28] The qualifying liability is a charge to be ranked ahead even of the administrator's own fees and expenses which otherwise form a first charge on the company's assets.[29]

As with liquidation, an administrator may make the company's officers and employees provide him with a statement of affairs about the company's affairs.[30] Assuming the proposals are accepted, commonly the administrator does what he can and fulfils his plan or proposals. He may sell off or close down parts of the company and what is left is often put into liquidation. When his purposes are fulfilled, he is discharged from his office, and the company either is saved for another day, in which case the directors would resume office, or what is left after the administration is left to be wound up[31] if that is worthwhile doing.

New-style administration under the Enterprise Act 2002

While the old-style administration was essentially a temporary measure **16–07** for sorting out some problem with the company before going on to a voluntary arrangement or a liquidation with more funds for everyone involved than would have been available on a quick winding up, the new regime permits the administrator to pay secured and unsecured creditors, but only after he has tried to rescue the company. Note that it is the company—not the business—that is to be rescued. As from September 15, 2003, unless the company in question comes within the eight exceptions stated in the IA 1986 ss.72B–724A, any company granting a floating charge must grant a new type of floating charge known as a "qualifying" floating charge. This entitles the floating charge holder to appoint a new-style administrator, whose task will be, if possible, to save the company.

---

[24] IA 1986 s.24(2).
[25] IA 1986 s.24(4).
[26] IA 1986 s.24(5).
[27] IA 1986 s.27.
[28] IA 1986 s.19(6).
[29] IA 1986 s.19(4).
[30] IA 1986 s.22.
[31] It would also be possible to have the remnant of the company dealt with by a company voluntary arrangement.

However, it is not just qualifying floating charge holders who may appoint administrators: as will be seen shortly, the company, the directors and other creditors may do so as well.

The primary aim of the new legislation

16–08   The intention of the new legislation, as its name suggests, is to encourage enterprise. It does this by making the primary task of the administrator to rescue the company, and by setting aside sums for the benefit of unsecured creditors (the "prescribed sum") out of funds that traditionally would have gone to the floating charge holder. The legislation is designed to give a lifeline to unsecured creditors so that they will not themselves go out of business when one of their major customers collapses. To help in this process the Government has renounced its position as a preferential creditor. From a floating charge holder's point of view, it has reduced his ability to obtain through a receiver all or most of a company's assets out of which to repay his loan, but the Government's renunciation of its former preferential rights has enabled, or should enable, the floating charge holders to be no worse off, at least for the time being.

The new legislation

16–09   New rules for administration were introduced by the disapplication of what was Pt II of the IA 1986 and by the insertion of a new Sch.BI to the IA 1986, with effect from September 15, 2003. The Insolvency (Scotland) Rules 1986 ("the ISR") have been amended to take account of the new provisions.

The function of the administrator

16–10   The IA 1986 Sch.B1 para.3(1) states that the administrator of a company must perform his functions in the following order of priority with the objective of:

(a) rescuing the company as a going concern;

(b) achieving a better result for the company's creditors as a whole than would be likely to be achieved if the company were wound up (without first being in administration); or

(c) realising property in order to make a distribution to one or more secured or unsecured creditors.

This task must be carried out, "in the interests of the company's creditors as a whole".[32] He is also to carry out his functions as quickly and efficiently as is reasonably practicable.[33] He is supposed to pursue objective: (a) unless he thinks that that is not reasonably practicable and that (b)

---

[32] IA 1986 Sch.B1 para.3(2).
[33] IA 1986 Sch.B1 para.4.

would be better in the interests of the company's creditors as a whole[34]; and he may only pursue objective (c) if neither (a) nor (b) is reasonably practicable and provided he does not "unnecessarily harm the interests of the company as a whole".[35]

The Government's own notes on the legislation suggest that (a) is appropriate where there is a short-term problem and where the administrator thinks the company can trade itself out of its difficulties and thereby eventually generate a greater return for its creditors; that (b) is appropriate where a going concern sale would be a better return for its creditors than a break up sale; and that (c) in practice is not much different from a winding up: the assets are sold as best they may be; there may be a part-payment to the secured creditors and the ring-fenced payment of the prescribed part to the unsecured creditors.

The benefit to the floating charge holder

Qualifying floating charge holders undoubtedly lose some of the former control that they had with old-style floating charges. They will also find that the assets of a company in administration and which would otherwise have been caught by the crystallised floating charge are reduced by the "prescribed part"[36] payable to the unsecured creditors. This loss is compensated for by the renunciation of the Crown's status as a preferential creditor. The taxpayers' loss becomes the banks' gain. **16–11**

The benefit to the directors

Administration should make no difference to the directors. They do not necessarily demit office on administration, though the administrator may remove or appoint them if he sees fit to do so.[37] An administrator does not have the automatic right to investigate fraudulent trading, wrongful trading, etc.[38] **16–12**

The benefit to the company

A skilled administrator may enable the company to survive without the need for the break-up or liquidation of the company, particularly if he uses the moratorium well. This may enable employees to retain their positions. **16–13**

---

[34] IA 1986 Sch.B1 para.3.3.
[35] IA 1986 Sch.B1 para.3.4.
[36] See para.16–34.
[37] IA 1986 Sch.B1 para.61.
[38] IA 1986 ss.212–217. Administrators could possibly obtain the right to investigate these matters by applying to court for permission to do so, but it might be easier to wait until the administration is finished and then ask the liquidator to carry out these investigations.

The position of the administrator

16–14　There will be little change from the previous position, though the administrator does now become an officer of the court.[39]

The position of unsecured creditors

16–15　The unsecured creditors should be able to get their portion of the "prescribed part" which, with a maximum of £600,000, may not always be generous, but is better than nothing. The administration in its own right may also generate a return for the unsecured creditors.

Qualifying floating charges

16–16　With effect from September 15, 2003, apart from the eight exceptions at the IA 1986 ss.72B–72GA,[40] lenders seeking security for their loans by way of a floating charge must use a new type of floating charge, known as a qualifying floating charge. This must refer to the IA 1986 Sch.B1 para.14(2) and banks changed their standard wording in floating charge documentation to reflect this. The wording must state that para.14(2) applies to the floating charge, and that it purports to "empower the holder of the floating charge to appoint an administrator". To cover the position where the holder of an old-style floating charge might wish to appoint an administrator rather than an receiver, para.14(2)(c) allows a floating charge holder to do just that.

When may a qualifying floating charge holder appoint an administrator?

16–17　A qualifying floating charge holder, to be qualified to appoint an administrator, must under para.14(3) hold one or more debentures of the company secured:

- by a qualifying floating charge which relates to the whole or substantially the whole of the company's property;
- by a number of qualifying floating charges which together relate to the whole or substantially the whole of the company's property; or
- by charges and other forms of security which together relate to the whole or substantially the whole of the company's property and at least one of which is a qualifying floating charge.

Accordingly, if the debenture holder only holds fixed charges over the company's assets, this paragraph does not apply and no administrator may be appointed. In Scotland, the word "debenture" is not a term of

---

[39] IA 1986 Sch.B1 para.5. The significance of being an officer of the court is that a higher ethical standard is expected of officers of the court than of certain other persons. Some of the less reputable insolvency professionals or corporate restructurers make a virtue of the fact that if they were appointed to sort out a company's difficult position, they would not recommend administration because it would mean that they were officers of the court, and could not therefore battle so strongly for their client's interests.

[40] See para.15–32.

law, but what is meant is a loan note or bond. A "debenture" in English law is the written acknowledgment of a loan, indicating the terms on which the loan is made.

Out of court appointment of an administrator by the qualifying floating charge holder

Assuming that the floating charge is indeed a qualifying floating **16–18** charge, the qualifying floating charge holder has the following rights under para.15 to appoint an administrator *out of court* at anytime, and without prior notice provided:

- the qualifying floating charge itself is an enforceable one[41];
- the company is not in provisional liquidation or in liquidation[42]; and
- the company is not in administrative receivership.[43]

If, however, the qualifying floating charge holder's floating charge is postponed to the charge of any prior ranking[44] floating charge holder or prior ranking qualifying floating charge holder, he must give at least two business days' written notice to the holders of any prior ranking floating charges or prior ranking qualifying floating charges.[45] Alternatively, the prior ranking charge holder (of either type) must have consented in writing to the making of the appointment of the administrator at the instance of the postponed floating charge holder.[46] If the prior ranking charge holder does not consent, he may apply for the appointment of his own choice of administrator instead. The significant point about being a prior ranking charge holder is that if the prior ranking charge holder does not object within two days, he has missed his opportunity.

The significance of the appointment *out of court* is not to be underrated. The virtue of the *out of court* procedure is that it is quick and easy and although the court needs to be informed, and prior ranking floating charge holders (of either type) need to be informed, the qualifying floating charge holder can act swiftly.

If the company is in liquidation, provisional liquidation or administrative receivership, the out of court procedure is not applicable,[47] and the

---

41 IA 1986 Sch.B1 para.16.
42 IA 1986 Sch.B1 para.17(a).
43 IA 1986 Sch.B1 para.17(b).
44 IA 1986 Sch.B1 para.15(3) explains that "prior ranking" means created earlier, or treated as having been given priority by means of a ranking agreement.
45 IA 1986 Sch.B1 para.15(1)(a).
46 IA 1986 Sch.B1 para.15(1)(b).
47 IA 1986 Sch.B1 para 25. The Deregulation Bill 2014 (if enacted) proposes to introduce a s.25A to clarify that the prohibition on appointing an administrator when a winding-up petition has been presented and not disposed of applies only to a petition for winding-up presented before an interim moratorium comes into effect.

qualifying floating charge holder would have to go to court[48] (of which more later) to obtain the appointment.

Notice of appointment

16–19   The qualifying floating charge holder, once he has appointed his administrator under para.14 must lodge in triplicate with the court a notice of appointment. Under para.18(2) the notice of appointment must include the following:

- a statutory declaration by the qualifying floating charge holder making the appointment stating that he is a qualifying floating charge holder;
- a statement that each floating charge being relied on is enforceable; and
- a statement that the appointment is in accordance with Sch.B1 to the IA 1986.

Under para.18(3) the administrator himself must provide a statement indicating:

- that he consents to the appointment;
- details of any previous professional relationships with the company to which he will be appointed administrator; and
- his opinion that the purpose of the administration is reasonably likely to be achieved.

The court, on receipt of these documents will apply its seal to them and endorse them with the date and time, returning two copies to the applicant, one of which is for the administrator. Under ISR r.2.12 there are mechanisms to enable the application to be made to court by fax if the court is closed. The fax number is available on the Insolvency Service website. There needs to be good reason for using the fax procedure and it must be followed up that day or the next working day for sealing and endorsement by the court.

Appointment by the court of an administrator at the instance of the qualifying floating charge holder

16–20   It could be that there is some defect in the qualifying floating charge documentation, whereby out of court appointment is not possible. Alternatively, an administrator may need to show some sceptical foreign judiciary that he is properly appointed. In this case, under para.10 there is a power for a qualifying floating charge holder to obtain an order from the courts for the appointment of the administrator. There is no need to prove that the company cannot pay its debts (as would be the case if a

---

[48] Under IA 1986 Sch.B1 paras 10, 37.

creditor were petitioning for administration) but the qualifying floating charge holder would still need to be qualified to appoint an administrator under para.14.

Secondly, if a creditor, the company or the directors had applied to court for the administration of the company under para.22, the holder of a qualifying floating charge may go to court to have his own administrator appointed, unless the court thinks otherwise.[49]

Thirdly, if the company is wound up by order of the court, the qualifying floating charge holder may go to court and apply for administration instead.[50]

Fourthly, it would be possible for the qualifying floating charge holder under para.12(1)(c) to apply to the court for an order for the appointment of an administrator if the company was unable, or was likely to be unable, to pay its debts, and if the administration order was reasonably likely to be able to achieve the purpose of administration.[51] However, where the company is in receivership the qualifying floating charge holder may not ask the court to put the company into administration unless the receivership is flawed by being, say voidable under the IA 1986 s.245 (invalidity of certain floating charges) or ss.242–243 (gratuitous alienations and unfair preferences),[52] or the floating charge holder who appointed the receiver agrees to discharge the receiver and have an administrator instead.[53]

If the court does permit the floating charge holder to appoint his own administrator under any of the above four circumstances, the appointment can be made there and then by the court or such other time as the court sees fit.[54]

Out of court appointment by the company or its directors under para.22

The rules applicable to the company's appointment and the directors' **16–21** appointment for an administrator are much the same. In each case either the members or the directors will be of the view that administration is the solution to the company's problems. It is not permissible for an administrator to be appointed by either the company or its directors if:

- the application is within a period of 12 months from the end of a previous administration[55];
- the application is within a period of 12 months from the end of a company voluntary arrangement[56];

---

[49] IA 1986 Sch.B1 para.36.
[50] IA 1986 Sch.B1 para.37.
[51] IA 1986 Sch.B1 para.11.
[52] IA 1986 Sch.B1 para.39(1)(b), (c).
[53] IA 1986 Sch.B1 para.39(1)(a).
[54] IA 1986 Sch.B1 para.13(2).
[55] IA 1986 Sch.B1 para.23.
[56] IA 1986 Sch.B1 para.24.

- a petition for the winding up of the company has been presented but not yet disposed of[57];
- a petition for administration has been made but not yet disposed of[58]; or
- an administrative receiver is in office.[59]

The purpose of the first two prohibitions is to prevent administration being used as a quick and easy way of fending off creditors whenever life gets difficult for a company. In a manner similar to a qualifying floating charge holder's out of court application, the company or its directors must give notice of the application to anyone who may be entitled to appoint an administrative receiver or to a qualifying floating charge holder—but the notice in this case is of at least five days. The notice, which is a notice of intention to appoint an administrator, must also be sent to:

- anyone entitled to appointed a receiver[60];
- any qualifying floating charge holder[61];
- any supervisor of a company voluntary arrangement[62]; and
- the company itself if it has not made the application[63].

A copy of the notice of intention to appoint must also be sent to the court, accompanied by a statutory declaration made by the person giving notice of intention to appoint, and made within five business days before the filing of the notice with the court.[64] Under para.27(2) the statutory declaration must state that:

- the company is or is likely to be unable to pay its debts;
- the company is not in liquidation;
- the appointment is outside the 12 month time limits specified above.

If the company has applied for the administration order, the copy resolution approving the application must be produced; if the directors have applied, their board resolution must be produced.[65] The court must see these resolutions.

The administrator cannot be appointed until the five-day period has expired or those who have received notice of the intended appointment

---

[57] IA 1986 Sch.B1 para.25(a).
[58] IA 1986 Sch.B1 para.25(b).
[59] IA 1986 Sch.B1 para.25(c).
[60] IA 1986 Sch.B1 para.26(1)(a).
[61] IA 1986 Sch.B1 para.26(1)(b).
[62] IA 1986 Sch.B1 para.27 and ISR r.2.13(2)(a).
[63] ISR r.2.13(2)(b). The Deregulation Bill 2014 proposes to do away with these four requirements on the grounds that they are time-consuming and unnecessary.
[64] ISR r.2.20(3).
[65] ISR r.2.15.

have consented to the appointment.[66] Even so, the appointment must then be made within a total of 10 days from the date of filing of the notice of appointment with the court.[67] Under para.29, once the appointment has been made, the person making the application must then file the notice of appointment with the court in triplicate together with the administrator's written consent (confirming his consent to appointment), details of any prior professional relationship with the company and his opinion that it is reasonably likely that the purpose of the administration will be achieved[68] and the written consent of all those who consented to the appointment as above.[69]

As before, the court will certify the notices of appointment, noting the date and time.[70]

Appointment of an administrator by the court at the behest of the creditors, the company or its directors.

An old-style non-qualifying floating charge holder who did not wish to **16–22** put the company into receivership might wish to obtain an order from the courts for the appointment of an administrator. For an unsecured creditor, the only way that it could put the company into administration is through the courts[71]—though it is arguable that most creditors would go straight for liquidation, and then it would be open to any qualifying floating charge holders to appoint an administrator over the head of the petitioning creditor. The company itself may apply to court for the appointment, as may the directors, under para.12(1), but in each case the court must be satisfied that the company is or is likely to become unable to pay its debts, and that the administration order is reasonably likely to achieve the purpose of administration.[72]

The process of application to the court

The applicant (usually an elected or chosen representative of the **16–23** company, the directors, the creditors, etc.) will complete the relevant application form. The proposed administrator will complete a form indicating his acceptance of the appointment, disclosing any details of prior professional relationship with the company about to go into administration and giving his opinion that it is likely that the purpose of the administration will be achieved.[73]

The applicant must provide a statement of the applicant's belief in the company's inability to pay its debts (except where the applicant is a qualifying floating charge holder under para.35, in which case the

---

[66] IA 1986 Sch.B1 para.28(1).
[67] IA 1986 Sch.B1 para.28(2).
[68] IA 1986 Sch.B1 para.29(3) and ISR r.2.23(2)(b).
[69] ISR r.2.16(3).
[70] ISR r.2.18.
[71] IA 1986 Sch.B1 para.12(1)(c).
[72] IA 1986 Sch.B1 para.11.
[73] ISR r.2.2(2).

company's inability to pay its debts is not an issue to be considered)[74] and an affidavit outlining the company's financial position . If there is an extra-territorial element (i.e. EU insolvency regulations are applicable), this must be explained.[75] The forms are filed with the court and a date for the hearing will be organised. Copies are then served on all those who might have an interest in the hearing (administrators, liquidators, receivers, creditors petitioning for winding up, the company, supervisors under a CVA and others).[76] The court will then hold the hearing and grant or dismiss the application, make the order appointing the administrator, make an interim order, wind up the company or make such other order as it thinks appropriate.[77]

The practice of new-style administration

Moratorium

16–24   The effect of the court order for the appointment of an administration, or out of court appointment by the qualifying floating charge holder, the company, or the directors, of an administrator is that once the administrator is appointed, there is a moratorium[78] on both insolvency proceedings (subject to certain exceptions)[79] and any other legal process, save with the consent of the administrator or the court.[80]

There are also provisions for interim moratoria if necessary should there be a delay in the granting of the court order or the process of application. This also prevents insolvency proceedings (with the exception of a public interest petition under the IA 1986 s.124A and a FSA petition) and any other enforcement, execution or distress against the company.[81] Broadly speaking the courts are reluctant to lift the moratorium unless this will cause significant loss to the claimant or the claimant is effectively having to subsidise the administration of the company for the unsecured creditors.[82]

---

[74] ISR r.2.4(1).
[75] ISR r.2.2(3).
[76] IA 1986 Sch.B1 para.13 and ISR r.2.3(1).
[77] IA 1986 Sch.B1 para.13(1).
[78] A moratorium is a period during which creditors may not enforce their claims, although the claims themselves remain extant.
[79] Such as a public interest petition under IA 1986 s.124A or an FSA petition as above (s.42(4)).
[80] IA 1986 Sch.B1 paras 42, 43.
[81] IA 1986 Sch.B1 para.44.
[82] *Re Atlantic Computer Systems Plc* [1992] Ch. 505. See also *Scottish Exhibition Centre Ltd v Mirestop Ltd*, 1993 S.L.T. 1034. Criminal proceedings may also be precluded by the moratorium, in the absence of leave: *Re Rhondda Waste Disposal Ltd (In Administration)* [2001] Ch. 57.

Publicity for the appointment of the administrator

Once the administrator is appointed, he must ensure that all future **16–25** business documentation from the company states that the company is in administration[83] and under para.46 must as soon as reasonably practicable send a notice of his appointment to all the creditors. Also as soon as reasonably practicable the administrator must obtain a "statement of affairs" about the company from any officers of the company or any employees (whether by contract of service or contract for services)[84] all within 11 days of being asked to supply the information (though the period may be extended if necessary).[85] Those who do not co-operate without good cause with the administrator may suffer criminal penalties.[86] The information should give particulars of the company's property, debts, liabilities, creditors, securities given and any other useful information.[87] If the administrator thinks that open disclosure of all or some part of the statement of the company's affairs might be prejudicial to the conduct of the administration, he may go to court to obtain an order permitting him not to file the relevant statement or the part thereof with the Registrar of Companies.[88] Creditors may, however, challenge such permission for cause shown.[89]

The administrator's proposals

The administrator is required to produce proposals which will satisfy **16–26** at least one of the three statutory purposes of administration in terms of para.3(1). The proposals must be sent to the company's creditors, members and the Registrar of Companies normally no later than eight weeks after the company has entered into administration.[90] Rule 2.25(1) contains a list of the items that must be contained in the statement, namely much information about the company and its directors, a summary of the problems that gave rise to administration, a summary of the statement(s) of the company's affairs, a list of the creditors, information about the administrator's remuneration, the extent of the prescribed part potentially available to unsecured creditors, how the administrator sees the purpose of the administration being achieved, how the company has been managed since administration, the reasons for any disposal of assets, and any other information which the administrator believes will help creditors to decide whether or not to vote for the adoption of his proposals. The administrator will have his own views which of the statutory purposes under para.3(1) he should adopt. These were that the administrator of a company must perform his functions with the objective of:

---

[83] IA 1986 Sch.B1 para.45.
[84] IA 1986 Sch.B1 para.47(3).
[85] IA 1986 Sch.B1 para.48.
[86] IA 1986 Sch.B1 para.48(4).
[87] IA 1986 Sch.B1 para.47(2).
[88] ISR r.22.1.
[89] ISR r.2.22(4).
[90] IA 1986 Sch.B1 para.49.

- rescuing the company as a going concern, which failing
- achieving a better result for the company's creditors as a whole than would be likely to be achieved if the company were wound up (without first being in liquidation), which failing
- realising property in order to make a distribution to one or more secured or unsecured creditors.

The administrator's decision must be explained in the proposals.[91] If a rescue under (a) is chosen, the administrator may recommend a scheme of arrangement under the CA 2006 s.985 or a company voluntary arrangement.[92]

Although this is what the law requires, in practice increasingly administrators settle for a "pre-pack" which is where the administrators sell what is left of the business to people whom they have sounded out beforehand. This is discussed shortly.

The creditors' view of the proposals

16–27   The creditors are invited to a creditors' meeting to discuss the proposals; this should normally be held within 10 weeks of the company's entering administration.[93]

There is no need to have a creditors' meeting if:

- the creditors can be paid in full;
- there are only funds available for secured creditors and for the prescribed part for the unsecured creditors; or
- company rescue is not possible and administration would not produce any more funds than a winding up.[94]

Despite this, creditors holding 10 per cent of the company's total debts may requisition a meeting if necessary.[95] It is possible to hold meetings by correspondence.[96] If a meeting is held, the administrator presides over the meeting. The creditors consider the administrator's proposals and either approve them or approve them with any modifications to which the administrator consents.[97] Voting is by majority[98] and the result must be communicated to the court.[99] If the creditors reject the proposals, this too must be reported to the court and the court has considerable discretion as to what to do next (such as wind up the company, remove the administrator, etc.). Revisions to the proposals may be entertained provided suitable notice is given to the creditors[100] and there should be regular

---

[91] IA 1986 Sch.B1 para.49(2).
[92] IA 1986 Sch.B1 para.49(3).
[93] IA 1986 Sch.B1 para.51(2).
[94] IA 1986 Sch.B1 para.52(1).
[95] IA 1986 Sch.B1 para.52(2)–(4).
[96] ISR r.2.28.
[97] IA 1986 Sch.B1 para.53.
[98] ISR r.2.27(2).
[99] IA 1986 Sch.B1 para.53(2).
[100] ISR r.2.34.

progress reports on the conduct of the administration to the creditors.[101] The administrator may be advised, if he chooses, by a creditors' committee under para.57 and the ISR r.2.36, but the rules are silent as to the extent to which he is bound by the creditors' committees' decisions.

The administrator's powers and duties

The administrator, acting as agent for the company[102] has considerable **16–28** powers to "do anything expedient for the management, affairs, business and property of the company",[103] and under the IA 1986 Sch.1 he has extensive powers identical to those used by a receiver. These include the following:

- he may remove and appoint directors[104];
- he is required within six months of the onset of administration to report to the Secretary of State any matters relating to potential disqualification of any of the company's directors in terms of the Company Directors' Disqualification Act 1986 s.7(3)(c);
- he may investigate antecedent transactions and apply to the court to redress any gratuitous alienations, transactions at an undervalue,[105] unfair preferences,[106] extortionate credit transactions[107] and improper floating charges[108]; and
- he may dispose of company assets subject to a floating charge.[109]

As regards disposing of the company's assets subject to a floating charge, the charge holder's rights are transferred to the proceeds of sale or the new assets acquired, so that the floating charge holder is no worse off.

The sale by the administrators of assets subject to a fixed charge or to a hire purchase agreement needs the consent of the court.[110] In this context hire purchase agreement includes a conditional sale agreement, chattel leasing agreement and retention of title agreement.[111] The court will give consent for this, but only where it is necessary for the promotion of the purpose of the administration.[112]

One difficulty for the administrator is that the process of preparing proposals, writing to creditors, and having a meeting all within 10 weeks is quite burdensome; and in the meantime a commercial opportunity to have a quick sale of the company's assets may be lost. Normally it would

---

[101] ISR r.2.38.
[102] IA 1986 Sch.B1 para.69.
[103] IA 1986 Sch.B1 para.59.
[104] IA 1986 Sch.B1 para.61.
[105] IA 1986 s.242.
[106] IA 1986 s.243.
[107] IA 1986 s.244.
[108] IA 1986 s.245; *Power v Sharp Investments Ltd* [1993] B.C.C. 609; [1994] 1 B.C.L.C. 111.
[109] IA 1986 Sch.B1 para.70.
[110] IA 1986 Sch.B1 para.72.
[111] IA 1986 Sch.B1 para.111.
[112] IA 1986 Sch.B1 para.72(2).

be necessary to have a creditors' meeting first to approve this. However, *Re T & D Industries Plc*[113] deals with this point and Neuberger J. (as he then was) gave seven principles that may be used to help administrators:

- normally a creditors' meeting should be held;
- sometimes as administrators will have to make swift decisions, and that is a job for them and not the courts; equally the courts cannot be used a "sort of bomb shelter";
- administrators should not take advantage of the creditors, but where possible some consultation should be made, particularly with the major creditors;
- application to court may well be necessary if, say, creditors do not agree with their proposed plans, or guidance is needed on some matter;
- even if there is an application to court, the courts would be very likely to expect some degree of consultation between the parties, and the courts would not make any administrative or commercial decisions;
- the courts if necessary could order a creditors' meeting to be held at short notice; and
- if an administrator does sell all the company's assets without a creditors' meeting, it makes a subsequent meeting slightly pointless.

The effect of this is that if a quick sale is necessary it may be done, but it should be carefully thought about in the light of the above, and if the decision that administrator makes is not reasonable under the circumstances, he may be liable for breach of his duty to the company. His actions are open to challenge anyway under para.74, which allows any creditor or member of the company to apply to court if he thinks that the administrator proposes to act, has acted or is acting in such a way as to unfairly harm the applicant's interests, or is not performing his actions as quickly or as efficiently as possible. Paragraph 75 also allows the court, creditors, official receiver, liquidator, administrator and others to examine the conduct of the administrator (or any purported administrator) if he has breached his duty to the company; and if found liable he must compensate the company for its loss or restore assets to the company.

A further duty for the administrator is that he is expected to complete his administration within 12 months[114] though this may be extended if necessary under procedures outlined in that paragraph, either by the court or by consent of the creditors.

---

[113] *Re T & D Industries Plc* [2000] B.C.C. 956.
[114] IA 1986 Sch.B1 para.76(1).

The administrator's own remuneration

The rules for the administrator's own remuneration are shown in the **16–29** Insolvency (Scotland) Rules 1986 Ch.8. His remuneration and expenses are payable out of property of which he had custody or control before he ceases to hold office and are paid in priority to payment to any floating charge holder.

The administrator's contracts

Continuing contracts

The administrator is the agent of the company[115] though the company **16–30** is not at liberty to terminate the appointment. He is not personally liable on contracts that he continues on behalf of the company. If he decides not to pay what is due under continuing contracts, the moratorium prevents the contractors enforcing rights against the company without going to court; the contractors could bring an action under para.74 saying that he was unfairly harming their interests; or they may refuse to do any more work. If he does pay them, and if they are treated as administrator's expenses, they will be an allowable expense of the administration. Many contracts provide that if a company goes into administration, the contract automatically terminates anyway.

New contracts

An administrator does not incur personal liability on new contracts **16–31** entered on behalf of the company. However, contracts that he makes the company enter into in the course of his administration are allowable expenses of the administration in priority to paying the administrator himself.[116]

Employment contracts

An administrator incurs no personal liability on an adopted contract of **16–32** employment. If an administrator keeps an employee on for more than 14 days after the start of the administration, the administrator is deemed to have adopted the contract of employment.[117] The administrator may of course if he chooses adopt the contract before that time. The employee is thereupon entitled to his wages and salary with effect from the adoption of his employment[118] and these may be paid out of assets subject to a floating charge in priority to the administrator's own remuneration and expenses.[119] "Wages and expenses" mean holiday pay, illness pay, sums in lieu of holiday, certain sums treated as earnings in respect of holiday pay and illness in connection with social security requirements, and

---

[115] IA 1986 Sch.B1 para.69.
[116] IA 1986 Sch.B1 para.99(4).
[117] IA 1986 Sch.B1 para.99(5)(a).
[118] IA 1986 Sch.B1 para.95(5)(b).
[119] IA 1986 Sch.B1 para.99(4)(b).

contributions to occupational pension schemes.[120] However, the administrator is not responsible for payments from before he adopted the contracts of employment.

Employees may also be entitled to certain payments (up to £800) in their position as preferential creditors. It would appear, following *Allders Department Stores*[121] that redundancy payments do not count as necessary disbursements under the Insolvency Rules r.2.67(1)(f)[122] giving them a priority over the other items referred to, such as the administrator's fees, corporation tax arising out of chargeable gains on the realisation of any assets of the company, and the fees of those employed by the administrator.

The termination of the administration

16–33   Paragraph 65 permits the administrator to act as a liquidator and make payments to preferential creditors and/or secured creditors, and may make payment to unsecured creditors with the court's approval, if it will help the purpose of the administration. The "relevant" date under the new rules is the date the company entered into liquidation by whichever method. Payment is subject to the IA 1986 s.175 (the main provision about payment of preferential debts and their equal ranking).

Payment to the creditors

16–34   On the assumption that creditors are satisfied with the administrator's proposals, and there are funds in the administrator's hands which are designed for the creditors, the administrator will pay the preferential creditors what they are due and then must pay the unsecured creditors their "prescribed part". The prescribed part, referred to in the IA 1986 s.176A(3)(a), is to be found in the Insolvency Act 1986 (Prescribed Part) Order 2003,[123] and is as follows:

- where the company's net property is less than £10,000, the prescribed part is 50 per cent of that property;
- where the company's net property is more than £10,000, the prescribed part is 50 per cent of the first £10,000's worth of property;
- 20 per cent of the remainder in excess of that first £10,000's worth of property; and
- all subject to a maximum overall prescribed part of £600,000.

If the company's net property is less than £10,000, and the administrator believes that the cost of making a distribution to the unsecured creditors would be greater than its benefits, the payment to the unsecured creditors

---

[120] IA 1986 Sch.B1 para.99(6).
[121] *Re Allders Department Stores (In Administration)* [2005] B.C.C. 289.
[122] The Scottish equivalent is ISR r.4.67, with the wording being, "any outlays properly chargeable or incurred".
[123] Insolvency Act 1986 (Prescribed Part) Order 2003 (SI 2003/2097).

need not be made.[124] The administrator may also apply to the court if necessary to seek approval for non-payment on those grounds.[125] Net property in these circumstances means all the property that would otherwise be available to a qualifying floating charge holder if the prescribed part did not exist.[126] Only after the prescribed part has been paid may the qualifying floating charge holder start to receive what he is due. This may exhaust the funds in the administrator's hands.

In *Re Airbase International Services Ltd*[127] a creditor with the benefit of a security over assets of the company, and whose realisation of the security failed to repay him the sums due to him, attempted to get a second bite of the cherry by claiming as a creditor under the prescribed part. This was not held to be permissible. A similar decision arose in *Re Permacell Finesse Ltd*.[128] However, In *Liquidators of PAL SC Realisations 2007 Ltd v Inflexion Fund 2 Limited Partnerships*,[129] floating chargeholders whose charge was worthless released their charge, successfully enabling them to apply as unsecured creditors and to claim their share of the prescribed part.

Entering into a creditors' voluntary liquidation

Alternatively once the preferential creditors have received their due, **16–35** the prescribed part has been paid, and the secured creditors have received their funds, or as much as is available to them, the administrator may put the company into a creditors' voluntary liquidation under para.83, having intimated as much to creditors, the court and others. It is anticipated that the administrator will normally change hats and become the liquidator, dividing what is left of the assets, after payment of his own fees and expenses, between the unsecured creditors, having already taken account in particular of the prescribed part that will already have been paid to them and which was taken out of the net assets that would otherwise have been payable to the floating charge holder. He will then send his final accounts and return in terms of the IA 1986 s.106 and within three months the company will be dissolved.[130]

Dissolution of the company

Alternatively the administrator may, if there are no assets to be realised **16–36** for unsecured creditors, go straight into dissolution of the company under para.84. The company is then dissolved as above.

---

[124] IA 1986 s.176A(3)(a), (b).
[125] IA 1986 s.176A(5).For an example of this taking place, see *Stephen and Hill, joint administrators of QMD Hotels Ltd* [2010] CSOH 168.
[126] IA 1986 s.176A(6).
[127] *Re Airbase International Services Ltd* [2008] EWHC 124 Ch.
[128] *Re Permacell Finesse Ltd* [2008] B.C.C. 208.
[129] [2010] EWHC 2850 (Ch); [2011] B.C.C. 93.
[130] IA 1986 s.201(2).

Rescue achieved

16–37   It is in addition possible for an out of court appointed administrator to decide that the purpose of the administration has been achieved and that, say, the company has been rescued or no further action needs to be taken. Under para.80, and the ISR r.2.45 the administrator lodges the requisite form and a final progress report with the court, and tells all the creditors of this. The administration then comes to an end. If the company has been successfully rescued, alternative options are for a company voluntary arrangement to deal with the process of repaying the creditors in an agreed manner, or possibly a scheme of arrangement under the CA 20065 s.895.

Rescue mission failed

16–38   Equally, the administrator may be of the view that the purpose of the administration cannot be achieved, or that the company should not have entered into administration. He can then apply to the court for the termination of the administration.[131] This would generally be followed by a petition for winding up under the IA 1986 s.124. Likewise a creditor, if he believes that the administrator is acting improperly, may apply to court for termination of the administration,[132] and the administration may also be terminated by means of a winding up in the public interest under the IA 1986 s.124A or a petition by the FSA in terms of the Financial Services and Markets Act 2000 s.367.

Prepacks

16–39   Many companies are well aware that they are in financial difficulties before they opt for administration. Prudent directors will have been looking at the options other than liquidation and within the last few years an increasingly common remedy is the "prepack". A prepack is the swift sale by the administrator of the business to people who have been set up beforehand to buy the business. In the run-up to administration it is quite usual for the company or its bankers to invite insolvency practitioners to look over the company to see what can be salvaged. The insolvency practitioners will sound out what interest there might be in someone buying the business.[133] Acting under conditions of considerable secrecy and discretion, potential buyers are approached, due diligence quietly carried out, confidentiality letters signed, new funders put in place and if a suitable purchaser is found, a draft contract may be drawn up. When everything is ready, the company or its bankers will appoint an administrator who, acting under the powers indicated above, will then swiftly

---

[131] IA 1986 Sch.B1 para.79 and ISR r.2.46.

[132] IA 1986 Sch.B1 para.81.

[133] Cobra beer has achieved the considerable feat of having been through four administrations, being sold on in each case.

sell the worthwhile parts of the business to the purchaser who has been waiting in the wings, while leaving the worthless parts of the business in the now collapsed company. The advantages of this are the following:

- the purchaser takes over the business free of the company's liabilities;
- the price should reflect full going concern value as the company is still operational;
- the employees will keep their jobs;
- suppliers still have a customer;
- the company keeps the goodwill of the business;
- the name of the company may be retained without falling foul of the phoenix trading rules[134];
- creditors may continue to get paid;
- customers still can obtain their products; and
- the proceeds of sale are paid to the administrator to be distributed properly, as opposed to being left to the whim of the directors.

Points to note about are prepack are that quite often the purchasers are the directors of the company now in administration. This is not necessarily a bad thing, as the amount of due diligence is minimal, and the directors may be best placed to make a quick offer.

One of the main negotiating tools of the administrator is to point out to creditors that they have a choice: they could put the company into liquidation, which would be time-consuming and not necessarily guarantee much of a repayment; or they could cut their losses, agree to do business with the people who buy out the company's business, and that way still continue to receive their products, supply their raw materials, obtain rent or continue a good business relationship. Liquidation benefits few people, whereas a prepack benefits most people.[135]

The main disadvantage of the prepack is that some liabilities remain in the now defunct company, which means that some creditors are left stranded, in particular lenders and HM Revenue and Customs.[136] They are in a difficult position, because quite commonly they are the largest creditors, and have most to lose. On the other hand, if a prepack saves jobs, that in its own right is a desirable objective and it would not reflect well on HM Revenue and Customs if in order to recoup money for the taxpayer it deprived a large number of employees of jobs. There are sometimes complaints that insolvency practitioners, in their zeal for carrying out the deal, and to get their own fees, do not test the market fully enough and are content to sell to those who have already indicated

---

[134] Insolvency (Scotland) Rules 1986 (SI 1986/1915), rr.4.78–4.82.

[135] The prepack does not need to be the best price if it is the best deal: *Re Hellas Telecommunications (Luxembourg) SA* [2011] B.C.C. 295.

[136] In *DKLL Solicitors v HM Revenue and Customs* [2007] EWHC 2067 the judge ruled against HM Revenue and Customs saying that a prepack was a valid course of action, not least in the interest of preserving jobs.

their interest, and indeed sell at less than best price. Furthermore, it is sometimes alleged that they do not consult with creditors as much as some creditors think they should. On the other hand, however unsatisfactory a quick prepack may be, it is not necessarily the case that delaying matters for a possible better price later would be a better course of action.

In order to allay these fears, insolvency practitioners are required to follow a standard set of rules known as Statement of Insolvency Practice 16. This requires clear explanation to the creditors of what is taking place, the positive marketing of the company in administration for at least three days, proper valuation of assets, including intellectual property and goodwill, and overall transparency in the process.

Another disadvantage of a prepack, from a purchaser's point of view, is that insolvency practitioners will be most unlikely to give the sort of warranties that would be expected in a normal purchase of a business. The purchaser buys the business at his own risk, even if that is reflected in the price he pays for it. A purchaser needs to be alert to any TUPE provisions when taking over the employment of staff and to be alert to any covenants with lenders or landlords that may be breached on a change of ownership. Stock may be subject to retention of title agreement and sellers' approval may be required.

Is administration better than old-style receivership?

16–40   One aim of administration was to be fairer to unsecured creditors who under receivership commonly received nothing; and another was to try to keep companies going where under receivership the receiver did often not greatly care whether the company collapsed or not as long as the floating charge holder was repaid his loan. This resulted in job losses and caused consequential damage to other businesses dependent on the company in receivership. It was thought that administration, by requiring administrators actively to try to rescue the company, might make a difference to business within the United Kingdom.

As with many attempts by politicians to influence business behaviour, the legislation has worked to some extent, but not as well as might be hoped. There is a general recognition that some small businesses have benefited from the prescribed part.

Perhaps where the legislation has been less successful is in the process of maintaining the company as a going concern. The unkind view is that if a company is collapsing, because its products are not what the market wants at the price that they are being offered, no amount of administration will save it and to attempt to rescue an ailing company in that fashion is a waste of time and effort. There are those who say it should be allowed to collapse, the worthwhile parts should be sold on and the rest just put into liquidation. This is what happened with Woolworths where no buyer could be found, although the shop premises still contained some value. A second problem is that floating charges nowadays are less all-encompassing than they once were. Fifty years ago, it was not unusual for companies to own their own premises outright, without any secured loan over the heritage, and for stock and book debts to be unencumbered assets of the company. In those days, a floating charge over the company's assets was a valuable security for a lender. Nowadays, many businesses do not own their own sites; large items are often on lease agreements or other forms of asset financing; book debts are factored. It can sometimes be the case that there is not actually very much by way of assets wholly owned (without any form of security over them) to which a floating charge could usefully attach.

However, the research of Dr Sandra Frisby,[137] the leading expert in this field, suggests that the Enterprise Act and the use of prepacks have made some small beneficial differences to unsecured creditors, that returns to the banks are not greatly different from what they were before the Act was passed, but that broadly speaking jobs have been saved by the swift use of prepacks. While companies may not necessarily have been saved as going concerns, at least employees are still in work.

COMPANY VOLUNTARY ARRANGEMENTS

Voluntary arrangements are the unloved poor relations of the insolvency **16–41** methods. Insolvency practitioners are not as familiar with them as the Government might wish because voluntary arrangements tend to involve small companies and are not as financially rewarding as receiverships, administrations and liquidations where the insolvency practitioner's fees will usually be met out of the company's assets. The advantages of a voluntary arrangement are that it need not be expensive; it is relatively informal; it binds even those who have not voted in favour of it; and it may keep the company going, particularly in the light of the moratorium provisions to be discussed shortly. Compared to the use of the IA 1986 s.110 it is useful in that not every member need consent to it; compared to a s.895 scheme of arrangement it is cheap.

The practice of the voluntary arrangement without a moratorium

The directors[138] of a company in financial difficulty, but not necessarily **16–42** insolvent, may suggest to its creditors that they wish to make a "proposal" for the payment of its debts. The proposal will effectively be a rescheduling of the company's debts, in the hope that by rearranging the debts and marshalling the payments in a coherent manner all the creditors will either get more than they would otherwise, or will actually get something as opposed to getting nothing. The proposal may not, however, propose anything which may affect the right of a secured creditor to enforce his security without his consent[139] or a preferential creditor to lose his preferential right without his consent.[140] As part of the proposal a

---

[137] Reader in Commercial Law, University of Nottingham.
[138] Or indeed the liquidator or administrator (IA 1986 s.1(3)).
[139] IA 1986 s.4(3).
[140] IA 1986 s.4(5).

"nominee" will be put in charge of it. The nominee used to have to be an insolvency practitioner but now other professional bodies involved in recovery of companies may be eligible.[141] If the nominee is not already the liquidator or administrator but has been appointed by the directors, he is required within 28 days after he has been given notice of the proposal, and having received a suitable report from the directors outlining the state of the company's finances,[142] to give to the court a report indicating whether the members and the creditors should be invited to separate meetings to consider the proposal.[143] The report effectively is a statement saying whether or not the proposal is viable. If the nominee makes the report to the court, where it is filed, and indicates that the meeting should be summoned, the meetings should be convened.[144] If the nominee is the liquidator or administrator, he may summon the meetings anyway.[145] The two separate meetings may approve the report or suggest modifications. Approval is indicated by three-quarters of the creditors voting at their meeting doing so in favour of the resolution[146] and a bare majority for the members.[147] The creditors and members may both suggest modifications, but among the modifications that are not permitted are those that would affect the rights of a secured creditor without the consent of that creditor,[148] or that would affect the rights of any preferential creditor without the consent of that creditor.[149] The results of the meetings will be reported to the court. If both meetings approve, the proposal takes effect and is deemed to bind every person who was entitled to appear at the meetings[150] and if the court is in liquidation or administration at the time of the approvals, the courts may sist the liquidation or administration in order to allow the proposal to be implemented.[151] The proposal may still be challenged in the court, by a member, creditor or contributory if such a person may be unfairly prejudiced by the proposal or there has been some irregularity at the meeting[152] in which case the court may revoke the proposal or arrange further meetings to resolve the difficulty. If the members reject the proposal but the creditors accept it, strictly speaking the creditors have the right to impose their wishes on the company, subject to a right of objection to the court by any member.[153] Although this begs the question of why members are consulted at all, the reason is

---

[141] IA 1986 s.1(2).
[142] IA 1986 s.2(3).
[143] IA 1986 s.2(2).
[144] IA 1986 s.3(1).
[145] IA 1986 s.3(2).
[146] ISR r.7.12(2).
[147] ISR r.7.12(1).
[148] IA 1986 s.4(3).
[149] IA 1986 s.4(4).
[150] IA 1986 s.5(2).
[151] IA 1986 s.5(3).
[152] IA 1986 s.6. The challenge must be brought within 28 days of the arrival of the first report with the court: *Inland Revenue Commissioners v Adams and Partners Ltd* [1999] 2 B.C.L.C. 730. See also *Prudential Assurance Co Ltd v PRG Powerhouse Ltd* [2007] B.C.C. 500.
[153] IA 1986 s.4A.

that if the company is solvent, the members still have an interest in the company, and even if the company is likely to become insolvent, there is always the possibility that it may turn out solvent after all.

Once the proposal has been approved, the nominee is known as the supervisor, he reports the outcome of the meetings to the Registrar of Companies and he implements the proposal, which now becomes known as the CVA.[154] The CVA binds all creditors[155] including those who may not have voted in its favour or not turned up to the meetings to vote.[156] Commonly the proposal will include terms that prevent the creditors raising actions against the company provided the company adheres to the terms of the CVA. The CVA will stay in existence until all payments have been made or any required time limit has expired. If the CVA has not been successful, the supervisor may then petition for a winding up order or an administration order.[157] The supervisor will inform the Registrar of Companies, the court and all the creditors of the termination.[158]

Company voluntary arrangement with a moratorium

As part of the Government's attempts to introduce a rescue culture for **16–43** small businesses, and partly because CVAs were not proving popular, when the Insolvency Act 2000 was brought into force, it became open to small private companies to apply for a moratorium of 28 days (though it may be extended) from its debts, during which time the directors may put forward their proposal to a nominee for a company voluntary arrangement.[159] It is believed that the moratorium, by insulating a financially troubled company from its creditors temporarily, will enable it more easily to come forward with a coherent plan for its rescue. Certain companies in the financial world are not permitted to apply for any moratorium,[160] and neither is any company already subject to insolvency proceedings.[161] In addition to be eligible for a CVA with a moratorium the company must be a small company within the terms of the CA 2006 s.382[162] and must not be a holding company for a group of companies which is neither a small group nor a medium-sized group.[163]

The directors prepare a document outlining why they believe a moratorium in conjunction with the company voluntary arrangement would

---

[154] IA 1986 s.7.
[155] With the exception of the secured creditors and preferential creditors, who are still entitled to their respective rights unless they consent to waive or reduce them.
[156] There are rights under s.6 to challenge the proposals if there is some procedural irregularity or a member, creditor or contributory of the company is unfairly prejudiced; and under s.7(3) if any of the above is dissatisfied with any act, omission or decision of the supervisor in the implementation of the CVA.
[157] IA 1986 s.7(4)(b).
[158] ISR r.1.23
[159] IA 1986 s.1A and Sch.A1.
[160] IA 1986 Sch.A1 para.2(2) and para.4 exclude insurance companies, deposit-taking institutions, a project company in a public private partnership and certain finance or other companies with a contractual liability of more than £10 million.
[161] IA 1986 Sch.A1 para.4(1).
[162] See para.7–46.
[163] IA 1986 Sch.A1 para.3.

be useful, and the nominee gives his opinion on both the voluntary arrangement and on the continued viability of the company during the proposed moratorium.[164] If his opinion is favourable, the directors lodge with the court all the supporting documentation for their request for a moratorium, the nominee's written consent to being the supervisor, the nominee's approval of the company voluntary arrangement and moratorium, and his opinion that members' and creditors' meetings should be summoned to approve the proposed voluntary arrangement.[165] On filing all these documents with the court the moratorium will come into place[166] and lasts for 28 days, though the Secretary of State may choose to extend or shorten it if necessary[167] and the members and creditors may choose to make it last two further months.[168] The moratorium may be brought to an end by the expiry of the 28 day period, the decision of the creditors or members, by the nominee's withdrawal from acting or by the court.[169] Creditors, the court and the Registrar of Companies must all be kept informed of these extensions or cessations of the moratorium.[170]

16–44 During the moratorium, without the consent of the court no creditor may touch the company's assets, nor take any steps to enforce any rights against the company. All actions against the company are stayed except with the leave of the court.[171] The company may continue to trade in the ordinary course of business.[172] During the moratorium the nominee will continue to assess whether or not the proposed voluntary arrangement is still viable[173] and he may withdraw from acting if he thinks that it is no longer viable.[174] If it is in his view viable, he may summon meetings of the members and creditors to approve the voluntary arrangement as in an ordinary company voluntary arrangement as described above.[175]

A significant feature of the moratorium is that a company may enter a moratorium even if a floating charge holder does not want it to. Under the IA 1986 Sch.A1 para.43 any provision in a floating charge that attempts to prevent a company entering a moratorium, or causes the floating charge to crystallise if the company either starts a moratorium or takes any steps towards a moratorium is automatically void. Once the moratorium is over, the charge may crystallise—but not until then.

If the members or creditors are dissatisfied with the nominee's actions, they may apply to the court for redress.[176] As directors remain involved in

---

[164] IA 1986 Sch.A1 para.6.
[165] IA 1986 Sch.A1 para.7.
[166] IA 1986 Sch.A1 para.8(1).
[167] IA 1986 Sch.A1 para.8(8).
[168] IA 1986 Sch.A1 para.32.
[169] IA 1986 Sch.A1 para.8(6).
[170] IA 1986 Sch.A1 para.11.
[171] IA 1986 Sch.A1 paras 12–14.
[172] IA 1986 Sch.A1 para.18, but any disposals must be of benefit to the company and receive approval by a specially set up moratorium committee or if there is no committee, by the nominee.
[173] IA 1986 Sch.A1 para.24.
[174] IA 1986 Sch.A1 para.25.
[175] IA 1986 Sch.A1 paras 29–31.
[176] IA 1986 Sch.A1 paras 26, 27.

the company during the period of the moratorium, there are also powers to enable creditors or members to take action against the directors.[177]

Although CVAs with a moratorium were designed to effect a rescue culture amongst small companies, they have not been greatly used, partly because of the eligibility criteria, the potential for liability for the nominee (which makes nominees reluctant to carry out the task) and the requirement to write to all creditors, thereby alerting them to the company's financial difficulties and making them withdraw their custom. It is true that a bank cannot exercise its rights under a floating charge, but equally the company may need the bank's goodwill to survive the moratorium anyway. With the increasing use of qualifying floating charges that permit the bank to appoint an administrator instead, it is quite likely that CVAs with moratoria will be little entertained. On advantage of the CVA, never to be underestimated from a director's point of view, is that there is normally no enquiry into the director's conduct or the company's affairs. Furthermore, while the supervisor may be keeping an eye on the company, the directors do not relinquish control of the company. In these respects CVAs have much to recommend them.

Further Reading

Donna Mckenzie Skene, *Insolvency Law in Scotland* (London: Tottel, 1999).

Greene and Fletcher on The Law and Practice of Receivership in Scotland, edited by I.M. Fletcher and Roy Roxburgh, 3rd edn (Haywards Heath: Tottel, 2005).

Kerr and Hunter on Receivers and Administrators, 19th edn (London: Sweet and Maxwell, 2004).

St Clair and the Hon. Lord Drummond Young, *The Law of Corporate Insolvency in Scotland*, 4th edn (Edinburgh: W. Green, 2011).

---

[177] IA 1986 Sch.A1 para.40.

CHAPTER 17

WINDING UP

17–01 The purpose of winding up is to ensure a fair distribution of a company's assets to those who are entitled to them, in the first place to the creditors and in the second place to the members in accordance with the terms of the articles. If the process of winding up did not exist, the keener and fiercer creditors would seize all the company's assets at the expense of other more patient creditors, and there would be no opportunity for directors to have a second chance. Winding up also enables unresolved company business to be terminated in everyone's interests.

Summary of winding up procedure

17–02   In essence, when a company is wound up by whichever means:

(1) the company is put into liquidation;
(2) an (initial)[1] liquidator is appointed;
(3) creditors are invited to submit their claims;
(4) a liquidator is appointed at a meeting of the members and creditors;
(5) the liquidator gathers in the company's assets in all the permissible ways;
(6) the liquidator then pays out funds to the creditors, in full if possible, otherwise in proportion to their claims;
(7) if there are still funds, the shareholders are repaid their capital, in full if possible, otherwise in proportion to their shareholding;
(8) the liquidator applies to have the company struck off, if necessary;
(9) occasionally companies may be revived if undiscovered assets or liabilities emerge later.

It is important in liquidation that various forms and copies of resolutions are sent to the Registrar of Companies, the *Edinburgh Gazette* and the Accountant in Bankruptcy. The required forms and procedures are well explained in a booklet produced by the Registrar of Companies, entitled *Liquidation and Insolvency (Scotland)—GPO8s* and available from its website.

---

[1] The word "initial" is used here because although he will be appointed as liquidator, it is possible that he may be replaced at the creditors' meeting. The word "initial" here has no legal meaning in this context.

The distinction between a liquidator and a receiver

The liquidator can be contrasted with the receiver. The receiver is **17–03** primarily interested in the assets subject to the floating charge and in satisfying the floating charge holder under the pre-Enterprise Act 2002 rules. He is not unduly concerned about the claims of other creditors, though he should not take them lightly. The liquidator is interested in all the assets of the company, in the first place for the creditors' benefit and thereafter for the members', though he has no rights in assets subject to the prior claims of secured creditors such as standard security holders, floating charge holders or preferential creditors. The secured and pre-ferential creditors take what they are entitled to, and the liquidator gets the rest.

Liquidation triggers the attachment of a floating charge, and entitles fixed charge holders (such as standard security holders) to exercise their rights too. Where there are no charges, the liquidator may deal with all the company's assets himself, subject to the claims of any preferential creditors.

Liquidation ensures the demise of the company, though the liquidator **17–04** may sell on the business itself. This can have severe effects on employees, customers and suppliers. Receivership is not necessarily the demise of the company, since a good receiver could possibly turn the company around, repay the floating charge holder and return the operational company to the directors again, although in practice this is rare.

A liquidator has the right to challenge antecedent transactions and make the directors compensate the company for its losses. A receiver does not have this right.

A liquidator is an officer of the court, and therefore must not stoop to any "dirty tricks". This means that he can be trusted to deal with all the interests involved in a wound-up company and should not be favouring any one interest over another. For example, any assets that came into his hands in the process of winding up the company, and which properly belonged to a secured creditor, must be passed by him to the secured creditor. When a liquidator and a receiver have both been appointed to a company the rights of the receiver take precedence over those of the liquidator irrespective of whether he was appointed before or after the commencement of the winding-up, and the liquidator is bound to deliver to the receiver the property which is covered by the floating charge.[2] If he does so, the receiver is primarily liable for the payment of the secured creditors and those who have preferential claims against the company, although otherwise this would be the task of the liquidator.

Both receivers' and liquidators' appointments are registered at the Register of Insolvencies at the office of the Accountant in Bankruptcy.

---

[2] *Manley, Petitioner*, 1985 S.L.T. 42. Note also *McGuiness v Black*, 1990 S.L.T. 156 regarding the position of a judicial factor and a provisional liquidator.

The distinction between a liquidator and an administrator

17–05 As indicated above, liquidation terminates the company, whereas the whole point of administration is to salvage some of the company and where possible keep it going. An administrator once appointed is potentially able to insulate the company from its creditors, to give it a breathing space while the administrator sorts the company out, and if done well, can ensure the survival of a good deal of the company, for the benefit of all its stakeholders, in a way that is not always feasible in a liquidation.

An administrator has the right to challenge antecedent transactions[3] but not to make the directors compensate the company unless he specifically asks the court for permission to do so.

Administrators' appointments are not registered within the Register of Insolvencies at the office of the Accountant in Bankruptcy though they are shown at the Registrar of Companies.

Methods of winding up

17–06 There are three types of winding up:

- members' voluntary winding up;
- creditors' voluntary winding up; and
- compulsory winding up by the court.

Voluntary Winding Up

Provisions applicable to both types of voluntary winding up

17–07 Winding up is voluntary where the members choose to wind up the company, by ordinary resolution if the company has reached its expiry event or expiry date in terms of its articles,[4] or by special resolution.[5] Before a company passes a resolution to wind itself up voluntarily it must give written notice of the proposed resolution to the holder of any qualifying floating charge.[6] This is to enable the qualifying floating chargeholder to appoint an administrator if he so wishes. The resolution may only be passed after a period of five business days beginning with the day the notice was given, or if the person to whom the notice was given consented to the passing of the resolution.[7] Assuming the resolution is passed, the company must send a copy of the resolution to the Registrar of Companies and Accountant in Bankruptcy within 15 days[8] of the passing of the resolution, and send a copy to the *Edinburgh Gazette*

---

[3] Insolvency Act 1986 ("IA 1986") ss.242–245.

[4] IA 1986 s.84(1)(a).

[5] IA 1986 s.84(1)(b).

[6] IA s.84(2A).

[7] IA s.84(2B).

[8] IA 1986 s.84(3).

within 14 days.[9] The winding up is deemed to commence on the time of the passing of the resolution.[10] The appointment of the liquidator must be intimated to the Registrar of Companies and the *Edinburgh Gazette* within 14 days of his appointment.[11]

Once the resolution has been passed, the business of the company ceases except to the extent required to wind the company up,[12] but the company still stays in existence until it is dissolved.[13] There may be no more share transfers.[14] If for some reason no liquidator is appointed or nominated by the company the company must take steps to dispose of the company's perishable assets and safeguard the rest.[15] The liquidator's fees will always be paid out of the company's assets in priority to all other claims.[16] It should be noted that voluntary winding up does not terminate the employees' contracts of employment, although the liquidator may terminate contracts of employment if he wishes to do so.[17]

On the completion of the voluntary winding up by either method, the **17–08** liquidator may write to the Registrar of Companies with the final accounts and three months later the company will be dissolved.[18]

Members' voluntary winding up

A members' voluntary winding up means that the company is believed **17–09** to be solvent at the time of winding up and so there should be funds repayable to the members after payment in full, first to the preferential creditors and then to the other creditors.[19] The winding up is therefore primarily for the members' benefit and the members are in charge of the proceedings. As the creditors will be paid in full, creditors will not be so anxious about the procedure. If the directors believe that the company would be able to pay its debts in full within the succeeding 12 months, the directors should make a statutory declaration of solvency to that effect.[20] The declaration must be made no more than five weeks before the resolution to wind up the company[21] and forwarded to the Registrar of Companies within 15 days of the resolution. If no statutory declaration is made it becomes a creditors' voluntary winding up.[22] If it turns out that the declaration was unjustified, and the directors had no reasonable grounds for making it and the company's debts were not paid within the

---

[9] IA 1986 s.85(1).
[10] IA 1986 s.86. This may be significant when it comes to calculating the periods for the adjustment of antecedent transactions.
[11] IA 1986 s.109. The time of appointment varies according to the type of winding up.
[12] IA 1986 s.87(1).
[13] IA 1986 s.87(2).
[14] IA 1986 s.88.
[15] IA 1986 s.114.
[16] IA 1986 s.115.
[17] This is different from a compulsory winding up where the employees lose their jobs unless the liquidator keeps them on: *Laing v Gowans* (1902) 10 S.L.T. 461 OH.
[18] IA 1986 s.201.
[19] IA 1986 s.107.
[20] IA 1986 s.89(1). If the company is insolvent, the directors will not make the declaration.
[21] IA 1986 s.89(2)(a).
[22] IA 1986 s.90.

succeeding 12 months, the directors may be fined, though they will not be personally liable.[23] In addition the members' voluntary winding up will have to convert into a creditors' voluntary winding up.

17–10   At the resolution for the members' voluntary winding up, the members will appoint one or more liquidators.[24] The directors' powers all cease[25] and the liquidator will then gather in the company's assets,[26] pay all the creditors out of them, repay the members and having prepared final accounts, call a final meeting of the members to explain what he has done.[27] He will then send in his final account to the Registrar of Companies[28] and if necessary, apply for the company's dissolution as above.

Technically any repayments of surplus funds or assets in the hands of the members will be liable to Capital Gains Tax. The members' liability for the company's debts is also extinguished on the dissolution of the company.

Creditors' voluntary winding up

17–11   A creditors' voluntary winding up means that although the members still choose to put the company into liquidation there will be no funds repayable to the members but there should be some for the creditors. Consequently a creditors' voluntary winding up is for the creditors' benefit and the creditors have the major say in the conduct of the liquidation.

In a creditors' voluntary winding up the company must convene a meeting of all its creditors to take place within 14 days of the resolution to wind up the company, having advertised the notice of the meeting in the local newspapers and the *Edinburgh Gazette*.[29] The notice of the meeting will contain the name and address of an insolvency practitioner who will supply the creditors with information about the company in liquidation. Meanwhile, the directors will prepare a statement about the accounts of the company, its creditors and securities,[30] which will be laid before the meeting of the creditors under the chairmanship of one of the directors.[31]

17–12   Both the members, at their initial meeting at which they resolve to wind

---

[23] IA 1986 s.89(4), (5).

[24] IA 1986 s.91(1). The director must inform the Registrar of Companies and the *Edinburgh Gazette* of his appointment (IA 1986 s.109(1)). The Accountant in Bankruptcy will need to be informed as well so that there may be an entry in the Register of Insolvencies.

[25] Except insofar as the liquidator or the members collectively permit otherwise (IA 1986 s.91(2)).

[26] In order to do this, he is given powers under the IA 1986 s.165 and Sch.4 Pts I, II and III. Part I powers require him to seek the approval of the members first, since he may be compromising their rights or otherwise reducing the amount of money available to them. Parts II and III do not require the sanction of the members and allow the liquidator to carry on the business of the company, defend or raise actions, etc.

[27] IA 1986 s.94(1).

[28] IA 1986 s.94(3).

[29] IA 1986 s.98.

[30] IA 1986 s.99(2).

[31] IA 1986 s.99(1). The meeting is not invalid because none of the directors are present: *Re Salcombe Hotel Development Co Ltd* [1991] B.C.L.C. 44.

up the company, and the creditors at their initial meeting, may appoint a liquidator,[32] but unless the creditors do not choose a liquidator[33] or the courts decide otherwise,[34] the creditors' choice prevails.[35] The creditors may decide to appoint a committee of not more than five persons to advise the liquidator.[36] The company members may also decide that they wish to appoint five of their members to the liquidation committee,[37] but the creditors may object to the members' choices unless the court decides otherwise.[38]

Once the liquidator has been appointed by the relevant committee, the directors' powers cease[39] and the notice of the appointment of the liquidator is forwarded to the Registrar of Companies for publication in the *Gazette*.[40]

The liquidator will then manage the liquidation in terms of the **17–13** Insolvency Act 1986 ("IA 1986") ss.165 and 167. This enables the liquidator to get in all the company's assets in much the same manner as a members' voluntary winding up, with slight variations to take account of the fact that the creditors' meeting may wish to choose its own liquidator and so no disposals or dealings with the company's assets (except where they might disappear or perish) may be undertaken by any liquidator until after the creditors' meeting.[41] The liquidator should have regular annual meetings to explain the conduct of the liquidation.[42] At the end of the liquidation, there will be a final meeting[43] before the liquidator applies to have the company dissolved. As with members' voluntary winding-up, the members' potential liability for any company debts is extinguished on dissolution.

Voluntary winding up as a method of disposing of a company's property

Although it is a slightly cumbersome method of disposing of the whole **17–14** or part of a company's business or property to another company, it is possible, following a voluntary winding up of the company, for the liquidator, having paid off all the creditors or secured their agreement, to transfer the company's assets to another company[44] in exchange for shares in the purchasing company. In the case of a members' voluntary winding up, a special resolution will be required to approve this[45]; in the

---

[32] IA 1986 s.100(1).
[33] IA 1986 s.100(2).
[34] IA 1986 s.100(3).
[35] IA 1986 s.100(2).
[36] IA 1986 s.101(1).
[37] IA 1986 s.101(2).
[38] IA 1986 s.101(3).
[39] IA 1986 s.103.
[40] IA 1986 s.109.
[41] IA 1986 s.167.
[42] IA 1986 s.105. The longest known liquidation apparently lasted over 100 years and saw two liquidators die in office.
[43] IA 1986 s.105.
[44] IA 1986 s.110(1).
[45] IA 1986 s.110(3)(a).

case of a creditors' voluntary winding up, the court's or the creditors' committee's approval is needed.[46] The shares in the purchasing company will then be paid as a final dividend to the members of the company just wound up. This can be used either to merge companies, so that one company is absorbed into another, or to merge two companies into a third new company, or equally to demerge companies (as for example, where a liquidated holding company sells off its assets to various little companies and the shareholders of the holding company receive shares in all the little companies). There is protection built in for shareholders who dissent from the arrangement,[47] but this dissent mechanism is precisely why it is not much used by companies except where everyone is agreed.

COMPULSORY WINDING UP BY THE COURT

Jurisdiction

17–15   In Scotland, a company may be wound up compulsorily in the Court of Session or, if the company's share capital is less than £120,000, in the sheriff court in which the company's registered office is situated.[48]

Grounds under which a company may be wound up compulsorily

17–16   A company may be wound up by the courts if:

- the company has resolved by special resolution to be wound up by the court[49];
- it was registered as a public company on incorporation, and has not obtained a s.761 trading certificate within a year of registration[50];
- the company does not commence its business within a year of incorporation or suspends its business for a year[51];
- the company is unable to pay its debts;[52]
- at the time at which a moratorium for a company voluntary arrangement expires without the arrangement having been approved[53]; or
- the court is of the opinion that it is just and equitable that the company should be wound up.[54]

---

[46] IA 1986 s.110(3)(b). The creditors' approval is very important: without it a creditor could petition for the liquidation of the company and collapse the reconstruction.

[47] IA 1986 s.111. The normal way to deal with the dissent is to pay the dissenting shareholders off, or to put their shares in a trust for their benefit. There is also the possibility of arbitration.

[48] IA 1986 s.120.

[49] IA 1986 s.122(1)(a). This would be an expensive way of being wound up.

[50] IA 1986 s.122(1)(b). This is very rare indeed.

[51] IA 1986 s.122(1)(d). This too is rare, and would need a member to feel strongly enough about the matter to incur the expense of going to court.

[52] IA 1986 s.122(1)(f).

[53] IA 1986 s.122(1)(fa).

[54] IA 1986 s.122(1)(g).

Of these grounds only the last two are in practice significantly used.

Although it too is very unlikely to be used, as a remnant of the old provisions whereby a floating charge holder in Scotland could not appoint a receiver, but instead have the company wound up, s.122(2) preserves a Scottish floating chargeholder's right to wind up the company.

The company's inability to pay its debts

The company's inability to pay its debts is defined in s.123(1) as: **17–17**

- a failure to pay a debt of £750 or more, either in cash or by granting a security, when given three weeks' notice to do so following delivery of prescribed written demand (sometimes known as a statutory demand)[55];
- in England and Wales, execution issued on a judgment, decree or order of any court is returned unsatisfied in whole or in part[56];
- a failure to pay within the *induciae* of a charge (15 days) following an extract decree, extract registered bond or extract protested bill[57];
- the company's inability to pay its debts as they fall due.[58] This means that the company cannot pay its bills when they should be paid even though technically it may be solvent—it is just that it has a cash flow problem; or
- that the company's assets are less than its liabilities taking into account all its contingent and prospective liabilities.[59] This is effectively a balance sheet test.

As regards the failure to pay a debt of £750 or more, it is possible for various creditors to combine together to demand payment provided that the total is at least £750, but where there is a demand for £750 or more, that demand must be justified. If a company's terms of trade were that it

---

[55] IA 1986 s.123(1)(a). Use Form 4.1.

[56] IA 1986 s.123(1)(b).

[57] IA 1986 s.123(1)(c). The *induciae* of a charge are the number of days between a sheriff officer's serving of a charge (a demand for payment) on the debtor company during which the debtor must pay or face the first steps in the public sale of its goods. An "extract" decree is a form of certified copy decree from the courts. A registered bond is a bond or debt instrument that has been registered in the Books of Council and Session or the Sheriff Court Books and a certified copy thereof is an "extract". An extract registered protest is a certified copy of a document proving that a bill of exchange was not honoured by the person on whom the bill was drawn when it should have been, the process of the bill not being honoured and a public record being made of this being known as a protest. It is very rare nowadays. The charge, decree, etc. may be for less than the sum of £750 indicated in s.123(1)(a) (*Spiers & Co v Central Building Co Ltd*, 1911 S.C. 330).

[58] IA 1986 s.123(1)(e). *Macplant Services Ltd v Contract Lifting Services (Scotland) Ltd* [2008] CSOH 158; *Blue Star Security Services (Scotland) Ltd, Petitioners*, 1992 S.L.T. (Sh Ct) 80.

[59] IA 1986 s.123(2). A contingent liability is a liability that is dependent on something else happening and so may not necessarily take place; a prospective liability is one that probably will arise but it is not known when it may do so.

did not pay its bills for 45 days, and the creditor accepted those terms, the creditor would be premature if he petitioned under s.122(1)(f) a mere 10 days after the account was rendered. Equally, if the debt is genuinely disputed, a petition for liquidation will be unjustified.[60] Furthermore, if a creditor is acting in bad faith, or there is evidence that the other creditors are unhappy about the prospect of the company being wound up, the court may ascertain the other creditors' and contributories' views,[61] though the courts are not bound to pay any attention to employees' interests or the public interest.[62] If there is no genuine dispute as to the debt, the debtor company should not advance, "a cloud of objections on affidavits" in an attempt to dissuade the creditor from pursuing a valid claim or to avoid or postpone an otherwise justified winding up.[63] Just because a company's assets are all secured in favour of creditors or the company has no assets does not mean that the company cannot be wound up.[64] Nevertheless, where the debt is due, courts in general have no compunction about putting companies in liquidation if those companies are not paying their creditors when required to do so.[65]

The cash-flow test and the balance sheet test

17–18   The cash-flow test normally takes precedence over the balance sheet test. If a company clearly is able to pay its debts as they fall due, the courts will be reluctant to close it down, since many a business might have trouble meeting all its liabilities all at once because its assets are not easily realisable—but in the meantime it is managing to meet its debts. However, in *Macplant Services Ltd v Contract Lifting Services (Scotland) Ltd*,[66] ample evidence from the provisional liquidator, a letter from a director of the debtor company offering to pay by instalments and a statement of account with unpaid invoices all suggested an inability to pay debts as they fell due. By contrast the balance sheet test takes a broader view. The leading case at present is *BNY Corporate Trustee Services Ltd v Eurosail*.[67] This was a complex case arising out of the collapse of Lehman Brothers. Despite the collapse of its various hedging arrangements, Eurosail was managing to pay its debts as they fell due. The Supreme Court held that the test to be applied was not whether or not Eurosail had reached "the point of no return" (as the Court of Appeal put it) but whether on a balance of probabilities Eurosail had sufficient assets to meet its considerable liabilities, some of which were not due to mature for many years. It was held that Eurosail did have

---

[60] *Cunninghame v Walkingshaw Oil Co Ltd* (1886) 14 R. 87; *Landauer & Co v W H Alexander & Co Ltd*, 1919 S.C. 492.

[61] IA 1986 s.195.

[62] *Re Craven Insurance Co. Ltd* [1968] 1 All E.R. 1140.

[63] *Re Claybridge Shipping Co SA* [1981] Com L.R. 107, per Oliver L.J. at 109.

[64] IA 1986 s.125(1).

[65] See also the Late Payment of Commercial Debts (Interest) Act 1998 which requires the payment of interest on outstanding debts.

[66] [2008] CSOH 158.

[67] [2013] UKSC 28. See also *J & A Construction (Scotland) Ltd v Windex Ltd* [2013] CSOH 170.

sufficient assets to meet its liabilities, and that given its particular circumstances there should be a discount for its long term contingencies and future liabilities. It was stated that courts should in principle be wary of pronouncing that a company is balance-sheet insolvent and it is for the creditor to prove that the debtor company is insolvent. It is an inexact test, with room for judicial discretion, and there also needs to be careful weighing of the significance of the company's contingent and future liabilities.

The just and equitable grounds for winding up a company

The "just and equitable" grounds are used by the courts when in the **17–19** light of the circumstances surrounding the company the fairest thing to do with it is to wind it up. The just and equitable grounds are entirely separate from issues of the company's solvency, and indeed, there is no virtue in winding up the company on the just and equitable grounds unless the company is solvent, since the members would not get any money back. The courts will also have to be satisfied that the members of the company seeking the winding up order are not acting unreasonably in not seeking a better remedy.[68]

Occasions where the courts have wound up companies on the just and equitable grounds include the following:

- loss of substratum of the company[69];
- illegality of the company's activities[70];
- deadlock in the management of the company[71];

---

[68] IA 1986 s.125(2). If the company were insolvent, a cheaper method than winding up through the courts would be to put the company into a creditors' voluntary winding up.

[69] The substratum is the primary purpose for which the company was set up, as shown in the objects clause: *Re German Date Coffee Co Ltd* (1882) 20 Ch. D. 169. With the decline in significance of the objects clause, this particular ground is very unlikely to be used now, but it has never technically been overruled, though nowadays the matter would almost certainly be remitted to the shareholders for their decision rather than a winding up order being granted. See also *Galbraith v Merito Shipping Co*, 1947 S.C. 446; *Levy v Napier*, 1962 S.C. 468.

[70] *Re Thomas Brinsmead Sons Ltd* [1897] 1 Ch. 45. Again, this is very unlikely nowadays, since a company set up as a fraud would generally be wound up on the grounds of public interest under the IA 1986 s.124A. Nevertheless, this case is still good law.

[71] *Re Yenidje Tobacco Co Ltd* [1935] Ch. 693. In this case two traders sold their businesses to a company in which they each had 50 per cent of the shares. The two traders started bickering and were unable to work together despite the profitability of their company. As the poorly drafted articles of association of their company had no arbitration clause, their only remedy was to have the company wound up. Nowadays special articles, known as deadlock articles, usually prevent this type of situation arising. Nonetheless, the principle of winding up where there is no other resolution of conflict is still valid. See *Baird v Lees*, 1924 S.C. 83; *Lewis v Haas*, 1971 S.L.T. 57.

- quasi-partnership cases[72]; and
- oppressive conduct by the majority shareholders or directors.[73]

Who may petition to wind up the company?

17–20   Those who may petition to wind up the company are:

- the company itself[74];
- the directors[75];
- creditors[76];
- contributories[77];
- the Secretary of State, on public interest grounds,[78] or where a public company incorporated as such does not have a trading certificate and has been in existence for over a year[79];
- an administrator[80];
- a receiver in Scotland[81];
- an administrative receiver in England[82]; and
- the Lord Advocate if the company is a charitable company.[83]

Creditors are likely to be the ones who petition on the grounds of the company's inability to pay its debts, but under certain circumstances, a contributory may petition as well. A contributory—broadly speaking—is a member or very occasionally past member of a company who holds or

---

[72] *Ebrahimi v Westbourne Galleries Ltd* [1973] A.C. 360; *Virdi v Abbey Leisure Ltd* [1990] B.C.L.C. 342; *Jesner v Jarrad Properties Ltd*, 1993 S.C. 34; [1993] B.C.L.C. 1032. A quasi-partnership is a company which before its business was incorporated was run as a partnership, and a sense of the partnership ethos and mutual trust has been carried forward to the company. Where this has been lost by taking legal but unfair advantage of some rule applicable to companies, it is appropriate to have the company wound up on the grounds that the trust that used to be maintained by the partners towards each other, and which should be maintained by the directors to the members, has been lost. The courts will not be eager to grant a winding up order on these grounds since there may be other members of the company who are not involved in the issue of loss of trust, and the court will wish to be sure that their concerns are not ignored.

[73] *Loch v John Blackwood Ltd* [1924] A.C. 783. In this case the majority shareholders deliberately made it difficult for the minority to find out what was happening in the company and how much the company was worth, in the hope that the minority would become fed up and sell their shares to the majority. Were such a situation to arise nowadays, the minority would almost certainly use a CA 2006 s.994 minority protection petition instead. See also *Re Lundie Bros* [1965] 1 W.L.R. 1051; *Re Fildes Bros* [1970] 1 W.L.R. 592.

[74] IA 1986 s.124(1).
[75] IA 1986 s.124(1).
[76] IA 1986 s.124(1).
[77] IA 1986 s.124(1).
[78] IA 1986 s.124A(1).
[79] IA 1986 s.124(4)(a).
[80] IA 1986 s.14(1).
[81] IA 1986 s.55(2) and Sch.2 para.21.
[82] IA 1986 s.42(1) and Sch.1 para.21.
[83] Law Reform (Miscellaneous Provisions) (Scotland) Act 1990 s.14.

used to hold partly paid shares,[84] or in the case of a guarantee company has not paid his guarantee to the liquidator.[85] In addition, directors, who within a year of the winding up authorised payments out of capital on the redemption or repurchase of shares in a private company, may be contributories to the extent of the company's loss if the company's funds turn out to be insufficient.[86] Past or present members who received payments out of capital as indicated above will also be contributories[87] to the same extent together with those directors. Past or present directors who have unlimited liability may be contributories under limited circumstances.[88] Past members of an unlimited company which converted to a limited company or a public company may also be contributories and liable if the new limited company or public company went into insolvent liquidation within three years of the conversion.[89]

A director who is found liable for wrongful trading under IA 1986 s.214, or any officer or member found liable for fraudulent trading under the IA 1986 s.213, is not deemed to be a contributory.[90]

If the contributory is a member, past member or director involved in **17–21** the purchase or redemption of shares in a private company out of capital,[91] he may petition on either the grounds of inability to pay debts[92] or the just and equitable grounds[93] without any further qualification; but if the contributory is not a member, past member or director involved in a purchase or redemption of shares out of capital as above, the contributory may only petition on the grounds of inability to pay debts or the just and equitable grounds if the number of members in a public company has dropped below two,[94] or he was allotted the shares or inherited the shares and thereby held the shares for at least six out of the preceding 18 months before the commencement of the winding up.[95]

The Secretary of State regularly petitions to wind up companies in the

---

[84] There is an extensive definition under the IA 1986 s.76, of which this is a brief summary. A past member may be liable where he transferred partly paid shares within 12 months before the winding up of the company, but he will only be liable in respect of debts contracted by the company while he was still a member, and he can only be found liable when the other members' funds are inadequate.

[85] IA 1986 s.79(1).

[86] IA 1986 s.76(2)(b).

[87] IA 1986 s.76(2)(a).

[88] IA 1986 s.75.

[89] IA 1986 s.77.

[90] IA 1986 s.79(1).

[91] IA 1986 s.124(3).

[92] IA 1986 s.122(1)(f).

[93] IA 1986 s.122(1)(g).

[94] IA 1986 s.124(2)(a).

[95] IA 1986 s.124(2)(b).

public interest under the IA 1986 s.124A, common examples being illegal lotteries[96] and dodgy pyramid trading ventures.

The procedure for the petition

17–22   The details of the procedure may be found in the Insolvency (Scotland) Rules 1986 ("the ISR").[97] Assuming the petition has been properly served by a suitable petitioner, and there has been advertisement in the newspapers and the *Edinburgh Gazette* of the forthcoming hearing, the courts will entertain the petition. In cases of emergency, it may be possible to obtain a provisional liquidator at any time after the presentation of the petition[98] but before the granting of the order for winding up. A provisional liquidator may be used where there is a danger of the company's assets disappearing.[99] If the winding up petition is ultimately dismissed he demits office. Again, during the time between the presentation of the petition and the granting of the order for winding up, the company, any creditor or contributory may apply for the petition to be sisted (stopped or delayed) if there is action being taken against the company elsewhere in the United Kingdom.[100] On the hearing of the actual petition for winding up, the court may make such decision as it sees fit[101] but as indicated above, the courts will not grant to members or contributories a winding up order if there is some better, more reasonable remedy.[102]

Where the petition is granted, the time of commencement of the winding up is deemed to be the time of the presentation of the petition for winding up[103] unless the company has passed a resolution for winding up beforehand, in which case (in the absence of fraud or mistake) the time of commencement of the winding up is the time of the passing of the resolution.[104] With effect from the commencement of the winding up any dispositions of the company's property or transfers of shares are void.[105]

Once a winding up order has been given, the Registrar of Companies

---

[96] *Secretary of State for Trade and Industry v Hasta International Ltd*, 1998 S.L.T. 73 OH. For a more colourful example, in 1996 the DTI closed down on the ground of public interest the Ostrich Farming Corp Ltd, which invited gullible investors to buy interests in young ostriches which would be reared in Belgium for their meat. Each ostrich was sold many times over to different owners, but because of the remoteness of the farm few investors knew this; those who did visit the farm were easily convinced when told that one particular ostrich was "their" ostrich. Many of the ostriches died of disease. The perpetrators of the fraud were jailed for up to five years and banned from being company directors.

[97] Insolvency (Scotland) Rules 1986 (SI 1986/1915) ("the ISR") rr.4.1–4.82.

[98] IA 1986 s.135. Quite often the provisional liquidator becomes the liquidator.

[99] In *Purewal Enterprises Ltd, Petitioner* [2008] CSOH 127 the appointment of the provisional liquidator was recalled.

[100] IA 1986 s.126.

[101] IA 1986 s.125(1).

[102] IA 1986 s.125(2).

[103] IA 1986 s.129(2).

[104] IA 1986 s.129(1). *Haig v Lord Advocate*, 1976 S.L.T. (Notes) 16.

[105] IA 1986 s.127. *Site Preparations v Buchan Development Co*, 1983 S.L.T. 317; *United Dominions Trust, Noters*, 1977 S.L.T. (Notes) 56; *Hollicourt (Contracts) Ltd (In Liquidation) v Bank of Ireland* [2001] 1 W.L.R. 895.

and Accountant in Bankruptcy must be informed within seven days[106] and thereafter no-one may raise an action against the company except with leave of the court.[107] Within 28 days of appointment notices are sent to the creditors and/or put in the newspapers and the *Edinburgh Gazette* intimating the winding up and the name and address of the liquidator.[108]

Once the liquidator (or indeed provisional liquidator) is appointed, he **17–23** may obtain statements of affairs from the officers, promoters, employees and recent past employees of the company concerning the company's assets and liabilities, creditors and their securities, and any other useful information.[109] The liquidator may apply to the court for a public examination of any officer, receiver, manager, liquidator, administrator or promoter of the company[110]; and if anyone summoned to appear for a public examination absconds, he may be arrested and his papers and records seized.[111]

The liquidator will within 42 days[112] of the winding up order summon separate meetings of the creditors and contributories (if there are any, which is unusual) in order to choose who the liquidator will be.[113] If there is disparity between the two meetings' choices, the creditors' choice will prevail unless the court can be persuaded otherwise.[114] If the company has been in administration or a company voluntary arrangement the court may appoint the administrator or the supervisor to be the liquidator.[115]

The liquidator may set up a liquidation committee to advise him.[116] The members of the committee are not paid for their trouble.[117]

Once appointed and in office, the liquidator proceeds to get in the **17–24** company's property. He takes control of it all,[118] makes inventories of it[119] and he may apply to court to have it vested in him so that he may dispose of it or raise proceedings to recover it.[120] He may obtain payment from any contributories[121] and make creditors prove their debts.[122] The liquidator has extensive powers under IA 1986 Sch.4 Pts I, II and III to deal

---

[106] IA 1986 s.130(1) and the ISR rr.4.18, 4.19.

[107] IA 1986 s.130(2).

[108] This liquidator is the one appointed by the court at the court hearing. At the creditors' or contributories' meeting a different insolvency practitioner may be appointed as the liquidator (as opposed to the first liquidator).

[109] ISR Pt 4 Ch.2 (referring to the IA 1986 s.131).

[110] IA 1986 s.133.

[111] IA 1986 s.134.

[112] ISR r.4.12(2A).

[113] IA 1986 s.138. The liquidator who calls the meeting may be replaced by another liquidator, or he may remain in place, depending on what the decisions of the creditors and contributories are.

[114] IA 1986 s.139.

[115] IA 1986 s.140.

[116] IA 1986 s.142. Note that a committee should consist of more than one individual: *Souter, Petitioner*, 1981 S.L.T. (Sh Ct) 89. See also the ISR Pt 4 Ch.7.

[117] *Liquidator of Pattisons* (1902) 4 F. 1010.

[118] IA 1986 s.144.

[119] ISR r.4.22.

[120] IA 1986 s.145.

[121] IA 1986 ss.148, 149.

[122] ISR r.4.15.

with the company's assets, most without the sanction of the court, but some, being the more problematic issues that may affect members' or creditors' rights, need the approval of the court. There is no specific provision, as there is in England, entitling the liquidator to repudiate contracts,[123] but by doing so the insolvent company may be liable in damages to the other party. The liquidator must make regular returns to the Registrar of Companies and Accountant in Bankruptcy, as well as keeping the creditors and contributories informed.[124] The liquidator has extensive powers to see company documentation and to investigate directors' behaviour.

There are extensive provisions relating to the replacement of liquidators and the proper conduct of the liquidation.

17–25 If an order for winding up has been made by the court, but it is apparent to the liquidator that the company's assets are insufficient to justify the expenses of the winding up, the liquidator may apply to the court to have the company dissolved.[125]

"Getting in" or gathering in the insolvent company's estate

17–26 The liquidator assesses what assets the company still has, and then tries to get in all the debts the company is due. Having done that, he has further means of swelling the company's estate. In particular he can:

(1) have certain forms of diligence against the company's assets set aside under the "equalisation of diligence rules"[126] whereby any attachments[127] or arrestments[128] within a period of 60 days prior to the appointment of the liquidator are all treated as taking place at the same time: the creditors then have to hand back what they have received from the company and then can reclaim as ordinary creditors later though they are entitled to their expenses of attachment, arrestment, etc.;

(2) set aside certain antecedent transactions if they are *gratuitous alienations* or *unfair preferences*:

---

[123] *The Scottish Coal Company (in provisional liquidation)*; sub nom. *Scottish Environment Protection Agency v Joint Liquidators of the Scottish Coal Co Ltd*, 2014 S.L.T. 259; [2013] CSIH 108. A liquidator may choose not to realise an asset with a negative value, in which case it will remain in the company until the company is dissolved. What he cannot do is disclaim ownership of land with associated liabilities (in this case the requirement to adhere to the terms of certain environmental protection licences).

[124] IA 1986 s.170.

[125] IA 1986 s.204. In practice, quite a few companies in Scotland are not worth putting into liquidation because the cost of liquidation would be too great. For details of what should be considered before going down this route, see *Redmount Properties Ltd* Unreported December 11, 2009 Edinburgh Sheriff Court.

[126] IA 1986 s.185, referring to the Bankruptcy (Scotland) Act 1985 s.37.

[127] Attachment is the diligence whereby creditors seize the debtor's assets and ultimately sell them at a public auction.

[128] Arrestment is the diligence whereby creditors seize the debtor's assets or funds in the hands of a third party and prevent the third party returning them to the debtor. By an action of furthcoming the debtor's assets can be made over to the creditors.

(a) a gratuitous alienation[129] is a gift or transfer at less than full value of an asset of the company's within a period of five years of the commencement of the winding up if the recipient is an associate[130] or within a period of two years for any other person; any such recipient will have to restore the asset to the company (or other redress as may be appropriate) unless he can prove:
   (i) the company's assets were greater than its liabilities at the time of the alienation[131];
   (ii) the alienation was made for adequate consideration[132];
   (iii) the alienation was a birthday, Christmas or other conventional gift, or a charitable gift which in either case it was reasonable for the company to make[133];
   In England the equivalent rule is known as a "transaction at an undervalue".[134]

(b) an unfair preference[135] is the early repayment of a loan or payment of a creditor which has the effect of prejudicing other creditors. Any such early repayments within six months of the liquidation may be recalled. An unfair preference can be the granting of a floating charge. The following are not unfair preferences:
   (i) transactions in the ordinary course of business[136];
   (ii) transactions in cash when the debt was due and payable, with no collusive purpose[137];
   (iii) reciprocal transactions unless collusive[138];
   (iv) the grant of a mandate authorising an arrestee to pay over sums to the arresting creditor.[139]

---

[129] IA 1986 s.242. *Nova Glaze Replacement Windows Ltd v Clark Thomson & Co*, 2001 S.C. 815, *John E Rae (Electrical Services) Linlithgow Ltd v Lord Advocate*, 1994 S.L.T. 788, *McLuckie Bros Ltd v Newhouse Contracts Ltd*, 1993 S.L.T. 641. There is also a common law form of gratuitous alienation but it is very rarely used. It has the advantage that the two year rule does not apply but the disadvantage that the challenger to the transaction has to prove that the company was both insolvent at the time of the gratuitous alienation (which in practice may be difficult to establish) and at the time of the challenge as well (*Stuart Eves (In Liquidation) v Smiths Gore*, 1993 S.L.T. 1274 OH).

[130] In terms of the Bankruptcy (Scotland) Act 1985 s.74. An associate is very similar to a "connected" person referred to above, being close family, employer, employee, fellow partners or companies with which the company is connected.

[131] IA 1986 s.242(4)(a).

[132] IA 1986 s.242(4)(b). For the meaning of "adequate" see *Lafferty Construction Ltd v McCombe*, 1994 S.L.T. 858 and *Rankin v Meek*, 1995 S.L.T. 526 OH.

[133] IA 1986 s.242(4)(c).

[134] IA 1986 s.238.

[135] IA 1986 s.243. See *Craiglaw Developments Ltd v Gordon Wilson & Co*, 1997 S.C. 356; 1998 S.L.T. 1046; 1997 S.C.L.R. 1157; [1998] B.C.C. 530; 1993 S.L.T. 533; 1992 S.C.L.R. 332; *Baillie Marshall Ltd (In Liquidation) v Avian Communications Ltd*, 2002 S.L.T. 189; *Anderson v Dickens* [2008] CSOH 134.

[136] IA 1986 s.243(2)(a).

[137] IA 1986 s.243(2)(b). *R Gaffney and Sons Ltd v Davidson*, 1996 S.L.T. (Sh Ct) 36.

[138] IA 1986 s.243(2)(c). *Nicoll v Steel Press (Supplies) Ltd*, 1992 S.C. 119.

[139] IA 1986 s.243(2)(d).

Unfair preferences may be challenged by a creditor or the liquidator and the recipient required to repay the loan. The recipient then claims for the value of his loan as an ordinary creditor.[140] In England a similar rule is known as a "preference".[141]

(3) set aside certain extortionate credit transactions[142];

(4) have a floating charge set aside as invalid. This will take place if:

    (a) the floating charge is granted to a connected person within two years of the onset of the company's insolvency[143]; or

    (b) it is granted to any person at any time between the presentation of a petition for the making of an administration order and the making of that order.[144]

    A "connected" person is a director or shadow director of the company, an associate of the company, or an associate of a director or shadow director.[145] An associate is extensively defined in the IA 1986 s.435, but in essence is a close relative or spouse of a director, a partner of the director, an employer or employee either of the director or the company.[146]

Where the charge is granted within 12 months to someone not connected with the company, the charge will be invalid if:

    (c) at the time of granting the security the company was unable to pay its debts in terms of the IA 1986 s.123[147]; or

    (d) the company became unable to pay its debts because of the transaction for which the charge was granted.[148]

Despite the above, a charge in favour of either a connected person or an unconnected person will still be valid if the charge was granted in respect of:

    (e) monies paid, or goods or services supplied at the same time or after the creation of the charge[149]; or

---

[140] IA 1986 s.243(4).

[141] IA 1986 s.239.

[142] IA 1986 s.244.

[143] IA 1986 s.245(3)(a). The "onset of insolvency" means the commencement of the winding up or the date of the presentation of the petition on which an administration order was made (IA 1986 s.245(5)).

[144] IA 1986 s.245(3)(c).

[145] IA 1986 s.249.

[146] This is not a full definition: reference should be made to the actual section. An "associate" for the purpose of a floating charge is not necessarily the same as an associate in terms of a gratuitous alienation.

[147] IA 1986 s.245(4)(a).

[148] IA 1986 s.245(4)(b).

[149] IA 1986 s.245(2)(a). *Power v Sharp Investments Ltd* [1993] B.C.C. 609 [1994] 1 B.C.L.C. 111.

(f) the value of any reduction or discharge of debt of the company in exchange for which the charge was granted[150]; or

(g) any interest payable in respect of (e) or (f) above.[151]

If the company is insolvent at the time an *unconnected* person gets the **17–27** floating charge (or becomes so as a result of the transaction involving the floating charge) (and provided the charge was granted within the 12-month period prior to the onset of insolvency) the unconnected person does not obtain the benefit of the floating charge except to the extent of (e), (f) and (g) above. If the company was solvent at the time of granting the floating charge, even if it was within the 12-month period, an unconnected person can have the entire benefit of the floating charge, including money lent before the granting of the charge, as well as the sums under (e), (f) and (g).

On the other hand, it makes no difference whether the company is **17–28** solvent or not as far as the granting of a floating charge to a *connected* person is concerned: within the two-year period the connected person can only get the benefit of the floating charge to the extent of (e), (f) or (g).

Outside the time periods above the charges will be valid.

Liability of directors on insolvent liquidation[152]

Directorial liability can extend to: **17–29**

(1) make directors repay or return to the company in liquidation such sums of money or other assets as they may have misappropriated or been otherwise liable for under the misfeasance provisions of the IA 1986 s.212[153];

(2) make anyone involved in fraudulent trading reimburse the company in liquidation[154];

(3) make any officer of the company who had caused the company to trade wrongfully to contribute to the company's assets[155];

(4) make any director involved in the management of a phoenix company contribute to the company in liquidation.[156]

---

[150] IA 1986 s.245(2)(b).

[151] IA 1986 s.245(2)(c).

[152] Reference should be made to Ch.9 where directors' liability on insolvency is explored in much greater depth.

[153] *Re DKG Contractors Ltd* [1990] B.C.C. 903; *Re Barton Manufacturing Co Ltd* [1999] 1 B.C.L.C. 740.

[154] IA 1986 s.213. Actual dishonesty must be proved: *Re Patrick and Lyon Ltd* [1933] Ch. 786. See *Goldfarb v Higgins and Ors* [2010] EWHC 613 (Ch.), a complex missing trader VAT fraud.

[155] IA 1986 s.214. *Re Produce Marketing Consortium Ltd (No.2)* [1989] B.C.L.C. 520. The money ingathered should be used for the benefit of the unsecured creditors: *Re Oasis Merchandise Services Ltd* [1998] 1 Ch.170.

[156] IA 1986 s.216.

Although all these methods are open to liquidators, they are not always used in practice because of the cost of raising the actions against the directors and following the Enterprise Act 2002 s.253, such action may only be commenced with the sanction of the court, the creditors' committee or in the absence of a creditors' committee, the creditors generally.[157] The creditors generally will probably wish to be convinced that they are not throwing good money after bad in pursuing directors who in many cases will not be worth suing after the collapse of their companies. What sometimes also happens in practice is that the liquidator may enter into a conditional fee arrangement with a firm of lawyers or takes out insurance to cover the costs.

17–30   Scots corporate insolvency law does not have certain useful mechanisms available to English law, such as the Official Receiver, or a specific statutory provision dealing with transactions by subsequently insolvent companies defrauding creditors.[158] However, it is submitted that it would be possible for the court to use the *nobile officium* if no other remedy were available to trace money that had been fraudulently removed from the company by a director.

Liquidators may report directors of insolvent companies to the Secretary of State who may then apply for the disqualification of those directors if the directors' behaviour justifies it.[159]

Distribution of the company's assets

17–31   Once the liquidator has amassed as much as he is able to, he may begin the distribution, though he may also pay interim distributions as funds arrive. The order of payment to the creditors (on the assumption that there are no secured creditors) is as follows,[160] with each category being paid in full until there are insufficient assets to pay in full the next category: in that event debts within the same category have the same priority and abate in equal proportions[161]:

(1) the expenses of the liquidation, being the liquidator's own fees and expenses[162];

---

[157] See IA 1986 ss.165(2) and 167(1), Sch 4 Pt 1 para.3A. This has the effect, at least in England, of ensuring the litigation expenses of actions against directors are treated as a legitimate expense incurred by the liquidator and does not have to come from the liquidator's own pocket. It is submitted that a similar outcome could be achieved by the use of Insolvency (Scotland) Rules 1986 (SI 1986/1915) r.4.32.

[158] IA 1986 ss.423–425.

[159] Company Directors Disqualification Act 1986 s.7.

[160] ISR r.4.66.

[161] ISR r.4.66(4).

[162] See IA 1986 s.115 (at least as regards voluntary winding up). ISR r.4.67, details these rules, and includes the provisional liquidator's fees and expenses, and the petitioning creditor's or member's expenses.

(2) if at the time when a winding up order was granted there was already a company voluntary arrangement, the expenses of the company voluntary arrangement;
(3) preferential debts in terms of the IA 1986 s.386 and Sch.6[163];
(4) ordinary (unsecured) debts;
(5) interest on the preferential debts;
(6) interest on the ordinary debts;
(7) postponed debts, such as debts due to the recipient of a gratuitous alienation which has been reduced or restored to the company's assets.

The prescribed part, referred to in previous chapters in connection with administration and receivership, does not apply to liquidation.

In the event of the company being solvent, the surplus is repaid to the members proportionately to their shareholdings and subject to any requirements of the articles.[164]

In the event of the company having granted securities to charge holders, on the liquidation of the company, standard security holders and other fixed charge holders would be able to exercise their rights over the secured assets, recouping their loans, interest and expenses in priority to the liquidator, but if the sums realised were insufficient, the fixed charge holders would rank as unsecured creditors for the unpaid amounts.[165] Equally, should the fixed charge holders make a surplus, the surplus is handed to any receiver, whom failing the liquidator.

Where a creditor of the company in liquidation owes money to the **17–32** company, on the equitable principle of compensation, a creditor is allowed to offset what he owes against what he is owed. So a bank owed money by a company in liquidation may be able to set off the company's overdrawn current account against a deposit account held by the company with the same bank. On a company's insolvent liquidation, a liquid claim by one creditor may set off against an illiquid one[166] and a current debt may set against a future or contingent one.[167]

There are cross-border provisions to ensure that orders for winding up made in one part of the United Kingdom are enforceable in other parts[168] subject to the *lex situs* in respect of any property. The courts are required to assist one another where possible.

The liquidator is able to insist on delivery of any papers, books or other records of the company in liquidation notwithstanding any lien

---

[163] These no longer include outstanding PAYE, customs and excise duty and national insurance contributions.
[164] For an example of distribution of the surplus to some members in circumstances where others could not be traced, see *Joint Liquidation of Automatic Oil Tools Ltd, Noters*, 2001 S.L.T. 279. For the costs of havers of documents in producing those documents, see *Phoenicia Asset Management SAL v Steven Alexander* [2010] CSOH 71.
[165] Bankruptcy (Scotland) Act 1985 s.22(9) and Sch.1, as applied by the ISR r.4.16.
[166] *Scott's Trustees v Scott* (1887) 14 R. 1043 at 1051.
[167] See Bell's *Commentaries*, II, 122.
[168] IA 1986 s.426.

over those papers unless they happen to be documents giving a title to property.[169]

Methods of defeating a liquidator

17–33   The liquidator's reach will not extend to all assets being used by the company. Goods subject to retention of title, to hire purchase or conditional sale agreements may not be seized by the liquidator.[170] Goods held on trust for someone unconnected with the company, or goods borrowed from another person are not goods owned by the company and must be returned to their true owners.

Dissolution of the company

The Registrar's dissolution of a company

17–34   The Registrar of Companies may strike a defunct company[171] off the register if it fails to reply to correspondence from him, and appears not to be carrying on any business.[172] Eventually, usually after some months, the company's name will be struck from the register and publication of the company's demise will be published in the *Edinburgh Gazette*. The directors may still be liable for any claims against them until the five-year period of prescription expires. If the company is being wound up, but the Registrar believes that either no liquidator is acting or the affairs of the company are wound up, and there have been no returns by the liquidator, the Registrar may strike off the company.[173]

Dissolution on application

17–35   The company itself, whether public or private, may apply to the Registrar for its own dissolution under the Companies Act 2006 ("the CA 2006") ss.1003–1011, provided the appropriate documentation is supplied, including the Form DS01. However the company must genuinely have ceased trading except to the extent of paying any liabilities, must not have changed its name recently, and there may be no insolvency proceedings taking place against the company or s.895 schemes of arrangement being presented to the court. The company will be removed from the register three months after the application. The directors and members still remain potentially liable for the company's debts for a period of up to five years as if the company had not been dissolved.[174]

---

[169]   IA 1986 s.246.
[170]   *Armour v Thyssen Edelstahlwerke*, 1990 S.L.T. 891; *Vale Sewing Machines v Robb*, 1997 S.C.L.R. 797.
[171]   Or a company in liquidation of which the liquidation may have been abandoned as not being worth continuing.
[172]   CA 2006 s.1000. This is supposed to come into force on October 1, 2009.
[173]   CA 2006 s.1001. The Registrar of Companies has a helpful guide to the overall process, known as GP4, *Strike-off, Dissolution and Restoration*, available from its website.
[174]   CA 2006 s.1003(6).

Bona vacantia

If no-one can be found who should be entitled to the assets of the **17–36** company after its dissolution, the company's goods can be seized by the Crown as bona vacantia and the Lord Treasurer's Remembrancer will take them over.[175] That official may disclaim those goods should someone appear within three years to claim the goods.[176]

Restoration to the register

A director or former member of the company may apply to the **17–37** Registrar to have the company administratively restored to the Register.[177] This should normally be done within six years of the dissolution although under certain circumstances the six year rule may be waived.[178] Someone who wishes to bring an action against the company in respect of a claim for damages for personal injury or for damages under the Fatal Accidents Act 1976 or the Damages (Scotland) Act 1976,[179] must do so by an application to the court in which case there is no time limit.[180] There will need to be a waiver letter from the Crown in respect of any property subject to bona vacantia and any outstanding annual returns and accounts will need to be filed to bring the company's records up to date.

Cross-border insolvency

Cross-border insolvency, a notoriously difficult area, is regulated by **17–38** the EU Insolvency Regulations (1346/2000), effective from May 31, 2002. It is implemented by the Cross-Border Insolvency Regulations 2006 (SI 2006/1030). This allows the cross-border effect of insolvency proceedings throughout the European Union. This subject is beyond the ambit of this book.

Further Reading

Donna Mckenzie Skene, *Insolvency Law in Scotland*, (London: Tottel, 1999).

John St Clair and the Hon. Lord Drummond Young, *The Law of Corporate Insolvency in Scotland*, 4th edn. (Edinburgh: W. Green, 2011).

---

[175] CA 2006 s.1012.
[176] CA 2006 ss.1013, 1014.
[177] CA 2006 s.1024–1034. Form RT01 is required. The Registrar of Companies has a helpful guide to the overall process, known as GP4, *Strike-off, Dissolution and Restoration*, available from its website.
[178] CA 2006 s.1030(5).
[179] CA 2006 s.1030(6).
[180] CA 2006 s.1030(1).

INDEX

Accountant in Bankruptcy
notification of winding up
compulsory winding up, 17–22
voluntary winding up, 17–07
Accounting reference date
application for registration, 3–08
meaning, 7–31
Accounts
see also **Auditors**
accounting reference date, 3–08, 7–31
accumulated profits, 7–03
balance sheet
audit exemption, 7–50
inclusion of, 7–29
medium-sized companies, 7–51
micro-entity companies, 7–47
small companies, 7–46
capitalisation, 7–09
defective accounts, revision of, 7–56
depreciation, 7–07—7–08
directors' report, 7–35—7–41
distributable profits, 7–01, 7–13
distributions in kind
determination of amount, 7–14
non-cash dividends, 7–15
revaluation of assets, 7–15
dividends
directors' liability for improper, 7–27
initial accounts, 7–21
interim accounts, 7–22
non-cash dividends, 7–15
dormant companies, 7–55
financial reporting standards, 7–05
group companies
consolidated accounts, 7–52
medium-sized groups, 7–53—7–54
small groups, 7–53—7–54
initial accounts, 7–21
interim accounts, 7–22
keeping records, 7–28
micro-entity companies, 7–47—7–48
notes to accounts, 7–29
preparation
accounting reference date, 7–31
auditors, 7–33—7–34
balance sheet, 7–29
directors' report, 7–35—7–41
notes to accounts, 7–29
subsequent financial years, 7–32
summary accounts, 7–45
time for lodging, 7–42—7–43

true and fair view, 7–30
unlimited companies, 7–44
public limited companies
directors' liability for improper
dividend, 7–27
dividends, 7–25
generally, 3–30
members' liability for improper
distribution, 7–26
net assets rule, 7–23
uncalled share capital, 7–24
undistributable reserves, 7–24
publication, 7–29
medium-sized companies, 7–51
medium-sized groups, 7–53—7–54
realised losses, 7–04—7–08
realised profits, 7–04—7–08
reduction, 7–11
relevant accounts, 7–20
reorganisation, 7–12
research and development expenditure,
7–16—7–19
retained profit, 7–13
revaluation of assets, 7–15
small companies
audit exemption, 7–49—7–50
meaning, 7–46
micro-entity companies, 7–47—7–48
publication of accounts, 7–46
small groups, 7–53—7–54
statements of standard accounting
practice, 7–05
summary accounts, 7–45
true and fair view, 7–30
undistributed reserves, 7–13
unlimited companies, 7–44
written off, 7–10
Acting within powers
directors' duties, 9–10
Addresses
directors, 3–04, 3–05
registered office, 3–05
service address, 3–05
Administration
administrators
appointment, 16–17—16–23, 16–25
contracts, 16–30—16–32
functions of, 16–10
position of, 16–14
powers and duties, 16–28
proposals, 16–26—16–27

remuneration, 16–29
applying for, 16–04—16–06
company, benefit to, 16–13
creditors, payment to, 16–34
creditors' voluntary liquidation
dissolution, 16–36
introduction, 16–35
rescue achieved, 16–37
rescue mission failed, 16–38
directors, benefit to, 16–12
dissolution, 16–36
floating charge holders
appointment of administrator, 16–17
benefits to, 16–11
floating charges, qualifying, 16–16
need for, 16–01
new style
introduction of, 16–07—16–09
moratoriums, 16–24
publicity, 16–25
old-style administration
applying for, 16–04—16–06
process of, 16–03
retention of, 16–02
payment to creditors, 16–34
prepacks, 16–39
receivership, and, 16–40
rescue achieved, 16–37
rescue mission failed, 16–38
termination of, 16–33
unsecured creditors, position of, 16–15
Administrative receivers
appointment, 16–18, 16–21
capital markets, 15–25
meaning, 15–08
right to petition for winding up,
17–20
Administrators
see also **Administration**
appointment
application process, 16–23
court appointment, 16–20, 16–22
notice of appointment, 16–19
out of court appointment, 16–18,
16–21
publicity for, 16–25
qualifying charge holders, by,
16–17—16–18, 16–20
contracts, 16–30—16–32
functions of, 16–10
position of, 16–14
powers and duties, 16–28
proposals, 16–26—16–27
remuneration, 16–29
winding up petitions, 17–20
Agency
piercing the corporate veil, 2–17
Agenda
annual general meetings, 13–07

Allotment of shares
see also **Shares**
CREST, 5–21
directors' authority for, 5–12—5–13
intimation of, 5–19
members' pre-emption rights,
5–14—5–15
payment for shares, 5–16—5–18
piercing the corporate veil under statute,
2–11
procedure, 5–11
purpose, 5–10
registration of new shares, 5–20
Alternative Investment Market
insider dealing, 12–14
issue of shares to public, 3–27
Annual general meetings
agenda, 13–07
members' demand for, 13–09
private companies, 13–08
public companies, 13–10
Application for registration
see **Incorporation**
Appointments
administrators
application process, 16–23
court appointment, 16–20, 16–22
notice of appointment, 16–19
out of court appointment, 16–18,
16–21
publicity for, 16–25
qualifying charge holders, by,
16–17—16–18, 16–20
auditors
private companies, 10–08
public companies, 10–09
replacement auditors, 10–13
company secretary, 10–03
directors, 8–15
liquidators, 17–12
receivers, 15–33—15–34
Articles of association
classes of shares, 4–21—4–22
conduct of meetings, 13–17
entrenchment, provisions for,
4–23—4–24
founding documents, 4–01—4–03
function of, 4–18—4–20
memorandum of association, and,
4–02
objects clause
charitable companies in Scotland,
4–16
directors acting in their own interests,
4–17
generally, 4–04
parliament's solution, 4–08—4–15
reform, 4–05—4–07
shareholders agreements, 4–25—4–26

shares
  rights and duties under, 5–03
Assets
  compulsory winding up by court
    distribution, 17–31—17–32
    gathering in, 17–26—17–28
  ownership in takeovers, 14–04
  revaluation, 7–15
Assumption of responsibility
  piercing the corporate veil, 2–18
Auditors
  accountability, 10–19
  appointment
    private companies, 10–08
    public companies, 10–09
    replacement auditors, 10–13
  breach of duty, 10–17—10–18
  demands for EGM, 13–12
  directors
    duties to, 9–7, 10–10
    prohibition against being, 8–14
  duties, 10–16
  eligibility as, 10–07
  fraud, 10–16, 10–18
  liability, 10–17
  meetings
    attendance at, 10–10
    resignation, 10–13
  offences, 10–16
  private companies
    appointment, 10–08
    replacement auditors, 10–13
  public companies
    appointment, 10–09
    replacement auditors, 10–13
  Registrar of Companies
    appointments, 10–08
    removal, 10–12
    resignation, 10–13
    statement, 10–14
  removal of, 10–12
  remuneration, 10–11
  replacement auditors, 10–13
  reports, 7–33—7–34, 10–16
  requirement for, 10–07
  resignation, 10–13—10–15
  rights of, 10–10—10–11
  role of, 7–33, 10–16
  transparency, 10–19

Balance sheet
  audit exemption, 7–50
  inclusion of, 7–29
  medium-sized companies, 7–51
  micro-entity companies, 7–47
  small companies, 7–46
Balance sheet test
  compulsory winding up by court,
    17–18

Bearer shares
  see also **Shares**
  meaning, 5–09
Beneficial interests
  defeating receivership, 15–47
BIS investigations
  circumstances leading to, 11–44—11–46
  entitlement to apply, 11–43
  inspectors' report, 11–47
  introduction, 11–42
  powers of investigation, 11–48—11–49
  requisition and seizure of books and
    papers, 11–50
Board meetings
  chairman, 8–09
  scope of, 13–21
Bona vacantia
  dissolution of company, 17–36
Bonus issues
  meaning, 5–23
Bonus shares
  see also **Shares**
  financial assistance, 6–21
  meaning, 5–09
Breach of contract
  directorship, termination of, 8–21
Breach of duty
  auditors, 10–17—10–18
  criminal responsibility
    piercing the corporate veil,
      2–31—2–32
  directors
    discovery of, 9–30
    liabilities, 9–63—9–65
    prevention of, 9–30
    ratification, 9–28—9–29, 9–59
    relief, 9–59
    remedies, 9–27
Bribery
  piercing the corporate veil, 2–34
Burden of proof
  insider dealing, 12–20

Cancellation of shares
  see also **Purchase of own shares;
    Redemption of shares**
  requirement for, 6–31
  treasury shares, 6–32
Capital
  public limited companies, 3–22
  statement of, 3–03
Capital account
  types of, 6–04
Capital maintenance
  see also **Shares**
  alteration of capital, 6–05
  cancellation of shares
    requirement for, 6–31
    treasury shares, 6–32

capital account, types of, 6–04
capital redemption reserve
  meaning, 6–04
  purchase of own shares, 6–43—6–44
financial assistance
  exceptions, 6–21—6–22
  management buy-outs, 6–20
  meaning, 6–18
  penalties, 6–23
  principle purpose, 6–24—6–27
  private companies, 6–28—6–29
  private equity firms, 6–20
  prohibition, 6–18—6–19
  public companies, 6–21, 6–26, 6–28
group reconstruction relief, 6–53
loss of capital, 6–51
private companies
  financial assistance, 6–28—6–29
  purchase of own shares, 6–45—6–49
  redemption of shares, 6–45—6–49
private equity firms, 6–20
public companies
  financial assistance, 6–21, 6–26,
    6–28
  reduction of capital, 6–06—6–07,
    6–11, 6–16
purchase of own shares
  assignment of right, 6–38
  capital redemption reserve,
    6–43—6–44
  contingent purchases, 6–39
  disclosure, 6–40
  failure to, 6–50
  financial assistance, 6–21
  generally, 6–30—6–31
  payment for, 6–41—6–42
  private companies, 6–45—6–49
  procedure, 6–35—6–37
  reasons for, 6–33
  treasury shares, 6–32
reality of, 6–03
redemption of shares
  capital redemption reserve,
    6–43—6–44
  failure to, 6–50
  financial assistance, 6–21
  generally, 6–34
  payment for, 6–41—6–42
  private companies, 6–45—6–49
reduction of capital
  distribution of reserve, 6–17
  meaning, 6–06
  procedure for private companies,
    6–13—6–16
  procedure for public companies,
    6–11—6–12
  reduction of capital, 6–06—6–07,
    6–11, 6–16
  reasons for, 6–07—6–09

solvency statement, 6–14—6–15
  types of, 6–10
reserve capital, 6–04
revaluation reserve, 6–04
serious loss of capital, 6–51
share premium account
  meaning, 6–04
  reliefs, 6–52—6–53
  use of, 6–52
  theory behind, 6–01—6–02
Capital markets
  receivership, 15–25
Capital redemption reserve
  meaning, 6–04
  purchase of own shares, 6–43—6–44
Capitalisation
  meaning, 7–09
Cash-flow test
  compulsory winding up by court, 17–18
Certificate of registration
  charges, 15–13
  companies, 3–07
Chairman
  conduct of meetings, 13–17
  role of, 8–09
Charges
  concept, 15–01—15–02
  debentures over, 5–37
  fixed charges
    advantages of, 15–04
    disadvantages of, 15–05
    floating charges distinguished, 15–07
    meaning, 15–04
    ranking in receivership, 15–46
  floating charge holders
    appointment of administrator,
      16–16—16–20
    benefits to, 16–11
    right to wind up company, 17–16
  floating charges
    fixed charges distinguished, 15–07
    invalidity, 15–18—15–22
    meaning, 15–06
    priorities, 15–07
    registration, 15–11
    Scotland, 15–08—15–09
  qualifying floating charges, 16–16
  ranking
    fixed charges, 15–46
    floating charges, 15–07
  reform, 15–03
  registration
    certificate, 15–13
    copies, 15–15
    electronic filing, 15–12
    failure to register in time, 15–14
    floating charges, 15–11
    intimation of, 15–11
    persons eligible to register, 15–12

ranking agreements, 15–17
relief, entries of, 15–16
requirements, 15–10
satisfaction, entries of, 15–16
standard securities, 15–11
Scotland
fixed charges, 15–05
floating charges, 15–08—15–09
shares, over, 5–33
Charitable companies
characteristics of, 1–28
objects clause, 4–16
petition for winding up, 17–20
City Code on Takeovers
see also **Takeovers**
basis of, 14–07
benefits of, 14–08
Competition Commission, 14–13
mandatory bids, 14–09
minorities, buying out, 14–10—14–12
Office of Fair Trading, 14–13
sanctions for non-compliance, 14–07
sell outs, 14–10—14–12
squeeze outs, 14–10—14–12
Takeover Panel, 14–07
Class meetings
see **Meetings**
Classes of shares
see also **Shares**
articles of association, 4–21—4–22
bearer shares, 5–09
bonus shares, 5–09
convertible shares, 5–01, 5–07
deadlock shares, 5–09
deferred shares, 5–09
employee shares, 5–08
non-voting shares, 5–09
ordinary shares, 5–04
preference shares, 5–05
redeemable shares, 5–06
statement of capital, 3–03
treasury shares, 5–09, 5–23
weighted shares, 5–09
Clean hands
unfair prejudice remedy, 11–19
Commerce
promotion of, 1–06
Community interest companies
characteristics of, 1–28, 3–45
Companies
charities, 1–28
community interest companies, 1–27
disclosure principle, 1–07
dormant, 3–38
EU law, 1–13—1–16
European Economic Interest Groupings,
3–43
fraud, 1–09
incorporation, 1–02

jurisprudence, 1–30
legal personality, 1–01
limited liability
advantages, 1–25
disadvantages, 1–25
features, 1–26
scope of, 1–04—1–05
universality of, 1–11
limited liability partnerships compared,
1–20—1–23
limited partnerships compared, 1–24
medium-sized companies, 7–51
micro-entity companies, 7–47—7–48
overseas, 3–42
partnerships compared, 1–18—1–19
private, 3–33—3–37
professional standards, 1–08
promotion of commerce, 1–06
public, 3–21—3–32
registration, 1–03
Scotland, 1–29
small companies, 7–46—7–50
Societas Europaea, 1–15
Societas Privata Europaea, 1–15
sole traders, 1–17
UK legislation, 1–12
unlimited, 3–37
wealth creation, 1–10
Company name
change of
continuing obligations, 3–19
deceit, 3–13
misleading information, 3–15
prohibited names, 3–13
special resolution, 3–14
disclosure of, 3–11
display of, 3–11—3–12
limit of liability, 3–10
passing off, 3–17—3–18
tribunal, 3–16
uniqueness, 3–09
Company secretary
appointment, 10–03
conduct of meetings, 13–17
disclosure of interests, 10–03
duties of, 10–05—10–06
execution of documents, 10–03
officer of company, as, 10–01
power to bind company, 10–03
private companies, 10–03—10–04
professional body, 10–02
public companies, 10–02
register of, 10–03
sole directors, 10–02
statement of proposed officers,
3–04
status as employee, 10–03
Company voluntary arrangements
financial assistance, 6–21

introduction, 16–41
moratorium
  with, 16–43—16–44
  without, 16–42
Competition Commission
takeovers, 14–13
Competition law
directors' disqualification, 8–26
Compliance
statement of, 3–06
Compulsory winding up by court
cross-border insolvency, 17–38
defeating liquidator, 17–33
directors' liability, 17–29—17–30
dissolution of company, 17–34—17–36
distribution of company assets,
    17–31—17–32
entitlement to petition, 17–20—17–21
gathering in estate, 17–26—17–28
grounds
  balance sheet test, 17–18
  cash-flow test, 17–18
  generally, 17–16
  inability to pay debts, 17–17
  just and equitable grounds, 17–19
jurisdiction, 17–15
procedure, 17–22—17–25
restoration to register, 17–37
Concert parties
meaning, 5–32
Conduct of meetings
any other business, 13–19
articles of association, 13–17
chairman, 13–17
company secretary, role of, 13–17
minutes, 13–17
voting, 13–18
Conflicts of interest
directors' duties, 9–16—9–21
Connected persons
liquidations, 17–26—17–28
Contributories
right to petition for winding up, 17–20
Conversion of company
generally, 3–46
private limited company to unlimited,
    3–49
private to public, 3–47
public limited to private unlimited,
    3–51
public to private, 3–48
purpose, 5–25
unlimited to limited, 3–50
Convertible shares
see also **Shares**
meaning, 5–01, 5–07
Copies
charges, 15–15

Corporate manslaughter
piercing the corporate veil, 2–31
Corporate veil
criminal responsibility
  bribery, 2–34
  corporate manslaughter, 2–31
  deferred prosecution agreements, 2–34
  generally, 2–30
  gross breach of duty, 2–31—2–32
  non-fatal matters, 2–33
  punishment, 2–34
  regulatory offences, 2–33
  relevant duty of care, 2–31
involuntary creditors, 2–35
meaning, 2–04
piercing the veil
  see also **Piercing the corporate veil**
  civil matters, 2–25—2–29
  generally, 2–05—2–06
  under common law, 2–12—2-2–24
  under statute, 2–08—2–11
separate legal entity, 2–01—2–03
Credit transactions with directors
connected persons, 9–44
exemptions, 9–42—9–43
generally, 9–34
meaning, 9–40
preventing evasion of rules, 9–41
private companies, 9–38
public companies, 9–39
unauthorised, 9–45—9–46
Creditors
directors' duties to, 9–52—9–54
payment under administration, 16–34
right to petition for winding up, 17–20
Creditors' meetings
see also **Meetings**
takeovers
  notice, 14–16
  requirement for, 14–15
Creditors' voluntary winding up
see **Voluntary winding up**
CREST
use of, 5–21
Criminal activities
piercing the corporate veil, 2–22—2–23
Criminal law
insider dealing
  defences, 12–20—12–23
  effectiveness of criminalisation,
      12–27—12–28
  generally, 12–06
  investigations, 12–19
  market abuse, 12–26
  offence, 12–07—12–14
  professional intermediary,
      12–15—12–18
Criminal liability
piercing the corporate veil

bribery, 2–34
corporate manslaughter, 2–31
deferred prosecution agreements, 2–34
generally, 2–30
gross breach of duty, 2–31—2–32
non-fatal matters, 2–33
punishment, 2–34
regulatory offences, 2–33
relevant duty of care, 2–31
Cross-border insolvency
compulsory winding up by court,
17–38
Cross-border receivership
Scotland, 15–42

Deadlock shares
see also **Shares**
meaning, 5–09
Dealing
see also **Insider dealing**
meaning, 12–13
Debentures
charges over, 5–37
meaning, 5–01, 5–35
register of debenture-holders, 5–36
transfer of, 5–35
Deceit
company name, 3–13
De facto directors
see also **Directors**
meaning, 8–11
Defective accounts
revision of, 7–56
Defences
insider dealing
burden of proof, 12–20
jurisdiction, 12–23
special defences, 12–22
specific defences, 12–21
Deferred prosecution agreements
piercing the corporate veil, 2–34
Deferred shares
see also **Shares**
meaning, 5–09
**Department of Business, Innovation and
Skills investigations**
circumstances leading to, 11–44—11–46
entitlement to apply, 11–43
inspectors' report, 11–47
introduction, 11–42
powers of investigation, 11–48—11–49
requisition and seizure of books and
papers, 11–50
Depreciation of assets
treatment of, 7–07—7–08
Derivative proceedings
continuation as, 11–33
effect of, 11–37
generally, 9–50

grounds, 11–34—11–36
leave to raise, 11–32
minority protection, 11–30
minority rights, 11–38
purpose of, 11–37
Scottish procedure, 11–31
Development expenditure
accounting treatment of, 7–16—7–19
Diligence, effectually executed
defeating receivership, 15–45
Directors
accounts, report on, 7–35—7–41
acting in own interests, 4–17
acting within powers, 9–10
address
change of, 3–05
disclosure, 3–04
administration, benefits of, 16–12
age, 8–01
appointment, 8–15
approval from members, 9–31
auditors, duty to, 9–57, 10–10
authority, 8–02
board of directors
chairman, 8–09
generally, 8–01
breach of duty
discovery of, 9–30
prevention of, 9–30
ratification, 9–28—9–29, 9–59
relief, 9–59
remedies, 9–27
chairman of the board, 8–09
conflicts of interest, 9–16—9–21
connected persons, 9–44
credit transactions
connected persons, 9–44
exemptions, 9–42—9–43
generally, 9–34
meaning, 9–40
preventing evasion of rules, 9–41
private companies, 9–38
public companies, 9–39
unauthorised, 9–45—9–46
creditors, duty to, 9–52—9–54
de facto directors, 8–11
definition, 8–01
management rights
receivership, 15–36
disclosure
interests in contracts, 8–19
interests in proposed transactions or
arrangements, 9–23—9–26
interests in securities, 8–18
members, to, 9–31
Registrar of Companies, to, 8–17
disqualification orders
consequences of, 8–33—8–34
difficulties with, 8–23

duration of disqualification,
    8–31—8–32
generally, 8–24
grounds, 8–25—8–26
law governing, 8–23
unfit directors, 8–27—8–30
duties
    acting within powers, 9–10
    approval from members, 9–31
    auditors, to, 9–57, 10–10
    breach of duty, 9–27—9–30
    Companies Act 2006, 9–03—9–05
    conflicts of interest, 9–16—9–21
    creditors, to, 9–52—9–54
    declaring interests in proposed
        transactions or arrangements,
        9–23—9–26
    disclosure to members, 9–31
    employees, to, 9–55
    exercising independent judgment,
        9–14
    fiduciary, 9–02, 9–06
    insolvency practitioners, cooperation
        with, 9–58
    interpretation of, 9–07—9–09
    introduction, 9–02
    members, to, 9–56
    non-statutory duties, 9–71—9–73
    promote success of company,
        9–11—9–13
    reasonable skill, care and diligence,
        9–15
    scope and nature of, 9–06
    third parties, benefits from, 9–22
    UK Corporate Governance Code,
        9–71—9–73
employees, duty to, 9–55
excluded persons, 8–14
executive directors, 8–07
fitness for office, 8–27—8–30
independent judgment, 9–14
insolvency practitioners, cooperation
    with, 9–58
liabilities
    generally, 9–49
    insolvency, 9–60—9–70
    unlawful dividend, 7–27
loans
    approval, 9–35
    connected persons, 9–44
    exemptions, 9–42—9–43
    generally, 9–34
    preventing evasion of rules, 9–41
    unauthorised, 9–45—9–46
loss of office, payments on, 9–47
managing directors, 8–06
members, disclosure to, 9–56
nominee directors, 8–10
non-executive directors, 8–08

non-statutory duties, 9–71—9–73
payments on loss of office, 9–47
political donations, 9–51
powers and rights, 9–01
private companies
    credit transactions, 9–38
    loans, 9–35
    quasi-loans, 9–36
promote success of company,
    9–11—9–13
public companies
    credit transactions, 9–39
    loans, 9–35
    quasi-loans, 9–37
quasi-loans
    connected persons, 9–44
    exemptions, 9–42—9–43
    generally, 9–34
    preventing evasion of rules, 9–41
    private companies, 9–36
    public companies, 9–37
    unauthorised, 9–45—9–46
reasonable skill, carer and diligence,
    9–15
remedies for breach of duty, 9–27
remuneration, 8–16, 9–47
reports, 7–35—7–41, 10–16
retirement, 9–47
role, 8–03
service contracts, 9–32
shadow directors, 8–12
share allotment
    authority for, 5–12—5–13
significance of being, 8–04
single member companies, 9–48
sole directors, 10–02
statement of proposed officers, 3–04
substantial property transactions, 9–33
termination of directorship
    dismissal, 8–22
    methods, 8–21
    unsatisfactory directors, 8–20
third parties, benefits from, 9–22
transfer of property, payments on,
    9–47
types
    chairman of the board, 8–09
    de facto directors, 8–11
    executive directors, 8–07
    generally, 8–05
    managing directors, 8–06
    nominee directors, 8–10
    non-executive directors, 8–08
    shadow directors, 8–12
    unrecognised directors, 8–13
UK Corporate Governance Code,
    9–71—9–73
unrecognised directors, 8–13
winding up, liability on

avoidance of penalties if not wound
up, 9–61
breach of duty, 9–63—9–65
civil sanctions, 9–62
compulsory winding up by court,
17–29—17–30
fraudulent trading, 9–66
introduction, 9–60
phoenix trading, 9–70
wrongful trading, 9–67—9–69
winding up petitions, 17–20
Disclosure
companies' duties, 1–07
company name, 3–11
company secretaries' interests, 10–03
concert parties' interests, 5–32
directors
appointment, 8–17
interests, 8–18—8–19, 9–23—9–26
members, to, 9–31
Dismissal
directors, 8–22
Disqualification orders
directors
consequences of, 8–33—8–34
difficulties with, 8–23
duration of disqualification,
8–31—8–32
generally, 8–24
grounds, 8–25—8–26
law governing, 8–23
unfit directors, 8–27—8–30
Dissolution of company
compulsory winding up by court
bona vacantia, 17–36
on application, 17–35
Registrar's dissolution, 17–34
creditors' voluntary liquidation, 16–36
directorship, termination of, 8–21
Distributable profits
accumulated, 7–03
capitalisation, 7–09
depreciation, 7–07—7–08
development expenditure, 7–16—7–19
distribution, 7–02
distribution in kind
determination of amount, 7–14
non-cash dividends, 7–15
revaluation of assets, 7–15
dividends
directors' liability for improper,
7–27
initial accounts, 7–21
interim accounts, 7–22
non-cash dividends, 7–15
financial reporting standards, 7–05
meaning, 7–01, 7–13
private companies, 7–20
public limited companies

directors' liability for improper
dividend, 7–27
dividends, 7–25
members liability for improper
distribution, 7–26
net assets rule, 7–23
uncalled share capital, 7–24
undistributable reserves, 7–24
realised losses, 7–04—7–08
realised profits, 7–04—7–08
reduction, 7–11
relevant accounts, 7–20
reorganisation, 7–12
research and development expenditure,
7–16—7–19
retained profit, 7–13
statements of standard accounting
practice, 7–05
undistributed reserves, 7–13
unlawful distributions, 2–11, 7–26, 7–27
written off, 7–10
Distribution in kind
determination of amount, 7–14
non-cash dividends, 7–15
revaluation of assets, 7–15
Distribution of company assets
compulsory winding up by court,
17–31—17–32
Dividends
see also **Distributable profits**
directors' liability for improper dividend,
7–27
financial assistance, 6–21
initial accounts, 7–21
interim accounts, 7–22
non-cash dividends, 7–15
Dormant companies
accounting records, 7–55
nature of, 3–38
Duty of care
directors' duties, 9–15
gross breach of duty
piercing the corporate veil, 2–31

Electronic filing
charges, registration of, 15–12
Employee share schemes
financial assistance, 6–22
Employee shares
see also **Shares**
meaning, 5–08
Employees
directors' duties to, 9–55
receivership, 15–38
Entrenchment, provisions for
articles of association, 4–23—4–24
EU law
Directives, 1–13—1–14
level playing field, 1–16

Regulations, 1–15
Societas Europaea, 1–15
Societas Privata Europaea, 1–15
European economic interest groupings
characteristics, 3–43
Execution of documents
company secretaries, 10–03
incorporation of company, 3–56—3–57
Executive directors
see also **Directors**
meaning, 8–07
Existing business
incorporation of, 3–54—3–55
Extraordinary general meetings
auditors' demand, 13–12
meaning, 13–11
notice, 13–11
public companies suffering fall in net
asset value, 13–13

Façade concealing true facts
see **Corporate veil**
Financial assistance
bonus shares, 6–21
company voluntary arrangements, 6–21
dividends, 6–21
employee share schemes, 6–22
exceptions, 6–21—6–22
foreign subsidiaries, 6–22
management buy-outs, 6–20
meaning, 6–18
penalties, 6–23
piggybacking, 6–27
principle purpose
private companies, 6–28—6–29
public companies, 6–24—6–27
private equity firms, 6–20
prohibition, 6–18—6–19
purchase of shares, 6–21
redemption of shares, 6–21
schemes of arrangement, 6–21
subsidiaries, 6–28
"whitewash" procedure, 6–29
winding up, 6–21
Financial markets
receivership, 15–30
Financial reporting standards
distributable profits, 7–05
Fixed charges
advantages of, 15–04
disadvantages of, 15–05
floating charges distinguished, 15–07
meaning, 15–04
receivership
prior ranking, 15–46
Floating charge holders
appointment of administrator
circumstances permitting, 16–17
court appointment, 16–20

notice of appointment, 16–19
out of court appointment, 16–18
qualifying floating charges, 16–16
benefits to, 16–11
Floating charges
fixed charges distinguished, 15–07
holders' right to wind up company,
17–16
meaning, 15–06
priorities, 15–07
registration, 15–11
Scotland, 15–08—15–09
Foreign subsidiaries
financial assistance, 6–22
Forfeiture
shares, 5–34
Foss v Harbottle
exceptions, to, 11–06—11–08
rule in, 11–04—11–05
Fraud
auditors, 10–16, 10–18
limited liability, and, 1–09
piercing the corporate veil, 2–24
Fraudulent trading
directors
disqualification, 8–26
liabilities, 9–66
qualification as contributory, 17–21

Gathering in estate
compulsory winding up by court,
17–26—17–28
General duties
see **Directors**
General meetings
public limited companies, 3–29
Golden parachute
takeovers, 14–19
Golden shares
takeovers, 14–19
Good faith
objects clause, 4–15
Gratuitous alienations
liquidation, and, 17–26
Group companies
accounting records
consolidated accounts, 7–52
medium-sized groups, 7–53—7–54
small groups, 7–53—7–54
Group entity theory, demise of
piercing the corporate veil, 2–15
Group reconstruction relief
share premium account, 6–53
Guarantee
statement of, 3–03
Guarantee, limited by
nature of company, 3–35
statement of guarantee, 3–03

Holding companies
auditors' liability to, 10–17
meaning and purpose of, 3–39—3–41
Hostile takeover
meaning, 14–01

Incapacity
directorship, termination of, 8–21
Incorporation
accounting reference date, 3–08
address
directors, 3–04, 3–05
registered office, 3–05
service address, 3–05
application for registration
contents, 3–01, 3–02
errors, 3–06
capital, statement of, 3–03
certificate of registration, 3–07
compliance, statement of, 3–06
date of registration, 3–07
directors
change of address, 3–05
execution of documents, 3–56—3–57
existing business of directors,
3–54—3–55
guarantee, statement of, 3–03
initial documentation
accounting reference date, 3–08
address of registered office, 3–05
application for registration, 3–01,
3–02
certificate of registration, 3–07
date of registration, 3–07
errors, 3–06
initial shareholding, 3–03
memorandum of association, 3–02
service address, 3–05
statement of capital, 3–03
statement of compliance, 3–06
statement of guarantee, 3–03
statement of proposed officers,
3–04
unlawful purpose, 3–07
introduction, 1–02
memorandum of association, 3–02
name of company
change of, 3–13—3–15, 3–19
disclosure of, 3–11
display of, 3–11—3–12
limit of liability, 3–10
passing off, 3–17—3–18
tribunal, 3–16
uniqueness, 3–09
off the shelf companies, 3–53
officers, statement of proposed, 3–04
operating new companies
acquisition of existing business from
directors, 3–54—3–55

introduction, 3–52
off the shelf companies, 3–53
practicalities of, 3–52—3–55
pre-incorporation contracts, 3–60
private limited companies
conversion from, 3–48
conversion to, 3–47, 3–49
introduction, 3–33
limited by guarantee, 3–35
limited by shares, 3–34
single member companies, 3–36
unlimited companies, 3–37
promoters, 3–58—3–59
public limited companies
accounting requirements, 3–30
benefit of, 3–32
capital, 3–22
conversion from, 3–47
conversion to, 3–48, 3–51
general meetings, 3–29
generally, 3–21
issue of shares to public, 3–27—3–28
non-cash consideration for shares,
3–24
officers, 3–25
purpose of, 3–31
single member companies, 3–26
trading certificates, 3–23
service address, 3–05
shareholding
initial shareholding, 3–03
statement of capital, 3–03
statement of capital, 3–03
statement of compliance, 3–06
statement of guarantee, 3–03
statement of proposed officers, 3–04
unlawful purpose, 3–07
Independent judgment
directors' duties, 9–14
Index of members
requirement for, 5–30
Initial accounts
see **Accounts**
Inside information
meaning, 12–08
Inside source
meaning, 12–10
Insider
meaning, 12–09
Insider dealing
access to information, 12–03
arguments in favour of, 12–04—12–05
burden of proof, 12–20
civil penalties, 12–24—12–25
criminal law
defences, 12–20—12–23
effectiveness of criminalisation,
12–27—12–28
generally, 12–06

investigations, 12–19
market abuse, 12–26
offence, 12–07—12–14
professional intermediary,
  12–15—12–18
defences
  burden of proof, 12–20
  jurisdiction, 12–23
  special defences, 12–22
  specific defences, 12–21
introduction, 12–01
investigations, 12–19
market abuse, 12–26
offence
  "dealing", 12–13
  generally, 12–07
  "inside information", 12–08
  "inside source", 12–10
  "insider", 12–09
  "public", 12–12
  "regulated market", 12–14
  "securities", 12–11
professional intermediary
  application of Criminal Justice Act
    1993, 12–18
  issuer, 12–17
  meaning, 12–15
  price-affected, 12–16
  price-sensitive, 12–16
victims, 12–02
Insolvency practitioners
directors' cooperation with, 9–58
**Institute of Chartered Secretaries and
  Administrators**
company secretaries
  raising profile of, 10–06
  representation of, 10–02
Interim accounts
see **Accounts**
Investigations
insider dealing, 12–19
Issuer
insider dealing, 12–17

Judicial factors
Scotland, 11–41
Jurisdiction
compulsory winding up by court,
  17–15
insider dealing, 12–23
Jurisprudence
generally, 1–30
Just and equitable
compulsory winding up by court, 17–19

Legal personality
status of companies, 1–01
Legitimate expectation
unfair prejudice remedy, 11–27—11–28

Liability limitation agreements
auditors, 10–18
Liabilities
auditors, 10–17—10–18
receivers, 15–37
Liens
shares, over, 5–34
Limit of liability
company name, 3–10
Limited by guarantee
nature of company, 3–35
Limited by shares
nature of company, 3–34
Limited liability
companies
  advantages, 1–25
  disadvantages, 1–25
  features, 1–26
  scope of, 1–04—1–05
  universality of, 1–11
partnerships, 1–20—1–23
Limited liability partnerships
characteristics, 1–20—1–23
Limited partnerships
characteristics, 1–24
Liquidation
see **Winding up**
Liquidation committee
use of, 17–23
Liquidators
administrators, distinction from, 17–05
appointment
  voluntary winding up, 17–12
defeating
  compulsory winding up by court,
    17–33
powers, 17–24
provisional liquidator
  use of, 17–22
receivers, distinction from,
  17–03—17–04
Loans to directors
approval, 9–35
connected persons, 9–44
exemptions, 9–42—9–43
generally, 9–34
preventing evasion of rules, 9–41
unauthorised, 9–45—9–46
London Stock Exchange
allotment of shares, 5–11, 5–19
convertible shares, 5–07
insider dealing, 12–04, 12–04, 12–26
issue of shares to public, 3–27
limited liability companies, 1–25
prospectuses, 5–27
substantial property transactions, 9–33
wealth creation, 1–10
Loss of capital
procedure following, 6–51

Loss of office
payments to directors on, 9–47

Managing directors
see also **Directors**
meaning, 8–06
Management buy-outs
financial assistance, 6–20
takeovers, 14–13
Market abuse
see **Insider dealing**
Medium-sized companies
accounting records, 7–51
Medium-sized groups
accounting records, 7–53—7–54
Meetings
annual general meetings
agenda, 13–07
members' demand for, 13–09
private companies, 13–08
public companies, 13–10
auditors
attendance at, 10–10
resignation, 10–13
board meetings, 8–01, 13–21
class meetings, 13–20
compulsory winding up, 17–23
conduct of
any other business, 13–19
articles of association, 13–17
chairman, 13–17
company secretary, role of, 13–17
minutes, 13–17
voting, 13–18
creditors' meetings
compulsory winding up, 17–23
creditors' voluntary winding up, 17–11
takeovers, 14–15—14–16
creditors' voluntary winding up, 17–11
extraordinary general meetings
auditors' demand, 13–12
meaning, 13–11
notice, 13–11
public companies suffering fall in net
asset value, 13–13
members' statements, 13–16
notices
AGM of public company, 13–10
contents, 13–14
extraordinary general meetings, 13–11
resolutions requiring special notice,
13–15
proxies
notice of meetings, 13–14
reasons for, 13–01—13–04
resolutions
ordinary resolutions, 13–23
special notice, 13–15
special resolutions, 13–24
types, 13–22
written resolutions, 13–25—13–26
shareholder democracy, 13–27
types
annual general meetings,
13–07—13–10
extraordinary general meetings,
13–11—13–13
generally, 13–06
voting rights
generally, 13–05
shareholder democracy, 13–27
Members
contributories demand for AGM,
13–09
directors' duties to, 9–56
liabilities
creditors' voluntary winding up, 17–13
members' voluntary winding up,
17–10
past members of unlimited companies,
17–20—17–21
unlawful dividends, 7–26
register of
access to, 5–31
contents, 5–30
statements, 13–16
Members' voluntary winding up
see **Voluntary winding up**
Memorandum of association
articles of association, and, 4–02
initial documentation, 3–02
Mergers
takeovers contrasted, 14–01
Micro-entity companies
accounting records, 7–47—7–48
Minorities, buying out
takeovers, 14–10—14–12
Minority protection
derivative claims
continuation of proceedings as,
11–33
effect of, 11–37
generally, 11–30
grounds, 11–34—11–36
leave to raise, 11–32
minority rights, 11–38
purpose of, 11–37
Scottish procedure, 11–31
Foss v Harbottle
exceptions, to, 11–06—11–08
rule in, 11–04—11–05
generally, 11–02—11–02
historically, 11–03
Minutes
conduct of meetings, 13–17
Misleading information
company name, 3–15
prospectuses, 5–26

Money laundering
piercing the corporate veil under statute,
2–11
Moratorium
administration, 16–24
company voluntary arrangement,
16–42—16–44
grounds for liquidation, 17–16

Name of company
change of
continuing obligations, 3–19
deceit, 3–13
misleading information, 3–15
prohibited names, 3–13
special resolution, 3–14
disclosure of, 3–11
display of, 3–11—3–12
limit of liability, 3–10
passing off, 3–17—3–18
tribunal, 3–16
uniqueness, 3–09
Negative pledge
floating charges, 15–07, 15–17
Nominal value
limited liability, and, 1–04
shareholder's duties, 5–02
statement of capital, 3–03
Nominee companies
CREST, 5–21
Nominee directors
see also **Directors**
meaning, 8–10
Non-executive directors
see also **Directors**
meaning, 8–08
Non-voting shares
see also **Shares**
meaning, 5–09
No-par value shares
limited liability, 1–04
meaning, 6–03
Notices
AGM of public company, 13–10
appointment of administrators, 16–19
contents, 13–14
extraordinary general meetings, 13–11
resolutions requiring special notice,
13–15
takeovers, 14–16

Objects clause
charitable companies in Scotland, 4–16
directors acting in their own interests,
4–17
generally, 4–04
parliament's solution
external policy, 4–12—4–15
generally, 4–08

good faith, 4–15
internal policy, 4–10—4–11
overriding statute, 4–09
reform, 4–05—4–07
Off the shelf companies
operating new companies, 3–53
Offences
auditors, 10–16
insider dealing
"dealing", 12–13
generally, 12–07
"inside information", 12–08
"inside source", 12–10
"insider", 12–09
"public", 12–12
"regulated market", 12–14
"securities", 12–11
Office of Fair Trading
takeovers, 14–13
Office of the Scottish Charity Regulator
governance of charities in Scotland, 1–28
Officers
company secretaries, 10–01
public limited companies, 3–25
statement of proposed, 3–04
Ordinary resolutions
meaning, 13–23
Ordinary shares
see also **Shares**
meaning, 5–04
Overseas companies
nature of, 3–42

Pacman defence
takeovers, 14–01
Partnerships
characteristics
generally, 1–18—1–19
limited liability partnerships,
1–20—1–23
limited partnerships, 1–24
Passing off
company name, 3–17—3–18
Penalties
directors' liabilities, 9–62
financial assistance, 6–23
insider dealing, 12–24—12–25
Phoenix trading
directors' liabilities, 3–13, 9–70, 17–29
Piercing the corporate veil
see also **Corporate veil**
civil matters
difficulties with overall decision,
2–29
generally, 2–25—2–26
Lord Neuberger's views, 2–28
Lord Sumption's decision, 2–27
common law
agency, 2–17

alternative remedy in statute,
2–19—2–21
assumption of responsibility, 2–18
criminal activities, 2–22—2–23
evasion of responsibilities, 2–13
fraud through a company, 2–24
generally, 2–12
group entity theory, demise of, 2–15
public policy, 2–14
subsidiaries, 2–16
generally, 2–05—2–06
statute
directors' disqualification, 2–10
generally, 2–07
insolvency, 2–09
other circumstances, 2–11
trading certificate, absence of, 2–08
Piggybacking
financial assistance, 6–27
Poison pills
takeovers, 14–19
Political donations
directors, 9–51
Post office box numbers
registered office, 3–05
Power to bind company
company secretaries, 10–03
receivers, 15–37
Pre-emption rights
disapplication of, 5–15
meaning, 5–14
piercing the corporate veil under statute,
2–11
use of, 5–14
Preference shares
see also **Shares**
meaning, 5–05
Preferential debts
defeating receivership, 15–39
Pre-incorporation contracts
post-incorporation position, 3–60
Prepacks
administration, 16–39
Price-affected
meaning, 12–16
Price-sensitive
meaning, 12–16
Priorities
fixed charges, 15–46
floating charges, 15–07
ranking agreements, 15–17
Private companies
annual general meetings, 13–08
auditors
appointment, 10–08
replacement auditors, 10–13
company secretaries, 10–03—10–04
directors
credit transactions, 9–38

loans, 9–35
quasi-loans, 9–36
financial assistance, 6–28—6–29
generally, 3–33—3–37
Private equity firms
financial assistance, 6–20
Private limited companies
conversion
from public, 3–48
to public, 3–47
to unlimited, 3–49
introduction, 3–33
limited by guarantee, 3–35
limited by shares, 3–34
single member companies, 3–36
unlimited companies, 3–37
Private unlimited companies
conversion from public limited, 3–51
Professional intermediary
insider dealing
application of Criminal Justice Act
1993, 12–18
issuer, 12–17
meaning, 12–15
price-affected, 12–16
price-sensitive, 12–16
**Professional Oversight Board of the
Financial Reporting Council**
auditors
statement on resignation, 10–14
Professional standards
maintenance of, 1–08
Profits, distributable
accumulated, 7–03
capitalisation, 7–09
depreciation, 7–07—7–08
distribution, 7–02
distribution in kind
determination of amount, 7–14
non-cash dividends, 7–15
revaluation of assets, 7–15
dividends
directors' liability for improper, 7–27
initial accounts, 7–21
interim accounts, 7–22
non-cash dividends, 7–15
financial reporting standards, 7–05
meaning, 7–01, 7–13
piercing the corporate veil under statute,
2–11
public limited companies
directors' liability for improper
dividend, 7–27
dividends, 7–25
members liability for improper
distribution, 7–26
net assets rule, 7–23
uncalled share capital, 7–24
undistributable reserves, 7–24

realised losses, 7–04—7–08
realised profits, 7–04—7–08
reduction, 7–11
relevant accounts, 7–20
reorganisation, 7–12
research and development expenditure,
    7–16—7–19
retained profit, 7–13
statements of standard accounting
    practice, 7–05
undistributed reserves, 7–13
written off, 7–10
Prohibited names
company name, 3–13
Project finance
receivership, 15–29
Promote success of company
directors' duties, 9–11—9–13
Promoters
incorporation, 3–58—3–59
Promotion of commerce
companies' duties, 1–06
Property
disposal of, 17–14
substantial property transactions, 9–33
transfer, payments on, 9–47
Prospectuses
listed companies, 5–27
piercing the corporate veil under statute,
    2–11
public non-listed companies, 5–26
purpose, 5–26
Protected railway companies
receivership, 15–32
Provisional liquidator
use of, 17–22
Proxies
notice of meetings, 13–14
Public companies
accounting requirements, 3–30
annual general meetings, 13–10
auditors
    appointment, 10–09
    replacement auditors, 10–13
benefit of, 3–32
capital, 3–22
company secretaries, 10–02
conversion
    from private, 3–47
    to private, 3–48
    to private unlimited, 3–51
directors
    credit transactions, 9–39
    loans, 9–35
    quasi-loans, 9–37
distributable profits
    directors' liability for improper
        dividend, 7–27
    dividends, 7–25

members liability for improper
    distribution, 7–26
net assets rule, 7–23
uncalled share capital, 7–24
undistributable reserves, 7–24
extraordinary general meetings, 13–13
fall in net asset value, 13–13
financial assistance, 6–24—6–27
general meetings, 3–29
generally, 3–21—3–32
issue of shares to public, 3–27—3–28
non-cash consideration for shares, 3–24
officers, 3–25
purpose of, 3–31
single member companies, 3–26
trading certificates, 3–23
Public interest
petition for winding up, 17–20
Public policy
piercing the corporate veil, 2–14
Public-private partnerships
receivership, 15–26
Punishment
piercing the corporate veil, 2–34
Purchase of own shares
assignment of right, 6–38
cancellation, 6–31
capital redemption reserve, 6–43—6–44
contingent purchases, 6–39
disclosure, 6–40
failure to, 6–50
financial assistance, 6–21
generally, 6–30
payment for, 6–41—6–42
private companies
    conditions for payment out of capital,
        6–48—6–49
    funding arrangements, 6–45
    permissible capital payment,
        6–45—6–47
procedure
    generally, 6–35
    market purchase, 6–37
    off-market purchase, 6–36
reasons for, 6–33
redemption of shares
    capital redemption reserve,
        6–43—6–44
    failure to, 6–50
    generally, 6–34
    payment for, 6–41—6–42
    private companies, 6–45—6–49
treasury shares, 6–32

Qualifying floating charges
appointment of administrator, 16–16
Quasi-loans to directors
connected persons, 9–44
exemptions, 9–42—9–43

generally, 9–34
preventing evasion of rules, 9–41
private companies, 9–36
public companies, 9–37
unauthorised, 9–45—9–46
Quasi-partnerships
winding up, 17–19

Railway companies
receivership, 15–32
Ranking
fixed charges, 15–46
floating charges, 15–07
ranking agreements, 15–17
Ratification
directors' breach of duty, 9–28—9–29,
9–59
Realised losses
meaning, 7–04—7–08
Realised profits
meaning, 7–04—7–08
Reasonable skill, care and diligence
directors' duties, 9–15
Receivers
right to petition for winding up,
17–20
Receivership (pre-Enterprise Act)
administration, and, 16–40
capital markets, 15–25
financial markets, 15–30
introduction, 15–23
project finance, 15–29
protected railway companies, 15–32
public-private partnerships, 15–26
registered social landlords, 15–31
urban regeneration projects, 15–28
use of old rules, 15–24
utilities, 15–27
Receivership (Scotland)
appointment, 15–33—15–34
cross-border receivership, 15–42
defeating
beneficial interests, 15–47
effectually executed diligence, 15–45
generally, 15–43
prior ranking fixed charges, 15–46
retention of title, 15–44
directors' management rights, 15–36
disbursal of sums gathered,
15–40—15–41
duties, 15–35
employees, 15–38
introduction, 15–23
liabilities, 15–37
power to bind company, 15–37
powers, 15–35
preferential debts, 15–39
problems with, 15–48
reports, 15–35

Redeemable shares
see also **Shares**
meaning, 5–06
Redemption of shares
capital redemption reserve, 6–43—6–44
failure to, 6–50
financial assistance, 6–21
generally, 6–34
payment for, 6–41—6–42
private companies
conditions for payment out of capital,
6–48—6–49
funding arrangements, 6–45
permissible capital payment,
6–45—6–47
Reduction of capital
distribution of reserve, 6–17
meaning, 6–06
procedure for private companies,
6–13—6–16
procedure for public companies,
6–11—6–12
reasons for, 6–07—6–09
solvency statement, 6–14—6–15
types of, 6–10
Reform
charges, 15–03
objects clause, 4–05—4–07
Regeneration projects
receivership, 15–28
Registered social landlords
receivership, 15–31
Registers
company secretaries, 10–03
debenture-holders, 5–36
members
access to, 5–31
contents, 5–30
restoration to, 17–37
Registrar of Companies
auditors
appointment of, 10–08
removal of, 10–12
resignation of, 10–13
statement of, 10–14
company secretaries
duties of, 10–05
notification of new, 10–03
compulsory winding up
notification of order, 17–22
directors' disclosure to, 8–17
dissolution of company, 17–34
restoration to register, 17–37
schemes of arrangement, 14–16
voluntary winding up
appointment of liquidator,
17–07
copy of resolution, 17–07
final accounts, 17–08

Registration
see also **Incorporation**
application for
contents, 3–01, 3–02
errors, 3–06
certificate of, 3–07
charges
certificate, 15–13
copies, 15–15
electronic filing, 15–12
failure to register in time, 15–14
floating charges, 15–11
intimation of, 15–11
persons eligible to register,
15–12
ranking agreements, 15–17
relief, entries of, 15–16
requirements, 15–10
satisfaction, entries of, 15–16
standard securities, 15–11
date of, 3–07
generally, 1–03
shares, 5–20
Regulatory offences
piercing the corporate veil, 2–33
Relief, entries of
register of charges, 15–16
Removal
auditors, 10–12
directors, 8–16
Remuneration
administrators, 16–29
auditors, 10–11
directors, 9–47
Reorganisation
distributable profits, 7–12
Reports
auditors, 10–16
receivers, 15–35
Research and development expenditure
treatment in accounts of, 7–16—7–19
Reserves
meaning, 6–04
undistributed reserves, 7–13
Resolutions
ordinary resolutions, 13–23
special notice, 13–15
special resolutions, 13–24
types, 13–22
voluntary winding up, 17–07, 17–10
written resolutions, 13–25—13–26
Resignation
auditors, 10–13—10–15
Restoration to register
procedure, 17–37
Retained profit
meaning, 7–13
Retention of title
defeating receivership, 15–44

Retirement
directors, 8–21, 9–47
Revaluation reserve
meaning, 6–04
Rights issues
meaning, 5–22

Sale and purchase agreements
takeovers, 14–03
Sanctions
City Code on Takeovers, non-
compliance with, 14–07
Satisfaction, entries of
register of charges, 15–16
Schemes of arrangement
advantages of, 14–17
court powers, 14–17
creditors' meetings, 14–15
disadvantages of, 14–17
explanatory note, 14–16
financial assistance, 6–21
meaning, 14–14
notice of meeting, 14–16
Scotland
charitable companies
objects clause, 4–16
company law, 1–29
fixed charges, 15–05
floating charges, 15–08—15–09
judicial factors, 11–41
receivership
appointment, 15–33—15–34
cross-border receivership, 15–42
defeating, 15–43—15–47
directors' management rights, 15–36
disbursal of sums gathered,
15–40—15–41
duties, 15–35
employees, 15–38
introduction, 15–23
liabilities, 15–37
power to bind company, 15–37
powers, 15–35
preferential debts, 15–39
problems with, 15–48
reports, 15–35
Scottish Charitable Incorporated
Associations
governance of charities in Scotland, 1–28
Scrip issues
meaning, 5–24
Secretary, company
see **Company secretary**
Securities
see also **Shares**
bonus issues, 5–23
concert parties, 5–32
convertible shares, 5–01, 5–07
conversion of share capital, 5–25

debentures
  charges over, 5–37
  meaning, 5–01, 5–35
  register of debenture-holders, 5–36
  transfer of, 5–35
disclosure of interests, 5–32
index of members, 5–30
meaning, 5–01
options, 5–01
prospectuses
  listed companies, 5–27
  public non-listed companies, 5–26
  purpose, 5–26
register of members
  access to, 5–31
  contents, 5–30
rights issues, 5–22
scrip issues, 5–24
transfer and transmission, 5–28—5–29
warrants, 5–01
Sell outs
  takeovers, 14–10—14–12
Sequestration
  directorship, termination of, 8–21
Serious loss of capital
  procedure following, 6–51
Service address
  initial documentation, 3–05
Service contracts
  directors, 9–32
Shadow directors
  see also **Directors**
  meaning, 8–12
Share allotment
  piercing the corporate veil under statute,
    2–11
Share for asset offers
  takeovers, 14–05
Share premium account
  meaning, 6–04
  reliefs, 6–52—6–53
  use of, 6–52
Shareholder democracy
  meetings, 13–27
Shareholders agreements
  articles of association, 4–25—4–26
Shares
  see also **Capital maintenance**
  allotment
    CREST, 5–21
    directors' authority for, 5–12—5–13
    intimation of, 5–19
    members' pre-emption rights,
      5–14—5–15
    payment for shares, 5–16—5–18
    procedure, 5–11
    purpose, 5–10
    registration of new shares, 5–20

articles of association
  classes of shares, 4–21—4–22
  shareholders agreements, 4–25—4–26
bonus issues, 5–23
cancellation of
  requirement for, 6–31
  treasury shares, 6–32
charges over, 5–33
classes
  articles of association, 4–21—4–22
  bearer shares, 5–09
  bonus shares, 5–09
  convertible shares, 5–01, 5–07
  deadlock shares, 5–09
  deferred shares, 5–09
  employee shares, 5–08
  non-voting shares, 5–09
  ordinary shares, 5–04
  preference shares, 5–05
  redeemable shares, 5–06
  statement of capital, 3–03
  treasury shares, 5–09
  weighted shares, 5–09
consolidation, 5–25
conversion, 5–25
CREST, 5–21
forfeiture, 5–34
initial shareholding, 3–03
legal status, 5–02
lien over, 5–34
meaning, 5–01, 5–02
nominal value, 3–03
payment for, 5–16—5–18
pre-emption rights, 5–14—5–15
public limited companies
  issue to public, 3–27—3–28
  non-cash consideration, 3–24
purchase of own shares
  assignment of right, 6–38
  capital redemption reserve,
    6–43—6–44
  contingent purchases, 6–39
  disclosure, 6–40
  failure to, 6–50
  generally, 6–30—6–31
  payment for, 6–41—6–42
  private companies, 6–45—6–49
  procedure, 6–35—6–37
  reasons for, 6–33
  treasury shares, 6–32
redemption of shares
  capital redemption reserve,
    6–43—6–44
  failure to, 6–50
  generally, 6–34
  payment for, 6–41—6–42
  private companies, 6–45—6–49
registration, 5–20
rights from, 5–02—5–03

rights issues, 5–22
scrip issues, 5–24
shareholders agreements, 4–25—4–26
statement of capital, 3–03
subdivision, 5–25
transfers
  charges over shares, 5–33
  concert parties, 5–32
  disclosure of interests, 5–32
  forfeiture, 5–34
  index of members, 5–30
  liens, 5–34
  register of members, 5–30, 5–31
  right to transfer, 5–28
  transmission, 5–29
  wrongful inducement to issue share
    certificate, 5–28
Single member companies
  directors, 9–48
  private limited companies, 3–36
  public limited companies, 3–26
Skill
  directors' duties, 9–15
Small companies
  accounting records
    audit exemption, 7–49—7–50
    meaning, 7–46
    micro-entity companies, 7–47—7–48
    publication of accounts, 7–46
Small groups
  accounting records, 7–53—7–54
Social landlords
  receivership, 15–31
Societas europaea
  characteristics, 1–15, 3–44
Societas Privata Europaea
  characteristics, 1–15
Sole directors
  company secretaries, requirement for,
    10–02
Sole traders
  characteristics, 1–17
Solvency statement
  reduction of capital, 6–14—6–15
Special resolutions
  company name, 3–14
  meaning, 13–24
Squeeze outs
  takeovers, 14–10—14–12
Stamp duty land tax
  takeovers, 14–03
Standard securities
  registration, 15–11
Statement of affairs
  liquidators, 17–23
Statement of capital
  initial documentation, 3–03
Statement of compliance
  initial documentation, 3–06

Statement of guarantee
  initial documentation, 3–03
Statement of proposed officers
  initial documentation, 3–04
Statements of standard accounting practice
  distributable profits, 7–05
Subsidiaries
  financial assistance
    foreign subsidiaries, 6–22
    generally, 6–28
  meaning and purpose of, 3–39—3–41
  piercing the corporate veil, 2–16
Substantial property transactions
  directors, 9–33

Takeover Panel
  role of, 14–07
Takeovers
  asset ownership, 14–04
  City Code
    basis of, 14–07
    benefits of, 14–08
    Competition Commission, 14–13
    mandatory bids, 14–09
    minorities, buying out, 14–10—14–12
    Office of Fair Trading, 14–13
    sanctions for non-compliance, 14–07
    sell outs, 14–10—14–12
    squeeze outs, 14–10—14–12
    Takeover Panel, 14–07
  commercial significance, 14–06
  golden parachute, 14–19
  golden shares, 14–19
  hostile takeover, 14–01
  impediments to
    free market, 14–18
    poison pills, 14–19
    post credit crunch climate, 14–24
    Takeover Directive, 14–20—14–23
  law relating to, 14–02
  management buy-outs, 14–13
  meaning, 14–01
  merger contrasted, 14–01
  Pacman defence, 14–01
  sale and purchase agreement, 14–03
  schemes of arrangement
    advantages of, 14–17
    court powers, 14–17
    creditors' meetings, 14–15
    disadvantages of, 14–17
    explanatory note, 14–16
    meaning, 14–14
    notice of meeting, 14–16
  share for asset offers, 14–05
  stamp duty land tax, 14–03
  target company, 14–21
Target company
  takeovers, 14–21

Taxation
piercing the corporate veil under statute, 2–11
Terrorism
piercing the corporate veil under statute, 2–11
Third parties, benefits from
directors' duties, 9–22
Trade marks
company names, 3–19
Trading certificates
public limited companies, 3–23
Transactions at an undervalue
liquidation, and, 17–26
Transfers
debentures, 5–35
property
payments to directors on, 9–47
shares
charges over shares, 5–33
concert parties, 5–32
disclosure of interests, 5–32
forfeiture, 5–34
index of members, 5–30
liens, 5–34
register of members, 5–30, 5–31
right to transfer, 5–28
transmission, 5–29
wrongful inducement to issue share certificate, 5–28
Transparency
auditors, 10–19
Treasury shares
see also **Shares**
meaning, 5–09
Tribunals
company name, 3–16
Types of companies
community interest companies, 3–45
conversion
generally, 3–46
private limited company to unlimited, 3–49
private to public, 3–47
public limited to private unlimited, 3–51
public to private, 3–48
unlimited to limited, 3–50
dormant companies, 3–38
European economic interest groupings, 3–43
holding companies, 3–39—3–41
introduction, 3–20
overseas companies, 3–42
private limited companies
conversion to unlimited, 3–49
introduction, 3–33
limited by guarantee, 3–35
limited by shares, 3–34
single member companies, 3–36
unlimited companies, 3–37
public limited companies, 3–21—3–32
societas europaea, 1–15, 3–44
societas privata europaea, 1–15
subsidiaries, 3–39—3–41

UK Corporate Governance Code
directors' duties, 9–71—9–73
Ultra vires
charitable companies in Scotland, 4–16
directors acting in own interests, 4–17
external policy, 4–12, 4–13
internal policy, 4–10—4–11
objects clause, 4–04—4–05
Undistributed reserves
meaning, 7–13
Unfair preferences
liquidation, and, 17–26
Unfair prejudice remedy
appropriate remedy, 11–22
clean hands, 11–19
controlling position
use of to weaken minority, 11–23—11–29
court's remedies, 11–16—11–17
definitions
actual or proposed act or omission, 11–15
are being or have been conducted, 11–12
interests of members, 11–14
manner that is unfairly prejudicial, 11–13
member, 11–10
order, 11–11
fair value, 11–18
former majority shareholders, 11–21
introduction, 11–09
legitimate expectation, 11–27—11–28
looking after own interests, 11–20
unreasonable behaviour, 11–20
Unlawful distribution of profits
piercing the corporate veil under statute, 2–11
Unlawful purpose
incorporation, 3–07
Unlimited companies
accounting records, 7–44
conversion
private limited company to unlimited, 3–49
public limited to private unlimited, 3–51
unlimited to limited, 3–50
nature of, 3–37
past members' liability, 17–20—17–21
Unquoted companies
websites, 5–21

Urban regeneration projects
receivership, 15–28
Utilities
receivership, 15–27

Vending agreement
meaning, 3–54
Voluntary arrangements
see **Company voluntary arrangements**
Voluntary winding up
creditors' voluntary winding up
dissolution, 16–36
generally, 17–11—17–13
introduction, 16–35
rescue achieved, 16–37
rescue mission failed, 16–38
disposal of company property, and,
17–14
generally, 17–07
liquidators, appointment of, 17–12
meaning, 17–07
members' voluntary winding up,
17–09—17–10
Voting
conduct of meetings, 13–18
Voting rights
generally, 13–05
shareholder democracy, 13–27
shares, 5–02

Warrant
securities, 5–01, 12–11
Websites
requirement for, 5–21
Weighted shares
see also **Shares**
meaning, 5–09
"Whitewash" procedure
financial assistance, 6–29
Winding up
compulsory winding up by court
cross-border insolvency, 17–38
defeating liquidator, 17–33
directors' liability, 17–29—17–30

dissolution of company,
17–34—17–36
distribution of company assets,
17–31—17–32
entitlement to petition, 17–20—17–21
gathering in estate, 17–26—17–28
grounds, 17–16—17–19
jurisdiction, 17–15
procedure, 17–22—17–25
restoration to register, 17–37
directors' liability
avoidance of penalties if not wound
up, 9–61
breach of duty, 9–63—9–65
civil sanctions, 9–62
fraudulent trading, 9–66
introduction, 9–60
phoenix trading, 9–70
wrongful trading, 9–67—9–69
financial assistance, 6–21
just and equitable grounds,
11–39—11–40
liquidator/administrator distinction,
17–05
liquidator/receiver distinction,
17–03—17–04
methods, 17–06
procedure, 17–02
voluntary winding up
creditors' voluntary winding up,
17–11—17–13
disposal of company property, and,
17–14
generally, 17–07
meaning, 17–07
members' voluntary winding up,
17–09—17–10
Written off
meaning, 7–10
Written resolutions
meaning, 13–25—13–26
Wrongful trading
directors
disqualification, 8–26
liabilities, 9–67—9–69
qualification as contributory, 17–21